THE NEW CFO
FINANCIAL LEADERSHIP
MANUAL

Second Edition

THE NEW CFO
FINANCIAL LEADERSHIP
MANUAL

SECOND EDITION

STEVEN M. BRAGG

Library of Congress Cataloging-in-Publication Data:

Bragg, Steven M.
   The new CFO financial leadership manual / Steven M. Bragg. – 2nd ed.
      p. cm.
   Includes index.
   ISBN-13: 978-0-470-08200-3 (cloth)
   ISBN-10: 0-470-08200-3 (cloth)
   1. Chief financial officers–Handbooks, manuals, etc. 2.
Corporations—Finance—Management—Handbooks, manuals, etc. I. Title.
II. Title: CFO financial leadership manual.
   HG4027.35.B73 2007
   658.15—dc22

                                                    2006042123

Printed in the United States of America.

10 9 8 7 6 5 4 3 2

Electrician, locksmith, and woodworker, the first in the family to finish college, an indisputable genius, and our provider—I would not be where I am without you, Dad. But couldn't you let me win at Scrabble just once?

CONTENTS

PREFACE

The second edition of the *New CFO Financial Leadership Manual* is designed to give the Chief Financial Officer (CFO) a complete overview of his or her place in the corporation, and to provide strategies for how to handle strategic decisions related to a variety of financial, tax, and information technology issues. Some of the questions that Chapters 1 through 4 answer include:

- What should I do during my first days on the job?
- What are my specific responsibilities?
- How do I reduce my foreign currency exposure?
- How do I increase the company's return on assets?
- When should I issue convertible securities?
- What factors should I consider in regard to a step costing decision?
- When can I use net operating loss tax carryforwards?
- How do I decide which products to eliminate?
- How can I use transfer pricing to reduce income taxes?
- What specific information technologies should I install for a certain type of business, such as a low-cost producer or rapid product innovator?

The CFO must also become involved in a variety of accounting topics, though not at the transactional level of detail with which a controller will be occupied. Key areas of concern are the development and maintenance of performance measurement and control systems. The CFO must also interact with the internal and external auditors, while also (if the company is publicly held) making regular reports to the Securities and Exchange Commission (SEC). Chapters 5 through 8 address these topics, and yield answers to all of the following questions, as well as many more:

- How do I set up a performance measurement system?
- What are the best performance measurements to install for tracking a variety of accounting and financial issues?
- What types of fraud can be committed, and what kinds of controls can reduce their likelihood of occurrence?
- Which key controls should I install?
- How do I identify and eliminate unnecessary controls?
- What is the impact of Sarbanes-Oxley on my company?
- Who serves on the audit committee, and what is its role?
- How do I deal with the external and internal auditors?
- Which reports do I file with the SEC, and what information should I include in them?

One of the CFO's primary tasks is the analysis of a wide range of financial issues, resulting in recommendations for action to the management team. Chapters 9 through 11 address such topics as the cost of capital, capital budgeting, risk analysis, capacity utilization, and breakeven. With these chapters in hand, one can answer the following questions:

- How do I calculate my company's cost of capital?
- How can I modify the cost of capital to increase shareholder value?
- What are the various methods for determining the value of proposed capital projects?
- How do I calculate net present value, the internal rate of return, and the payback period?
- How do I allocate funding to research and development projects?
- How do I determine capacity utilization, and what decisions can I make with this information?
- How can breakeven analysis be used to optimize profitability?

A CFO is sometimes given the primary task of obtaining funding, leaving all other activities up to the controller or treasurer. In this role, the CFO must know how to manage existing cash flows, invest excess funds, obtain both debt and equity financing, conduct an initial public offering, and take a company private. These topics are addressed by Chapters 12 through 17, which provide answers to all of the following questions, and more:

- How do I construct a cash forecasting model and measure its accuracy?
- How do I control cash flows?
- How do I construct natural hedges?
- What investment restrictions should I recommend to the Board of Directors?
- What are good short-term investment options?
- What is the role of credit rating agencies?
- What are the various types of available debt financing?
- How do I conduct a private placement of stock?
- How do I arrange a private investment in public equity?
- What information goes into an offering memorandum?
- How do I place a value on offered stock?
- Which steps do I follow to complete an initial public offering?
- How do I create a reverse merger?
- Why are companies using the Alternative Investment Market as their stock exchange of choice?
- How do I file with the SEC to take a company private?

Though a CFO can certainly be of great value to a company by properly managing its flow of funds, there are also a number of management areas in which he or she can enhance operations. These are addressed in Chapters 18 through 22, which discuss risk management, outsourcing, operational best practices, mergers and acquisitions, and electronic commerce. By perusing them, one can find answers to the following questions:

- How do I engage in risk planning?

- What types of company-wide policies and procedures should I install to mitigate risks?

- How do I evaluate insurance carriers?

- What are the advantages and disadvantages of outsourcing various aspects of the accounting and finance functions, and which contractual and transitional issues should I be aware of?

- What are some of the best practices I can implement in the accounting and finance functions to improve their efficiency?

- How do I evaluate acquisition targets?

- How do I place a value on an acquisition target?

- How do I value prospective synergies resulting from an acquisition?

- How does the e-commerce business model work, and how do I restructure the business to incorporate it?

There are also several topics that may require some degree of expertise by the CFO from time to time. One is employee compensation, which is addressed in Chapter 23. It covers such topics as deferred compensation, life insurance, stock appreciation rights, stock options, and the bonus sliding scale. One issue that a CFO certainly hopes never to experience is bankruptcy, which is described in Chapter 24. This chapter describes the sequence of events in a typical bankruptcy proceeding, as well as special bankruptcy rules, payment priorities, the parties that typically become involved in the process, and the impact of the Bankruptcy Act of 2005.

The CFO may also require checklists to perform certain aspects of the job. Toward this end, Appendix A contains a checklist that itemizes the usual priority of action items required during the first days of fitting into a new CFO position. Appendix B contains a summary-level list of performance measurements that are useful as a reference for those CFOs who are constructing performance measurement systems. Finally, Appendix C contains an extensive due diligence checklist that is most helpful for reviewing the operations of a potential acquisition candidate.

In total, this book is a comprehensive guidebook for the CFO who needs an overview of strategies, measurement and control systems, financial analysis tools, funding sources, and management improvement tips that will help provide the greatest possible value to the company. If you have any comments about this book, or would like to see additional chapters added in future editions, contact the author at bragg.steven@gmail.com. Thank you!

Steven M. Bragg
Centennial, Colorado
December 2007

ACKNOWLEDGMENTS

The real work of preparing a book for publication begins only after the rough manuscript appears at the publisher's doorstep. It is generally greeted with gasps of dismay by the group of editors who must review it in more detail than I ever did, working through several colored correction pencils to achieve a version that will not be immediately rejected with snorts of derision by the reading public. Thank you for making all the corrections that turn my words into a smoothly flowing and intelligible document.

ABOUT THE AUTHOR

Steven Bragg, CPA, CMA, CIA, CPM, CPIM, has been the chief financial officer or controller of four companies, as well as a consulting manager at Ernst & Young and auditor at Deloitte & Touche. He received a master's degree in Finance from Bentley College, an MBA from Babson College, and a bachelor's degree in Economics from the University of Maine. He has been the two-time president of the Colorado Mountain Club and is an avid alpine skier, mountain biker, and certified master diver. Mr. Bragg resides in Centennial, Colorado. He has written the following books published by John Wiley & Sons:

Accounting and Finance for Your Small Business
Accounting Best Practices
Accounting Control Best Practices
Accounting Reference Desktop
Billing and Collections Best Practices
Business Ratios and Formulas
Controller's Guide to Costing
Controller's Guide to Planning and Controlling Operations
Controller's Guide: Roles and Responsibilities for the New Controller
Controllership
Cost Accounting
Design and Maintenance of Accounting Manuals
Essentials of Payroll
Fast Close
Financial Analysis
GAAP Guide
GAAP Implementation Guide
Inventory Accounting
Inventory Best Practices
Just-in-Time Accounting
Managing Explosive Corporate Growth
Outsourcing
Payroll Accounting
Payroll Best Practices
Sales and Operations for Your Small Business
Throughput Accounting
The Controller's Function
The New CFO Financial Leadership Manual
The Ultimate Accountants' Reference

Other titles by Mr. Bragg include:

Advanced Accounting Systems (Institute of Internal Auditors)
Run the Rockies (CMC Press)

Free On-Line Resources by Steve Bragg

Steve issues a free bimonthly accounting best practices newsletter, as well as an accounting best practices podcast. You can sign up for free delivery of the newsletter and/or podcast (also available through iTunes) at www.stevebragg.com.

PART 1

OVERVIEW

CHAPTER 1

CFO'S PLACE IN THE CORPORATION

Years ago, Chief Executive Officers (CEOs) were satisfied with finance chiefs who could manage Wall Street analysts, implement financial controls, manage initial public offerings (IPOs), and communicate with the Board of Directors—who, in short, possessed strong financial skills. However, in today's business environment, the ability to change quickly has become a necessity for growth, if not for survival. CEOs are no longer satisfied with financial acumen from their CFOs. They are demanding more from their finance chiefs, looking instead for people who can fill a multitude of roles: business partner, strategic visionary, communicator, confidant, and creator of value. This chapter addresses the place of the CFO in the corporation, describing how to fit into this new and expanded role.

FIRST DAYS IN THE POSITION

You have just been hired into the CFO position and have arrived at the offices of your new company. What do you do? Though it is certainly impressive (to you) to barge in like Napoleon, you may want to consider a different approach that will calm down your new subordinates as well as make them feel that you are someone they can work with. Here are some suggestions for how to handle the critical first few days on the job:

- *Meet with employees.* This is the number-one activity by far. Determine who the key people in the organization are and block out lots of time to meet with them. This certainly includes the entire management team, but it is even better to build relationships far down into the corporate ranks. Get to know the warehouse manager, the purchasing staff, salespeople, and engineers. Always ask who else you should talk to in order to obtain a broad-based view of the company and its problems and strengths. By establishing and maintaining these linkages, you will have great sources of information that circumvent the usual communication channels.

- *Do not review paperwork.* Though you may be tempted to lock yourself up in an office and pore through management reports and statistics, meeting people is the top priority. Save this task for after hours and weekends, when there is no one on hand to meet with.

- *Wait before making major decisions.* The first few months on the job are your assigned "honeymoon period," where the staff will be most accepting of you. Do not shorten the period by making ill-considered decisions. The best approach is to come up with possible solutions, sleep on them, and discuss them with key staff before making any announcements that would be hard to retract.

- *Set priorities.* As a result of your meetings, compile an initial list of work priorities, which should include both efficiency improvements and any needed departmental restructurings. You can communicate these general targets in group meetings, while revealing individual impacts on employees in one-on-one meetings. Do not let individual employees be personally surprised by your announcements at general staff meetings—always reveal individual impacts *prior to* general meetings, so these people will be prepared.

- *Create and implement a personnel review system.*   If you intend to let people go, early in your term is the time to do it. However, there is great risk of letting strong performers go if you do not have adequate information about them, so install a personnel review system as soon as possible and use it to determine who stays and who leaves.

The general guidelines noted here have a heavy emphasis on communication, because employees will be understandably nervous when the boss changes, and you can do a great deal to assuage those feelings. Also, setting up personal contacts throughout the organization is a great way to firmly insert yourself into the organization in short order and makes it much less likely that you will be rejected by the organization at large.

SPECIFIC CFO RESPONSIBILITIES

We have discussed how to structure the workday during the CFO's initial hiring period, but what does the CFO work on? What are the primary tasks to pursue? These targets will vary by company, depending on its revenue, its industry, its funding requirements, and the strategic intentions of its management team. Thus, the CFO will find that entirely different priorities will apply to individual companies. Nonetheless, some of the most common CFO responsibilities are:

- *Pursue shareholder value.*   The usual top priority for the CFO is the relentless pursuit of the strategy that has the best chance of increasing the return to shareholders. This also includes a wide range of tactical implementation issues designed to reduce costs.

- *Construct reliable control systems.*   A continuing fear of the CFO is that a missing control will result in problems that detrimentally impact the corporation's financial results. A sufficiently large control problem can quite possibly lead to the CFO's termination, so a continuing effort to examine existing systems for control problems is a primary CFO task. This also means that the CFO should be deeply involved in the design of controls for new systems, so they go on-line with adequate controls already in place. The CFO typically uses the internal audit staff to assist in uncovering control problems.

- *Understand and mitigate risk.*   This is a major area of concern to the CFO, who is responsible for having a sufficiently in-depth knowledge of company systems to ferret out any risks occurring in a variety of areas, determining their materiality and likelihood of occurrence, and creating and monitoring risk mitigation strategies to keep them from seriously impacting the company. The focus on risk should include some or all of the following areas:

  — *Loss of key business partners.*   If a key supplier or customer goes away, how does this impact the company? The CFO can mitigate this risk by lining up alternate sources of supply, as well as by spreading sales to a wider range of customers.

— *Loss of brand image.* What if serious quality or image problems impact a company's key branded product? The CFO can mitigate this risk by implementing a strong focus on rapid management reactions to any brand-related problems, creating strategies in advance for how the company will respond to certain issues, and creating a strong emphasis on brand quality.

— *Product design errors.* What if a design flaw in a product injures a customer, or results in a failed product? The CFO can create rapid-response teams with preconfigured action lists to respond to potential design errors. There should also be product design review teams in place whose review methodologies reduce the chance of a flawed product being released. The CFO should also have a product recall strategy in place, as well as sufficient insurance to cover any remaining risk of loss from this problem.

— *Commodity price changes.* This can involve price increases from suppliers or price declines caused by sales of commodity items to customers. In either case, the CFO's options include the use of long-term fixed-price contracts, as well as a search for alternative materials (for suppliers) or cost cutting to retain margins in case prices to customers decline.

— *Pollution.* Not only can a company be bankrupted by pollution-related lawsuits, but its officers can be found personally liable for them. Consequently, the CFO should be heavily involved in the investigation of all potential pollution issues at existing company facilities, while also making pollution testing a major part of all facility acquisition reviews. The CFO should also have a working knowledge of how all pollution-related legislation impacts the company.

— *Foreign exchange risk.* Investments or customer payables can decline in value due to a drop in the value of foreign currencies. The CFO should know the size of foreign trading or investing activity, be aware of the size of potential losses, and adopt hedging tactics if the risk is sufficiently high to warrant incurring hedging costs.

— *Adverse regulatory changes.* Changes in local, state, or federal laws—ranging from zoning to pollution controls and customs requirements—can hamstring corporate operations and even shut down a company. The CFO should be aware of pending legislation that could cause these changes, engage in lobbying efforts to keep them from occurring, and prepare the company for those changes most likely to occur.

— *Contract failures.* Contracts may have clauses that can be deleterious to a company, such as the obligation to order more parts than it needs, to make long-term payments at excessive rates, to be barred from competing in a certain industry, and so on. The CFO should verify the contents of all existing contracts, as well as examine all new ones, to ensure that the company is aware of these clauses and knows how to mitigate them.

— *System failures.* A company's infrastructure can be severely impacted by a variety of natural or man-made disasters, such as flooding, lightning, earthquakes, and wars. The CFO must be aware of these possibilities and have disaster recovery plans in place that are regularly practiced, so the organization has a means of recovery.

— *Succession failures.* Without an orderly progression of trained and experienced personnel in all key positions, a company can be impacted by the loss of key personnel. The CFO should have a succession planning system in place that identifies potential replacement personnel and grooms them for eventual promotion.

— *Employee practices.* Employees may engage in sexual harassment, stealing assets, or other similar activities. The CFO should coordinate employee training and set up control systems that are designed to reduce the risk of their engaging in unacceptable activities that could lead to lawsuits against the company or the direct incurrence of losses.

— *Investment losses.* Placing funds in excessively high-risk investment vehicles can result in major investment losses. The CFO should devise an investment policy that limits investment options to those vehicles that provide an appropriate mix of liquidity, moderate return, and a low risk of loss (see Chapter 13, Investing Excess Funds).

— *Interest rate increases.* If a company carries a large amount of debt whose interest rates vary with current market rates, then there is a risk that the company will be adversely impacted by sudden surges in interest rates. This risk can be reduced through a conversion to fixed interest-rate debt, as well as by refinancing to lower-rate debt whenever shifts in interest rates allow this to be done.

- *Link performance measures to strategy.* The CFO will likely inherit a companywide measurement system that is based on historical needs, rather than the requirements of its strategic direction. He or she should carefully prune out those measurements that are resulting in behavior not aligned with the strategic direction, add new ones that encourage working on strategic initiatives, and also link personal review systems to the new measurement system. This is a continuing effort, since strategy shifts will continually call for revisions to the measurement system.

- *Encourage efficiency improvements everywhere.* The CFO works with all department managers to find new ways to improve their operations. This can be done by benchmarking corporate operations against those of other companies, conducting financial analyses of internal operations, and using trade information about best practices. This task involves great communication skills to convince fellow managers to implement improvements, as well as the ability to shift funding into those areas needing it in order to enhance their efficiencies.

- *Clean up the accounting and finance functions.* While most of the items in this list involve changes throughout the organization, the CFO must create an ongoing system of improvements within the accounting and finance functions—otherwise the managers of other departments will be less likely to listen to a CFO who cannot practice what he preaches. To do this, the CFO must focus on the following key goals:

— *Staff improvements.* All improvement begins with the staff. The CFO can enhance the knowledge base of this group with tightly focused training, cross-training between positions, and encouraging a high level of communication within the group.

— *Process improvements.* Concentrate on improving both the accuracy of information that is released by the department as well as the speed with which it is released. This can be accomplished to some extent through the use of increased data-processing automation, as well as through the installation of more streamlined access to data by key users. There should also be a focus on designing controls that interfere with core corporate processes to the minimum extent possible while still providing an adequate level of control. Also, information should be provided through simple data-mining tools that allow users to directly manipulate information for their own uses.

— *Organizational improvements.* Realign the staff into project-based teams that focus on a variety of process improvements. These teams are the primary implementers of process changes and should be tasked with the CFO's key improvement goals within the department.

- *Install shared services.* The CFO has considerable control over many administrative tasks, and so can encourage cost reductions in those areas through the use of shared services (where the same task is completed from a central location for multiple company locations). This can result in major cost savings, and is typically completed in coordination with the Chief Operating Officer (COO), who may be responsible for some of the areas being consolidated.

- *Examine outsourcing possibilities.* A company should focus the attention of its management team on its core activity. The CFO can assist this effort by determining which noncore areas are absorbing large amounts of management time and/or funding, and seeing if they can be prudently outsourced. Though certainly not all noncore areas can be handled in this fashion, the CFO can conduct periodic reviews to see how the attractiveness of this option changes over time.

- *Allocate resources.* In its simplest form, the CFO is expected to review the net present value of proposed capital expenditures and pass judgment on whether funding should be allowed. However, the CFO can take a much more proactive stance. For example, he can set aside a block of cash for more radical projects that would not normally make it past the rigorous capital expenditure review process, thereby adding high-risk, high-return projects to the company's portfolio of capital projects. Under this approach, the CFO becomes an internal venture capitalist and mentor to the teams undertaking these high-risk projects.

- *Encourage innovation.* The CFO can modify internal measurement, reporting, and budgetary systems to ensure that some original ideas are allowed to percolate through the company, potentially resulting in the implementation of high-return ideas. It is particularly important to take this approach in mature businesses that are most highly concerned with cost reductions, since an excessive focus on this area can drive out innovation.

Most of the responsibilities noted here rarely fall entirely within the capabilities of the CFO. Instead, he or she must coordinate activities with other department managers, including such specialized areas as the legal and human resources departments, to ensure that these target areas are addressed. This calls for a strong ability to work with other members of the company who are probably not directly supervised by the CFO.

OVERVIEW OF THE CHANGE MANAGEMENT PROCESS*

Becoming the business partner that CEOs demand means facilitating change that not only affects finance but also directly impacts the operating units. To accomplish this end, CFOs must become skilled in the following key management practices:

- *Develop and communicate a compelling finance agenda.*   Based on both his own perceptions of a company's situation and the recommendations of others, the CFO should create a list of bullet points for short-term and long-term accomplishments and memorize them so that he can repeat them to anyone at any time during the workday. Compressing the finance agenda in this manner is an excellent tool for communicating the CFO's work to others. Review the list regularly, and spread any changes to the list around the organization on a regular basis.

- *Build a commitment to change within the finance function.*   Besides talking about the agenda to everyone in the company, the CFO must reinforce the message with his behavior, which means demonstrating a full commitment of the time and money required to make the agenda a reality. This also means that the CFO must be seen personally working on the agenda for a significant proportion of his time. Building staff commitment also means listening to their views and letting this shape the CFO's opinion of what should be included in the agenda.

- *Change executive management practices.*   The director of strategic planning at a Fortune 500 company once pointed out that she spent 25% of her time determining the corporate direction, and 75% of her time convincing everyone in the organization that this was the right direction to follow. Though this sort of time distribution is extreme, the CFO must understand that many of the changes he advocates will impact other functional areas outside the accounting and finance functions, and so will require a hefty allocation of time to communicate the change vision. This requires regular meetings with managers throughout the organization, as well as strong listening skills to learn of any issues that may impact the implementation of the agenda. These meetings must be effective, requiring meeting agendas that are closely followed, have resultant minutes that identify who is responsible for the implementation of decisions reached, and a follow-up process to ensure that implementations are completed promptly.

- *Enlist the support of the CEO.*   Work with the CEO to develop his role in creating and implementing the agenda. This requires frequent meetings to go over the agenda. In order to obtain the CEO's full support, it is most useful to ask the CEO to assist in jointly solving problems arising from the agenda implementation effort.

- *Mobilize the organization.*   With the CEO firmly supporting the CFO's agenda, the rest of the organization must be mobilized to follow it as well. This calls for the creation of measurement and reward systems that are specifically designed to channel activities into the correct areas, plus visible and prolonged involvement by the senior management team and ongoing "communication events," such as general or team meetings, that describe the company's progress toward the completion of various items on the CFO's agenda.

---

*   Summarized with permission from pp. 7–23 of *Controllership, 2003 Cumulative Supplement* by Willson et al. (John Wiley & Sons, 2003).

- *Institutionalize continuous improvement.*   Once the agenda has been achieved, the CFO should continue to review and question the functions of all systems to see if better ways can be found to operate the company. If so, and changes are made, then he must alter the corporate measurement and reward system to ensure that the new initiatives are properly supported by the staff on an ongoing basis.

DIFFERENCES BETWEEN THE CONTROLLER AND CFO POSITIONS

Having already discussed what the CFO position *should* do, it is also worthwhile to point out those areas that the position should *not* become involved in. This issue is of particular concern to controllers who have been promoted to the CFO position, but who are having difficulty relinquishing their old chores in order to take up new ones. The result is that, with twice the workload, the newly promoted CFO does both the CFO and controller jobs poorly. Exhibit 1.1 describes the tasks that are most commonly assigned to the CFO and controller.

The exhibit indicates that there are a few areas in which the two roles may become jointly involved in the accounting area. However, their levels of involvement are entirely different. For example, when external auditors review the company's accounting records, the CFO is most likely to maintain relations with the audit partner, and deal with any reportable audit issues uncovered. The controller, however, is more likely to be directly involved with the auditors in presenting the accounting books, explaining the reasons for specific accounting transactions, and providing labor for more menial tasks that the auditors would otherwise have to perform themselves.

The same issue arises in other accounting areas, such as the issuance of management reports, financial statements, or Securities and Exchange Commission (SEC) reports. The controller creates the reports, but the CFO must review them prior to their release, since the CFO is the one who must explain their contents to readers. The CFO also needs the information in order to see how the presented information fits into any other analyses being created; for example, if the CFO is building a case for an increased emphasis on product quality, a management report on material scrap trends would fit directly into this analysis.

The CFO and controller also have different roles in the budgeting process. The controller usually manages the nuts and bolts of obtaining information from other departments and incorporating it into a master budget. Meanwhile, the CFO is examining the data presented by the various departments to see how they have changed from the past year, how revenues and expenses reflect any changes in the company's strategic direction, and the reasons for capital expenditure requests.

A primary part of the CFO's job is to conduct financial analyses on various topics anywhere in the company, as well as to drive operational improvements, at least partially based on the results of the financial analyses. The CFO decides on which analyses to create and which improvements to push, while also presenting this information and proselytizing in favor of operational improvements with other department managers. Conversely, the controller is more likely to create the analyses mandated by the CFO and to implement improvements within the accounting function. Thus, there is a dual role for the CFO and controller in these areas, but on different levels.

Control systems also attract the attention of both positions. The CFO is extremely interested in controls, since any control problems reflect poorly on his or her performance. The controller is also interested, partially to spot problems for the CFO's attention, but

Area of Responsibility	CFO	Controller
Accounting		
Assist with the annual audit	X	X
Pay accounts payable on time		X
Collect accounts receivable		X
Take discounts on accounts payable		X
Issue billings promptly		X
Calculate job costs		X
Complete bank reconciliations		X
Issue management reports	X	X
Issue financial statements	X	X
File information with the SEC	X	X
Maintain policies and procedures		X
Maintain the chart of accounts		X
Manage outsourced functions		X
Manage the accounting staff		X
Manage the budgeting process	X	X
Review capital requests	X	
Process payroll		X
Implement operational best practices	X	X
Provide financial analysis	X	X
Develop performance measurements	X	
Maintain performance measurements		X
Review control weaknesses	X	X
Finance		
Formulate financial strategy	X	
Formulate tax strategy	X	
Formulate risk management strategy	X	
Negotiate acquisitions	X	
Maintain banking relations	X	
Arrange for debt financing	X	
Conduct equity placements	X	
Invest funds	X	
Invest pension funds	X	
Issue credit to customers		X
Maintain insurance coverage	X	
Monitor cash balances		X
Maintain investor relations	X	

Exhibit 1.1   Position Responsibilities

mainly to ensure that the existing set of controls are functioning as planned. The CFO can be of particular assistance in setting up or changing controls impacting other departments, since the CFO is responsible for building relations between the accounting function and other areas of the company.

The finance area calls for minimal attention by the controller, who is only responsible for day-to-day activities in the areas of issuing credit and monitoring cash balances, which are simple activities that can easily be handled at the clerical level. In all other respects, financial activities involve a specialized knowledge of banking relationships, overall corporate strategy, and funds investment and procurement that falls directly within the CFO's area of expertise.

The main point to be gained from this comparison of the controller and CFO positions is that the controller is responsible primarily for the daily administration of accounting activities, whereas the CFO must cordon himself off from these activities and concentrate instead on the general design of control systems, strategic direction, and funding issues. Anyone who attempts to perform both jobs, except in a small company where a lack of funding usually calls for the merger of both positions, will be overwhelmed by the multitude of tasks to be completed. Realistically, someone who combines the positions will tend to concentrate on the daily activities of the controller and not attend to CFO tasks because of the perception that daily transactional activities *must* be completed, whereas strategic issues can always be addressed when there is spare time. Though this may work for a short interval, improper attention to the CFO part of the job will eventually lead to stagnation, inefficiency, and poor development of potential funding sources.

RELATIONSHIP OF THE CONTROLLER TO THE CFO*

In a larger company, there is a clear division of tasks between the controller and CFO. However, there is no clear delineation of these roles in a smaller company, because there is usually no CFO. As a company grows, it acquires a CFO, who must then wrestle away some of the controller's tasks that traditionally belong under the direct responsibility of the CFO. This transition can cause some conflict between the controller and CFO, which is discussed in this section. In addition, the historical promotion path for the controller has traditionally been through the CFO position; when that position is already occupied, and is likely to stay that way, there can be some difficulty with the controller. This section also discusses that issue.

In a small company, the controller usually handles all financial functions, such as setting up and maintaining lines of credit, cash management, determining credit limits for customers, dealing with investors, handling pension plan investments, and maintaining insurance policies. These are the traditional tasks of the CFO, and when a company grows to the point of needing one, the CFO will want to take them over from the controller. This can turn into a power struggle, though a short-lived one, because the controller always reports to the CFO and will not last long if there is no cooperation. Nonetheless, this is a difficult situation, for the controller has essentially taken a step down in the organizational structure upon the arrival of the CFO. For example, the CFO replaces the controller on the executive committee. If the controller is ambitious, this will probably lead to that person's departure in the near term. If the controller is good, this is a severe loss, for someone with a detailed knowledge of a company's processes and operating structure is extremely difficult to replace.

The controller should take a job elsewhere if he or she perceives that the person newly filling the CFO position is a roadblock to further advancement. However, this does not have to be a dead-end position. The controller should talk to the CFO about career prospects within the company and suggest that there may be other responsibilities that can replace those being switched to the CFO. For example, a small minority of controllers supervise the materials management department; this will become increasingly common as controllers realize that much of the paperwork they depend on originates in that area and that they can acquire better control over their processes by gaining experience in

*   Adapted with permission from pp. 18–19 of *Controllership* by Willson et al. (John Wiley & Sons, 2004).

this area. There may also be possibilities in the areas of administration, human resources, and computer services, which are sometimes run by controllers. The fact that there is a new CFO does not mean that a controller should immediately quit; there may be other opportunities involving related tasks that can shift the controller's career in other directions.

The CFO position is one with an extreme emphasis on money management, involving such tasks as determining the proper investment vehicles for excess cash, dealing with lenders regarding various kinds of debt, making presentations to financial analysts, and talking to investors. None of these tasks are ones that the controller is trained to perform. Instead, the traditional controller training involves handling transactions, creating financial statements, and examining processes. The requirements for the CFO position and the training for the CFO position are so different that it seems strange for the controller to be expected to advance to the CFO position, and yet that is a common expectation among accountants, which regularly causes problems between the controller and CFO when a CFO is initially hired.

SUMMARY

It may have become apparent in this chapter that the key attributes of the CFO do not lie in the area of accounting competency. If a CEO wanted skills in that area, he would hire a great controller and never fill the CFO position. Instead, the key CFO attributes are that person's ability to find innovative ways to solve problems, and then to use change management skills to implement them. By focusing on these key areas, the CFO brings the greatest positive impact to overall corporate value.

In addition, the CFO must concentrate a great deal of his time on the formulation and implementation of appropriate strategies in the areas of accounting, taxation, and (if responsible for this area) information technology. These issues are addressed in Chapter 2, Financial Strategy; Chapter 3, Tax Strategy; and Chapter 4, Information Technology Strategy.

FINANCIAL STRATEGY

This book is built around the concepts of financial management, analysis, and accounting, as well as the procurement of funding. However, the true test of the CFO is in the quality of decisions made on topics that impact a company's finances. For the other topics, the CFO can hire quality controllers and financial analysts who can take care of matters quite nicely from an operational perspective. But in the area of making financial strategy decisions, the buck stops at the CFO's desk. In this chapter, we will review a number of common decision areas that a CFO is likely to face. They are generally grouped in the order in which the topics can be found on the balance sheet and then the income statement. The chapter finishes with the discussion of throughput analysis, and how it can change your way of thinking about financial decisions.

CASH

Reducing Foreign Currency Exposure. A CFO whose company engages in international trade must be concerned about potential changes in the value of its trading partners' currencies. For example, if a company sells products to a French company and receives payment after the euro loses value, then the company absorbs the reduction in value of the euro, creating a loss. Any one or a combination of the following approaches may be used to avoid incurring such a loss:

- If selling to a foreign customer, avoid long customer payment terms. If long terms are necessary in order to secure a sale, then offset the potential currency risk by charging interest on overdue payments, or encourage early payments with a discount.

- If buying from a foreign supplier, make purchases on the longest possible credit terms in order to pay later with less expensive funds.

- If buying from a foreign supplier, avoid advance payments to it. By waiting to make the payment, the company can pay in potentially less expensive currency.

- If running an operation in a foreign location, avoid storing excess cash there; instead, invest the funds in stronger currencies.

- If running multiple operations in many foreign locations, hedge the risk of exchange loss on one transaction by creating offsetting transactions in the opposite direction. For example, if one transaction calls for the conversion of euros to dollars in 90 days, then create another transaction, possibly with a different subsidiary, that calls for the conversion of roughly the same amount of dollars to euros in about the same time frame.

- In general, hedge potential exposure by purchasing a forward exchange contract.

If foreign currency transaction volumes are small, the potential risk of loss will be correspondingly small, and so is not worth much review by the CFO. However, the CFO should certainly review these issues if large foreign contracts are contemplated. If a company engages in substantial foreign trade, then reducing foreign currency exposure is so large an issue that the CFO should consider creating a hedging department that does nothing but track and mitigate this issue.

Decision to Change a Banking Relationship.   A good banking relationship is extremely important to the CFO. It should involve excellent responsiveness by all departments of the bank, minimal transaction-processing errors, moderate fees, reasonable levels of asset collateralization on loans, on-line access to transactional data, and the ability to process more advanced transactions, such as letters of credit. Larger companies with massive transaction volumes and lending needs are the most likely to find all of these needs fulfilled. However, smaller entities will not represent enough business to a bank to warrant this level of service, and so will most likely suffer in the areas of customer service and advantageous loan terms.

Of particular concern to the CFO of an expanding business is growing beyond the capabilities of a small local bank that it may have begun doing business with when it first started. Smaller banks may offer reasonable attentiveness, but are most unlikely to offer on-line transaction processing or any form of international transaction support.

Given these issues, there are several key factors in deciding when to change a banking relationship. The first is a simple lack of responsiveness by the bank, which seems most common with large banks that service thousands of business customers—one gets lost in the shuffle. This is primarily a problem when special transactions are needed that require a bank officer, such as letters of credit or wire transfers. If no one picks up the phone or returns a call within a reasonable time frame, and these actions result in significant business problems, then the bank must go. A second reason is outgrowing the capabilities of the bank, as noted above. One should be certain that additional capabilities are truly needed before switching banks for this reason, given the difficulty of severing a banking relationship (see below). The third and least justifiable reason for changing banks is the cost of the relationship. When compared to the cost of other business expenses, banking fees are comparatively inexpensive, and so should only be a reason to sever a banking relationship when combined with some other factor, such as poor service.

A CFO may have multiple reasons for switching to a different bank, but must bear in mind the extreme difficulty of stopping all banking transactions with one bank and starting them up with another. The following list highlights the number of changes required to switch banks:

- Adopt a corporate resolution to switch banks.
- Open up accounts at the new bank.
- Order check stock for the new accounts.
- Contact suppliers who take direct deductions from the old accounts and have them switch to the new accounts.
- Create bank reconciliations for the old accounts until all checks have cleared.
- Wire funds from the old accounts to the new accounts.
- Close the old accounts.
- Shred all remaining old check stock.
- Have auditors review the old accounts as well as the new ones at year-end.

- Arrange for new loan agreements with the new bank.
- Draw down new loans and pay off old loans.
- Cancel old loans.

Clearly, the number of steps required to shift a banking relationship should give the CFO pause before proceeding. It is much easier to leave well enough alone unless there are significant factors favoring a change.

INVESTMENTS

Maximizing Return on Assets.   A CFO can gain an excellent understanding of a company's efficiency through close attention to the return on assets (ROA) measurement. Since this measure is also tracked by analysts and investors, it is wise to understand its components, how they can be manipulated to enhance the ROA, and how these changes should be made in light of overall company strategy.

As shown in Exhibit 2.1, the ROA measure is comprised of margins (on the left side of the exhibit) and asset turnover (on the right side of the exhibit). Multiplying the earnings percentage by asset turnover yields the return on assets. Many companies have a long tradition of squeezing every possible cost out of their operations, which certainly addresses the first half of the ROA equation. However, asset turnover is either ignored or given a much lower priority. The CFO should investigate this latter portion of the calculation to see what asset reductions, both in the areas of working capital and fixed assets, can be achieved in order to achieve a higher ROA.

Working capital reduction techniques are addressed in the "Working Capital" section later in this chapter. Fixed asset reductions can be achieved through a well-managed capital budgeting process (see Chapter 10, Capital Budgeting), as well as through constant investigation and disposal of potentially unused assets and the investigation of outsourcing in order to shift expensive facility and equipment costs to suppliers.

When investigating ROA improvement opportunities, the CFO should be aware that an excessive degree of cost and asset reduction can *hurt* a company by such means as reducing the quality of its products, giving it minimal excess production capacity to use during high-volume periods, and reducing the size of its research and development activities. Thus, improving ROA should not be taken to extremes, though it certainly requires continuing attention.

Bond Refunding Decision.   A company can buy bonds back from investors prior to their due dates, but only if there is a call provision on the bond or if it was originally issued as a serial bond. The call provision gives the company the right to buy the bond back on a specific series of dates over the life of the bond, while the serial bond approach sets different maturity dates on sets of bonds within a total bond offering. Thus, the call provision gives a company the option to refund bonds, whereas the serialization feature requires the company to refund them. In either instance, the presence of these refunding features on a bond will decrease its value, resulting in a higher effective interest rate that the company must pay.

In this instance, the CFO must make a decision *in advance* of a bond offering to add refunding features to the bonds. If there is no reasonable prospect of having funds available to pay off the bonds early, and if the interest rate being paid appears reasonable, then there is no particular need for the refunding features. However, if this is not the case, the CFO would be well advised to add a call provision, since this option gives

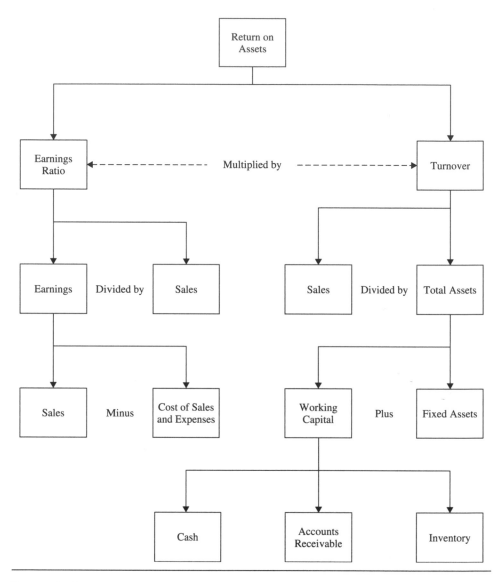

EXHIBIT 2.1   COMPONENTS OF THE RETURN ON ASSETS

the firm the ability to refund the bonds without necessarily being required to do so. A serialization feature is less useful, since it incorporates a direct requirement to make cash payments at regular intervals to refund specific bonds, whereas the CFO may have better uses for these funds.

If the CFO is concerned that the presence of either type of call feature will result in a more expensive interest rate, then she can add other features to the bonds, such as convertibility or warrants, that will increase the value of the bonds to investors, thereby keeping the effective interest rate from being increased.

WORKING CAPITAL

Working Capital Reduction Methodology.   The typical CFO is constantly in search of a ready source of inexpensive funding for the company. One of the best sources is working capital, which is accounts receivable plus inventory, minus accounts payable. These are the "float" funds required to keep the business operating from day to day. By reducing the amount of accounts receivable and inventory or extending the payment terms on accounts payable, the CFO has access to a ready source of cash. Some of the actions one can take to access these funds are:

ACCOUNTS RECEIVABLE

- *Automate collection record keeping.*   Tracking of collection calls, including who was reached, when the call occurred, and what was promised, is a time-consuming chore that is highly subject to error. By obtaining a computerized database that is linked to a company's accounts receivable records, the collections staff can greatly increase its collection efficiency.

- *Bill recurring invoices early.*   If a customer subscribes to a long-term service or maintenance contract, then it can be billed slightly earlier in the hopes of receiving payment sooner.

- *Change the terms of commission payments.*   The sales staff should be paid commissions based on cash received from customers rather than on sales made to them. By doing so, the sales staff has a vested interest in finding creditworthy customers and in collecting from them.

- *Encourage ACH payments.*   If a customer has a long-term relationship with the company, request that it set up Automated Clearing House (ACH) payments so that payments are wired directly into the company's bank account, thereby avoiding any mail float.

- *Encourage credit card payments.*   If billings are relatively small, note on the invoices that the company accepts a variety of credit card payments so that customers will be encouraged to use this approach to accelerate cash flow.

- *Factor accounts receivable.*   Arrange with a lender to pay the company at the time of billing, using accounts receivable as collateral.

- *Grant early payment discounts.*   Offer discounts to customers if they pay within a few days of receiving the invoice.

- *Install lockboxes.*   Set up bank lockboxes near customer sites, and have them mail their payments to the lockboxes. By doing so, one can greatly reduce the mail float associated with the payments.

- *Stratify collections.*   Stratify accounts receivable by size and assign the bulk of the collection staff's time to the largest items so that the full force of the collections department is brought to bear on those items yielding the largest amount of cash.

- *Tighten credit.*   Closely review the payment histories of existing customers and run more intensive checks on new customers, thereby cutting back on the amount of bad debt.

INVENTORY

- *Consolidate storage locations.*   If there are many warehouses, then the company is probably storing the same inventory items in multiple locations. By consolidating storage locations, some of this duplication can be eliminated.

- *Install a materials planning system.*   A material requirements planning system (MRP) will allow a company to determine exactly what material it needs, and by what date. These systems typically result in massive drops in inventory levels and the elimination of overpurchases.

- *Install just-in-time (JIT) manufacturing techniques.*   There are many manufacturing practices that comprise the general JIT concept, such as rapid setup times, cell-based manufacturing, and minimal production runs. These techniques require minimal work-in-process (WIP) inventory, and also generate far less scrap.

- *Maintain accurate bills of material.*   It is impossible to create a working MRP or JIT system without knowing exactly what parts are required to manufacture a product. Consequently, a bill of material accuracy rate of at least 98% is the foundation for other initiatives that will greatly reduce inventory levels.

- *Return parts to suppliers.*   If parts are not needed, return them to suppliers for cash or credit.

- *Stock fewer finished goods.*   The distribution of product sales follows a bell curve, where the bulk of all sales are concentrated into only a few inventory items. The CFO should review the inventory items that rarely sell to see if they should be stocked at all.

- *Store subassemblies rather than finished goods.*   Inventory subassemblies can potentially be configured into a multitude of finished goods, whereas a finished good must be sold "as is." Consequently, a strategy to keep inventory at the subassembly level until the last possible moment will result in fewer stock-keeping units (SKUs), and therefore a smaller inventory investment.

ACCOUNTS PAYABLE

- *Avoid prepayments.*   If a supplier insists that the company make prepayments on various goods or services, try to reduce the amount of the prepayments or spread out the payment intervals, thereby reducing the up-front cash commitment.

- *Draw checks on remote banks.*   One can set up an account at a bank in a remote location and pay checks from that account. By doing so, checks will take slightly longer to clear, allowing the company to have use of its cash for one or two additional days.

- *Extend payments a reasonable amount.*   Suppliers typically do not start collection efforts on an overdue invoice until a number of days have passed beyond the invoice due date. A company can take advantage of this grace period by judiciously extending payment dates for a few additional days. However, this strategy can result in lower reported credit levels by credit reporting agencies, and certainly will not endear the company to its suppliers.

- *Negotiate longer payment terms.*   It may be possible to negotiate longer payment terms with suppliers, though this may involve offsetting terms, such as larger order commitments or higher product prices.

- *Pay with a charge card to extend payments.*   Many suppliers allow their invoices to be paid with credit cards. By doing so on the payment due date and then waiting to pay the credit card bill until the cycle closing date for the credit card, payment terms can be substantially extended.

Though a CFO could simply implement the entire checklist to break free a large amount of cash, there are a number of issues to be considered before doing so. For example, tightening credit may run counter to an overall corporate strategy to accept higher bad debt losses in exchange for greater sales to high-risk customers. Similarly, unilaterally extending payment terms to a key supplier can damage the operating relationship between the business partners, perhaps resulting in higher prices charged by the supplier or a lower shipment priority. As another example, the decision to stock fewer finished goods can damage customer service, especially when a company has built its reputation on having a wide range of inventory items available for customers at all times. Further, a company in a low-margin business may be unable to factor its receivables or accept credit card payments, because the resulting credit fees will eat into their margins too much. Thus, the CFO must implement the preceding suggestions only after due consideration of their impact on overall company strategy.

The inventory reduction decision is covered in more detail in the next section.

INVENTORY: INVENTORY REDUCTION DECISION

A truly cost-conscious CFO who wants to also increase cash flow will militantly demand continual reductions in inventory by any means possible, since this can potentially free up a considerable quantity of cash, thereby eliminating the expenses associated with inventory carrying costs. However, there are other issues to consider before running rampant with continual inventory reductions.

First, one must consider the classes of inventory involved, and only target those inventory types that will not have an adverse affect on other company operations. For example, a reduction in finished goods inventory can severely impact sales, since customers may only purchase from stock, not wanting to wait for something to be ordered or produced. This is particularly important for service-intensive retail businesses, such as those that claim to have *all* parts on hand, *all* the time. Costs may also go up in this situation if lower stocks are kept on hand, because the company may be forced to pay overnight shipping fees to obtain needed stock for customer orders. However, finished goods inventory levels can still be reduced by tracking usage trends by product and reducing safety stock levels for those items that show declining sales trends.

Work-in-process inventory can be an enormous working capital burden for companies having inefficient manufacturing processes, but inventory reductions can still wreak havoc in this area unless managed properly. Large WIP balances in front of bottleneck operations may be mandatory, since the cost of bottleneck production may be higher than the cost of the buffering inventory (see the throughput discussion at the end of this chapter). Also, in the absence of a proper shop floor production system, large quantities of WIP may be the only way to run the manufacturing process with any semblance of order. Consequently, it is better to first review the manufacturing operations in detail to see where there are legitimate excessive WIP quantities, and then install manufacturing systems, such as manufacturing resources planning (MRP II) or JIT systems that can be used to gradually reduce WIP levels as the manufacturing process becomes more highly structured and easier to manage. The

CFO should also be aware that old piles of WIP frequently disguise large proportions of obsolete or out-of-specification parts that no one wants to discard. Consequently, an inventory write-down is a common result of reductions in the WIP inventory area.

Raw materials is one of the best areas in which to implement an inventory reduction. This is where the full force of an MRP II or JIT implementation is felt, clearly exposing any inventory items that are not currently required for planned production needs. However, this analysis may reveal a number of raw material items that are obsolete and therefore have minimal or reduced value, resulting in a significant write-down in the inventory valuation. Alternatively, the CFO may be forced to accept significant restocking fees to convince a supplier to take back unwanted goods. It may be useful to have the purchasing staff create a list of which unused products can be returned to suppliers, as well as the restocking fees that will be charged, so the CFO can have a general idea of the costs involved with this form of inventory reduction.

There are several issues for the CFO to be aware of when attempting to reduce inventories. First, as just noted, the odds of successfully reducing inventory vary by inventory type. Second, reducing inventory without proper consideration of the net impact on other parts of the business, such as in reduced customer service, may actually increase costs. Third, there is a limit to how much inventory can be squeezed out of a company without an offsetting investment in manufacturing planning systems whose efficiencies will help drive the inventory reduction. Thus, inventory reduction is not an easy decision; cutbacks require careful consideration of offsetting costs, as well as their impact on other parts of the business.

FIXED ASSETS: LEASE VERSUS BUY DECISION

In a leasing situation, the company pays a lessor for the use of equipment that is owned by the lessor. Under the terms of this arrangement, the company pays a monthly fee, while the lessor records the asset on its books and takes the associated depreciation expense, while also undertaking to pay all property taxes and maintenance fees. The lessor typically takes back the asset at the end of the lease term, unless the company wishes to pay a fee at the end of the agreement period to buy the residual value of the asset and then record it on the company's books as an asset.

A leasing arrangement tends to be rather expensive for the lessee, since it is paying for the interest cost, profit, taxes, maintenance, and decline in value of the asset. However, it would have had to pay for all these costs except the lessor's profit and the interest cost if it had bought the asset, so this can be an appealing option, especially for the use of those assets that tend to degrade quickly in value or usability, and which would therefore need to be replaced at the end of the leasing period anyway.

The cost of a lease tends to be high, since the number of variables included in the lease calculation (e.g., down payment, interest rate, asset residual value, and trade-in value) makes it very difficult for the lessor to determine the true cost of what it is obtaining. Consequently, when using leasing as the financing option of choice, a CFO must be extremely careful to review the individual costs that roll up into the total lease cost, probably using a net present value analysis to ensure that the overall expenditure is reasonable (see Chapter 10, Capital Budgeting).

PAYABLES

EARLY PAYMENT DISCOUNT DECISION.   Some suppliers note on their invoices that a discount will be granted to the customer if it pays the invoice early. An example of such an offer is "2/10 N/30," which stands for "take 2% off the price if you pay within 10 days, or pay the full amount in 30 days." The CFO should know how to calculate the savings to be gained from such offers. The basic calculation is:

$$\frac{\text{Discount Lost}}{\begin{array}{c}\text{Dollar Proceeds Useable by}\\ \text{Not Taking Discount}\end{array}} \times \frac{360}{\begin{array}{c}\text{Number of Days Can Use Money}\\ \text{by Not Taking Discount}\end{array}}$$

For example, the Columbia Rafting Company has an opportunity to take a 1% discount on an invoice for a new raft if it makes the payment in 10 days. The invoice is for $12,000, and is normally payable in 30 days. The calculation is:

$$\frac{\$120}{\$11,880} \times \frac{360}{20}$$

$$1.01\% \times 18 = 8.2\% \text{ Interest Rate on the Proffered Discount}$$

In the example, the 18.2% interest rate on the early payment discount probably makes it an attractive deal to the CFO. However, one should consider the availability of cash before taking such an offer. For example, what if there are no funds available, or if the corporate line of credit cannot be extended to make the early payment? Even if the cash is available, but there is a risk of a cash shortfall in the near term, the CFO may still be unable to take such an offer. In short, no matter how attractive the offer may be, near-term cash shortages can interfere with taking an early payment discount.

PAYMENT FACTORY DECISION.   In a typical accounts payable environment, a company allows its subsidiaries to manage their own payables processes, payments, and banking relationships. The results are higher transaction costs and banking fees, since each location uses its own staff and has little transaction volume with which to negotiate reduced banking fees.

The CFO should be aware of an improvement on this situation, which is the payment factory. It is a centralized payables and payment processing center, and is essentially a subset of an enterprise resources planning (ERP) system, specifically targeted at payables. It features complex software with many interfaces, since it must handle incoming payment information in many data formats, workflow management of payment approvals, a rules engine to determine the lowest-cost method of payment, and links to multiple banking systems.

Key payment factory benefits include a stronger negotiating position with the company's fewer remaining banks, better visibility into funding needs and liquidity management, and improved control over payment timing.

The payment factory is especially effective when the payables systems of multinational subsidiaries are centralized, as cross-border banking fees can be significantly reduced. For example, it can automatically offset payments due between company subsidiaries, which results in smaller cash transfers and similarly reduced foreign exchange charges, wiring costs, and lifting fees (a fee charged by the bank receiving a payment), while also routing payments through in-country accounts to avoid these international fees.

There are several problems with payment factories—the seven-figure cost of the software, gaining the cooperation of the various subsidiaries who will no longer have direct control over their payment systems, and more centralized banking relationships.

It is also possible to emulate a payment factory in a low-budget situation. First, centralize all accounts payable operations. Second, minimize the number of banking relationships. Third, try outsourcing the foreign exchange operations with one of the remaining banks.

SPEND MANAGEMENT DECISION.   Spend management systems allow a company to monitor its expenditures and potentially save a great deal of money through improved purchasing. Using these systems, companies can analyze their expenditures in a number of ways—by commodity, supplier, business unit, and so on. They then summarize this information for centralized procurement negotiations with suppliers, thereby reducing costs. Spend management suppliers usually add contract management capabilities and even set up electronic supplier catalogs, so that users can conduct on-line ordering with a predefined set of suppliers. They also impose better controls over spending, since their systems require access passwords, approval cycles, contract compliance alerts, and supplier performance measurements.

However, these systems are extremely expensive to install and maintain—costs start at $1 million and rapidly increase from there. Some suggestions for creating a low-budget spend management solution are:

- *Identify unauthorized purchases with exception reports.*   The reason for centralizing procurement contracts is to negotiate lower prices in exchange for higher purchasing volumes, so anyone purchasing from an unauthorized supplier is reducing a company's ability to rein in its costs. To identify these people, create a table of approved suppliers and match it against the vendor ledger for each period, yielding a report that lists how much was spent with various unauthorized suppliers. It is also useful to record in an empty purchasing or payables field the name of the requisitioning person, who can then be tracked down and admonished for incorrect purchasing practices.

- *Impose a penalty system.*   People resist centralization, especially when it involves eliminating their favorite suppliers. Though penalties may be considered a coercive approach to solving the problem, the imposition of a graduated penalty scale will rapidly eliminate unauthorized spending. For example, a department may incur a $100 penalty for one unauthorized expenditure, $1,000 for the next, and $10,000 for the next.

- *Restrict procurement cards to specific suppliers.*   If there is a procurement card system in place, it may be possible to restrict purchases to specific suppliers, thereby achieving centralized purchasing without any central oversight of the process. If there is no procurement card system, then consider obtaining a credit card from each designated supplier, and restrict purchases to those cards.

- *Require officer-level approval of all contracts.*   Department and division managers love to retain control over supplier relationships by negotiating their own deals with local suppliers. By enforcing a corporatewide policy that all purchasing contracts be countersigned by a corporate officer, contract copies can be collected in one place for easier examination by a central purchasing staff.

- *Add granularity to the chart of accounts.* To gain a better knowledge of costs, consider altering the chart of accounts to subdivide expenses by individual department, and then go a step further by adding subcodes that track costs at an additional level of detail. For example, if the existing account code is 5020 for the travel expense account, and the revised code is 5020-01 to track travel costs for just the engineering department, then consider adding a set of subcodes, such as 5020-01-XX, to track more detailed expenditures within the travel category, such as airfare (code 5020-01-01), hotels (code 5020-01-02), and rental cars (code 5020-01-03). This approach requires careful definition of spending categories and can result in data entry errors if there are too many subcategories of expenses. Also, it will not be of much use if reports cannot be created to properly interpret and present this extra level of expense information.

These suggestions will not result in a seamless in-house spend management system. However, they will yield somewhat greater control over expenses and more visibility into the nature of a company's expenditures.

DEBT

Decision to Acquire More Debt. A CFO should regularly review the need to acquire more debt as part of an overall funding strategy that can include other forms of financing, such as reducing working capital requirements or conducting an equity offering. The following factors should be considered as part of the debt decision:

- *Existing loan covenants.* A legal agreement for an existing loan may allow no further debt until the current debt is either paid off or reduced to a specific level. Covenants may also limit the debt/equity ratio (see next item), making it impossible to obtain more debt without first adding equity.
- *Current debt level in relation to equity.* Lenders will look askance at additional requests for debt if there is not a counterbalancing amount of equity. A company with a high debt/equity ratio is likely to be told to find more equity before being granted additional debt.
- *Debt due dates.* Try not to obtain new debt having a due date identical to that of existing debt, so there will be less risk of having to refinance large amounts of debt at the same time.
- *Business cycle.* Some businesses have natural revenue peaks and valleys that will greatly reduce their ability to pay loans during slow periods. This type of business needs a higher proportion of equity in order to avoid the risk of loan defaults.
- *Product cycles.* If a company's product lines are aging and facing cancellation, then it may have little ability to pay off loans that come due after the projected termination date of the products.
- *Net operating loss (NOL) carryforwards.* If a business has large NOLs that it can use to offset its income, it will have no immediate use for the tax deductibility of interest, though using debt can still delay the use of NOLs into later years.
- *Need for a borrowing reserve.* The CFO should always plan to have more debt available through a line of credit than is actually needed, so unforeseen cash requirements can be easily handled.

Realistically, the CFO will be stymied more by the first two bullet points than the remaining ones. If there is too much debt already on the balance sheet, or if legal provisions of existing loans are too restrictive, there will be no way to obtain more debt in the short term. The remaining bullet points are more advisory in nature, where the CFO should take them into account, but in reality may have to take any deal offered if obtaining debt in the short term is a critical priority.

Refinancing Decision.   The CFO should regularly review the cost of all types of company debt to see if it is too expensive and therefore worthy of refinancing. Though this may seem like a simple matter, there are several issues to take into consideration. First, the company may have a very tight relationship with a single lender who has extended all of the company's debt to it—if so, paying off the most expensive loan in the debt portfolio will not endear this critical lender to the company. Under this scenario, it may not even be possible to refinance a single loan within the portfolio, because the lender has cross-collateralized all of the company's assets on the various loan documents. Because no collateral is available to secure a loan with a different lender, the company can only refinance the debt by shifting the entire loan package to a new lender.

Another consideration is that the debt the CFO wishes to replace has a fixed interest rate, but the least expensive replacement debt carries a variable interest rate. The decision to switch from the security of a fixed rate to a situation where the rate could increase substantially should be subject to considerable debate. The CFO can reduce the risk of a rapid rate increase by negotiating an annual cap on any rate increases during the term of the new loan. The decision to adopt a variable loan is frequently driven by the expected loan payoff date, such that maximum interest rate increases would still not exceed the current fixed loan rate by the time the loan should be paid off. For example, The International Pickle Company has a long-term loan that carries a 10% interest rate. The CFO expects to pay off this loan in five years. In the meantime, he has been offered a 6% variable-rate loan with an annual rate cap increase of 1.5% that would not take effect until the end of each year. He calculates that, even if interest rates skyrocketed over the next five years, the new loan would still be less expensive than the existing loan until the end of the fourth year of the loan, and agrees to refinance the debt.

Convertible Security Issuance Decision.   A convertible security is a bond that can be converted into common stock. The common stock price at which the bond can be converted is based on the conversion ratio, which is the ratio of the number of shares that can be purchased with each bond. For example, if a $1,000 bond has a conversion ratio of 10, then it can be converted into ten shares, which translates into a share price of $100. This does not mean that the holder of a bond will immediately convert to shares, however—that will only happen when the market price of the stock equals or exceeds the amount indicated by the conversion ratio. If the market price of the common stock exceeds the price indicated by the conversion ratio, the price of the bond will also rise, since its value, based on its convertibility, is now greater than its price based on the stream of future interest payments from the company in payment for the bond.

A convertible security is worthy of much attention by the CFO if a company does not want to pay back the underlying principal on its bonds. This is most common in a high-growth situation where all cash will be needed for the foreseeable future. Also, by converting debt over to equity, a company can improve its debt/equity ratio, which will improve relations with lenders, while also eliminating the need to pay interest on the bonds that no longer exist. Further, the CFO can make a debt offering look more attractive to investors by giving them some upside potential if the common stock subsequently increases in value, which should result in a reduction in the interest rate on the debt. This is particularly important if market conditions would otherwise necessitate a high interest rate. Finally, a company can convert a group of existing debt holders into a group of shareholders, which means that it has a (presumably) friendly and long-term group of investors now holding its stock. The only downsides of this approach are that the increased number of shares will reduce the earnings per share, and that control will be spread over a larger group of investors, which may weaken the stake of a majority owner.

Disclosure Reporting Decision.   An established company with a mature business model discloses a different set of performance metrics to investors and analysts than does a newer company that is on a more rapid growth path. The CFO must decide at what point the types of disclosures change to match the current or expected business model. For example, a mature company should emphasize the disclosure of such basic financial performance information as gross and net margins and cash flow, as well as such basic operational issues as customer retention, capacity utilization, and revenue per employee. Conversely, a company on a rapid growth path should place more emphasis in its disclosures on the level of expenditures for R&D and marketing, as well as sales from new products, patents granted, and share of market.

EQUITY

Debt versus Equity Funding Decision.   Debt is almost always a less expensive source of funding than equity, because investors expect significant returns on their investments, while the interest cost of debt is tax-deductible, rendering debt less expensive. Furthermore, during the usual periods of inflation, a company pays back its debt with less expensive dollars, making this an even less expensive source of funding. However, there are several other issues to consider when determining whether to pursue debt or equity as the next source of funding.

The first issue is that the senior management team or the company owners may be uncomfortable with the prospect of obtaining more debt, no matter how available or inexpensive it may be. This happens most frequently in privately owned firms with later-generation owners who are most concerned with maintaining their long-term source of income. It is less common with entrepreneurs who are willing to take more risks, or with public companies where the CFO is allowed to balance the risk of debt default with the reduced cost of using more debt than equity.

Even if the owners and managers are willing to obtain more debt, the lenders may not be willing to do so. This problem arises when a company has poor or highly variable cash flows, is already highly leveraged, or has a history of either not paying off its debts in a timely manner or of violating its loan covenants. If so, the company will probably have to turn to an equity offering with incentive clauses (see the next section).

Even if lenders are ready and willing to issue more debt, there may be no collateral left on the balance sheet to assuage their levels of anxiety about repayment risk. If so, the company may be forced to accept a high interest rate, an early payoff date, highly restrictive covenants, or allow the lender to take a junior position on any corporate assets. If these options do not work for the lender, then the company will once again be forced to shift to an equity offering.

It is evident from this discussion that debt is generally the preferred source of funding, with the CFO only seriously considering the procurement of equity when it is either impractical to obtain more debt or if it would put the company at serious risk of defaulting on its loans.

Type of Equity Offering Decision.   The CFO can recommend the issuance of two types of equity—common or preferred stock. The terms of common stock are typically laid down in the articles of incorporation, and include specific terms required by the state in which the company is incorporated. The CFO usually recommends a common stock offering only when several circumstances apply. First, the existing shareholders must not be concerned about a dilution in their ownership interests through this new issuance (unless the new shares are being sold to them, in which case ownership percentages will only change among the existing shareholders). This is a major concern in cases where the bulk of a company's stock is owned by a small number of individuals.

The second circumstance is that the company's lenders are becoming uncomfortable with a high level of debt, and wish to balance it with more equity. This pressure may also come from the Board of Directors, which may not want to run the risk of default if there are large loans outstanding.

The CFO generally recommends a common stock issuance only when all other sources of less expensive funds have been exhausted, because shareholders typically have a much higher expectation of return on investment than is the case for other fund providers.

A variation on a common stock offering is preferred stock. This equity instrument can come in a variety of flavors, including a fixed or variable interest rate that may or may not be cumulative, a conversion feature to common stock, the ability to be called by the company at any time or at fixed intervals—the range of possible features is endless. The exact terms of a preferred stock issuance should be tailored to the perceived needs of the pool of potential investors. For example, if a company's stock has a history of being highly variable, investors may want the option to convert it to common stock in order to take advantage of a possible increase in the stock price at a later date.

Onerous terms can also be added to a preferred stock issuance in order to ensure that investors will accept the offering at an acceptable price. For example, its terms can state that, in the event of a company sale, the preferred shareholders will receive 100% of their investment back before common shareholders receive anything. In order to protect their rights in this regard, the preferred shareholders may also have an override vote on any contemplated mergers, acquisitions, or significant asset sales. These additional terms may seem onerous, but they can ensure a high price for the stock. In the meanwhile, avoiding the need for any collateral improves the debt/equity ratio to the point where lenders may be willing to issue additional credit.

For example, the Xtreme Running Shoe Company's CFO is attempting to obtain additional debt financing, but the company's lenders are concerned about the debt/equity ratio and insist on an additional equity infusion prior to granting any additional loans. Unfortunately, it is also a bear market, and the company's valuation has been driven lower than normal, so any sale of common stock would result in an excessive degree of dilution for the existing shareholders in relation to the amount of equity obtained. Accordingly, the CFO recommends issuing a special class of preferred stock, containing an above-market interest rate on annual dividend payments, as well as a guaranteed conversion at the investors' option to common stock at a favorable rate in five years' time. Thus, potential investors are willing to pay more for the stock, which gives them short-term dividend income, plus a potential equity kicker in the medium term.

Dividend Issuance Decision.   The CFO plays a significant role in convincing the Board of Directors to issue dividends, and the amount paid out per share. The decision to issue dividends requires consideration of many issues. First, one must consider that investors prefer to see a *steady and reliable* stream of dividends. Thus, a well-meaning initial dividend issuance could spark calls from investors who expect to keep seeing it. If so, the Board may feel obligated to continue the payments, even if the company needs the money for other purposes.

Another issue is the impact of loan restrictions on dividends. Many lenders allow no dividends at all as part of their loan requirements, or at least no increase in the preexisting level of dividends. Their reasoning is obvious, since a company might otherwise take out a loan to pay their shareholders, thereby leaving fewer assets for the lender to attach in the event of a bankruptcy. Thus, the lending situation has a major impact on the decision to issue dividends, and typically precludes an issuance when a company's debt load is so heavy that lenders would begin to restrict dividends in any event.

A related problem with dividends is that dividend payments represent a reduction of retained earnings. When dividends are paid, equity is reduced, which will create a higher debt to equity ratio. If a lender has imposed a maximum debt/equity ratio as part of a loan agreement, then it is possible that a dividend issuance will place the company in a state of noncompliance with its loan covenants.

Another consideration regarding the dividend issuance decision is the company's ability to obtain debt. If it has ready access to credit markets, then corporate management will be more likely to issue dividends, since the company is reasonably assured of obtaining replacement funding. Conversely, if credit sources are scarce, a company will be more inclined to hoard its cash in order to provide a buffer for any future financial problems; this leaves less cash available for a dividend.

A key concern is cash flow. If a company has an extremely unstable cash flow, perhaps shifting from cash drains during some months to major inflows during others, or tied to a major short-term project, then a potentially long-term obligation such as a dividend issuance is a bad idea. Though there may appear to be enough cash on hand to make the payment, the company may need the cash in the short term.

From the taxation perspective, dividends are not deductible as an expense, as opposed to interest payments on debt. This makes equity a more expensive form of funding than debt by the amount of a corporation's incremental tax rate.

A reason in favor of issuing dividends is that the Internal Revenue Service (IRS) will penalize a company for accumulating an excessive amount of earnings. The IRS considers accumulated earnings of less than $150,000 to be sufficient for the working needs of service businesses, such as accounting, engineering, architecture, and consulting firms. It considers accumulations of anything under $250,000 to be sufficient for most other types of businesses. A company can argue that it needs a substantially larger amount of accumulated earnings if it can prove that it has specific, definite, and feasible plans that will require the use of the funds within the business. Another valid argument is that a company needs a sufficient amount of accumulated earnings to buy back the company's stock that is held by a deceased shareholder's estate. If these conditions are not apparent, then the IRS will declare the accumulated earnings to be taxable at a rate of 39.6%. The severity of this tax is designed to encourage organizations to issue dividends on a regular basis to their shareholders, so that the IRS can tax the shareholders for this form of income.

Perhaps the chief reason for avoiding a dividend is a high-growth situation where a company must pour all available funds into its working capital in order to sustain its rate of growth in new customer orders. In such cases, the rapidly increasing value of the firm will be reflected in an increased stock price that should more than compensate investors for any lost dividends. Alternatively, if a company has minimal growth prospects, a better use of the funds may be to return them to investors in the form of dividends.

An alternative to a dividend issuance is to buy back shares from investors. By accepting this buyout, investors will (depending on their circumstances) probably claim a long-term capital gain on the transaction, which is taxed at a lower rate than dividend income. This approach is especially good for situations where a company has obtained a temporary increase in its cash flows, but does not necessarily have prospects for future cash flows of a similar size, and so does not want to set investor expectations for a long series of dividend payments.

As an example of how this concept may be used, the Breakout Software Company, maker of prison databases, has two components to its business, which are long-term database subscriptions and software consulting. The database portion of the business generates a steady stream of cash flows that can be predicted with great reliability for the next few years. The consulting business, however, is tied to short-term contracts, and so results in highly variable cash flows. Based on this information, the CFO recommends a dividend that is based on a percentage of the subscription cash flows, while recommending a stock buyback based on the short-term cash flows from the consulting business. This dual approach links the appropriate dividend policy to the nature of the firm's underlying cash flows.

PRODUCTS: PRODUCT ELIMINATION DECISION. Pareto analysis holds that 80% of the activity in a given situation is caused by 20% of the population. This rule is strongly applicable to the profitability of a company's products, where 80% of the total profit is generated by 20% of the products. Of the remaining 80% of the product population, it is reasonable to assume that some make no profit at all. Consequently, financial analysis should encompass the regularly scheduled review of all company product offerings to determine which products should be withdrawn from the marketplace. This is a valuable analysis for the following reasons:

- *Complexity.* In general, too many products lead to an excessive degree of system complexity within a company in order to support those products.

- *Excessive inventory.* Each inventory item usually contains some unique parts, which require additional storage space in the warehouse, as well as a working capital investment in those parts, and the risk of eventual obsolescence. Further, the presence of unique parts in a product may be the sole reason why the purchasing department continues to deal with a supplier; canceling the product allows the company to reduce the number of suppliers it uses, thereby gaining greater volume discounts with the remaining suppliers.

- *Engineering time.* If there are changes to products, the engineering staff must update the bill of material and labor routing records, all of which takes time.

- *Marketing literature.* The marketing department usually maintains a unique set of literature for each product, which requires periodic updating and reprinting.

- *Servicing cost.* The customer support staff must be trained in the unique features of each product, so they can adequately answer customer questions.

- *Warranty cost.* Some products have a considerable warranty cost, possibly due to design flaws or inadequate materials that require sizeable warranty reserves.

When conducting a product withdrawal analysis, care must be taken not to assume that some expenses will be eliminated along with a product. Instead, an expense may have been allocated to a product, but will still remain once the product is gone. For example, the servicing cost of the customer support staff is unlikely to result in the actual elimination of a customer support position just because a single product has been canceled. Instead, customer support overhead will now be assigned to the smaller remaining pool of products. Thus, it is extremely important to only include direct costs in a product withdrawal analysis, and exclude any overhead allocations. To be certain that a product cancellation is not merely shifting overhead costs elsewhere, it is useful to develop before-and-after pro forma financial statements to see if there is really an improvement in profitability resulting from the cancellation.

As noted, only direct costs should be used in calculating the profitability of a product for purposes of the cancellation decision. This results in the following formula:

$$
\begin{aligned}
&\text{Standard list price (1)}\\
&-\text{Commission (2)}\\
&-\text{Buyer discounts (3)}\\
&-\text{Material cost (4)}\\
&-\text{Scrap cost (5)}\\
&-\text{Outsourced processing (6)}\\
&-\text{Inventory carrying cost (7)}\\
&-\text{Packaging cost (8)}\\
&-\text{Unreimbursed shipping cost (9)}\\
&\underline{-\text{Warranty cost (10)}}\\
&=\underline{\underline{\text{Profit (loss)}}}
\end{aligned}
$$

Comments regarding this formula are as follows, and match the numbers next to each line item in the formula:

1. *Standard list price.* If a product has a number of prices based on volume discounts or other criteria, it may be necessary to create a model using the costs itemized in the model to determine the breakeven price below which no profit is earned. The result may be a decision not necessarily to cancel the product, but rather to not sell it at less than a certain discounted price, below which it makes no profit.

2. *Commission.* Salespeople sometimes earn a commission on product sales. If these commissions are clearly identifiable with a specific product and will not be earned if the product is not sold, then include the commission in the product cost.

3. *Buyer discount.* The inclusion of buyer discounts in the calculation calls for some judgment. It should not be included if discounts are a rare event and comprise only a small dollar amount. If discounts are common, then calculate an average discount amount and deduct it from the standard list price.

4. *Material cost.* This is the cost of any materials included in the manufacture of a product.

5. *Scrap cost.* If a standard amount of scrap can be expected as part of the production process that is specifically identifiable with a product, then include this cost in the profitability calculation.

6. *Outsourced processing.* If any production work related to the product is completed by an outside entity, then the cost of this work should be included in the calculation

on the grounds that the entire cost of the outsourced processing will be eliminated along with the product.

7. *Inventory carrying cost.*   This should only be the incremental inventory carrying cost, which is usually only the interest cost of the company's investment in inventory specifically related to the product. It should not include the cost of warehouse storage space or insurance, since both of these costs are fixed in the short term and are very unlikely to change as a result of the elimination of a single product. For example, a company may lease a warehouse, and is obligated to make monthly lease payments irrespective of the amount of storage space being taken by inventory used for a specific product.

8. *Packaging cost.*   Include the cost of any packaging materials used to contain and ship the product, but only if those materials cannot be used for other products.

9. *Unreimbursed shipping cost.*   If the company is absorbing the cost of shipments to customers, then include this cost, net of volume discounts from the shipper.

10. *Warranty cost.*   Though normally a small expense on a per-unit basis, an improperly designed product or one that includes low-quality parts may have an extremely high average warranty cost. If significant, this cost should be included in the profitability analysis.

In addition, note that production labor costs are *not* included in the above calculation. The reason is that production labor rarely varies directly with the level of production; instead, a fixed number of workers will be in the production area every day, irrespective of the level of work performed. Thus, the cancellation of a product will not impact the number of workers employed. However, if a product cancellation will result in the verifiable and immediate elimination of labor positions, then the incremental cost of the eliminated labor should be included in the above calculation.

Even if a product is clearly unprofitable, it may be needed by a key customer who orders other, more profitable products from the company. If so, combine the profits of all sales made to that customer to ensure that the net combined profit is sufficiently high to warrant the retention of the unprofitable product. If this is not the case, consider canceling the unprofitable product and negotiating with the customer for a price reduction on other products in order to retain the customer.

Another cancellation issue is the presence of dependent products. There may be ancillary products that are supplements to the main product, and which provide additional profits to the overall product line. For example, the profit margin on a cell phone may be negative, but there may be a sufficiently high profit level on extra cell phone batteries, car chargers, headsets, and phone covers to more than offset the loss on the initial product sale. In these cases, the margins on all ancillary products should be included in the profitability analysis.

Finally, the frequency of product profitability reviews will be greatly dependent on product life cycles. If products have very short life cycles, then sales levels will drop rapidly once products enter the decline phase of their life cycles, potentially leaving the company with large stocks of excess inventory. In these situations, it is critical to conduct frequent reviews in order to keep a company's investment in working capital from becoming excessive.

There are also two nonfinancial reasons for retaining unprofitable products that must be considered before canceling a product. First, a company may want to offer to customers a full range of product offerings so they can purchase anything they need from the company without having to go to a competitor. This may require the retention of a product whose absence would otherwise create a hole in the corporate product line. Second, it may be necessary to offer a product in a specific market niche in order to keep competitors from entering a market that the company considers to be crucial to its ongoing viability.

FIXED EXPENSES: STEP COSTING DECISION

A key decision for the CFO is whether to recommend the incurrence of a step cost. This is an incremental fixed cost, such as the creation of a new overhead position, that will permanently increase a company's cost base. Adding such costs may be required if the current staff is simply unable to address the needs of existing sales and production levels, and needs the help. Nonetheless, the CFO must review this decision in light of its impact on profitability. One of the best ways to do so is through breakeven analysis of the step costing decision, which is discussed in Chapter 11, Other Financial Analysis Topics. This analysis frequently shows that profits are maximized just *prior to* the incurrence of a step cost, since it may require significant additional sales to offset the step cost.

There are several key factors for a CFO to consider when mulling over this decision. One is the sales point at which profits will match the level just prior to the incurrence of the step cost. For example, a printing plant is experiencing a ramp-up in sales and its CFO decides to invest in a new press to meet the demand. The press is leased, and costs $250,000 per year. Gross margins are 30%, so the plant must generate $833,333 per year in additional sales just to cover the step cost represented by the new press.

Another factor leads from the last point, which is to determine the maximum sales level that a facility can possibly support under the best of circumstances. To continue with the last example, if the printing plant's other departments can only support incremental new sales of an additional $500,000 without the incurrence of even more step costs, then it is impossible to achieve the $833,333 sales level required to pay for the printing press.

Yet another factor to consider is the stability of incremental new sales required to pay for a step cost. To continue with the example, the CFO should decline to lease the press if the incremental sales driving the decision are for a short-term deal with a firm expiration date, or with an uncertain future that is not supported by a long-term purchase order. A hard look at the market served by a company, the level of competition, potential price wars, and related factors should all be carefully considered before making the step costing decision.

The examples shown thus far relate to major step costing decisions. However, most step costs are much more minor, with small jumps in costs that have a minimal incremental impact on the bottom line. Nonetheless, these additions gradually eat away at profits over time. To gain control over them, the CFO should require elaborate approval mechanisms for any step costs incurred outside of the standard budgeting process. For those costs included in the budget, the CFO has more time to conduct an analysis of why each step cost is needed, how improved efficiencies might avoid the cost, whether to outsource rather than incur the cost, and so on. The step costing decision is one of the most crucial to a company on an ongoing operating basis, and therefore deserves a substantial proportion of a CFO's time.

PAYROLL EXPENSES: TEMPORARY LABOR VERSUS PERMANENT STAFFING DECISION

In many organizations, particularly those in the service industry, the largest expense by far is for payroll. Consequently, the CFO should become deeply involved in decisions to alter the size of the workforce. This is a particular concern in areas where the business is highly seasonal, requires experienced personnel, operates under a union agreement, or is subject to burdensome state unemployment taxes. Some of the key decision points to consider are:

- *Seasonality.*   If a business has a highly variable sales season, this is a key indicator in favor of using temporary labor during the peak season, leaving only a small core of seasoned employees for the remainder of the year. A classic example is the amusement park, where temporary staffers know in advance that they will only be employed for a few months. However, this is not such a simple decision when the experience level required of the staff is relatively high, since it may be difficult to obtain new help with the requisite knowledge base when sales ramp up again. In such situations, the CFO should consider level-loading the production facility, balancing this cost against an increase in inventory levels during low sales periods. If this is not an option, then a corporate investment in a significant training program to ramp up new employees quickly may be a reasonable alternative.

- *Turnover rate of existing in-house staff.*   There may be no decision to make between the use of temporary versus in-house full-time staff if the full-time staff turns over with great regularity. This is a common problem in low-skill, highly repetitive environments, such as base-level positions on the manufacturing floor.

- *Union agreements.*   A labor force represented by a union can greatly restrict a company's ability to lay off the regular workforce. This may tend to lead a CFO to recommend extensive use of temporary employees for short-term requirements, rather than run the risk of hiring more staff into the union who will then be difficult to let go. The union may suggest giving its members high-cost overtime rather than bring in temporary employees, thereby increasing their total pay. However, quality problems can arise after employees work too many hours, making this a choice of diminishing returns.

- *Unemployment taxes.*   If a company constantly hires and fires staff as it experiences rapid changes in its required staffing levels, it will experience increasing state unemployment tax rates. State unemployment agencies annually review the amount of unemployment payments made to a company's former employees and alter the company's prospective tax rate for the next year to make the company foot the bill for these payments. If a company creates a large pool of former employees who are drawing unemployment benefits, it is setting itself up for an increase of potentially several percent in its payroll taxes.

- *Technical skill requirements.*   Temporary labor agencies used to specialize in providing low-skill staff to companies. However, these agencies now offer pools of very experienced, technically capable people who can step into almost any position. Nonetheless, a strategically critical position should be brought in house and provided with a proper benefits package, on the grounds that the company wants to retain the person in that position for as long as possible. In this case, cost issues are secondary to retention.

- *Terms of agreements with temporary labor agencies.*   A temporary labor agency charges a substantial markup on the hourly fees it charges for a company's use of people provided to it by the agency. This fee covers not only the agency's profit, but also its recruiting costs, payroll taxes, and benefits (if any) that it may offer its temporary workforce. A company using a recruiting agency will usually have to sign a contract with the agency, agreeing not to hire any of its temporary workers without paying a search fee, or else only after a number of months have passed (during which time the agency will have earned a large profit). This type of fee structure frequently leads the CFO to recommend either running an in-house temporary work agency or only using temporary labor agencies for very specific requirements.

For example, the CFO of the SecureTech Consulting Company is faced with the decision whether to bring in temporary labor for a government system security consulting project, or to hire the personnel directly. The company has a long tradition of not laying off personnel, so the CFO wants to be sure that these people will be needed after the current government contract has been completed. Accordingly, she talks to the business development vice president to see if the government contract may be extended past its current one-year term. The response is that the government will make a firm commitment for extended funding after it has reviewed the quality of SecureTech's work for the first three months of the contract. Based on this information, she elects to hire personnel through an IT temporary services agency for the first three months of the contract and then pay a small recruiting fee to hire them full-time if the contract is extended. If the contract is not extended, then she will keep them on temporary status and let them go at the end of the contract.

As another example, the CFO of the Stereo Devices Company must make a recommendation about hiring stereo systems installers for the crucial holiday season. A good stereo installer with above-average customer skills is considered a key employee worth retaining, but the company can afford to keep only half the installer staff during slower parts of the year. A major consideration is the quality of work provided to customers by the installers, which has proven to be of a lower standard when short-term staff were used in the past. Accordingly, the CFO recommends authorizing a considerable jump in overtime hours allowed during the holiday season by the more experienced staff, while only hiring a minimum number of personnel who act as assistants to the more experienced staff.

In both of the examples, monetary concerns were not the only reasons for the decisions being made. On the contrary, the consulting firm wanted to avoid breaking a long company tradition of avoiding layoffs, while the installation company wanted the best possible customer service. Less expensive alternatives were available, but the CFOs both decided that key company values came first.

ENTITIES: DIVESTITURE DECISION

A company will occasionally consider the divestiture of some portion of the business, for a variety of reasons. For example, the CFO may feel that the company will be worth more to investors if it is broken into pieces, though this approach is difficult to prove. Another reason is that the management team is having difficulty allocating capital between various portions of the entity, or that one business segment is using most of the capital, essentially "starving" other business segments of funds. The same reasoning can apply to the time of the management team, which may be unreasonably allocated to fix the problems of one business unit; in this case, the management team may be of the opinion that managing a smaller firm will be easier on them, and better for the company as a whole. A divestiture may also seem attractive if the management team decides to steer the company in a different strategic direction, which may call for the divestiture of all business segments that are considered to be unrelated to the new direction. In a few cases, a company may even be forced by the government to divest because of antitrust issues. Whatever the initial reason given, the CFO should explore the issue by focusing on the inherent value of the subject business segment to the company, what kind of effort or funding it would take to more fully achieve the benefits of that segment within the company, and what would happen to the company's competitive position if the segment were divested. By reviewing these issues, the CFO should be able to arrive at a defensible conclusion regarding the best action to be taken.

If the CFO is asked to look into the size and structure of a divestiture, there are several issues to consider. First, is there a clearly identifiable entity that can be broken away from the company? For example, separate facilities and staff should be clearly identifiable as belonging to the business segment to be divested. Second, the business segment must be one that can operate profitably on its own, which means that it must address a clearly identifiable market, have an appropriate infrastructure for that market, and therefore be able to successfully compete in it.

If these conditions apply, then the CFO can consider the type of structure that the divestiture should follow. For example, the business segment can be spun off to existing shareholders. This is an excellent approach from the perspective of the shareholders, who will avoid an income tax liability by receiving qualified shares in the new entity. A spin-off also allows the management team to avoid the hassle of dealing with a buyer, setting its own terms for the divestiture instead. A variation on the spin-off is a carve-out, where the company makes shares in the new entity available through an initial public offering (IPO), rather than as a stock distribution to shareholders. Yet another variation is a sale to the management team of the business segment, which typically structures the deal as a leveraged buyout (LBO), involving little capital and large amounts of debt. Finally, a divestiture can be accomplished through a sale to another company, though this approach can involve a painful amount of negotiation, legal fees, contingent fees, and a lower price than might be achieved by other means.

Systems: When to Use Throughput Costing*

Throughput costing requires an understanding of some new accounting terminology. *Throughput* is the contribution margin that is left after a product's price is reduced by the amount of its totally variable costs. There is no attempt to allocate overhead costs to a product, nor to assign to it any semivariable costs. As a result, the amount of throughput for most products tends to be quite high. *Totally variable costs* are the costs that will only be incurred if a product is created. In many instances, this means that only direct materials are considered to be a totally variable cost. Direct labor is not totally variable unless employees are only paid if a product is produced. A *capacity constraint* is a resource within a company that limits its total output. For example, it may be a machine that can only produce a specified amount of a key component in a given time period, thereby keeping overall sales from expanding beyond the maximum capacity of that machine. *Operating expenses* are the sum total of all company expenses, excluding totally variable expenses.

The primary focus of throughput costing is on how to force as many throughput dollars as possible through a capacity constraint, pure and simple. It does this by first determining the throughput dollars per minute of every production job scheduled to

---

*   Adapted with permission from Chapter 14 of *Cost Accounting* by Bragg (John Wiley & Sons, 2001).

run through the capacity constraint, and then rearranging the order of production priority so that the products with the highest throughput dollars per minute are produced first. The system is based on the supposition that only a certain amount of production can be squeezed through a bottleneck operation, so the production that yields the highest margin must come first in order of manufacturing priority to ensure that profits are maximized. The concept is most easily demonstrated in the example shown in Exhibit 2.2.

In the example, we have four types of products that a company can sell. Each requires some machining time on the company's capacity constraint, which is the circuit board manufacturing process (CBMP). The first item is a 19-inch color television, which requires 10 minutes of the CBMP's time. The television sells for $150, and has associated direct materials of $68.90, which gives it a throughput of $81.10. We then divide the throughput of $81.10 by the ten minutes of processing time per unit on the capacity constraint to arrive at the throughput dollars per minute of $8.11 that is shown in the second column of Exhibit 2.2. We then calculate the throughput per minute for the other three products, and sort them in high-low order, based on which ones contribute the most throughput per minute. This leaves the 19-inch television at the top of the list. Next, we multiply the unit demand for each item by the time required to move it through the capacity constraint point. We do not care about the total production time for each item, only the time required to push it through the bottleneck. Next, we determine the total amount of time during which the capacity constraint can be operated, which in the example is 62,200 minutes, and which is noted in bold at the top of the example. We then fill in the total number of minutes required to produce each product in the fifth column, which also shows that we will not have enough time available at the capacity constraint to complete the available work for the high-definition television, which was listed as having the lowest priority. Then, by multiplying the throughput per minute by the number of minutes for each product, and then multiplying the result by the total number of units produced, we arrive at the total throughput for the entire production process for the period, which is $405,360. However, we are not done yet. We must still subtract from the total throughput the sum of all operating expenses for the facility. After

Product	Maximum Constraint Time: 62,200				
	Throughput $$/Minute of Constraint	Required Constraint Usage (min.)	Unit Demand/ Actual Production	Cumulative Constraint Utilization	Cumulative Throughput/ Product
19" Color Television	$8.11	10	1,000/1,000	10,000	$81,100
100-Watt Stereo	7.50	8	2,800/2,800	22,400	168,000
5" LCD Television	6.21	12	500/500	6,000	37,260
50" High-Definition Television	5.00	14	3,800/1,700	23,800	119,000
		Throughput Total			$405,360
		Operating Expense Total			375,000
		Profit			30,360
		Profit Percentage			7.5%
		Investment			500,000
		Return on Investment			6.1%

EXHIBIT 2.2   THROUGHPUT MODEL

Product Description	Price	Totally Variable Cost	Overhead Allocation	Gross Margin
19″ Color Television	$150.00	$68.90	$49.20	$31.90
100-Watt Stereo	125.50	65.50	18.00	38.00
5″ LCD Television	180.00	105.48	41.52	33.00
50″ High-Definition Television	900.00	830.00	20.00	50.00

EXHIBIT 2.3   FULLY ABSORBED PRODUCT COSTS

they are subtracted from the total throughput, we find that we have achieved a profit of 7.5% and a return on investment of 6.1%. This is the basic throughput accounting model.

So far, this looks like an ordinary analysis of how much money a company can earn from the production of a specific set of products. However, there is more here than is at first apparent. The issue is best explained with another example. Let us say that the CFO arrives on the scene, does a thorough costing analysis of all four products in the preceding exhibit, and determines that, after all overhead costs are properly allocated, the high-definition television actually has the highest gross margin, and the 19-inch television has the least. The relative positions of the other two products do not change. The CFO's summary of the product costs appears in Exhibit 2.3.

According to the cost accounting scenario, we should actually be producing as many high-definition television sets as possible. To test this theory, we will duplicate the throughput analysis shown earlier in Exhibit 2.2, but this time we will move the high-definition television to the top of the list and produce all 3,800 units that are on order, while dropping the 19-inch television to the bottom of the list, and only producing as many units as will still be available after all other production has been completed. All other variables will stay the same. This analysis is shown in Exhibit 2.4.

	Maximum Constraint Time: 62,200				
Product	Throughput $$/Minute of Constraint	Required Constraint Usage (min.)	Unit Demand/ Actual Production	Cumulative Constraint Utilization	Cumulative Throughput/ Product
50″ High-Definition Television	$5.00	14	3,800/3,800	53,200	$266,000
100-Watt Stereo	7.50	8	2,800/1,125	9,000	67,500
5″ LCD Television	6.21	12	500/0	0	0
19″ Color Television	8.11	10	1,000/0	0	0
		Throughput Total			$333,500
		Operating Expense Total			375,000
		Profit			−41,500
		Profit Percentage			−12.4%
		Investment			500,000
		Return on Investment			−8.3%

EXHIBIT 2.4   THROUGHPUT ANALYSIS USING PRIORITIES BASED ON OVERHEAD COSTS

According to this analysis, which is based on the best cost allocation principles, where we have carefully used activity-based costing to ensure that overhead is closely matched to actual activities, we have altered the mix of products and realized a net *reduction* in profits of $53,360! How can this be possible?

This issue is caused by three major problems with the traditional cost accounting methodology, all of which are corrected through the use of throughput accounting. All three of these issues contributed to the problem just noted in Exhibit 2.4. The first is that you cannot really allocate overhead costs to products and expect to use the resulting information in any meaningful way for incremental decisions of any kind. To do so would be to make the erroneous assumption that overhead costs vary directly with every unit of a product that is produced or sold. In reality, the only cost that varies directly with a product is the cost of its direct material. That is all. Even direct labor is no longer so direct. In how many companies can one find a situation where the staff immediately goes home when the last product is completed? Instead, the staff is employed on various projects during downtime periods, to ensure that the same experienced staff is available for work the next day. There is an even less tenuous linkage between machine costs and products. Will a company immediately sell a machine if there is one less unit of production running through it? Of course not. The machine will sit on the factory floor and accumulate depreciation and preventive maintenance costs until some other job comes along that requires its services. In short, nearly all of the costs of any company can be lumped into a general category called "operating expenses" or some similar category. These are simply the costs that a company incurs to maintain a given level of capacity, rather than a disaggregated group of costs that are closely tied to specific products. The reason why this concept has such a large bearing on Exhibit 2.4 is that the high-definition television was assumed to have a much higher margin than the 19-inch television on the basis of allocated costs. However, for the purposes of the production runs used in the throughput example, the overhead cost pools that were assigned to these two products will still become valid expenses, whether either of the products is produced at all. Consequently, it is detrimental to use overhead as a factor in the determination of product throughput, no matter what traditional cost accounting principles may state.

The second major problem with traditional cost accounting is that it completely ignores the concept of limited production capacity. Instead, the primary goal of a costing analysis is to determine which products have the highest gross margins and which have the least. This information is then used to pursue two goals—to sell oodles of the high-margin products while either dumping or improving the margins on the low-margin products. Unfortunately, the real world states that there is a limited production capacity available, so one must choose between the best set of customer orders that are available at the moment, only some of which can be run through the capacity constraint—and possibly none of which may be the highest-margin products that the company is capable of producing. Therefore, a simple categorization of which products are the "best" or "worst" has no meaning on a day-to-day basis. The real world forces one to choose between a set of possible product sales, which requires one to continually reevaluate a mix of product orders for different products and quantities in relation to one another. In Exhibit 2.4, ignoring the capacity constraint would have led to the much higher profit of $177,360 (assuming that all production is completed for all four products), but of course this was rendered impossible by the capacity constraint.

The final problem, and the one that is clearly the largest inherent flaw in traditional cost accounting, is that it ignores the fact that a company is one large, interactive system, and instead strives to achieve lots of local improvements in efficiency. The flaw that we just saw in Exhibit 2.4 was that the CFO determined the fully absorbed cost of each product on its own, not realizing that, to a significant degree, each of those products shares in the use of many overhead costs. Any type of allocation system will result in locally optimized profitability levels for individual products, but does not address the fact that the overhead cost pool really services the capacity of the company as a whole, not an individual product. For example, the cost of a production scheduler's salary may be allocated to a product based on the amount of scheduling time required to insert it into the production schedule. However, does this added cost really "belong" to the product? If the product were not to be produced at all, the scheduler would still be there, being paid a salary, so it is evident that, for the purposes of the throughput model, there is no point in assigning such overhead costs to products. This means that, because so many costs are not assignable to products, it is valid to only charge totally variable costs to a specific product; all other costs must be paid for by the combined throughput of *all* products produced, since the overhead applies to all of them. In short, we cannot look at the individual profitability levels of products; but rather at how the throughput of all possible product sales, when combined, can be used to offset the total pool of overhead costs.

What we have just seen is that traditional cost accounting methodologies make the multiple mistakes of applying overhead to products for incremental decision-making purposes, ignoring the role of capacity constraints, and not thinking of the entire set of products and related operating expenses as a complete system, for which various combinations of products must be considered in order to determine the highest possible level of profitability. However, we are still dealing with throughput accounting at an abstract level. We will now work through a few examples to clarify the concepts presented thus far.

HIGH-VOLUME, LOW-PRICE SALE DECISION USING THROUGHPUT COSTING

The sales manager of the electronics company in our previous example runs into the corporate headquarters, flush from a meeting with the company's largest account, Electro-Geek Stores (EGS). He has just agreed to a deal that drops the price of the 100-watt stereo system by 20%, but which guarantees a doubling in the quantity of EGS orders for this product for the upcoming year. The sales manager points out that the company may have to hold off on a few of the smaller-volume production runs of other products, but no problem—the company is bound to earn more money on the extra volume. To test this assumption, the CFO pulls up the throughput model on his computer, shifts the stereo to the top of the priority list, adjusts the throughput to reflect the lower price, and obtains the results shown in Exhibit 2.5.

To be brief, the sales manager just skewered the company. By dropping the price of the stereo by 20%, much of the product's throughput was eliminated, while so much of the capacity constraint was used up that there was little room for the production of any other products that might generate enough added throughput to save the company. This example clearly shows that one must carefully consider the impact on the capacity constraint when debating whether to accept a high-volume sales deal. This is a particularly dangerous area in which to ignore throughput accounting, for the acceptance of a really large-volume deal can hog all of the time of the capacity constraint, eliminating any chance for the company to manufacture other products, and thereby eliminating any chance of offering a wide product mix to the general marketplace.

Product	Maximum Constraint Time: 62,200				
	Throughput $$/Minute of Constraint	Required Constraint Usage (min.)	Unit Demand/ Actual Production	Cumulative Constraint Utilization	Cumulative Throughput/ Product
100-Watt Stereo	$4.36	8	5,600/5,600	44,800	$195,328
19″ Color Television	8.11	10	1,000/1,000	10,000	81,100
5″ LCD Television	6.21	12	500/500	6,000	37,260
50″ High-Definition Television	5.00	14	3,800/100	1,400	7,000
		Throughput Total			$320,688
		Operating Expense Total			375,000
		Profit			−54,312
		Profit Percentage			−16.9%
		Investment			500,000
		Return on Investment			−10.9%

EXHIBIT 2.5 THROUGHPUT MODEL WITH VOLUME DISCOUNTS

CAPITAL BUDGETING DECISION USING THROUGHPUT COSTING

The production and cost accounting managers have been reviewing a number of work-stations in the production area, and find that they can speed up the production capacity of the circuit board insertion machine, which is the next workstation in line *after* the capacity constraint operation. They can double the speed of the insertion machine if the company is willing to invest an extra $28,500. To see if this is a good idea, we once again look at the throughput model. In this instance, the only number we change is the investment amount. The results are shown in Exhibit 2.6.

By making the extra investment, the only change in the company's situation is that its return on investment has dropped by four-tenths of a percent. The reason is that any

Product	Maximum Constraint Time: 62,200				
	Throughput $$/Minute of Constraint	Required Constraint Usage (min.)	Unit Demand/ Actual Production	Cumulative Constraint Utilization	Cumulative Throughput/ Product
19″ Color Television	$8.11	10	1,000/1,000	10,000	$81,100
100-Watt Stereo	7.50	8	2,800/2,800	22,400	168,000
5″ LCD Television	6.21	12	500/500	6,000	37,260
50″ High-Definition Television	5.00	14	3,800/1,700	23,800	119,000
		Throughput Total			$405,360
		Operating Expense Total			375,000
		Profit			30,360
		Profit Percentage			7.5%
		Investment			528,500
		Return on Investment			5.7%

EXHIBIT 2.6 THROUGHPUT MODEL AND INVESTMENT ANALYSIS

investment used to improve any operation besides the capacity constraint is a waste of money. *The only thing that a company achieves by making such an investment is improving the efficiency of an operation that will still be controlled by the speed of the capacity constraint.* In reality, the situation is even worse, for any newly upgraded subsidiary operation will now have greater efficiency, and can therefore produce in even greater quantities—all of which will turn into WIP that will pile up somewhere in front of the bottleneck operation, which increases the amount of a company's WIP investment. Thus, an investment in a nonbottleneck operation may actually worsen the overall financial results of the company, because its investment in inventory will increase.

This is an important concept for investment analysis, for the typical CFO is trained to examine each investment proposal strictly on its own merits, with no consideration of how the investment fits into the entire production system. If the impact of the capacity constraint were also to be factored into investment analyses, very few of them would ever be approved, because they do not have a positive impact on the capacity constraint.

MAKE VERSUS BUY DECISION USING THROUGHPUT COSTING

One of the company's key suppliers has offered to take over the entire production of the 5-inch LCD television, package it in the company's boxes, and drop ship the completed goods directly to the company's customers. The catch is that the company's cost will increase from its current fully burdened rate of $147 (as noted in Exhibit 2.3) to $165, which only leaves a profit of $15. A traditional cost accounting review would state that the company will experience reduced profits of $18 if this outsourcing deal is completed (the difference between the current and prospective costs of $147 and $165. To see if this is a good deal, we turn once again to the throughput model, which is reproduced in Exhibit 2.7. In this exhibit, we have removed the number from the "Cumulative Constraint Utilization" column for the LCD television, since it can now be produced without the use of the capacity constraint. However, we are still able to put a cumulative throughput dollar figure into the final column for this product, since there is some margin to be made by outsourcing it through the supplier. By removing the LCD television's usage of the

	Maximum Constraint Time: 62,200				
Product	Throughput $$/Minute of Constraint	Required Constraint Usage (min.)	Unit Demand/ Actual Production	Cumulative Constraint Utilization	Cumulative Throughput/ Product
19″ Color Television	$8.11	10	1,000/1,000	10,000	$81,100
100-Watt Stereo	7.50	8	2,800/2,800	22,400	168,000
5″ LCD Television	6.21	12	500/500	N/A	7,500
50″ High-Definition Television	5.00	14	3,800/2,129	29,806	149,030
		Throughput Total			$405,630
		Operating Expense Total			375,000
		Profit			30,630
		Profit Percentage			7.5%
		Investment			500,000
		Return on Investment			6.1%

EXHIBIT 2.7   THROUGHPUT MODEL WITH AN OUTSOURCING OPTION

capacity constraint, we are now able to produce more of the next product in line, which is the high-definition television set. This additional production allows the company to increase the amount of throughput dollars, thereby creating $270 more in profits than was the case before the outsourcing deal.

Once again, the traditional cost accounting approach would have stated that profits would be lowered by accepting an outsourcing deal that clearly cost more than the product's internal cost. However, by using this deal to release some capacity at the bottleneck, the company is able to earn more money on the production of other products.

SUMMARY

This chapter presented a multitude of financial strategy decisions that a CFO is likely to encounter. It may at first appear that some of these decisions need to be addressed only after long intervals, when there is an immediate need. For example, the decision to offer a particular type of equity is only needed when a new offering is anticipated—right? Not at all. On the contrary, a forward-thinking CFO should review this chapter at regular intervals as part of his or her ongoing strategic planning process, perhaps as much as on a quarterly basis. By doing so, the CFO can constantly review the background information used to make earlier decisions, test them in light of new information, and incrementally (or substantially) revise the decisions. To use the previous example, the CFO can continually evaluate the types of equity being offered, even if there is no immediate need for new equity, in order to see if the firm's capital structure requires revision. Similarly, a regular review of the inventory liquidation decision is needed to test inventory levels in light of any new manufacturing systems or customer service goals, while the early payment discount decision must be reviewed in light of any changes in the corporate cost of capital or short-term cash flow requirements. Similar reasons apply to the regular review of all other decisions noted in this chapter. In short, the CFO must continually test all assumptions used to make key financial decisions, and revise those decisions as needed.

CHAPTER 3

TAX STRATEGY

The obvious objective of tax strategy is to minimize the amount of cash paid out for taxes.* However, this directly conflicts with the general desire to report as much income as possible to shareholders, since more reported income results in more taxes. Only in the case of privately owned firms do these conflicting problems go away, since the owners have no need to impress anyone with their reported level of earnings, and would simply prefer to retain as much cash in the company as possible by avoiding the payment of taxes.

For those CFOs who are intent on reducing their corporation's tax burdens, there are five primary goals to include in their tax strategies, all of which involve increasing the number of differences between the book and tax records, so that reportable income for tax purposes is reduced. The five items are:

1. *Accelerate deductions.* By recognizing expenses sooner, one can force expenses into the current reporting year that would otherwise be deferred. The primary deduction acceleration involves depreciation, for which a company typically uses the modified accelerated cost recovery system (MACRS), an accelerated depreciation methodology acceptable for tax reporting purposes, and straight-line depreciation, which results in a higher level of reported earnings for other purposes.

2. *Take all available tax credits.* A credit results in a permanent reduction in taxes, and so is highly desirable. Unfortunately, credits are increasingly difficult to find, though one might qualify for the research and experimental tax credit, which is available to those companies that have increased their research activities over the previous year. The only type of expense that qualifies for this credit is that which is undertaken to discover information that is technical in nature, and its application must be intended for use in developing a new or improved business component for the taxpayer. Also, all of the research activities must be elements of a process of experimentation relating to a new or improved function, or which enhance the current level of performance, reliability, or quality. A credit cannot be taken for research conducted after the beginning of commercial production, for the customization of a product for a specific customer, the duplication of an existing process or product, or for research required for some types of software to be used internally.

    There are more tax credits available at the local level, where they are offered to those businesses willing to operate in economic development zones, or as part of specialized relocation deals (normally only available to larger companies).

---

* Adapted with permission from pp. 615–616 of *Ultimate Accountants' Reference* by Bragg (John Wiley & Sons, 2005).

3. *Avoid nonallowable expenses.*   There are a few expenses, most notably meals and entertainment, that are completely or at least partially not allowed for purposes of computing taxable income. A key company strategy is to reduce these types of expenses to the bare minimum, thereby avoiding any lost benefits from nonallowable expenses.

4. *Increase tax deferrals.*   There are a number of situations in which taxes can be deferred, such as when payments for acquisitions are made in stock or when revenue is deferred until all related services have been performed. This can shift a large part of the tax liability into the future, where the time value of money results in a smaller present value of the tax liability than would otherwise be the case.

5. *Obtain tax-exempt income.*   The CFO should consider investing excess funds in municipal bonds, which are exempt from both federal income taxes and the income taxes of the state in which they were issued. The downside of this approach is that the return on municipal bonds is less than the return on other forms of investment, due to their inherent tax savings.

There is no single tax strategy that will be applicable to every company, since the tax laws are so complex that the CFO most construct a strategy that is tailored to the specific circumstances in which her company finds itself. Nonetheless, there are a number of taxation areas that a CFO must be aware of when creating a tax strategy using the preceding five goals. Those areas are listed in alphabetical order through the remainder of this chapter, ranging from the accumulated earnings tax to unemployment taxes. The CFO should carefully peruse these topics to see if they should be incorporated into her overall tax strategy.

ACCUMULATED EARNINGS TAX*

There is a double tax associated with a company's payment of dividends to investors, because it must first pay an income tax from which dividends *cannot* be deducted as an expense, and then investors must pay income tax on the dividends received. Understandably, closely held companies prefer not to issue dividends in order to avoid the double taxation issue. However, this can result in a large amount of capital accumulating within a company. The Internal Revenue Service (IRS) addresses this issue by imposing an accumulated earnings tax on what it considers to be an excessive amount of earnings that have not been distributed to shareholders.

The IRS considers accumulated earnings of less than $150,000 to be sufficient for the working needs of service businesses, such as accounting, engineering, architecture, and consulting firms. It considers accumulations of anything under $250,000 to be sufficient for most other types of businesses. A company can argue that it needs a substantially larger amount of accumulated earnings if it can prove that it has specific, definite, and feasible plans that will require the use of the funds within the business. Another valid argument is that a company needs a sufficient amount of accumulated earnings to buy back the company's stock that is held by a deceased shareholder's estate.

If these conditions are not apparent, then the IRS will declare the accumulated earnings to be taxable at a rate of 39.6%. Also, interest payments to the IRS will be due from

---

*   Adapted with permission from p. 616 of *Ultimate Accountants' Reference* by Bragg (John Wiley & Sons, 2005).

the date when the corporation's annual return was originally due. The severity of this tax is designed to encourage organizations to issue dividends on a regular basis to their shareholders, so that the IRS can tax the shareholders for this form of income.

CASH METHOD OF ACCOUNTING*

The normal method for reporting a company's financial results is the accrual basis of accounting, under which expenses are matched to revenues within a reporting period. However, for tax purposes, it is sometimes possible to report income under the cash method of accounting. Under this approach, revenue is not recognized until payment for invoices is received, while expenses are not recognized until paid.

The cash basis of accounting can result in a great deal of manipulation from the perspective of the IRS, which discourages its use, but does not prohibit it. As an example of income manipulation, a company may realize that it will have a large amount of income to report in the current year, and will probably have less in the following year. Accordingly, it prepays a number of supplier invoices at the end of the year, so that it recognizes them at once under the cash method of accounting as expenses in the current year. The IRS prohibits this type of behavior under the rule that cash payments recognized in the current period can only relate to current-year expenses. Nonetheless, it is a difficult issue for the IRS to police. The same degree of manipulation can be applied to the recognition of revenue, simply by delaying billings to customers near the end of the tax year. Also, in situations where there is a sudden surge of business at the end of the tax year, possibly due to seasonality, the cash method of accounting will not reveal the sales until the following year, since payment on the invoices from customers will not arrive until the next year. Consequently, the cash method tends to underreport taxable income.

In order to limit the use of this method, the IRS prohibits it if a company has any inventories on hand at the end of the year. The reason for this is that expenditures for inventory can be so large and subject to manipulation at year-end that a company could theoretically alter its reported level of taxable income to an enormous extent. The cash basis is also not allowable for any C corporation, partnership that has a C corporation for a partner, or a tax shelter. However, within these restrictions, it is allowable for an entity with average annual gross receipts of $5 million or less for the three tax years ending with the prior tax year, as well as for any personal service corporation that provides at least 95% of its activities in the services arena.

The IRS imposes some accrual accounting concepts on a cash-basis organization in order to avoid some of the more blatant forms of income avoidance. For example, if a cash-basis company receives a check at the end of its tax year, it may be tempted not to cash the check until the beginning of the next tax year, since this would push the revenue associated with that check into the next year. To avoid this problem, the IRS uses the concept of *constructive receipt*, which requires one to record the receipt when it is made available to one without restriction (whether or not it is actually recorded on the company's books at that time). Besides the just-noted example, this would also require a company to record the interest on a bond that comes due prior to the end of the tax year, even if the associated coupon is not sent to the issuer until the next year.

---

*   Adapted with permission from pp. 621–622 of *Ultimate Accountants' Reference* by Bragg (John Wiley & Sons, 2005).

INVENTORY VALUATION

It is allowable to value a company's inventory using one method for book purposes and another for tax purposes, except in the case of the last-in first-out (LIFO) inventory valuation method. In this case, the tax advantages to be gained from the use of LIFO are so significant that the IRS requires a user to employ it for both book and tax purposes. Furthermore, if LIFO is used in any one of a group of financially related companies, the entire group is assumed to be a single entity for tax reporting purposes, which means that they must all use the LIFO valuation approach for both book and tax reporting. This rule was engendered in order to stop the practice of having LIFO-valuation companies roll their results into a parent company that used some other method of reporting, thereby giving astute companies high levels of reportable income and lower levels of taxable income at the same time.

MERGERS AND ACQUISITIONS*

A key factor to consider in corporate acquisitions is the determination of what size taxable gain will be incurred by the seller (if any), as well as how the buyer can reduce the tax impact of the transaction in the current and future years. In this section, we will briefly discuss the various types of transactions involved in an acquisition, the tax implications of each transaction, and whose interests are best served by the use of each one.

There are two ways in which an acquisition can be made, each with different tax implications. First, one can purchase the acquiree's stock, which may trigger a taxable gain to the seller. Second, one can purchase the acquiree's assets, which triggers a gain on sale of the assets, as well as another tax to the shareholders of the selling company, who must recognize a gain when the proceeds from liquidation of the business are distributed to them. Because of the additional taxation, a seller will generally want to sell a corporation's stock rather than its assets.

When stock is sold to the buyer in exchange for cash or property, the buyer establishes a tax basis in the stock that equals the amount of the cash paid or fair market value of the property transferred to the seller. Meanwhile, the seller recognizes a gain or loss on the eventual sale of the stock that is based on its original tax basis in the stock, which is subtracted from the ultimate sale price of the stock.

It is also possible for the seller to recognize no taxable gain on sale of a business if it takes some of the acquiring company's stock as full compensation for the sale. However, there will be no tax only if *continuity of interest* in the business can be proven by giving the sellers a sufficient amount of the buyer's stock to prove that they have a continuing financial interest in the buying company. A variation on this approach is to make an acquisition over a period of months, using nothing but voting stock as compensation to the seller's shareholders, but for which a clear plan of ultimate control over the acquiree can be proven. Another variation is to purchase at least 80% of the fair market value of the acquiree's assets solely in exchange for stock.

When only the assets are sold to the buyer, the buyer can apportion the total price among the assets purchased, up to their fair market value (with any excess portion of the price being apportioned to goodwill). This is highly favorable from a taxation perspective, since the buyer has now adjusted its basis in the assets substantially higher; it can now

---

* Adapted with permission from pp. 647–648 of *Ultimate Accountants' Reference* by Bragg (John Wiley & Sons, 2005).

claim a much larger accelerated depreciation expense in the upcoming years, thereby reducing both its reported level of taxable income and tax burden. From the seller's perspective, the sale price is allocated to each asset sold for the purposes of determining a gain or loss; as much of this as possible should be characterized as a capital gain (since the related tax is lower) or as an ordinary loss (since it can offset ordinary income, which has a higher tax rate).

The structuring of an acquisition transaction so that no income taxes are paid must have a reasonable business purpose besides the avoidance of taxes. Otherwise, the IRS has been known to require tax payments on the grounds that the structure of the transaction has no reasonable business purpose besides tax avoidance. Its review of the substance of a transaction over its form leads the CFO to consider such transactions in the same manner, and to restructure acquisition deals accordingly.

There is a specialized tax reduction available for the holders of stock in a small business, on which they experience a gain when the business is sold. Specifically, they are entitled to a 50% reduction in their reportable gain on sale of that stock, though it is limited to the greater of a $10 million gain or 10 times the stockholder's basis in the stock. This exclusion is reserved for C corporations, and only applies to stock that was acquired at its original issuance. There are a number of other exclusions, such as its inapplicability to personal service corporations, real estate investment trusts, domestic international sales corporations, and mutual funds. This type of stock is called *qualified small business stock*. The unique set of conditions surrounding this stock make it clear that it is intended to be a tax break specifically for the owners of small businesses.

NET OPERATING LOSS CARRYFORWARDS*

Since income taxes can be the largest single expense on the income statement, the CFO should carefully track the use and applicability of net operating loss (NOL) carryforwards that were created as the result of reported losses in prior years. An NOL may be carried back and applied against profits recorded in the 2 preceding years, with any remaining amount being carried forward for the next 20 years, when it can be offset against any reported income. If there is still an NOL left after the 20 years have expired, then the remaining amount can no longer be used. One can also irrevocably choose to ignore the carryback option and only use it for carryforward purposes. The standard procedure is to apply all of the NOL against the income reported in the earliest year, with the remainder carrying forward to each subsequent year in succession until the remaining NOL has been exhausted. If an NOL has been incurred in each of multiple years, then they should be applied against reported income (in either prior or later years) in order of the first NOL incurred. This rule is used because of the 20-year limitation on an NOL, so that an NOL incurred in an earlier year can be used before it expires.

The NOL is a valuable asset, since it can be used for many years to offset future earnings. A company buying another entity that has an NOL will certainly place a high value on the NOL, and may even buy the entity strictly in order to use its NOL. To curtail this type of behavior, the IRS has created the Section 382 limitation, under which there is a limitation on its use if there is at least a 50% change in the ownership of an entity that has an unused NOL. The limitation is derived through a complex formula that essentially multiplies the acquired corporation's stock times the long-term tax-exempt

---

*   Adapted with permission from pp. 522–523 of *Accounting Reference Desktop* by Bragg (John Wiley & Sons, 2002).

bond rate. To avoid this problem, a company with an unused NOL that is seeking to expand its equity should consider issuing straight preferred stock (no voting rights, no conversion privileges, and no participation in future earnings) in order to avoid any chance that the extra equity will be construed as a change in ownership.

If a company has incurred an NOL in a short tax year, it must deduct the NOL over a period of six years, starting with the first tax year after the short tax year. This limitation does not apply if the NOL is for $10,000 or less, or if the NOL is the result of a short tax year that is at least 9 months long and is less than the NOL for a full 12-month tax year beginning with the first day of the short tax year. This special NOL rule was designed to keep companies from deliberately changing their tax years in order to create an NOL within a short tax year. This situation is quite possible in a seasonal business where there are losses in all but a few months. Under such a scenario, a company would otherwise be able to declare an NOL during its short tax year, carry back the NOL to apply it against the previous two years of operations, and receive a rebate from the IRS.

NEXUS*

A company may have to complete many more tax forms than it would like, as well as remit taxes to more government entities, if it can be established that it has nexus within a government's area of jurisdiction. Consequently, it is very important to understand how nexus is established.

The rules vary by state, but nexus is generally considered to have occurred if a company maintains a facility of any kind within a state, or if it pays the wages of someone within that state. In some locales, the definition is expanded to include the transport of goods to customers within the state on company-owned vehicles (though nexus is not considered to have occurred if the shipment is made by a third-party freight carrier). A more liberal interpretation of the nexus rule is that a company has nexus if it sends sales personnel into the state on sales calls or training personnel there to educate customers, even though they are not permanently based there. To gain a precise understanding of how the nexus rules are interpreted by each state, it is best to contact the department of revenue at each state government.

A recent issue that is still being debated in the courts is that Internet sales may be considered to have occurred within a state if the server used to process orders or store data is kept within that state, even if the server is only rented from an Internet hosting service.

If nexus has been established, a company must file to do business within the state, which requires a small fee and a refiling once every few years. In addition, it must withhold sales taxes on all sales within the state. This is the most laborious issue related to nexus, since sales taxes may be different for every city and county within each state, necessitating a company to keep track of potentially thousands of different sales tax rates. Also, some states may require the remittance of sales taxes every month, though this can be reduced to as little as once a year if the company predicts that it will have minimal sales taxes to remit, as noted on its initial application for a sales tax license.

Some states or local governments will also subject a company to property or personal property taxes on all assets based within their jurisdictions, which necessitates even more paperwork.

---

*   Adapted with permission from pp. 648–649 of *Ultimate Accountants' Reference* by Bragg (John Wiley & Sons, 2005).

Though the amount of additional taxes paid may not be that great, the key issue related to the nexus concept is that the additional time required to track tax liabilities and file forms with the various governments may very well require additional personnel in the accounting department. This can be a major problem for those organizations in multiple states, and should be a key planning issue when determining the capacity of the accounting department to process tax-related transactions. Some organizations with a number of subsidiaries will avoid a portion of the tax filing work by only accepting the nexus concept for those subsidiaries that are clearly established within each governmental jurisdiction, thereby avoiding the tax filing problems for all other legal entities controlled by the parent corporation.

PROJECT COSTING

A company that regularly develops large infrastructure systems, such as enterprise resource planning (ERP) systems, for its own use will usually cluster all costs related to that project into a single account and then capitalize its full cost, with amortization occurring over a number of years. Though this approach will certainly increase reported income over the short term, it also increases income taxes. If the avoidance of income taxes is a higher priority for the CFO than reported profits, then it would be useful to separate the various components of each project into different accounts, and expense those that more closely relate to ongoing operational activities. For example, a strong case can be made for expensing all training associated with a major system installation, on the grounds that training is an ongoing activity.

Another approach is to charge subsidiaries for the cost of a development project, especially if the charging entity is located in a low-tax region and the subsidiaries are in high-tax regions. This transfer pricing approach would reduce the reported income in high-tax areas, effectively shifting that income to a location where the tax rate is lower. However, these cost-shifting strategies must be carefully documented with proof that the systems are really being used by subsidiaries and that the fees charged are reasonable.

A variation on the last approach is to create a data center in a tax haven that stores and analyzes company data, and then issues reports back to other corporate divisions for a substantial fee. This approach has to involve more than simply locating a file server in a low-tax location, since the IRS will claim that there is no business purpose for the arrangement. Instead, a small business must be set up around the data center that provides some added value to the information being collected and disseminated. This approach is especially attractive if a company acquires another entity with a data center in a low-tax location and simply shifts its own facilities to the preestablished location.

S CORPORATION*

The S corporation is of considerable interest to the CFO, because it generally does not pay taxes. Instead, it passes reported earnings through to its shareholders, who report the income on their tax returns. This avoids the double taxation that arises in a C corporation,

---

* Adapted with permission from pp. 660–661 of *Ultimate Accountants' Reference* by Bragg (John Wiley & Sons, 2005).

where a company's income is taxed, and then the dividends it issues to its shareholders are taxed as income to them a second time. The amount of income is allocated to each shareholder on a simple per-share basis. If a shareholder has held stock in the corporation for less than a full year, then the allocation is on a per-share, per-day basis. The per-day part of this calculation assumes that a shareholder still holds the stock through and including the day when the stock is disposed of, while a deceased shareholder will be assumed to retain ownership through and including the day that he or she dies.

An S corporation has unique taxation and legal protection aspects that make it an ideal way to structure a business if there are a small number of shareholders. Specifically, it can only be created if there are no more than 75 shareholders, if only one class of stock is issued, and if all shareholders agree to the S corporation status. All of its shareholders must be either citizens or residents of the United States. Shareholders are also limited to individuals, estates, and some types of trusts and charities. Conversely, this means that C corporations and partnerships cannot be shareholders in an S corporation. The requirement for a single class of stock may prevent some organizations from organizing in this manner, for it does not allow for preferential returns or special voting rights by some shareholders.

There are a few cases where an S corporation can owe taxes. For example, it can be taxed if it has accumulated earnings and profits from an earlier existence as a C corporation and its passive income is more than 25% of total gross receipts. It can also be liable for taxes on a few types of capital gains, recapture of the old investment tax credit, and LIFO recapture. If any of these taxes apply, then the S corporation must make quarterly estimated income tax payments. On the other hand, an S corporation is not subject to the alternative minimum tax.

If the management team of an S corporation wants to terminate its S status, the written consent of more than 50% of the shareholders is required, as well as a statement from the corporation to that effect. If the corporation wants to become an S corporation at a later date, there is a five-year waiting period from the last time before it can do so again, unless it obtains special permission from the IRS.

SALES AND USE TAXES*

Sales taxes are imposed at the state, county, and city level—frequently by all three at once. It is also possible for a special tax to be added to the sales tax and applied to a unique region, such as for the construction of a baseball stadium or to support a regional mass transit system. The sales tax is multiplied by the price paid on goods and services on transactions occurring within the taxing area. However, the definition of goods and services that are required to be taxed will vary by state (not usually at the county or city level), and so must be researched at the local level to determine the precise basis of calculation. For example, some states do not tax food sales, on the grounds that this is a necessity whose cost should be reduced as much as possible, while other states include it in their required list of items to be taxed.

A company is required to charge sales taxes to its customers and remit the resulting receipts to the local state government, which will split out the portions due to the local county and city governments and remit these taxes on the company's behalf to those entities. If the company does not charge its customers for these taxes, it is still liable for

---

* Adapted with permission from pp. 661–662 of *Ultimate Accountants' Reference* by Bragg (John Wiley & Sons, 2005).

them, and must pay the unbilled amounts to the state government, though it has the right to attempt to bill its customers after the fact for the missing sales taxes. This can be a difficult collection chore, especially if sales are primarily over the counter, where there are few transaction records that identify the customer. Also, a company is obligated to keep abreast of all changes in sales tax rates and charge its customers for the correct amount; if it does not do so, then it is liable to the government for the difference between what it actually charged and the statutory rate. If a company overcharges its customers, the excess must also be remitted to the government.

The state in which a company is collecting sales taxes can decide how frequently it wants the company to remit taxes. If there are only modest sales, the state may decide that the cost of paperwork exceeds the value of the remittances, and will only require an annual remittance. It is more common to have quarterly or monthly remittances. The state will review the dollar amount of remittances from time to time, and adjust the required remittance frequency based on this information.

All government entities have the right to audit a company's books to see if the proper sales taxes are being charged, and so a company can theoretically be subject to three sales tax audits per year—one each from the city, county, and state revenue departments. Also, since these audits can come from any taxing jurisdiction in which a company does business, there could literally be thousands of potential audits.

The obligation to collect sales taxes is based on the concept of nexus, which was covered earlier in this chapter. If nexus exists, then sales taxes must be collected by the seller. If not, the recipient of purchased goods instead has an obligation to compile a list of items purchased and remit a use tax to the appropriate authority. The use tax is in the same amount as the sales tax. The only difference is that the remitting party is the buyer instead of the seller. Use taxes are also subject to audits by all taxing jurisdictions.

If the buyer of a company's products is including them in its own products for resale to another entity, then the buyer does not have to pay a sales tax to the seller. Instead, the buyer will charge a sales tax to the buyer of *its* final product. This approach is used under the theory that a sales tax should only be charged one time on the sale of a product. However, it can be a difficult chore to explain the lack of sales tax billings during an audit, so sales taxes should only be halted if a buyer sends a sales tax exemption form to the company, which should then be kept on file. The sales tax exemption certificate can be named a resale certificate instead, depending on the issuing authority. It can also be issued to government entities, which are generally exempt from sales and use taxes. As a general rule, sales taxes should always be charged unless there is a sales tax exemption certificate on file—otherwise, the company will still be liable for the remittance of sales taxes in the event of an audit.

TRANSFER PRICING*

Transfer pricing is a key tax consideration, because it can result in the permanent reduction of an organization's tax liability. The permanent reduction is caused by the recognition of income in different taxing jurisdictions that may have different tax rates.

The basic concept behind the use of transfer pricing to reduce one's overall taxes is that a company transfers its products to a division in another country at the lowest possible price if the income tax rate is lower in the other country, or at the highest

---

*   Adapted with permission from pp. 668–670 of *Ultimate Accountants' Reference* by Bragg (John Wiley & Sons, 2005).

possible price if the tax rate is higher. By selling to the division at a low price, the company will report a very high profit on the final sale of products in the other country, which is where that income will be taxed at a presumably lower income tax rate.

For example, Exhibit 3.1 shows a situation in which a company with a location in countries Alpha and Beta has the choice of selling goods either in Alpha or transferring them to Beta and selling them there. The company is faced with a corporate income tax rate of 40% in country Alpha. To permanently avoid some of this income tax, the company sells its products to another subsidiary in country Beta, where the corporate income tax rate is only 25%. By doing so, the company still earns a profit ($60,000) in country Alpha, but the bulk of the profit ($125,000) now appears in country Beta. The net result is a consolidated income tax rate of just 28%.

The IRS is well aware of this tax avoidance strategy, and has developed tax rules that do not eliminate it, but that will reduce the leeway that a CFO has in altering reportable income. Under Section 482 of the IRS Code, the IRS's preferred approach for developing transfer prices is to use the market rate as its basis. However, very few products can be reliably and consistently compared to the market rate, with the exception of commodities, because there are costing differences between them. Also, in many cases, products are so specialized (especially components that are custom-designed to fit into a larger product) that there is no market rate against which they can be compared. Even if there is some basis of comparison between a product and the average market prices for similar products, the CFO still has some leeway in which to alter transfer prices, because the IRS will allow one to add special charges that are based on the cost of transferring the products, or extra fees, such as royalty or licensing fees that are imposed for the subsidiary's use of the parent company's patents or trademarks, or for administrative charges related to the preparation of any documentation required to move products between countries. It is also possible to slightly alter the interest rates charged to subsidiaries (though not too far from market rates) for the use of funds sent to them from the parent organization.

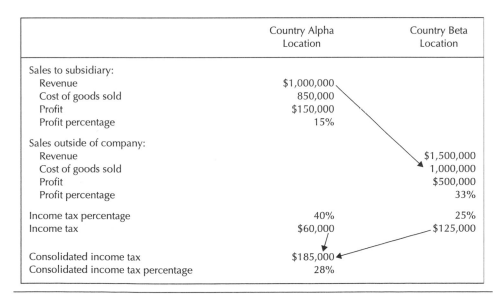

	Country Alpha Location	Country Beta Location
Sales to subsidiary:		
Revenue	$1,000,000	
Cost of goods sold	850,000	
Profit	$150,000	
Profit percentage	15%	
Sales outside of company:		
Revenue		$1,500,000
Cost of goods sold		1,000,000
Profit		$500,000
Profit percentage		33%
Income tax percentage	40%	25%
Income tax	$60,000	$125,000
Consolidated income tax	$185,000	
Consolidated income tax percentage	28%	

Exhibit 3.1 Income Tax Savings from Transfer Pricing

If there is no basis on which to create prices based on market rates, then the IRS's next most favored approach is to calculate the prices based on the *work-back method*. Under this approach, one begins at the end of the sales cycle by determining the price at which a product is sold to an outside customer, and then subtracts the subsidiary's standard markup percentage and its added cost of materials, labor, and overhead, which results in the theoretical transfer price. The work-back method can result in a wide array of transfer prices, since a number of different costs can be subtracted from the final sale price, such as standard costs, actual costs, overhead costs based on different allocation measures, and overhead costs based on cost pools that contain different types of costs.

If that approach does not work, then the IRS's third most favored approach is the *cost plus method*. As the name implies, this approach begins at the other end of the production process and compiles costs from a product's initiation point. After all costs are added before the point of transfer, one then adds a profit margin to the product, thereby arriving at a transfer cost that is acceptable to the IRS. However, once again, the costs that are included in a product are subject to the same points of variation that were noted for the work-back method. In addition, the profit margin added should be the standard margin added for any other company customer, but can be quite difficult to determine if there are a multitude of volume discounts, seasonal discounts, and so on. Consequently, the profit margin added to a product's initial costs can be subject to a great deal of negotiation.

An overriding issue to consider, no matter what approach is used to derive transfer prices, is that taxing authorities can become highly irritated if a company continually pushes the outer limits of acceptable transfer pricing rules in order to maximize its tax savings. When this happens, a company can expect continual audits and penalties on disputed items, as well as less favorable judgments related to any taxation issues. Consequently, it makes a great deal of sense to consistently adopt pricing policies that result in reasonable tax savings, are fully justifiable to the taxing authorities of all involved countries, and that do not push the boundaries of acceptable pricing behavior.

Another transfer pricing issue that can modify a company's pricing strategy is the presence of any restrictions on cash flows out of a country in which it has a subsidiary. In these instances, it may be necessary to report the minimum possible amount of taxable income at the subsidiary, irrespective of the local tax rate. The reason is that the only way for a company to retrieve funds from the country is through the medium of an account receivable, which must be maximized by billing the subsidiary the highest possible amount for transferred goods. In this case, tax planning takes a back seat to cash-flow planning.

Yet another issue that may drive a company to set pricing levels that do not result in reduced income taxes is that a subsidiary may have to report high levels of income in order to qualify for a loan from a local credit institution. This is especially important if the country in which the subsidiary is located has restrictions on the movement of cash, so that the parent company would be unable to withdraw loans that it makes to the subsidiary. As was the case for the last item, cash-flow planning is likely to be more important than income tax reduction.

A final transfer pricing issue to be aware of is that the method for calculating taxable income may vary in other countries. This may falsely lead one to believe that another country has a lower tax rate. A closer examination of how taxable income is calculated might reveal that some expenses are restricted or not allowed at all, resulting in an actual tax rate that is much higher than originally expected. Consultation with a tax expert for the country in question prior to setting up any transfer pricing arrangements is the best way to avoid this problem.

UNEMPLOYMENT TAXES*

Both the state and federal governments will charge a company a fixed percentage of its payroll each year for the expense of unemployment funds that are used to pay former employees who have been released from employment. The state governments administer the distribution of these funds and will compile an experience rating on each company, based on the number of employees it has laid off in the recent past. Based on this experience rating, it can require a company to submit larger or smaller amounts to the state unemployment fund in future years. This can become a considerable burden if a company has a long history of layoffs. Consequently, one should consider the use of temporary employees or outsourcing if this will give a firm the ability to retain a small number of key employees and avoid layoffs while still handling seasonal changes in workloads. Also, if a company is planning to acquire another entity, but plans to lay off a large number of the acquiree's staff once the acquisition is completed, it may make more sense to only acquire the acquiree's assets and selectively hire a few of its employees, thereby retaining a pristine unemployment experience rating with the local state government.

The federal unemployment tax is imposed on a company if it has paid employees at least $1,500 in any calendar quarter, or had at least one employee for some portion of a day within at least 20 weeks of the year. In short, nearly all companies will be required to remit federal unemployment taxes. For the 2006 calendar year, the tax rate is 6.2% of the first $7,000 paid to each employee. This tends to concentrate most federal unemployment tax remittances into the first quarter of the calendar year. In many states, one can take a credit against the federal unemployment tax for up to 5.4% of taxable wages, which results in a net federal unemployment tax of only 0.8%.

If a company is shifting to a new legal entity, perhaps because of a shift from a partnership to a corporation, or from an S corporation to a C corporation, it will have to apply for a new unemployment tax identification number with the local state authorities. This is a problem if the organization being closed down had an unusually good experience rating, since the company will be assigned a poorer one until a new experience rating can be built up over time, which will result in higher unemployment taxes in the short term. To avoid this problem, one should contact the local unemployment taxation office to request that the old company's experience rating be shifted to the new one.

SUMMARY

This chapter presented a set of general tax-planning goals, and then proceeded directly into a series of specific tax topics that should be considered when creating and updating a tax strategy. For example, the presence of an accumulated earnings tax may force a CFO to recommend the issuance of enough dividends to avoid the tax, while the "Mergers and Acquisitions" section shows how the CFO must structure an acquisition in order to minimize the incurrence of income taxes for all parties. From a tax-processing perspective, a firm understanding of the "Nexus" and "Sales and Use Taxes" sections

---

*   Adapted with permission from pp. 671–672 of *Ultimate Accountants' Reference* by Bragg (John Wiley & Sons, 2005).

is crucial for maximizing the efficiency with which tax forms are filed, while the CFO should thoroughly understand the transfer pricing topic in order to realize permanent reductions in federal income taxes. Thus, the CFO must have a broad-based knowledge of a variety of taxation topics, which in turn allows her to construct a tax strategy that considers all aspects of company operations, financing methods, locations, and corporate structure.

CHAPTER 4

INFORMATION TECHNOLOGY STRATEGY

The CFO is sometimes assigned to supervise the information technology (IT) function. Even if she is not, the CFO should have a strong interest in this area, since it can require a great deal of capital investment. Companies tend to invest too much money in IT, or at least spend it on the wrong projects, because they do not invest the time up-front to determine how IT can most effectively dovetail into the overall business strategy. In this chapter, we will look at why IT strategy is important to the CFO, how to properly develop an IT strategy, and what specific IT projects are likely to be of value, depending on the general type of business strategy that a company intends to follow.

REASONS FOR DEVISING AN INFORMATION TECHNOLOGY STRATEGY

The standard corporate approach to the development of an IT strategy is to continue the funding of existing projects, and to approve funding for additional projects as presented by the IT manager until a predetermined cap on expenditures is reached. This approach completely avoids any linkage of IT investments to a company's overall business strategy, likely resulting in lost opportunities to improve the business. However, there are several IT decision points at which a CFO could insert the need for a complete evaluation of the IT strategy, thereby creating a closer fit between IT projects and the general business direction. They are:

- *When merging entities.* When a company acquires another company, there will be questions about whose systems will be used for various functions, or whether systems should be kept separate. This is an excellent time to conduct a thorough review of the reasons why either company's systems should be used, allowing for the "best of breed" to be retained.

- *When major cost reductions are needed.* When a company finds itself losing so much money that it must conduct a detailed review of all costs companywide, this is a good excuse for an IT strategy review, though the review will be heavily skewed in the direction of cost reductions rather than toward how strategy can be used to enhance the business.

- *When there is an IT project request overload.* This is one of the most common reasons for creating an IT strategy. The IT manager is completely overwhelmed by the number of requests being dropped on his department, and complains to senior management for assistance in sorting through the requests; this results in an IT strategy that is primarily used as a sorting device for picking the most necessary projects.

- *When current IT systems are failing.*   When in-house legacy systems are beginning to fail for any number of reasons—loss of key programmers, excessive transaction volume, and so on—the CFO can push for the development of an IT strategy to use as a framework for the creation of replacement systems. The only problem is that the systems may be failing so rapidly that the strategy development process is rushed.

- *When the company's organizational structure is being changed.*   From time to time, senior management may decide to reorganize a company based on geographical locations, new managers running different functions, and so on. The existing IT systems may be overburdened by the information requirements of the new structure, which is an ideal time for an IT strategy review.

- *When existing systems interfere with functional efficiency.*   This problem arises most frequently in companies whose main target is to continually reduce costs in order to be the low-cost producer. They will eventually reduce costs to the point where the procedures surrounding the existing IT systems are interfering with further cost improvements, resulting in a strategy review just to see how the systems can be altered from a cost-reduction standpoint.

- *When new management is hired.*   When a new CEO is installed and brings in her own staff to run a company, they may conduct a complete "spring cleaning" of the entire company, which may include existing IT systems. This is an excellent opportunity for an IT strategy review, since new directions can be determined without any interference from the old management team.

No matter which of the above circumstances is used as an excuse to create an IT strategy, the CFO must be sure to incorporate it into an ongoing schedule of IT strategy reviews, so that incremental adjustments can be made to the plan over time as the overall business strategy changes.

DEVELOPING THE INFORMATION TECHNOLOGY STRATEGY

The first step in the development of an IT strategy is the formation of an IT steering committee that is given responsibility for creating the strategy. It is essential that this group be comprised of people from all key functional areas of the company, so that its decisions have a better chance of being accepted by the entire company. The CFO should attend these meetings, as should the manager of the IT function. However, there should be no additional IT representatives, unless required for special information, since a heavy IT-weighting will tend to skew decisions in the direction of what is technically needed, rather than what the entire business needs.

The committee is responsible for creating IT strategies and prioritizing IT projects based on those strategies, but must forward this work to the executive committee for final approval. It is also responsible for the review and approval of new IT projects that are submitted from around the company. In order to avoid having the committee be bogged down by the review of *all* requested IT projects, it should limit its scope to reviews of only the largest and most expensive projects, letting the IT manager handle all smaller issues.

Once assembled, the steering committee should first spend considerable time learning about the overall corporate strategies, which it will use to formulate the IT strategy. This initial learning stage can take as little as one day if a formal strategy document has already been created. However, it is more likely that the company operates without one, in which case the committee must interview members of senior management to gather information that they can then assemble into a strategy.

The process of learning about the business strategy will likely require a considerable amount of education about the general operating framework of the company. For example, the committee members should know if the company uses make-to-order or make-to-stock production, whether it uses single or multiple warehouses, back flushes its production records, processes transactions in multiple currencies, has special government reporting requirements, outsources various functions, swaps product designs with its suppliers, and so on. This level of detailed knowledge about operations is crucial for later determining the types of IT projects that can be implemented to most effectively assist the company's overall strategy.

With a general business strategy in hand, the committee can then create an IT strategy that supports the business strategy by shoring up weak areas that are considered important to the business, as well as by increasing the capabilities of areas where the company wishes to maintain a strong competitive posture. To this end, the strategy should include a detailed list of corporate strengths and weaknesses, and how the IT strategy will impact them. In addition, it should anticipate the need to compete with the IT projects currently under development at competing firms, to the extent that this information can be ascertained. Another approach for developing possible strategies is to conduct a benchmarking review of other companies' IT projects, possibly of organizations located completely outside the company's industry. For ideas about what types of strategies can be implemented, see the later "Specific Applications" section. This step is an ongoing process that is constantly updated in light of changes to the general strategy, and so tends to require incremental adjustments to the priorities assigned to various projects.

With an IT strategy in place, the steering committee must next determine what specific IT projects need to be completed in order to implement the strategy. This requires a detailed knowledge of precisely what IT functionality is already present, as well as the types of projects required to bridge the gap between current and desired capabilities. The analysis should also consider the technical ability of the in-house IT department in order to understand how much outside assistance may be required for certain projects. This review of in-house talent must break down the capabilities of personnel into such categories as subject matter experts, process experts, application development experts, and systems maintenance personnel. By doing so, the committee can spot those areas in which a lack of personnel skills could make it exceedingly difficult to implement a new project. The committee should also determine the proportion of IT staff time currently being used to maintain existing IT systems, since this tends to absorb most staff time, leaving little for new development efforts of any kind. This problem can sometimes be overcome by the judicious replacement of custom-developed software with packaged software that is supported by an outside party, thereby reducing the maintenance efforts of the IT department.

Further, the committee should include a detailed examination of the projects currently under development and the amount of resources and time required to complete them. In many cases, it may make sense to complete projects that are already under development, even if they fall well outside the requirements of the IT strategy, simply because they require minimal effort to finish.

This detailed level of review can be a massive effort, especially if the company has many product lines, locations, or divisions. In order to complete at least some portion of the work as soon as possible, the committee can limit its scope by focusing on only specific areas. The limitation criterion can be whether the resulting information will be critical to business operations, if it will be used by more than one functional area, or if it results in information sharing with other business partners. Of course, the overriding criterion will be if the business strategy states that a specific target area is considered the primary opportunity for the business as a whole. If the IT plan's scope is limited in this manner, the committee should prioritize the value of the remaining parts of the business and add them to the IT strategy as time allows.

Even with an IT strategy in place that clearly defines what types of projects should be approved, it will still be difficult for the committee to assign exact priorities to different IT projects, due to the wide variety of possible projects. Any or all of the following techniques can be used to accomplish this prioritization:

- *Building-block approach.*   Assign high priorities to those projects needed as building blocks for later projects that cannot be completed until the first projects are implemented. For example, a companywide network must be completed before an enterprise resource planning (ERP) system can be installed throughout a company.

- *Portfolio approach.*   When cash resources are reduced, a company tends to cancel all high-risk IT projects and focus its efforts on just those with a clear and likely payoff. However, this approach runs the risk of never achieving a breakthrough technical advantage. A better approach is to identify those projects with potentially high payoffs and assign a small proportion of the IT budget to them, even if there is a strong risk of failure.

- *Competing standards approach.*   If a project requires the use of one of a set of competing industry standards, it may be worthwhile to delay the implementation until it becomes more clear as to which of the standards will emerge as the dominant one. Otherwise, a company may find itself having invested funds in a technology for which there is a shrinking base of support expertise.

- *Forced ranking.*   Sequentially compare the value of each project to every other proposed project in order to create a ranking. For example, Project A is compared to all other proposed projects. If the committee considers it to be the top priority, it is assigned that ranking. Then the committee individually compares all remaining projects to determine the next most critical project. Once priorities have been assigned using this approach, the committee takes another pass at the list and compares each project on it to the one immediately below, and reiterates this process until it is satisfied with the ranking.

- *Payoff approach.*   Every project proposal should be accompanied by a cost-benefit proposal. Though the committee can choose to ignore this information in the interests of long-term strategy, the ability of an IT project to generate a profit, especially when prioritizing among short-term projects, should not be ignored.

Of the prioritization methods just described, strong consideration should be given to the forced ranking approach, but within the larger framework of specific business strategies. For example, if a massive jump in sales through the use of a more efficient, wireless-enabled sales force is considered the primary business strategy, then all key projects related to this strategy can be ranked higher than those of the next most important strategy. The building-block prioritization approach can then be used to determine the initial prioritization of projects within each group of projects, while a forced ranking can then be conducted on the remaining projects.

Throughout the process of defining the IT strategy, conducting a gap analysis, and assigning priorities to specific projects, the steering committee must be mindful of the need for in-depth communication of its activities with the executive committee, the IT department, and the company as a whole. This is necessary to ensure the highest level of support and cooperation by all parties when it comes time to implement the set of projects that the steering committee recommends to the executive committee.

TECHNICAL STRATEGIES

The primary point of this chapter is the development of a list of IT projects that will support a company's overall business strategy. Nonetheless, the IT department itself is likely to have a few thoughts about the underlying structure of IT systems to be used. These are technical issues that a CFO is not likely to be conversant with, so the following few points should be kept in mind when discussing technical strategies with the IT staff:

- *Use scaleable components.*   If a company has any prospects of expanding, it will eventually run the risk of outgrowing its existing computer infrastructure. Thus, the CFO should ask about the scalability of any new systems that the IT staff wants to install. A truly scaleable system should easily handle substantially more transaction volume, or at least do so through a logical upgrade path.

- *Use open standards.*   The CFO should avoid the use of proprietary systems whenever possible, since these systems are linked to the fortunes of their suppliers. They also tend to be more expensive than open systems, and attract fewer independent developers who provide add-on applications. This tends to be a long-term and sometimes expensive goal, and so must be reviewed in light of other targets and how this goal will impact them.

- *Use the same architecture for as long as possible.*   Despite the preceding recommendation to switch to open standards, the CFO also faces the problem of keeping the IT investment as low as is prudent. One approach for doing so is to force the IT department to prolong the use of existing standards for as long as possible. Once the architecture changes, a slew of related expenses will arise, such as training, software, and hardware, so the CFO should force the IT staff to carefully consider the likely longevity of any IT architecture it wants to adopt.

- *Use packaged software.*   Many companies suffer from the "not invented here" syndrome, and prefer to sink large amounts of cash into the development of IT systems that could have been purchased from a supplier. The advantage of using a packaged system is its lower cost, support by the supplier, and relative absence of bugs (since many customers are testing it and feeding back their comments to the supplier). Packaged software should only be avoided when a prospective application is so company-specific that no packaged solutions are available.

- *Use an enterprise resources planning (ERP) system.*   Even if a company installs packaged software, as just described, it may install different packages in each part of the company. Each of these packages may be written in a different software language, operate on a different hardware platform, require special maintenance skills, or not have an interface with other systems within the company. The result is silos of information for which manual or customized interfaces must be used. An alternative is to install a single ERP system that addresses the computing needs of all functions within the company. Though highly complex to install and operate, an ERP system uses a single underlying database so that information can be more easily exchanged throughout the company.

- *Use object-oriented programming.* When in house programming must be used, the CFO should emphasize object-oriented programming, which allows one to easily move blocks of code into different applications and link them together again. This approach greatly reduces the amount of programming required on an ongoing basis.

- *Use few suppliers.* IT suppliers love to pin the blame for a system failure on other suppliers. The obvious solution is to concentrate IT purchases with the smallest possible number of suppliers. Another reason for using few suppliers is that volume purchases can result in purchase discounts. If there is no way to avoid hiring many suppliers, then the CFO should at least designate a lead supplier, to whom other suppliers act as subcontractors and who is responsible for fixing system problems.

- *Use relational databases.* The most efficient method for storing data is the relational database, which is a set of separate tables linked by indexing fields, so that information can be easily cross-referenced and extracted without storing the same data in multiple locations. Using a relational database allows a company to store a specific data item only once, which makes it much easier to update and maintain.

- *Use dashboards.* The management team is most likely receiving the bulk of its operational and financial information at lengthy intervals from the accounting department, probably no more frequently than once a week, if not once a month. A better approach is to push selected operational information out from the corporate databases to managers' computers with dashboards. A dashboard is a computer display that summarizes key operational and financial information that is as current as the underlying database information. Thus, a dashboard can present real-time information. The more comprehensive dashboards also include a drill-down capability, so that managers can view more detailed information.

- *Centralize only the most important information.* Data warehouses are touted as a wonderful way to centralize and organize all of a company's key information, but they are also expensive and labor-intensive to create and maintain. Consequently, the CFO should carefully examine the need to store various types of information in this repository, as well as the incremental cost of doing so, and only include those data items for which a clear value can be seen.

There are many more considerations in the development of a technical strategy that supports the overall IT strategy, but they are well beyond the scope of this book. The bullet points noted here are most useful to the CFO as general guidelines to consider when discussing technical strategy issues with the IT department.

SPECIFIC APPLICATIONS

Thus far, we have looked at the general structure that a CFO should pursue when developing an IT strategy. However, the question remains: What specific IT activities are most worthwhile for a company that is pursuing a specific type of strategy? Circumstances will vary widely by individual company, but the following list of activities will generally be most useful when conducted under the indicated strategies:

- *Explosive sales growth strategy.* In this instance, a company has chosen to increase sales at the highest possible rate, ignoring cost efficiencies, product improvements, or other internal efficiencies in the short term. It should consider installing computer systems for its dealers and sales representatives that give them direct access to the company's quote and order status database. It may wish to provide wireless access to its sales representatives, so they can access information more easily from the field. It can also create a quoting system for the sales staff that tracks which quotes are under development, which have been submitted, and which have been won, as well as the reasons for lost quotes. Senior management will want daily access to sales information, especially for new sales regions. Also, the strategy could include a complete standardization of systems installed at all new company locations, in order to reduce the maintenance workload of the IT staff. In general, the company should consider installing packaged customer relationship management (CRM) software for use by its sales staff in order to have a centralized database of customer information.

- *Great customer service strategy.*   In this case, a company chooses to expend extra effort to ensure top-level service to its customers, probably combined with higher product costs that customers are willing to pay in exchange for the service. It should consider giving its customers electronic access to information about their orders, perhaps through an Internet connection. It should also allow them to place electronic orders, either through the Internet or an electronic data interchange (EDI) connection. Further, if computer access is not possible, it can consider dial-up access to obtain the same information through the telephone system. In addition, there should be in-house databases to track the status of customer complaints, as well as product or service quality issues and the status of all field service orders. These systems can also be integrated with global positioning systems, so that customers can see exactly where their shipments are located around the world. Company management should have immediate access to these databases to see where problems are arising; this approach could be advanced to "push" technology, where management is notified automatically by the system when a problem arises. The company should also have a product recall system in place, perhaps including tracking by production lots, so that product problems can be dealt with rapidly and efficiently. The system should also have a linkage between the order entry and part ordering or manufacturing systems, so that delivery commitments can be made automatically and on-line, with access to this information to customers.

- *Product improvement strategy.*   In this instance, a company elects to constantly upgrade its products and develop new ones, on the assumption that customers will pay a premium for them. It should consider installing systems that allow it to easily swap drawings and other product documents electronically with its business partners. It can also implement project management systems that allow for concurrent product development by multiple departments. Further, systems should allow the management team to track time to market on all product development projects, as well as development problems. There should also be a database of product component costs that stores cost information for a variety of product configurations and purchasing or production volumes, which is useful for meeting target costing goals. In addition, there should be advanced cost accounting systems for accumulating product costs at any stage of the development process. Also, a prototyping system should allow for rapid product designs and modeling applications. Finally, systems may be needed for tracking all stages of product patent applications, as well as for product licensing agreements with other companies.

- *Low-cost strategy.* In this case, a company chooses to limit its service level and range of product offerings, concentrating instead on selling products at the absolute lowest cost possible. One possible application under this strategy is the acquisition of a manufacturing resources planning (MRP II) package, which creates an orderly flow of resources through a manufacturing facility, resulting in much better use of materials, equipment, and personnel. Another option is the installation of a just-in-time (JIT) manufacturing system, though this involves fewer computer systems, with a greater emphasis on the reconfiguration of the shop floor, reducing the size of production runs, and altering the size and timing of supplier deliveries. Another possibility is the use of supply chain management (SCM) software, which gives suppliers a transparent view of what customer orders have reached the company and when they must send in parts in order for the company to meet its product schedule. A mandatory system to have in place is a comprehensive bill of materials database that is maintained with the highest degree of accuracy, since this information is needed to drive a variety of parts ordering systems. Also, if IT is considered a less strategic capability, some portions of it can be outsourced overseas to take advantage of lower labor costs.

In addition to the basic strategies just noted, there are general types of operations or situations where certain types of IT projects are more likely to be found. For example, a publicly held company may be interested in a rapid closing of its financial transactions at the end of each quarter, and so may be more interested in advanced software systems that will allow it to do so. A public company may also want fast access to key metrics in order to be able to pass this information along to its investors, so it may be more inclined to invest in an executive information system. For the same reason, other projects high on its list may be a data warehouse, a CRM system containing up-to-date forecasting capabilities, and an accurate backlog tracking system.

Another type of company operation is the international corporation. This entity requires accounting software with multicurrency capabilities, as well as worldwide electronic meeting capabilities that can be provided through instant messaging, a wide-area network, and videoconferencing. Also, if company management wishes to centralize selected worldwide transactions, it can invest in an ERP system, or at a lower level, just the customer service and purchasing functions.

A company type requiring significantly different IT systems is the service business. In this case, taking care of key employees and tracking who has key knowledge are critical to corporate success. Consequently, IT systems should track employee training, benefits, hiring, rewards, performance reviews, and turnover, as well as applicants for specific positions. If the people in this business are knowledge-intensive, such as consultants, they should also be supplied with wireless communications to other employees, so they can quickly obtain information relevant to their clients.

Finally, the classic manufacturing operation requires many of the systems previously noted under the low-cost strategy. The previously noted MRP or JIT systems can also be integrated into a companywide ERP system in order to share information across all departments that may be of the most use to the manufacturing function. Further, IT systems should allow the manufacturing operation to create products in a make-to-order mode, which is the least inventory-intensive form of production. There can also be supplier certification systems that allow the receiving department to cancel incoming inspections for prequalified goods, while a cost estimation system is critical for the design of new products. There should also be an engineering changes tracking database that notes the times when product modifications will be swapped into the existing production process.

Clearly, the types of systems installed will vary widely depending on the type of business strategy that the management team chooses to pursue. Even when the range of choices are narrowed down into any of the preceding strategic directions, there may still be too many possible projects from which to pick. If so, the selection criteria noted earlier in the "Developing the Information Technology Strategy" section should be used to locate those few projects with the greatest potential to give the company's strategy a boost.

SUMMARY

As may have become evident in this chapter, a company with a proper IT strategy is well on its way to devising an extremely successful overall business strategy. The selection of the proper set of IT project priorities requires considerable time and the involvement of all parts of the company, but results in excellent use of limited capital to support the most important business activities. When these strategies are created in light of what is being done at competing firms, a company has a good chance of establishing a strong competitive position from which it can only be dislodged with great difficulty.

PART 2

ACCOUNTING

CHAPTER 5

PERFORMANCE MEASUREMENT SYSTEMS

This chapter contains the 28 most important performance measurement ratios for a CFO to use, covering asset utilization, operating performance, cash flow, liquidity, solvency, return on investment (ROI), and market performance. Each measurement description includes an overview, notes on how to derive the calculation, and how it is used in an example.

CREATING A PERFORMANCE MEASUREMENT SYSTEM

If a CFO were in favor of using all 28 of the measurements listed in this chapter, he or she might spend a great deal of time compiling the calculations, which is not a good use of time. Instead, one should see if the accounting software currently in use can automatically calculate this information. If not, then the task should be handed off to a financial analyst to calculate on an electronic spreadsheet.

Another issue for a performance measurement system is consistency of calculations. It is a simple matter to show enhanced performance measurements simply by deleting a few elements from a calculation; to avoid this, the CFO should spend a considerable amount of time formally laying out the precise definition and calculation methodology for each performance measurement. If there is some perceived risk that the measurements will be altered even with these instructions in place, then the internal audit team should be asked to review the measurements from time to time. If there is a good reason for altering a calculation at some point in the future, then the new calculation should be used to modify the same measurement for all previous periods for which the measure is reported, so there is reporting consistency across all periods.

The CFO should be prepared to handle criticism from other department managers if the performance measurement system shows them to have subpar performance. A common reaction is that the measurements are being made incorrectly, with the "correct" version undoubtedly yielding improved results for the department in question. The CFO can avoid this problem to some extent by spending time at the front end of the performance measurement system implementation, working with the department managers to derive the best measurements possible. By giving department managers a voice in the calculation methodology in advance, they are less likely to complain later on.

ASSET UTILIZATION MEASUREMENTS*

The six ratios noted in this section primarily focus on the level of a company's sales in relation to other key operating variables of a company, such as working capital, head count, and total expenses. They are designed to give the CFO a quick overview of the sufficiency of sales being generated.

Sales to Working Capital Ratio.   It is exceedingly important to keep the amount of cash used by an organization at a minimum, so that its financing needs are reduced. One of the best ways to determine changes in the overall usage of cash over time is the ratio of sales to working capital. This ratio shows the amount of cash required to maintain a certain level of sales. It is most effective when tracked on a trend line, so that management can see if there is a long-term change in the amount of cash required by the business in order to generate the same amount of sales. For instance, if a company has elected to increase its sales to less creditworthy customers, it is likely that they will pay more slowly than regular customers, thereby increasing the company's investment in accounts receivable. Similarly, if the management team decides to increase the speed of order fulfillment by increasing the amount of inventory for certain items, then the inventory investment will increase. In both cases, the ratio of sales to working capital will worsen due to specific management decisions. An alternative usage for this ratio is for budgeting purposes, since budgeted working capital levels can be compared to the historical amount of this ratio to see if the budgeted working capital level is sufficient.

The formula is to compare sales to working capital, which is accounts receivable, plus inventory, minus accounts payable. One should not use annualized *gross* sales in the calculation, since this would include in the sales figure the amount of any sales that have already been returned, and are therefore already included in the inventory figure. The formula is:

$$\frac{\text{Annualized Net Sales}}{(\text{Accounts Receivable} + \text{Inventory} - \text{Accounts Payable})}$$

As an example, the Jolt Power Supply Company has elected to reduce the amount of inventory it carries for some of its least-ordered stock items, with a goal of increasing inventory turnover from twice a year to four times a year. It achieves its inventory goal quite rapidly by selling back some of its inventory to its suppliers in exchange for credits against future purchases. Exhibit 5.1 shows portions of its operating results for the first four quarters after this decision was made.

The accounts receivable turn over at a rate of once every 30 days, which does not change through the term of the analysis. Inventory dropped in the second quarter to arrive at the new inventory turnover goal, while the amount of accounts payable stays at one-half of the revenue level, reflecting a typical distributor's gross margin of 50% throughout all four periods. The resulting ratio shows that the company has indeed improved its ratio of sales to working capital, but at the price of some lost sales to customers who were apparently coming to the company because of its broad inventory selection.

---

*   Adapted with permission from Chapters 2 to 8 of *Business Ratios and Formulas* by Bragg (John Wiley & Sons, 2002).

	Quarter 1	Quarter 2	Quarter 3	Quarter 4
Revenue	$320,000	$310,000	$290,000	$280,000
Accounts Receivable	107,000	103,000	97,000	93,000
Inventory	640,000	320,000	320,000	320,000
Accounts Payable	53,000	52,000	48,000	47,000
Total Working Capital	694,000	371,000	369,000	366,000
Sales: Working Capital Ratio	1:.54	1:.30	1:.32	1:.33

EXHIBIT 5.1 SAMPLE SALES AND WORKING CAPITAL DATA

Days of Working Capital.   A company can use a very large amount of working capital to generate a small volume of sales, which represents a poor use of assets. The inefficient asset use can lie in any part of working capital—excessive quantities of accounts receivable or inventory in relation to sales, or very small amounts of accounts payable. The days of working capital measure, when tracked on a trend line, is a good indicator of changes in the efficient use of working capital. A low number of days of working capital indicates a highly efficient use of working capital. However, working capital levels will vary throughout the year, depending on a company's business cycle, which will alter the days of working capital figure depending on the month of the year. For example, if a firm has a Christmas selling season, then it will build inventory until its prime selling season, resulting in a gradual increase in the days of working capital measure for most of the year.

The formula is to add together the current balance of accounts receivable and inventory, and subtract accounts payable. Then divide the result by sales per day (annual sales divided by 365). The formula is:

$$\frac{(\text{Accounts Receivable} + \text{Inventory} - \text{Accounts Payable})}{\text{Net Sales}/365}$$

As an example, the Electro-Therm Company, maker of electronic thermometers, has altered its customer service policy to guarantee a 99% fulfillment rate within one day of a customer's order. To do that, it has increased inventory levels for many stockkeeping units. Electro-Therm's CFO is concerned about the company's use of capital to sustain this new policy; she has collected the information in the following table to prove her point to the company president:

Time Period	Accounts Receivable	Inventory	Accounts Payable	Working Capital	Net Sales	Sales per Day	Days of Working Capital
Year before policy change	602,000	1,825,000	493,000	2,920,000	5,475,000	15,000	195
Year after policy change	723,000	2,760,000	591,000	4,074,000	6,570,000	18,000	226

The table reveals that Electro-Therm's management has acquired an additional $1,095,000 of revenue (assuming that incremental sales are solely driven by the customer service policy change) at the cost of a nearly equivalent amount of investment in inventory. Depending on the firm's cost of capital, inventory obsolescence rate, and changes in customer retention rates, the new customer service policy may or may not be considered a reasonable decision.

Sales per Person.   This is one of the most closely watched of all performance measures. It is based on the assumption that employees are at the core of a company's profitability, and so high degrees of efficiency in this area are bound to result in strong profitability. It is also a standard benchmark in many industries.

The formula is to divide revenue for a full year by the total number of full-time equivalents (FTEs) in the company. An FTE is the combination of staffing that equals a 40-hour week. For example, two half-time employees would be counted as one FTE. The formula is:

$$\frac{\text{Annualized Revenue}}{\text{Total Full-Time Equivalents}}$$

As an example, the operations manager of the Twirling Washing Machine Company wants to determine the sales per person for his company. The company has annual revenues of $4,200,000. Its head count is:

Department	Head Count
Direct labor department	22
Direct labor part-time staff	6
Production supervisors	2
Materials handling department	4
Sales, general, & administrative	10
Administrative part-time staff	2
Engineering department	8

In total, the company has 54 employees. However, if we assume that the part-time staff all work half time, then the eight part-time positions can be reduced to four FTEs, which decreases the total head count to 50 personnel. The calculation results in overall sales per employee of $84,000, which is $4,200,000 in revenues, divided by 50 employees.

Sales Backlog Ratio.   This ratio is an extremely useful tool for determining a company's ability to maintain its current level of production. If the ratio is dropping rapidly over several consecutive months, then it is likely that the company will shortly experience a reduction in sales volume, as well as overcapacity in its production and related overhead areas, resulting in imminent losses. Conversely, a rapid jump in the ratio indicates that a company cannot keep up with demand and may soon experience both customer relations problems from delayed orders and a need for additional capital expenditures and staff hirings to increase its productive capacity.

The formula is to divide the most current total backlog of sales orders by sales. It is generally best not to use annualized sales in the denominator, since sales may vary considerably over that period, due to the influence of seasonality. A better denominator is sales over just the preceding quarter. The formula is:

$$\frac{\text{Backlog of Orders Received}}{\text{Sales}}$$

	January	February	March
Rolling 3-month sales	$4,500,000	$4,750,000	$4,800,000
Month-end backlog	2,500,000	2,000,000	1,750,000
Sales backlog ratio	.55:1	.42:1	.36:1

Exhibit 5.2 Sample Sales and Backlog Data

A variation on this formula is to determine the number of days of sales contained within the backlog, which is achieved by comparing the backlog to the average daily sales volume that a company typically produces. This formula is:

$$\frac{\text{Total Backlog}}{\text{Annual Sales}/360 \text{ Days}}$$

As an example, Exhibit 5.2 shows the sales and backlog data for the Jabber Phone Company. The data reveals that the company's sales are continuing to increase over time, while its backlog is decreasing. The change was caused by an increase in the company's productive capacity for additional cell phones. As a result, the company is gradually clearing out its backlog and converting it into sales. However, the management team must be aware that, if the present trend continues, the company will eventually clear out its entire backlog and find itself with a sudden reduction in sales unless it greatly increases its sales and marketing efforts to build the backlog back up to a higher level.

Breakeven Point.   This measurement determines the sales level at which a company exactly breaks even. This figure is useful for determining how much extra productive capacity is available after breakeven sales have been manufactured, which tells the management team how much profit can theoretically be generated at maximum capacity levels. It is also good for determining changes in the breakeven point resulting from decisions to add fixed costs (especially when replacing variable production costs with fixed automation costs). It can also be used to determine changes in profits when the sales staff is contemplating making changes in product prices.

The formula is to divide the average gross margin percentage into total operating costs. Be sure to include all operating costs outside of the cost of goods sold in this calculation—only extraordinary items that are in no way related to ongoing operations should be excluded from this formula, which is:

$$\frac{\text{Total Operating Expenses}}{\text{Average Gross Margin Percentage}}$$

As an example, the Reef Shark Acquisition Company is looking into the purchase of a sewing thread company. Its two key concerns are the breakeven point of the acquiree and the presence of any overhead costs that it can eliminate by centralizing functions at its corporate headquarters. Its due diligence team constructs the table of information in Exhibit 5.3.

This exhibit clearly shows that the acquiree currently has a breakeven point so high that it is essentially incapable of ever turning a profit, since the breakeven level is the same as its maximum productive capacity. However, the removal of some key overhead costs reduces the breakeven point to such an extent that the acquirer will be able to

	Before Acquisition
Maximum sales capacity	$10,000,000
Current average sales	9,500,000
Gross margin percentage	35%
Total operating expenses	3,500,000
Breakeven point	$10,000,000
Operating expense reductions	750,000
Revised breakeven level	$7,857,000
Maximum profits with revised breakeven point	$750,050

Exhibit 5.3   Sample Breakeven Data

generate a significant return from the existing sales level. The revised breakeven level is determined by subtracting the operating expense reductions of $750,000 from the existing operating expenses of $3,500,000, and then dividing the remaining $2,750,000 in operating expenses by the gross margin of 35% to arrive at a new breakeven point of $7,857,000. The maximum potential profit figure of $750,050 is derived by subtracting the revised breakeven point from the maximum possible sales capacity level of $10,000,000 and then multiplying the result by the gross profit percentage.

Margin of Safety.   This is the amount by which sales can drop before a company's breakeven point is reached. It is particularly useful in situations where large portions of a company's sales are at risk, such as when they are tied up in a single customer contract that can be cancelled. Knowing the margin of safety gives one a good idea of the probability that a company will find itself in difficult financial circumstances caused by sales fluctuations.

The formula is to subtract the breakeven point from the current sales level, and then divide the result by the current sales level. To calculate the breakeven point, divide the gross margin percentage into total fixed costs. This formula can be broken down into individual product lines for a better view of risk levels within business units. The formula is:

$$\frac{\text{Current Sales Level} - \text{Breakeven Point}}{\text{Current Sales Level}}$$

As an example, the Fat Tire Publishing House, Inc., is contemplating the purchase of several delivery trucks to assist in the delivery of its *Fat Tire Weekly* mountain biking magazine to a new sales region. The addition of these trucks will add $200,000 to the operating costs of the company. Key information related to this decision is noted in Exhibit 5.4.

This exhibit shows that the margin of safety is reduced from 21% to 19% as a result of the truck acquisition. However, profits are expected to increase by $20,000, so the management team must weigh the risk of adding expenses to the benefit of increased profitability.

OPERATING PERFORMANCE MEASUREMENTS

The four measurements noted in this section focus on the margins derived when certain types of expenses are included. The most highly recommended one is the operating profit

	Before Truck Purchase	After Truck Purchase
Sales	$2,300,000	$2,700,000
Gross margin percentage	55%	55%
Fixed expenses	$1,000,000	$1,200,000
Breakeven point	$1,818,000	$2,182,000
Profits	$265,000	$285,000
Margin of safety	21%	19%

EXHIBIT 5.4 SAMPLE MARGIN OF SAFETY DATA

percentage, especially when tracked on a trend line, since it shows operating results before any special adjustments are added that might otherwise cloud the picture of a company's true underlying performance.

Core Growth Rate. Companies regularly trumpet their ability to increase revenues year after year. But how much of that growth is due to acquisitions, accounting changes, or product price increases? By stripping out these forms of manufactured revenue, it is much easier to see if a company's core operations are actually growing, and by how much. However, the information used in this formula can be difficult to obtain, and may involve the use of approximations, especially for the determination of changes caused by revenue recognition policies and the determination of an average annual price increase. Consequently, the results should be considered approximations of the actual core growth rate.

The formula is to subtract from the current annual revenue the annual revenue from five years ago, as well as revenue from acquisitions at the point of acquisition, and any revenue changes arising from altered revenue recognition policies. Divide the result by the annual revenue from five years ago, then divide this result by five to annualize it, and then subtract the company's average annual price increase over the five-year measurement period. The formula is:

$$\frac{((\text{Current Annual Revenue} - \text{Annual Revenue 5 Years Ago} - \text{Acquired Revenue} - \text{Revenue Recognition Changes}))/(\text{Annual Revenue Five Years Ago})}{5} - \frac{\text{Average Annual Price}}{\text{Increase}}$$

If information about the company's average annual price increase is not available, then consider using the change in price of the underlying commodity or industry segment, as measured by either the Consumer Price Index or the Product Price Index.

As an example, the president of the Premier Concrete Group (PCG) has recently claimed that the company has experienced average annual compounded growth of 12%. An outside analyst wants to verify this claim by calculating PCG's core growth rate. PCG's current revenue is $88 million, and its revenue five years ago was $50 million. During that period, PCG acquired companies having a total of $27 million in revenues when they were acquired. Also, PCG benefited from altered revenue recognition policies that increased its revenue by $5 million. The analyst also learns that the concrete industry's average annual price increase during the measurement period was 2%. The analyst determines PCG's core growth rate with the following calculation:

$$\frac{\begin{array}{c} ((\$88 \text{ Million Current Revenue}) - (\$50 \text{ Million Revenue 5 Years Ago}) \\ - \$27 \text{ Million Acquired Revenue}) - (\$5 \text{ Million From Revenue} \\ \text{Recognition Changes}))/(\$50 \text{ Million Revenue 5 Years Ago}) \end{array}}{5 \text{ Years}}$$

$$- 2\% \text{ Average Annual Price Increase} = 0.4\%$$

Gross Profit Percentage.   This measurement reveals the profit left over from operations after all variable costs have been subtracted from revenues. In essence, it shows the efficiency of the production process in relation to the prices and unit volumes at which products are sold.

There are two ways to measure the gross margin. The most common approach is to add together the costs of overhead, direct materials, and direct labor, subtract them from revenue, and then divide the result by revenue. This approach takes into account all costs that can be reasonably associated with the production process. The formula is:

$$\frac{\text{Revenue} - (\text{Overhead} + \text{Direct Materials} + \text{Direct Labor})}{\text{Revenue}}$$

The trouble with this approach is that many of the production costs are not truly variable. Under a much more strictly defined view of variable costs, only direct materials should be included in the formula, since this is the only cost that truly changes in lockstep with changes in revenue. All other production costs are then shifted into other operational and administrative costs, which typically yields a very high gross margin percentage. The formula is:

$$\frac{\text{Revenue} - \text{Direct Materials}}{\text{Revenue}}$$

As an example, the Spanish Tile Company bases its sales quoting system on the gross margin assigned to its products—prices quoted must have a gross margin of at least 25% in order to cover administrative costs and create a modest profit. Recently, the Iberian Tile Company has been taking business away from the Spanish Tile Company through more aggressive pricing. Investigation of its competitor's quoting practices reveals that it uses an alternative gross margin model that uses only direct material costs as a deduction from revenues. This means that its competitor is always in a position to offer lower prices, since it does not incorporate direct labor and overhead costs into its pricing model. The Iberian Tile Company is in danger of quoting excessively low prices if it continues to use its gross margin model, so it focuses on how prospective sales will impact its bottleneck operation, which is the tile kiln. If a prospective sale requires a great deal of kiln time, then it is charged a much higher price than other quotes that do not use as much of this valuable resource. As a result of this survey, the Spanish Tile Company realizes that its competitor has a more precise and aggressive quoting model that will likely result in more lost sales for Spanish Tile in the future.

Revenue	$1,428,000
Cost of goods sold	−571,000
Gross margin	857,000
Operating costs	−849,000
Interest expense	−23,000
Operating profit/loss	−$15,000
Operating profit percentage	−1%

EXHIBIT 5.5 SAMPLE OPERATING PROFIT DATA

Operating Profit Percentage. The operating profit percentage reveals the return from standard operations, excluding the impact of extraordinary items and other comprehensive income. Use of this percentage reveals the extent to which a company is earning a profit from standard operations, as opposed to resorting to asset sales or unique transactions to post a profit.

The formula is to subtract the cost of goods sold, as well as all sales, general, and administrative expenses, from sales. In order to obtain a percentage that is strictly related to operational results, be sure to exclude interest income and expense from the calculation, since these items are related to a company's financing decisions rather than its operational characteristics. Expense totals used in the ratio should exclude all extraordinary transactions, as well as asset dispositions, since they do not relate to continuing operations. The formula is:

$$\frac{\text{Sales} - (\text{Cost of Goods Sold} + \text{Sales, General \& Administrative Expenses})}{\text{Sales}}$$

As an example, the Swiss Mountain Chocolate Company has a loan with the local bank whose covenants include the stipulation that the loan will be immediately callable if the company's operating profit percentage drops below zero. In the current month, it will incur an operating loss of $15,000, which will allow the bank to call its loan. The calculation it is using to derive the operating loss is shown in Exhibit 5.5.

Since there is no specification in the loan agreement of the operating loss calculation, the CFO defines it as excluding financing activities, removes the interest expense from the calculation, and achieves an operating profit of $8,000. To be ethically correct, the CFO also specifies the exact contents of the calculation in her next report to the bank.

Net Profit Percentage. This percentage is used to determine the proportion of income derived from all operating, financing, and other activities that an entity has engaged in during an accounting period. It is the one most commonly used as a benchmark for determining a company's performance, even though it does not necessarily reflect a company's cash flows, which may be negative even when net profits are reported.

The formula is to divide net income by revenue.

$$\frac{\text{Net Income}}{\text{Revenue}}$$

If this percentage is being tracked on a trend line, it may be useful to eliminate from the calculation any extraordinary income items, such as losses from disasters, since they do not yield comparable period-to-period information.

	Per-Store Results
Sales	$350,000
Wages	260,000
Supplies	75,000
Assets < $1,000	42,000
Net income	$15,000
Net income percentage	4%

Exhibit 5.6   Sample Net Profit Data

As an example, the Quick Cuts Hair Salon is a franchise operation that pays for the initial fixed assets required by each franchisee. This involves an investment of about $200,000 per hair salon. The management team is determined to grow the operation as fast as possible while still reporting healthy profits. To do so, it sets the capitalization limit very low, at just $250, so that nearly everything it purchases is capitalized. Because it uses a ten-year depreciation period for all fixed assets, this results in the recognition of costs over many future periods that would normally be recognized at once if a higher capitalization limit were used. Its operating results for a typical store are shown in Exhibit 5.6.

The key line item in the exhibit is the assets costing less than $1,000; if the company had set a higher capitalization limit, these costs would have been recognized as expenses at once, which would have yielded a loss on operations of $27,000 per store. As a result, the company's accounting policy is creating false profits. When combined with the high initial setup cost of each store, it is apparent that this seemingly healthy franchise operation is actually burning through its cash reserves at a prodigious rate.

CASH-FLOW MEASUREMENTS

The three measurements noted in this section focus on a company's cash sufficiency in order to sustain operations. If a CFO does not pay attention to these measures, it is possible for an organization to quite suddenly find itself in need of outside funding. Consequently, cash-flow measures should be parked near the top of a CFO's list of "must have" measurements.

Cash Flow from Operations.   Under generally accepted accounting principles (GAAP), a company can quite easily report a large income figure, even while its cash reserves are draining away. The cash flow from operations ratio can be used to determine the extent to which cash flow differs from the reported level of either operating income or net income. Any difference in the ratio that varies significantly from one is indicative of substantial noncash expenses or sales in the reported income figures. Cash-flow problems are likely if the ratio is substantially less than one.

The formula can be generated in two formats. One is to divide operational cash flow by income from operations, while the second format is to divide cash flow from all transactions (including extraordinary items) by net income. The first format yields a more accurate view of the proportion of cash being spun off from ongoing operations, while the second version shows the impact of any transactions that are unrelated to operations.

	Current Year	Next Year	Following Year
Sales	$5,000,000	$10,000,000	$15,000,000
Net income	1,000,000	2,000,000	3,000,000
Revenue recognition of future insurance payments	800,000	1,600,000	2,400,000
Annual cash flow	200,000	400,000	600,000
Cash flow from operations ratio	20%	20%	20%

EXHIBIT 5.7 SAMPLE CASH FLOW FROM OPERATIONS DATA

Both formulas are shown below:

$$\frac{\text{Income from Operations} + \text{Noncash Expenses} - \text{Noncash Sales}}{\text{Income from Operations}}$$

$$\frac{\text{Net Income} + \text{Noncash Expenses} - \text{Noncash Sales}}{\text{Net Income}}$$

As an example, the Bargain Basement Insurance Company (BBIC) is opening new stores at a rapid clip, trying to gain premium locations before its key competitor, Super Low Premiums, Inc., grabs the same spots. The company is reporting net income of 20% from its operations, which is considered reasonable in the insurance business. However, it cannot understand why its bank continues to refuse additional loans to fund ongoing operational needs. The bank is concerned about BBIC's cash flow from operations ratio. The company's relevant projections are shown in Exhibit 5.7.

The exhibit reveals the key problem for BBIC, which is that the company is recognizing insurance as revenue prior to the receipt of cash from policyholders in some cases. Consequently, its rapid growth is only resulting in modest positive cash flow, which translates into a poor cash flow from operations ratio of 20%. The bank correctly finds this ratio to be probably indicative of BBIC's future inability to pay back a loan, and so refuses to extend one.

Cash-Flow Return on Assets.   This calculation is used to determine the amount of cash that a company is generating in proportion to its asset level. This can be used as a substitute for the popular return on assets measure, since the net income figure used in the return on assets calculation is subject to greater manipulation through the use of noncash accounting entries.

The formula is to add together net income and any noncash expenses, such as depreciation and amortization. Then subtract from this amount any noncash sales, such as revenue that has been recognized but is unbilled. Then divide the result by the *net* value of all assets; this should include accounts receivable net of a bad debt reserve, inventory net of an obsolescence reserve, and fixed assets net of depreciation. The formula is:

$$\frac{\text{Net Income} + \text{Noncash Expenses} - \text{Noncash Sales}}{\text{Total Assets}}$$

As an example, the CFO of the Glowering Taillight Company, resellers of 1950s-era taillights, has been told by his controller for several years that the company has a sterling return on assets. He would like to verify this by comparing the measure to the cash-flow return on assets. He collects the information shown in Exhibit 5.8.

	Return on Assets	Cash-Flow Return on Assets
Net income	$1,000,000	$1,000,000
Depreciation		+$105,000
Pension fund gains		−$45,000
Bill and hold revenue		−$132,000
Percentage of completion revenue		−$154,000
Total assets	$3,250,000	$3,250,000
Measurement	30.8%	23.8%

EXHIBIT 5.8   SAMPLE CASH-FLOW RETURN ON ASSETS DATA

The return on assets figure listed at the bottom of the exhibit is derived by dividing net income of $1,000,000 by total assets of $3,250,000. To arrive at the cash-flow return on assets, the CFO must add back the noncash depreciation expense and then subtract a series of noncash accounting entries that have artificially increased the revenue level. The result is:

$$\frac{\$1,000,000 \text{ Net Income} + \$105,000 \text{ Noncash Expenses} - \$331,000 \text{ Noncash Sales}}{\$3,250,000 \text{ Total Assets}}$$

$$=$$

$$\frac{\$774,000 \text{ Cash Flow}}{\$3,250,000 \text{ Total Assets}}$$

$$=$$

$$\underline{23.8\%} \text{ Cash-Flow Return on Assets}$$

Though the cash-flow return on assets percentage is quite acceptable, it is also considerably less than the reported return on assets.

Cash to Working Capital Ratio.   This ratio is useful for determining the proportion of working capital that is made up of either cash or investments that can be readily converted into cash. If this ratio is low, then this can be an indication that a company may have trouble meeting its short-term commitments, due to a potential lack of cash. If this is the case, the next formula to calculate would be the number of expense coverage days (see earlier measurement in this chapter) in order to determine exactly how many days of operations can be covered by existing cash levels.

The formula is to add together the current cash balance, as well as any marketable securities that can be liquidated in the short term, and divide it by current assets, less current liabilities. The key issue is which investments to include in the measurement—since this is intended to be a measure of short-term cash availability, any investments that cannot be liquidated in one month or less should be excluded from the calculation. The formula is:

$$\frac{\text{Cash} + \text{Short-Term Marketable Securities}}{\text{Current Assets} - \text{Current Liabilities}}$$

As an example, the Arbor Valley Tree Company has a large inventory of potted plants and trees on hand, which comprises a large proportion of its inventory, and is recorded

Fund Type	Amount	Liquidity
Cash	$55,000	Immediately available
Money market funds	180,000	Available in one day
Officer loan	200,000	Due in 90 days
Accounts receivable	450,000	Due in 45 days
Inventory	850,000	Turnover every 4 months
Current liabilities	450,000	Due in 30 days

EXHIBIT 5.9   SAMPLE CASH TO WORKING CAPITAL DATA

as part of current assets. However, they turn over only three times per year, which does not make them very liquid for the purposes of generating short-term cash. The CFO wants to know what proportion of the current ratio is really comprised of cash or cash equivalents, since it appears that a large part of working capital is skewed in the direction of this slow-moving inventory. She has the information shown in Exhibit 5.9.

Based on this information, she calculates the cash to working capital ratio as:

$$\frac{\text{Cash} + \text{Short-Term Marketable Securities}}{\text{Current Assets} - \text{Current Liabilities}}$$

$$=$$

$$\frac{\$55,000 + \$180,000}{(\$55,000 + \$180,000 + \$200,000 + \$450,000 + \$850,000) - (\$450,000)}$$

$$=$$

$$\frac{\$235,000}{\$1,285,000}$$

$$=$$

$$\underline{18.3\%}$$

She did not include the note receivable from the company officer, since it would be available for 90 days. This nearly halved the amount of the ratio to 18.3%, which reveals that the company should be extremely careful in its use of cash until more of the accounts receivable or inventory balances can be liquidated.

LIQUIDITY MEASUREMENTS

The five measurements noted in this section are critical to a CFO's short-term reporting on the liquidity of assets. The days of accounts receivable measure should certainly be reviewed no less than once a week to verify that the credit and collections function is working properly. The collection effectiveness index provides a good overview of the efficiency of the collections function. Inventory turnover is worthy of a monthly review, preferably on a trend-line basis, to ensure that a company is not investing too much in its on-hand inventories. Similarly, a weekly review of accounts payable days will inform the CFO if bills are being paid either too early or too late. The quick ratio is more useful as a summary-level review of the four other liquidity measures, of which they are key components.

Average Receivable Collection Period.   The speed with which a company can obtain payment from customers for outstanding receivable balances is crucial for the reduction of cash requirements. A very long accounts receivable collection period indicates that a company's credit and collections function is very good at avoiding potentially delinquent customers, as well as collecting overdue funds. This format is particularly useful when it is compared to the standard number of days of credit granted to customers. For example, if the average collection period is 60 days and the standard days of credit is 30, then customers are taking much too long to pay their invoices. A sign of good performance is when the average receivable collection period is only a few days longer than the standard days of credit.

The formula is to divide annual credit sales by 365 days, and divide the result into average accounts receivable. The formula is:

$$\frac{\text{Average Accounts Receivable}}{\text{Annual Sales/365}}$$

As an example, the new CFO of the Flexo Paneling Company, makers of modularized office equipment, wants to determine the company's accounts receivable collection period. In the June accounting period, the beginning accounts receivable balance was $318,000 and the ending balance was $383,000. Sales for May and June totaled $625,000. Based on this information, the CFO calculates the average receivable collection period as:

$$\frac{(\$318,000 \text{ Beginning Receivables} + \$383,000 \text{ Ending Receivables})/2}{(\$625,000 \times 6)/365}$$

$$=$$

$$\frac{\$350,500 \text{ Average Accounts Receivable}}{\$10,274 \text{ Sales per Day}}$$

$$=$$

$$\underline{\underline{34.1}} \text{ Days}$$

Note that the CFO derived the annual sales figure used in the denominator by multiplying the two-month sales period in May and June by six. Since the company has a stated due date of 30 days after the billing date, the 34.1-day collection period appears reasonable.

Collection Effectiveness Index.   Most liquidity measurements for receivables, such as accounts receivable turnover or the days of delinquent sales outstanding, are easily impacted by spikes or declines in sales, so they are not valid measures of collection performance. Instead, use the collection effectiveness index (CEI), which more precisely determines the effectiveness of the credit and collections staff. This measure compares what was collected in a given period to what was available to collect. A score close to 100% indicates a high degree of collection effectiveness.

The formula is to add together the beginning receivables for the measurement period, plus credit sales during the period, and subtract ending total receivables. Then divide this number by the sum of beginning receivables and credit sales and subtract ending current receivables. Finally, multiply the result by 100 to obtain a percentage. The formula is:

$$\frac{\text{Beginning Receivables} + \text{Credit Sales} - \text{Ending Total Receivables}}{\text{Beginning Receivables} + \text{Credit Sales} - \text{Ending Current Receivables}} \times 100$$

As an example, the sales and receivable information for Moonlight Productions is as follows:

Beginning receivables	$4,500,000
Credit sales	3,200,000
Ending current receivables	2,800,000
Ending total receivables	5,000,000

Based on this information, Moonlight's CEI is as follows:

$$\frac{\$4,500,000 + \$3,200,000 - \$5,000,000}{\$4,500,000 + \$3,200,000 - \$2,800,000} \times 100 = 55\% \text{ CEI}$$

The credit sales in this calculation are assumed to be generated over a one-month period. If the calculation were to cover a longer period, then divide the credit sales figure by the number of months being measured. For example, to measure the CEI for a quarter, divide the credit sales for the quarter by three before using it in the formula.

Inventory Turnover. Inventory is frequently the largest component of a company's working capital; in such situations, if inventory is not being used up by operations at a reasonable pace, then a company has invested a large part of its cash in an asset that may be difficult to liquidate in short order. Accordingly, keeping close track of the rate of inventory turnover is a significant function of management. This section describes several variations on the inventory turnover measurement, which may be combined to yield the most complete turnover reporting for management to peruse. In all cases, these measurements should be tracked on a trend line in order to see if there are gradual reductions in the rate of turnover, which can indicate to management that corrective action is required in order to eliminate excess inventory stocks.

The most simple turnover calculation is to divide the period-end inventory into the annualized cost of sales. One can also use an *average* inventory figure in the denominator, which avoids sudden changes in the inventory level that are likely to occur on any specific period-end date. The formula is:

$$\frac{\text{Cost of Goods Sold}}{\text{Inventory}}$$

A variation on the preceding formula is to divide it into 365 days, which yields the number of days of inventory on hand. This may be more understandable to the layman; for example, 43 days of inventory is more clear than 8.5 inventory turns, even though they represent the same situation. The formula is:

$$365 / \frac{\text{Cost of Goods Sold}}{\text{Inventory}}$$

Balance Sheet Line Item	Amount
Cost of goods sold	$4,075,000
Direct materials expense	$1,550,000
Raw materials inventory	$388,000
Total inventory	$815,000

EXHIBIT 5.10   SAMPLE INVENTORY TURNOVER DATA

As an example, the Rotary Mower Company, maker of the only lawn mower driven by a Wankel rotary engine, is going through its annual management review of inventory. Its CFO has the information shown in Exhibit 5.10.

To calculate total inventory turnover, the CFO creates the following calculation:

$$\frac{\$4,075,000 \text{ Cost of Goods Sold}}{\$815,000 \text{ Inventory}}$$

$$=$$

$$\underline{5} \text{ Turns per Year}$$

To determine the number of days of inventory on hand, the CFO divides the number of turns per year into 365 days:

$$365 \Big/ \frac{\$4,075,000 \text{ Cost of Goods Sold}}{\$815,000 \text{ Inventory}}$$

$$=$$

$$\underline{73} \text{ Days of Inventory}$$

Accounts Payable Days.   A calculation of the days of accounts payable gives an outside observer a fair indication of a company's ability to pay its bills on time. If the accounts payable days are inordinately long, this is probably a sign that the company does not have sufficient cash flow to pay its bills, and may find itself out of business in short order. Alternatively, a small amount of accounts payable days indicates that a company is either taking advantage of early payment discounts or is simply paying its bills earlier than it has to.

The formula is to divide total annualized purchases by 360 days, and then divide the result into the ending accounts payable balance. An alternative approach is to use the *average* accounts payable for the reporting period, since the ending figure may be disproportionately high or low. The amount of purchases should be derived from all nonpayroll expenses incurred during the year; payroll is not included, because it is not a part of the accounts payable listed in the numerator. Also, depreciation and amortization should be excluded from the purchases figure, since they do not involve cash payments. The formula is:

$$\frac{\text{Accounts Payable}}{\text{Purchases}/360}$$

As an example, the Drain-Away Toilet Company has beginning accounts payable of $145,000 and ending accounts payable of $157,000. On an annualized basis, its total expenses are $2,400,000, of which $600,000 is payroll and $50,000 is depreciation. To determine its accounts payable days, we plug this information into the following formula:

$$\frac{(\text{Beginning Accounts Payable} + \text{Ending Accounts Payable})/2}{(\text{Total Expenses} - \text{Payroll} - \text{Depreciation})/360}$$

$$=$$

$$\frac{(\$145,000 \text{ Beginning Payables} + \$157,000 \text{ Ending Payables})/2}{(\$2,400,000 \text{ Total Expenses} - \$600,000 \text{ Payroll} - \$50,000 \text{ Depreciation})/360}$$

$$=$$

$$\frac{\$151,000 \text{ Average Accounts Payable}}{\$1,750,000 \text{ Purchases}/360} = \underline{\underline{31}} \text{ Days}$$

Quick Ratio. This ratio excludes inventory from the current assets portion of the current ratio. By doing so, one can gain a better understanding of a company's very short-term ability to generate cash from more liquid assets such as accounts receivable and marketable securities.

The formula is to add together cash, marketable securities, and accounts receivable, and divide the result by current liabilities. Be sure to only include those marketable securities that can be liquidated in the short term, and those receivables that are not significantly overdue. The formula is:

$$\frac{\text{Cash} + \text{Marketable Securities} + \text{Accounts Receivable}}{\text{Current Liabilities}}$$

As an example, the Huff-Puff Shed Company, makers of sheds that are guaranteed not to blow down in any wind under 100 miles per hour, appears to have a comfortably high current ratio of 2.5:1. The components of that ratio are broken down in Exhibit 5.11.

This more detailed analysis reveals that the presence of an excessive amount of inventory is making the company's liquidity look too high with the current ratio. Only by switching to the quick ratio is this problem revealed.

SOLVENCY MEASUREMENTS

The two measures noted in this section address the ability of a firm to pay off its debts. This is applicable not only to high-debt situations, but also to prospective ones where

Account	Amount
Cash	$120,000
Marketable securities	$53,000
Accounts receivable	$418,000
Inventory	$2,364,000
Current liabilities	$985,000
Current ratio	3:1
Quick ratio	.6:1

EXHIBIT 5.11 SAMPLE QUICK RATIO DATA

	January	February	March
Interest expense	$45,000	$43,000	$41,000
Net income	83,500	65,000	47,000
Depreciation	17,000	17,250	17,500
Amortization	2,500	2,500	2,500
Net cash flow	103,000	84,750	67,000
Times interest earned	2.3	2.0	1.6

EXHIBIT 5.12   SAMPLE INTEREST EARNED DATA

the CFO must model the level of corporate solvency that will result from some major financing activity, such as an acquisition that is paid for with debt.

Times Interest Earned.   The times interest earned ratio reveals the amount of excess funding that a company still has available after it has paid off its interest expense. If this ratio is close to one, then the company runs a high risk of defaulting on its debt, while any higher ratio shows that it is operating with a comfortable amount of extra cash flow that can cushion it if its business falters.

The formula is to divide the average interest expense by the average cash flow. Cash flow is a company's net income, to which all noncash expenses (such as depreciation and amortization) have been added back. This ratio should be run on a monthly basis, rather than annually, since short-term changes in the amount of debt carried or cash flow realized can have a sudden and dramatic impact on it. The formula is:

$$\frac{\text{Average Cash Flow}}{\text{Average Interest Expense}}$$

As an example, the Cautious Bankers Corporation (CBC) is investigating the possibility of lending money to the Grasp & Sons Door Handle Corporation (GSR). It collects the information in Exhibit 5.12 for the last few months of GSR's operations.

The exhibit reveals that, though GSR's interest expense is dropping, its cash flow is dropping so much faster that the company will soon have difficulty meeting its interest payment obligations. The CBC examiner elects to pass on providing the company with any additional debt.

Debt Coverage Ratio.   A key solvency issue is the ability of a company to pay its debts. This can be measured with the debt coverage ratio, which compares reported earnings to the amount of scheduled after-tax interest and principal payments to see if there is enough income available to cover the payments. If the ratio is less than one, this indicates that a company will probably be unable to make its debt payments. The measure is of particular interest to lenders, who are concerned about a company's ability to repay them for issued loans.

The formula is to divide the scheduled amount of principal payments by the inverse of the corporate tax rate. This yields the amount of after-tax income required by a company to pay back the principal. Then add the interest expense to be paid, and divide the sum into the net amount of earnings before interest and taxes. An alternative treatment of the numerator is to use earnings before interest, taxes, depreciation, and amortization, since this yields a closer approximation of available cash flow. The formula is:

$$\frac{\text{Earnings Before Interest and Taxes}}{\text{Interest} + \dfrac{\text{Scheduled Principal Payments}}{(1 - \text{Tax Rate})}}$$

As an example, the Egyptian Antiques Company's CFO wants to be sure that earnings will be sufficient to pay upcoming debt requirements, prior to implementing the owner's suggested round of Christmas bonuses. The expected operating income for the year, prior to bonuses, is $135,000. The interest expense is expected to be $18,500. The tax rate is 34%. Upcoming principal payments will be $59,000. The CFO uses the following debt coverage calculation to see if Christmas bonuses can still be paid:

$$\frac{\$135,000 \text{ Operating Income}}{\$18,500 \text{ Interest} + \dfrac{\$59,000 \text{ Principal Payments}}{(1 - 34\% \text{ Tax Rate})}}$$

$$=$$

$$\frac{\$135,000 \text{ Operating Income}}{\$107,894 \text{ Debt Payments}} = \underline{125\%} \text{ Debt Coverage Ratio}$$

The ratio indicates that extra funds will be available for Christmas bonuses since operating income exceeds the amount of scheduled debt payments.

RETURN ON INVESTMENT MEASUREMENTS

Investors want to know what kind of return they are getting on their investment in a company, and the CFO must be prepared to tell them. This section contains four measures that address the same issue in different ways. The return on assets employed as well as the return on equity are the two most commonly used measurements for return on investment, both of which the CFO should be thoroughly familiar with. The economic value-added measure is a more recent attempt at defining the value added to underlying assets by a company, while the dividend payout ratio addresses the needs of those investors who are only interested in the amount of cash paid directly to them by the company.

Return on Assets Employed. A company is deemed efficient by investors if it can generate an adequate return while using the minimum amount of assets to do so. This also keeps investors from having to put more cash into the company, and allows the entity to shift its excess cash to investments in new endeavors. Consequently, the return on assets employed measure is considered a critical one for determining a company's overall level of operating efficiency.

The formula is to divide net profits by total assets. Though the assets figure is sometimes restricted to just fixed assets, it should include accounts receivable and inventory, since both these areas can be major users of cash. The amount of fixed assets included in the denominator is typically net of depreciation; it can also be recorded at its gross value, as long as the formula derivation is used consistently over multiple time periods, thereby ensuring consistent long-term reporting. The formula is:

$$\frac{\text{Net Profit}}{\text{Total Assets}}$$

	Year-End Results	Days on Hand
Sales	$3,070,000	
Net profit	215,000	—
Accounts receivable	512,000	60
Inventory	461,000	90
Fixed assets	1,950,000	—
Total assets	$2,923,000	—

Exhibit 5.13   Sample Return on Assets Data

As an example, Mr. Willston is the new CFO of Southern Sheet Metal, a metal stamping company. He purchased the company for $3 million, and wants to retrieve as much of these funds as possible by increasing the company's return on assets. He creates the table of information shown in Exhibit 5.13 about company income and assets. Based on the exhibit, the calculation of net assets employed is:

$$\frac{\text{Net Profit}}{\text{Total Assets}} = \frac{\$215,000}{\$2,923,000} = \underline{\underline{7.4\%}}$$

Mr. Willston is not certain which of the fixed assets can be safely eliminated while maintaining productive capacity. However, he is quite sure that the days of accounts receivable and inventory, as noted in the table, are much too high. Accordingly, he improves collection activities and early payment discounts, and drops the outstanding accounts receivable balance from 60 days to 45, reducing this asset to $384,000. He also installs an improved inventory management system, reducing the on-hand inventory balance from 90 to 60 days and this asset to $309,000. By taking these actions, he has eliminated $280,000 of assets, which he can take out of the business. He has also improved the net assets employed measurement to 8.1%, which is calculated as:

$$\frac{\text{Net Profit}}{\text{Total Assets}} = \frac{\$215,000}{(\$2,923,000 - \$280,000)} = \underline{\underline{8.1\%}}$$

Return on Equity Percentage.   This calculation is used to determine the amount of return investors are receiving from their investment in a company. The measure can be misleading, because a management team that is eager to increase a company's return on equity can do so easily by incurring new debt and using these funds to buy back stock. Though the amount of equity is thereby reduced, making the ratio more favorable, this also means that the company has an obligation to pay back the debt and related interest. An overly zealous pursuit of this approach can result in such a large debt load that a small downturn in sales will not allow it to pay off the debt, possibly ending in bankruptcy.

The formula is to divide net income by total equity. To obtain a better picture of the ability of a company to generate a return from operating activities only, the measure can be modified to be net income *from operations*, divided by total equity. The basic formula is:

$$\frac{\text{Net Income}}{\text{Total Equity}}$$

	Before Stock Buyback	After Stock Buyback
Sales	$5,000,000	$5,000,000
Expenses	4,850,000	4,850,000
Debt interest expense	—	24,000
Profits	150,000	126,000
Equity	1,000,000	700,000
Return on equity	15%	18%

Exhibit 5.14 Sample of Return on Equity Data

As an example, Mr. Mo Funds, CFO of the Lounger Chairs Furniture Company, has been provided with a bonus plan that is largely based on his ability to increase the return on equity for the shareholders. There is $1,000,000 of equity on the books, of which $400,000 is closely held and the other $600,000 is held by a variety of small investors. He estimates that he can buy back $300,000 of the stock from small investors by obtaining a loan, which has an after-tax interest rate of 8%. He compiles the information in Exhibit 5.14 to see if the stratagem makes sense.

The strategy appears to be a good one. Though expenses will be driven up by the interest cost of the debt, the amount of equity will be reduced to such an extent that the return on equity will increase by 3%. However, before implementing this strategy, the CFO should investigate the company's ability to generate enough cash flow to pay off or at least maintain the debt.

Economic Value Added.   Economic value added shows the incremental rate of return in excess of a firm's total cost of capital. Stated differently, this is the surplus value created on an initial investment. It is *not* just the difference between a firm's percentage cost of capital and its actual rate of return percentage, since it is designed to yield a *dollar* surplus value. If the measurement is negative, then a company is not generating a return in excess of its capital costs. It is extremely important to break down the drivers of the measurement in order to determine what parts of a company are keeping the measure from reaching its maximum potential.

Economic value added has become the most fashionable measurement for determining the ability of a company to generate an appropriate rate of return, thanks in part to the efforts of several consulting firms that specialize in installing the systems that roll up into this measurement. Some studies have shown that a favorable economic value-added measurement correlates closely with the market price achieved by a company's stock, so it can become the cornerstone of a company's efforts to increase its market value. It can also be linked to a company's compensation system, so that managers are paid (or not) based on their ability to combine efficient asset utilization with profitable operating results.

The formula is to multiply the net investment by the difference between the actual rate of return on assets and the percentage cost of capital. The three elements of the calculation are:

1. *Net investment.* The net investment figure used in the formula is subject to a great deal of variation. In its most limited form, one can use the net valuation for all fixed assets. However, some assets may be subject to accelerated depreciation calculations, which greatly reduce the amount of investment used in the calculation; a better approach is to use the straight-line depreciation methodology for all assets,

Type of Funding		Amount of Funding	Cost of Funding
Debt		$2,500,000	8.5%
Preferred stock		$4,250,000	12.5%
Common stock		$8,000,000	16.0%
	Total	$14,750,000	**13.7%**

EXHIBIT 5.15   SAMPLE COST OF CAPITAL DATA

with only the depreciation *period* varying by type of asset. A variation on this approach is to also add research and development (R&D), as well as training costs, back into the net investment, on the grounds that these expenditures are made to enhance the company's value over the long term. Also, if assets are leased rather than owned, they should be itemized as assets at their fair market value and included in the net investment figure, so that managers cannot use financing tricks to enhance their return on investment.

2. *Actual return on investment.*   When calculating the return on investment, R&D, as well as training expenses, should be shifted out of operating expenses and into net investment (as noted in the last point). In addition, any unusual adjustments to net income that do not involve ongoing operations should be eliminated. This results in an income figure related to just those costs that can be legitimately expensed within the current period.

3. *Cost of capital.*   The formulation of the cost of capital is complex; rather than repeat what has been covered elsewhere see Chapter 9, Cost of Capital.

The formula is:

(Net Investment) × (Actual Return on Investment − Percentage Cost of Capital)

As an example, the CFO of the Miraflores Manufacturing Company wants to see if the company has a positive economic value added. Based on her calculation of outstanding debt, preferred stock, and common stock, as noted in Exhibit 5.15, she estimates that the firm's cost of capital is 13.7%.

She then takes the balance sheet and income statement, and redistributes some of the accounts in them in accordance with Exhibit 5.16 so that some items that are usually expensed under GAAP are shifted into the investment category.

The return on investment, as based on the net income and investment figures in the preceding table, is 13.5% (net income divided by the total net investment). Using this information, she derives the following calculation to determine the amount of economic value added:

(Net Investment) × (Actual Return on Assets − Percentage Cost of Capital)

= ($3,115,000 Net Investment) × (13.5% Actual Return − 13.7% Cost of Capital)

= $3,115,000 Net Investment × −.2% = −$6,230 Economic Value Added

In short, the company is destroying its capital base by creating actual returns that are slightly less than its cost of capital.

Account Description	Performance	Net Investment
Revenue	$8,250,000	
Cost of goods sold	5,950,000	
General and administrative	825,000	
Sales department	675,000	
Training department		$100,000
Research and development		585,000
Marketing department	380,000	
Net income	**$420,000**	
Fixed assets		2,080,000
Cost of patent protection		125,000
Cost of trademark protection		225,000
Total net investment		**$3,115,000**

Exhibit 5.16 Sample Net Investment Data

Dividend Payout Ratio. The dividend payout ratio tells an investor what proportion of earnings are being paid back in the form of dividends. This is particularly important when the ratio is greater than one, since it indicates that a company is dipping into its cash reserves in order to pay dividends, which is not a sustainable trend. Alternatively, if only a small proportion of earnings are being paid back as dividends, one can assume that the remaining cash is being plowed back into operations, which should result in an increase in the stock price. If the stock price is stagnant or declining, then investors have a valid concern regarding the proper use of corporate earnings.

The formula is to divide the dividend per share by the earnings per share. It is allowable to include the cash flow from nonoperating items in the earnings per share figure, since they will impact the amount of cash available for distribution as dividends. However, if nonoperating items having no immediate cash-flow impact, such as restructuring reserves, are included in the earnings per share figure, then they should be removed; such items do not properly reflect a company's ability to pay dividends. Also, it may be necessary to add expected capital expenditures to the earnings per share figure, if this is expected to require a significant proportion of the cash provided by earnings. The formula is:

$$\frac{\text{Dividend per Share}}{\text{Earnings per Share}}$$

As an example, Mr. Jones has invested a large part of his savings in the stock of Illinois Gas Distribution Company, operator of a nationwide gas pipeline. He wants to see if the company can continue to issue its semiannual dividend of $4.00 per share, based on its most recent earnings report. The report contains the information shown in Exhibit 5.17.

Mr. Jones adjusts the $15,430,000 by adding back $7,000,000 in goodwill amortization, depreciation of $3,500,000, and a restructuring reserve of $4,500,000, since none of them involves cash flows (though the restructuring reserve may require a cash outflow at some point in the future). He also adds back $3,750,000 of capital expenditures. The net income after all of these adjustments is $34,180,000. He then calculates the dividend

Net income	$15,430,000
Goodwill amortization	$7,000,000
Depreciation	$3,500,000
Capital expenditures	$3,750,000
Restructuring reserve	$4,500,000
Number of shares outstanding	5,450,000

EXHIBIT 5.17   SAMPLE DIVIDEND PAYMENT DATA

payout ratio using the following formula:

$$\frac{\text{Dividend per Share}}{\text{Earnings per Share}}$$

$$=$$

$$\frac{\$4.00 \text{ Dividend per Share}}{\$34,180,000 \text{ Adjusted Net Income}/5,450,000 \text{ Shares}} = 64\% \text{ Dividend Payout Ratio}$$

The ratio reveals that the company is capable of paying out dividends from its earnings per share. However, nearly all of the funds acquired through earnings are being paid out, so there may be some danger of a cutback in dividends in the future if the company's profit level drops by a small amount, or if it needs to use its earnings to fund an increase in its rate of growth.

MARKET PERFORMANCE MEASUREMENTS

The CFO of a publicly held company must be aware of the organization's key market performance measurements on a daily basis, in order to field calls from analysts about them. The sales to stock price ratio reveals the expectations of investors about an organization's ability to increase its sales volume, the price/earnings ratio reveals investors' same expectations regarding corporate profits, and the quality of earnings ratio provides some indication of the level of artificial bolstering of reported results.

Sales to Stock Price Ratio.   This ratio indicates the opinion of investors regarding a company's ability to increase its sales volume. If sales increase and there is no change in the stock price, then the rate of growth in sales falls within the expectations of investors. If there is an increase in the stock price, then sales have exceeded their expectations; a drop in the stock price is indicative of sales levels that do not meet their expectations.

The formula is to divide annualized net sales by the average common stock price for the reporting period. The annualized net sales figure used in this calculation should be the prospective sales figure for the current reporting year, since this represents the announced sales figure that company management has released to investors, and is the number on which they are basing their decisions to buy or hold the stock. The average common stock price should be used instead of the ending stock price, since this removes some fluctuation from the price.

$$\frac{\text{Annual Net Sales}}{\text{Average Common Stock Price}}$$

Most recent stock price	$32.87
Number of shares outstanding	3,875,000
Net income	$8,500,000
Extraordinary income	$2,250,000

EXHIBIT 5.18   SAMPLE PRICE/EARNINGS DATA

As an example, the CFO of the Gonging Clock Company has been given a stock compensation package that will reward him richly if he can double the stock price within one year. He elects to do so by focusing solely on increases in sales. The display clocks that the company produces are sold almost entirely within the Christmas selling season. To increase sales, he allows customers to pay for their clocks within 180 days, instead of the usual 30 days, and also offers discounts for bulk purchases. As a result, the company experiences a massive increase in sales, investors bid up the stock price, and the CFO retires with a large stock bonus. Unfortunately, the CFO's actions so thoroughly clog the company's distribution pipeline with product that its sales volume in the following year dives down to less than one-quarter of the sales level in the preceding year. The Board of Directors learns its lesson from this experience, and subsequently revises its senior management incentive plan to focus on more long-term-value objectives.

Price/Earnings Ratio.   By comparing earnings to the current market price of the stock, one can obtain a general idea of the perception of investors of the quality of corporate earnings. For example, if this ratio is substantially lower than the average rate for the industry, it can indicate an expectation among investors that a company's future earnings are expected to trend lower. Alternatively, a high ratio could indicate the excitement of investors over a new patent that a company has just been granted, or the expected favorable results of a lawsuit—the possible explanations are legion. The key point when using this ratio is that a result that varies from the industry average probably indicates a change in investor perceptions from the rest of the industry in regard to a company's ability to continue to generate income.

The formula is to divide the average common stock price by the net income per share. The net income per share figure is typically used on a fully diluted basis, accounting for the impact of options, warrants, and conversions from debt that may increase the number of shares outstanding. The formula is:

$$\frac{\text{Average Common Stock Price}}{\text{Net Income per Share}}$$

As an example, an investment analyst wants to determine the price/earnings ratio for the Mile-High Dirigible Company. The industry average price/earnings ratio for lighter-than-air transport manufacturers is 18:1. She accumulates the information shown in Exhibit 5.18.

If she chooses to leave the extraordinary income in the total net income figure, then she uses the following calculation to derive the price/earnings ratio:

$$\frac{\$32.87 \text{ Stock Price}}{(\$8,500,000 \text{ Net Income}/3,875,000 \text{ Shares Outstanding})} = \underline{\underline{15{:}1}} \text{ Price/Earnings}$$

So far, the price/earnings ratio appears to compare favorably to the industry average. However, if she excludes the extraordinary gain from net income, the earnings per share figure drops to \$1.61 per share. When incorporated into the price/earnings formula, this change increases the ratio to 20:1, which is higher than the industry average. Accordingly, she considers the stock to be overpriced relative to the industry, and forbears from recommending it to her clients.

QUALITY OF EARNINGS RATIO

It can be extremely difficult for an outsider such as a stock analyst, bank officer, or investor, to determine if the earnings reported by a company are based on a foundation of solid operational earnings, or if the company is taking advantage of a broad array of accounting tricks that are allowable under generally accepted accounting principles in order to artificially bolster its earnings. A simple ratio for determining the quality of reported earnings is the quality of earnings ratio. This measurement essentially compares the reported earnings level to reported cash flow from operations; if the numbers are close, then the reported earnings number probably fairly reflects actual results. Even if the ratio appears to indicate that there is considerable divergence between cash flow and earnings, there may be a good reason for the change. However, if cash flow from operations is persistently well below the level of reported earnings, then some degree of accounting trickery is likely to be occurring.

The formula is to subtract cash from operations from net earnings, and divide the result by average total assets. The formula follows:

$$\frac{\text{Earnings} - \text{Cash from Operations}}{(\text{Beginning Assets}) + (\text{Ending Assets})/2}$$

The percentage resulting from this formula show be very low, with a number close to zero indicating a high quality of earnings. Any number higher than 6% indicates a low quality of earnings.

As an example, Bonzo Pranks Company, operator of a chain of publicly held joke shops, has issued annual financial statements showing earnings of \$20 million and cash flow from operations of \$4 million. The total assets it reports at the beginning of the year are \$94 million, and \$106 million at the end of the year. Its quality of earnings ratio is:

$$\frac{\$20 \text{ Million Earnings} - \$4 \text{ Million Cash from Operations}}{(\$94 \text{ Million Beginning Assets} + \$106 \text{ Ending Assets})/2} = 16\%$$

Bonzo appears to be playing a prank on its investors! Bonzo's earnings are much higher than its cash from operations, resulting in an inordinately high quality of earnings ratio.

SUMMARY

The 28 ratios covered in this chapter should be on a CFO's short list of potential measurements. However, other ratios may make more sense under certain circumstances, such as the type of industry, the presence (or not) of manufacturing versus service operations, or whether a company is privately or publicly held. For a more complete list of ratios from which to choose, refer to Appendix B, which contains more than 120 ratios.

CHAPTER 6

CONTROL SYSTEMS*

One of the chief roles of the CFO is to examine each process that involves financial transactions to see where there is a risk of losing assets, and installing control points that will prevent those losses from occurring. For example, a major potential weakness in the billing process is that the shipping department may never inform the accounting staff of a shipment, resulting in no invoice being sent to a customer. In this chapter, we review the need for control systems, the types of fraudulent activities that make the use of controls particularly important, and describe over 85 controls that can be added to the typical accounting system.

Since controls frequently have a cost associated with them, it is also possible to take them *out of* an accounting system in order to save money; we will discuss the process of spotting these controls and evaluating their usefulness prior to removing them.

NEED FOR CONTROL SYSTEMS

The most common situation in which a control point is needed is when an innocent error is made in the processing of a transaction. For example, an accounts payable clerk neglects to compare the price on a supplier's invoice to the price listed on the authorizing purchase order, which results in the company paying more than it should. Similarly, the warehouse staff decides to accept a supplier shipment, despite a lack of approving purchasing documentation, resulting in the company being obligated to pay for something that it does not need. These types of actions may occur based on poor employee training, inattention, or the combination of a special set of circumstances that were unforeseen when the accounting processes were originally constructed. There can be an extraordinary number of reasons why a transactional error arises, which can result in errors that are not caught, and which in turn lead to the loss of corporate assets.

Controls act as review points at those places in a process where these types of errors have a habit of arising. The potential for some errors will be evident when a process-flow expert reviews a flowchart that describes a process, simply based on his or her knowledge of where errors in similar processes have a habit of arising. Other errors will be specific to a certain industry—for example, the casino industry deals with enormous quantities of cash, and so has a potential for much higher monetary loss through its cash-handling processes than do similar processes in other industries. Also, highly specific circumstances within a company may generate errors in unlikely places. For example, a manufacturing company that employs mostly foreign workers who do not speak English will experience extra errors in any processes where these workers are required to fill out paperwork, simply due to a reduced level of comprehension of what they are writing. Consequently,

---

*   Adapted with permission from Chapter 28 of *Ultimate Accountants' Reference* by Bragg (John Wiley & Sons, 2005).

the typical process can be laced with areas in which a company has the potential for loss of assets.

Many potential areas of asset loss will involve such minor or infrequent errors that accountants can safely ignore them and avoid the construction of any offsetting controls. Others have the potential for very high risk of loss, and so are shored up with not only one control point, but a whole series of multilayered cross-checks that are designed to keep all but the most unusual problems from arising or being spotted at once.

The need for controls is also driven by the impact of their cost and interference in the smooth functioning of a process. If a control requires the hiring of an extra person, then a careful analysis of the resulting risk mitigation is likely to occur. Similarly, if a highly efficient process is about to have a large and labor-intensive control point plunked down into the middle of it, it is quite logical that an alternative approach should be found that provides a similar level of control, but from outside the process.

The controls installed can be of the preventive variety, which are designed to spot problems as they are occurring (such as on-line pricing verification for the customer order data entry staff), or of the detective variety, which spot problems after they occur, so that the accounting staff can research the associated problems and fix them after the fact (such as a bank reconciliation). The former type of control is the best, since it prevents errors from ever being completed, whereas the second type results in much more labor by the accounting staff to research each error and correct it. Consequently, the type of control point installed should be evaluated based on its cost of subsequent error correction.

All of these factors—perceived risk, cost, and efficiency—will have an impact on a company's need for control systems, as well as the preventive or detective type of each control that is contemplated.

TYPES OF FRAUD

The vast majority of transactional problems that controls guard against are innocent errors that are caused by employees. These tend to be easy to spot and correct, when the proper control points are in place. However, the most feared potential loss of assets is not through these mistakes, but through deliberate fraud on the part of employees, since these transactions are deliberately masked, making it much more difficult to spot them. The most common types of fraud that are perpetrated are:

- *Cash and investment theft.* The theft of cash is the most publicized type of fraud, and yet the amount stolen is usually quite small, when compared to the byzantine layers of controls that are typically installed to prevent such an occurrence. The real problem in this area is the theft of investments, when someone sidesteps existing controls to clean out a company's entire investment account. Accordingly, the CFO should spend the most time designing controls over the movement of invested funds.

- *Expense account abuse.* Employees can use fake expense receipts, apply for reimbursement of unapproved items, or apply multiple times for reimbursement through their expense reports. Many of these items are so small that they are barely worth the cost of detecting, while others, such as the duplicate billing to the company of airline tickets, can add up to very large amounts. Controls in this area tend to be costly and time-consuming.

- *Financial reporting misrepresentation.* Though no assets appear to be stolen, the deliberate falsification of financial information is still fraud, because it impacts a company's stock price by misleading investors about financial results. Controls in this area should involve internal audits to ensure that processes are set up correctly, as well as full audits (not reviews or compilations) by external auditors.

- *Fixed assets theft.*   Though the fixed assets name implies that every asset is big enough to be immovable, many items—particularly computers—can be easily stolen and then resold by employees. In many instances, there is simply no way to prevent the loss of assets without the use of security guards and surveillance equipment. Given that many organizations do not want to go that far, the most common control is the purchase of insurance with a minimal deductible, so that losses can be readily reimbursed.

- *Inventory and supplies theft.*   The easiest theft for an employee is to remove inventory or supplies from a storage shelf and walk away with them. Inventory controls can be enhanced through the use of fencing and limited access to the warehouse, but employees can still hand inventory out through the shipping and receiving gates. The level of controls installed in this area will depend on the existing level of pilferage, and the value of inventory and supplies.

- *Nonpayment of advances.*   The employees who need advances, either on their pay or for travel, are typically those who have few financial resources. Consequently, they may not pay back advances unless specifically requested to do so. This requires detailed tracking of all outstanding advances.

- *Purchases for personal use.*   Employees with access to company credit cards can make purchases of items that are diverted to their homes. Controls are needed that require one to have detailed records of all credit card purchases, rather than relying on a cursory scan and approval of an incoming credit card statement.

- *Supplier kickbacks.*   Members of the purchasing staff can arrange with suppliers to source purchases through them in exchange for kickback payments directly to the purchasing staff. This usually results in a company paying more than the market rate for those items. This is a difficult type of fraud to detect, since it requires an ongoing review of prices paid as compared to a survey of market rates.

Fraud problems are heightened in some organizations, because the environment is such that fraud is easier to commit. For example, a rigorous emphasis on increasing profits by top management may lead to false financial reporting in order to "make the numbers." Problems can also arise if the management team is unwilling to pay for controls or for a sufficient number of supervisory personnel, if it is dominated by one or two people who can override existing controls, or if it has high turnover, so that new managers have a poor grasp of existing controls. Fraud is also common when the organizational structure is very complex or the company is growing rapidly, since both situations tend to result in fewer controls, which create opportunities to remove assets. Consequently, fraud is much more likely if there are unrealistic growth objectives, there are problems within the management ranks, or if controls are not keeping pace with changes in the organizational structure.

KEY CONTROLS

There are thousands of possible controls that can be used to ensure that a company maintains proper control over its assets. The following list represents the most common controls found in most organizations. These can be supplemented by additional controls in cases where the potential for loss of assets is considered to be exceptionally high, with the reverse being true in other instances. The controls are:

1. *Cash.* The handling of cash is considered to be rife with control issues, resulting in perhaps an excessive use of controls. Though many potential controls are listed below, one should attempt to create a mix of controls that balances their cost against incremental gains in the level of control achieved. They are:

   - *Compare check register to actual check number sequence.* The computer's list of checks printed should exactly match the checks that have actually been used. If not, this can be evidence that someone has removed a check from the check stock in hopes that it will not be noticed. This irregularity is most common for laser check stock, since these checks are stored as separate sheets, rather than as a continuous roll of check stock, and so can be more easily pilfered.

   - *Conduct spot audits of petty cash.* It is possible to misrepresent the contents of a petty cash box through the use of miscellaneous receipts and IOU vouchers. By making unscheduled audits, one can sometimes spot these irregularities.

   - *Control check stock.* The check stock cannot be stored in the supply closet along with the pencils and paper, because anyone can remove a check from the stack, and then is only a forged signature away from stealing funds from the company. Instead, the check stock should be locked in a secure cabinet, to which only authorized personnel have access.

   - *Control signature plates.* If anyone can access the company's signature plates, then it is not only possible to forge checks, but also to stamp authorized signatures on all sorts of legal documents. Accordingly, these plates should always be kept in the company safe.

   - *Create a checklist in the mail room.* If there is any chance that someone in the accounting department is removing customer checks before they are included in the daily deposit records, then the mail room staff can be asked to create a separate list, which can later be compared to the deposit slip list to see if there are any differences.

   - *Review restrictive endorsements before cashing checks.* A customer could insert a restrictive clause on a check payment that limits a company's ability to legally collect additional funds. Restrictive endorsements are rare, so most organizations do not conduct this review. However, if there is a reasonable probability of losses, then train the cashier to examine checks for restrictive endorsements and withhold them from the daily deposit until the company lawyer can review them.

   - *Deposit all checks daily.* If checks are kept on hand for several days, there is an increased likelihood that someone will gain access to them and cash them into his or her own account. Consequently, bank deposits should be made every day.

   - *Transport cash in locked cash pouch.* To reduce the risk of unauthorized access to any cash being transported for deposit, always store it in a locked cash pouch. The most elaborate extension of this concept is to hire an armored truck to transport the cash, which is mandatory for larger quantities of cash.

- *Reconcile the validated deposit slip to the original bank deposit ticket.* Once deposited, the bank will issue a validated receipt for the cash. Someone other than the person who made the deposit should compare the original deposit ticket to the validated receipt and investigate any differences. This control is needed to ensure that the person making the deposit does not remove cash during delivery to the bank.

- *Divert incoming cash to a lockbox.* If cash or checks from customers never reach a company, then a host of control problems related to the potential misuse of that cash goes away. To do this, a lockbox can be set up that is controlled by the company's bank, and customers can be asked to send their payments to the lockbox address.

- *Fill in empty spaces on checks.* If the line on a check that lists the amount of cash to be paid is left partially blank, a forger can insert extra numbers or words that will result in a much larger check payment. This can be avoided by having the software that prints checks insert a line or series of characters in the spaces.

- *Fill out petty cash vouchers in ink.* Petty cash receipts can be modified to make it appear that they are larger than was really the case, with the perpetrator removing the difference from the cash box. This issue can be resolved by requiring that all vouchers be filled out in ink.

- *Limit petty cash reserves.* If there is little money in a petty cash box, then there is less incentive for anyone to steal the box. If there is a large amount of cash volume flowing through the box, then a useful alternative is procurement cards.

- *Install a petty cash contact alarm.* A simple battery-powered contact alarm can be installed on a petty cash drawer that triggers a buzzer or flashing light. If the petty cash box is located in a relatively public location, this may act as a deterrent to anyone attempting to access petty cash.

- *Require supervisory approval of cash refunds.* One way to steal cash is to take money from the cash register and record a refund on the cash register tape. By requiring a supervisory password or key entry every time a refund is issued, the cash register operator has no opportunity to steal cash by this method. If there is a minimum level above which supervisory approval is needed for a refund, then review the cash register tape for an unusually large number of cash refunds just below the approval limit.

- *Mutilate voided checks.* A voided check can be retrieved and cashed. To keep this from happening, a stamping device that cuts the word "void" into the surface of the check should be used, thereby sufficiently mutilating it so that it cannot be used again.

- *Perform bank reconciliations.* This is one of the most important controls anywhere in a company, for it reveals all possible cash inflows and outflows. The bank statement's list of checks cashed should be carefully compared to the company's internal records to ensure that checks have not been altered once they leave the company or that the books have not been altered to disguise the amount of the checks. It is also necessary to compare the bank's deposit records to the books to see if there are discrepancies that may be caused by someone taking checks or cash out of the batched bank deposits.

Further, one should compare the records of all company bank accounts to see if any check kiting is taking place. In addition, it is absolutely fundamental that the bank reconciliation be completed by someone who is entirely unassociated with the accounts payable, accounts receivable, or cash receipts functions, so that there is no way for anyone to conceal their wrongdoings by altering the bank reconciliation. Finally, it is now possible to call up on-line bank records through the Internet, so that a reconciliation can be conducted every day. This is a useful approach, since irregularities can be spotted and corrected much more quickly.

- *Use metrics analysis to detect skimming.*   Skimming is the removal of cash prior to its entry into the accounting system, usually involving the removal of cash from a sale transaction and then destroying all evidence of the sale. If there is a significant amount of skimming, its presence can be indicated through several metrics: decreasing cash to total current assets, decreasing ratio of cash to credit card sales, and flat or declining sales with an increasing cost of sales.

- *Review uncashed checks.*   If checks have not been cashed, it is possible that they were created through some flaw in the accounts payable system that sent a check to a nonexistent supplier. An attempt should be made to contact these suppliers to see if there is a problem.

- *Update signature cards.*   A company's bank will have on file a list of check signatories that it has authorized to sign checks. If one of these people leaves the company for any reason, he or she still has the ability to sign company checks. To avoid this control problem, the bank's signature card should be updated as soon as a check signer leaves the company.

- *Stamp incoming checks with "deposit to account number xxx."*   It is possible that employees with access to customer checks will try to cash them, as might anyone with access to the mail once it has left the company. This can be made more difficult by stamping the back of the check with "deposit to account number xxx," so that they would have to deface this stamp in order to cash the check.

- *Require cash application staff to take vacations.*   Lapping involves taking money paid by customer A, then using cash from customer B to pay customer A's account, and so on. This type of fraud tends to be difficult to maintain, requiring constant attention by the person perpetrating the fraud. Requiring employees to take their designated vacations will frequently bring lapping situations to light while they are absent.

2. *Investments.*   The shifting of investment funds is the area in which a person has the best chance for stealing large quantities of company funds, or of placing them in inappropriate investments that have a high risk of loss. The following controls are designed to contain these risks:

- *Impose investment limits.*   When investing its excess funds, a company should have a policy that requires it to only invest certain amounts in particular investment categories or vehicles. For example, only the first $100,000 of funds are insured through a bank account, so excess funding beyond this amount can be shifted elsewhere. As another example, the Board of Directors may feel that there is too much risk in junk bond investments, and so will place a general prohibition on this type of investment. These sorts of policies can be programmed into a treasury workstation, so that the system will automatically flag investments that fall outside a company's preset investment parameters.

- *Obtain and document quotes for each investment.* An investment officer may have a favorite bank and will continue to invest with it, even if its rates are not competitive. It is also common for the investment staff to not want to go through the effort of obtaining multiple quotes on a regular basis. By requiring them to complete a quotation sheet, this control ensures that the best investment rate is obtained.

- *Require authorizations to shift funds among accounts.* A person who is attempting to fraudulently shift funds out of a company's accounts must have approval authorization on file with one of the company's investment banks to transfer money out to a noncompany account. This type of authorization can be strictly controlled through signatory agreements with the banks. It is also possible to impose strict controls over the transfer of funds *between* company accounts, since a fraudulent person may uncover a loophole in the control system whereby a particular bank has not been warned *not* to allow fund transfers outside of a preset range of company accounts, and then shifts all funds to that account and thence to an outside account.

3. *Accounts Receivable.* Controls are needed in the accounts receivable area to ensure that employees do not take payments from customers and then hide the malfeasance by altering customer receivable records. The most common controls are:

- *Compare checks received to applications made against accounts receivable.* It is possible for an accounts receivable clerk with the dual responsibility of cash application to cash a check to his or her personal account, and then hide evidence of the stolen funds by continually applying subsequent cash received against the oldest accounts receivable. This can be spotted by conducting an occasional comparison of checks listed on the deposit slip for a given day to the accounts against which the funds were credited.

- *Confirm receivables balances.* If an employee is falsely applying cash from customers to different accounts in order to hide the loss of some cash that he or she has extracted from the company, it is possible to detect this problem by periodically sending out a confirmation form to customers to verify what they have paid to the company.

- *Require approval of bad debt expenses.* A manager should approve any bad debt write-offs from the accounts receivable listing. Otherwise, it is possible for someone to receive a check from a customer, cash it into their own account, and write off the corresponding account receivable as a bad debt. This control can be greatly enhanced by splitting the cash receipts function away from the collections function, so that it would require collusion to make this type of fraud work.

- *Require approval of credits.* It is possible for someone in the accounts receivable area to grant a credit to a customer in exchange for a kickback from the customer. This can be prevented through the use of approval forms for all credits granted, as well as a periodic comparison of credits granted to related approval forms. It is acceptable to allow the accounting staff to grant very small credits in order to clean up miscellaneous amounts on the accounts receivable listing, but these should be watched periodically to see if particular customers are accumulating large numbers of small credits.

- *Audit credit memos and supporting documentation.*   The internal audit staff should periodically schedule an examination of a sample of all issued credit memos, as well as the supporting documentation for each one, and the security of any unused prenumbered credit memo forms. Audit tasks should include a review for the presence of an authorized approval signature, as well as for a received item that matches the quantity indicated on the credit memo.

4. *Inventory.*   A company's inventory can be so large and complex that extensive controls are needed simply to give it any degree of accuracy at all. Consequently, virtually all of the following controls are recommended to achieve a high level of inventory record accuracy:

- *Conduct inventory audits.*   If no one ever checks the accuracy of the inventory, it will gradually vary from the book inventory, as an accumulation of errors builds up over time. To counteract this problem, one can either schedule a complete recount of the inventory from time to time or else an ongoing cycle count of small portions of the inventory each day. Whichever method is used, it is important to conduct research in regard to why errors are occurring, and attempt to fix the underlying problems.

- *Investigate negative-balance perpetual records.*   A record in the perpetual inventory database contains a running balance of the current on-hand inventory quantity. If this number ever reaches a negative balance, always investigate to determine what transaction or counting error caused the problem, and take steps to ensure that it does not happen again.

- *Control access to bill of material and inventory records.*   The security levels assigned to the files containing bill of material and inventory records should allow access to only a very small number of well-trained employees. By doing so, the risk of inadvertent or deliberate changes to these valuable records will be minimized. The security system should also store the keystrokes and user access codes for anyone who has accessed these records, in case evidence is needed to prove that fraudulent activities have occurred.

- *Keep bill of material accuracy levels at a minimum of 98%.*   The bills of material are critical for determining the value of inventory as it moves through the work-in-process stages of production and eventually arrives in the finished goods area, since they itemize every possible component that comprises each product. These records should be regularly compared to actual product components to verify that they are correct, and their accuracy should be tracked.

- *Conduct receiving inspections with a receiving checklist.*   The receiving staff is responsible for inspecting all delivered items. If they perform only a perfunctory inspection, then the company is at risk of having accepted goods with a variety of problems. To ensure that a complete inspection is made, create a receiving checklist describing specific inspection points, such as timeliness of the delivery, quality, quantity, and the presence of an authorizing purchase order number. Require the receiving staff to initial each item on the receiving checklist and then file it with the daily receiving report.

- *Require approval to sign out inventory beyond amounts on pick list.* If there is a standard pick list used to take raw materials from the warehouse for production purposes, then this should be the standard authorization for inventory removal. If the production staff requires any additional inventory, they should go to the warehouse gate and request it, and the resulting distribution should be logged out of the warehouse. Furthermore, any inventory that is left over after production is completed should be sent back to the warehouse and logged in. By using this approach, the CFO can tell if there are errors in the bills of material that are used to create pick lists, since any extra inventory requisitions or warehouse returns probably represent errors in the bills.

- *Require transaction forms for scrap and rework transactions.* A startling amount of materials and associated direct labor can be lost through the scrapping of production or its occasional rework. This tends to be a difficult item to control, since scrap and rework can occur at many points in the production process. Nonetheless, the manufacturing staff should be well trained in the use of transaction forms that record these actions, so that the inventory records will remain accurate.

- *Restrict warehouse access to designated personnel.* Without access restrictions, the company warehouse is like a large store with no prices—just take all you want. This does not necessarily mean that employees are taking items from stock for personal use, but they may be removing excessive inventory quantities for production purposes, which leads to a cluttered production floor. Also, this leaves the purchasing staff with the almost impossible chore of trying to determine what is in stock and what needs to be bought for immediate manufacturing needs. Consequently, a mandatory control over inventory is to fence it in and closely restrict access to it.

- *Segregate customer-owned inventory.* If customers supply a company with some parts that are used when constructing products for them, it becomes very easy for this inventory to be mingled with the company's own inventory, resulting in a false increase in its inventory valuation. Though it is certainly possible to assign customer-specific inventory codes to these inventory items in order to clearly identify them, a more easily discernible control is to physically segregate these goods in a different part of the warehouse.

- *Review inventory for obsolete items.* The single largest cause of inventory valuation errors is the presence of large amounts of obsolete inventory. To avoid this problem, periodically print a report that lists which inventory items have *not* been used recently, including the extended cost of these items. A more accurate variation is to print a report itemizing all inventory items for which there are no current production requirements (only possible if a material requirements planning system is in place). Alternatively, create a report that compares the amount of inventory on hand to annual historical usage of each item. With this information in hand, one should then schedule regular meetings with the materials manager to determine what inventory items should be scrapped, sold off, or returned to suppliers.

- *Move obsolete inventory to segregated area.* It is much easier to review and disposition obsolete inventory if it is congregated in a single area, rather than scattered throughout the warehouse.

5. *Employee Advances.*   Employees may ask for advances on their next paycheck, or to cover the cost of their next trip on the company's behalf. In either case, it is easy to lose track of the advance. The following controls are needed to ensure that an advance is eventually paid back:

   - *Continually review all outstanding advances.*   When advances are paid to employees, it is necessary to continually review and follow up on the status of these advances. Employees who require advances are sometimes in a precarious financial position, and must be issued constant reminders to ensure that the funds are paid back in a timely manner. A simple control point is to have a policy that requires the company to automatically deduct all advances from the next employee paycheck, thereby greatly reducing the work of tracking advances.

   - *Require approval of all advance payments to employees.*   When employees request an advance for any reason—as a draw on the next paycheck or as funding for a company trip—this should always require formal signed approval from their immediate supervisors. The reason is that an advance is essentially a small, short-term loan, which would also require management approval. The accounts payable supervisor or staff should only be allowed to authorize advances for very small amounts.

6. *Fixed Assets.*   The purchase and sale of fixed assets require special controls to ensure that proper authorization has been obtained to conduct either transaction, and also to ensure that the funds associated with fixed assets are properly accounted for. All of the following controls should be implemented to ensure that these goals are achieved:

   - *Ensure that fixed asset purchases have appropriate prior authorization.*   A company with a capital-intensive infrastructure may find that its most important controls are over the authorization of funds for new or replacement capital projects. Depending on the potential amount of funding involved, these controls may include a complete net present value (NPV) review of the cash flows associated with each prospective investment, as well as multilayered approvals that reach all the way up to the Board of Directors. A truly comprehensive control system will also include a post-completion review that compares the original cash flow estimates to those actually achieved, not only to see if a better estimation process can be used in the future, but also to see if any deliberate misrepresentation of estimates was initially made.

   - *Conduct a post-completion project analysis.*   Managers have been known to make overly optimistic projections in order to make favorable cases for asset acquisitions. This issue can be mitigated by conducting regular reviews of the results of asset acquisitions in comparison to initial predictions, and then tracing these findings back to the initiating managers. This approach can also be used at various milestones during the construction of an asset to ensure that costs incurred match original projections.

   - *Assign responsibility for assets.*   There is a significant risk that assets will not be carefully tracked through the company once they are acquired. To avoid this, formally assign responsibility for each asset to the department manager whose staff uses the asset, and send all managers a quarterly notification of which assets are under their control. Even better, persuade the human resources manager to include "asset control" as a line item in the formal performance review for all managers.

- *Verify that correct depreciation calculations are being made.* Though there is no potential loss of assets if incorrect depreciation calculations are being made, it can result in an embarrassing adjustment to the previously reported financial results at some point in the future. This control should include a comparison of capitalized items to the official corporate capitalization limit, in order to ensure that items are not being inappropriately capitalized and depreciated. The control should also include a review of the asset categories in which each individual asset has been recorded, in order to ensure that an asset has not been misclassified, and therefore incorrectly depreciated.

- *Verify that fixed asset disposals are properly authorized.* A company does not want to have a fire sale of its assets taking place without any member of the management team knowing about it. Consequently, the sale of assets should be properly authorized prior to any sale transaction being initiated, if only to ensure that the eventual price paid by the buyer is verified as being a reasonable one.

- *Verify that cash receipts from asset sales are properly handled.* Employees may sell a company's assets, pocket the proceeds, and report to the company that the asset was actually scrapped. This control issue can be reduced by requiring that a bill of sale or receipt from a scrapping company accompany the file for every asset that has been disposed of.

- *Compare fixed asset serial numbers to the existing serial number database.* There is a possibility that employees are acquiring assets, selling them to the company, then stealing the assets and selling them to the company again. To spot this behavior, always enter the serial number of each acquired asset in the fixed asset master file, and then run a report comparing serial numbers for all assets to see if there are duplicate serial numbers on record.

- *Verify that fixed assets are being utilized.* Many fixed assets are parked in a corner and neglected, with no thought to their being profitably sold off. To see if this problem is occurring, the accounting staff should conduct a periodic review of all fixed assets, which should include a visual inspection and discussion with employees to see if assets are no longer in use.

- *Test for asset impairment.* There are a variety of circumstances under which the net book value of an asset should be reduced to its fair value, which can result in significant reductions in the recorded value of an asset. This test requires a significant knowledge of the types of markets in which a company operates, the regulations to which it is subject, and the need for its products within those markets. Consequently, only a knowledgeable person who is at least at the level of a controller or CFO should be relied upon to detect the presence of assets whose values are likely to have been impaired.

7. *Accounts Payable.* This is one of the most common areas in which the misuse of assets will arise, as well as the one where transactional errors are most likely to occur. Nonetheless, an excessive use of controls in this area can result in a significant downgrading in the performance of the accounts payable staff, so a judiciously applied blend of controls should be used.

- *Audit credit card statements.* When employees are issued company credit cards, there will be some risk that the cards will be used for noncompany expenses. To avoid this, one can spot-check a few line items on every credit card statement, if not conduct a complete review of every statement received. For those employees who have a history of making inappropriate purchases, but for whom a credit card is still supplied, it is also possible to review their purchases on-line (depending on what services are offered by the supplying bank) on the same day that purchases are made, and alter credit limits at the same time, thereby keeping tighter control over credit card usage.

- *Compare payments made to the receiving log.* With the exception of payments for services or recurring payments, all payments made through the accounts payable system should have a corresponding record of receipt in the receiving log. If not, there should be grounds for investigation into why a payment was made. This can be a difficult control to implement if there is not an automated three-way matching system already in place, since a great deal of manual cross-checking will otherwise be needed.

- *Compare the invoice numbers of supplier invoices received.* When suppliers are not paid promptly, they will probably send another copy of an invoice to the company, on the grounds that the first one must have been lost. If the first invoice is just being processed for payment, there is a good chance that the company will pay for both the original invoice and its copy. Consequently, the accounting software should automatically compare the invoice numbers of all invoices received, to see if there are duplications.

- *Impose limitations on credit card purchases.* When credit cards are issued to employees, a company has a number of possible restrictions it can place on the cards that will help to keep employee spending within certain predefined limits. For example, if the card is issued by a specific store, then purchases can be limited to that entity. However, since this can result in a large number of credit card types, a more popular alternative is the procurement (or purchasing) card. This is a credit card for which a number of additional limits are imposed. This can include a maximum dollar amount for individual transactions, or maximum amounts per day, or be restricted to stores that have a certain SIC code. Depending on the level of service offered through the procurement card, the monthly charge statement can also list the general category of product purchased.

- *Require approval of all invoices that lack an associated purchase order.* If the purchasing department has not given its approval to an invoice, then the accounting staff must send it to the supervisor of the department to which it will be charged, so that this person can review and approve it.

- *Require supervisory review and approval of credit card statements.* Even with the restrictions just noted for procurement cards, it is still possible for purchases to be made that are not authorized. If it seems necessary to verify employee spending habits, then copies of credit card statements can be sent to employee supervisors for review. This does not have to be for payment approval, but at least to ensure that supervisors are aware of the types of charges being made.

- *Verify authorizations with a three-way match.* Though extremely labor-intensive, it is important to compare a supplier's invoice to the authorizing purchase order to ensure that the details of each one match, while also matching the billed amount to the receiving documentation to ensure that the company is only paying for the amount received. Some computer systems can automate this matching process. An alternative is to have the receiving staff approve the amounts received from suppliers by comparing them to purchase orders, which then allows the accounting staff to pay suppliers from the authorizing purchase order, rather than the supplier invoice.

- *Separate the supplier record creation and payment approval functions.* A strong risk of fraud arises when the same person can create supplier records in the vendor master file, as well as approve payments to the same suppliers, since this person is capable of creating a fake supplier and approving payments to it. Instead, split these two responsibilities among different employees.

- *Require independent review of additions to the vendor master file.* To reduce the risk of having an employee create a shell company to which payments are made by the company, have a person not associated with the payables process review all additions to the vendor master file, and confirm that they are acceptable prior to any payments being made. Under this approach, only collusion that involves the reviewer will result in shell company fraud.

- *Use the universal payment identification code (UPIC).* The UPIC is a banking address used to receive electronic credit payments. It is a unique number that is assigned to a company's bank account, and is essentially a mask for the real account number. It is combined with a universal routing/transit (URT) number, which routes all incoming payment information for the associated UPIC to The Clearing House Payments Company, which in turn translates this information into the company's actual bank account information for payment purposes. With the UPIC, only ACH credits can be initiated, with all debits blocked. Given this high level of security, a company can print its UPIC on invoices or display it on the Internet with no fear that the information will be used to extract money from its account. The company keeps the same UPIC even if it changes bank accounts within the same bank, changes banking relationships entirely, or if its bank is involved in a merger. To do so, the company merely links its new bank account number to the existing UPIC. Finally, the UPIC also protects a company from someone using the number to create fraudulent checks or demand drafts, because the UPIC cannot be used to clear a paper item.

8. *Notes Payable.* The acquisition of new debt is usually a major event that is closely watched by the CFO, and so requires few controls. Nonetheless, the following control points are recommended as general corporate policies.

- *Require approval of the terms of all new borrowing agreements.* A senior corporate manager should be assigned the task of reviewing all prospective debt instruments to verify that their interest rate, collateral, and other requirements are not excessively onerous or conflict with the terms of existing debt agreements. It may also be useful from time to time to see if a lending institution has inappropriate ties to the company, such as partial or full ownership in its stock by the person responsible for obtaining debt agreements.

- *Require supervisory approval of all borrowings and repayments.* As was the case with the preceding control point, high-level supervisory approval is required for all debt instruments—except this time it is for final approval of each debt commitment. If the debt to be acquired is extremely large, it may be useful to have a policy requiring approval by the Board of Directors, just to be sure that there is full agreement at all levels of the organization regarding the nature of the debt commitment. To be a more useful control, this signing requirement should be communicated to the lender, so that it does not inadvertently accept a debt agreement that has not been signed by the proper person.

9. *Revenues.* The key controls concern related to revenues is that all shipments be invoiced in a timely manner. A controls failure in this area can lead to a major revenue shortfall and threaten overall company liquidity.

   - *Compare all billings to the shipping log.* There should be a continual comparison of billings to the shipment log, not only to ensure that everything shipped is billed, but also to guard against illicit shipments that involve collusion between outside parties and the shipping staff. Someone who is handing out products at the shipping dock will rarely be obliging enough to record this transaction in the shipping log, so the additional step of carefully comparing finished goods inventory levels to physical inventory counts and reviewing all transactions for each item must be used to determine where inventory shrinkage appears to be occurring.

   - *Compare discounts taken to return authorizations granted.* Customers will sometimes take deductions when paying company invoices, on the grounds that they have returned some products to the company. The problem is that the company may never have authorized the returns, much less received them. A comparison of the returns authorization log to the list of discounts taken in the cash receipts journal will provide evidence that a customer is not paying for its obligations.

   - *Identify shipments of product samples in the shipping log.* A product that is shipped with no intention of being billed is probably a product sample being sent to a prospective customer or marketing agency. These should be noted as product samples in the shipping log, and the internal audit staff should verify that each of them was properly authorized, preferably with a signed document.

10. *Cost of Goods Sold.* There are many ways in which a company can lose control over its costs in the cost of goods sold area, since it involves many personnel and the largest proportion of company costs. The application of the following suggested controls to a production environment will rely heavily on the perceived gain that will be experienced from using them, versus the extent to which they will interfere with the smooth functioning of the production department.

    - *Compare the cost of all completed jobs to budgeted costs.* A company can suffer from major drops in its gross margin if it does not keep an eagle eye on the costs incurred to complete jobs. To do so, the CFO should compare a complete list of all costs incurred for a job to the initial budget or quote, and determine exactly which actual costs are higher than expected. This review should result in a list of problems that caused the cost overruns, which in turn can be addressed by the management team so that they do not arise again. This process should also be performed while jobs are in process (especially if the jobs are of long duration) so that these problems can be found and fixed before job completion.

- *Compare projected manning needs to actual direct labor staffing.*   The production manager will have a tendency to overstaff the production area if this person is solely responsible for meeting the requirements of the production plan, since an excess of labor will help to ensure that products are completed on time. This tendency can be spotted and quantified by using labor routings to determine the amount of labor that should have been used, and then comparing this standard to the actual labor cost incurred.

- *Pick from stock based on bills of material.*   An excellent control over material costs is to require the use of bills of material for each item manufactured, and then requiring that parts be picked from the raw materials stock for the production of these items based on the quantities listed in the bills of material. By doing so, a reviewer can hone in on those warehouse issuances that were *not* authorized through a bill of material, since there is no objective reason why these issuances should have taken place.

- *Purchase based on blanket purchase orders and related releases.*   The purchasing staff is already doing its job if all purchases are authorized through purchase orders. However, they will be doing this work more efficiently if repeating purchase orders can be summarized into blanket purchase orders, against which releases are authorized from time to time. The internal audit staff should periodically determine if there are opportunities for the use of additional blanket purchase orders, if current ones are being used properly, and if the minimum quantity commitments listed on existing blanket orders are being met, thereby keeping the company from paying penalties for missing minimum order totals.

- *Reject all purchases that are not preapproved.*   A major flaw in the purchasing systems of many companies is that all supplier deliveries are accepted at the receiving dock, irrespective of the presence of authorizing paperwork. Many of these deliveries are verbally authorized orders from employees throughout the company, many of whom are not authorized to make such purchases, or who are not aware that they are buying items at high prices. This problem can be eliminated by enforcing a rule that all items received must have a corresponding purchase order on file that has been authorized by the purchasing department. By doing so, the purchasing staff can verify that there is a need for each item requisitioned, and that it is bought at a reasonable price from a certified supplier.

11. *Travel and Entertainment Expenses.*   Employee expense reports can involve dozens of line items of requested expense reimbursements, a few of which may conflict with a company's stated reimbursement policies. In order to ensure that these "gray area" expense line items are caught, many accountants will apply a disproportionate amount of clerical time to the minute examination of expense reports. The need for this level of control will depend on the CFO's perception of the amount of expenses that will be reduced through its use. In reality, some

lesser form of control, such as expense report audits, are generally sufficient to keep expense reports "honest."

- *Audit expense reports at random.*   Employees may be more inclined to pass through expense items on their expense reports if they do not think that the company is reviewing their expenses. This issue can be resolved fairly inexpensively by conducting a few random audits of expense reports, and following up with offending employees regarding any unauthorized expense submissions. Word of these activities will get around, resulting in better employee self-monitoring of their expense reports. Also, if there is evidence of repeat offenders, the random audits can be made less random by requiring recurring audits for specific employees.

- *Issue policies concerning allowable expenses.*   Employees may submit inappropriate expenses for reimbursement simply because they have not been told that the expenses are inappropriate. This problem can be resolved by issuing a detailed set of policies and procedures regarding travel. The concept can be made more available to employees by posting the information on a corporate intranet site. Also, if there is an on-line expense report submission system in place, these rules can be incorporated directly into the underlying software, so that the system will warn employees regarding inappropriate reimbursement submissions.

- *Require supervisory approval of all expense reports.*   If there are continuing problems with expense reimbursement submissions from employees, it may be necessary to require supervisory approval of all expense reports. This has the advantage of involving someone who presumably knows why an employee is submitting a reimbursement form, and who can tell if the company should pay for it. The downside is that expense reports tend to sit on managers' desks for a long time, which increases the time before an employee will receive payment.

12.   *Payroll Expenses.*   The controls used for payroll cover two areas—the avoidance of excessive amounts of pay to employees, and the avoidance of fraud related to the creation of paychecks for nonexistent employees. Both types of controls are addressed here.

- *Require approval of all overtime hours worked by hourly personnel.*   One of the simplest forms of fraud is to come back to the company after hours and clock out at a later time, or have another employee do it on one's behalf, thereby creating false overtime hours. This can be resolved by requiring supervisory approval of all overtime hours worked. A more advanced approach is to use a computerized time clock that categorizes each employee by a specific work period, so that any hours worked after his or her standard time period will be automatically flagged by the computer for supervisory approval. They may not even allow an employee to clock out after a specific time of day without a supervisory code first being entered into the computer.

- *Require approval of all pay changes.*   Pay changes can be made quite easily through the payroll system if there is collusion between a payroll clerk and any other employee. This can be spotted through regular comparisons of pay rates *paid* to the approved pay rates *stored* in employee folders. It is best to require the approval of a high-level manager for all pay changes, which should include that person's signature on a standard pay change form. It is also useful to audit the deductions taken from employee paychecks, since these can be altered downward to effectively yield an increased rate of pay. This audit should include a review of the amount and timing of garnishment payments, to ensure that these deductions are being made as required by court orders.

- *Require approval of all negative deductions.*   A negative deduction from a paycheck is essentially a cash payment to an employee. Though this type of deduction is needed to offset prior deductions that may have been too high, it can be abused to artificially increase a person's pay. Consequently, all negative deductions should be reviewed by a manager.

- *Look for paychecks having no tax or other deductions.*   A paycheck that has no tax deductions or personal deductions is more likely to be a check issued for a ghost employee, where the perpetrator wants to receive the maximum amount of cash. The easiest way to spot these checks is to create a custom report that runs automatically with each payroll, and which only itemizes checks of this nature.

- *Issue checks directly to recipients.*   A common type of fraud is for the payroll staff to either create employees in the payroll system, or to carry on the pay of employees who have left the company, and then pocket the resulting paychecks. This practice can be stopped by ensuring that every paycheck is handed to an employee who can prove his or her identity.

- *Paymaster retains unclaimed paychecks.*   The person who physically hands out paychecks to employees is sometimes called the paymaster. This person does not prepare the paychecks or sign them, and his sole responsibility in the payroll area is to hand out paychecks. If an employee is not available to accept a paycheck, then the paymaster retains that person's check in a secure location until the employee is personally available to receive it. This approach avoids the risk of giving the paycheck to a friend of the employee who might cash it, and also keeps the payroll staff from preparing a check and cashing it themselves.

- *Issue lists of paychecks issued to department supervisors.*   It is useful to give supervisors a list of paychecks issued to everyone in their departments from time to time, because they may be able to spot payments being made to employees who are no longer working there. This is a particular problem in larger companies, where any delay in processing termination paperwork can result in continuing payments to ex-employees. It is also a good control over any payroll clerk who may be trying to defraud the company by delaying termination paperwork and then pocketing the paychecks produced in the interim.

- *Compare the addresses on employee paychecks.*   If the payroll staff is creating additional fake employees and having the resulting paychecks mailed to their home addresses, then a simple comparison of addresses for all check recipients will reveal duplicate addresses. (So that employees cannot get around this problem by having checks sent to post office boxes, a policy should be created to prohibit payments to post office boxes.)

- *Review report showing multiple direct deposit payments to the same bank account.*   Under a direct deposit system, a payroll clerk could create ghost employees and then have their payments sent directly to his or her bank account through the direct deposit system. This type of fraud is easily detected by running a custom report in the payroll software that only shows employees for whom more than one direct deposit payment has been made as part of a single payroll cycle. An even more effective control is to run the same report for multiple payroll cycles, in case a canny employee only creates ghost employees who are located in different pay cycles.

- *E-mail employees with change information.* Whenever an employee uses a self-service screen to alter information, the system should send a confirming e-mail message detailing the change. This gives employees the opportunity to spot errors in their entries while also notifying them if someone else has gained access to the payroll system using their access codes and has altered their payroll information.

13. *Occupancy Expenses.* Though a relatively minor item, the following control is intended to ensure that employees are prudent in their acquisition of furnishings for company offices:

- *Compare the cost of employee furnishings to company policy.* Employees may obtain furnishings at a cost that is well beyond what would be obtained by a prudent manager. This issue can be addressed by promulgating a policy that outlines the maximum cost of furnishings per employee, and by enforcing it with occasional internal audits of costs incurred. Another means of enforcement is to authorize a standard set of furnishings for the purchasing staff to procure, with any furnishings outside this list requiring special approval.

14. *General.* A few continuing payments to suppliers are based on long-term contracts. Most of the following controls are associated with having a complete knowledge of the terms of these contracts, so that a company does not make incorrect payment amounts:

- *Monitor changes in contractual costs.* This is a large source of potential expense reductions. Suppliers may alter the prices charged to the company on their invoices from the rates specified on either purchase orders, blanket purchase orders, or long-term contracts, in hopes that no one at the receiving company will notice the change in prices. Of particular concern should be prices that the supplier can contractually change in accordance with some underlying cost basis, such as the price of oil, or the consumer price index. Suppliers will promptly increase prices based on these escalator clauses, but will be much less prompt in reducing prices in accordance with the same underlying factors. The internal audit team can review these prices from time to time, or the accounting computer system can automatically compare invoice prices to a database of contract terms. Another alternative is to only pay suppliers based on the price listed in the purchase order, which entirely negates the need for this control.

- *Monitor when contracts are due for renewal.* A company may find itself temporarily paying much higher prices to a supplier if it inadvertently lets a long-term contract containing advantageous price terms expire. To avoid this difficulty, a good control is to set up a master file of all contracts that includes the contract expiration date, so that there will be fair warning of when contract renegotiations must be initiated.

- *Require approval for various levels of contractually based monetary commitment.* There should be a company policy that itemizes the levels of monetary commitment at which additional levels of management approval are required. Though this may not help the company to disavow signed contracts, it is a useful prevention tool for keeping managers from signing off on contracts that represent large or long-term monetary commitments.

- *Obtain bonds for employees in financially sensitive positions.* If there is some residual risk that, despite all the foregoing controls, corporate assets will still be lost due to the activities of employees, it is useful to obtain bonds on either specific employees or for entire departments, so that the company can be reimbursed in the event of fraudulent activities.

The preceding set of recommended controls only encompasses the most common ones. These should be supplemented by reviewing the process flows used by a company to see if there is a need for additional (or fewer) controls, depending on how the processes are structured. Controls will vary considerably by industry, as well—for example, the casino industry imposes multilayered controls over cash collection, since it is a cash business. Thus, these controls should only be considered the foundation for a comprehensive set of controls that must be tailored to each company's specific needs.

WHEN TO ELIMINATE CONTROLS

Despite the lengthy list of controls noted in the last section, there are times when one can safely take controls away. By doing so, one can frequently eliminate extra clerical costs, or at least streamline the various accounting processes. To see if a control is eligible for removal, the following steps should be used:

1. *Flowchart the process.* The first step is to create a picture of every step in the entire process in which a control fits by creating a flowchart. This is needed in order to determine where other controls are located in the process flow. With a knowledge of redundant control points or evidence that there are no other controls available, one can then make a rational decision regarding the need for a specific control.

2. *Determine the cost of a control point.* Having used a flowchart to find controls that may no longer be needed, we must then determine their cost. This can be a complex calculation, for it may not just involve a certain amount of labor, material, or overhead costs that will be reduced; it is also possible that the control is situated in the midst of a bottleneck operation, so that the presence of the control is directly decreasing the capacity of the process, thereby resulting in reduced profits. In this instance, the incremental drop in profits must be added to the incremental cost of operating the control in order to determine its total cost.

3. *Determine the criticality of the control.* If a control point is merely a supporting one that backs up another control, then taking it away may not have a significant impact on the ability of the company to retain control over its assets. However, if its removal can only be counteracted by a number of weaker controls, it may be better to keep it in operation.

4. *Calculate the control's cost benefit.* The preceding two points can be compared to see if a control point's cost is outweighed by its criticality, or if the current mix

of controls will allow it to be eliminated with no significant change in risk, while stopping the incurrence of its cost.

5. *Verify the use of controls targeted for elimination.*   Even when there is a clear-cut case for the elimination of a control point, it is useful to notify everyone who is involved with the process in which it is imbedded, in order to ascertain if there is some other purpose for which it is being used. For example, a control that measures the cycle time of a manufacturing machine may no longer be needed as a control point, but may be an excellent source of information for someone who is tracking the percentage utilization of the equipment. In these cases, it is best to determine the value of the control to the alternate user of the control before eliminating it. It may be necessary to work around the alternate use before the control point can be removed.

This control evaluation process should be repeated whenever there is a significant change to a process flow. Even if there has not been a clear change for some time, it is likely that a large number of small changes have been made to a process, whose cumulative impact will necessitate a controls review. The period of time between these reviews will vary by industry, since some have seen little process change in many years, while others are constantly shifting their business models, which inherently requires changes to their supporting processes.

If there are any significant changes to a business model, such as the addition of any kind of technology, entry into new markets, or the addition of new product lines, a complete review of all associated process flows should be conducted both prior to and immediately after the changes, so that unneeded controls can be promptly removed or weak controls enhanced.

SUMMARY

The main focus of this chapter has been on the specific control points that can be attached to an accounting system in order to reduce the risk of loss. The selection of these controls should be contingent on an evaluation of the risks to which an accounting system is subject, as well as the cost of each control point and its impact on the overall efficiency of each accounting process. In a larger organization, the continuing examination, selection, and installation of control points can easily become a full-time job for a highly trained process expert. Smaller organizations that cannot afford the services of such a person will likely call on the in-house accounting staff to provide such control reviews, which should be conducted on a fixed schedule in order to ensure that ongoing incremental changes to processes are adequately supported by the correct controls.

CHAPTER 7

AUDIT FUNCTION

The audit function is crucial for ensuring the integrity of a company's financial systems, which includes not only its financial results but also the control systems and code of ethics that are the cornerstones of an accurate financial reporting system. The CFO plays a major role in the audit function, given the position's ability to allocate resources to or from audits as well as to influence the annual internal audit plan. However, the key player in this area is the audit committee, which is comprised of independent directors who report directly to the Board of Directors. This committee is described in the next section.

COMPOSITION OF THE AUDIT COMMITTEE

The audit committee should be a standing committee of the Board of Directors, and should be comprised primarily of nonofficer directors. These directors should not be involved in the management of the company, nor have previously been its officers. These restrictions are intended to create the most independent overview environment possible for the committee.

The committee is generally comprised of between three and five members, not all of whom must have an accounting, auditing, or finance background. It can be more useful to have some directors with a solid operational knowledge of the industry in which the company operates; these people can spot potential control weaknesses, based on their knowledge of how transactions flow in an industry-specific environment. Nonetheless, at least one committee member should have considerable training or experience in the accounting and finance arena. The committee should be expected to meet on at least a quarterly basis.

The CFO is rarely a member of this committee. Instead, she will sometimes be asked to attend its meetings in order to advise committee members on specific issues, or to answer questions about problems that the committee has uncovered through its review activities. The CFO should certainly maintain a strong line of communication with committee members, in order to inform them of possible accounting rule changes or prospective policy changes that may impact the reporting of financial information. The CFO should also educate committee members about key financial topics, such as corporate lines of business, accounting policies, legal obligations, regulatory filings, and industry accounting practices.

The director of the internal audit function usually reports to the CFO, but can report instead to the audit committee. The most common reporting relationship is for the internal audit director to be supervised by the CFO, but to have unimpeded access to the audit committee at any time; this reporting system is designed to give committee members direct access to the results of internal audits, while at the same time giving the internal audit director the ability to go around the CFO if that person appears to be obstructing the dissemination of internal audit results.

In short, the audit committee's structure is intended to be as independent of the management team as possible, while still giving it direct access to key accounting and audit personnel within the management team.

ROLE OF THE AUDIT COMMITTEE

The goal of the audit committee is to assist the Board of Directors by providing oversight of the financial reporting process and related controls. The committee is not empowered to make any decisions—rather, it recommends actions to the full Board, which may then vote on its recommendations. The exact range of tasks granted to the audit committee will vary, but are generally confined to the following issues:

TASKS RELATED TO COMPANY MANAGEMENT

- *Review expenses incurred by the management team.*   Used to spot any excessive use of corporate funds by managers.
- *Review business transactions between the company and the management team.* Used to ensure that managers are neither enriching themselves at the expense of the company nor holding their personal interests above those of the company.

TASKS RELATED TO EXTERNAL AUDITORS

- *Recommend the hiring of external auditors.*   Used to ensure that a truly independent auditor is used, rather than one having connections with the company in some way that may influence its review of the company's financial statements. The audit committee should also base this recommendation on the auditor's expertise in the industry, the quality of its services, the extent to which it performs other services for the company, and the amount of its quoted fees for the audit.
- *Review auditor recommendations.*   Used to ensure that control issues spotted by the auditors are properly dealt with by the management team, resulting in a stronger control environment.
- *Review disputes between the external auditors and management.*   Used to determine if the management team is attempting to force the auditors to agree with an alternative accounting treatment for transactions.
- *Review the use of external auditors for other services.*   Used to determine if the external auditor has obtained such a significant amount of extra business with the company that it may be less inclined to issue an unfavorable audit opinion, due to the risk of losing the additional business.

TASKS RELATED TO INTERNAL AUDITS

- *Review the replacement of the internal audit director.*   Used to verify that the internal audit director is being replaced for reasonable cause, rather than because the CFO wants to install a more malleable director.
- *Review the internal audit staff's objectives, work plans, training, and reports.* Used to verify that the internal audit staff is appropriately targeted at those areas

of the company that are at greatest risk of control problems, and that the audit staff is appropriately trained to handle the audits. A detailed review of the annual work plan will reveal if the internal audit director has allocated a sufficient amount of time to each audit, or has sufficient staff available to complete all goals.

- *Review the cooperation received by the internal auditors.* Used to spot possible areas of fraudulent activities, since minimal cooperation is a signal that an auditee may be hiding information from audit teams.

- *Review disaster recovery plans.* Used to ensure that adequate recovery plans have been created and tested for the most likely disaster scenarios.

TASKS RELATED TO FINANCIAL SYSTEMS

- *Investigate fraud and other forms of financial misconduct.* Used as the grounds for a direct investigation of any situation possibly involving deliberately inaccurate financial reporting or the misuse of company assets.

- *Review corporate policies for compliance with laws and ethics.* Used to ensure that all corporate policies, irrespective of their relationship to financial systems, are constructed in accordance with local regulations and meet the restrictions of the corporate statement of ethical activities.

- *Verify that financial reports address all information requirements of lenders.* Used to ensure that lender-required financial information is reported to them at the appropriate times and in the correct formats, so there is minimal risk of losing vital credit lines as a result of missing information.

- *Review all reports to shareholders, including special reports, for consistency of information.* Used to verify that all reports present a consistent picture of corporate financial health to investors. This is of particular concern for special reports, which tend to include different types of measures (such as Earnings Before Interest, Taxes, Depreciation, and Amortization [EBITDA] instead of the net income figure found on financial statements) and bullish statements by management that do not always match the tenor of information presented in the standard set of financial reports.

Of special interest is the audit committee's emphasis on the *review* of a wide range of financial activities—with the exception of one item. The audit committee is empowered to *investigate* fraud and other forms of financial misconduct, rather than review the results of such an investigation by someone else. The reason for this direct action is that employees are probably involved in the fraudulent activities, which may possibly involve members of management, so the audit committee can only obtain an unbiased review of the situation by investigating it itself.

Thus, in all cases besides the investigation of financial misconduct, the audit committee's role is to examine the results of a variety of audits and other investigations to ensure that the company's system of financial reporting fairly represents actual operating results.

PURPOSE OF THE EXTERNAL AUDITORS

The primary role of external auditors is to arrive at an opinion on the fairness of the information presented in a company's financial statements. If they do not approve of the financial statements, then they must note any exceptions in a letter accompanying the financial statements. Opinions can be of the following three types:

1. *Unqualified.* This opinion states that the financial statements are a fair representation of a company's financial position, results of operations, and cash flows.

2. *Qualified.* This opinion states that, with the exception of specified issues, the financial statements are a fair representation of a company's financial position, results of operations, and cash flows.

3. *Adverse.* This opinion states that the financial statements are not a fair representation of a company's financial position, results of operations, and cash flows. When this opinion is made, the auditors must list the reasons for their opinion and their impact on the financial statements.

Auditors may also be asked to review selected portions of a public company's quarterly financial reports. This type of examination is much less limited in scope than a full audit, and is more concerned with the proper presentation of information and the consistency of presentation in relation to information that was disclosed at an earlier date, which may involve the use of comparative ratio analysis. Auditors may also review interim Board or stockholder meeting minutes to see if any issues were discussed that may require disclosure in the quarterly statements. They can also make inquiries about any changes to the assemblage of accounting controls that are used to derive the financial statements.

The external auditors usually issue a management letter alongside their opinion of the financial statements. The management letter contains control problems the auditors uncovered during their audit, along with recommended changes. Auditors always review this letter in advance with the management team in order to prune out any inaccuracies, so the CFO will have time to implement them or prepare a response before the letter goes to the Board of Directors.

Part of the external auditors' job is to evaluate a company's system of internal controls in order to see if they are adequate for properly recording financial transactions. They need this information to determine the extent to which they can rely on existing controls to replace some portion of their audit work. Thus, if they judge internal controls to be weak, audit testing will be more substantial, and vice versa. Auditors conduct internal control tests by tracing a set of actual transactions through the accounting records to see if they have been properly and consistently handled. If they find significant weaknesses in the system of controls (i.e., those that could adversely affect a company's ability to present accurate financial statements), they should report them to either the audit committee or Board of Directors. However, reviewing internal controls is not a primary task of external auditors, so one should not place complete reliance on a statement by them regarding the adequacy of controls. Instead, the internal audit staff is used to provide additional assurance of the adequacy of internal controls.

External auditors have a close working relationship with the audit committee, since it recommends their hiring to the Board of Directors and is the first to hear from them about any audit-related issues. As such, the presence of the audit committee reinforces the independence of the external auditors from the management team. For larger companies requiring a continual audit presence, the external auditors should meet with the audit committee at least once a quarter on a private basis to go over any issues uncovered by the auditors, as well as to discuss the level of cooperation received during the conduct of audit work. The auditors can also take this opportunity to educate the audit committee members about applicable areas of Generally Accepted Accounting Principles (GAAP), where subjectivity can be used in reporting financial information, and how the management team is using these gray areas. The external auditors should discuss with the audit committee not whether an accounting treatment being used by the management team is acceptable, but rather if it is the right thing to do. These ongoing discussions should hopefully result in instructions from the Board to the CFO regarding the proper use of GAAP and the avoidance of any gray areas in the accounting regulations.

DEALING WITH EXTERNAL AUDITORS

Because of the tight linkage between the external auditors and the audit committee, the CFO has little direct control over which auditors are hired or the nature of their review. Because of this arrangement, the CFO's best course for dealing with the auditors is to work with them to the greatest extent possible. This strategy should include assigning members of the internal audit staff to them as helpers during the audit, which not only concludes the audit with greater speed, but also leaves expert internal auditors on hand to answer external auditor questions and also reduces the auditors' final billing (since the internal audit staff is doing part of the work). Another tactic under the same strategy is to lay out all changes in accounting policies for the current year and go over them in detail with the external auditors, so there will be no surprises during the audit in regard to these changes. An even more proactive approach is to communicate with the auditors throughout the year prior to the audit, consulting with them in advance before any prospective accounting policy changes are implemented.

Once the audit is completed, the auditors may be prepared to issue an unqualified or adverse opinion on the financial statements. This is cause for great concern to a CFO, since it essentially states that the CFO is unable to manage a financial system that generates accurate results, or else that the CFO is using an accounting treatment that departs significantly from GAAP. Since investors and lenders will see the auditors' report, the CFO should generally accept whatever changes are recommended by the auditors in order to earn an unqualified opinion.

A CFO may think that these recommendations essentially require the CFO to raise the white surrender flag and accept anything recommended by the auditors. This is not the case, since dealing with auditors throughout the year allows the CFO time to share opinions with them prior to the formal audit and perhaps influence their thinking about how GAAP should be applied to the company's particular circumstances. Thus, cooperation with the external auditors is crucial.

IMPACT OF THE SARBANES-OXLEY ACT ON THE AUDIT FUNCTION

The Sarbanes-Oxley Act of 2002 (Sarbanes) is one of the most extensive enhancements of the federal securities laws since the 1930s. Given the far-reaching nature of its provisions, every CFO should have a grasp of its general requirements. This section provides that information by splitting a summary of its provisions into three categories: issues for the external auditor, public company, and private company.

ISSUES FOR THE EXTERNAL AUDITOR.   Sarbanes strengthens the oversight of public accountants with the creation of an oversight board and by requiring lengthy documentation retention, while also improving auditor independence from clients by prohibiting certain activities and rotating partners off audits. Key provisions are:

- *Public accounting oversight board.* Sarbanes created the Public Accounting Oversight Board, which is responsible for establishing rules and quality control standards for auditors who deliver audit reports for publicly held companies.

- *Document retention.* Auditors who perform an audit or review must retain the documents and all related correspondence for seven years. It is also a felony to knowingly destroy or create documents if that action will obstruct or influence a federal investigation.

- *Auditor independence.* Auditors must establish their independence from audit clients by not providing bookkeeping services, financial system design or implementation services, valuation services, fairness opinions, actuarial services, legal or expert services, investment banking assistance, or actuarial services to those clients.

- *Partner rotation.* Sarbanes requires the lead and concurring audit partners to rotate off the audit team after five years. Once off the audit, they cannot be involved with it for another five years, when the requirements begin anew.

- *Auditors hired by clients.* If a client hires the lead or concurring partner from the previous year's audit team and that person oversees the reporting of financial information for the client, then the auditor is not considered to be independent.

ISSUES FOR THE PUBLIC COMPANY.   The bulk of the Sarbanes provisions are targeted at public companies, specifically at the enhancement of both control systems and financial reporting. Control improvements include the establishment of an audit committee, management certification of the financial statements and supporting control system, issuance of a controls report, and whistleblower protection. Disclosure improvements include coverage of off-balance sheet arrangements, a code of ethics, and insider stock trades. Miscellaneous provisions include penalties for document destruction and the prohibition of loans to officers. Key provisions are:

- *Audit committee.* Sarbanes requires the various stock exchanges to adopt rules requiring listed companies to have audit committees whose directors are independent of the company. Independence is defined as receiving no compensatory fees from the company, such as from consulting engagements.

- *Disclosure of financial experts on the audit committee.* Companies must note whether there is a financial expert on the audit committee. If there is not one, the discussion should indicate why the company has not added such a person.

- *Management certification of financial statements.* The chief executive officer and chief financial officer of the reporting company must personally certify that the company's financial statements do not contain material misstatements or omissions, that the statements fairly reflect the company's financial position, that control systems will bring material issues to the attention of the officers, and they have conducted an evaluation of the company's disclosure controls and procedures within the past 90 days.

- *Additional SEC-required report.* The Securities and Exchange Commission has issued release number 33-8238 under Section 404 of Sarbanes, in which it requires public companies to file an annual internal report that identifies the internal control framework that a company is using, states whether controls are effective as of the end of its fiscal year, discloses material control weaknesses, describes the management team's responsibility for establishing and maintaining an adequate system of internal controls, and notes that the company's external auditors have issued an audit report on management's assessment of its internal controls.

- *Whistleblower protection.* If an employee is discharged or disciplined as a result of disclosing information about fraudulent activities as part of a federal investigation or several other specific categories, he or she can file a complaint with the Department of Labor (DOL), and then file a lawsuit in federal court if the DOL does not issue a ruling within 180 days. Under Sarbanes, it is a criminal violation to retaliate against a whistleblower for revealing information to a law enforcement officer regarding any federal offense.

- *Disclosure of off-balance-sheet arrangements.* Companies must include a discussion of their off-balance-sheet reporting in a separately captioned section of the financial statements.

- *Disclosure of code of ethics.* Companies must disclose if they have issued a code of ethics for their senior managers and accounting managers, and publicly issue changes to the code.

- *Reporting of insider stock trades.* Companies must disclose insider stock trades by directors, officers, and principal shareholders no later than the end of the second business day after the trade took place.

- *Document destruction.* It is a felony to knowingly destroy or create documents if that action will obstruct or influence a federal investigation.

- *Loans to directors or officers.* Companies are prohibited from extending credit to directors or executive officers.

- *Forfeiture of officer compensation.* If a company officer earns a bonus or a profit on stock sales through the issuance of misstated financial statements, the officer must forfeit the amount of the bonus earned during the 12-month period beginning on the date of issuance of the misstated financial statements.

Several of the above provisions have proven so onerous for some public companies that they have either delisted from a stock exchange in order to avoid some requirements, or have gone private (which makes them subject to only the few Sarbanes provisions noted below).

ISSUES FOR THE PRIVATE COMPANY. Only two Sarbanes provisions apply to privately held companies, which are as follows:

- *Document destruction.* It is a felony to knowingly destroy or create documents if that action will obstruct or influence a federal investigation.

- *Whistleblower protection.* It is a criminal violation to retaliate against a whistleblower for revealing information to a law enforcement officer regarding any federal offense.

ROLE OF THE INTERNAL AUDIT FUNCTION

The internal audit director usually sorts through a number of requests from the audit committee, CFO, CEO, and other members of management, and assembles a proposed schedule of audits to conduct over the course of the upcoming year. If these are approved, the director then creates a work schedule for the various audit teams. After the work is completed, the audit team writes a report on its findings, which works its way back through the director and eventually to the various members of management, where its findings are usually cause for systemic changes that either eliminate or mitigate any uncovered control problems. The audit teams will sometimes conduct post-audit reviews to see if subsequent system changes have resulted in better controls.

Some suggested audits that the teams can review, and which will give the CFO much better information about how to resolve control issues, are:

- *Accounts payable.*   Verify that all payments are properly authorized and supported by receiving documentation. Also verify that there are no late payment fees being paid, and that early payment discounts are taken when the discounts exceed the corporate cost of capital.

- *Accounts receivable credits.*   Verify that all accounts receivable credits are properly authorized, and that bad debts are expensed to the bad debt allowance, rather than reduced with a credit to sales. Verify that customers are not taking early payment discounts and still paying at longer terms than those required by the early payment discount deal.

- *Advertising credits.*   Verify that all credits issued to customers for advertising are supported by copies of advertisements, clearly showing the dates when the advertisements were run, as well as accompanying documentation for advertising fees.

- *Contracts.*   Verify that there is an updated file containing all current contracts, as well as an accurate summary-level contract listing that itemizes key dates for each contract, such as termination dates, penalty clauses, and review dates.

- *Debt.*   Verify that debt payments are made on time, and that no penalty payments are incurred. Also verify that the interest rates charged by lenders are in agreement with the rates listed on loan documentation, and that no additional fees are being charged.

- *Expense reports.*   Verify that submitted expenses meet company guidelines for approved travel and entertainment expenses. Also verify that all expense reports have been approved in advance by department managers, and that expense reports do not include expenses for an excessively large number of time periods.

- *Fixed assets.*   Verify that all capitalized assets are above the capitalization limit, and that they are being expensed at the correct rate of depreciation. Also verify that capital expenditures were properly authorized, and that a net present value analysis was conducted, reviewed, and approved for each one.

- *Freight revenue.*   Verify that customers are charged the correct amounts for freight. Also verify that freight billings are reconciled against actual shipments by freight carriers.

- *Inventory.*   Verify that inventory accuracy is at least 95%. Also verify that cycle counts are being completed in a timely manner, and that counters are investigating the root causes of any errors they find. Verify that customer-owned inventory is properly segregated and that it is not included in the inventory that has received a valuation. Verify that all inventory costs are properly supported by backup documentation regarding actual product costs.

- *Payroll.* Verify that all employee pay changes and bonuses have been properly authorized, and that all legal requirements for employee files, such as I-9 form verification, have been completed and are present in employee files. Also verify that all employee garnishment deductions are properly supported by legal documentation, and that the payroll staff is aware of the dates on which the garnishments are to be terminated.

- *Pricing.* Verify that customers are being charged the correct prices, based on pricing tables for quantities and dates shipped.

- *Product invoicing.* Verify that all items shipped are invoiced, and vice versa. Also verify that all invoices are printed within one day of shipment.

- *Service invoicing.* Verify that all service invoices are billed within one day of the completion of work, or in accordance with a prearranged invoicing schedule, and that services billed are matched by supporting documentation.

The recommended internal audits itemized here are only the standard ones that apply to most industries. A CFO should also review specialized systems within the company that require special attention and design additional audit programs to ensure that their controls are also adequate.

The internal audit director may also be asked to conduct a variety of *operational* audits. These audits can cover any topic, resulting in a report on the efficiency and effectiveness of operations in a selected area, along with improvement recommendations. Examples of operational audits include examinations of procurement practices, hiring standards, and management reviews. An operational audit may be conducted at the request of a manager who wants an outside opinion on the performance of his department, or by senior management, which may be looking for areas of improvement within the company.

Another type of audit is the *compliance* audit. This audit requires the internal audit staff to review a company's compliance not only with internal policies, but also with those of such external regulatory agencies as the Securities and Exchange Commission, the Internal Revenue Service, and the Department of Labor. These reviews are rarely requested by anyone within a company; instead, the internal audit director should block out a standard amount of space for them within the annual audit work plan, and continually rotate through compliance examinations of all internal and external policies on an ongoing basis.

The internal audit staff may also be asked to recommend the *elimination* of controls, on the grounds that they are too expensive to maintain in proportion to the level of control provided. If so, internal auditors should determine the level of offsetting control provided by other control points in the financial system. If other controls can "back fill" for a deleted control, then it can possibly be eliminated. However, internal auditors must also consider the gravity of a control breakdown in the subject area. If the level of potential risk is in the millions of dollars, then it may be more prudent to retain the targeted control point. Finally, some estimation of the cost of the targeted control should be made in order to determine the cost-effectiveness of elimination. Determining a control's cost-effectiveness can include a discussion of its impact on efficient transaction processing—if it significantly impedes efficiency enhancements, this can be grounds for elimination. In short, internal auditors must balance a number of offsetting issues when deciding if controls can be eliminated.

In addition to its other tasks, the internal audit staff is frequently called upon to assist the external auditors in their review of a company's financial statements. The internal staff may be asked to complete any tasks that will reduce the workload of the external auditors, thereby reducing the fees charged by them. For large audits, this can represent a substantial reduction in the fee charged. Tasks that may be shifted to the internal audit staff include the gathering of data for analysis by the external auditors, filling out boilerplate audit forms, and assisting with transaction confirmations.

MANAGING THE INTERNAL AUDIT FUNCTION*

The internal audit director most commonly reports to the CFO, and is also allowed direct access to the audit committee. It is also common to see the director reporting straight to the audit committee, which eliminates any chance that the CFO can stall an auditing program through the withholding of budgeted funds.

Within the internal audit department, there will usually be a set of managers reporting to the internal audit director who are specialists in different auditing areas. For example, information technology audits are almost always handled by a highly trained subgroup, while financial, compliance, and operational audits are typically funneled to separate teams. If there are many corporate locations, there may also be regional audit managers who are responsible for all auditing activities within their regions, and who coordinate auditing work with the managers of other departments for projects that span large areas.

The primary tool for managing the internal audit function is the annual audit plan. This is usually a document that lists every audit to be completed during the year, as well as a brief description of the objectives of each audit. An example of a possible set of objectives is:

> Review the method for recording additions, changes, and deletions of fixed assets to and from the accounting records for the Andersonville facility. The audit will verify that the correct capitalization limit is being observed, that there are documented and justified reasons for making alterations to the fixed asset records subsequent to additions, that deletions are recorded properly, and that the sale amounts of assets are reasonable.

Though this audit description gives one a good idea of what will happen during the audit, it does not yield a sufficient degree of additional information, such as the number of hours budgeted for the work, who will be assigned to the project, or when it will take place. This requires a more detailed audit budget for the year, such as the one shown in Exhibit 7.1. The primary items contained in this budget are the budgeted hours scheduled for each job and the estimated range of dates during which work will be completed. When constructing the plan, the internal audit director should verify that there are sufficient funds to complete it, that there is no duplication of effort between audit teams (or from recently completed audits), and that the assigned tasks are reasonable in relation to the size of the systems to be reviewed.

With the internal audit budget in hand, the CFO can exercise a much greater degree of control over the department. The budget information allows one to use the following controls:

- Compare budget to actual hours worked.
- Compare budget to actual project start and completion dates.
- Compare budget to actual staffing requirements.

---

* Adapted with permission from pp. 136–138 of *Controllership* by Willson, Roehl-Anderson, and Bragg (John Wiley & Sons, 2004).

Division	Project	Hours	Start Date	End Date	Personnel
Denver	Fixed assets	240	01/01/xx	02/15/xx	Smith/Jones
Denver	Billings	280	01/01/xx	02/21/xx	Barnaby/Granger
Boston	Expense reports	120	02/16/xx	03/31/xx	Smith/Jones
Chicago	Payroll	320	04/01/xx	05/15/xx	Smith/Jones
Chicago	Fixed assets	280	02/22/xx	03/07/xx	Barnaby/Granger
Atlanta	Expense reports	120	05/16/xx	06/30/xx	Smith/Jones
Atlanta	Billings	240	03/08/xx	04/21/xx	Barnaby/Granger

EXHIBIT 7.1 SAMPLE INTERNAL AUDIT BUDGET

In addition to these quantitative control points, there are a variety of supplemental controls that a CFO can use for specific situations. They are:

PLANNING CONTROLS

- Compare the written objectives of the department to its actual activities.
- Ensure that there is an up-to-date policies and procedures manual that clearly shows how audit work is to be conducted.
- Verify that auditors have a sufficient educational background to conduct specific types of audits.
- Verify that the department is sufficiently large to accomplish all planned goals.
- Review the mix of scheduled reviews to see if there is a lack of attention to specific areas, such as reviews of accounting, computer, or operational controls.
- Verify that the department is reviewing the controls being built into new computer system projects.
- Verify that there are scheduled reviews of the company's ethical standards.
- Ensure that the internal audit staff coordinates its work to support that of the external auditors.

PERFORMANCE CONTROLS

- Review work papers to ensure that audits were completed in as thorough a manner as possible.
- Review audit reports for activities conducted, findings noted, and recommendations given.
- Review comments from departments that were the subject of audits.
- Verify that the audit committee is satisfied with departmental performance, and follow up on any shortcomings.

FOLLOW-UP CONTROLS

- Verify that there have been no restrictions of departmental activities due to intransigence by auditees, and bring up exceptions with the audit committee for action.
- Verify that audit recommendations are being acted on.

By using the appropriate mix of the preceding controls, a CFO can create an efficient and effective management system that will result in a high-performance internal audit department.

SUMMARY

Auditing is about the verification of financial systems that are already in place. As such, auditors are really reviewing the systems for which the CFO is responsible. Because of this overview role, it is inappropriate for the CFO to be responsible for the hiring of an external audit firm or to have direct control over the work plan of the internal audit staff. Otherwise, a CFO would be reviewing herself, resulting in very few adverse audit findings. Though this book is intended to assist the CFO with his or her job, this chapter has really described why the CFO should *not* have direct control over the audit function. A discerning CFO will realize that this lack of control is not only good, but also should be trumpeted to investors as solid proof of the strength and integrity of a company's financial systems.

CHAPTER 8

REPORTS TO THE SECURITIES AND EXCHANGE COMMISSION

The CFO of any publicly held company must deal with the Securities and Exchange Commission (SEC) certainly on a quarterly basis, and frequently as much as once a week on a variety of topics. Given the frequency of interaction, it is useful to have an overview of the SEC, as well as learn about the principal legislation under which it gains its authority, its primary regulations, and the most common forms submitted by public companies to the SEC.

OVERVIEW*

The SEC was created as a direct result of the stock market crash of October 1929. Given the massive loss of net worth as a result of the plunge in stock market prices at that time, the federal government felt that a considerable degree of regulation over the securities industry was necessary in order to ensure that the resulting increase in public confidence in the markets would eventually draw them back to it.

After a series of hearings to determine what specific forms of regulation would meet this goal, Congress passed the Securities Act and the Securities Exchange Act in 1933 and 1934, respectively. As noted next in this chapter, the two acts were designed to greatly increase the information reported by an entity issuing securities (especially the nature of its business and any associated investment risks), as well as the amount of oversight by the government. The oversight function was centered on the regulation of the markets in which securities were sold, as well as the brokers and investment advisers who worked with investors to buy and sell securities. The reporting of information by securities issuers has blossomed into a key function of the SEC, which requires timely filings to it of all material financial information by issuers, which it promptly makes available to the public through its Electronic Data Gathering, Analysis, and Retrieval system (EDGAR) on-line database (see later section).

Congress created the SEC as part of the 1934 act to administer the new acts. Its powers later increased as other acts were also passed, eventually giving it regulatory authority over public utility holding companies and mutual funds, too. It has a significant amount of enforcement authority to back up its regulatory oversight function, typically bringing about 500 civil enforcement actions per year against any person or business entity that breaks the securities laws.

---

* Descriptions of the SEC, securities acts, and regulations in this chapter were adapted with permission from Chapter 6 of *Ultimate Accountants' Reference* by Bragg (John Wiley & Sons, 2005).

SECURITIES ACT OF 1933

The Securities Act of 1933 requires companies issuing securities for public purchase to issue financial and other significant information to investors, while also prohibiting fraud or misrepresentations of financial information. The issuance of information is accomplished through the registration of information about the securities with the SEC, which will review submitted information to ensure that disclosure requirements under this act have been met. A key item is that this act is primarily concerned with the issuance of information related to the initial offering of securities only, rather than with ongoing updates to securities-related information (which is covered by the Securities Exchange Act of 1934).

There are a few instances where the mandated disclosure requirements do not have to be met. If a securities offering is of a limited size, it is issued by a municipal, state, or federal government, or if the offering is limited to a small number of investors, then it is exempted from registration with the SEC.

The information sent to the SEC provides essential details about the issuing company's properties and business, securities available for sale, information about the management team, and audited financial statements.

If the information provided by the issuing company can be proven by an investor to be incomplete or inaccurate, then investors may have the right to recover their invested funds from the company.

SECURITIES EXCHANGE ACT OF 1934

This act created the SEC, giving it authority to regulate many players in the securities industry, such as stock exchanges (e.g., the New York Stock Exchange and National Association of Securities Dealers), clearing agencies, brokerage firms, and transfer agents. The act requires these market players to register with the SEC, which involves the filing of regularly updated disclosure reports. It prohibits the trading of securities on unregistered exchanges. Also, self-regulatory organizations (such as the National Association of Securities Dealers) are required to set up rules under which they can ensure that investors are adequately protected while conducting transactions with members of the self-regulatory organizations.

The act requires firms with more than $10 million in assets, and whose securities are held by greater than 500 investors, to file both annual reports and a variety of other supplemental reports. The act also requires anyone who wishes to acquire more than 5% of a company's securities by tender offer or direct purchase to disclose information to the SEC (this provision was added through a 1970 amendment to the act).

The act also creates rules for the types of information included in proxy solicitations that are used to obtain shareholder votes regarding the election of directors and other corporate matters. In brief, the solicitations must disclose all important facts regarding the topics about which the shareholders are being asked to vote. It requires that these solicitations be filed with the SEC prior to their issuance to the shareholders in order to ensure that their content complies with the disclosure rules of the act.

The act also gave the Federal Reserve System's Board of Governors the power to determine the allowable credit limits that could be used to purchase securities through margin trading. It also requires broker-dealers to obtain the written permission of investors before lending any securities carried on the investor's account. The intention behind these actions was to avoid the massive loss of wealth that occurred during the 1929 stock market crash, when investors who had purchased heavily on margin lost all of their net worth.

It also prohibits insider trading activities, which occur when a person trades a security based on nonpublic information, particularly when that person has a fiduciary duty to refrain from trading. A 1984 amendment to the act prohibited the officers and directors of a company from short-selling the securities issued by their companies. They are also required to report the amount of securities they hold in their companies, and any changes in those holdings, as long as the amount held is more than 10% of the total of registered securities.

The act specifically prohibits market manipulation through such means as giving a false impression of high levels of trading activity in a stock, issuing false information about possible changes in a stock's price, price fixing, and making false statements in regard to a security.

REGULATION S-X

This regulation is the principal one used by the SEC to oversee the form and content of financial statements submitted by the issuers of securities. It presents a standard format for the presentation of financial statements to be filed with the SEC's various reporting forms, as well as for the dates when these reports are to be filed.

This is a very important regulation for a publicly held company; to peruse its entire content, one can access it on the SEC's web site at www.sec.gov/divisions/corpfin/forms. The regulation separately itemizes the financial reporting formats for a few niche industries, such as investment companies, bank holding companies, and insurance companies, that for the sake of brevity are not included here. Selected summary descriptions from the more commonly used articles from the regulation are:

- *Article 2: Qualifications and reports of accountants.* The SEC will not recognize as a CPA any person who is not currently registered to practice in the state where his or her home or office is located. It will also not recognize a CPA as being independent if the CPA has a financial interest in the entity being audited, or was a manager or promoter of an auditee at the time of the audit. It requires a CPA's report to be dated and manually signed, state that generally accepted accounting principles (GAAP) was followed, state an audit opinion, and clearly itemize any exceptions found.

- *Article 3: General instructions as to financial statements.* Balance sheets must be submitted for the last two year-ends, as well as statements of income and cash flow for the preceding three years. If interim financial statements are provided, then standard year-end accruals should also be made for the shorter periods being reported on. Changes in stockholders' equity shall be included in a note or a separate statement. The financial statements of related businesses can be presented to the SEC in a single consolidated format if the companies are under common control and management during the period to which the reports apply. There are a number of tests to determine whether or not consolidated results are required, as well as for how many time periods over which the combined financial statements must be reported. If a registrant is inactive (revenues and expenses of less than $100,000, and no material changes in the business or changes in securities) during the period, then its submitted financial statements can be unaudited. There are also special reporting requirements for foreign private issuers, real estate investment trusts, and management investment companies.

- *Article 3a: Consolidated and combined financial statements.*   For financial statement reporting purposes, a registrant shall consolidate financial results for business entities that are majority owned, and shall not do so if ownership is in the minority. A consolidated statement is also possible if the year-end dates of the various companies are not more than 93 days apart. Intercompany transactions shall be eliminated from the consolidated reports. If consolidating the results of a foreign subsidiary, then the impact of any exchange restrictions shall be made.

- *Article 4: Rules of general application.*   Financial statements not created in accordance with GAAP will be presumed to be misleading or inaccurate. If the submitting entity is foreign-based, it may use some other set of accounting standards than GAAP, but a reconciliation between its financial statements and those produced under GAAP must also be submitted. Footnotes to the statements that duplicate each other may be submitted just once, as long as there are sufficient cross-references to the remaining footnote. The amount of income taxes applicable to foreign governments and the U.S. government shall be shown separately, unless the foreign component is no more than 5% of the total. There must also be a reconciliation between the reported amount of income tax and the amount as computed by multiplying net income by the statutory tax rate. This article also contains an extensive review of the manner in which oil and gas financial results must be reported.

- *Article 5: Commercial and industrial companies.*   This article describes the specific line items and related footnotes that shall appear in the financial statements. On the *balance sheet*, this shall include:

  — Cash
  — Marketable securities
  — Accounts and notes receivable
  — Allowance for doubtful accounts
  — Unearned income
  — Inventory
  — Prepaid expenses
  — Other current expenses
  — Other investments
  — Fixed assets and associated accumulated depreciation
  — Intangible assets and related amortization
  — Other assets
  — Accounts and notes payable
  — Other current liabilities
  — Long-term debt
  — Minority interests (footnote only)
  — Redeemable and nonredeemable preferred stock
  — Common stock

— Other stockholder's equity

On the *income statement*, this includes:

— Gross revenues

— Costs applicable to revenue

— Other operating costs

— Selling

— General & administrative expenses

— Other general expenses

— Nonoperating income

— Interest

— Nonoperating expenses

— Income or loss before income taxes

— Income tax expense

— Minority interest in income of consolidated subsidiaries

— Equity in earnings of unconsolidated subsidiaries

— Income or loss from continuing operations

— Discontinued operations

— Income or loss before extraordinary items

— Extraordinary items

— Cumulative effect of changes in accounting principles

— Net income or loss

— Earnings per share data

- *Article 6A: Employee stock purchase, savings, and similar plans.*   These types of plans must present a statement of financial condition that includes:

    — Investments in securities of participating employers

    — Investments in securities of unaffiliated issuers

    — Investments

    — Dividends and interest receivable

    — Cash

    — Other assets

    — Liabilities

    — Reserves and other credits

    — Plan equity and close of period

These plans must include in their statements of income and changes in plan equity the following line items:

— Net investment income

— Realized gain or loss on investments

— Unrealized appreciation or depreciation on investments

    —   Realized gain or loss on investments

    —   Contributions and deposits

    —   Plan equity at beginning of period

    —   Plan equity at end of period

- *Article 10: Interim financial statements.* An interim statement does not have to be audited. Only major line items need to be included in the balance sheet, with the exception of inventories, which must be itemized by raw materials, work-in-process, and finished goods either in the balance sheet or in the accompanying notes. Any assets comprising less than 10% of total assets, and which have not changed more than 25% since the end of the preceding fiscal year, may be summarized into a different line item. If any major income statement line item is less than 15% of the amount of net income in any of the preceding three years, and if its amount has not varied by more than 20% since the previous year, it can be merged into another line item. Disclosure must also be made in the accompanying footnotes of any material changes in the business since the last fiscal year-end.

- *Article 11: Pro forma financial information.* Pro forma information is required in cases where a business entity has engaged in a business combination or roll-up under the equity method of accounting, or under the purchase method of accounting, or if a company's securities are to be used to purchase another business. It is also required if there is a reasonable probability of a spin-off, sale, or abandonment of some part or all of a business. The provided information should consist of a pro forma balance sheet, summary-level statement of income, and explanatory notes. The presented statements shall show financial results on the assumption that the triggering transaction occurred at the beginning of the fiscal year, and shall include a net income or loss figure from continuing operations prior to noting the impact of the transaction.

- *Article 12: Form and content of schedules.* This article describes the format in which additional schedules shall be laid out in submitted information, including layouts for valuation and qualifying accounts. It also itemizes formats for the display of information for management investment companies, which include the following formats: investments in securities of unaffiliated issuers, investments in securities sold short, open option contracts written, investments other than securities, investments in and advances to affiliates, summary of investments, supplementary insurance information, reinsurance, and supplemental information.

REGULATION S-K

This regulation contains the instructions for filing forms with the SEC under the rules set by the Securities Act of 1933, the Securities Exchange Act of 1934, and the Energy Policy and Conservation Act of 1975. It concentrates primarily on the content of the nonfinancial statements that must be filed, dwelling in particular on the following topics:

- Description of the general development of the business during the past five years
- Financial information and a narrative description about individual segments of the business for each of the last three years
- Financial information about geographic areas for each of the last three years

- The general types of property owned by the company, as well as where it is located
- Estimates of oil or gas reserves
- Any legal proceedings currently under way, either at the company's initiation or to which it is subject
- The primary markets in which each class of the company's common stock is being traded
- The approximate number of holders of each type of common stock
- The amount and timing of the cash dividends declared on each class of common stock for the last two years
- Description of all securities to be offered for sale
- Key financial information in a columnar format for the last five years
- Selected quarterly financial information for the last two years
- Management's discussion of liquidity, capital resources, and the results of operations
- Material changes during interim reporting periods
- Any change in the outside auditing firm in the last two years
- The market risks associated with trading instruments, as well as how these risks are managed
- Terms and information about derivative financial instruments
- The name, age, and position of each company director
- The name, age, and position of each executive officer
- The compensation of the CEO and the four most highly paid individuals besides the CEO (but only if their total pay exceeds $100,000). This statement shall separately itemize salary, bonus, option, and pension remuneration.

The regulation also sets forth the reporting requirements for a prospectus, and cross-references a series of industry guides that detail additional, and more specific, reporting requirements. The industry guides are for the oil and gas, bank holding company, real estate limited partnership, property-casualty underwriting, and mining businesses. Regulation S-K provides the foundation for much of the information reporting requirements that publicly held companies must file, and so should be perused in detail by those entities.

REGULATION S-B

This regulation is similar to Regulation S-K in that it lays out the specific information that issuers must periodically send to the SEC. However, this regulation has a somewhat reduced set of filing requirements that are targeted at small companies that cannot afford the more in-depth filing requirements of S-K. As a qualified small business issuer, a company will file its registration statement under Form SB-2 or Form 10-SB. In order to qualify for these reduced requirements, a company must have revenues of less than $25 million, be an American or Canadian-based issuer, and not be an investment company. Also, if it is a subsidiary, its corporate parent must also qualify as a small business issuer. Furthermore, its market capitalization must be no more than $25 million, based on the price of its securities within 60 days of its most recent fiscal year-end. Finally, the business must meet these requirements for two consecutive years before qualifying as a small business.

REGULATION FD

The SEC recently released a new regulation, which is the Regulation Fair Disclosure (Regulation FD). The new regulation is designed to curb the disclosure of material information by companies to selected individuals, such as securities analysts, that is not revealed to the general investing public. The regulation will also supposedly reduce a security analyst's incentive not to disclose this information to the general public (on the grounds that the analyst might no longer be given the privileged information). By imposing Regulation FD, this may curb the amount of insider trading that has arisen based on the nonpublic information.

In essence, the regulation requires that an issuer of material information must do so publicly, either by filing the disclosure with the SEC, or by some other broad, nonexclusionary method, such as an Internet Webcast or press release. If material information is disseminated by mistake, then the issuer must act promptly to publicly disclose the information. The regulation does not apply to issuer communications with the press, rating agencies, and communications during the ordinary course of business with business partners, such as customers and suppliers, nor does it apply to any foreign issuers. It *does* apply to all communications with anyone who is involved with the securities markets on a professional basis, as well as with the holders of any securities issued by the company. Also, to keep a company from having to monitor the communications of its entire staff, the regulation only applies to senior management, its investor relations staff, and anyone else who works for the company and who regularly communicates with holders of company securities or anyone involved with the securities markets.

If an issuer violates the regulation, the SEC can initiate an administrative proceeding resulting in a cease-and-desist order, or can go further to seek an injunction or even civil penalties.

Thus far, public companies have adapted to this regulation in two ways. Under the first approach, some companies have reduced the amount of information given out to anyone—analysts or the public—on the theory that no disclosure to anyone will meet the guidelines of Regulation FD. This has been particularly common in regard to no longer giving earnings guidance and in limiting one-on-one discussions with analysts. As an example of this approach, some have imposed a quiet period on the weeks leading up to an earnings announcement, so there is no chance that management will leak the news in advance to anyone.

The second approach is to flood the market with information, on the theory that analysts will have so much information available through general disclosures to the public that they will no longer need any additional information, thereby avoiding any chance of one-on-one meetings where the FD guidelines could be violated. This approach has led to the release of far more 8-K reports, detailing all possible items of interest to investors. By doing so, they have certainly increased the volume of information available, though not necessarily the quality.

A variation on the two basic approaches has been to have analysts submit questions in writing, with responses to the questions being posted on the corporate web site within a few days. This interesting approach avoids the risk of ever answering a verbal question with more information than would be released to the public by other means, while ensuring that all investors are informed of answers to analyst questions.

Without further guidance from the SEC, a CFO can take either approach. Given that the supposed need for FD was the curtailment of the flow of restricted information to a small number of analysts, one can take the position that this is best accomplished by not revealing information to anyone, thereby keeping information releases to a minimum. However, in the interests of full and fair disclosure to all investors, the better approach is to pursue a path of full disclosure to all investors, while still retaining enough information to keep competitors from capitalizing on any released information.

SEC FORMS

The SEC requires public companies to file a variety of forms with it, based on the occurrence of certain transactions. In this section, we will describe the most commonly used forms. This includes a matrix showing what information is required for each form, followed by details regarding the contents of each requirement noted in the matrix. For a thorough treatment of the requirements for these forms, one can access Title 17, Chapter II of the Code of Federal Regulations. This information is available on the Internet at www.access.gpo.gov, and can be downloaded in both text and PDF formats.

The *Form 10-K* is the primary annual reporting form required by the SEC for most companies that have registered securities for public sale under the Securities Exchange Act of 1934. It must be submitted to the SEC within 90 days of a company's fiscal year-end, though an amended form can be filed 30 days later. The quarterly *Form 10-Q* updates changes in a company's financial position, as well as a variety of other events, since the filing of the last Form 10-K, and is due within 45 days of the end of the first three fiscal quarters. The periodic *Form 8-K* is filed immediately after any significant event occurs, such as a bankruptcy, merger or acquisition, director resignation, change in corporate control, change of auditors, or initiation of a lawsuit. In general, the form should be filed immediately after any event occurs that would be of interest to a prudent investor. While the form must be filed within 5 days of a director resignation or a change in the certifying accountants, in most other cases it can be filed within 15 days of the reportable event.

A series of "S" forms are filed in connection with the issuance of securities. The *Form S-1* is used by companies selling securities, and which have only been subject to SEC reporting requirements for the past three years or less. It is the principal form used for the filing of initial public offerings (see Chapter 16, Initial Public Offering). The *Form S-2* is a short form used for the same reason, but by companies that have reported to the SEC for more than three years, and which have voting stock of less than $150 million. The *Form S-3* is used if there is voting stock of more than $150 million, or if the company issues $100 million of securities and the annual trading volume is at least 3 million shares. It can only be used for investment-grade offerings exceeding $75 million, for which securities of the same class are already listed on a national securities exchange. The *Form S-4* is used when reporting on changes in securities resulting from business combination transactions. The types of information required to be included in each of these forms are noted in Exhibit 8.1.

An overview of the informational requirements noted in Exhibit 8.1 for each of the seven primary SEC reporting forms is discussed, in alphabetical order, in the following bullet points. These descriptions only include the primary information requirements for

	8-K	10-K	10-Q	S-1	S-2	S-3	S-4
Acquisition or disposition of assets	X						
Bankruptcy	X						
Business		X		X			
Capitalization				X			
Certain relationships and related transactions		X					
Change in certifying accountants	X						
Change in corporate control	X						
Change in fiscal year	X						
Changes in and disagreements with accountants on accounting and financial disclosure		X					
Changes in securities			X				
Defaults on senior securities			X				
Description of securities to be registered					X	X	
Determination of the offering price					X	X	
Dilution				X	X	X	
Directors and executive officers		X		X		X	
Executive compensation		X					
Exhibit, financial statement schedules, and reports on Form 8-K		X	X				
Experts				X			
Financial statements and supplementary data	X	X	X	X			
Interest of named experts and counsel					X	X	X
Legal proceedings		X	X	X			
Management's discussion and analysis of financial/operational condition		X	X	X			
Market for registrant's common stock and related matters		X					
Other information	X		X	X			X
Plan of distribution					X	X	
Principal shareholders				X			
Properties		X					
Prospectus summary				X	X	X	X
Resignation of directors	X						
Risk factors				X			X
Sale of equity securities	X						
Security of ownership of certain beneficial owners and management		X					
Selected financial data		X		X			
Selling security holders					X	X	
Shares eligible for future sale				X			
Submission of matters to a vote of security holders		X	X				
Transaction terms							X
Underwriting				X			
Use of proceeds				X	X	X	

Exhibit 8.1   Information Requirements for SEC Forms

each item, so one should consult the exact requirements as listed in the Code of Federal Regulations before completing any of the forms.

- *Acquisition or disposition of assets.*   Describe any major asset acquisitions or dispositions outside those enacted in the ordinary course of business. Information provided should include the date and amount of each transaction, the parties involved, the description of the assets being transferred, and the source and use of funds.

- *Bankruptcy.*   If the company enters bankruptcy, note the court in which it applied for bankruptcy, as well as all pertinent information about the case.

- *Business.*   Discuss the development of the business since the beginning of the fiscal year, as well as its financial information by industry segment, major products, market areas, competition, customers, supply sources, order backlog, and other information in which a discerning investor would be interested.

- *Capitalization.*   Note the structure of the current corporate capitalization, as well as any significant new borrowings, or modifications of existing financial arrangements.

- *Certain relationships and related transactions.*   Describe transactions and relationships between the company and certain officers, directors, and other specific parties as defined in the S-K regulations.

- *Change in certifying accountants.*   Describe the reason why the certifying accountant left, and whether there was any kind of qualified or adverse opinion issued by that accountant, as well as any other disagreements or reportable events by the accountant within the preceding two years.

- *Change in corporate control.*   Note the identity of both the selling and acquiring entities, plus the consideration used to effect the change in control, and its amount. Also include the percent ownership of the new owner, as well as any related-party transactions.

- *Change in fiscal year.*   Note the date of the new fiscal year, when the decision was made to use it, and whether a Form 10-K or 10-Q will be used to describe the results of the remaining portion of the year.

- *Changes in and disagreements with accountants on accounting and financial disclosure.*   Identify changes in independent accountants during the previous two years, along with reasons for the change.

- *Changes in securities.*   Disclose any change to any class of registered securities, as well as the impact of the changes on shareholder rights.

- *Defaults on senior securities.*   Disclose any default on the interest or principal payments on securities, but only those not fixed within 30 days of the due date. This reporting also applies to defaults on preferred stock dividends.

- *Description of securities to be registered.*   Describe all rights associated with the securities to be registered, such as voting rights, dividend rights, preemptive rights, and liquidation distribution rights.

- *Determination of the offering price.*   Describe the factors considered in determining the offering price of securities.

- *Dilution.*   When equity securities are offered to the public at a price substantially different from the price paid by officers, note the net tangible book value per share both before and after the distribution of securities.

- *Directors and executive officers.* Provide a list of company officers and directors and pertinent information about them.

- *Executive compensation.* Furnish the amount of compensation earned by the CEO and each of the four other most highly compensated executives and report earnings of all other officers as a group. The compensation and pension plans of officers must be described.

- *Exhibits, financial statement schedules, and reports on form 8-K.* List documents filed as part of the report, including financial statements, supplemental disclosures, and reference to Form 8-K, if it has been filed.

- *Experts.* Note the names of any third-party experts used to develop or certify information used in the report, and state that management relies on this information.

- *Financial statements and supplementary data.* Include the balance sheet for the past two years, as well as statements for income, cash flows, and shareholders' equity for the past three years.

- *Interest of named experts and counsel.* Describe the nature and amount of any financial interest in the company by anyone certifying information provided by the company to the investing public, as long as that amount exceeds $50,000.

- *Legal proceedings.* Describe any material legal issues to which the company is a party, including the filing date, location, and parties to each litigation case. Briefly note the nature of each dispute and the amount or type of relief sought.

- *Management's discussion and analysis of financial condition and results of operations.* Discuss the financial condition, results of operations and changes in financial condition, liquidity, significant trends, and events that are expected to occur in sufficient detail to provide an understanding of the business.

- *Market for registrant's common stock and related matters.* Note the company's types of securities, the markets in which they are traded, and market pricing information during the reporting period. List the total number of holders of each security type, as well as the amount of dividends declared and their frequency and future probability of recurrence.

- *Other information.* Include any information that would otherwise have been reported on a Form 8-K. If reported here, it does not have to be reported again on a Form 8-K.

- *Plan of distribution.* List the names of underwriters accepting securities, as well as the proportion of the total securities offered that they will accept, plus the terms under which they are accepted.

- *Principal shareholders.* List the shares held and proportion of total ownership for all beneficial shareholders of at least 5% of company stock, as well as all executive officers and directors.

- *Property.* Describe the location and nature of the company's primary facilities, as well as the industry segments for which they are used and their levels of capacity and utilization.

- *Prospectus summary.* Most parts of the prospectus issued to investors should be included as an appendix to the filed form.

- *Resignation of directors.* Note the circumstances of any director resignation related to disagreements about company operations, as well as the company's position on the dispute.

- *Risk factors.* Describe all risks to which a securities holder may be subject, which may be caused by such issues as dilution, competitive pressure, reliance on key individuals, product liability, and environmental litigation.

- *Sale of equity securities.* Note the dates on which securities are sold, as well as the type and amount sold, payment received, and the name of the security recipient.

- *Security of ownership of certain beneficial owners and management.* Provide information about ownership of voting securities for directors and certain other owners.

- *Selected financial data.* List in columnar format for the last five years total revenues, profits, assets, debt, and cash dividends declared. Describe all business changes that impact the comparability of the presented information.

- *Selling security holders.* List the name and relationship to the company of any entity selling securities as part of an offering, as well as the amount offered, and the entity's remaining ownership interest subsequent to the sale.

- *Shares eligible for future sale.* Note the number of shares held and the identities of their owners for all shares that cannot currently be sold on the open market. Also note the dates when they can be sold, the amounts available for sale at that time, and the dilution impact on existing shareholders.

- *Submission of matters to a vote of security holders.* Describe any issues that were submitted to the shareholders for a vote during the reporting period, as well as the results of the vote.

- *Transaction terms.* Describe the number and class of securities sought, the date by which the offer expires, the amount of consideration, the procedure for tendering securities, and the transaction's accounting treatment and income tax consequences.

- *Underwriting.* List the underwriters handling the stock offering, as well as the number of shares apportioned to each one. Also describe the main points of the agreements signed with these underwriters, as well as the compensation and expense reimbursements the company expects to pay to the underwriters.

- *Use of proceeds.* State in general terms the uses to which management plans to put the proceeds of the offering.

EDGAR FILING SYSTEM

EDGAR is the SEC's primary on-line tool for automating the collection, validation, indexing, and forwarding of forms filed by companies that are legally required to do so with the SEC. Not only does EDGAR nearly eliminate the paperwork burden on the SEC, but it is also a superior tool for investors and analysts, who have almost immediate on-line access to the forms being filed. The rules and guidelines under which companies are required to make submissions to EDGAR are codified under the SEC's Regulation S-T.

The SEC requires all publicly held companies with more than $10 million in assets and 500 shareholders to file their registration statements and periodic reports through

EDGAR. However, Form 144 (Notice of Proposed Sale of Securities), Forms 3, 4, and 5 (which are reports related to security ownership and transaction reports for corporate insiders), and the annual report to shareholders (except for investment companies) only have to be filed through EDGAR at the filer's option. Foreign companies do not have to file forms through EDGAR.

Transmissions may be sent to the SEC, either by dial-up modem or directly through the Internet, between the hours of 8 A.M. and 10 P.M., eastern standard time, on any business day except federal holidays. The following types of documents must be filed in an electronic format:

- Registration statements and prospectuses
- Statements and applications required by the Trust Indenture Act
- Statements, reports, and schedules required by the Exchange Act
- Documents required by the Investment Company Act
- Documents required by the Public Utility Act

It is not necessary (or allowable) to make electronic submissions for some documents, where paper-based filings are still necessary. At the moment, these include:

- Applications for deregistration, filed under the Investment Company Act
- Confidential treatment applications
- Regulation A filings and any other offering that is exempt from Securities Act registration
- No-action, exemptive, and interpretive requests
- Shareholder proposal filings
- Litigation information filed under the Investment Company Act

If a company is attempting to meet a filing deadline with the SEC, an electronic submission that is filed on or before 5:30 P.M., eastern standard time, will be presumed to have been filed on that business day, whereas any filing submitted after that time will be presumed to have been filed on the next business day. However, this assumption shifts to 10 P.M. for the filing of registration statements.

Official submissions to EDGAR must be in either HTML (version 3.2 is the standard as of this writing) or plain text. Anyone who chooses to make a submission in the HTML format is allowed to use hyperlinks between different sections of the same HTML document, and may also include hyperlinks to exhibits that have been included in the same filing. One can also include links to other official filings within the EDGAR database if submissions are made with the new EDGARLink version; however, it is not allowable to include links to documents located outside of the EDGAR database. Hyperlinks are not allowed as a substitute for information that is required to be included in a specific document, even if the required information could be located through a linkage to another document that is also filed through EDGAR.

The SEC does not currently allow video or audio material to be included in submissions to EDGAR, though it is acceptable to include graphic and image material within HTML documents.

It is also possible to make a submission in a PDF (Acrobat) format, but this is considered an unofficial filing that must be accompanied by one of the other two formats. If a PDF file is submitted, only its formatting and graphics may differ from the official filing.

If the submitting entity makes an electronic submission that contains errors solely due to errors in the transmission, and if the submitter corrects the errors as soon as possible after becoming aware of the difficulty, then there shall be no liability under the antifraud portions of the federal securities laws.

In order to protect itself from computer viruses, the SEC will suspend the filing of any document that appears to contain executable code. If such a document is accepted and the code is discovered at a later date, then it may be deleted from EDGAR and the filer will be required to make a new submission of the required data.

There are two cases in which a company can plead hardship and avoid making an electronic submission of data. In the first instance, Rule 201 of Regulation S-T allows a temporary exemption for an electronic filer that is having unanticipated trouble in submitting a report, such as in cases where the transmitting computer fails. A paper-based filing, using Form TH (Notification of Reliance on Temporary Hardship Exemption) is still required in this instance, and must be followed within six days by an electronic submission. In the second case, Rule 202 of Regulation S-T allows a permanent exemption for a few cases where the information to be filed is so large that the filer would be caused undue hardship to do so. The first case requires no SEC approval, whereas the second case does.

The primary document needed for preparing an electronic document for the SEC is its *EDGAR Filing Manual.* One can download it at www.sec.gov/info/edgar/filermanual.htm, or order it from the Public Reference Room, Securities and Exchange Commission, 450 5th Street, N.W., Washington, D.C. 20549-0102.

SUMMARY

The information noted in this chapter is applicable in other areas of this book. For example, Chapter 15, Obtaining Equity Financing, discusses the use of a prospectus that is modeled on the disclosure statement to the SEC described in this chapter. Similarly, Chapter 16, Initial Public Offering, notes the use of a registration statement that is also discussed here. Finally, Chapter 17, Taking a Company Private, is almost entirely concerned with the proper completion of the SEC's Schedule 13-E3. Thus, it is evident that the CFO of a public company must deal with the SEC on a variety of topics.

PART **3**

FINANCIAL ANALYSIS

CHAPTER 9

COST OF CAPITAL*

Many companies make decisions to build new facilities, invest in new machinery, or expend sums for other large projects without any idea of whether the return to be expected from these projects will exceed the cost of capital needed to fund them. As a result, a company may find that it is working furiously on any number of new projects, but seeing its ability to generate cash flow to repay debt or pay stockholders decline over time. To avoid this situation, it is necessary to calculate the return on investment, which is covered in the next chapter. In this chapter, we discuss the first part of the investment decision, which is the calculation of the cost of capital against which investment decisions must be compared. The chapter describes the primary components of a company's capital, how the cost of each kind is combined to form a weighted cost of capital, and how this information should be most appropriately used when evaluating the return on new projects that require funding, as well as for discounting the cash flows from existing projects.

COMPONENTS

Before determining the amount of a company's cost of capital, it is necessary to determine its components. The following two sections describe in detail how to arrive at the cost of capital for these components. The weighted average calculation that brings together all the elements of the cost of capital is then described in the "Calculating the Weighted Cost of Capital" section.

The first component of the cost of capital is debt. This is a company's commitment to return to a lender both the interest and principal on an initial or series of payments to the company by the lender. This can be short-term debt, which is typically paid back in full within one year, or long-term debt, which can be repaid over many years, either with continual principal repayments, large repayments at set intervals, or a large payment when the entire debt is due, which is called a *balloon* payment. All these forms of repayment can be combined in an infinite number of ways to arrive at a repayment plan that is uniquely structured to fit the needs of the individual corporation.

The second component of the cost of capital is preferred stock. This is a form of equity that is issued to stockholders and which carries a specific interest rate. The company is only obligated to pay the stated interest rate to shareholders at stated intervals, but not the initial payment of funds to the company, which it may keep in perpetuity, unless it chooses to buy back the stock. There may also be conversion options, so that a shareholder can convert the preferred stock to common stock in some predetermined proportion. This type of stock is attractive to those companies that do not want to dilute earnings per

---

* Adapted with permission from Chapter 16 of *Financial Analysis* by Bragg (John Wiley & Sons, 2000).

share with additional common stock, and which also do not want to incur the burden of principal repayments. Though there is an obligation to pay shareholders the stated interest rate, it is usually possible to delay payment if the funds are not available, though the interest will accumulate and must be paid when cash is available.

The third and final component of the cost of capital is common stock. A company is not required to pay anything to its shareholders in exchange for the stock, which makes this the least risky form of funding available. Instead, shareholders rely on a combination of dividend payments, as authorized by the Board of Directors (and which are entirely at the option of the Board—authorization is not required by law), and appreciation in the value of the shares. However, since shareholders indirectly control the corporation through the Board of Directors, actions by management that depress the stock price or lead to a reduction in the dividend payment can lead to the firing of management by the Board of Directors. Also, since shareholders typically expect a high return on investment in exchange for their money, the actual cost of these funds is the highest of all the components of the cost of capital.

As will be discussed in the next two sections, the least expensive of the three forms of funding is debt, followed by preferred stock and common stock. The main reason for the differences between the costs of the three components is the impact of taxes on various kinds of interest payments. This is of particular concern when discussing debt, which is covered in the next section.

CALCULATING THE COST OF DEBT

This section covers the main factors to consider when calculating the cost of debt, and also discusses how these factors must be incorporated into the final cost calculation. We also note how the net result of these calculations is a form of funding that is less expensive than the cost of equity, which is covered in the next section.

When calculating the cost of debt, it is important to remember that the interest expense is tax deductible. This means that the tax paid by the company is reduced by the tax rate multiplied by the interest expense. An example is shown in Exhibit 9.1, where we assume that $1,000,000 of debt has a basic interest rate of 9.5% and the corporate tax rate is 35%.

The example clearly shows that the impact of taxes on the cost of debt significantly reduces the overall debt cost, thereby making this a most desirable form of funding.

If a company is not currently turning a profit, and therefore not in a position to pay taxes, one may question whether the company should factor the impact of taxes into the interest calculation. The answer is still yes, because any net loss will carry forward

$$\frac{(\text{Interest Expense}) \times (1 - \text{Tax Rate})}{\text{Amount of Debt}} = \text{Net After-Tax Interest Expense}$$

Or,

$$\frac{\$95,000 \times (1 - .35)}{\$1,000,000} = \text{Net After-Tax Interest Expense}$$

$$\frac{\$61,750}{\$1,000,000} = 6.175\%$$

EXHIBIT 9.1   CALCULATING THE INTEREST COST OF DEBT, NET OF TAXES

$$\frac{(\text{Interest Expense}) \times (1 - \text{Tax Rate})}{(\text{Amount of Debt} - \text{Fees} - \text{Discount on Sale of Debt})} = \text{Net After-Tax Interest Expense}$$

Or,

$$\frac{\$95,000 \times (1 - .35)}{\$1,000,000 - \$25,000 - \$20,000} = \text{Net After-Tax Interest Expense}$$

$$\frac{\$61,750}{\$955,000} = 6.466\%$$

Note: There can also be a premium on sale of debt instead of a discount, if investors are willing to pay extra for the interest rate offered. This usually occurs when the rate offered is higher than the current market rate, or if the risk of nonpayment is so low that this is perceived as an extra benefit by investors.

EXHIBIT 9.2 CALCULATING THE INTEREST COST OF DEBT, NET OF TAXES, FEES, AND DISCOUNTS

to the next reporting period, when the company can offset future earnings against the accumulated loss to avoid paying taxes at that time. Thus, the reduction in interest costs caused by the tax deductibility of interest is still applicable even if a company is not currently in a position to pay income taxes.

Another issue is the cost of acquiring debt, and how this cost should be factored into the overall cost of debt calculation. When obtaining debt, either through a private placement or simply through a local bank, there are usually extra fees involved, which may include placement or brokerage fees, documentation fees, or the price of a bank audit. In the case of a private placement, the company may set a fixed percentage interest payment on the debt, but find that prospective borrowers will not purchase the debt instruments unless they can do so at a discount, thereby effectively increasing the interest rate they will earn on the debt. In both cases, the company is receiving less cash than initially expected, but must still pay out the same amount of interest expense. In effect, this raises the cost of the debt. To carry forward the example in Exhibit 9.1 to Exhibit 9.2, we assume that the interest payments are the same, but that brokerage fees were $25,000 and the debt was sold at a 2% discount. The result is an increase in the actual interest rate.

When compared to the cost of equity that is discussed in the following section, it becomes apparent that debt is a much less expensive form of funding than equity. However, though it may be tempting to alter a company's capital structure to increase the proportion of debt, thereby reducing the overall cost of capital, there are dangers involved in incurring a large interest expense. These dangers are discussed in the "Modifying the Cost of Capital to Enhance Shareholder Value" section.

CALCULATING THE COST OF EQUITY

This section shows how to calculate the cost of the two main forms of equity, which are preferred stock and common stock. These calculations, as well as those from the preceding section on the cost of debt, are then combined in the following section to determine the weighted cost of capital.

Preferred stock stands at a midway point between debt and common stock. It requires an interest payment to the holder of each share of preferred stock, but does not require repayment to the shareholder of the amount paid for each share. There are a few special cases where the terms underlying the issuance of a particular set of preferred shares will require an additional payment to shareholders if company earnings exceed a specified level, but this is a rare situation. Also, some preferred shares carry provisions that allow delayed interest payments to be cumulative, so that they must all be paid before dividends can be paid out to holders of common stock. The main feature shared by all kinds of preferred stock is that, under the tax laws, interest payments are treated as dividends instead of interest expense, which means that these payments are not tax deductible. This is a key issue, for it greatly increases the cost of funds for any company using this funding source. By way of comparison, if a company has a choice between issuing debt or preferred stock at the same rate, the difference in cost will be the tax savings on the debt. In the following example, a company issues $1,000,000 of debt and $1,000,000 of preferred stock, both at 9% interest rates, with an assumed 35% tax rate:

$$\text{Debt Cost} = \text{Principal} \times (\text{Interest Rate} \times (1 - \text{Tax Rate}))$$
$$\text{Debt Cost} = \$1,000,000 \times (9\% \times (1 - .35))$$
$$\$58,500 = \$1,000,000 \times (9\% \times .65)$$

If the same information is used to calculate the cost of payments using preferred stock, we have the following result:

$$\text{Preferred Stock Interest Cost} = \text{Principal} \times \text{Interest Rate}$$
$$\text{Preferred Stock Interest Cost} = \$1,000,000 \times 9\%$$
$$\underline{\underline{\$90,000 = \$1,000,000 \times 9\%}}$$

The above example shows that the differential caused by the applicability of taxes to debt payments makes preferred stock a much more expensive alternative. This being the case, why does anyone use preferred stock? The main reason is that there is no requirement to repay the stockholder for the initial investment, whereas debt requires either a periodic or balloon payment of principal to eventually pay back the original amount. Companies can also eliminate the preferred stock interest payments if they include a convertibility feature into the stock agreement that allows for a conversion to common stock at some preset price point for the common stock. Thus, in cases where a company does not want to repay principal any time soon, but does not want to increase the amount of common shares outstanding, preferred stock provides a convenient, though expensive, alternative.

The most difficult cost of funding to calculate by far is common stock, because there is no preset payment from which to derive a cost. Instead, it appears to be free money, since investors hand over cash without any predetermined payment or even any expectation of having the company eventually pay them back for the stock. Unfortunately, the opposite is the case. Since holders of common stock have the most at risk (they are the last ones paid off in the event of bankruptcy), they are the ones who want the most in return. Any management team that ignores its common stockholders and does nothing to give them a return on their investments will find that these people will either vote in a new Board of Directors that will find a new management team, or else they will sell off their shares at a loss to new investors, thereby driving down the value of the stock and opening up the company to the attentions of a corporate raider who will also remove the management team.

One way to determine the cost of common stock is to make a guess at the amount of future dividend payments to stockholders, and discount this stream of payments back into a net present value. The problem with this approach is that the amount of dividends paid out is problematic, since they are declared at the discretion of the Board of Directors. Also, there is no provision in this calculation for changes in the underlying value of the stock; for some companies that do not pay any dividends, this is the only way in which a stockholder will be compensated.

A better method is called the capital asset pricing model (CAPM). Without going into the very considerable theoretical detail behind this system, it essentially derives the cost of capital by determining the relative risk of holding the stock of a specific company as compared to a mix of all stocks in the market. This risk is composed of three elements. The first is the return that any investor can expect from a risk-free investment, which is usually defined as the return on a U.S. government security. The second element is the return from a set of securities considered to have an average level of risk. This can be the average return on a large "market basket" of stocks, such as the Standard & Poor's 500, the Dow Jones Industrials, or some other large cluster of stocks. The final element is a company's beta, which defines the amount by which a specific stock's returns vary from the returns of stocks with an average risk level. This information is provided by several of the major investment services, such as Value Line. A beta of 1.0 means that a specific stock is exactly as risky as the average stock, while a beta of 0.8 would represent a lower level of risk, and a beta of 1.4 would be higher. When combined, this information yields the baseline return to be expected on any investment (the risk-free return), plus an added return that is based on the level of risk that an investor is assuming by purchasing a specific stock. This methodology is totally based on the assumption that the level of risk equates directly to the level of return, which a vast amount of additional research has determined to be a reasonably accurate way to determine the cost of equity capital. The main problem with this approach is that a company's beta will vary over time, since it may add or subtract subsidiaries that are more or less risky, resulting in an altered degree of risk. Because of the likelihood of change, one must regularly recompute the equity cost of capital to determine the most recent cost.

A major problem with the use of beta for calculating a company's cost of equity capital is that it is based on past results, which may not accurately reflect a company's future prospects. Also, the beta calculation can result in drastically different results if the calculation period varies by as little as a few days, sometimes resulting in changes in beta of more than 100%. Given these problems, it has been proposed that the traded price of a company's equity options be used instead as the foundation for the beta calculation, since these prices are based on the market's best estimate of the future price volatility of the stock. This alternative method will only work if a company's equity options are publicly traded, though it may be possible to impute option data by using similar options issued by comparable companies.

The calculation of the equity cost of capital using the CAPM methodology is relatively simple, once one has accumulated all the components of the equation. For example, if the risk-free cost of capital is 5%, the return on the Dow Jones Industrials is 12%, and ABC Company's beta is 1.5, the cost of equity for ABC Company would be:

Cost of Equity Capital = Risk-Free Return + Beta (Average Stock Return

−Risk-Free Return)

Cost of Equity Capital = 5% + 1.5 (12% − 5%)

Cost of Equity Capital = 5% + 1.5 × 7%

Cost of Equity Capital $= 5\% + 10.5\%$

Cost of Equity Capital $= \underline{\underline{15.5\%}}$

Though the example uses a rather high beta that increases the cost of the stock, it is evident that, far from being an inexpensive form of funding, common stock is actually the *most* expensive, given the size of returns that investors demand in exchange for putting their money at risk with a company. Accordingly, this form of funding should be used the most sparingly in order to keep the cost of capital at a lower level.

CALCULATING THE WEIGHTED COST OF CAPITAL

Now that we have derived the costs of debt, preferred stock, and common stock, it is time to assemble all three costs into a weighted cost of capital. This section is structured in an example format, showing the method by which the weighted cost of capital of the Canary Corporation is calculated. Following that, there is a short discussion of how the cost of capital can be used.

The CFO of the Canary Corporation, Mr. Birdsong, is interested in determining the company's weighted cost of capital, to be used to ensure that projects have a sufficient return on investment, which will keep the company from going to seed. There are two debt offerings on the books. The first is $1,000,000, which was sold below par value and garnered $980,000 in cash proceeds. The company must pay interest of 8.5% on this debt. The second is for $3,000,000 and was sold at par, but included legal fees of $25,000. The interest rate on this debt is 10%. There is also $2,500,000 of preferred stock on the books, which requires annual interest (or dividend) payments amounting to 9% of the amount contributed to the company by investors. Finally, there is $4,000,000 of common stock on the books. The risk-free rate of interest, as defined by the return on current U.S. government securities, is 6%, while the return expected from a typical market basket of related stocks is 12%. The company's beta is 1.2, and it currently pays income taxes at a marginal rate of 35%. What is the Canary Company's weighted cost of capital?

The method we will use is to separately compile the percentage cost of each for of funding, and then calculate the weighted cost of capital, based on the amount of funding and percentage cost of each of the above forms of funding. We begin with the first debt item, which was $1,000,000 of debt that was sold for $20,000 less than par value, at 8.5% debt. The marginal income tax rate is 35%. The calculation is:

$$\text{Net After-Tax Interest Percent} = \frac{((\text{Interest Expense}) \times (1 - \text{Tax Rate})) \times \text{Amount of Debt}}{(\text{Amount of Debt}) - (\text{Discount on Sale of Debt})}$$

$$\text{Net After-Tax Interest Percent} = \frac{((8.5\%) \times (1 - .35)) \times \$1,000,000}{\$1,000,000 - \$20,000}$$

$$\text{Net After-Tax Interest Percent} = \underline{5.638\%}$$

We employ the same method for the second debt instrument, for which there is $3,000,000 of debt that was sold at par. Legal fees of $25,000 were incurred to place the debt, which pays 10% interest. The marginal income tax rate remains at 35%.

Type of Funding	Amount of Funding	Percentage Cost	Dollar Cost
Debt number 1	$980,000	5.638%	$55,252
Debt number 2	2,975,000	7.091%	210,957
Preferred stock	2,500,000	9.000%	225,000
Common stock	4,000,000	13.200%	528,000
Totals	$10,455,000	9.75%	$1,019,209

Exhibit 9.3   Weighted Cost of Capital Calculation

The calculation is:

$$\text{Net After-Tax Interest Percent} = \frac{((\text{Interest Expense}) \times (1 - \text{Tax Rate})) \times \text{Amount of Debt}}{(\text{Amount of Debt}) - (\text{Discount on Sale of Debt})}$$

$$\text{Net After-Tax Interest Percent} = \frac{((10\%) \times (1 - .35)) \times \$3,000,000}{\$3,000,000 - \$25,000}$$

$$\text{Net After-Tax Interest Percent} = \underline{7.091\%}$$

Having completed the interest expense for the two debt offerings, we move on to the cost of the preferred stock. As noted earlier, there is $2,500,000 of preferred stock on the books, with an interest rate of 9%. The marginal corporate income tax does not apply, since the interest payments are treated like dividends and are not deductible. The calculation is the simplest of all, for the answer is 9%, since there is no income tax to confuse the issue.

To arrive at the cost of equity capital, we take from the example a return on riskfree securities of 6%, a return of 12% that is expected from a typical market basket of related stocks, and a beta of 1.2. We then plug this information into the following formula to arrive at the cost of equity capital:

$$\text{Cost of Equity Capital} = \text{Risk-Free Return} + \text{Beta (Average Stock Return}$$

$$-\text{Risk-Free Return)}$$

$$\text{Cost of Equity Capital} = 6\% + 1.2(12\% - 6\%)$$

$$\text{Cost of Equity Capital} = \underline{13.2\%}$$

Now that we know the cost of each type of funding, it is a simple matter to construct a table, such as the one shown in Exhibit 9.3, that lists the amount of each type of funding and its related cost, which we can quickly sum to arrive at a weighted cost of capital.

When combined into the weighted average calculation shown in Exhibit 9.3, we see that the weighted cost of capital is 9.75%. Though there is some considerably less expensive debt on the books, the majority of the funding is comprised of more expensive common and preferred stock, which drives up the overall cost of capital.

Thus far, we have discussed the components of the cost of capital, how each one is calculated, and how to combine all the various kinds of capital costs into a single weighted cost of capital. Now that we have it, what do we use it for?

INCREMENTAL COST OF CAPITAL

Having gone to the effort of calculating a company's weighted cost of capital, we must ask ourselves if this information is of any use. Certainly, we now know the cost of all corporate funding, but this is the cost of funding that has already been incurred. How does this relate to the cost of capital for any upcoming funding that has not yet been obtained? What if a company wants to change its blend of funding sources, and how will this impact the cost of capital? What about using it to discount the cash flows from existing projects?

The trouble with the existing weighted cost of capital is that it reflects the cost of debt and equity only at the time the company obtained it. For example, if a company obtained debt at a fixed interest rate during a period in the past when the prime rate offered by banks for new debt was very high, the resulting cost of capital, which still includes this debt, will be higher than the cost of capital if that debt had been retired and refunded by new debt obtained at current market rates, which are lower. The same issue applies to equity, for the cost of equity can change if the underlying return on risk-free debt has changed, which it does continually (just observe daily or monthly swings in the cost of U.S. government securities, which are considered to be risk-free). Similarly, a company's beta will change over time as its overall risk profile changes, possibly due to changes in its markets, or internal changes that alter its mix of business. Accordingly, a company may find that its carefully calculated weighted cost of capital does not bear even a slight resemblance to what the same cost would be if recalculated based on current market conditions.

Where does this disturbing news leave us? If there is no point in using the weighted cost of capital that is recorded on the books, there is no reason why we cannot calculate the incremental weighted cost of capital based on current market conditions and use that as a hurdle rate instead. By doing so, a company recognizes that it will obtain funds at the current market rates and use the cost of this blended rate to pay for new projects. For example, if a company intends to retain the same proportions of debt and equity, and finds that the new weighted cost of capital is 2% higher at current market rates than the old rates recorded on the company books, then the hurdle rate used for evaluating new projects should use the new, higher rate.

It is also important to determine management's intentions in regard to the new blend of debt and equity, for changes in the proportions of the two will alter the weighted cost of capital. If a significant alteration in the current mix is anticipated, the new proportion should be factored into the weighted cost of capital calculation. For example, management may be forced by creditors or owners to alter the existing proportion of debt and equity. This is most common when a company is closely held, and the owners do not want to invest any more equity in the company, thereby forcing it to resort to debt financing. Alternatively, if the debt-to-equity ratio is very high, lenders may force the addition of equity in order to reduce the risk of default, which goes up when there is a large amount of interest and principal to pay out of current cash flow. In short, the incremental cost of capital is the most relevant hurdle rate figure when using new funds to pay for new projects.

The concept of incremental funds costs can be taken too far, however. If a company is only initiating one project in the upcoming year and needs to borrow funds at a specific rate to pay for it, then a good case can be made for designating the cost of that funding as the hurdle rate for the single project under consideration, since the two are inextricably intertwined. However, such a direct relationship is rarely the case.

Instead, there are many projects being implemented, which are spread out over a long time frame, with funds being acquired at intervals that do not necessarily match those of the funds requirements of individual projects. For example, a CFO may hold off on an equity offering in the public markets until there is a significant upswing in the stock market, or borrow funds a few months early if he or she can obtain a favorably low, long-term fixed rate. When this happens, there is no way to tie a specific funding cost to a specific project, so it is better to calculate the blended cost of capital for the period and apply it as a hurdle rate to all of the projects currently under consideration.

All this discussion of the incremental cost of capital does not mean that the cost of capital that is derived from the book cost of existing funding is totally irrelevant—far from it. Many companies finance all new projects out of their existing cash flow, and have no reason to go to outside lenders or equity markets to obtain new funding. For these organizations, the true cost of debt is indeed the same as the amount recorded on their books, since they are obligated to pay that exact amount of debt, irrespective of what current market interest rates may be. However, the weighted cost of capital does not just include debt—it also includes equity, and this cost *does* change over time. Even if a company has no need for additional equity, the cost of its existing equity will change, because the earnings expectations of investors will change over time, as well as the company's beta. For example, the underlying risk-free interest rate can and will change as the inflation rate varies, so that there is some return to investors that exceeds the rate of inflation. Similarly, the average market rate of return on equity will change over time as investor expectations change. Further, the mix of businesses and markets in which a company is involved will inevitably lead to variation in its beta over time, as the variability of its cash flows becomes greater or lower. All three of these factors will result in alterations to the weighted cost of capital that will continue to change over time, even if there is no new equity that a company sells to investors. Consequently, the book cost of debt is still a valid part of the weighted cost of capital as long as no new debt is added, whereas the cost of equity *will* change as the expectation for higher or lower returns by investors changes, which results in a weighted cost of capital that can blend the book and market costs of funding in some situations.

So far, the discussion in this chapter has assumed that the reader is only interested in using the weighted cost of capital as a hurdle rate for determining the viability of new projects that will generate a stream of cash flows. It can also be used as the discounting factor when arriving at the net present value of cash flows from existing projects, as is discussed in the next chapter. When this is the case, the cost of capital based on the book value of debt is more appropriate than using the current market rates for new debt, since the cash flows being discounted are for existing projects that were already funded by debt and equity already recorded on the books.

This section noted how the incremental market cost of capital is the more accurate way to arrive at a hurdle rate for new projects when new funding must be secured to pay for the projects. If a company can fund all cash flows for new projects internally, however, a company can use the book cost of debt and the market-based return on equity to derive the weighted cost of capital that is most accurately used to judge the acceptability of cash flows from prospective new projects. This later version is also most appropriate for discounting the cash flows from existing and previously funded projects.

USING THE COST OF CAPITAL IN SPECIAL SITUATIONS

There are a few situations in which companies frequently modify the cost of capital for special purposes. This section notes two of the more common cases, and how to handle them.

When management is considering whether or not to authorize a project through the capital request process, it should give some thought to the risk of not achieving the estimated returns for it. For example, if management is considering funding two projects with identical cash flows, where one is in an established industry where returns are relatively certain and another is in a "high-technology" field where product obsolescence is the norm, it is a fair bet that the cash-flow considerations will not form the basis of its decision—the project in the high-technology area will almost certainly be eliminated from consideration on the grounds that the risk of not achieving the projected cash flow is too high. How can one quantify this risk? The short answer is—not easily. Many organizations simply assign a higher cost of capital hurdle rate to risky projects. Unfortunately, it is very difficult to reliably determine what this higher hurdle rate should be. Is a premium of 1% over the cost of capital sufficient, or is 5% closer to the desired level? The problem is that the increase in the cost of capital cannot be reliably calculated to reflect the exact increase in risk. Instead, this is more a matter of management determining its own comfort level with the risk, and making a decision at that point. To do so, management will need additional information to supplement the cost of capital hurdle rate, such as:

- *Timing of cash flows.* If the positive cash flows from a proposed project are clustered toward the end of a project, perhaps five years away, this sort of project is riskier than one that returns positive cash flows right away.

- *Payback period.* The sooner a project pays back its projected cash outflows, the less risky the project is perceived to be, even if the chance of having large positive cash flows is relatively small. The point here is that the risk of loss is reduced with a quick payback.

- *Level of expected competition.* If a number of competitors are clustering their efforts in the same area, it is a fair bet that there will be price competition when everyone's projects are completed and start to spew new products into the marketplace, resulting in reduced profits for all competitors. One can quantify this risk somewhat by modeling a range of profit scenarios based on a number of different product price points. A further degree of sophistication is to include in the cash-flow analysis the estimated dates at which product pricing is anticipated to drop, based on when competing projects are estimated to be completed, resulting in high competition.

- *History of previous projects in this area.* If a company has funded a number of projects in the same area, and the majority of them have not done well, this is certainly a consideration in determining the level of project risk. Unless management thinks it can improve the situation by bringing in new project managers or doing something else to improve the probability of success, a project with this type of history should be assigned a higher degree of risk.

Thus, it is not necessary to blindly increase the hurdle rate, as defined by the cost of capital, to evaluate a new capital project, since a higher hurdle rate does not sufficiently define the level of risk. Instead, it is better to provide management with a range of supplemental data, as noted above, that provide more information about the likely level of project riskiness.

Another special situation in which the cost of capital can be modified is when it is used in a large corporation with multiple divisions that bear no close relationship to one another in terms of the markets they serve, the products they sell, or their methods of obtaining funding. The most common example of this is a conglomerate, which is an assemblage of unrelated businesses that are frequently brought together under one corporate umbrella because they have uniformly high returns on investment, or because they have offsetting cash flows—in other words, one subsidiary may have strong cash flows that match swings in the business cycle, while a fellow subsidiary has cash flows that track the inverse of the business cycle. When combined, the cash flows of the two entities theoretically result in even cash flows at all times, and a reduced level of risk for the conglomerate as a whole. In such situations, the conglomerate is the entity that obtains financing, and this results in a specific cost of capital. However, the levels of risk of all the component subsidiaries may diverge wildly from the overall level of risk, resulting in the application of a conglomerate-wide hurdle rate to all subsidiaries that is either too high or too low for each individual subsidiary. For example, a subsidiary with a very high risk of return on its projects will be subject to a hurdle rate that is compiled from the conglomerate as a whole, which may have been assembled for the express purpose of achieving a very low level of variability in cash flows, which of course results in a low cost of equity, and consequently a low cost of capital. When this happens, nearly all the projects of the risky subsidiary will be approved, since the hurdle rate is so low, without any consideration for the high degree of risk. A probable outcome is that the cash flows from many of these projects will be substandard, resulting in low future performance by this subsidiary. Alternatively, using the same hurdle rate for a different subsidiary with extremely low-risk projects will result in the rejection of some projects that are quite capable of generating an adequate return on investment. Thus, using an average hurdle rate for subsidiaries is not a good idea.

Instead, one can determine an average hurdle rate from information about the competitors in each subsidiary's industry, which is available from public sources such as 10-K or 10-Q reports, or the investment analyses of any of the major brokerage firms. By doing so, one can compile the cost of capital of the industry, or of selected competitors within each industry, and use that as the hurdle rate for applicable subsidiaries. Though not as accurate as determining the specific cost of capital of the subsidiary (which is not possible, since it has no equity or debt of its own—that is held by the corporate parent), it is still much more accurate than the overall cost of capital of the entire organization. This is the preferred method for calculating the cost of capital of a corporate subsidiary.

MODIFYING THE COST OF CAPITAL TO ENHANCE SHAREHOLDER VALUE

The preceding sections make it clear that shareholders can expect a higher return on their investment if the bulk of a company's funding is obtained through debt instead of equity, since debt costs are partially offset by tax-deductible interest expenses. In this section, we cover the extent to which shareholders can increase their returns by this means, as well as the risks of following this approach to an excessive degree.

When company management or owners examine ways to improve the return on equity, one relatively easy method that stands out is buying back some portion of the equity from stockholders with borrowed funds. What this does is reduce the amount of equity that is divided into the earnings, resulting in a greater amount of earnings per share. Exhibit 9.4 shows what happens when XYZ Company, with $150,000 in earnings, $500,000 in equity, and no debt, decides to buy back shares with funds that are obtained by borrowing.

Pre-Debt Earnings	Pre-Debt Equity	Amount of Buyback	Amount of After-Tax Interest Expense	Net Earnings	Return on Equity
$150,000	$500,000	$25,000	$2,000	$148,000	31.2%
150,000	500,000	50,000	4,000	146,000	32.4%
150,000	500,000	75,000	6,000	144,000	33.8%
150,000	500,000	100,000	8,000	142,000	35.5%
150,000	500,000	125,000	10,000	140,000	37.3%
150,000	500,000	150,000	12,000	138,000	39.4%
150,000	500,000	175,000	14,000	136,000	41.8%
150,000	500,000	200,000	16,000	134,000	44.7%
150,000	500,000	225,000	18,000	132,000	48.0%

EXHIBIT 9.4   ITEMIZATION OF CHANGES IN RETURN ON EQUITY WITH STOCK BUYBACK

The net after-tax cost of the new debt is assumed to be 8%, which reduces the amount of reported earnings somewhat.

As Exhibit 9.4 shows, there are major benefits to be had by introducing some debt into the capital structure in order to reduce the amount of equity. The example could be continued to the point where only one share of stock is outstanding, which can yield an extraordinarily high return on equity figure. The method is especially appealing for those companies whose shares are held by a small group of owners who cannot or will not invest additional equity in the business, and who prefer to strip out equity for their own uses as frequently as possible. Accordingly, if the return on equity percentage is considered important, altering the cost of capital by buying back stock is one of the easiest ways to do so.

However, there is a great risk that this strategy can backfire. The problem with shifting the capital structure strongly in the direction of debt and away from equity is that debt requires repayment, whereas equity does not. Because of this, a company's cash flow is impeded by the required debt and principal repayments to lenders, which can be a dangerous situation whenever the business cycle declines or company cash flow drops for other reasons, such as increased competition. When this happens, a company may not be able to meet the payment demands of its lenders, possibly resulting in bankruptcy and the loss of all owner equity.

Management can anticipate this problem by examining the variability of both existing and projected cash flows, and determining the likelihood and extent of potential drops in cash flow. This is obviously a highly judgmental process, since it is only the opinion of management (which may vary considerably by manager) as to how far down cash flow can go during lean times. Nonetheless, the consensus minimum cash flow should be agreed on. Then the controller or CFO can use this information to determine the amount of debt that can safely be added to the balance sheet while still ensuring that all debt payments can be made. A key factor in this calculation is determining management's level of comfort with the proportion of debt payments that will take up the minimum level of cash flow. For example, many managers are not at all comfortable with the thought of having virtually all of the minimum cash flow being allocated to debt payments, since there is no room left for capital or working capital additions that may be needed to improve the business. Consequently, some reduced proportion of the minimum cash flow level is normally used when determining the level of debt that can be taken on. An example of how this maximum debt level is determined is shown in Exhibit 9.5, where

Minimum Cash Flow	Debt Level	Debt-Related Payments (Principal and Interest)	Proportion of Cash Flow Used by Debt Payments	Percentage of Return on Equity
$50,000	$25,000	$8,000	16%	31.2%
50,000	50,000	16,000	32%	32.4%
50,000	75,000	24,000	48%	33.8%
50,000	100,000	32,000	64%	35.5%
50,000	125,000	40,000	80%	37.3%
50,000	150,000	48,000	96%	39.4%
50,000	175,000	56,000	112%	41.8%
50,000	200,000	64,000	128%	44.7%
50,000	225,000	72,000	144%	48.0%

EXHIBIT 9.5 TABLE OF CASH USAGE VERSUS RETURN ON EQUITY

the minimum cash-flow level is assumed to be $50,000. The rest of the table determines the return on equity using a range of debt levels taken from the preceding Exhibit 9.4 that fall within this minimum cash-flow level. Management can then review the table and select the combination of earnings level, return on equity, and risk that it feels most comfortable with, and then proceed to attain that level by using debt to buy back stock.

In Exhibit 9.5, it would be very unwise to increase the amount of debt to anything beyond the minimum possible cash-flow level, even though it is possible to increase the return on equity to stratospheric levels by doing so. A better option is to adopt one of the lower debt levels that still leaves room in the minimum amount of cash flow to cover other operating needs.

For those industries such as amusement parks, where cash flow varies widely from month to month, or the airlines, where it varies in longer cycles, it is generally not a good idea to increase the proportion of debt to excessive levels. The reason is that cash flows are more likely to bottom out during slow periods at extremely low levels, quite possibly requiring that more debt be incurred just to keep operations running. When this happens, a large amount of cash flow that is tied up in the servicing of debt makes it extremely likely that a company will have difficulty in meeting its debt payment obligations, which raises the specter of bankruptcy. Alternatively, if there is an exceptionally steady and predictable level of cash flow that is minimally impacted by long business cycles, the company fortunate enough to experience this situation is ideally positioned to take advantage of an increased degree of leverage and a correspondingly higher return on equity. The key is to be sensitive to swings in cash flow, and to model the appropriate mix of debt and capital to match these swings.

STRATEGIZE COST OF CAPITAL REDUCTIONS

A fair number of companies know how to calculate the cost of capital and have done so at some point in the past. However, how frequently do they recalculate the cost of capital, and (especially) do they ever discuss the ways in which it can be reduced? This is a particular problem for debt-heavy companies who have more than the optimal debt levels. For these organizations, the primary concern is that the next dollar of debt will become increasingly difficult to obtain, requiring an incremental cost of capital that could be sky high.

Even for those companies with more moderate debt levels, it is certainly worthwhile to regularly strategize over how the corporate cost of capital can be reduced, since even a decline of a few basis points drops straight into net profits.

Shrinking the cost of capital usually requires one of two approaches: either obtain guarantees that will allow lenders to reduce their rates, or free up enough cash to pay off higher-cost debt. Obtaining guarantees is a difficult proposition, and will require the cooperation of either a wealthy individual or a corporate parent. However, improving cash flow is a more viable alternative for nearly everyone. Here are some possible ways to do so:

- Review the capital spending plan to determine which planned purchases do not involve increases in the capacity of bottleneck operations, and eliminate them if they do not.

- Aggressively pursue early payment discounts for a few large-dollar customer accounts in order to squeeze more funds out of accounts receivable.

- Sort the inventory records by turnover for each item, and research the reasons why low-turnover items are still in stock. Chances are good that some policy changes are needed regarding buying in excessively large quantities, implementing engineering change orders before raw material stocks have been exhausted, and having production runs longer than what are actually needed by customers.

These approaches are useful for locating cash within working capital, which can be used to draw down debt balances and thereby shrink the cost of capital.

SUMMARY

In this chapter, we reviewed the various components of the weighted cost of capital, and how the cost components vary due to the applicability (or inapplicability) of taxes.

Because of taxes, there is a strong incentive to use debt instead of equity, but this can lead to considerable additional risk if a company is unable to cover the principal or interest payments on that debt. We also noted how the current market cost of capital is superior to the book method when using the cost of capital to evaluate new projects. When used with a full knowledge of the consequences of miscalculation or misuse, the weighted average cost of capital is an excellent benchmark for determining the ability of a proposed new project to provide positive cash flow to a corporation, as well as the discounted cash flows from existing projects. We also covered the use of long-term planning to reduce the cost of capital.

CHAPTER 10

CAPITAL BUDGETING*

One of the most common financial analysis tasks with which a CFO is confronted is evaluating capital investments. In some industries, the amount of money poured into capital improvements is a very substantial proportion of sales, and so is worthy of a great deal of analysis to ensure that a company is investing its cash wisely in internal improvements. In this section, we review the concept of the hurdle rate, as well as the three most common approaches for evaluating capital investments. We also discuss problems with the capital budget approval process and cash flow modeling issues, and then finish with reviews of the capital investment proposal form and the post-completion project analysis, which brings to a close the complete cycle of evaluating a capital project over the entire course of its acquisition, installation, and operation.

HURDLE RATE

When a CFO is given a capital investment proposal form to review, he or she needs some basis on which to conduct the evaluation. What makes a good capital investment? Is it the project with the largest net cash flow, or the one that uses the least capital, or some other standard of measure?

The standard criterion for investment is the hurdle rate. This is the discounting rate at which all of a company's investments must exhibit a positive cash flow. It is called a hurdle rate because the summary of all cash flows must exceed, or hurdle, this rate, or else the underlying investments will not be approved. The use of a discount rate is extremely important, for it reduces the value of cash inflows and outflows scheduled for some time in the future, so that they are comparable to the value of cash flows in the present. Without the use of a discount rate, we would judge the value of a cash flow ten years in the future to be the same as one that occurs right now. However, the difference between the two is that the funds received now can also earn interest for the next ten years, whereas there is no such opportunity to invest the funds that will arrive in ten years. Consequently, a discount rate is the great equalizer that allows us to make one-to-one comparisons between cash flows in different periods.

The hurdle rate is derived from the cost of capital, which is covered in depth in Chapter 9, Cost of Capital. This is the average cost of funds that a company uses, and is based on the average cost of its debt, equity, and various other funding sources that are combinations of these two basic forms of funds. For example, if a company has determined its cost of capital to be 16%, then the discounted cash flows from all of its new capital investments, using that discount rate, must yield a positive return. If they do not, then the funds flow resulting from its capital investments will not be sufficient for

---

* Adapted with permission from Chapter 3 of *Financial Analysis* by Bragg (John Wiley & Sons, 2000).

the company to pay for the funds it invested. Thus, the primary basis on which a CFO reviews potential capital investments is the hurdle rate.

A company may choose to use several hurdle rates, depending on the nature of the investment. For example, if the company must install equipment to make its production emissions compliant with federal air quality standards, then there is no hurdle rate at all—the company must complete the work, or be fined by the government. At the opposite extreme, a company may assign a high hurdle rate to all projects that are considered unusually risky. For example, if capital projects are for the extension of a current production line, there is very little perceived risk, and a hurdle rate that matches the cost of capital is deemed sufficient. However, if the capital expenditure is for a production line that creates equipment in a new market, where the company is the first entrant, and no one knows what kind of sales will result, the hurdle rate may be set a number of percentage points higher than the cost of capital. Thus, different hurdle rates can apply to different situations.

Having now given the reasons why the hurdle rate is the fundamental measuring stick against which all capital investments are evaluated, we will deal with the one exception to the rule—the payback period.

PAYBACK PERIOD

We have just seen how the primary criterion for evaluating a capital investment is its ability to return a profit that exceeds a hurdle rate. However, this method misses one important element, which is that it does not fully explain investment risk in a manner that is fully understandable to managers. Investment risk can be defined as the chance that the initial investment will not be earned back, or that the rate of return target will not be met. Discounting can be used to identify or weed out such projects, simply by increasing the hurdle rate. For example, if a project is perceived to be risky, an increase in the hurdle rate will reduce its net present value, which makes the investment less likely to be approved by management. However, management may not be comfortable dealing with discounted cash-flow methods when looking at a risky investment—they just want to know how long it will take until they get their invested funds back. Though this is a decidedly unscientific way to review cash flows, the author has yet to find a management team that did not insist on seeing a payback calculation alongside other, more sophisticated, analysis methods.

There are two ways to calculate the payback period. The first method is the easiest to use, but can yield a skewed result. That calculation is to divide the capital investment by the average annual cash flow from operations. For example, in Exhibit 10.1 we have a stream of cash flows over five years that is heavily weighted toward the time periods that are furthest in the future. The sum of those cash flows is $8,750,000, which is an average of $1,750,000 per year. We will also assume that the initial capital investment was $6,000,000. Based on this information, the payback period is $6,000,000 divided by $1,750,000, which is 3.4 years. However, if we review the stream of cash flows in Exhibit 10.1, it is evident that the cash inflow did not cover the investment at the 3.4-year mark. In fact, the actual cash inflow did not exceed $6,000,000 until shortly after the end of the fourth year. What happened? The stream of cash flows in the example was so skewed toward future periods that the annual *average* cash flow was not representative of the annual actual cash flow. Thus, we can use the averaging method only if the stream of future cash flows is relatively even from year to year.

Year	Cash Flow
1	$1,000,000
2	1,250,000
3	1,500,000
4	2,000,000
5	3,000,000

Exhibit 10.1   Stream of Cash Flows for a Payback Calculation

The most accurate way to calculate the payback period is to do so manually. This means that we deduct the total expected cash inflow from the invested balance, year by year, until we arrive at the correct period. For example, we have recreated the stream of cash flows from Exhibit 10.1 in Exhibit 10.2, but now with an extra column that shows the net capital investment remaining at the end of each year. We can use this format to reach the end of year four; we know that the cash flows will pay back the investment sometime during year five, but we do not have a month-by-month cash flow that tells us precisely when. Instead, we can assume an average stream of cash flows during that period, which works out to $250,000 per month ($3,000,000 cash inflow for the year, divided by 12 months). Since there was only $250,000 of net investment remaining at the end of the fourth year, and this is the same monthly amount of cash flow in the fifth year, we can assume that the payback period is 4.1 years.

As already stated, the payback period is not a highly scientific method, because it completely ignores the time value of money. Nonetheless, it tells management how much time will pass before it recovers its invested funds, which can be useful information, especially in environments, such as high technology, where investments must attain a nearly immediate payback before they become obsolete. Accordingly, it is customary to include the payback calculation in a capital investment analysis, though it must be strongly supplemented by discounted cash-flow analyses, which are described in the next two sections.

NET PRESENT VALUE

The typical capital investment is composed of a string of cash flows, both in and out, that will continue until the investment is eventually liquidated at some point in the future. These cash flows are comprised of many things: the initial payment for equipment, continuing maintenance costs, salvage value of the equipment when it is eventually sold,

Year	Cash Flow	Net Investment Remaining
0	0	$6,000,000
1	$1,000,000	5,000,000
2	1,250,000	3,750,000
3	1,500,000	2,250,000
4	2,000,000	250,000
5	3,000,000	—

Exhibit 10.2   Stream of Cash Flows for a Manual Payback Calculation

tax payments, receipts from product sold, and so on. The trouble is, since the cash flows are coming in and going out over a period of many years, how do we make them comparable for an analysis that is done in the present? As noted earlier in the section on hurdle rates, we can use a discount rate to reduce the value of a future cash flow into what it would be worth right now. By applying the discount rate to each anticipated cash flow, we can reduce and then add them together, which yields a single combined figure that represents the current value of the entire capital investment. This is known as its net present value.

For an example of how net present value works, we have listed in Exhibit 10.3 the cash flows, both in and out, for a capital investment that is expected to last for five years. The year is listed in the first column, the amount of the cash flow in the second column, and the discount rate in the third column. The final column multiplies the cash flow from the second column by the discount rate in the third column to yield the present value of each cash flow. The grand total cash flow is listed in the lower-right corner of the exhibit.

Notice that the discount factor in Exhibit 10.3 becomes progressively smaller in later years, since cash flows further in the future are worth less than those received sooner. The discount factor is published in present value tables, which are listed in many accounting and finance textbooks. They are also a standard feature in mid-range handheld calculators. Another variation is to use the following formula to manually compute a present value:

$$\text{Present Value of a Future Cash Flow} = \frac{\text{Future Cash Flow}}{(1 + \text{Discount Rate})^{(\text{Number of Periods of Discounting})}}$$

Using the above formula, if we expect to receive $75,000 in one year, and the discount rate is 15%, then the calculation is:

$$\text{Present Value} = \frac{\$75,000}{(1 + .15)^1}$$

$$\text{Present Value} = \$65,217.39$$

The example shown in Exhibit 10.3 was of the simplest possible kind. In reality, there are several additional factors to take into consideration. First, there may be multiple cash inflows and outflows in each period, rather than the single lump sum that was shown in the example. If a CFO wants to know precisely what is the cause of each cash flow, then it is best to add a line to the net present value calculation that clearly identifies the

Year	Cash Flow	Discount Factor*	Present Value
0	− $100,000	1.0000	− $100,000
1	+ 25,000	.9259	+ 23,148
2	+ 25,000	.8573	+ 21,433
3	+ 25,000	.7938	+ 19,845
4	+ 30,000	.7350	+ 22,050
5	+ 30,000	.6806	+ 20,418
		Net Present Value	+ $6,894

*Discount factor is 8%.

EXHIBIT 10.3   SIMPLIFIED NET PRESENT VALUE EXAMPLE

nature of each item and discounts it separately from the other line items. Another issue is which items to include in the analysis and which to exclude. The basic rule of thumb is that it must be included if it impacts cash flow, and stays out if it does not. The most common cash-flow line items to include in a net present value analysis are:

- *Cash inflows from sales.*   If a capital investment results in added sales, then all gross margins attributable to that investment must be included in the analysis.

- *Cash inflows and outflows for equipment purchases and sales.*   There should be a cash outflow when a product is purchased, as well as a cash inflow when the equipment is no longer needed and is sold off.

- *Cash inflows and outflows for working capital.*   When a capital investment occurs, it normally involves the use of some additional inventory. If there are added sales, then there will probably be additional accounts receivable. In either case, these are additional investments that must be included in the analysis as cash outflows. Also, if the investment is ever terminated, then the inventory will presumably be sold off and the accounts receivable collected, so there should be line items in the analysis, located at the end of the project time line, showing the cash inflows from the liquidation of working capital.

- *Cash outflows for maintenance.*   If there is production equipment involved, then there will be periodic maintenance needed to ensure that it runs properly. If there is a maintenance contract with a supplier that provides the servicing, then this too should be included in the analysis.

- *Cash outflows for taxes.*   If there is a profit from new sales that are attributable to the capital investment, then the incremental income tax that can be traced to those incremental sales must be included in the analysis. Also, if there is a significant quantity of production equipment involved, the annual personal property taxes that can be traced to that equipment should also be included.

- *Cash inflows for the tax effect of depreciation.*   Depreciation is an allowable tax deduction. Accordingly, the depreciation created by the purchase of capital equipment should be offset against the cash outflow caused by income taxes. Though depreciation is really just an accrual, it does have a net cash flow impact caused by a reduction in taxes, and so should be included in the net present value calculation.

The net present value approach is the best way to see if a proposed capital investment has a sufficient rate of return to justify the use of any required funds. Also, because it reveals the amount of cash created in excess of the corporate hurdle rate, it allows management to rank projects by the amount of cash they can potentially spin off, which is a good way to determine which projects to fund if there is not enough cash available to pay for an entire set of proposed investments.

In the next section, we look at an alternative discounting method that focuses on the rate of return of a capital investment's cash flows, rather than the amount of cash left over after being discounted at a standard hurdle rate, as was the case with the net present value methodology.

INTERNAL RATE OF RETURN

The end result of a net present value calculation is the amount of money that is earned or lost after all related cash flows are discounted at a present hurdle rate. This is a

Year	Cash Flow	Internal Rate of Return = 7%	Present Value
0	− $250,000	1.000	− $250,000
1	+ 55,000	.9345	+ 51,398
2	+ 60,000	.8734	+ 52,404
3	+ 65,000	.8163	+ 53,060
4	+ 70,000	.7629	+ 53,403
5	+ 75,000	.7130	+ 53,475
		Net Present Value	+ $13,740

EXHIBIT 10.4   INTERNAL RATE OF RETURN CALCULATION, LOW ESTIMATE

good evaluation method, but what if management wants to know the overall return on investment of the same stream of cash flows? Also, what if the net present value was negative, but only by a small amount, so that management wants to know how far off a project's rate of return varies from the hurdle rate? Also, what if management wants to rank projects by their overall rates of return, rather than by their net present values? All of these questions can be answered by using the internal rate of return (IRR) method.

The IRR method is very similar to the net present value method, because we use the same cash-flow layout, itemizing the net inflows and outflows by year. The difference is that, using the IRR method, we use a high-low approach to find the discount rate at which the cash flows equal zero. At that point, the discount rate equals the rate of return on investment for the entire stream of cash flows associated with the capital investment. To illustrate how the method works, we will begin with the standard net present value format that was listed in the last section. This time, we have a new set of annual cash flows, as shown in Exhibit 10.4. The difference between this calculation and the one used for net present value is that we are going to guess at the correct rate of return and enter this amount in the "Internal Rate of Return" column. We enter the discount rates for each year, using a low-end assumption of a 7% rate of return.

The end result of the calculation is that we have a positive net present value of $13,740. Since we are shooting for the IRR percentage at which the net present value is zero, this means that we must increase the IRR. If the net present value had been negative, we would have reduced the IRR percentage instead. We will make a higher guess at an IRR of 9%, and run the calculation again, which is shown in Exhibit 10.5.

The result of the calculation in Exhibit 10.5 is very close to a net present value of 9%. If we want to try a few more high-low calculations, we can zero in on the IRR more precisely. In the example, the actual IRR is 8.9%.

Year	Cash Flow	Internal Rate of Return = 9%	Present Value
0	− $250,000	1.000	− $250,000
1	+ 55,000	.9174	+ 50,457
2	+ 60,000	.8417	+ 50,502
3	+ 65,000	.7722	+ 50,193
4	+ 70,000	.7084	+ 49,588
5	+ 75,000	.6499	+ 48,743
		Net Present Value	− $517

EXHIBIT 10.5   INTERNAL RATE OF RETURN CALCULATION, HIGH ESTIMATE

This approach seems like a very slow one, and it is. A different approach, if the reader has access to an electronic spreadsheet, such as Microsoft Excel, is to enter the stream of cash flows into it and enter a formula that the computer uses to instantly calculate the internal rate of return. For example, the screen printout shown in Exhibit 10.6 contains the same stream of cash flows shown earlier in Exhibits 10.4 and 10.5. In this case, we have used the Excel formula for the internal rate of return to give us the IRR automatically. For the sake of clarity, we have duplicated the formula in a text format immediately below the main formula.

The internal rate of return is best used in conjunction with the net present value calculation, because it can be misleading when used by itself. One problem is that it favors those capital investments with very high rates of return, even if the total dollar return is rather small. An example of this is when a potential investment of $10,000 has a return of $3,000, which equates to a 30% rate of return, and is ranked higher than a $100,000 investment with a return of $25,000 (which has a 25% rate of return). In this case, the smaller project certainly has a greater rate of return, but the larger project will return more cash in total than the smaller one. If there were only enough capital available for one of the two projects, perhaps $100,000, and the smaller project were selected because of its higher rate of return, then the total return would be less than optimal, because much of the funds are not being invested at all. In this situation, only $3,000 is being earned, even though $100,000 can be invested, which yields only a 3% return on the total pool of funds. Thus, if there are too many capital investments chasing too few funds, selecting investments based on nothing but their IRR may lead to suboptimal decisions.

Another issue is that the IRR calculation assumes that all cash flows thrown off by a project over the course of its life can be reinvested at the same rate of return. This is not always a valid assumption, since the earnings from a special investment that yields a uniquely high rate of return may not be investable at anywhere close to the same rate of return.

Despite its shortcomings, the IRR method is a scientifically valid way to determine the rate of return on a capital investment's full stream of cash flows. However, because it does not recognize the total amount of cash spun off by an investment, it is best used in conjunction with the net present value calculation in order to yield the most complete analysis of a capital investment.

PROBLEMS WITH THE CAPITAL BUDGET APPROVAL PROCESS

A significant problem with the capital budget approval process is that the senior-level managers who are chiefly responsible for approving new capital expenditures are also

Year	Cash Flow
0	($250,000)
1	55,000
2	60,000
3	65,000
4	70,000
5	75,000
Internal Rate of Return (IRR):	8.9%
Text of IRR Formula:	= IRR(E6:E11)

EXHIBIT 10.6 INTERNAL RATE OF RETURN CALCULATION

responsible for generating an adequate return on investment from the company's existing capital base. This means that they will be less likely to approve the construction of any radical new systems that will render the older infrastructure obsolete. Consequently, new projects will probably only be approved if they involve the enhancement of existing systems, which will likely only involve modest improvements in productivity.

One way to resolve this problem is to set aside a large amount of cash to be handed out by a lower-level group of employees. This group should not be responsible for the existing infrastructure, and should preferably be younger and of an entrepreneurial mind-set. This group should be oriented toward the funding of project startups, with funds being allocated to prototype development, market trials, or expansions of a business case.

Another solution is to offer significant cash payouts if new ideas succeed in the marketplace. The prospect of large personal rewards may push managers to take greater risks than would normally be the case. Also, this tends to create a feedback loop where evidence of actual cash payouts breeds even more ideas, which generates more payouts, and so on.

Yet another approach is to fund an in-house venture capital firm. The company can give this group general strategic directions and then let it search for funding opportunities both inside and outside the company. By shifting investment authority away from the management team and onto a group of trained venture capitalists, it is likely that funding decisions will be different.

Finally, alter the capital budgeting guidelines so that riskier projects will be more easily approved at lower funding levels. This allows potentially high-return projects to at least receive initial funding to see if the concept works.

All of these variations on project funding are designed to keep a company from reinvesting in minor efficiency improvements to their existing infrastructures, instead allowing themselves an opportunity to create major improvements in their return on investment.

CASH FLOW MODELING ISSUES

The cash flow concepts used for most net present value or internal rate of return projects assume a simplified decision process where funding occurs once at the beginning of the project, after which a steady and predictable series of cash flows occurs over a multiyear period. In reality, there is a possibility for several additional decisions occurring during the investment period that can dramatically alter the value of a project. They are:

- *Deferred start date.* There may be a sufficient level of uncertainty regarding a project that it makes sense to hold off on its initiation until additional research can be conducted. However, delaying the project may also result in a reduction in the level of market share attained, since competitors will have a better opportunity to position their products in the market first. Thus, additional variables in the cash flow scenario are a combination of a delay in cash outflow and reduced long-term revenues.

- *Early cancellation.* If the expenditure of funds occurs over a lengthy period of time or requires additional investments at discrete intervals, then management has the option to cancel the project early in order to minimize potential losses. If there appears to be a significant probability of early cancellation, then consider creating an additional cash flow model that includes this scenario.

- *Add more capital later in project.* If there is a possibility that a project may yield additional profits through additional investments at various points in the future, then an added scenario may include the amount of any additional investments and the cash flows to be gained from them. Conversely, more cash may be needed when the project being created is of the experimental variety, and there is a risk that construction and implementation problems will require an additional investment. If considered significant, these options should be included in the cash flow model.

- *Alter project cost structure.* It may be possible to pay less cash up front in exchange for higher variable costs over the remainder of the project, as would be the case when more staffing is used instead of automated equipment (or vice versa). Depending on the changes in the timing and amounts of cash flows resulting from such decisions, it may be necessary to construct a separate cash flow forecast for each option.

The scenarios noted above bring up the prospect of having multiple possible variations on the cash flows from a prospective new project. Which one should be included in the formal cash flow analysis that is presented to management for approval? All of them. To do so, create a decision tree that outlines all cash flow options, with each option assigned a probability of occurrence. For each node on the decision tree, calculate its probability times its value outcome, and then sum all the nodes. This approach gives management valuable insight into the probability of different cash flow alternatives. The only problem with the decision tree model is that the calculation becomes cumbersome after more than a few cash flow options are added to it.

FUNDING DECISIONS FOR RESEARCH AND DEVELOPMENT PROJECTS

The traditional approach to R&D funding is to require all R&D proposals to pass a minimum return-on-investment hurdle rate. However, when there is limited funding available and too many investments passing the hurdle rate to all be funded, managers tend to pick the most likely projects to succeed. This selection process usually results in the least risky projects being funded, which are typically extensions of existing product lines or other variations on existing products that will not achieve breakthrough profitability. An alternative that is more likely to achieve a higher return on R&D investment is to apportion investable funds into multiple categories—a large percentage that is only to be used for highly risky projects with associated high returns, and a separate pool of funds specifically designated for lower risk projects with correspondingly lower levels of return. The exact proportions of funding allocated to each category will depend on management's capacity for risk, as well as the size and number of available projects in each category. This approach allows a company the opportunity to achieve a breakthrough product introduction that it would probably not have funded if a single hurdle rate had been used to evaluate new product proposals.

If this higher-risk approach to allocating funds is used, it is likely that a number of new product projects will be abandoned prior to their release into the market, on the grounds that they will not yield a sufficient return on investment or will not be technologically or commercially feasible. This is not a bad situation, since some projects are bound to fail if a sufficiently high level of project risk is acceptable to management. Conversely, if no projects fail, this is a clear sign that management is not investing in sufficiently risky investments. To measure the level of project failure, calculate R&D

waste, which is the amount of unrealized product development spending (e.g., the total expenditure on canceled projects during the measurement period). Even better, divide the amount of R&D waste by the total R&D expenditure during the period to determine the proportion of expenses incurred on failed projects. Unfortunately, this measure can be easily manipulated by accelerating or withholding the declaration of project termination. Nonetheless, it does give a fair indication of project risk when aggregated over the long term.

Though funding may be allocated into broad investment categories, management must still use a reliable method for determining which projects will receive funding and which will not. The standard approach is to apply a discount rate to all possible projects, and then to select those having the highest net present value (NPV). However, the NPV calculation does not include several key variables found in the expected commercial value (ECV) formula, making the ECV the preferred method. The ECV formula requires one to multiply a prospective project's net present value by the probability of its commercial success, minus the commercialization cost, and then multiply the result by the probability of technical success, minus the development cost. Thus, the intent of using ECV is to include all major success factors into the decision to accept or reject a new product proposal. The formula is:

$$(((\text{Project Net Present Value} \times \text{Probability of Commercial Success})$$

$$- \text{Commercialization Cost}) \times (\text{Probability of Technical Success}))$$

$$- \text{Product Development Cost}$$

As an example of the use of ECV, the Moravia Corporation collects the following information about a new project for a battery-powered lawn trimmer, where there is some technical risk that a sufficiently powerful battery cannot be developed for the product:

Project net present value	$4,000,000
Probability of commercial success	90%
Commercialization cost	$750,000
Probability of technical success	65%
Product development cost	$1,750,000

Based on this information, Moravia computes the following ECV for the lawn trimmer project:

$$(((\$4,000,000 \text{ Project Net Present Value} \times 90\% \text{ Probability of Commercial Success})$$

$$- \$750,000 \text{ Commercialization Cost}) \times (65\% \text{ Probability of Technical Success}))$$

$$- \$1,750,000 \text{ Product Development Cost}$$

$$\text{Expected Commercial Value} = \$102,500$$

Even if some projects are dropped after being run through the preceding valuation analysis, this does not mean that they should be canceled for good. On the contrary, these projects may become commercially viable over time, depending on changes in price points, costs, market conditions, and technical viability. Consequently, the R&D manager should conduct a periodic review of previously shelved projects to see if any of the factors just noted have changed sufficiently to allow the company to reintroduce a project proposal for development.

CAPITAL INVESTMENT PROPOSAL FORM

When a CFO is called upon to conduct an analysis of a potential capital investment, the largest task is collecting all necessary data about it. This can involve meeting with a number of employees who are working on the capital investment to determine the timing and cost of all up-front and continuing expenditures, as well as the timing and amount of all future cash inflows, not to mention the eventual salvage value of any equipment to be purchased. Once the CFO assembles this information, it may become apparent that there are a few items still missing, which will require another iteration of data gathering. In the end, the CFO may find that the data collection task has grossly exceeded the time needed to analyze the resulting information. If there are many capital proposals to review, the data collection phase of the analysis can easily turn into a full-time job.

A good way to entirely avoid the data collection phase of the investment proposal process is to make the department managers do it. The CFO can create a standard form, such as the one shown in Exhibit 10.7, that itemizes the exact information needed. This form can be created in a template format, perhaps in an electronic spreadsheet, and distributed by e-mail to all managers. They then fill out the necessary fields (all user-entered fields in the example are in italics), and e-mail it back to the CFO for review. This eliminates the data collection chore, while also putting the data into the exact format needed to yield basic calculations for the CFO, such as the payback period, net present value, and internal rate of return, thereby keeping not only the data collection work, but much of the related analysis, to a minimum.

The form shown in Exhibit 10.7 is divided into several key pieces. The first is the identification section, in which we insert the name of the project sponsor, the date on which the proposal was submitted, and the description of the project. For a company that deals with a multitude of capital projects, it may also be useful to include a specific identifying code for each one. The next section is the most important one—it lists all cash inflows and outflows, in summary form, for each year. The sample form has room for just five years of cash flows, but this can be increased for companies with longer-term investments. Cash outflows are listed as negative numbers, and inflows as positive ones. The annual depreciation figure goes into the box in the "Tax Effect of Annual Depreciation" column. The column of tax deductions listed directly below the depreciation box are automatic calculations that determine the tax deduction, based on the tax rate noted in the far right column. All of the cash flows for each year are then summarized in the far right column. A series of calculations are listed directly below this "Total" column that itemize the payback period, net present value, and internal rate of return, mostly based on the hurdle rate noted just above them. In the example, the rate of return on the itemized cash flows is 9.4%, which is just below the corporate hurdle rate of 10%. Since the discount rate is higher than the actual rate of return, the net present value is negative. Also, this can be considered a risky project, since the number of years needed to pay back the initial investment is quite lengthy. The next section of the form is for the type of project. The purpose of this section is to identify those investments that *must* be completed, irrespective of the rate of return; these are usually due to legal or safety issues. Also, if a project is for a new product, management may consider it to be especially risky, and so will require a higher hurdle rate. This section identifies those projects. The last section is for approvals by managers. It lists the level of manager who can sign off on various investment dollar amounts, and ensures that the correct number of managers have reviewed each investment. This format is comprehensive enough to give a CFO sufficient information to conduct a rapid analysis of most projects.

Name of Project Sponsor: H. Henderson   **Submission Date:**   09/09/07

Investment Description:
Additional press for newsprint.

Cash Flows:

Year	Equipment	Working Capital	Maintenance	Tax Effect of Annual Depreciation	Salvage Value	Revenue	Taxes	Total
0	−5,000,000	−400,000		800,000				−5,400,000
1			−100,000	320,000		1,650,000	−700,000	1,170,000
2			−100,000	320,000		1,650,000	−700,000	1,170,000
3			−100,000	320,000		1,650,000	−700,000	1,170,000
4			−100,000	320,000		1,650,000	−700,000	1,170,000
5		400,000	−100,000	320,000	1,000,000	1,650,000	−700,000	2,570,000
Totals	−5,000,000	0	−500,000	2,400,000	1,000,000	8,250,000		1,850,000

Tax Rate: **40%**

Hurdle Rate: **10%**

Payback Period: **4.28**

Net Present Value: **(86,809)**

Internal Rate of Return: **9.4%**

Type of Project (check one):
Legal requirement ____
New product-related ____
Old product extension   Yes
Repair/replacement ____
Safety issue ____

Approvals:

Amount	Approver	Signature
<$5,000	Supervisor	____
$5–19,999	General Mgr	____
$20–49,999	President	____
$50,000+	Board	____

EXHIBIT 10.7   CAPITAL INVESTMENT PROPOSAL FORM

Though the capital investment proposal form is a good way to have project sponsors assemble information for the CFO, it does not guarantee that the finished product will be free of errors—far from it. Department managers may not have a clear understanding of what information goes into each field of the form, so they may enter incorrect information which the CFO will then use to arrive at an incorrect analysis. To keep this from happening, there are several steps to take. One is to create a short procedure to accompany all forms when they are given to managers, which clearly describes what information goes into each field in the form. Another option is to meet with all new managers to go over the form, so that they have a clear understanding of how to fill it out. Yet another option, if the form is distributed in Excel, is to include instructions in a "Comments" field that can be attached to each cell in the spreadsheet; by positioning the cursor on the field, the comment appears on the screen, describing how to fill in each field. Finally, and of greatest importance, the CFO should meet with the sponsor of any large project to carefully review all aspects of the proposal form. For a large project, it is critical to verify all information, since even a small mistake can yield the wrong analysis results, possibly leading to significant and unexpected financial losses.

A final issue in regard to the use of capital investment proposal forms is that a bureaucratically minded person can create a behemoth of a form. This happens when the accounting department wants to see all possible underlying detail to justify every cash flow in the analysis. Though the accounting staff thinks it is just being careful, the managers who must fill out the novella-sized forms will certainly think otherwise. For them, creating a proposal form will become a major chore that is to be delayed or avoided at all costs. To keep this situation from arising, the CFO must remember that most capital requests are very small, usually hovering near the low-end capitalization limit, and so do not require a vast analysis. Only a few very large capital investments are worthy of in-depth review, and so should be treated as the exception, not the rule. Based on this logic, the investment proposal form should be a small one, which the CFO can investigate in greater detail if the size or uncertainty of the investment appears to warrant it.

The capital investment proposal form is a relatively easy one to create, and, with an accompanying procedure, is one of the best ways to improve the flow of information to the CFO for the analysis of capital investments.

POST-COMPLETION PROJECT ANALYSIS

The greatest failing in most capital review systems is not in the initial analysis phase, but in the post-completion phase, because there is not one. A CFO usually puts a great deal of effort into compiling a capital investment proposal form, educating managers about how to use it, and then setting up control points around the system to ensure that all capital requests make use of the approval system. However, if there is no methodology for verifying that managers enter accurate information into the approval forms, which is done by comparing actual results to them, then managers will eventually figure out that they can alter the numbers in the approval forms in order to beat the corporate hurdle rates, even if this information is incorrect. However, if managers know that their original estimates will be carefully reviewed and critiqued for some time into the future, then they will be much more careful in completing their initial capital requests. Thus, analysis at the back end of a capital project will lead to greater accuracy at the front end.

Analysis of actual expenditures can begin before a capital investment is fully paid for or installed. A CFO can subtotal the payments made by the end of each month and

Description	Actual	Projected Actual	Budget	Actual Present Value*	Budget Present Value*
Cash Outflows					
Capital Items	$1,250,000	—	$1,100,000	$1,250,000	$1,100,000
Working Capital	750,000	—	500,000	750,000	500,000
Total Outflows	$2,000,000	—	$1,600,000	$2,000,000	$1,600,000
Cash Inflows					
Year 1	250,000		$250,000	$229,350	$229,350
Year 2	375,000		400,000	315,638	336,680
Year 3	450,000		500,000	347,490	386,100
Year 4		450,000	500,000	318,780	354,200
Year 5		450,000	500,000	292,455	324,950
Total Inflows	$1,075,000	$900,000	$2,150,000	$1,503,713	$1,631,280
Net Present Value	—	—	—	− $496,287	+ $31,280

*Uses discount rate of 9%.

EXHIBIT 10.8   COMPARISON OF ACTUAL TO PROJECTED CAPITAL INVESTMENT CASH FLOWS

compare them to the total projected by the project manager. A total that significantly exceeds the approved expenditure would then be grounds for an immediate review by top management. This approach works best for the largest capital expenditures, where reviewing payment data in detail is worth the extra effort by the accounting staff if it can prevent large overpayments. It is also worthwhile when capital expenditures cover long periods of time, so that a series of monthly reviews can be made. However, it is not a worthwhile approach if the expenditure in question is for a single item that is made with one payment; however, this type of purchase can still be reviewed by comparing the company's purchase order total to the amount noted on the capital investment proposal form.

Once a project is completed, there may be cash inflows that result from it. If so, a quarterly comparison of actual to projected cash inflows is the most frequent comparison to be made, with an annual review being sufficient in many cases. Such a review keeps management appraised of the performance of all capital projects, and lets the project sponsors know that their estimates will be the subject of considerable scrutiny for as far into the future as they had originally projected. For those companies that survive based on the efficiency of capital usage, it may even be reasonable to tie manager pay reviews to the accuracy of their capital investment request forms.

An example of a post-completion project analysis is shown in Exhibit 10.8. In this example, the top of the report compares actual to budgeted cash outflows, while the middle compares all actual cash outflows to the budget. Note that the cash outflows section is complete, since these were all incurred at the beginning of the project, whereas the inflows section is not yet complete, because the project has only completed the third year of a five-year plan. To cover the remaining two years of activity, there is a column for estimated cash inflows, which projects them for the remaining years of the investment, using the last year in which there are actual data available. This projected information can be used to determine the net present value. We compare the actual and projected net present values at the bottom of the report, so that management can see if there are any problems worthy of correction. In this case, the initial costs of the project, both in terms of capital items and working capital, were so far over budget that the actual net present value is solidly in the red. In this case, management should take a hard look at reducing the working capital, since this is the single largest cash drain in excess of the budget, while also seeing if cash inflow can be increased to match the budgeted annual amounts for the last two years of the investment.

SUMMARY

In this chapter, we have gone over some of the most fundamental analyses that a CFO will see—the use of the payback period, net present value, and internal rate of return measures to determine whether or not a company should invest in a capital project (as well as special considerations for R&D projects). Just as important to this analysis, though unfortunately overlooked by all too many companies, is the post-implementation review of partially or fully completed capital investments, since this information tells a company which investments have succeeded and which have failed. Only by mastering all the techniques noted in this chapter can a CFO become an efficient analyzer of capital investment issues.

CHAPTER 11

OTHER FINANCIAL ANALYSIS TOPICS*

The cost of capital and capital budgeting are extensive topics, and so were accorded separate chapters preceding this one. However, the CFO has need of other analysis tools that can be explained more briefly, and which are contained within this chapter. The first is risk analysis, which addresses the variability of data the CFO uses to make decisions. Another is capacity utilization, which is of great importance when determining the ability of an organization to change the amount of revenue it produces and also monitors its bottleneck operations. Another analysis tool is the breakeven chart, which is addressed in increasing levels of complexity in order to show how it can be modified to incorporate a variety of variables. Finally, we cover the use of business cycle forecasting to assist with the budgeting process. The CFO will require all these tools in the conduct of his or her business.

RISK ANALYSIS

A CFO is sometimes called on to issue opinions based on *projected* information. This happens whenever a business forecast or sales projection is issued. In particular, it is a primary element of any cash-flow projection for a capital expenditure. If there is even a small difference between actual and projected cash flows from a project, it may result in a negative net present value, which means that an implemented project should not have been initially approved. To avoid this problem, one must have a good knowledge of the risk of any projection, which is essentially the chance that the actual value will vary significantly from the expected one.

There are several rough measures of data dispersion. They tell a CFO how spread out the projected outcomes are from a central average point. By reviewing the several measurements, one can obtain a good feel for the extent to which projections cluster together. If they are tightly clustered, then the risk of not meeting the estimated outcome is low, whereas a large degree of dispersion reflects considerable dissension over the projected outcome; a greater degree of risk is associated with this situation.

The first task when determining data dispersion is to determine the center, or midpoint, of the data, so that we can see how far the group of estimates vary from this point. There are several ways to arrive at this point. They are:

- *Arithmetic mean.* This is the summary of all projections, divided by the total number of projections. It rarely results in a specific point that matches any of the

---

* Adapted with permission from Chapters 8, 13, and 17 of *Financial Analysis* by Bragg (John Wiley & Sons, 2000).

underlying projections, since it is not based on any single projection—just the average of all points. It simply balances out the largest and smallest projections. It tends to be inaccurate if the underlying data includes one or two projections that are significantly different from the other projections, resulting in an average that is skewed in the direction of the significantly different projections.

- *Median.*   This is the point at which half of the projections are below, and half are above it. On the assumption that there are an even number of projections being used, the median is the average of the two middle values. By using this method, one can avoid the effect of any outlying projections that are radically different from the main group.

- *Mode.*   This is the most commonly observed value in a set of underlying projections. As such, it is not impacted by any extreme projections. In a sense, this represents the most popular projection.

When selecting which of the above measures to use for the midpoint of the data, we must remember why we are using the midpoint. With the determination of the level of risk being the goal, we want to determine how far apart the projections are from a midpoint. Since we will be including the extreme values in our next set of measurements, we do not have to include them in the determination of the center of the projections. Accordingly, we will use the median, which ignores the size of outlying values, as the measurement of choice for our determination of the middle of the set of projected outcomes.

The next step is to determine how far apart the projections are from the median. Given the small number of projections, this is easy enough. Just pick the highest and lowest values from the list of outcomes. Then we must determine the percentage by which the highest and lowest values vary from the median. To do so, we divide the difference between the lowest and median values by the median, and calculate the same variance between the median and the highest value. This is a good way to determine the range of possible outcomes. For example, the following cash-flow projections were collected as part of risk analysis determination:

- The set of projections for estimated cash flow is:
    $250, $400, $675, $725, $850, and $875

- The median is the average of the third and fourth values, which is:
    $700

- The percentage difference between the median and highest projection is:
    ($875 − $700)/$700 = 25%

- The percentage difference between the median and lowest projection is:
    ($700 − $250)/$700 = 64%

If the difference between the median and the highest possible estimate is only 25%, but the difference between the median and the lowest possible estimate is 64%, then we see that there is a modest chance that the actual result will be higher than the estimate, but that there is a significant risk that it may turn out to be lower than expected.

Another way to determine dispersion is to calculate the *standard deviation* of the data. This method measures the average scatter of data about the mean. In other words, it arrives at a number that is the amount by which the average data point varies from the midpoint, either above or below it. We can divide it by the mean of the data to arrive at a percentage that is called the *coefficient of variation*. This is an excellent way to convert the standard deviation, which is expressed in units, into a percentage. This is a much

---

1. The standard deviation formula in Excel, using data set, is as follows:

   $$= \text{STDEV}(250,400,675,725,850,875)$$

   $$= 252$$

2. The calculation of the mean of all data is:

   $$= (\text{Sum of All Data Items})/(\text{Number of Data Items})$$

   $$= (250 + 400 + 675 + 725 + 850 + 875)/6$$

   $$= 629$$

3. The calculation of the coefficient of variation is:

   $$= (\text{Standard Deviation})/(\text{Mean})$$

   $$= 252/629$$

   $$= 40\%$$

EXHIBIT 11.1 CALCULATING THE STANDARD DEVIATION AND COEFFICIENT OF VARIATION

better way of expressing the range of deviation within a group of projections, since one cannot always tell if a standard deviation of $23 is good or bad, but when converted into a percentage of deviation of 3%, we can see that the same number indicates a very tight clustering of data about the centerpoint of all data. In Exhibit 11.1, we use the data just noted to determine the standard deviation, the mean, and the coefficient of variation.

Thus, the calculations in Exhibit 11.1 reveal that the set of projections used as our underlying data vary significantly from the midpoint of the group, especially in a downward direction, which would make a CFO believe there is a high degree of risk that the expected outcome will not be achieved.

Sometimes, the management team to whom risk information is reported will not be awed by a reported coefficient of variation of a whopping 80%, nor by a standard deviation of 800 units. They do not know what these measures mean, and they do not have time to find out. For them, a graphical representation of data dispersion may be a better approach. They can see the spread of estimates on a graph, and then decide for themselves if there appears to be a problem with risk.

When constructing a graph that shows the dispersion of data, we can lay out the data set in terms of the percentage difference between each item and the midpoint. In Exhibit 11.2, we have taken the projection information used in Exhibit 11.1 and converted it into percentages from the median.

When translated into a graph, Exhibit 11.2 gives us a wide percentage distribution of data on either side of the x-axis, which gives a good indication of the true distribution of data about the mean. In Exhibit 11.3, we have restated the data in Exhibit 11.2 into the top graph.

Note that there are two additional graphs in Exhibit 11.3. The middle graph assumes that we have a number of projections clustered under each of the variance points. In the example, we have arbitrarily expanded the number of projections to 26, with 8 clustered

Projection	Percentage Variance from the Median
$250	− 64%
$400	− 43%
$675	− 4%
$700 (median)	**0%**
$725	4%
$850	21%
$875	25%

EXHIBIT 11.2 DATA DISPERSION, MEASURED IN PERCENTAGES

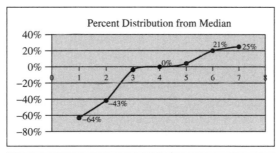

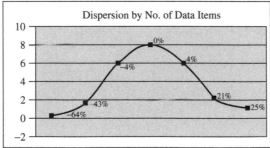

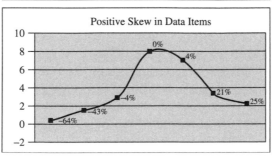

EXHIBIT 11.3 GRAPHICAL ILLUSTRATION OF DATA DISPERSION

at the median point, 6 each at the − 4% and + 4% variance points, and lesser amounts at the outlying variance points. This is close to a classic "bell curve" distribution, where the bulk of estimates are clustered near the middle, and a rapidly declining number are located at the periphery. This is an excellent way to present information, but for the types of projections that a CFO works with, there will rarely be a sufficient number of projections to present this type of graph. If there are, a variation that may arise is the final graph at the bottom of the exhibit, which shows data that is skewed toward the right-hand side of the chart. This indicates a preponderance of estimates that lean, or "skew," toward the higher end of the range of estimates. A reverse graph, which had "negative skew," would present a decided lean toward the left side of the graph. Of the graphs presented in Exhibit 11.3, only the first one, the "Percent Distribution from Median," is likely to see consistent use, because there are so few data points available for a CFO to work with in most situations. Nonetheless, any of these graphs should be used when making presentations to management about the riskiness of projections, since they are so easy to understand.

CAPACITY UTILIZATION

Capacity covers either human or machine resources. If those resources are not used to a sufficient degree, there are immediate grounds for eliminating them, either by a layoff (in the case of human capacity) or by selling equipment (in the case of machines). In the first case, a layoff usually has a short-term loss associated with it, which covers severance costs, followed by an upturn in profits, since there is no longer a long-term obligation to pay salaries. In the second case, the sale of a machine does not have much of an impact on profits, unless there is a gain or loss on sale of the asset, but it will result in an improvement in cash flow as sale proceeds come in; these funds can be used for a variety of purposes to increase corporate value, such as reinvestment in new machines, a loan payoff, a buyback of equity, and so on. Consequently, a CFO who keeps a close eye on capacity levels throughout a company, and who makes recommendations to keep capacity utilization close to current capacity levels, will have a significant impact on both profits and cash flows.

When making such analyses, the main issue to be aware of is that a CFO tends to be conservative—he or she wants to maximize the use of current capacity and get rid of everything not being used. This may not be a good thing when activity levels are projected to increase markedly in the near term. If management had followed a CFO's recommendation to eliminate excess capacity just prior to a large increase in production volumes, it would require some exceptional scrambling, possibly at high cost, to bring the newly necessary capacity back in house. Consequently, a CFO must work with the sales staff to determine future sales (and therefore production) trends before recommending any cuts in capacity.

Capacity utilization also reveals the specific spots in a production process where work is being held up. These bottleneck operations prevent a production line from attaining its true potential amount of revenue production. A CFO can use information about bottlenecks in two ways. One is to recommend improvements to bottleneck operations in order to increase the potential amount of revenue generation. The other is to point out that any capital improvements to other segments of a production operation are essentially a waste of money (from the perspective of increasing the flow of production), since all production is still going to create a log-jam in front of the bottleneck operation.

Another useful way for a CFO to use capacity utilization information is in the determination of pricing levels. For example, if a company has a large amount of surplus excess capacity and does not intend to sell it off in the near term, it makes sense (and cents) to offer pricing deals on incremental sales that only result in small margins. This is because there is no other use for the equipment or production personnel. If low-margin jobs are not produced, the only alternative is no jobs at all, for which there is no margin at all. However, if a CFO knows that a production facility is running at maximum capacity, it is time to be choosy on incremental sales, so that only those sales involving large margins are accepted. It may also be possible to stop taking orders for low-margin products in the future, thereby flushing low-margin products out of the current production mix, in favor of newer, higher-margin sales. Though a highly profitable approach, this can also irritate customers who are faced with "take it or leave it" answers by a company that refuses new orders unless higher prices are accepted by the customer. Consequently, incremental pricing for new sales is closely tied not only to how much production capacity a company has left, but also to its long-term strategy for how it wants to treat its customers.

A final area in which capacity analysis can be used to alter profit levels is in mergers and acquisitions. If an acquisition team is looking at buying another company, but can only justify it if there are significant synergies, then a hard look at the target company's capacity utilization may provide the needed profit increase. For example, if the target organization has a large amount of excess capacity, the acquiring company can assume that a large part of the excess equipment or production lines can be sold off, thereby garnering additional cash flow. Another approach is to purchase a company in order to make immediate use of its excess capacity. This approach has the added benefit of allowing a company to closely review the product margins on sales by both companies, eliminate those customers yielding meager profit margins, and keep the remaining high-margin accounts from both organizations, along with a repositioning of the needed capacity to match the requirements of these most desirable customers. Yet another reason is that building the needed capacity from scratch may be more expensive than acquiring a company that already has not only the facilities but also the expertise to run them. For all of these reasons, capacity utilization analysis should be a key part of any merger or acquisition strategy.

A company has a variety of activities that may be important enough to track the capacity utilization of. The area most commonly measured is machine utilization, since management teams are always interested in keeping expensive machinery running for as long as possible, so that the invested cost is not put to waste. Thus, capacity tracking for *expensive assets* is certainly a common activity. However, another factor that many organizations miss is the capacity utilization measurement for any *bottleneck operation*. This has nothing to do with a costly asset, but rather with determining whether or not a key operation in a process is interfering with the successful processing of a transaction. For example, if a number of production lines feed their products to a single person who must box and ship them, and this person cannot keep up with the volume of production arriving at her workstation, then she is a bottleneck operation that is interfering with the timely completion of the production schedule. Because she is a bottleneck, her capacity utilization should be tracked most carefully. This worker is not an expensive machine, and may in fact be paid very little, but she is potentially holding up the realization of a great deal of revenue that cannot be shipped to customers. Consequently, using a capacity utilization measure makes a great deal of sense in this situation.

To amplify on the concept of capacity planning for bottleneck operations, it is not sufficient to track the utilization of a single bottleneck operation, because the bottleneck will move to different steps in the production process as improvements are made to the system. For example, the key principle of the just-in-time concept is that management works to identify bottleneck operations and fix them. As a result, each specific bottleneck will be eliminated, but now the second most constrictive operation comes to the fore for review and improvement, which in turn will be followed by a third operation, and so on. Consequently, it is better to identify *every* work center and track the utilization of them all. By using this more comprehensive approach, management can spot upcoming bottleneck problems and address them before they become serious problems.

In the case of machinery, the tracking of utilization for virtually all of them is also useful, not just because they are also potential bottleneck operations, but because of the reverse problem—a machine that is *not* being used is a waste of invested capital, and should be sold off if possible. A detailed capacity utilization report will note those machines that are not being used, which tells management what can potentially be eliminated. This information is especially useful when machines are clustered on the report by type, so that a subtotal of capacity utilization is noted for each group of machines. If the machines within each cluster can be used interchangeably to complete similar work, management can then determine the total amount of work required of each cluster, and add or delete machines to meet that demand, which results in a very efficient use of capital. Such a report is described later in Exhibit 11.4.

A company frequently thinks of its production capacity only in terms of the current number of shifts being operated, and tracks its capacity utilization accordingly. For example, a production facility that operates for one eight-hour shift, and uses all machinery during that time, thinks that it is operating at 100% capacity utilization. In fact, it is only using one-third of the available hours in a day, which leaves lots of room for additional production. Accordingly, when developing a utilization measurement, one should always use the maximum amount of theoretical capacity as the baseline, rather than the amount of time during the day that is currently being used. For a single day, this means 24 hours, and for a week, it is 168 hours. On a monthly basis, the total number of hours will vary, since the number of days in a month can vary from 28 to 31. To get around this problem, it is easier to track capacity on a weekly basis, and use either four or five full weeks for individual months, depending on where the final month end dates fall, so that all months of the year (except the last) on the capacity report show full-week results for either four or five weeks.

Some companies will reduce the amount of available capacity due to holiday shutdowns, such as Thanksgiving or Christmas. Though these may be legal holidays, production capacity is still available during these periods, and can be used if a company can find any staff willing to work on those days. Consequently, though tradition says that these hours are not available, they can be if a company is willing to force staff to work then, and so they should still be included in the baseline capacity for all utilization measurements.

Once the decision is made to create a capacity utilization analysis, what format should be used to present it? Refer to the capacity report shown in Exhibit 11.4, which lists the utilization hours of 28 plastic injection and blow molding machines. The identification number of each machine is listed down the left column, with the tonnage of each machine noted in the next column. The next cluster of five columns shows the weekly utilization in hours for each machine. The final three columns show the average weekly utilization by machine for the preceding three months. In addition, there are subtotals for all blow molding machines and for five clusters of injection molding machines, grouped by tonnage size.

Machine ID	Machine Description	Run Hrs	Run Hrs	5/9– 5/15 Run Hrs	5/2– 5/8 Run Hrs	Apr. Run Hrs	Mar. Run Hrs	Feb. Run Hrs
							Month of	
B1100/BM04	Blow Mold	150	142	139	132	112	122	104
B2000/BM03	Blow Mold	149	135	137	152	114	154	119
		89%	**82%**	**82%**	**85%**	**67%**	**82%**	**66%**
01-25	25 Ton	123	125	126	132	138	125	111
02-90/TO11	90 Ton	150	158	152	137	117	132	144
03-90/TO10	90 Ton	129	168	164	129	126	111	120
04-90/TO09	90 Ton	75	50	94	138	142	167	147
16-55/AG01	55 Ton	132	168	163	59	125	109	102
		73%	**80%**	**83%**	**71%**	**61%**	**62%**	**61%**
05-150/TO08	150 Ton	141	150	147	162	133	139	133
06-150/TO07	150 Ton	119	130	137	152	122	124	127
07-198/TO06	198 Ton	147	135	133	77	114	132	54
08-200/TO05	200 Ton	110	120	124	141	117	101	113
17-190/TA05	190 Ton	138	141	127	116	97	106	91
		78%	**80%**	**80%**	**77%**	**69%**	**72%**	**62%**
09-300/TO04	300 Ton	168	168	168	133	148	125	148
10-300/TO03	300 Ton	0	50	79	143	135	142	129
11-330/TO02	330 Ton	148	149	129	136	93	125	100
20-390/TA04	390 Ton	110	127	121	158	128	136	154
21-375/C106	375 Ton	92	100	102	84	78	77	102
26-400/TO01	400 Ton	47	85	124	116	101	78	120
		56%	**67%**	**72%**	**76%**	**68%**	**68%**	**75%**
12-500/CI05	500 Ton	91	168	166	137	113	62	50
14-500/CI04	500 Ton	74	85	100	96	107	142	96
18-450/VN02	450 Ton	168	162	163	164	103	111	119
24-500/VN01	500 Ton	125	0	167	163	161	96	106
25-500/TA03	500 Ton	132	139	145	162	146	128	89
		70%	**66%**	**88%**	**86%**	**75%**	**64%**	**55%**
13-700/CI03	700 Ton	168	151	146	142	106	78	60
15-700/VN03	700 Ton	0	153	107	152	133	118	118
19-720/TA02	720 Ton	102	109	115	161	115	58	113
22-700/CI01	700 Ton	111	59	74	154	74	76	144
23-950/TA01	950 Ton	104	168	126	159	110	91	112
		58%	**76%**	**68%**	**91%**	**64%**	**50%**	**65%**
		66%	**74%**	**78%**	**80%**	**71%**	**66%**	**66%**
		68%	**74%**	**78%**	**81%**	**70%**	**67%**	**66%**

Exhibit 11.4 Capacity Utilization Report

This report format allows management to look across the report from left to right and determine any trends in capacity utilization, while also being able to look down the page and determine usage by clusters of machines. This second factor is of extreme importance in the molding business, since each machine is very expensive and must be eliminated if it is not being used to a sufficient degree. For example, look at the tonnage range of 300 to 400 tons, located midway through the report. A cluster of six machines is consistently showing between 68% and 76% percent of usage. Is it possible to eliminate one machine, thereby spreading the work over fewer machines and raising the overall usage percentage for all the machines? To determine the answer using data for the highest utilization reporting period, which is for the first week of May, at 76%, add up all the reported hours of usage for that cluster of machines, which is 770, and divide the total number of hours that the machine cluster has available, assuming that one machine has been removed. The total number of hours available for production will be 168 (which is 7 days multiplied by 24 hours per day) times five machines, which is 840. The result is a utilization of 92% for the maximum amount of work that has appeared in the last quarter of a year. Consequently, the answer is that it is theoretically possible to remove one machine from the 300- to 400-ton range of machines and still be able to complete all work.

However, when using a capacity report to arrive at such conclusions, there are several additional factors to consider. One is the reliability of the machines. If they have a history of failures, then a standard number of hours per operating period for repair work must be factored into the utilization formula, which will reduce the theoretical capacity of the machine. Another problem is that eliminating a machine is usually done in order to realize a cash inflow from sale of the machine—but what if the machines most likely to be sold will only fetch a minor amount in the marketplace? If so, it may make more sense to retain equipment, even if unused, so that it can take on additional work in the event of an increase in sales volume. Yet another issue is that there may be some difficulty in obtaining a sufficient number of staff to maintain or run a machine during all theoretical operating hours. For example, it is common for those organizations with a reduced number of maintenance personnel to cluster those staff on the day shift for maximum efficiency, which means that any machine failure during other hours will result in a shutdown machine until the maintenance staff arrives the next day. Finally, the preceding example shows management taking actual capacity utilization of its machinery to 92%. Is this wise, if management has essentially removed all remaining available capacity by selling off the excess machine? What if an existing customer suddenly increases an order and finds that the company cannot accommodate the work because all machines are booked? Not only lost revenues will result, but maybe even a lost customer.

One way in which a capacity analysis can be skewed is if there are either a large number of small jobs running through a process, each of which requires a small amount of downtime to switch over to the new job, or else a small number of jobs that require a very lengthy changeover process. In either case, the amount of reported capacity will never reach 100%, for the required setup time will take up the amount of capacity that is supposedly available. One action that management can take to alleviate this problem is to work on reducing the changeover time needed to switch to a new job. This typically involves videotaping the changeover process, and then reviewing the tape with the changeover team to identify and implement process alterations that will result in reduced setup times.

A revenue-related problem that arises when setup times eat up a large portion of total capacity is that the sales department may promise customers that work will begin very soon on their orders, because the capacity utilization report appears to reveal that there is lots of excess capacity. When it turns out that excessive changeover times do not leave any time for additional customer orders, it is possible that customers will take their business elsewhere. To counteract this problem, it is necessary to determine the amount of *practical capacity*, which is the total capacity, less the average amount of changeover time. If the setup reduction effort noted in the preceding paragraph is implemented, the practical capacity number will increase, since the time available for production will increase as changeover times go down. Consequently, a review of the practical capacity should be made fairly often to ensure that the correct figure is used.

A problem with using practical capacity as the standard measure of how much work can still be loaded into the production system is that it is based on an average of actual capacity information over several weeks or months. However, if there are one or more jobs scheduled for a changeover that require inordinate amounts of time to complete, the reported practical capacity measure will not reflect reality. Similarly, if the actual changeover times are quite small, the true capacity will be higher than the reported practical capacity. Because practical capacity is a historical average, the actual capacity will be somewhat higher or lower than this average nearly all of the time. Though a company with lots of excess capacity might call this hair-splitting, a company that is running at maximum production levels may find itself blindsided by a lack of available time, or some amount of unplanned downtime. In either case, there is a cost to having inaccurate capacity information. Those companies with well-maintained manufacturing resource planning (MRP II) software can avoid this problem by accurately scheduling jobs and changeover times, and updating the data as soon as changes are made.

BREAKEVEN ANALYSIS

There is usually a very narrow band of pricing and costs within which a company operates in order to earn a profit. If it does not charge a minimum price to cover its fixed and variable costs, it will quickly burn through its cash reserves and go out of business. In a competitive environment, prices drop to the point where they only barely cover costs, and profits are thin or nonexistent. At this point, only those companies with a good understanding of their own breakeven points and those of their competitors are likely to make the correct pricing and cost decisions to remain competitive. This section shows how breakeven (also known as the cost-volume-profit relationship) is calculated, as well as a variety of more complex variations on the basic formula.

The breakeven formula is an exceedingly simple one. To determine a breakeven point, add up all the fixed costs for the company or product being analyzed, and divide it by the associated gross margin percentage. This results in the sales level at which a company will neither lose nor make money—its breakeven point. The formula is:

Total fixed costs/Gross margin percentage = Breakeven sales level

For those who prefer a graphical layout to a mathematical formula, a breakeven chart can be informative. In the sample chart shown in Exhibit 11.5, we show a horizontal line across the chart that represents the fixed costs that must be covered by gross margins, irrespective of the sales level. The fixed cost level will fluctuate over time and in conjunction with extreme changes in sales volume, but we will assume no changes for the purposes of this simplified analysis. Also, there is an upward-sloping line that begins at the left end of the fixed cost line and extends to the right across the chart. This is the

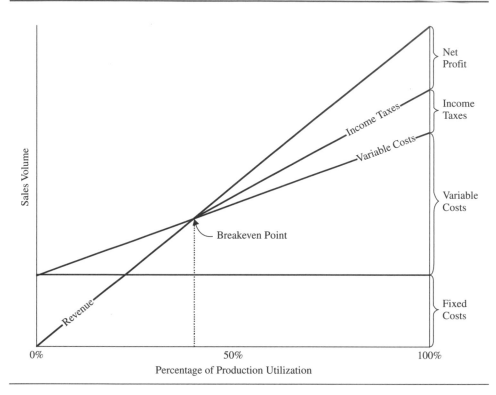

EXHIBIT 11.5   SIMPLIFIED BREAKEVEN CHART

percentage of variable costs, such as direct labor and materials, that are needed to create the product. The last major component of the chart is the sales line, which is based in the lower-left corner of the chart and extends to the upper-right corner. The amount of the sales volume in dollars is noted on the vertical axis, while the amount of production capacity used to create the sales volume is noted across the horizontal axis. Finally, there is a line that extends from the marked breakeven point to the right, and which is always between the sales line and the variable cost line. This represents income tax costs. These are the main components of the breakeven chart.

It is also useful to look between the lines on the graph and understand what the volumes represent. For example, as noted in Exhibit 11.5, the area beneath the fixed costs line is the total fixed cost to be covered by product margins. The area between the fixed cost line and the variable cost line is the total variable cost at different volume levels. The area beneath the income line and above the variable cost line is the income tax expense at various sales levels. Finally, the area beneath the revenue line and above the income tax line is the amount of net profit to be expected at various sales levels.

Though the previous breakeven chart appears quite simplistic, there are additional variables that can make a real-world breakeven analysis a much more complex endeavor to understand. One of these variables is fixed cost. A fixed cost is a misnomer, for any cost can vary over time or outside of a specified set of operating conditions. For example, the overhead costs associated with a team of engineers may be considered a fixed cost if a product line requires continuing improvements and enhancements over

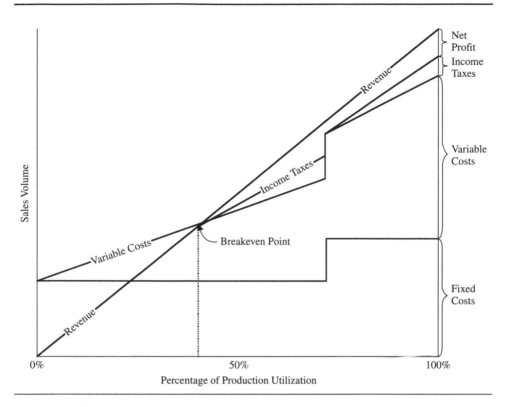

EXHIBIT 11.6   BREAKEVEN CHART INCLUDING IMPACT OF STEP COSTING

time. However, what if management decides to gradually eliminate a product line and milk it for cash flow, rather than keep the features and styling up-to-date? If so, the engineers are no longer needed, and the associated fixed cost goes down. Any situation where management is essentially abandoning a product line in the long term will probably result in a decline in overhead costs.

A much more common alteration in fixed costs is when additional personnel or equipment are needed in order to support an increased level of sales activity. As noted in the breakeven chart in Exhibit 11.6, the fixed cost will step up to a higher level (an occurrence known as step costing) when a certain capacity level is reached. An example of this situation is when a company has maximized the use of a single shift, and must add supervision and other overhead costs such as electricity and natural gas expenses in order to run an additional shift. Another example is when a new facility must be brought on line or an additional machine acquired. Whenever this happens, management must take a close look at the amount of fixed costs that will be incurred, because the net profit level may be less after the fixed costs are added, despite the extra sales volume. In Exhibit 11.6, the maximum amount of profit that a company can attain is at the sales level just *prior to* incurring extra fixed costs, because the increase in fixed costs is so high. Though step costing does not always involve such a large increase in costs as noted in the next exhibit, this is certainly a major point to be aware of when increasing capacity to take on additional sales volume. In short, more sales do not necessarily lead to more profits.

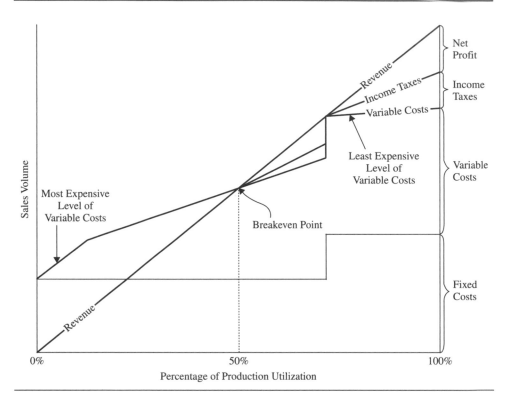

EXHIBIT 11.7   BREAKEVEN CHART INCLUDING IMPACT OF VOLUME PURCHASES

The next variable in the breakeven formula is the variable cost line. Though one would think that the variable cost is a simple percentage that is composed of labor and material costs and never varies, this is not the case. This percentage can vary considerably, and frequently drops as the sales volume increases. The reason for the change is that the purchasing department can cut better deals with suppliers when it orders in larger volumes. In addition, full truckload or railcar deliveries result in lower freight expenses than would be the case if only small quantities were purchased. The result is shown in Exhibit 11.7, where the variable cost percentage is at its highest when sales volume is at its lowest and gradually decreases in concert with an increase in volume.

Because material and freight costs tend to drop as volume increases, it is apparent that profits will increase at an increasing rate as sales volume goes up, though there may be step costing problems at higher capacity levels.

Another point is that the percentage of variable costs will not decline at a steady rate. Instead, and as noted in Exhibit 11.7, there will be specific volume levels at which costs will drop. This is because the purchasing staff can only negotiate price reductions at specific volume points. Once such a price reduction has been achieved, there will not be another opportunity to reduce prices further until a separate and distinct volume level is reached once again.

The changes to fixed costs and variable costs in the breakeven analysis are relatively simple and predictable, but now we come to the final variable, sales volume, which can shift for several reasons, making it the most difficult of the three components to predict.

The first reason why the volume line in the breakeven chart can vary is the mix of products sold. A perfectly straight sales volume line, progressing from the lower-left to the upper-right corners of the chart, assumes that the exact same mix of products will be sold at all volume levels. Unfortunately, it is a rare situation indeed where this happens, since one product is bound to become more popular with customers, resulting in greater sales and variation in the overall product mix. If the margins for the different products being sold are different, then any change in the product mix will result in a variation, either up or down, in the sales volume achieved, which can have either a positive or negative impact on the resulting profits. Since it is very difficult to predict how the mix of products sold will vary at different volume levels, most CFOs do not attempt to alter the mix in their projections, thereby accepting the risk that some variation in mix can occur.

The more common problem that impacts the volume line in the breakeven calculation is that unit prices do not remain the same when volume increases. Instead, a company finds that it can charge a high price early on, when the product is new and competes with few other products in a small niche market. Later, when management decides to go after larger unit volume, unit prices drop in order to secure sales to a larger array of customers, or to resellers who have a choice of competing products to resell. For example, the price of a personal computer used to hover around $3,000, and was affordable for less than 10% of all households. As of this writing, the price of a personal computer has dropped to as little as $400, resulting in more than 50% of all households owning one. Thus, higher volume translates into lower unit prices. The result appears in Exhibit 11.8, where

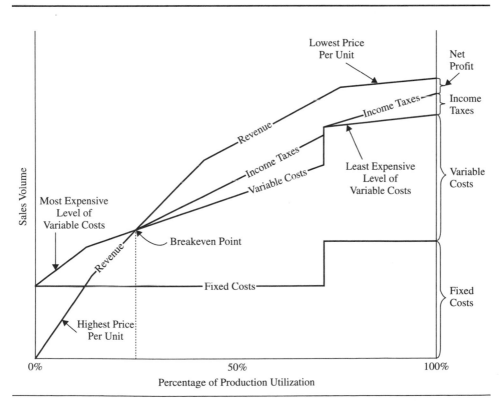

EXHIBIT 11.8 BREAKEVEN CHART INCLUDING IMPACT OF VARIABLE PRICING LEVELS

the revenue per unit gradually declines despite a continuing rise in unit volume, which causes a much slower increase in profits than would be the case if revenues rose in a straight, unaltered line.

The breakeven chart in Exhibit 11.8 may make management think twice before pursuing a high-volume sales strategy, since profits will not necessarily increase. The only way to be sure of the size of price discounts would be to begin negotiations with resellers or to sell the product in test markets at a range of lower prices to determine changes in volume. Otherwise, management is operating in a vacuum of relevant data. Also, in some cases the only way to survive is to keep cutting prices in pursuit of greater volume, since there are no high-priced market niches in which to sell.

The breakeven chart in Exhibit 11.8 is a good example of what the breakeven analysis really looks like in the marketplace. Fixed costs jump at different capacity levels, variable costs decline at various volume levels, and unit prices drop with increases in volume. Given the fluidity of the model, it is reasonable to periodically revisit it in light of continuing changes in the marketplace in order to update assumptions and make better calculations of breakeven points and projected profit levels.

BUSINESS CYCLE FORECASTING

The CFO may become involved in business cycle forecasting, which can be useful for overall corporate budgeting and capacity planning. This section presents a brief overview of what causes business cycles, what information can be used to make estimates of future changes in business cycles, and how this information can be used in a corporate setting.

A business cycle is a recurring series of expansions and contractions, involving and driven by many economic variables, that manifests itself as changes in the level of income, production, and employment. There are a great many theories regarding why the economy goes through these expansions and contractions. In the following bullet points, we briefly note a number of theories that have been raised in the past century regarding the reasons for business cycles. They are:

- *Consumer demand.* One theory states that a rise in consumer demand causes a demand for more production equipment so that manufacturers can meet the demand. Manufacturers then install an excessive amount of equipment, which leads to overcapacity. The manufacturers then cannot produce enough to pay for the new equipment, which causes debt defaults. Banks then tighten their lending policies, which causes a reduction in consumer demand.

- *Inventory expectations.* Another theory states that inventory is at the core of business cycles. Producers build inventories with the expectation of creating new sales volume. The added production increases the number of jobs in the economy, which spins off enough consumer demand to purchase the inventory. Once the inventory levels drop, producers expect more sales, so they hire more people to produce more inventory. Then, when the perception changes that consumers will no longer buy the inventory, producers cut back on production, which reduces the number of jobs, which reduces demand for the inventory.

- *Cost of capacity utilization.* Another theory holds that, as a company enters the late stages of a business expansion, the costs of operating at very high levels of capacity utilization will reduce profits, since the costs of overtime, machine maintenance, and high-demand supplies will rise. Due to the drop in cash flow caused by the reduced profits, businesses will have to curtail their capital spending, which reduces orders in the durable goods industries, which in turn reduces the level of activity in other supporting areas. This eventually cuts the level of activity in the entire economy.

- *Debt accumulation.* Another (and very similar) theory is that companies gradually burden themselves with more and more debt, which they need to build more capacity to fuel additional growth. Eventually, they are unable to pay back the debt, which causes lenders to tighten their credit terms, which in turn reduces lending on new projects until demand catches up with the current level of production capacity.

- *Money supply.* Yet another theory says that a moderate, positive growth rate in the money supply will avoid business contractions, while a reduction in the money supply will bring about a recession or depression. The money supply can be affected by government actions, as well as by the retention, investment, or spending of funds by consumers.

- *Innovation basis.* Another theory states that economic growth is founded upon bursts of innovation, which tends to be sector-specific and has a trickle-down effect on other parts of the economy. There tends to be immense growth within the sectors experiencing innovation, followed by speculation, overexpansion, and consolidation among the strongest remaining companies. Then there are layoffs as a result of the consolidations, and the economy enters a downward phase.

- *Long-term growth.* A final view is that long-term boom periods will eventually end due to a loss of investor prudence (when they assume that the growth period will go on forever), resulting in increasingly poor and risky investments, growing indebtedness, and a loss of liquidity. There will then be a rising tide of debt restructurings and defaults that drives lenders into tighter credit policies, which in turn reduces consumer demand, which causes an economic downturn.

There are two types of variables that cause business cycle changes to occur. The first is an *exogenous variable*. This is a variable that impacts the economic system, though it is not an integral component *of* the system. For example, a bad rainy season will impact the crop yields in the farming community, which in turn reduces the amount of purchases by farmers for the next season's crop, which in turn impacts the activity of the suppliers of those purchases, and so on. Another exogenous variable is a war, which can wreak enough destruction to entirely shatter an economy. These types of variables can, to some extent, be called "acts of God." The other type of variable is the *endogenous variable*. This is a variable that impacts an economic system from within. For example, overcapacity in the resin production industry causes suppliers to reduce their resin prices to plastic molding companies, which in turn can reduce the prices of their products, which creates an increase in sales, and contributes to an increase in the level of economic activity. Other examples of this type include the demand for products and pricing changes.

The typical company operates within a single sector of the economy, where a single major shock, either of the endogenous or exogenous variety, can cause immediate and massive changes, since individual sectors are much smaller than the national economy, and so can be severely impacted by smaller events. For example, an increase in the price of aviation jet fuel will cause the airlines to increase their prices, which reduces the number of seats filled, which drives down airline profits and forces them to postpone orders for new jets, which in turn harms the airline manufacturing companies and *their* supporting groups of suppliers—all due to an increase in the price of jet fuel, which is just a single variable.

Consequently, a CFO may not be overwhelmingly concerned with the operations of the entire national or international economy, since the typical economic contraction only corresponds to a drop in the gross national product of a few percentage points. However, industry-specific changes within that larger economy can be truly catastrophic, and it is within this smaller economic environment that a company operates and must make corresponding strategic and tactical changes.

If a downturn in the business cycle causes a company's sales to decline, management's first reaction is usually to contract the business. One of the first steps taken is to reduce inventories, so the company is not stuck with a large investment of products that will be at risk of becoming obsolete before they can be sold. One way to reduce inventories is to sell it at reduced prices, but this cuts into gross margins and also fills the distribution pipeline, so that no additional sales can be made until the pipeline clears. The more common approach is to reduce the production staff and all related overhead staff with a layoff, the extent of which will be driven by management's perception of the depth of the upcoming cyclical decline. Management will also likely curtail capital expenditures and increase controls over incidental expenses. Further, the CFO will be called upon to tighten credit to customers and heighten collection activities to ensure that accounts receivable do not include any bad debts, and that collections are made as soon as possible. If there are excess funds available, management will likely use them to pay down debt, so that fixed costs are reduced to the bare minimum in anticipation of poor sales conditions at the bottom of the economic cycle.

All of the changes noted here, for either an increase or decrease in the business cycle, call for changes in a company's operations that will certainly have some impact on profits, but even more so on the level of working capital and fixed assets. For example, waiting too long to cut back production will result in an excess investment in inventory, as well as any new capital projects that were not curtailed in time. The reverse problem arises during an economic upswing, when reacting too slowly will result in a cash inflow from the sale of all inventory, followed by the loss of additional profits because *all* of the inventory has been sold, and there is none left to sell. Thus proper management of working capital and fixed assets lies at the heart of management's decisions regarding how to deal with changes in the business cycle.

During business downturns, there will be a few adventurous companies that will buck the industry trend and *expand*. They do this because they anticipate a short downturn in the economy, and they want to pick up new business, either by undercutting competitors or (more commonly) by waiting until financially weaker companies begin to fail, and then buying them. They may also take advantage of lower real estate and equipment costs during these periods to add to their capacity with inexpensive new production facilities. This strategy is only possible if a company has substantial cash reserves or available debt, and has an aggressive management team that is willing to take chances.

When the economy begins to turn in an upward direction, management must make several difficult decisions. The first one is to ramp up existing production capacity, which may have been shuttered and now requires refurbishment before production can begin. Then management must determine the extent to which it wants to rebuild its inventory levels to anticipate renewed sales. This is a critical decision, for overproduction in a weakly rebounding economy will create more inventory than is needed, whereas producing too little in the midst of a strong economic rebound will result in sales being lost to more aggressive competitors. If the rebound is sudden, the company must spend more money on staff overtime and rush equipment deliveries to bring production back up to speed as soon as possible. Credit policies will likely be loosened in order to bring in new business, and management must decide on how much new capital equipment to purchase, and the most appropriate time to acquire it.

Some forecasting knowledge is required of the CFO in order to have sufficient information to make the preceding decisions. In many cases, the CFO purchases forecasts from specialists or relies upon a variety of indicators that are available from the government. Among the more popular indicators are:

- *Consumer Price Index (CPI).* The CPI measures the cost of a broad-ranging basket of goods that would typically be purchased by consumers, and is one of the more closely watched indicators of looming inflationary pressures on the economy. It is issued by the Department of Labor.

- *Gross Domestic Product (GDP).* GDP summarizes the value of all goods and services produced by the United States economy, and as such is the broadest available measure of economic activity. However, because it includes *all* output, it is difficult to translate into a projected measurable impact on a specific industry. It is only issued quarterly, so GDP information is not especially timely. It is issued by the Department of Commerce.

- *Housing Starts.* This is the total number of dwellings on which work has begun. It is a good leading indicator of consumer confidence, since consumers will not initiate construction unless there is reasonable confidence in the future. It is issued by the Census Bureau.

- *Producer Price Index (PPI).* The PPI measures the average change over time in the selling prices received by domestic producers for their output. This is a highly recommended measurement for CFOs to review, because it is an excellent early indicator of pricing changes, is broken down by a multitude of industries, and is easily available on the www.bls.gov/ppi Website. It is issued by the Department of Commerce.

- *Unemployment Rate.* This is the number of unemployed workers divided by the total of both employed and unemployed workers. It is a good indicator of pressures on employers to retain or release employees. It is issued by the Department of Labor.

An excellent Website containing many major economic indicators is www.stats.bls.gov, which is run by the Bureau of Labor Statistics. In most cases, considerable additional statistical information is available on other pages of this Website for most of the statistics listed on its home page.

If the CFO elects to use the services of a forecasting firm, then he or she should be aware of the principal approaches to forecasting that may be used by these firms. There are four primary methods. Since each one is based on different information and may arrive at somewhat different results, it is common for forecasters to blend the results of two or more methods to arrive at their estimates of future conditions. The methods are:

- *Anticipation surveys.* These are surveys of key people in the business community. The purpose of these surveys is to collect information about the intentions of the survey participants to engage in capital purchases, acquisitions, changes in headcount, or any other steps that may impact the economy, and then aggregate this information to arrive at general estimates of trends.

- *Time series models.*   These are trend lines that are based on historical information. For a forecast, one finds the trend line that fits a similar set of previous conditions, and fits it to the current conditions to arrive at a trend line of future expectations. These can be relatively accurate in the short run, but do not generate good results very far into the future.

- *Econometric models.*   These are highly complex and iterative models that simulate the real economy, and are frequently composed of hundreds of variables that interact with each other. These can yield good results over periods longer than those predicted by time series models. However, changes in the results of the models are difficult to explain, given the complexity of the underlying formulas.

- *Cyclical indicators.*   These are the leading, coincident, and lagging indicators that foretell changes in the economy. This method is a good way to confirm the existence of business cycle changes that have been predicted by other forecasting methods. A leading indicator is something that changes in advance of an alteration in a business cycle, such as the number of new business formations, new capital expenditure requests, construction contracts, the length of the average work week, layoff rate, unemployment insurance claims, profit margins, new orders, investments in residential structures, capacity utilization, and new bond or equity issues. These can change anywhere from a few months to over a year in advance of a related change in the phase of the business cycle. A lagging indicator is something that changes after an alteration in the business cycle has occurred, and is used by forecasters to confirm the business cycle change that was indicated by leading indicators. Examples of lagging indicators are investments in nonresidential structures, unit labor costs, and the amount of consumer credit outstanding.

Another item to review is the number of months by which leading indicators presage a change in the business cycle. Though there may be historical justification for using a certain number of months in a forecasting model, these periods can change, sometimes to the extent of having a leading indicator turn into a lagging indicator. Also, the selection process for variables needs to be very in-depth before they are added to a forecasting model. For example, a new variable should be thoroughly researched to determine the extent of its linkage to a business cycle, how well it predicts business cycle behavior, how consistently it does so, and also how frequently information about the variable is reported (so that it can be included in the forecast in a timely manner). Only if all these questions receive favorable answers should a new variable be included in a forecasting model.

For example, let us assume that a CFO of a sport rack company has elected to use the last of the above options for creating forecasting information. Sport racks is a very small niche market that creates and sells racks for skis, snowboards, bicycles, and kayaks that can be attached to the tops of most kinds of automobiles. The CFO wants to derive a forecasting system that will give management an estimate of the amount by which projected sales can be expected to vary. She decides to subdivide the market into four categories, one each for skis, snowboards, bicycles, and kayaks. Based on a historical analysis, she finds that 25% of ski purchasers, 35% of snowboard purchasers, 75% of bicycle purchasers, and 30% of kayak purchasers will purchase a car-top rack system to hold their new equipment. The typical delay in these purchases from the time when they bought their sports equipment to the time they bought sport racks was six months. The CFO finds that she can obtain new sports equipment sales data from industry trade groups every three months. Given the lag time before users purchase car-top racks, this means

Description	Sports Equipment Unit Sales	% Buying Sport Racks	Company Market Share	Forecasted Company Unit Sales	Original Company Forecast	Variance
Ski	3,200,000	25%	40%	320,000	300,000	+ 20,000
Snowboard	2,700,000	35%	40%	378,000	300,000	+ 78,000
Bicycle	2,500,000	75%	30%	562,500	550,000	+ 16,500
Kayak	450,000	30%	30%	40,500	45,000	− 4,500

EXHIBIT 11.9   INDUSTRY-SPECIFIC FORECASTING MODEL

that she can accumulate the underlying data that predicts sport rack sales and disseminate it to management with three months to go before the resulting sport rack sales will occur. Thus, she concludes that this is usable data. The next task is to determine the company's share of the sport rack market, which is readily obtainable from the industry trade group for sport racks, though this information is at least one year old. Given the stability of sales within the industry, she feels that this information is still accurate. She then prepares the report shown in Exhibit 11.9. It shows total sports equipment sales for the last quarter, uses historical percentages to arrive at the amount of resulting sport rack sales, and then factors in the company's market share percentage to determine the forecasted sales of each type of sport rack. By comparing this information to the previously forecasted sales information, the report reveals that the company should significantly ramp up its production of snowboard sport racks as soon as possible.

The example used was for an extremely limited niche market, but it does point out that a modest amount of forecasting work can yield excellent results that are much more company-specific than would be the case if a company relied solely on the forecasts of experts who were only concerned with general national trends. For most companies, there will be a number of additional underlying indicators that should be factored into the forecasting model; however, the work associated with tracking these added data must be compared to the benefit of more accurate results, so that a CFO arrives at a reasonable cost-benefit compromise. The level of precision into which a company can delve to arrive at an outstanding forecasting model can be overwhelming.

SUMMARY

From a practical perspective, the CFO should use capacity analysis regularly. This can involve the monitoring of revenue per person, usage levels of various machines, sales per salesperson, or the need for requested capital purchases. All of these issues involve changes in staffing or machinery, which are exceedingly expensive. Accordingly, the CFO should spend considerable time ensuring that the organization does not spend too much for excess capacity, instead keeping capacity levels at the highest possible level while ensuring that there is some excess capacity available for short-term growth.

Breakeven analysis should be a required part of any proposal to alter the underlying structure of a business. By reviewing it, the CFO can tell if any alterations, such as to price points, capital expenditures, or the incurrence of new expenses, will have a significant impact on the ability of the organization to exceed its breakeven point on a regular basis.

Business cycle forecasting can be the make-or-break analysis tool that gives managers sufficient foreknowledge of market conditions to allow a company to achieve superior performance.

PART 4

FUNDING

CHAPTER 12

CASH MANAGEMENT

Cash management is absolutely crucial to the operation of any but the most wealthy organizations. If there is ever a cash shortfall, payroll cannot be met, suppliers are not paid, scheduled loan payments will not be made, and investors will not receive dividend checks. Any one of these factors can either bring down a business or ensure a change in its management in short order.

In order to avoid these problems, this chapter covers how to construct a cash forecast and automate the creation of some of the information contained within it, as well as how to create a feedback loop for gradually increasing the accuracy of the forecast. We also describe a number of methods for controlling cash flows in order to avoid any shortfalls, how to invest excess funds, and how to use various cash management and natural hedging tools.

CASH FORECASTING MODEL

The core of any cash management system is the cash forecast. It is imperative for the management team to be fully apprised of any cash problems with as much lead time as possible. The sample model shown in Exhibit 12.1 is a good way to provide this information.

The cash forecast in the exhibit lists all cash activity on a weekly basis for the next nine weeks, which is approximately two months. These are followed by a partial month, which is needed in case the month that falls after the first nine weeks is also contained within the nine weeks. In the exhibit, the first week of May is listed, so the remaining three weeks of that month are described within a partial month column. There are also two more full months listed in the last two columns. By using this columnar format, the reader can see the expected cash flows for the next one-third of a year. The final two months on the forecast will tend to be much less accurate than the first two, but are still useful for making estimates about likely cash positions.

The top row on the report in the exhibit lists the date when the cash report was last updated. This is crucial information, for some companies will update this report every day, and the management team does not want to confuse itself with information on old reports. The next row contains the beginning cash balance. The leftmost cell in the row is encircled by heavy lines, indicating that the person responsible for the report should update this cell with the actual cash balance as of the first day of the report. The remaining cells in the row are updated from the ending cash balance for each period that is listed at the bottom of the preceding column. The next block of rows contains the expected receipt dates for sales that have not yet occurred. It is useful to break these down by specific customer and type of sale, rather than summarizing it into a single row, so that the sales staff can be held responsible for this information. The sales staff should

For the Week Beginning on

	11/4/06	11/11/06	11/18/06	11/25/06	12/2/06	12/9/06	12/16/06	12/23/06	12/30/06	Jan-07	Feb-07	Mar-07
Beginning Cash Balance	**$1,037,191**	$1,034,369	$968,336	$967,918	$918,082	$932,850	$918,747	$829,959	$834,924	$754,124	$808,592	$798,554
Receipts from Sales												
Projections:												
Coal Bed Drilling Corp.										$16,937	$174,525	
Oil Patch Kids Corp.								$12,965		$48,521		$28,775
Overfault & Sons Inc.									$2,500		$129,000	
Platte River Drillers									$3,000	$53,000		
Powder River Supplies Inc.									$8,700		$18,500	$14,500
Submersible Drillers Ltd.										$2,500	$16,250	$16,250
Commercial, Various											$25,000	$25,000
Uncollected Invoices:												
Canadian Drillers Ltd.	$1,823		$9,975							$18,510		
Coastal Mudlogging Co.			$6,686									
Dept. of the Interior				$11,629		$2,897						
Drill Tip Repair Corp.				$5,575								

Exhibit 12.1   Cash Forecast

		For the Week Beginning on										
	11/4/06	11/11/06	11/18/06	11/25/06	12/2/06	12/9/06	12/16/06	12/23/06	12/30/06	Jan-07	Feb-07	Mar-07
Overfault & Sons Inc.		$9,229										
Submersible Drillers Ltd.			$4,245									
U.S. Forest Service		$2,967	$812	$8,715								
Cash, Minor Invoices	$2,355	—	$3,668	—	$21,768							
Total Cash In	$4,178	$2,967	$30,370	$30,164	$21,768	$2,897	—	$12,965	$14,200	$139,468	$188,750	$259,050
Cash Out:												
Payroll + Payroll Taxes		$62,000		$65,000			$68,000		$71,000	$71,000	$138,000	$138,000
Commissions				$7,000					$7,000		$8,000	$9,000
Rent			$10,788				$10,788				$10,788	$10,788
Capital Purchases			$10,000			$10,000			$10,000		$10,000	$10,000
Other Expenses	$7,000	$7,000	$10,000	$8,000	$7,000	$7,000	$10,000	$8,000	$7,000	$14,000	$32,000	$32,000
Total Cash Out:	$7,000	$69,000	$30,788	$80,000	$7,000	$17,000	$88,788	$8,000	$95,000	$85,000	$198,788	$199,788
Net Change in Cash	$(2,822)	$(66,033)	$(418)	$(49,836)	$14,768	$(14,103)	$(88,788)	$4,965	$(80,800)	$54,468	$(10,038)	$59,262
Ending Cash:	$1,034,369	$968,336	$967,918	$918,082	$932,850	$918,747	$829,959	$834,924	$754,124	$808,592	$798,554	$857,816
Budgeted Cash Balance:				897,636				833,352		800,439	815,040	857,113

EXHIBIT 12.1 Continued

review this information regularly to see if the timing and amount of each expected cash receipt is still correct.

The next block of rows in the exhibit shows the specific weeks within which accounts receivable are expected to be collected. This section can become large and difficult to maintain if there are many accounts receivable, so it is better to only list the largest items by customer and then lump all others into a minor invoices row, as is the case in the exhibit. The input of the collections staff should be sought when updating these rows, since they will have the best insights into collection problems. The sum of all the rows thus far described is then listed in the "Total Cash In" row.

The next block of rows in the exhibit shows the various uses for cash. A service company is being used in this forecast, so the largest single use of cash is payroll, rather than the cost of goods sold, as would be the case in a manufacturing company. Other key cash outflows, such as monthly commission and rental payments, as well as capital purchases, are shown in the following rows. Being a service business, there are few other expenses, so they are lumped together in an "Other Expenses" row. In this case, cash payments have a slight tendency to be toward the beginning of the month, so the cash flows are adjusted accordingly. If the cost of goods sold had been a major component of the forecast, then it would have either been listed in aggregate and based on a percentage of total sales, or else split into a different cash outflow for each product line. The later case is more useful when the gross margin is significantly different for each product line, and when the sales by product line vary considerably over time.

There are a few other rows that could be added to the model, depending on the type of payments that a company makes. For example, there could be an annual dividend payment, quarterly income tax payment, or monthly principal and interest payments to lenders. These and other items can be added to enhance the basic model, if needed. However, the model requires considerable effort to update, so one should carefully consider the extra workload needed before adding more information requirements to it.

The bottom of the exhibit summarizes the end-of-period cash position, while also comparing it to the budgeted cash balance for the end of each month. The comparison is important, for it tells management if actual results are departing significantly from expectations.

The exhibit assumes a high degree of manual data entry, rather than automation, but it is certainly possible to use additional formulas in the model in order to reduce the work required to update it. For example, an aggregate assumption can be made regarding the days of receivables that are generally outstanding, and then the total amount of cash receipts from existing invoices can be determined based on that assumption. However, if the total amount of accounts receivable is skewed in favor of a few large invoices, any changes in the timing of cash receipts for those few invoices can significantly alter the aggregate assumption for the number of days outstanding. Similarly, a days of inventory assumption is generally acceptable for deriving a cash usage figure for inventory purchases, but this is highly dependent on the ability of the production department to manufacture exactly in accordance with the production schedule, so that actual inventory levels stay near their planned levels, while the purchasing staff buys components only in the quantities itemized by the manufacturing planning system.

MEASURING CASH FORECAST ACCURACY

A cash forecast is useless unless it can be relied on to yield accurate forecasts. There are a number of ways to improve the forecast, all involving the continuing comparison of past forecasts to actual results and correcting the system to ensure that better information is provided for future forecasts.

A key area in which the cash forecast can be wildly incorrect is in receipts from sales forecasts. A detailed review of this area will reveal that some salespersons do not want to forecast any sales, because then they will be held accountable for their predictions. This problem requires constant feedback with the sales staff to correct, and may require reinforcement by including the sales forecasting function in the annual review and compensation plan for them.

Another problem is in the accounts payable area, where actual cash outflows will typically exceed forecast cash outflows. This imbalance is caused by a faulty accounts payable data entry process, whereby invoices are initially mailed by suppliers to people outside of the accounts payable department, or because invoices are sent out for approval before they are logged into the accounting system, thereby resulting in their late appearance in the forecast, usually just before they need to be paid. These problems can be solved by asking suppliers to send invoices straight to the accounting department, and by entering all invoices into the accounting system before sending them out for approval. It is also possible to review open purchase orders to see if there are any missing invoices that are supposed to be currently payable, thereby proactively starting a search for the missing invoices.

A major cash-flow variance will arise if a fixed asset is suddenly purchased that was not included in the cash forecast. This problem is best resolved by giving the accounting staff complete access to the capital budgeting process, so that it can tell what capital requests are in queue for approval and when they are likely to require cash payments to obtain.

In short, the accuracy of the cash forecast requires great attention to processes that provide its source data. The accounting staff should regularly compare forecasted to actual results and work their way back through the underlying systems to determine what issues caused the error—and then correct them.

CASH FORECASTING AUTOMATION

The steps just noted to create a cash forecast can be quite cumbersome to accumulate, especially if there are multiple departments or subsidiaries spread out across many locations. When the cash forecast is generated on a regular basis, the required workload can be extraordinarily high. Automation can be used to avoid some of the most time-consuming steps.

Many off-the-shelf accounting software packages contain standard reports that itemize the daily or weekly time buckets in which payments are scheduled to be made, based on each supplier invoice date and the number of days before they are due for payment, including any requirements for early payment in order to take advantage of early payment discounts. The cash-flow information provided by this report is reliable, but tends to be less accurate for the time period several weeks into the future, because of delays in the entry of supplier invoice information into the accounting system. This delay is usually caused by the divergence of incoming invoices to managers for approval. By first entering the invoice information and *then* sending the invoices out for approval, this time delay can be avoided, thereby improving the accuracy of the automated accounts payable payment timing report.

If there is a well-managed purchase order system in place that is stored in a purchasing database, then the accounts payable report format can be stretched further into the future with some accuracy. Since purchase orders may be issued for some months into the future and involve specific delivery dates, this information can be compiled into a report that reveals when the payments to suppliers based on these purchase orders will be sent out. It is also useful for the purchase of fixed assets, since these orders are so large that suppliers will not normally process an order in the absence of a signed purchase order. However, a large asset purchase may require an up-front payment that will not become apparent until the purchase order is entered into the accounting system, which will result in the sudden appearance of a large cash requirement on the report in the near future.

There are some instances where invoice payments can be predicted for well into the future even in the absence of a purchase order. These are typically recurring payments in a constant amount, such as facility lease payments or maintenance payments that are prespecified under a long-term contract. If these payments are listed in the accounts payable system as recurring invoices, then the accounts payable payment timing report will include them.

The same report is available in many accounting software packages for accounts receivable, itemizing the day or week buckets in which invoice payments are scheduled to be received, based on their original issuance dates and the number of days before customers are required to pay for them. However, this report tends to be much less accurate, for any overdue invoice payments are scheduled for immediate payment in the current period, when in fact there may be collection problems that will delay receipt for quite some time. Also, the report does not account for the average delay in payments that varies by each customer, in accordance with each one's timeliness in making payments. Consequently, this report should be manually modified, especially for the largest outstanding invoices, to reflect the accounting staff's best estimates of when payments will actually be received.

In a few cases, software packages will also extend current payroll payments into the future by assuming that the existing salaries for current employees will continue at the same rates, and that hourly employees will be paid for a regular workweek for all future reporting periods. This is not a viable option for those companies that outsource their payroll, since the in-house software will not have any way to predict cash flows if it does not contain any information about payroll.

The preceding discussion shows that there are numerous ways in which elements of the cash forecast can be automated. However, there are so many variables, such as uncertain receipt dates for accounts receivable, changes in payroll levels, and the sudden purchase of fixed assets, that any automatically generated reports should be adjusted by the accounting staff's knowledge of special situations that will throw off the results of the reports. Also, the basis for automated reports is primarily very short-term accounts receivable and payable information that will rapidly become inaccurate for periods much greater than a month, so manual adjustments to the cash forecast will become increasingly necessary for later time periods.

CASH MANAGEMENT CONTROLS

Once a cash forecasting system is in place, one can tell if there will be cash-flow difficulties coming up in the short term and take steps to ensure that the problems are minimized. In this section, we look at a variety of methods for controlling the flow of cash, which involve not only a speeding up of the cash-handling process, but also an increased focus on reducing a company's cash requirements in all operational areas. The specific items are:

- *Avoid early payments.*   Though it seems obvious, the accounts payable department will pay suppliers early from time to time. This can occur because the accounting staff has already input a default payment interval into the accounting computer, and is not regularly reviewing supplier invoices to see if the payment terms have changed. It is also possible that only a few check runs are being printed per month, which results in some invoices being paid slightly early, simply because the next check run is not scheduled for some time; this can be avoided through the use of either more check runs or the implementation of a policy to only pay on or after the payment due date, thereby shifting these checks to a later check run.

- *Avoid engineering design changes.*   If minor modifications are allowed to be made to products currently in production, this probably means that some parts that were included in the old design will no longer fit in the new design. Unless great care is taken to use up all of the old parts prior to switching to the modified product, there will be a gradual buildup of parts in the warehouse that can no longer be used, thereby increasing the company's investment in raw materials inventory. For this reason, the value received from design changes must be clearly proven to outweigh their added inventory cost.

- *Avoid stuffing the distribution pipeline.*   One way to manufacture abnormally high sales is to offer especially good deals to one's customers, thereby dumping on them an excessive quantity of goods. However, doing so will eventually backfire on the company, since customers will not need to purchase from the company again for some time, resulting in reduced future sales. For the purposes of this discussion, the issue is particularly important if the deal offered to customers is delayed payment in exchange for their accepting goods immediately. By doing so, a company greatly increases the amount of cash that is needed to fund a much larger accounts receivable balance.

- *Conduct a prompt bank reconciliation.*   The management team can find itself scrambling for cash if the bank's and the company's cash records diverge significantly, due to delays in completing a bank reconciliation. To avoid this, it is possible to conduct a bank reconciliation every day through an on-line connection to the bank's database, or at least by immediately completing the reconciliation as soon as the report is received from the bank.

- *Eliminate excess checking accounts.*   Most checking accounts do not earn interest on the funds stored within them, so the presence of more than one account means that an excess volume of cash is being spread out in too many accounts. By evaluating the need for each checking account and consolidating as many as possible, one can reduce the amount of unused cash in the system. For a further refinement to this approach, see the later comment in this section about zero balance accounts.

- *Eliminate invoicing errors.*   An invoicing error of any type can result in a greatly delayed customer payment, while the problem is identified and corrected. To avoid this problem, the accounting department should keep a log of all errors encountered and assign a task force to the chore of altering the invoicing process in order to eliminate the errors in the future.

- *Improve sales forecast accuracy.*   If the forecasts on which the production schedule is based are inaccurate, then there is a strong chance that there will be some production overages, which will result in excess inventory that must be funded for a long time until the inventory can be sold off. This forecasting error can be improved on by obtaining direct access to the forecasts of the company's customers so that the production scheduling staff can see exactly what the demand levels are likely to be. It is also possible to switch to a just-in-time (JIT) manufacturing system, where the focus is on producing to order, rather than to a forecast (though by no means always achievable). At a minimum, one should compare sales forecasts to historical sales records at both the customer and product level to see if the forecasts have any basis in historical fact and investigate those with the greatest variances.

- *Install lockboxes.*   Most banks offer the service of opening one's mail, extracting customer payments, and depositing them directly into one's account, which can shave anywhere from one to three days off the transit time required to move cash into one's account. The savings is especially great if lockboxes are distributed throughout the country, so that customers are directed to send their payments to those lockboxes located nearest to them. This requires the company to contact all customers and request them to shift their payments to the lockbox address, which will be a post office box number. In exchange for this service, the bank will charge a small monthly service fee, plus a fee for each check processed. During the processing of cash, the bank will photocopy each incoming check and mail it to the company, so that the accounts receivable staff can record the cash receipt in the accounting computer system.

- *Install zero balance accounts.*   The concentration of all available cash can be heightened not only through the use of lockboxes, but also by keeping the resulting cash in investment accounts and then shifting the cash automatically to the checking accounts only when checks are drawn against them. This type of checking account is called a zero balance account. It can also be used for a payroll account.

- *Lengthen supplier payment terms.*   If a few key suppliers have required the company to pay on very short terms, then this can greatly reduce the amount of cash that a company has available. The purchasing staff should be asked to negotiate with these suppliers to lengthen terms, perhaps at the cost of committing to larger purchasing volumes or slightly higher prices. When this change takes place, the purchasing staff must notify the accounting department, or else it will continue to pay on the original shorter terms, which are already listed in the accounts payable system and will automatically be used for all future payments unless manually changed.

- *Outsource cash-intensive functions.*   Some activities, such as computer services, require considerable investments in capital equipment. To avoid this expenditure, those departments can be outsourced to a supplier, thereby not only avoiding additional asset investments, but also allowing the company to sell off any existing assets, perhaps to the supplier that takes over the function. This tends to be a longer-term solution, since shifting any function outside a company requires a great deal of transitional planning.

- *Reduce purchasing overages.*   An overly efficient purchasing department can buy greater quantities of items than are strictly needed in the short term, on the grounds that it does not want to issue a number of purchase orders for small quantities when a single order would have sufficed, thereby saving it a great deal of personnel time. These large purchases can lead to a considerable excess use of cash. A good way to avoid this problem is to invest in a materials management system, such as material requirements planning (MRP), under which the system specifies exactly what materials to buy and can even issue the required purchase orders. The purchasing staff can also be evaluated based on the number of raw material inventory turns, which will focus them away from making unnecessarily large purchases.

- *Sell fixed assets.* The accounting department should regularly review the complete list of fixed assets to see if there are any that are no longer in use, and so can be sold. Though this task should be left up to the department mangers, cash conservation is not one of their primary tasks, and so they tend to ignore old assets. One way around this performance problem is to measure department managers based on their return on assets; by doing so, they will constantly work to reduce the asset base for which they are responsible, which will lead to the increased conversion of old assets into cash.

- *Sell obsolete inventory.* The accounting staff should create a report that shows which inventory items have not been used recently, or which items are in such excessive quantities that they will not be drawn down for a long time. With this information, the purchasing department can contact suppliers to sell back the inventory or obtain credits against future purchases. If neither approach will work, the company may still be able to obtain a tax deduction by donating the inventory to a nonprofit organization.

- *Tighten customer credit.* If the accounts receivable balance appears to be disproportionately high or if the proportion of overdue accounts receivable is excessive, then reduce the amount of credit extended to selected customers. However, this can interfere with the corporate growth rate if the strategy involves increasing sales through the use of easy credit.

- *Tighten the process flow that results in cash.* The entire process of taking a customer order, building the product, delivering it, sending an invoice, and receiving payment can be an extraordinarily involved and lengthy one. If it is handled improperly, the inflow of cash once a customer order has been received will be greatly delayed. In order to avoid this problem, one should periodically reexamine the entire process with the objective of minimizing the time required to receive cash at the end of the process. For example, one can avoid queue times when orders are waiting in the in-boxes of employees by concentrating as many steps in the hands of one employee as possible (called process centering). Another possibility is to replace portions of the existing system with new technology, such as the use of lockboxes to accelerate the receipt of cash, or the use of a centralized ordering database that tracks the flow of orders through the system. (For information about tightening the process, refer to *Just-in-Time Accounting*, 2nd Edition by Steven M. Bragg (John Wiley & Sons, 2001).

- *Use a manufacturing planning system.* Any production planning system will greatly streamline the flow of materials through a manufacturing facility. Accordingly, any company engaged in production should invest in a material requirements planning (MRP), manufacturing resources planning (MRP II), or JIT system. Though all have differing underlying concepts and methods of operation, they will all result in reduced inventory levels. When properly installed, the JIT system is particularly effective in achieving this result.

- *Verify times when cash discounts are applicable.* Though it is standard practice to always take discounts in exchange for early payments to suppliers whenever

If Paid On:	1/10, N/30	2/10, N 30
Day 10	0%	0%
Day 20	36.9%	73.8%
Day 30	18.5%	36.9%
Day 40	12.3%	24.6%

Source: Reprinted with permission from p. 121 of *Accounting and Finance for Your Small Business,* 2nd Edition by Burton and Bragg (John Wiley & Sons, 2006).

Exhibit 12.2   Annual Interest Cost of Not Taking a Cash Discount

they are offered, one should verify that the discounts taken are worth their cost. As noted in Exhibit 12.2, there are situations where it does not make sense to take the discount. For example, the second column of the exhibit shows that an invoice paid on regular terms of 30 days, rather than at a discount of 1% after 10 days have passed, will have a net annualized interest cost to the company of 18.5%. We derive the 18% figure from the 1% interest cost that the company is incurring to wait an extra 20 days to make a payment; since there are roughly 18 20-day periods in a year, the annualized interest rate is about 18 times 1%, or 18%. To take the example a step further, if cash is in such short supply that the company cannot pay for the early discount, and in fact can only pay after 40 days have passed, its cost of funds will have dropped to 12.3%, which may be quite close to its existing cost of funds, and so it may appear to be a reasonable alternative to paying early.

A key issue in the preceding bullet points is that the opportunity to manage cash lies in all areas of a company, including the finance, accounting, production, sales, distribution, and engineering departments. Thus, the management of cash should not be considered the sole responsibility of the finance and accounting departments.

CASH MANAGEMENT SYSTEMS

Companies operating on an international scale frequently have trouble reconciling the need for efficient banking operations with the use of local banking partners with whom they may have long-standing relationships and valuable business contacts. The solution is the bank overlay structure.

A bank overlay structure consists of two layers. The lower layer is comprised of all in-country banks that are used for local cash transaction requirements. The higher layer is a group of regional banks, or even a single global bank, that maintains a separate bank account for each country or legal entity of the corporate structure. Cash balances in the lower layer of banks are zero-balanced into the corresponding accounts in the higher layer of banks on a daily basis (where possible, subject to cash flow restrictions). This approach allows funds to be consolidated on either a regional or global basis for greater visibility of cash positions, as well as for centralized management of cash flows.

FOREIGN EXCHANGE WITH THE CONTINUOUS LINK SETTLEMENT SYSTEM

Foreign exchange settlement has been a prolonged affair in which there is significant risk of one party defaulting before a transaction has been completed. To avoid this risk while also speeding up the settlement process, a number of major banks banded together to create the Continuous Link Settlement (CLS) system, which is operated by CLS Bank (of which the founding banks are shareholders). In essence, member banks submit foreign exchange transactions to CLS Bank, which matches up both sides of each transaction during a five-hour period (which represents the overlapping business hours of the participating settlement systems). If the exact settlement criteria are not met for each side of the trade during this time period, then no funds are exchanged.

How does CLS impact the corporation? It gives the cash manager exact information about the availability of funds in various currencies that had previously been difficult to predict with precision. With foreign exchange information, they can now optimize their short-term investment strategies.

Some of the better-known members of CLS Bank are Bank of America, CitiBank, Goldman Sachs, JP Morgan Chase, Mellon Bank, Morgan Stanley, and State Street Bank and Trust. Other banks can submit their foreign exchange transactions through these member banks, so access to the CLS system is quite broad.

NATURAL HEDGING TECHNIQUES

When a company engages in transactions that involve another currency, it incurs a transaction risk that currency fluctuations will adversely impact its cash flows. They frequently purchase derivatives to hedge against these transaction risks. However, some organizations are reluctant to follow this path, because (1) derivatives can be expensive, and (2) FAS Statement 133 requires a company to charge fluctuations in the value of a derivative to the current reporting period if it cannot prove that the derivative effectively hedges an exposure. The latter issue also requires a considerable amount of documentation work.

To avoid the use of derivatives, some companies have centralized their treasury operations, which gives the treasurer sufficient information about company-wide transaction flows to determine where transactions can offset each other. This information allows treasurers to create natural hedges, which require no FAS 133 documentation and are free. When using natural hedges, there will still be some residual exposure if revenues and costs do not exactly offset each other, but the remaining exposure is greatly reduced.

This technique is only possible if treasury operations are centralized or if the information needed to construct natural hedges can be obtained by other means, such as through a data warehouse that accumulates information from multiple sources.

SUMMARY

The cash management function is an important one that deserves the utmost attention from the CFO, since a cash shortfall can bring a company's operations to an abrupt halt in short order. The cash management process is based on a foundation of detailed and ongoing cash forecasting, which should be regularly compared to actual results in order to review and improve the accuracy of the overall process. Only by doing so can a company predict the amount and timing of cash problems and work to correct them in a timely manner.

CHAPTER 13

INVESTING EXCESS FUNDS

In most companies, surplus funds not needed for either operating purposes or compensating bank balances are available for investment. Prudent use of these funds can add to income, though the CFO must consider a range of investment criteria before selecting the appropriate investment vehicle. This chapter describes the major investment criteria, investment restrictions, and a variety of commonly used investment options.

INVESTMENT CRITERIA*

When considering various forms of cash investment, one should first consider the *safety of the principal* being invested. It would not do to invest company funds in a risky investment in order to earn extraordinarily high returns if there is a chance that any portion of the principal will be lost. Accordingly, a company policy should be approved by the Board of Directors that limits investments to a specific set of low-risk investment types. Also, some consideration should be given to the *maturity* and *marketability* of an investment. For example, if an investment in a block of apartment houses appears to generate a reasonably risk-free return and a good rate of return, it is still a poor investment from a cash management perspective, because the investment probably cannot be converted to cash on short notice. Accordingly, it is best to only make investments where there is a robust market available for their immediate resale. The final consideration when making an investment is its *yield*—and this is truly the last consideration after the previous items have already been reviewed. Within the boundaries of appropriate levels of risk, maturity, and marketability, one can then pick the investment with the highest yield. Since these criteria tend to limit one to very low-risk investments, the yield will be quite low. Nonetheless, it is still a better investment than leaving the cash in a checking account.

The investment criteria for a company that finds itself in a rapid growth situation are more circumscribed. It typically burns through its cash reserves quite rapidly, so the liquidity of its investments must be extremely high in order to allow rapid access to it. Unfortunately, high liquidity is commonly associated with low investment returns, so the CFO is forced to invest in low-yield investments. In addition, the company cannot run the risk of loss on its investments, because it is critically important to keep cash available to feed the company's growth engine. Since risk is also associated with return, the CFO must, once again, favor low-yield investments for minimal risk.

---

* Adapted with permission from pp. 538–540 of *Ultimate Accountants' Reference* by Bragg (John Wiley & Sons, 2005).

Objective: To invest excess cash in only top-quality short-term investments, for optimum total return, commensurate with corporate liquidity requirements.

Liquidity: Liquidity shall be provided by minimum and maximum limits as follows:

1. At least $80 million shall be invested in the overnight investments and in negotiable marketable obligations of major U.S. issuers.
2. No more than 50% of the total portfolio shall be invested in time deposits or other investments with a lack of liquidity such as commercial paper for which only the dealer and issuer make a market.

Diversification: Diversification shall be provided through a limit on each nongovernment issuer (as listed next). These are general limits, and in each case quality review may result in elimination of a lower limit for the issuer. Overnight or repurchase investments must meet quality criteria but are not subject to limits on the amount invested.

1. U.S. government and agencies—no limit.
2. Domestic bank certificates of deposit, time deposits, and banker's acceptances—$30 million limit for banks with capital accounts in excess of $800 million (top 10 banks); $20 million for banks with capital accounts of $350 to $800 million (second 11 banks); $5 million for all other banks with capital accounts in excess of $250 million (11 banks).
3. U.S. dollar (or fully hedged foreign currency) obligations of foreign banks, each with capital accounts exceeding $500 million—limited to $15 million each for Canadian banks and $10 million each for other foreign banks, subject to an aggregate limit of $75 million for non-Canadian foreign banks.
4. Domestic commercial paper with P-1/A-1 rating only—$20 million limit for issuers with long-term senior debt rating of Aa or better; $10 million for issuers with a debt rating of A; and $10 million for commercial bank holding companies with capital amounts in excess of $500 million, within the overall limit of the flagship bank described in item 2 above.
5. Foreign commercial paper unconditionally guaranteed by a prime U.S. issuer and fully hedged, subject to the guarantor's issuer limit described in item 4 above.
6. Obligations of savings and loan associations, each with capital accounts exceeding $250 million, and limited to $10 million each.

Operating procedure: Payments shall be made only against delivery of a security to a custodian bank. Securities shall be delivered from custody only against payment. Due bills by a bank will be accepted for delivery only under exceptional conditions. No due bills issued by a dealer will be accepted.

Maturity limits: The average maturity of the entire fund shall be limited to an average of two years. The maximum maturity for each category is as follows:

U.S. government	5 years
Municipal obligations	2 years
Bank certificates of deposit	1 year
Banker's acceptances	1 year
Bank time deposits	90 days
Commercial paper	270 days

Source: Adapted with permission from pp. 208–209 of *The Controller's Function* by Roehl-Anderson and Bragg (John Wiley & Sons, 2005).

Exhibit 13.1   Investment Guidelines

INVESTMENT RESTRICTIONS

Sometimes the Board of Directors or the CFO will place restrictions on how funds may be invested. Subjects covered should include maximum levels of investment security, the credit rating of the issuer, and the maximum allowable amount of investment in selected types of securities by issuer, type of instrument, country, and currency. An example of investment guidelines is shown in Exhibit 13.1.

Where the amount of funds invested is significant, the Board of Directors may want to see a summarization of the types of investment vehicles used, as well as the amounts

	Dollars Invested (millions)	Percent of Total
Resales and overnight time deposits	$18.0	10.3%
U.S. banks—U.S. dollar time deposits	$105.2	60.2%
Foreign banks—U.S. dollar certificates of deposit	$24.7	14.1%
U.S. banks—Eurodollar time deposits	$17.5	10.0%
Commercial paper	$9.3	5.4%
Totals	$174.7	100.0%

EXHIBIT 13.2   SAMPLE INVESTMENT REPORT

invested and expected yields on each one. Detailed investments by individual bank are not necessary, just a grouping by category. An example of such a report is shown in Exhibit 13.2.

INVESTMENT OPTIONS

Within the investment boundaries just noted, there are a number of available investment options available. The most common ones that have low risk levels, short maturity dates, and high levels of marketability are:

- *Bonds near maturity dates.*   A corporate bond may not mature for many years, but one can always purchase a bond that is close to its maturity date. There tends to be a minimal risk of loss (or gain) on the principal amount of this investment, since there is a low risk that interest rates will change enough to impact the bond's value in the short time period left before its maturity date. A variation on this type of investment is the municipal bond, for which there is no tax on the interest income; however, in consideration of this reduced liability, its yield also tends to be somewhat lower than on other types of bonds.

- *Certificate of deposit.*   Banks issue these certificates, usually in small-dollar amounts such as $1,000. A CD requires a minimum investment period and carries a rate slightly higher than what is found in a money market account. A CD does not allow one to write checks against it.

- *Commercial paper.*   Larger corporations issue short-term notes that carry higher yields than on government debt issuances. There is also an active secondary market for them, so there is usually no problem with liquidity. As long as one stays with the commercial paper issued by "blue-chip" organizations, there is also little risk of default.

- *Money market fund.*   This is a package of government instruments, usually comprised of Treasury bills, notes, and bonds, that is assembled by a fund management company. The investment is highly liquid, with many investors putting in funds for as little as a day. It is possible to write checks against a money market account, though the number may be limited by the fund operator in order to keep a company from using the fund as their main checking account.

- *Repurchase agreement.*   This is a package of securities that an investor buys from a financial institution, under the agreement that the institution will buy it back at a specific price on a specific date. It is most commonly used for the overnight investment of excess cash from one's checking account, which can be automatically handled by one's bank. The typical interest rate earned on this investment is equal to or less than the money market rate, since the financial institution takes a transaction fee that cuts into the rate earned.

- *U.S. Treasury issuances.* The U.S. government issues a variety of notes with maturity dates that range from less than a year (U.S. Treasury certificates) through several years (notes) to more than five years (bonds). The wide range of maturity dates gives one a broad range of investment options. Also, there is a strong secondary market for these issuances, and so they can be liquidated in short order. U.S. government debts of all types are considered to be risk-free, and so have somewhat lower yields than other forms of investment.

SUMMARY

The proper investment of excess funds is commonly overlooked by the CFO, who frequently delegates this task. However, by doing so she may be missing out on incremental improvements in investment income that can add up to substantial additional profits. Further, lack of attention to this area may result in a subordinate's investments in areas that present a risk of lost funds, or which are not sufficiently liquid to meet a company's short-term cash-flow requirements. Consequently, the CFO should create an investment policy such as the one described in this chapter and then arrange with the internal audit department to verify that actual investment performance matches the guidelines laid out within the policy.

CHAPTER 14

OBTAINING DEBT FINANCING*

A business of any size is likely to require extra funding at some point during its history that exceeds the amount of cash flow that is generated from ongoing operations. This may be caused by a sudden growth spurt that requires a large amount of working capital, an expansion in capacity that calls for the addition of fixed assets, a sudden downturn in the business that requires extra cash to cover overhead costs, or perhaps a seasonal business that requires extra cash during the off-season. Different types of cash shortages will call for different types of funding, of which this chapter will show that there are many types. In the following sections, we will briefly describe each type of financing and the circumstances under which each one can be used, as well as the management of financing issues and bank relations.

MANAGEMENT OF FINANCING ISSUES

The procurement of financing should never be conducted in an unanticipated rush, where the CFO is running around town begging for cash to meet its next cash need. A reasonable degree of planning will make it much easier to not only tell *when* additional cash will be needed, but also *how much*, and what means can be used to obtain it.

To achieve this level of organization, the first step is to construct a cash forecast, which is covered in detail in Chapter 12, Cash Management. With this information in hand, one can determine the approximate amounts of financing that will be needed, as well as the duration of that need. This information is of great value in structuring the correct financing deal. For example, if the company is expanding into a new region and needs working capital for the sales season in that area, then it can plan to apply for a short-term loan, perhaps one that is secured by the accounts receivable and inventory purchased for the store in that region. Alternatively, if the company is planning to expand its production capacity through the purchase of a major new fixed asset, it may do better to negotiate a capital lease for its purchase, thereby only using the new equipment as collateral and leaving all other assets available to serve as collateral for future financing arrangements.

Besides this advanced level of cash-flow planning, a company can engage in all of the following activities in order to more properly control its cash requirements and sources of potential financing:

- *Maximize the amount of loans using the borrowing base.* Loans that use a company's assets as collateral will offer lower interest rates, since the risk to the lender is much reduced. The CFO should be very careful about allowing a lender

---

* Adapted with permission from Chapter 34 of *Ultimate Accountants' Reference* by Bragg (John Wiley & Sons, 2005).

to attach all company assets, especially for a relatively small loan, since this leaves no collateral for use by other lenders. A better approach is to argue a lender into accepting the smallest possible amount of collateral, preferably involving specific assets rather than entire asset categories. The effectiveness of this strategy can be tracked by calculating the percentage of the available borrowing base that has been committed to existing lenders. Also, if the borrowing base has not yet been completely used as collateral, then a useful measurement is to determine the date on which it is likely to be fully collateralized, so that the planning for additional financing after that point will include a likely increase in interest costs.

- *Line up investors and lenders in advance.*   Even if the level of cash planning is sufficient for spotting shortages months in advance, it may take that long to find lenders willing to advance funds. Accordingly, the CFO should engage in a search for lenders or investors as early as possible. If this task is not handled early on, then a company may find itself accepting less favorable terms at the last minute. The effectiveness of this strategy can be quantified by tracking the average interest rate for all forms of financing.

- *Minimize working capital requirements.*   The best form of financing is to eliminate the need for funds internally, so that the financing is never needed. This is best done through the reduction of working capital, as is described later in the sections devoted to accounts receivable, accounts payable, and inventory reduction.

- *Sweep cash accounts.*   If a company has multiple locations and at least one bank account for each location, then it is possible that a considerable amount of money is lingering unused in those accounts. By working with its bank, a CFO can automatically sweep the contents of those accounts into a single account every day, thereby making the best use of all on-hand cash and keeping financing requirements to a minimum.

BANK RELATIONS

Part of the process of obtaining financing involves the proper care and feeding of one's banking officer. Since one of the main sources of financing is the bank with which one does business, it is exceedingly important to keep one's assigned banking officer fully informed of company activities and ongoing financial results. This should involve issuing at least quarterly financial information to the officer, as well as a follow-up call to discuss the results, even if the company is not currently borrowing any funds from the bank. The reasoning behind this approach is that the banking officer needs to become comfortable with the CFO and also gain an understanding of how the company functions.

Besides establishing this personal relationship with the banking officer, it is also important to centralize as many banking functions as possible with the bank, such as checking, payroll, and savings accounts, sweep accounts, zero balance accounts, and all related services, such as lockboxes and on-line banking. By doing so, the bank officer will realize that the company is paying the bank a respectable amount of money in fees, and so is deserving of attention when it asks for assistance with its financing problems.

The CFO should also be aware of the types of performance measurements that bankers will review when they conduct a loan review, so that they can work on improving these measurements in advance. For example, the lender will likely review a company's quick and current ratios, debt/equity ratio, profitability, net working capital, and number of days on hand of accounts receivable, accounts payable, and inventory. The banking officer may be willing to advise a company in advance on what types of measurements it will examine, as well as the preferred minimum amounts of each one. For example, it may require a current ratio of 2:1, a debt/equity ratio of no worse than 40%, and days of inventory of no worse than 70. By obtaining this information, a company can restructure itself prior to a loan application in order to ensure that its application will be approved.

Even by taking all of these steps to ensure the approval of financing, company management needs to be aware that the lender may impose a number of restrictions on the company, such as the ongoing maintenance of minimum performance ratios, the halting of all dividends until the loan is paid off, restrictions on stock buybacks and investments in other entities, and (in particular) the establishment of the lender in a senior position for all company collateral. By being aware of these issues in advance, it is sometimes possible to negotiate with the lender to reduce the amount or duration of some of the restrictions.

In short, a company's banking relationships are extremely important, and must be cultivated with great care. However, this is a two-way street that requires the presence of an understanding banking officer at the lending institution. If the current banking officer is not receptive, then it is quite acceptable to request a new one, or to switch banks in order to establish a better relationship.

CREDIT RATING AGENCIES

The debt of any publicly held company can be rated by either Moody's, Standard & Poor's, Fitch, or Dominion Bond Rating Service, which are credit rating agencies. These four firms are ranked as "nationally recognized statistical rating organizations" (NRSO) by the Securities and Exchange Commission (SEC), and as such are the only entities allowed by the SEC to issue debt ratings.

A credit rating agency's analysts are given a detailed review of the company's financial information and use it to derive a credit score. The scores of any of the four agencies are indicative of the perceived risk of default on the underlying debt, resulting in changing prices for the debt instruments on the open market. Changes in their ratings below "investment grade" can have startling adverse results, since many investment funds are prohibited by internal rules from owning anything with less than an investment grade, and must dump the debt at that point, resulting in massive price drops.

Credit agencies charge an issuing company a fee to rate its new debt, and also have a "relationship pricing" plan under which they charge a company an annual fee to rate virtually all of its bond issues. It is difficult for a public company to get out from under this arrangement, since any debt issuance that carries with it no credit rating at all is by default noninvestment grade, and will therefore have a much higher implicit interest rate, resulting in a lower sale price and fewer debt issuance proceeds flowing to the company. A concern with this payment system is that, because the credit rating agencies are paid by the companies being reviewed, there is an inherent conflict of interest that could result in excessively high credit ratings.

The remaining sections describe different types of financing that a company can potentially obtain, including the reduction of working capital in order to avoid the need for financing.

ACCOUNTS PAYABLE PAYMENT DELAY

Though not considered a standard financing technique, since it involves internal processes, one can deliberately lengthen the time periods over which accounts payable are paid. For example, if a payables balance of $1,000,000 is delayed for an extra month, then the company has just obtained a rolling, interest-free loan for that amount, financed by its suppliers.

Though this approach may initially appear to result in free debt, it has a number of serious repercussions. One is that suppliers will catch on to the delayed payments in short order, and begin to require cash in advance or on delivery for all future payments, which will forcibly tell the company when it has stretched its payments too far. Even if it can stay just inside of the time period when these payment conditions will be imposed, suppliers will begin to accord the company a lesser degree of priority in shipments, given its payment treatment of them, and may also increase their prices to it in order to offset the cost of the funds that they are informally extending to the company. Also, if suppliers are reporting payment information to a credit reporting bureau, the late payments will be posted for all to see, which may give new company suppliers reason to cut back on any open credit that they would otherwise grant it.

A further consideration that argues against this practice is that suppliers who are not paid will send the company copies of invoices that are overdue. These invoices may very well find their way into the payment process and be paid alongside the original invoice copies (unless there are controls in place that watch for duplicate invoice numbers or amounts). As a result, the company will pay multiple times for the same invoice.

Another concern is that any early payment discounts that a company could have obtained will be lost by following this late payment strategy. However, it is likely that a company finding itself in difficult cash-flow circumstances would have already skipped these early payments. Also, there are usually not many suppliers who offer discounts, so this would comprise only a small portion of accounts payable.

The only situation in which this approach is a valid one is when the purchasing staff contacts suppliers and negotiates longer payment terms, perhaps in exchange for higher prices or larger purchasing volumes. If this can be done, then the other problems just noted will no longer be issues.

Thus, unless payment delays are formally negotiated with suppliers, the best use of this financing option is for those organizations with no valid financing alternatives, who essentially are reduced to the option of irritating their suppliers or going out of business.

ACCOUNTS RECEIVABLE COLLECTION ACCELERATION

A great deal of corporate cash can be tied up in accounts receivable, for a variety of reasons. A company may have injudiciously expanded its revenues by reducing its credit restrictions on new customers, or it may have extended too much credit to an existing customer that has no way of repaying it in the short term, or it has sold products during the off-season by promising customers lengthy payment terms, or perhaps it is in an industry where the customary repayment period is quite long. Given the extent of the problem, a company can rapidly find itself in need of extra financing in order to support the amount of unpaid receivables.

This problem can be dealt with in a number of ways. One approach is to offer customers a credit card payment option, which accelerates payments down to just a few days. Another alternative is to review the financing cost and increased bad debt levels associated with the extension of credit to high-risk customers, and eliminate those customers who are not worth the trouble. A third alternative is to increase the intensity with which the collections function is operated by using automated dunning letter (and fax) generation software, collections software that interacts with the accounts receivable files, and ensuring that enough personnel are assigned to the collections task. Finally, it may be possible to reduce the number of days in the standard payment terms, though this can be a problem for existing customers who are used to longer payment terms.

The reduction of accounts receivable should be considered one of the best forms of financing available, since it requires the acquisition of no debt from an outside source.

CREDIT CARDS

A large company certainly cannot rely on credit cards as a source of long-term financing, since they are liable to be cancelled by the issuing bank at any time, nor are they inexpensive, because credit card rates consistently approach the legal interest limits in each state. Furthermore, they may require someone's personal guarantee. Nonetheless, the business literature occasionally describes accounts by small business owners who have used a large number of credit cards to finance the beginnings of their businesses, sometimes using cash advances from one card to pay off the minimum required payment amounts on other cards. Given the cost of these cards and the small amount of financing typically available through them, this is not a financing method that is recommended for any but the most risk-tolerant and cash-hungry businesses.

DIRECT ACCESS NOTES

An interesting financing option is to issue bonds to retail investors through brokers, rather than issuing to institutional investors. These bonds are called Direct Access Notes (DANs). This is an alternative source of funding that can be useful in tight credit markets. It is also a good long-term funding source, since bond durations can extend to 30 years. Furthermore, because offerings are usually relatively small and on a frequent basis, they are useful for companies wanting to fine-tune their cash and debt balances. Finally, holders do not usually flip their DAN holdings, preferring instead to hold them for the long term.

A DAN is usually sold in $1,000 increments, at par. They are attractive to investors, because they feature a survivor's option under which the notes can be put back to the issuer at par in the event of the holder's death; this eliminates any market risk caused by changes in interest rates.

A number of well-known organizations now issue DANs, including United Parcel Service, John Hancock Life Insurance, the Tennessee Valley Authority, Caterpillar Financial Services, and the City of Chicago.

The primary broker of DANs is LaSalle ABN AMRO, which runs an informative web site on the topic at www.directnotes.com.

EMPLOYEE TRADE-OFFS

In rare cases, it is possible to trade off employee pay cuts in exchange for grants of stock or a share in company profits. However, a company in severe financial straits is unlikely to be able to convince employees to switch from the certainty of a paycheck to the uncertainty of capital gains or a share in profits from a company that is not performing well. If this type of change is forced on employees, then it is much more likely that the best employees will leave the organization in search of higher compensation elsewhere. Another shortfall of this approach is that a significant distribution of stock to employees may result in employees (or their representatives) sitting on the Board of Directors. In short, this option is not recommended as a viable form of financing.

FACTORING

Under a factoring arrangement, a finance company agrees to take over a company's accounts receivable collections and keep the money from those collections in exchange for an immediate cash payment to the company. This process typically involves having customers mail their payments to a lockbox that appears to be operated by the company, but which is actually controlled by the finance company. Under a true factoring arrangement, the finance company takes over the risk of loss on any bad debts, though it will have the right to pick which types of receivables it will accept in order to reduce its risk of loss. A finance company is more interested in this type of deal when the size of each receivable is fairly large, since this reduces its per-transaction cost of collection. If each receivable is quite small, the finance company may still be interested in a factoring arrangement, but it will charge the company extra for its increased processing work. The lender will charge an interest rate (at least 2% higher than the prime rate), as well as a transaction fee for processing each invoice as it is received. There may also be a minimum total fee charged, in order to cover the origination fee for the factoring arrangement in the event that few receivables are actually handed to the lender. A company working under this arrangement can be paid by the factor at once, or can wait until the invoice due date before payment is sent. The later arrangement reduces the interest expense that a company would have to pay the factor, but tends to go against the reason why the factoring arrangement was established, which is to get money back to the company as rapidly as possible. An added advantage is that no collections staff is required, since the lender handles this chore.

A similar arrangement is accounts receivable financing, under which a lender uses the accounts receivable as collateral for a loan and takes direct receipt of payments from customers rather than waiting for periodic loan payments from the company. A lender will typically only loan a maximum of 80% of the accounts receivable balance to a company, and only against those accounts that are less than 90 days old. Also, if an invoice against which a loan has been made is not paid within the required 90-day time period, then the lender will require the company to pay back the loan associated with that invoice.

Though both variations on the factoring concept will accelerate a company's cash flow dramatically, it is an expensive financing option, and so is not considered a viable long-term approach to funding a company's operations. It is better for short-term growth situations where money is in short supply to fund a sudden need for working capital. Also, a company's business partners may look askance at such an arrangement, since it is an approach associated with organizations that have severe cash-flow problems.

FIELD WAREHOUSE FINANCING

Under a field warehousing arrangement, a finance company (usually one that specializes in this type of arrangement) will segregate a portion of a company's warehouse area with a fence. All inventory within it is collateral for a loan from the finance company to the company. The finance company will pay for more raw materials as they are needed, and is paid back directly from accounts receivable as soon as customer payments are received. If a strict inventory control system is in place, the finance company will also employ someone who will record all additions to and withdrawals from the secured warehouse. If not, then the company will be required to frequently count all items within the secure area and report this information back to the finance company. If the level of inventory drops below the amount of the loan, then the company must pay back the finance company the difference between the outstanding loan amount and the total inventory valuation. The company is also required under state lien laws to post signs around the secured area, stating that a lien is in place on its contents.

Field warehousing is highly transaction intensive, especially when the finance company employs an on-site warehouse clerk, and so is a very expensive way to obtain funds. This approach is only recommended for those companies that have exhausted all other less-expensive forms of financing. However, lenders typically do not require any covenants in association with these loans, giving corporate management more control over company operations.

FLOOR PLANNING

Some lenders will directly pay for large assets that are being procured by a distributor or retailer (such as kitchen appliances or automobiles) and be paid back when the assets are sold to a consumer. In order to protect itself, the lender may require that the price of all assets sold be no lower than the price the lender originally paid for it on behalf of the distributor or retailer. Since the lender's basis for lending is strictly on the underlying collateral (as opposed to its faith in a business plan or general corporate cash flows), it will undertake frequent recounts of the assets and compare them to its list of assets originally purchased for the distributor or retailer. If there is a shortfall in the expected number of assets, the lender will require payment for the missing items. The lender may also require liquidation of the loan after a specific time period, especially if the underlying assets run the risk of becoming outdated in the near term.

This financing option is a good one for smaller or underfunded distributors or retailers, since the interest rate is not excessive (due to the presence of collateral).

INVENTORY REDUCTION

A terrific drain on cash is the amount of inventory kept on hand. The best way to reduce it, and therefore shrink the amount of financing needed, is to install a manufacturing planning system, for which many software packages are available. The most basic is the material requirements planning system (MRP), which multiplies the quantities planned for future production by the individual components required for each product to be created, resulting in a schedule of material quantities to be purchased. In its most advanced form, MRP can schedule component deliveries from suppliers down to a time frame of just a few hours on specific dates. If its shop floor planning component is installed, it can also control the flow of materials through the work-in-process (WIP) area, which reduces WIP inventory levels by avoiding the accumulation of partially completed products at bottleneck operations. Understandably, such a system can make great inroads into a company's existing inventory stocks. A more advanced system, called manufacturing resources planning (MRP II) adds the capabilities of capacity and labor planning, but does not have a direct impact on inventory levels.

The just-in-time (JIT) manufacturing system blends a number of requirements to nearly eliminate inventory. It focuses on short equipment setup times, which therefore justifies the use of very short production runs, which in turn keeps excessive amounts of inventory from being created through the use of *long* production runs. In addition, the system requires that suppliers make small and frequent deliveries of raw materials, preferably bypassing the receiving area and taking them straight to the production workstations where they are needed. Furthermore, the production floor is rearranged into work cells, so that a single worker can walk a single unit of production through several production steps, which not only prevents WIP from building up between workstations, but also ensures that quality levels are higher, thereby cutting the cost of scrapped products. The key result of this system is a manufacturing process with very high inventory turnover levels.

The use of inventory planning systems to reduce inventory levels and hence financing requirements is an excellent choice for those organizations already suffering from a large investment in inventory, and which have the money and the time to install such a system. The use of MRP, MRP II, and JIT will not be of much help in alleviating short-term cash-flow problems, since they can require the better part of a year to implement and several more years to fine-tune.

LEASE

A lease covers the purchase of a specific asset, which is usually paid for by the lease provider on the company's behalf. In exchange, the company pays a fixed rate, which includes interest and principal, to the leasing company. It may also be charged for personal property taxes on the asset purchased. The lease may be defined as an *operating lease*, under the terms of which the lessor carries the asset on its books and records a depreciation expense, while the lessee records the lease payments as an expense on its books. This type of lease typically does not cover the full life of the asset, nor does the buyer have a small-dollar buyout option at the end of the lease. The reverse situation arises for a *capital lease*, where the lessee records it as an asset and is entitled to record all related depreciation as an expense. In the latter case, the lease payments are split into their interest and principal portions and recorded on the lessee's books as such.

The cost of a lease can be reduced by clumping together the purchases of multiple items under one lease, which greatly reduces the paperwork cost of the lender. If there are multiple leases currently in existence, they can be paid off and released through a larger single lease, thereby obtaining a lower financing cost.

The leasing option is most useful for those companies that only want to establish collateral agreements for specific assets, thereby leaving their remaining assets available as a borrowing base for other loans. Leases can be arranged for all but the most financially shaky companies, since lenders can always use the underlying assets as collateral, and rarely impose any other financing restrictions. Also, there is no issue with disposing of unneeded equipment at the end of a lease, since this is handled by the lender. Furthermore, future operating lease payments are not listed on the balance sheet as a liability.

However, unscrupulous lenders can hide or obscure the interest rate charged on leases so that less financially knowledgeable companies will pay exorbitant rates. Also, a company is obligated to make all payments through the end of a lease term, even if it no longer needs the equipment being leased.

LINE OF CREDIT

A line of credit is a commitment from a lender to pay a company whenever it needs cash, up to a present maximum level. It is generally secured by company assets, and for that reason bears an interest rate not far above the prime rate. The bank will typically charge an annual maintenance fee, irrespective of the amount of funds drawn down on the loan, on the grounds that it has invested in the completion of paperwork for the loan. The bank will also likely require an annual audit of key accounts and asset balances to verify that the company's financial situation is in line with the bank's assumptions. One problem with a line of credit is that the bank can cancel the line or refuse to allow extra funds to be drawn down from it if the bank feels that the company is no longer a good credit risk. Another issue is that the bank may require a company to maintain a compensating balance in an account at the bank; this increases the effective interest rate on the line of credit, since the company earns no interest on the funds stored at the bank.

The line of credit is most useful for situations where there may be only short-term cash shortfalls or seasonal needs that result in the line being drawn down to zero at some point during the year. If one's cash requirements are expected to be longer term, then a term note or bond is a more appropriate form of financing.

LOANS

Asset Based.   A loan that uses fixed assets or inventory as its collateral is a common form of financing by banks. Loans may also be issued that are based on other forms of collateral, such as the cash surrender value of life insurance, securities, or real estate. The bank will use the resale value of fixed assets (as determined through an annual appraisal) and/or inventory to determine the maximum amount of available funds for a loan. If inventory is used as the basis for the loan, a prudent lender will typically not lend more than 50% of the value of the raw materials and 80% of the value of the finished goods, on the grounds that it may have to sell the inventory in the event of a foreclosure and may not obtain full prices at the time of sale. Lenders will be much less likely to accept inventory as collateral if it has a short shelf life, is customized, is so seasonal that its value drops significantly at certain times of the year, or if it is subject to rapid obsolescence.

Given the presence of collateral, this type of loan tends to involve a lower interest rate. Also, lenders typically do not require any covenants in association with these loans, giving corporate management more control over company operations. However, the cost of an annual appraisal of fixed assets or annual audit by the bank (which will be charged to the company) should be factored into the total cost of this form of financing. Also, lenders require frequent reports on the status of underlying assets—sometimes as much as once a day for accounts receivable and once a week for inventory.

Bond.   A bond is a fixed obligation to pay, usually at a stated rate of $1,000 per bond, that is issued by a corporation to investors. It may be a *registered bond*, under which a company maintains a list of owners of each bond. The company then periodically sends interest payments, as well as the final principal payment, to the investor of record. It may also be a *coupon bond*, for which the company does not maintain a standard list of bondholders. Instead, each bond contains interest coupons that the bondholders clip and send to the company on the dates when interest payments are due. The coupon bond is more easily transferable between investors, but the ease of transferability makes them more susceptible to loss.

Bonds come in many flavors. The following list provides short descriptions of the most common ones:

- *Collateral trust bond.*   A bond that uses as collateral a company's security investments.

- *Convertible bond.*   A bond that can be converted to stock using a predetermined conversion ratio. The presence of conversion rights typically reduces the interest cost of these bonds, since investors assign some value to the conversion privilege. See the "zero coupon convertible bond" for a variation on this approach.

- *Debenture.*   A bond issued with no collateral. A subordinated debenture is one that specifies debt that is senior to it.

- *Deferred interest bond.*   A bond that provides for either reduced or no interest in the beginning years of the bond term, and compensates for it with increased interest later in the term. Since this type of bond is associated with firms having short-term cash-flow problems, the full-term interest rate can be high.

- *Floorless bond.*   A bond whose terms allow purchasers to convert it to common stock, as well as any accrued interest. The reason for its "death spiral" nickname is that bondholders can convert some shares and sell them on the open market, thereby supposedly driving down the price and allowing them to buy more shares, and so on. If a major bondholder were to convert all holdings to common stock, the result could be a major stock decline, possibly resulting in a change of control to the former bondholder. However, this conversion problem can be controlled to some extent by including conversion terms that only allow bondholders to convert at certain times or with the permission of company management.

- *Guaranteed bond.*   A bond whose payments are guaranteed by another party. Corporate parents will sometimes issue this guarantee for bonds issued by subsidiaries in order to obtain a lower effective interest rate.

- *Income bond.*   A bond that only pays interest if income has been earned. The income can be tied to total corporate earnings, or to specific projects. If the bond terms indicate that interest is cumulative, then interest will accumulate during nonpayment periods and be paid at a later date when income is available for doing so.

- *Mortgage bond.*   A bond offering can also be backed by any real estate owned by the company (real property mortgage bond), or by company-owned equipment (equipment bond), or by all assets (general mortgage bond).

- *Serial bond.*   A bond issuance where a portion of the total number of bonds are paid off each year, resulting in a gradual decline in the total amount of debt outstanding.

- *Variable rate bond.*   A bond whose stated interest rate varies as a percentage of a baseline indicator, such as the prime rate. CFOs should be wary of this bond type, because jumps in the baseline indicator can lead to substantial increases in interest costs.

- *Zero coupon bond.*   A bond with no stated interest rate. Investors purchase these bonds at a considerable discount to their face value in order to earn an effective interest rate.

- *Zero coupon convertible bond.*   A bond that offers no interest rate on its face, but that allows investors to convert to stock if the stock price reaches a level higher than its current price on the open market. The attraction to investors is that, even if the conversion price to stock is marked up to a substantial premium over the current market price of the stock, a high level of volatility in the stock price gives investors some hope of a profitable conversion to equity. The attraction to a company is that the expectation of conversion to stock presents enough value to investors that they require no interest rate on the bond at all, or at least will only purchase the bond at a slight discount from its face value, resulting in a small effective interest rate. A twist on the concept is a contingent conversion clause (or "co-co" clause), which requires the stock price to surpass the designated conversion point by some fixed amount before allowing investors to actually switch to stock, thereby making the conversion even more unlikely. This concept is least useful for a company whose stock has a history of varying only slightly from its current price, since investors will then see little chance to convert and so will place little value on the conversion feature, requiring instead a higher interest rate on the bonds.

There may be a bond indenture document that itemizes all features of the bond issue. It may contain restrictions that the company is imposing on itself, such as limitations on capital expenditures or dividends, in order to make the bond issuance as palatable as possible to investors. If the company does not follow these restrictions, the bonds will be in default.

A bond is generally issued with a fixed interest rate. However, if the rate is excessively low in the current market, then investors will pay less for the face value of the bond, thereby driving up the net interest rate paid by the company. Similarly, if the rate is too high, then investors will pay extra for the bond, thereby driving down the net interest rate paid.

A number of features may be added to a bond in order to make it more attractive for investors. For example, its terms may include a requirement by the company to set up a sinking fund into which it contributes funds periodically, thereby ensuring that there will be enough cash on hand at the termination date of the bond to pay off all bondholders. There may also be a conversion feature that allows a bondholder to turn in his or her bonds in exchange for stock; this feature usually sets the conversion ratio of bonds to stock at a level that will keep an investor from making the conversion until the stock price has changed from its level at the time of bond issuance, in order to avoid watering down the ownership percentages of existing shareholders. In rare instances, bonds may be backed by personal guarantees or by a corporate parent.

There are also features that bondholders may be less pleased about. For example, a bond may contain a call feature that allows the company to buy back bonds at a set price within certain future time frames. This feature may limit the amount of money that a bondholder would otherwise be able to earn by holding the bond. The company may also impose a staggered buyback feature, under which it can buy back some fixed proportion of all bonds at regular intervals. When this feature is activated, investors will be paid back much sooner than the stated payback date listed on the bond, thereby requiring them to find a new home for their cash, possibly at a time when interest rates are much lower than what they would otherwise have earned by retaining the bond. The bondholder may also be positioned last among all creditors for repayment in the event of a liquidation (called a subordinated debenture), which allows the company to use its assets as collateral for other forms of debt; however, it may have to pay a higher interest rate to investors in order to offset their perceived higher degree of risk. The typical bond offering will contain a mix of these features that impact investors from both a positive and negative perspective, depending on its perceived level of difficulty in attracting investors, its expected future cash flows, and its need to reserve assets as collateral for other types of debt.

Bonds are highly recommended for those organizations large enough to attract a group of investors willing to purchase them, since the bonds can be structured to precisely fit a company's financing needs. Bonds are also issued directly to investors, so there are no financial intermediaries, such as banks, to whom transactional fees must be paid. Also, a company can issue long-maturity bonds at times of low interest rates, thereby locking in modest financing costs for a longer period than would normally be possible with other forms of financing. Consequently, bonds can be one of the lowest-cost forms of financing.

Bridge.   A bridge loan is a form of short-term loan that is granted by a lending institution on the understanding that the company will obtain longer-term financing shortly that will pay off the bridge loan. This option is commonly used when a company is seeking to replace a construction loan with a long-term note that it expects to gradually pay down over many years. This type of loan is usually secured by facilities or fixtures in order to obtain a modest interest rate.

Debt-Equity Hybrid.   Also known as an enhanced trust-preferred, this new type of financial instrument is intended to take advantage of the best aspects of both debt and equity. It does this by having an extremely long term, usually in the range of 50 years, which makes it look like equity. It makes regular payments to investors with a fixed interest rate, which makes it look like debt, but the issuer does not have to pay the interest if the company's creditworthiness falls below a preset limit (which makes it look like equity). The reason for using this unusual mix of features is that the interest payments are deductible for tax purposes, while credit rating agencies treat portions of it as equity, which gives the issuer a better credit rating. It also allows an issuer to use the proceeds to buy back stock without significantly impacting its debt/equity ratio.

Though this complex financial instrument is great for the issuer, it can be dangerous for the investor, who could see all returns vanish during an economic downturn. Another risk is that the Internal Revenue Service has not yet issued a definitive ruling on the tax-deductibility of payments made by this type of financial instrument.

Economic Development Authority.   Various agencies of state governments are empowered to guarantee bank loans to organizations that need funds in geographic areas where it is perceived that social improvement goals can be attained. For example, projects that will result in increased employment or the employment of minorities in specific areas may warrant an application for this type of loan. It is usually extended to finance a company's immediate working capital needs. Given these restrictions, an economic development authority loan is only applicable in special situations.

Long-Term.   There are several forms of long-term debt. One is a long-term loan issued by a lending institution. These loans tend to be made to smaller companies that do not have the means to issue bonds or commercial paper. To reduce the risk to the lender, these typically require the company to grant the lender senior status over all other creditors in the event of liquidation. This is a standard requirement, because the lender is at much greater risk of default over the multiyear term of the loan, when business conditions may change dramatically. If there is no way for a lender to take a senior position on collateral, then the company should expect to pay a much higher interest rate in exchange for dropping the lender into a junior position in comparison to other creditors. If the lender also wants to protect itself from changes in long-term interest rates, it may attempt to impose a variable interest rate on the company. However, if the lender simply creates the loan and then sells it to a third party, it may be less concerned with future changes in the interest rate.

A long-term loan nearly always involves the use of fixed payments on a fixed repayment schedule, which will involve either the gradual repayment of principal or else the gradual repayment of interest, with the bulk of the principal being due at the end of the loan as a balloon payment. In the latter case, a company may have no intention of paying back the principal, but instead will roll over the debt into a new loan and carry it forward once again. If this is the case, the CFO may review the trend of interest rates and choose to roll over the debt to a new loan instrument at an earlier date than the scheduled loan termination date, when interest rates are at their lowest possible levels.

In summary, long-term debt is a highly desirable form of financing, since a company can lock in a favorable interest rate for a long time, which keeps it from having to repeatedly apply for shorter-term loans during the intervening years, when business conditions may result in less favorable debt terms.

Mezzanine Financing.　If a company wishes to avoid an excessive loss of control, but wants to obtain financing for multiple years, it could consider the use of mezzanine financing. This is a form of debt that can have a term of up to ten years, commonly with larger principal repayments towards the end of the loan period, and which is obtained from a single lender. Mezzanine financing requires a relatively high interest rate, usually in excess of 10%, as well as warrants to purchase company stock that can bring the total cost of the debt to somewhere in the range of 15% to 20%. This form of financing is generally subordinate to an existing bank loan, and so is intended to provide additional debt financing beyond the comfort level of the primary lender.

Purchase Order Financing.　A relatively rare form of debt financing can be obtained by using a customer purchase order as collateral. Under this approach, the lender advances funds to the company based on a proportion of the total amount of a purchase order received from a customer. The customer then remits payment directly to the lender, which extracts its principal and interest from the payment and forwards the remainder to the company.

Small Business Administration.　The Small Business Administration (SBA) provides guarantees on small loans to small businesses. These loans tend to carry reasonable interest rates, because of the backup guarantee. However, the loans are issued by local lending institutions that must still pass their standard loan approval processes, so it is not that easy to obtain SBA loans if a company is in severe financial straits. The SBA tends to give guarantees to loans originating in economically depressed areas or where unemployment is high. For these reasons, SBA loans will only be available in a minority of situations, and not in sufficiently large amounts to cover many business needs.

Short-Term.   The most common type of business loan extended by banks is the short-term loan. It is intended to be repaid within one year. The short time frame reduces the risk to the bank, which can be reasonably certain that the business's fortunes will not fall so far within such a short time period that it cannot repay the loan, while the bank will also be protected from long-term variations in the interest rate.

The short-term loan is intended to cover seasonal business needs, so that the cash is used to finance inventory and accounts receivable buildup through the main selling season, and is then repaid immediately after sales levels drop off and accounts receivable are collected. It can also be used for short-term projects, such as for the financing of the production requirements for a customer project that will be repaid as soon as the customer pays for the completed work. For these reasons, the timing of repayment on the loan should be right after the related business activity has been completed.

Commercial paper is debt that is issued directly by a company, typically in denominations of $25,000. It is generally unsecured and can be sold in a public market, since it is not registered to a specific buyer. Interest rates are typically at or slightly below the prime rate. Commercial paper is not an option for smaller companies, since the cost of placing the paper, as well as its level of acceptance in the public markets, will limit its use to only the largest organizations.

In some cases, a company may obtain such a loan if it really needs a long-term loan but feels that it will obtain lower interest rates on long-term debt if it waits for interest rates to come down. However, this strategy can backfire if interest rates are on an upward trend, since a company will be at risk of large changes in interest rates every time that it pays off a short-term debt instrument and rolls the funds over into a new short-term loan.

PREFERRED STOCK

Preferred stock contains elements of both equity and debt, since it generally pays interest on the amount of funding paid in. However, the interest may be withheld on a cumulative basis by order of the Board of Directors, the shares do not have to be repaid, and they may be convertible to common stock. Also, the interest on preferred stock is considered a dividend under the tax laws, and so is not tax deductible. As a result, the cost of preferred stock tends to be higher than other forms of debt, and, if the stock is convertible, shareholders may find that their ownership has been diluted by the preferred shareholders who have converted their shares to common stock.

Preferred stock is a good solution for those organizations looking for a long-term source of funds without a requirement to make fixed interest payments on *specific* dates (since preferred stock dividends can be deferred). It is also useful for companies being forced by their lending institutions to improve their debt/equity ratios, but who do not want to reduce the ownership percentages of their existing common stockholders through the infusion of new equity (only an option if the preferred shares are not convertible to common stock).

Preferred stock is becoming increasingly common as a form of purchase consideration for corporate mergers, due to the elimination of the pooling of interests accounting method. That approach used to require mergers to be paid for solely with common stock. With the demise of that approach to mergers, the fixed income component of preferred stock makes it the equity of choice for acquirees. It is especially attractive for establishing a merger's tax-free status, since acquirees will still maintain a "continuity of interest" in the acquirer. However, the tax-free status may not be allowed by the IRS if the preferred

Debt Financing Type	Features	Cost
Accounts payable payment delay	Short-term funding obtained by paying suppliers late	No direct cost, but impacts supplier relations
Accounts receivable collection acceleration	Short-term funding obtained by heightened collections activity and tighter credit policies	No direct cost, and one of the easiest sources of ready cash
Credit cards	Short-term funding, with small balances available per card	Very expensive, and may require personal guarantees
Direct Access Notes	Long-term funding sold directly to retail investors	Cost varies based on market conditions and bond terms
Employee trade-offs	Short-term funding based on exchanging employee wages for stock or profits	No immediate cost, but may lose employees, dilute investor shares
Factoring	Short-term funding based on accounts receivable	Expensive, but greatly accelerates cash flow
Field warehouse financing	Short-term funding based on inventory	Cost is somewhat higher than the prime rate, and may require detailed inventory tracking
Floor planning	Short-term funding based on retailer inventory	Cost is somewhat higher than the prime rate, and may require detailed inventory tracking
Inventory reduction	Short-term funding based on permanent inventory elimination	No credit cost, but requires better inventory planning and tracking systems
Lease	Medium-term funding that backs the purchase of specific assets	Cost can be hidden within lease agreement
Line of credit	Short-term revolving funding collateralized by a variety of assets	Cost is near the prime rate, but bank can refuse additional funding and it must be paid off in the short term
Loan, asset-based	Long-term funding with asset collateral	Cost is near the prime rate, but may require frequent reporting on collateral status
Loan, bond	Long-term funding based on obligations issued by the company	Cost varies based on market conditions and bond terms
Loan, bridge	Short-term funding used to carry a debt position until longer-term financing is found	Cost is near the prime rate, but secured by facilities
Loan, debt-equity hybrid	Very long-term funding, some equity features	Cost is near the prime rate
Loan, economic development authority	Short-term funding backed by the government in special social improvement situations	Cost is near the prime rate
Loan, long-term	Long-term funding issued by a lender	Cost is near the prime rate, but requires senior debt status and can involve balloon payments
Loan, mezzanine	Long-term funding that may include warrants	Cost is high when equity rights are added to the interest cost
Loan, purchase order	Short-term funding to support the working capital requirements of a specific purchase order	Cost is high, with significant administrative expenses
Loan, Small Business Administration (SBA)	Long-term funding from a lender, with an SBA guarantee	Cost is near the prime rate, but not usually available in large amounts
Loan, short-term	Short-term funding based on seasonal cash-flow needs	Cost is near the prime rate, but can require collateral
Preferred stock	Long-term funding from the sale of equity that carried a dividend	Higher cost, since dividends paid are not tax deductible, but improves debt/equity ratio
Sale and leaseback	Long-term funding from selling a building or major asset and leasing it back for a long period	Low cost, but requires a long-term ease commitment

Exhibit 14.1   Summary of Debt Financing Types

stock can be redeemed in the short-term, since this reduces the "equity attributes" of the stock.

SALE AND LEASEBACK

Under this arrangement, a company sells one of its assets to a lender and then immediately leases it back for a guaranteed minimum time period. By doing so, the company obtains cash from the sale of the asset that it may be able to more profitably use elsewhere, while the leasing company handling the deal obtains a guaranteed lessee for a time period that will allow it to turn a profit on the financing arrangement. A sale and leaseback is most commonly used for the sale of a corporate building, but can also be arranged for other large assets, such as production machinery.

A sale and leaseback is useful for companies in any type of financial condition, for a financially healthy organization can use the resulting cash to buy back shares and prop up its stock price, while a faltering organization can use the cash to fund operations. It has the added advantage of not burdening a company's balance sheet with debt; furthermore, it puts cash back *into* the balance sheet, allowing a company to obtain additional debt. It is especially useful when market conditions make other forms of financing too expensive. Obviously, it is only an option for those organizations that have substantial assets available for sale.

SUMMARY

The previous discussion shows that there are a large array of approaches available to solve the problem of obtaining financing. For the reader's convenience, the various types of debt financing are summarized in Exhibit 14.1.

The best types of debt financing by far involve the reduction of a company's working capital needs through internal management and process-oriented streamlining techniques, thereby reducing or eliminating the need for any financing. Once this approach has been maximized, a company that properly forecasts its cash needs and then makes long-range plans for the procurement of financing in the required amounts will be in a much better position to obtain the lowest-cost financing, as opposed to those organizations that must scramble for funding at the last minute.

CHAPTER 15

OBTAINING EQUITY FINANCING

A key function of the CFO is to acquire equity financing. This chapter is primarily concerned with the offering memorandum, which is the key document used by investors to determine if they wish to invest in a company. This memorandum is designed for private offerings; for more information on a public offering, refer to Chapter 16, Initial Public Offering.

Besides the offering memorandum, this chapter also covers the establishment of a valuation for the offering memorandum as well as equity financing alternatives, such as swapping stock for expenses or cash, issuing stock warrants or shares, private investments in public equity (PIPEs), or the use of Committed Long-Term Capital Solutions (CLOCS), which is a form of insurance that can provide equity financing. Finally, we cover the essential elements of a stock buyback, in case a company finds itself in the reverse situation of having more cash than it needs or wanting to increase earnings per share by reducing the number of shares outstanding.

In the first section, we briefly discuss the general features of common and preferred stock, which are relevant to the subsequent discussion.

TYPES OF STOCK

The owners of *common stock* are the true owners of the corporation. Through their share ownership they have the right to dividend distributions, to vote on various issues presented to them by the Board of Directors, to elect members to the Board, and to share in any residual funds left if the corporation is liquidated. If the company is liquidated, they will not receive any distribution from its proceeds until all creditor claims have been satisfied, as well as the claims of holders of all other classes of stock. There may be several classes of common stock, which typically have different voting rights attached to them; the presence of multiple types of common stock generally indicates that some shareholders are attempting some degree of preferential control over a company through their type of common stock.

Most types of stock contain a par value, which is a minimum price below which the stock cannot be sold. The original intent for using par value was to ensure that a residual amount of funding was contributed to the company that could not be removed from it until dissolution of the corporate entity. In reality, most common stock now has a par value that is so low (typically anywhere from a penny to a dollar) that its original intent no longer works.

Preferred stock comes in many flavors, but essentially is stock that offers a variety of incentives, such as guaranteed dividend payments and preferential distributions over common stock, to convince investors to buy them. The dividends can also be preconfigured to increase to a higher level at a later date, which is called *increasing rate preferred stock*. This is an expensive form of funds for a company, since the dividends paid to investors are not tax deductible as interest expense.

The dividends provided for in a preferred stock agreement can only be distributed after the approval of the Board of Directors (as is the case for dividends from common stock), and so may be withheld. If the preferred stock has a cumulative provision, then any dividends that were not paid to the holders of preferred shares in preceding years must be paid prior to dividend payments for any other types of shares. Also, some preferred stock will give its owners voting rights in the event of one or more missed dividend payments.

Because this stock is so expensive, many companies issue it with a call feature that states the price at which the company will buy back the shares. The call price must be high enough to give investors a reasonable return over their purchase price, or else no one will initially invest in the shares. Preferred stock may also be converted by the shareholder into common stock at a preset ratio, if the preferred stock agreement specifies that this option is available.

PRIVATE PLACEMENT OF STOCK

A company may find itself with an excessive proportion of debt in relation to its equity, or there is no way to obtain additional debt, forcing the CFO to go in search of equity. A private company accomplishes this through a private stock placement, where shares are sold to a limited number of individuals or business entities. It may be possible for company management to sell shares on an informal basis to friends and family, but this is at best a limited source of equity. When more equity is needed, the CFO must search outside this circle of acquaintances.

A formal private placement of stock may require the services of an investment banker whose connections are considerably more far-reaching than those of the CFO. A reputable investment banker will require an in-depth review of the company to ensure that it is an acceptable investment vehicle for potential investors. Next, the banker will work with the CFO to construct an offering memorandum, which describes the type and terms of stock to be offered, its price, the company, and how the company plans to use the funds. Details concerning an offering memorandum are described in the next section. The offering memorandum will then be sent to a group of prospective investors, followed by investment meetings where the CEO and CFO make presentations to investors. If all goes well, the investment banker then coordinates a closing where the investors pay the company for the proffered stock.

Sounds easy? It is not. Finding the right investment banker who works well with the company is difficult, as is the writing of an offering memorandum (mostly the CFO's chore), while presentations require long preparation and role playing. And do not forget the investment banker's fee. This can vary substantially, but expect some variation on the "Lehman Formula," which is 5% of the first million dollars raised, 4% of the second million, 3% of the third million, 2% of the fourth million, and 1% of all funds raised above that amount. For example, if an investment banker raises $5 million on behalf of the company, his fee will be $150,000. In addition, a banker may request a large number of warrants on the purchase of company stock, so he can take advantage of any potential increase in the company's value at a later date.

LAYOUT OF THE OFFERING MEMORANDUM

The offering memorandum is a crucial document that is the foundation of any successful effort to raise equity capital, since it contains all the information an investor needs in order to make an investment decision. A CFO will likely create such a document several times in his or her career, and so should be familiar with its content and general layout, which are described in detail in this section. The ten major components of the memorandum do not have to be addressed in the exact order or even in the format used here, but should be included somewhere in the document so that investors have a clear idea of the business, how it intends to use their money, and the general risks to which their funds will be subject. The general structure of the offering memorandum is to begin with contact information and an executive summary, which are the only parts many investors read; if the general concept does not interest them, they will not proceed past the summary. The next section covers the proposed offering and the rights to be accorded to investors. If an investor is interested in these terms, he or she will want to read more about the company, a description of which covers the remaining sections of the memorandum. The format of the memorandum, with selected textual examples for many sections, is:

1. *Contact information.* If an investment banker is being used, then contact information should be restricted to the personnel of that entity. If not, then the CEO and CFO are the most common contacts to list in this section.

2. *Executive summary.* Many investors do not have time to wade through a large prospectus in order to determine a general level of interest in making an investment. Instead, they need a quick summarization of the offering, from which they can decide if a more in-depth review is in order. The summary should include the following elements:

   a. *Proposed transaction.* Describe the amount of money needed, and the requested size of commitments from individual investors.

   b. *Use of proceeds.* Point out the general uses to which the funds will be put, including the proportions assigned to each use.

   c. *The exit.* Describe the range of possible exit strategies that the company is contemplating on behalf of its investors. Any discussion of timing should be extremely broad, so investors cannot claim reliance on a specific date.

   d. *The company.* Briefly address the company's general activities and products or services offered. It is appropriate to include a table showing revenues and profits for the past few years.

   e. *Customers.* Note the number of total customers, the distribution of revenues among them, and name some of the more prominent ones.

   f. *The management team.* Generally describe the management team's experience level, such as "the management team has a total of 128 years of experience in this industry." Do not get into individual resumes, which are listed later in the memorandum.

3. *Description of the offering.* This section contains the basic terms of the stock offering, including the minimum and maximum number of shares the company is willing to sell, the price per share, and other rights, which typically include:

a. *Information rights.* These rights entitle investors to receive financial and related explanatory information, which usually includes audited annual results as well as unaudited quarterly results. Sample text is:

> Investors will be entitled to receive, within 90 days following the fiscal year-end, audited annual financial statements accompanied by a general description of the company during the relevant period. Also, investors will be entitled to receive, within 45 days following the end of the quarter, unaudited quarterly financial statements accompanied by a description of material events during the relevant period.

b. *Registration rights.* A common feature is for the company to include investor shares in any future public placement of stock, at the company's expense. This allows investors to "piggyback" their shares onto an offering initiated by the company. Sample text is:

> In the event that the company proposes to register any of its equity securities under the Securities Act for sale in an underwritten public offering prior to the fifth anniversary of the Final Closing Date, the company would be obligated to permit any shares of Common Stock, upon request of the holders, to be included in the securities to be registered in such underwritten public offering; provided, that the company shall not be required to include any holders' shares in such public offering unless such holders accept the terms agreed upon between the company and the underwriters selected by it, and then only in such quantity as will not, in the opinion of the underwriters, jeopardize the success of the offering by the company. The company will bear the expenses of the registration of the holders' shares, except any underwriting discounts and commissions.

c. *Demand rights.* Demand rights are similar to the piggyback rights just discussed, except that investors can demand of the company a separate public registration of their stock, which they will then have the right to sell to the general public. Sample text is:

> In the event that the company completes an initial public offering of its equity securities prior to the fifth anniversary of the Final Closing Date, the holders of a majority of the shares of Common Stock may, by written request, demand one time that the company file a registration statement under the Securities Act, and to use its best efforts to cause such registration statement to become effective with respect to such Common Stock, and all holders of Common Stock shall be entitled to participate ratably in such registration. The company will bear the expenses of registration of the holders' Common Stock, except any underwriting discounts and commissions, and will pay the reasonable fees and expenses of one legal counsel for the holders.

d. *Conversion rights.* The holder of preferred stock may want the right to convert his or her shares into common stock, which may result in a higher return on investment. Typical wording is:

> Each Share of Preferred Stock will be convertible, at the holder's option, at any time into one Share of Common Stock (subject to adjustment for stock splits, combinations and other similar events).

e. *Dividends.* Company management may feel that a better stock price can be obtained if it promises a dividend payment on the sale of preferred stock to investors. More commonly, management does not anticipate doing so (since it creates a liability), so the best approach is to clearly state that dividend payments are not planned. Typical wording is:

> There are no stated dividends. Dividends are payable when, as, and if dividends are declared and payable on the Common Stock out of funds legally available and in an amount equal to the amount which the Preferred Stockholders would have been entitled to receive if they had converted their Shares of Preferred Stock into Common Stock and had been holders of Common Stock on the record date for such dividends on the Common Stock.

f. *Voting rights.* If preferred stock is being issued, the voting rights may vary from those of the common shareholders, and so should be enumerated within the offering memorandum. These rights may include final approval of the issuance of any other classes of stock, the incurrence of additional debt, sale of the business or large assets, or any other actions that may reduce the value of the shareholders' investment or increase the level of financial risk of the business. Typical wording is:

> Any proposed sale of the company or the sale of substantially all of its assets shall require the approval of the holders of at least two-thirds of the Preferred Stock then outstanding.

g. *Liquidation preference.* A preferred shareholder may be entitled to a flat-fee payment in the event of a corporate liquidation, which can be a significant incentive to purchase the stock if the business is expected to be sold in the near term. Less commonly, preferred shareholders may be offered a liquidation preference on a payment scale that slides in proportion to the total sale price of the business. Typical wording is:

> In the event of a liquidation, dissolution, or winding up of the company, all holders of Preferred Stock will be entitled to receive a liquidating distribution equal to $_____ per Share in preference to the Common Stock. Upon the payment of such liquidating distributions, the holders of the Preferred Stock will not be entitled to any further distribution from the Company.

h. *Preemptive rights.* Shareholders may want to avoid dilution of their ownership interests, in which case preemptive rights can be written into the stock agreement. These rights entitle existing shareholders to purchase enough shares in future stock issuances to ensure that they continue to retain the same percentage of ownership in the company. Typical wording is:

> In the event the company proposes to sell, or to grant rights or options to purchase, any shares of any class of capital stock or any securities convertible into or carrying rights or options to purchase any shares of any class of capital stock (collectively, "Other Securities"), each holder of Preferred Stock shall have the preemptive right to purchase that number of such Other Securities as shall enable the holder to retain its then current pro rata equity ownership interest in the company on a fully diluted basis, and at a price not less favorable than

the price at which such Other Securities are proposed to be offered by the company.

4. *Description of the company.* This description is meant to give an investor a general overview of a company's history, operations, and market positioning. It is not meant to be a lengthy essay, but rather a succinct review. An example is:

> The company was founded in 2006, experiencing first-year sales of $5 million that have since grown to $25 million, with all sales in the motorized garden products market. The company now has 40 major distributors in the United States, as well as 12 retail locations in California, Oregon, and Washington. Its products are designed and manufactured in a single facility in Salt Lake City. The company retains a tight focus on developing niche gardening products of the highest quality for professional and serious hobbyist gardeners.

5. *Risk factors.* This is an extremely important part of the offering memorandum. Investors must be informed of a wide range of potential risks that could impact the company's success in using their money to achieve the goals stated in this memorandum. It is best to include every conceivable risk, thereby avoiding the potential for a later lawsuit on the grounds that investors were not fully informed. The full list of potential risks should be preceded by the following general statement, in caps:

> ANY INVESTMENT IN THE COMPANY INVOLVES A HIGH DEGREE OF RISK AND ONLY PERSONS WHO CAN AFFORD TO SUSTAIN A TOTAL LOSS OF THEIR INVESTMENT SHOULD CONSIDER MAKING SUCH AN INVESTMENT. THERE CAN BE NO ASSURANCE THAT THE BUSINESS PLAN DESCRIBED HEREIN WILL BE COMMERCIALLY VIABLE. IN ADDITION, ACTUAL RESULTS OF OPERATIONS MAY REQUIRE SIGNIFICANT MODIFICATIONS OF ALL OR PART OF SUCH PLAN. PROSPECTIVE INVESTORS SHOULD CAREFULLY CONSIDER, AMONG OTHER FACTORS, THE FOLLOWING:

A sample of risks, with attendant sample text, is:

a. *Absence of dividends.* "The Company does not expect to declare or pay any cash dividends in the foreseeable future."

b. *Competitive risk.* "The Company will face competition in its chosen markets. There is no assurance that the Company can continue to compete successfully for business, or that Company products and services will be sold for a profit. Many potential competitors have substantially greater financial resources and significantly greater accumulated experience in marketing products."

c. *Dependence on key individuals.* "The success of the Company depends to a large degree upon the knowledge, personal efforts and ability of *(name)*, the loss of whose services may have a materially adverse effect on the Company."

d. *Dilution.* "In order to meet the projections set forth in the Financial Projections, the Company does not currently envision the need to raise additional capital or funds through the sale of equity securities or convertible debt instruments. If the Company is unable to achieve the requisite sales needed to achieve desired results within the required time frame, then the Company may attempt to raise additional rounds of private equity or convertible debt. In addition, the Company may determine it advisable to raise additional equity to support more rapid sales growth, product development, or other business needs. In any case, if the Company issues additional equity securities or convertible debt (and such securities were subsequently converted), investors who invest in the round contemplated within this document would sustain dilution, and said dilution may be substantial."

e. *Government contracting risks.* "Approximately _____% of the Company's total revenues are derived directly and indirectly from contracts with the government. Government contracts, by their terms, generally can be terminated at any time by the government, without cause, for the convenience of the government. In addition, all government contracts require compliance with various contract provisions and procurement regulations. The adoption of new or modified procurement regulations could adversely affect the Company or increase its costs of competing for or performing government contracts. Any violation (intentional or otherwise) of these regulations could result in the termination of such government contracts, imposition of fines, and/or debarment from the award of additional government contracts."

f. *Growth management.* "The Company expects to experience a period of significant revenue growth, which will result in new and increased responsibility for management personnel and place significant strain upon the Company's management, operating and financial systems, and resources. The Company's future success will depend to a significant extent on the ability of its current and future management personnel to operate effectively, both independently and as a group. There can be no assurance that the Company's personnel, systems, procedures, and controls will be adequate to support the Company's future operations."

g. *Need for additional financing.* "The Company may need additional financing to support its projected level of operations. No assurance can be given as to the availability of additional financing or, if available, the terms upon which it may be obtained. Any such additional financing will most likely result in dilution of an Investor's equity investment in the Company."

h. *No public market for shares.* "There is no public market for the Common or Series _____ Preferred Stock of the Company, and none will result from this offering. The sale of the _____ Stock is not being registered under the Securities Act of 1933, as amended (the "Securities Act"), and the Shares may not be resold or otherwise transferred unless they are subsequently registered under the Securities Act and qualified under applicable state laws or unless exemptions from registration and qualification are available. Accordingly, purchasers may not be able to readily liquidate their investment."

i. *Product liability.* "The Company has not experienced any product liability claims to date. However, the sale and support of its products by the Company may entail the risk of such claims. A successful product liability claim brought against the Company could have a material adverse effect upon the Company's business, operating results, and financial condition."

j. *Risk of infringement.* "The Company is not aware that it is infringing any proprietary rights of third parties. There can be no assurance, however, that third parties will not claim infringement by the Company of their intellectual property rights. Any such claims, with or without merit, could be time-consuming to defend, result in costly litigation, divert management's attention and resources, cause product shipment delays, or require the Company to enter into royalty or licensing agreements."

   k. *Technological change.* "Certain intellectual property is proprietary to the Company. However, new developments are occurring and there can be no assurance that such developments will not render the Company's products obsolete."

   l. *Uncertainties regarding new business.* "Although the Company has sold many of its products and services, there can be no assurance that the Company's products and services will continue to find market acceptance or will be saleable at a price that is profitable to the Company."

   m. *Uncertainty of future operating results.* "Revenues are not predictable with any significant degree of accuracy. Accordingly, the Company believes that period-to-period comparisons of its operating results are not necessarily meaningful and should not be relied upon as indications of future performance. Although the Company has recently experienced revenue growth, such growth should not be considered indicative of future revenue growth, if any, or as an indication of future operating results. Failure by the Company, for any reason, to increase revenues would have a material adverse effect on the Company's business, operating results and financial condition."

6. *Use of proceeds.* State in general terms the uses to which management plans to put the proceeds of the offering. Too much detail could cause legal problems later on, if investors sue for the return of their money on the grounds that the company has misappropriated funds. It is also important to note the types of investments in which the money will be placed until they are used. An example is:

> The principal purposes of this offering are to obtain additional working capital, to create a commercial product from existing technology, to bring these products to market, and to facilitate the Company's future entry into public equity markets. The Company expects to use the net proceeds of this offering for working capital and general corporate purposes. A portion of the net proceeds of the offering may also be used to acquire or invest in products, technologies, or businesses that broaden or enhance the Company's current product or service offerings. Pending such uses, the Company intends to invest the net proceeds in short-term, investment grade, and interest-bearing securities.

7. *Selected financial data.* A summary-level income statement and balance sheet should be included that shows company performance over at least the past three years, and preferably five. The level of summarization should be sufficient to group all of this information on a single page.

8. *Discussion of the business.* The intent of this section is to give investors a clear idea of what key success factors drive the business. This may include varying degrees of industry fragmentation, pricing or quality issues, as well as a discussion of the firm's product or service offerings. The discussion should include all key parts of the business, including the market in which the company operates, sales and distribution, legal issues, customers, and its investment in research. Possible areas to include in this section are:

a. *Industry background.*   Describe the general structure of the industry in which the company operates. If it crosses multiple boundaries, then describe the ones having primary impact on the company. The description can include the estimated total industry revenue, market segmentation, and key players. An example is:

> The land data market is an approximately $500 million market. It is comprised of several thousand ground surveying firms, several hundred aerial surveying firms, about two dozen land database firms, and two major purveyors of software for geographical information systems. The bulk of the profits in the industry flow to the two software firms, whose products are in a monopoly position. The database firms tend to be quite small, with occasional regional consolidation resulting in mid-size entities that are soon bought by the major oil and gas companies. The land and aerial surveying firms have minimal barriers to entry, resulting in low price points and minimal profit margins.

b. *Products.*   The memorandum should describe each major company product or service in a separate paragraph. It is not necessary to reveal sales by product—rather, the intent is to give investors a feel for the general areas in which products have been created, as well as their capabilities. An example is:

> The Lease Sale System provides a vastly improved approach to the tasks of researching and analyzing competitive Oil and Gas Lease Sale information. It combines a powerful search engine with government oil and gas lease sale information to enable the user to quickly identify areas of interest, track competitor trends, identify opportunities and potential partners, highlight overlooked parcels to acquire, and analyze costs of accruing prospective parcels. This product is designed for land professionals who nominate and acquire federal parcels, regularly attend government oil and gas lease sales, or expend time and effort to research and study oil and gas lease sale information.

c. *Customers.*   This statement should summarize the type and number of customers, as well as identify the major customers. For example:

> The company has obtained business from a total of 240 customers during the past two years, of which 180 purchase services from the company at least once a month. Of the total amount of business, 20% is spread among the top five customers, with 28% among the total ten customers. The top ten customers in terms of dollar purchases from the company are as follows...

d. *SWOT analysis.*   This acronym stands for the strengths, weaknesses, opportunities, and threats that the management team foresees. Each of these items should be listed in a table in summary format. Strengths should be paired with associated advantages, so investors can see how current strengths can be capitalized on. Weaknesses are similarly paired with curative actions, while opportunities are linked with harvesting strategies and threats are shown alongside defensive posturing. A sample is shown in the tables in Exhibit 15.1.

e. *Sales and marketing.* This section should reveal the basic structure of the sales and marketing function, including the use of different sales channels and geographical distribution of the sales effort. An example is:

> The company uses multiple distribution channels, including a direct sales force, co-marketing relationships with software manufacturers, and value-added resellers. The sales staff compensation is primarily based on commissions, thereby keeping the company's fixed costs low. Sales are conducted in the western United States, with current planning for new sales efforts in the northern midwest region.

f. *Teaming agreements.* If a company obtains significant sales from its teaming agreements, these should be stated. If there are teaming agreements but no significant results from them, this section can be omitted.

g. *Distribution.* If the company has obtained a competitive advantage through its distribution system, then this should be mentioned. An example is:

> The company operates 1,450 retail stores throughout the North American region, which exceeds the retail locations of its nearest competitor by a factor of three. This allows the company to roll out new products into a much larger geographical area than any of its competitors.

h. *Employees.* Employees are a key factor, both positively and negatively, in any business. Be sure to state any employee problems, such as high turnover rates or the presence of unions, as well as factors that investors may feel are key to its success, such as the presence of a high proportion of Ph.D. employees on the research staff. An example is:

> The company's Michigan production facility is unionized. This facility produces 45% of the company's furniture products, so a work shutdown or slowdown in this plant would have a major impact on company revenues. Labor costs in this facility are approximately 15% higher than in the company's other production facilities.

i. *Intellectual property.* If a company has a significant investment in research and development, it should state the size of this effort, or the percentage of revenues that are allocated to this function. If there are a number of patents, they should be mentioned in general terms. The presence of trademarks or copyrights are generally not worth stating. An example is:

> In an industry where research and development expenditures are typically 2% of gross revenues, the company's allocation of 11% of gross revenues to this activity shows its strong commitment to the creation of innovative new products. This significant investment supports a development team of two hundred scientists, who have generated 140 patents in the past three years.

j. *Competition.* This section is closely read by many investors. Be sure to note the company's position in the industry versus its primary competitors, noting market share when this information is available. Though speculative, it may be useful to project possible changes in market share as a result of likely structural changes within the industry. An example is:

Strengths ⟶	Associated Advantages
• Knowledge base • The company's products and services provide a unique and compelling value proposition in targeted markets. • Broad application potential in several government and commercial markets with a total market potential of over $ _____ million. • No direct competition in primary target markets. • Strong financial trend with multiyear history of solid revenue growth. • Experienced and industry knowledgeable management team in place.	• Competitive advantage • High client return on investment and therefore high client retention. • Excellent near- and long-term revenue growth potential. • Noncompetitive access to large and potentially lucrative markets. • Demonstrated market acceptance and company financial performance. • Ability to identify opportunities with capability to deliver quality products in a profitable manner.
Weaknesses ⟶	**Curative Action**
• Limited market size for existing products to current markets. • Limited number of employees to handle accelerated growth. • Limited resources	• Broadening of existing product capability to reach an expanded market by virtue of ease of access via the Internet and the addition of new products aimed at allied market segments. • New funding will allow for additional staffing. • Strategic marketing programs
Opportunities ⟶	**Harvesting Strategies**
• The newly completed e-commerce capability greatly expands the market accessibility of the company's products from major companies into a much larger number of mid-size companies. • The expanded sales force will open additional opportunities in existing and allied markets. • The impact of the new GSA contract is yet to be fully realized. • The recently signed teaming agreement with _____ provides access to millions of dollars in new business opportunities.	• Initiate marketing and public relations program aimed at mid-size companies in their respective markets. • Hire experienced sales personnel to pursue new and existing markets. • Promote awareness of the GSA contract throughout the federal government. • Assign a business development manager to this partner and selectively pursue opportunities.
Threats ⟶	**Defensive Posturing**
• Loss of one or more of the top employees could slow the progress of the company. • A competing product could be developed and released by another company. • Changes in the federal government's patent application laws could impact the amount of time over which the company will enjoy patent protection for its products.	• The company has obtained a $1 million life insurance policy on each of its key employees, with benefits payable to the company. • Being first to market with a high quality, effecient, and reasonably priced product has created a strong barrier to entry, which should allow the company to successfully defend its markets. • The company plans to hire additional legal staff in order to more vigorously pursue patent enforcement during the reduced period when are in effect.

EXHIBIT 15.1   STRENGTHS, WEAKNESSES, OPPORTUNITIES, AND THREATS

The industry in which the company operates is dominated by the eight largest oil and gas companies based in the Gulf Coast states, which extract roughly 45% of the oil and gas in the United States. This leaves a $120 billion share of the market that is split evenly between large independent drillers and much smaller "Mom and Pop" drilling operations that typically lease less than one thousand acres of land and operate fewer than ten wells. Recent improvements in oil extraction technologies make it likelier for the largest drillers to reenter smaller oil fields they had previously exited, thereby possibly increasing their share of the total market to 55% of the total.

k. *Regulatory issues.* If there is a modest chance that regulatory issues will impact the company, then they must be addressed in the memorandum. These issues can also be shifted to the "risks" section of the report. An example is:

The recent Clean Air Act requires coal-burning utility plants to install clean air scrubbers in their smokestacks. Given the time lines under which these changes must be implemented, the company expects to incur capitalized costs of $150 million over the next three years in order to bring itself into compliance with this federal law.

l. *Facilities.* Investors generally assume that company premises are leased over a modest time period and at market rates. If this is not the case, such as with company ownership of facilities, unusually high or low lease rates, or an especially long lease term, then this information should be revealed. An example is:

The company leases 50,000 square feet at $18.50 per square foot under a lease that expires in 12 years, with annual escalation clauses based on the Consumer Price Index.

9. *Management.* Investors will be extremely interested in this section of the memorandum, since they realize that the composition and experience of the management team are the key factors leading to company success. Investors will also be interested in any pay levels that depart substantially from current standards. Key disclosures are:

a. *Resumes.* There should be a brief resume describing each key member of the management team, which should address their experience and education. A sample resume would be:

Richard B. Smith, President & CEO: Mr. Smith is responsible for all operations of the Company. He has an MBA in Finance from the University of Florida, as well as a BS in Marketing from Iowa State University. Mr. Smith has demonstrated capabilities at officer-level executive positions in public and private corporations, including large multibillion-dollar corporate environments as well as smaller rapidly growing entrepreneurial environments. His previous experience includes: president of a farm cooperative, senior vice president of an insurance company, president of a plastic injection molding company, vice president of finance for a multibillion-dollar consulting company, and director of the strategic planning group for a multibillion-dollar shipping company.

Expect investors to spend a considerable amount of time poring through the resumes of those management team members in key positions. They will be

Name	Salary	Bonus	Total
Smith, Richard (CEO)	$175,000	$50,000	$225,000
Doe, John (COO)	$125,000	$35,000	$160,000
Alvin, James (CFO)	$110,000	$25,000	$135,000
Done, Davis (CTO)	$150,000	$40,000	$190,000

EXHIBIT 15.2   SAMPLE EXECUTIVE COMPENSATION TABLE

looking for a history of success in growing companies, while also looking for evidence of failure in the past. Canny investors may conduct independent inquiries about managers to verify what is stated in the offering memorandum.

b.   *Compensation.*   The memorandum does not need to include compensation levels, but in the interests of full disclosure it is better to note all forms of compensation earned by key members of the management team. The format in Exhibit 15.2 could be used.

c.   *Employment agreements.*   Investors want to know if there are any onerous payout requirements associated with employment agreements. If so, they must be disclosed. A sample disclosure is:

> An employment agreement exists between the company and Mr. Smith. Under its terms, he is guaranteed one year of pay in the event of termination for any reason, as well as fully paid medical insurance for a period of 18 months.

10.   *Benefits.*   Investors are primarily interested in the additional compensation aspect of employee benefits, so do not bother to itemize other types of benefits, such as medical insurance or vacation time. The key items are:

a.   *Stock option plans.*   Investors want to know not only if there are many options outstanding that could potentially reduce the value of their shares, but also the proportion vested (indicating how many could be converted in the near future) and the names of the principal option holders. A sample table of options held is shown in Exhibit 15.3.

b.   *401(k) plans.*   Investors are not interested in the general presence of a 401(k) plan, but rather in the presence of a substantial funds-matching facility that could result in a substantial drop in profits. Consequently, the wording of a 401(k) plan description could be:

Option Holder	Total Options	Options Vested	Vesting in 1 Year	Vesting in 2 Years
Smith, Richard	525,000	175,000	175,000	175,000
Doe, John	148,000	0	50,000	50,000
Alvin, James	73,000	0	0	24,000
Done, Davis	50,000	50,000	0	0
All Others	210,000	129,000	41,000	40,000
Totals	1,006,000	354,000	266,000	289,000

EXHIBIT 15.3   SAMPLE OPTION HOLDER TABLE

The company offers a 401(k) plan to those of its employees who have been with the company for at least one year. At that time, the company offers a 6% match to any funds employees contribute to the plan, with immediate vesting. The company contributed a total of $103,000 in matching funds to the plan in the past year; based on budgeted staffing levels and the past history of employee participation rates, the company expects its matching expense to be in the range of $110,000 to $130,000 in the upcoming year.

c.   *Bonus plans.*   As was the case with 401(k) plans, investors are most interested in the potential impact that bonuses may have on profits. As a secondary issue, they are also interested in who may be receiving bonuses and the general nature of the plans. A sample text for this item is:

The company operates two bonus plans. One is for the production staff, and pays out a maximum of $10,000 per month, based on reported levels of efficiency and the attainment of a minimum number of no-injury days. In the past year, payouts from this monthly pool were achieved in four months, resulting in a bonus expense of $40,000. The company expects similar bonus amounts to be paid out under the terms of this plan in the upcoming year.

The second bonus plan is a management incentive plan that pays out a maximum of $280,000 at year-end if the management team meets both its revenue and profit targets for the full year. At this time, the management team expects to achieve this bonus. A distribution of prospective bonus payments under this plan is:

Name	Bonus Payment
Smith, Richard	$110,000
Doe, John	$60,000
Alvin, James	$30,000
Done, Davis	$80,000
Total	$280,000

ESTABLISHING A VALUATION FOR THE OFFERING MEMORANDUM

The offering memorandum includes a fixed price at which shares are being offered to investors, which implies that the company must establish a valuation for itself prior to issuing the memorandum. There are a number of methods available for making this determination, as noted in the following bullet points:

- *Comparables method.*   In brief, this is the "what is everyone else worth?" method. The CFO determines the valuations of similar companies and assumes that her company is worth the same multiple of revenues. For example, if X Company's current stock price yields a total valuation of $200 million on sales of $40 million, then a CFO could apply its revenue multiple of 5 to her company's sales of $3 million to arrive at a valuation of $15 million. This approach does not work as well if there are no public companies against which a valuation can be measured. Also, if a company has few sales, then comparisons to other measurements, such as the customer base, number or value of patents, measured natural resources, or new products must be used. The resulting valuation for a private company may also suffer some discounting from a comparable generated from a public company, on the grounds that its shares are more difficult to sell. Investment bankers keep databases of the prices at which many privately held companies have sold, and so can give a good estimate of valid comparables.

- *Net present value (NPV) method.* Net present value was discussed in Chapter 10, Capital Budgeting. Discounting a company's cash flows is a valid valuation approach, but is of less use in cases where a company has not yet developed significant cash flows. For example, a company that has spent millions to develop a truly unique product would have no valuation under this approach up until the point when it begins selling it, even though the product may be quite valuable. Also, it is difficult to develop an accurate discount rate for the calculation of cash flows for a privately held company whose beta may be substantially different from that of a public company in the same industry. Further, the NPV method assumes a constant discount rate, which is not the case in highly leveraged buyout deals where rapid declines in the proportion of debt will result in a gradual increase in the cost of capital over time. For these reasons, it is best to develop a high-low NPV estimate using a range of discount rates, and then consider other factors, such as the comparables method, in narrowing down the valuation to a tighter valuation range.

- *Venture capital method.* This is a quick "back of the envelope" approach to deriving a valuation. First, the investor estimates a firm's value at the time of liquidation of the venture capitalist's shares. He then discounts this value back to the present using a target rate of return, which is high (40 to 50%). He then divides the amount of the proposed investment by the discounted value to determine his prospective ownership percentage in the company. He then incorporates the impact of dilution from future rounds of financing by dividing the required final ownership percentage by the percentage of ownership subsequent to dilution. An example is shown in Exhibit 15.4.

The main disadvantage of this approach is the extremely high (and arbitrary) discount rate, which gives the investor an unusually high ownership percentage in a company.

Assumptions	Venture Capital Valuation
Net earnings	$ 6,778,000
P/E multiple	15
Terminal value	$ 101,670,000
Discount rate	50%
Discounted terminal value	$45,186,667
Amount of proposed investment	$ 4,500,000
Required final percent ownership	10.0%
Additional percentages of firm to be sold in future rounds of financing	10%
Retention ratio	90.5%
Required current percent ownership	11.0%

EXHIBIT 15.4   CALCULATION OF THE VENTURE CAPITAL METHOD

Investment bankers tend to recommend a slightly lower valuation for the purposes of issuing stock on the grounds that this ensures a complete subscription of all shares offered. The fact that a stock offering was fully subscribed or (better yet) oversubscribed is a useful marketing tool for subsequent rounds of equity financing, and may therefore be worth the incremental loss in equity resulting from it.

SWAPPING STOCK FOR EXPENSES

Equity is frequently obtained in order to pay off short-term expenses. This is a two-step process of obtaining the equity from one party and then using the resulting cash to pay off suppliers. One can sometimes shortcut this process by issuing stock directly to suppliers in exchange for their services. Though it can be an effective way to eliminate debts, it also sends a clear message to suppliers that the company is short on cash. Thus, this approach usually only works once—when suppliers have already sent their bills to the company and it responds by negotiating a stock payment in lieu of cash. If a company tries to convince suppliers in advance to take stock as payment, it is unlikely to have many takers.

SWAPPING STOCK FOR CASH

An unusual approach for a privately held company to obtain cash is to buy another company with stock, with the intent of shutting down or scaling back the acquiree and taking its cash. This approach is most common when a company has venture capital (VC) funding, and the VC wants to merge a failing company from its portfolio of investments into the acquirer.

The primary difficulty in such a case is the potential presence of hidden liabilities on the books of the acquiree that may make the acquisition much more expensive than the value of the acquired cash. Nonetheless, this is an option in a limited number of situations.

STOCK WARRANTS

A stock warrant is a legal document that gives the holder the right to buy a specific amount of a company's shares at a specific price, and usually for a limited time period, after which it becomes invalid. The stock purchase price listed on the warrant is usually higher than the market price at the time of issuance.

A stock warrant can be used as a form of compensation instead of cash for services performed by other entities to the company, and may be attached to debt instruments in order to make them appear to be more attractive investments to buyers. For example, a CFO may be interested in obtaining debt at an especially low interest rate, and attaches stock warrants to a new bond offering in order to do so. Investors attach some value to the warrants, which drives them to purchase the bonds at a lower effective interest rate than would have been the case without the presence of the attached warrants.

A stock warrant is rarely sold on its own by a company in the expectation of receiving a significant amount of cash in exchange. Consequently, this is not a good approach for directly obtaining equity funding, but rather is used to reduce the cost of other types of funding or to reduce or eliminate selected supplier expenses.

STOCK SUBSCRIPTIONS

Stock subscriptions allow investors or employees to pay a company a consistent amount over time and receive shares of stock in exchange. When such an arrangement occurs, a receivable is set up for the full amount expected, with an offset to a common stock subscription account. When the cash is collected and the stock is issued, the funds are deducted from these accounts and shifted to the standard common stock accounts.

Stock subscriptions can be arranged for employees, in which case the amount invested tends not to be large and is not a significant source of new equity financing. When it is used with investors, it typically involves their up-front commitment to make payments to the company as part of a new share offering, and so tends to occur over a short time period rather than involve small incremental payments over a long time frame.

PRIVATE INVESTMENT IN PUBLIC EQUITY

A Private Investment in Public Equity (PIPE) involves the sale of a public company's equity to accredited private investors, usually at a discount of about 10 to 20% from the market price. Because a PIPE is a private investment, it does not require registration with the Securities and Exchange Commission, can be completed quickly, and involves less administrative expense than would be the case for a large public offering. Since stock is sold in large blocks under this method, a company tends to gain larger, more long-term investors, especially if the issuing company sells the shares directly, and so can select which investors it wants.

However, some PIPE agreements also require a company to pay out additional shares if its stock price falls within a certain time period, which can result in a considerable level of ownership dilution for other investors. It may also be necessary to sweeten the PIPE deal with warrants or a variety of conversion options that are highly favorable to the investor. Another problem arises when an investment bank is used to find investors, since the company no longer has control over who is buying its shares, which may result in an investor pool with short-term cash-out expectations. This last problem can be handled to some extent by forcing investors to sign agreements declaring they will not sell their shares for a certain period of time.

The worst-case scenario is when the PIPE agreement grants more shares to investors when the common stock price declines. When manipulated by short selling, a company may find that its share price declines precipitously, requiring more stock to be issued, followed by more short selling, and so on, until the company's ownership shifts to the PIPE investors. This is known as a "death spiral" PIPE. To avoid this problem, the PIPE agreement should specify a floor price below which no further shares of compensatory stock will be issued to investors.

COMMITTED LONG-TERM CAPITAL SOLUTIONS

A Committed Long-Term Capital Solutions (CLOCS) policy essentially gives a company access to cash at predetermined interest rates if an adverse event occurs that indicates an environment in which a company would probably have an increased level of difficulty in obtaining capital by traditional means, such as a drop in a country's gross domestic product. By using this approach, a company does not need to retain a large equity base as a reserve against difficult economic conditions in the future, since it can activate the credit line instead. A CLOCS transaction is not a form of equity, but rather a means of avoiding the need for it during difficult economic circumstances. Also, since it is a contingent source of debt, it is an off-balance-sheet arrangement until such time as debt is drawn down from the available balance.

A variation on the CLOCS concept is to pay an insurance company an ongoing premium in exchange for the right to have the insurance company purchase some form of preferred stock from the company during a future period of economic hardship, as defined by a predetermined set of trigger points. The insurance company obtains preferentially treated stock (typically involving a dividend and senior liquidation rights), while the company obtains guaranteed access to equity in the event of significant downturn in the business, which is precisely when obtaining equity financing would be the most difficult.

These innovative policies are custom-tailored to the needs of specific businesses. However, given the effort required to structure these deals, they are generally only available to firms having revenues in excess of $1 billion.

BUYING BACK SHARES

This chapter is about obtaining equity financing. However, sometimes a company's stock price drops so low that it becomes advantageous to do the reverse and buy back shares. By doing so, a company can reduce the number of shares outstanding without impacting its reported income, thereby increasing its earnings per share. One would then expect the price of the remaining outstanding shares to increase.

Unfortunately, this logic does not always hold. The underlying logic of a share buyback is that an increase in earnings per share should increase the value of the company and therefore the price of all remaining shares. However, the company must use cash to buy back outstanding shares, so cash flow declines as a result of this action, and a reduction in cash flow reduces the value of a company. Also, a share buyback announcement sends a signal to investors that a company has no better use for its money, which may lead them to believe that the company's future prospects are bleak. This is a particular concern when company managers sell their shares back to the company as part of the general buyback program, which sends a clear signal to investors that the management team does not feel the share price can go any higher. Thus, a good approach to retaining the value of all remaining stock after a buyback is to inform the market that the management team is not allowing the company to buy back *any* of its shares.

One situation in which earnings can be expected to rise as a result of a buyback is when debt is acquired and the proceeds are used to buy back shares. By doing so, company management swaps high-cost equity for lower-cost debt, and also obtains the tax deduction associated with interest expenses. However, this approach should only be used if there is clearly enough future cash flow to support the extra debt burden.

If management decides to buy back shares, it has the following three methods available for doing so:

1. *Buy shares through a tender offer.* The company sets a fixed price, typically somewhat above the current market rate, at which it is willing to buy back shares during a fixed time period of usually one month.

2. *Buy shares on the open market.* The company can buy back shares on the open market, but this approach is limited by SEC rules to one-quarter of the average daily traded volume for the past four weeks on a rolling basis, so it can take a very long time to complete a large stock buyback.

3. *Buy shares through an auction.*   Under this approach, shareholders can post the prices at which they will sell their shares back to the company and the number of shares they will sell at those prices. The company then selects those shares offered at the lowest prices until it has bought enough shares to meet its goal. This approach is described more fully in Chapter 16, Initial Public Offering.

The auction approach is the most cost-effective way to buy back large quantities of shares, since the prices paid tend to be lower than what a company will realize through a tender offer. For small volume buybacks, open market purchases are the most cost effective.

SUMMARY

This chapter has dealt with the principal means of obtaining equity financing, which is a private placement via an offering memorandum. This option is available to far more companies than the public offering, which requires one to navigate the difficult initial public offering (IPO) process, which is described in the next chapter.

CHAPTER 16

INITIAL PUBLIC OFFERING

The initial public offering (IPO) is considered by many business owners to be the true sign of success—they have grown a business to the point where its revenue volume and profitability are large enough to warrant public ownership. However, the road to an IPO is both expensive and time-consuming and requires significant changes to a company. This chapter describes the pluses and minuses of going public, as well as the steps required and costs to be incurred in order to achieve that goal.

REASONS TO GO PUBLIC

Though a management team may not say it, a major reason for going public is certainly to create a market for the shares they already own. Though these shares may not be available for sale for some time after the IPO (see the "Restrictions on Stock in a Publicly Traded Company" section), they will eventually be able to cash in their shares and options, potentially generating considerable profits from doing so. This reason is not publicized to the public, since they will be less likely to invest if they think the management team is simply cashing in and then leaving the business.

A slight variation on the wealth creation theme is that, by having a broad public market for their shares, original shareholders are likely to see a rise in the value of their shares even if they have no intention of selling the shares. The reason is that there is no longer a penalty for not having a ready market for the shares, which adds a premium to what the shares would have been worth if the company had remained privately held.

The same logic can be used as a tool for employee retention. A private company can issue options to its employees, but they are worth little to the employees unless there is a market in which they can sell the shares. By going public, a company may experience increased employee retention, since they wish to wait until their options vest so they can cash in the resulting shares for a profit.

Going public is also useful from the estate planning perspective. If the owner of a private company dies, his or her heirs are frequently forced to sell the entire business in order to pay estate taxes (though with proper planning, life insurance payouts can be used instead). By taking the company public, the heirs are only forced to sell a portion of the company to pay estate taxes, at least leaving them some portion of the business as a residual.

From an operating perspective, going public gives a company a large pot of cash, which it can use to increase its competitiveness by increasing its asset base, improving marketing, hiring qualified staff, funding more product research, and so on. This can be such a competitive advantage that other companies in the same market segment may be forced to go public as well, just to raise enough funds to survive against their newly funded competitor.

Along the same lines, having publicly held shares allows a company to more readily include its shares in the purchase price of an acquisition. The acquiree is much more willing to accept this form of compensation, since it can sell the shares for cash to other investors. This is a powerful tool for some companies, who use it as the primary method for consolidating a group of small, privately held organizations within an industry.

From a financing perspective, going public lowers a company's cost of capital. The main reason is that investors are willing to pay a higher price for a company's stock than if the shares had been privately issued, since they can easily sell the shares. This premium can reduce the cost of capital by several percent. In addition, issuing shares to the public reduces the power that private investors previously may have had over the business, which could have included restrictions on operations, guaranteed dividend payments, or their prior approval of a potential sale of the business. Also, by being publicly held, it is much less time-consuming and expensive to raise funds through subsequent rounds of financing.

Another financing reason to go public is that new equity drastically lowers the proportion of debt to equity that is recorded on the corporate balance sheet, which is looked on with great favor by lenders. With the new equity in hand, a company can then ask lenders for a larger amount of debt, which they will be likely to lend until the amount handed over results in a significantly higher debt/equity ratio.

Thus, there are excellent wealth-creating, operating, and financing reasons to pursue an IPO. However, there are just as many reasons *not* to do so, which are itemized in the next section.

REASONS NOT TO GO PUBLIC

One of the best reasons for not going public is its cost. These costs are detailed in the following section, while the fees for trading on an exchange are listed later in the "Trading on an Exchange" section. In brief, a small company will be fortunate indeed to incur less than $.5 million in up-front fees as part of an IPO. A large company can expect to pay many times these base-level expenses. Also, a company conducting a small offering will find that the proportional cost of obtaining equity funding is extremely high, since the underwriter will charge a higher fee as a percentage of the amount raised in order to cover its costs and still earn a profit on the transaction.

Besides the initial cost of going public, there will be incremental increases in ongoing expenses. Most obviously, additional staff must be hired into the accounting department, whose job will be to keep up with all reports required by the Securities and Exchange Commission (SEC). In addition, the cost of directors' and officers' (D&O) insurance will skyrocket from what would have been paid when a company was privately held, assuming that the insurance can be obtained at all. The reason for this increase is the vastly increased pool of investors who may be tempted to sue the company on the grounds of material misstatements in its public comments (such as its registration statement for the IPO) in the event that the stock price drops. One can reasonably expect the cost of this insurance to increase by a factor of at least ten.

Another problem is that a smaller company with a modest market capitalization will have difficulty establishing a market for its stock. If it is too small, institutional investors (who like to buy and sell in large blocks of stock) will have minimal interest in making an investment. Because of this small market, a company's stock will be more likely to be subject to manipulation by a small number of investors, who can short-sell it to drive the stock down and then purchase large blocks of stock at a reduced price in order to gain some measure of control over the company.

Loss of control is possible unless the owner has retained a large proportion of corporate stock or unless a separate class of super voting stock has been established that gives the owners additional votes at shareholder meetings. Otherwise, outside investors can either buy up shares to create large voting blocks or band together to create the same result.

Information disclosure is yet another problem. In addition to the expense of having additional accounting staff to organize and report this information, there is the problem of disclosing information to a company's competitors, who only need to go to the SEC's web site to access all required reports filed by the company. Though many pundits claim that the types of information disclosed will not harm the competitive posture of a public company, competitors can tell from its financial statements when it has put itself out on a financial limb by obtaining too much debt and can easily start a price war at this point that could cause the company to miss debt payments and therefore possibly go into bankruptcy.

A serious concern is the risk of shareholder class action lawsuits. These arise when there is a drop in the stock price that shareholders claim was the result of material misstatements in the registration statement or in any other information releases thereafter. These lawsuits are the reason for much more expensive D&O insurance. They will be targeted at the company as a whole, the corporate directors, whoever signed the registration statement, any experts who have given statements on behalf of the company, and its underwriters. The threat of lawsuits is one of the main reasons why IPO prices are frequently set somewhat low—there is less chance that the price will drop further, giving investors no reason to sue.

Another issue is the constant pressure from investors and analysts to show improved results every quarter. If a company were private, it could easily stand lower profits for a year or so while it ramped up new products and markets, but being public makes this completely practical approach to growing a business more difficult to implement. Investors can attempt to unseat the management team by approving a different Board of Directors if they feel that growth rates are below their expectations. This issue can only be dealt with by continually informing the investing public of management's intentions for corporate growth so that investors will adopt a longer-term perspective.

Finally, the management team must understand that they now exist not to serve itself, but to serve the investing public. This major shift in focus calls for the elimination of unusually high compensation packages to the managers, as well as a commitment to increasing shareholder value over other objectives that may have been in vogue at the company prior to going public. Management may be uncomfortable with this paradigm shift, resulting in investor unhappiness with a perceived lack of attention to their needs by management.

There are so many negative reasons for going public that the managements of many perfectly good private companies have elected to stay away from the public markets. In addition, a great many companies that have gone public find these issues to be so burdensome that they have elected to take themselves private once again.

COST OF AN IPO

Even a small company should expect to pay a minimum of $.5 million to complete an IPO. This expense is comprised of a number of fees. Accounting and legal fees will consume the largest proportion of the total. Expect to pay at least $250,000 in legal fees. Audit fees will vary, depending on the size and complexity of the company, but certainly expect to pay at least three times the cost of a normal audit. This figure will increase if there are weak internal control systems that require the auditors to conduct more extensive audit tests. Further, printing costs for the prospectus will exceed $100,000 for all but the most "Plain Jane" documents, which will increase if a large number of revisions to the registration statement are required prior to printing. Also, initial filing fees with a number of government and regulatory bodies will likely consume a minimum of another $25,000.

In addition to these professional fees, the underwriter requires a significant payment that is based on the percentage of capital raised. The usual fee is in the range of 6 to 7% if an offering exceeds $20 million, with the percentage gradually increasing to as much as 15% of the total offering if it is quite small (in the $1 to $3 million range). This cost can be reduced if a company accepts "best efforts" marketing by the underwriter, whereby it does not guarantee a full sale of the entire stock offering. In this case, the percentage fee will drop by 2 to 3%.

To make the situation worse, with the exception of the underwriter fee, most of these costs are incurred prior to the sale of any stock, so a company will be charged with the full expense of an IPO even if it is never completed. If the company withdraws from the IPO process, it must pay the fees incurred to that point by its underwriter, though this obligation is not usually required when the underwriter withdraws. Furthermore, if the IPO is merely delayed, many of the costs must be incurred again, since the underlying operational and financial information on which the original offering was contemplated will have changed and must be reexamined by the lawyers and accountants.

PREPARING FOR THE IPO

Preparing for an IPO begins years before the actual event because the company must "clean up" prior to being presented to the investing public as a quality investment. The steps to this housecleaning are:

- *Increase the competence of the management team.* The single greatest driver of corporate value is the quality of the management team. The owners must evaluate each management position and replace anyone who is not a team player, who does not drive efficiency and effectiveness throughout his or her department, and who does not have a tight strategic vision. Obtaining a manager who is well known at a national level can have a startling positive impact on the perceived value of the company as a whole. A key point is that a management team is not a one-man show. Investors need to see a competent supporting team that can readily take over the business in the event that one key manager dies or leaves the company.

- *Create a reward system that is tied to strategy.* With the assistance of a compensation expert, design a reward system not only for the management team but for the entire company that motivates them to focus their activities on those areas of the business that must be improved prior to the IPO (as described in all the points in this section). A key area is in the use of stock options, which can be issued several years prior to the IPO, when the company's value is substantially lower, resulting in significant gains for the recipients after the company goes public. To do this, one should set aside a large pool of stock for option conversions well in advance of the IPO in order to avoid having the new shareholders vote to create it.

- *Obtain audited financials.*   A reputable audit firm, and preferably one with a national presence, should audit the financial statements for the three years prior to the IPO. A review or compilation is not acceptable—these less expensive and less thorough forms of an audit will be rejected by the underwriter and the SEC when the registration statement is filed.

- *Obtain a top securities law firm.*   Though there may be little perceived need for a law firm well in advance of an IPO, it is useful to have such a firm examine the legal structure of the business and recommend changes that will properly position the company for the IPO. The need for this firm will rise dramatically during the IPO filing period, when its lawyers will review the company's prospectus and registration statement to ensure its completeness in accordance with SEC regulations. The lawyers will also channel all communications to and from the SEC in regard to both the initial registration and filings subsequent to the IPO.

- *Strip out personal transactions.*   The owners of a private business typically mesh their personal affairs with those of the company to a considerable extent. This can include keeping personal servants on the company payroll, having the company guarantee personal loans, loaning company money to their other businesses, and giving themselves inordinate levels of compensation. Stopping these practices can be quite difficult for an owner, whose overall level of compensation may drop substantially as a result.

- *Show 25% annual growth.*   Potential investors want to invest in companies with a record of strong growth, preferably at least 25% for each of the last few years. To create a business in line with these expectations, the business owner must close down or sell off those portions of the business that have no reasonable near-term prospect for growth, or (worse) those areas that are not only *not* growing, but that also require substantial cash infusions that could be better applied to higher-growth business segments.

- *At least show breakeven profitability.*   Investors understand that extra expenses must be incurred in order to ramp up sales, so they are not looking for inordinate profit levels in addition to high sales growth rates. However, there should be no losses appearing on the income statement for the past few years, since this would imply an inability by management to control costs, which brings into question the viability of the entire business model. This may also require a business to switch away from some tax reduction strategies that it may have pursued as a private company in order to reduce its tax liability in favor of ensuring that some degree of profitability appears in the financial statements. Another alternative for ensuring some profitability is a tighter focus on cost controls, perhaps through the use of benchmarking or best practices implementations that are recommended by consultants.

- *Fill the product pipeline.*   Investors want to see a company that has established a clear competitive differentiation in the marketplace. This can be done through the advance funding of research and development projects that lead to the creation of a stream of new products. Since it takes a long time to create new products, the investment in this activity should begin far in advance of the IPO. It is particularly important not to appear like a "one hit wonder," with only a single winning product—be sure to create a process that reliably generates a continuing stream of products.

- *Achieve critical mass.* In order to attract the attention of institutional investors, a company must have a market capitalization of at least $100 million. At this point, their participation will yield an active market for the stock, which can help to drive up the stock price. To reach this capitalization level, a company requires substantial revenue volume. Though roughly one-quarter of all public companies have revenues of less than $10 million, a much higher level is required to reach the crucial $100 million capitalization level. In order to do this, company management may need to concentrate on making acquisitions in the years leading up to the IPO, with the objective of building enough critical mass for the IPO.

- *Expand high-growth segments.* Investors want to see a high rate of growth in areas where other public companies have been rewarded with high price/earnings (P/E) multiples. To do this, the management team should be aware of P/E multiples for all companies in its market segment and allocate funding to those areas of the business that will reward the company with a high P/E multiple when it goes public. This capital allocation process is a difficult one, for the market can increase or decrease P/E multiples in a very short time period, depending on its perception of how "hot" a market segment may be.

- *Pick an independent Board.* Investors want a majority of the Board of Directors to be independent from the management team in order to place investor interests ahead of those of the management team. Though this group can be selected just prior to the IPO, it is better to do so at least a year in advance in order to give this group time to settle into their roles and learn about company operations.

- *Protect owner wealth.* The owner of a company that has just gone public and who has sold some proportion of his or her shares to the public should expect to be paying a large amount of taxes. To reduce this tax burden, the owner can spend the previous few years gifting company stock to heirs, which can be given tax-free in blocks of $10,000 per year to each recipient (or $20,000 if the owner is married). In addition, if there are potential capital losses on any investments, this is the year in which they should be recognized in order to offset the gains from the IPO.

The main point of this section is to impress upon the CFO the need for advance planning for an IPO, preferably beginning a minimum of three years prior to it. Only by taking this long view to going public can a company position itself properly to achieve the maximum value for its shareholders, while minimizing the tax impact for its original owners.

FINDING AN UNDERWRITER

The process of becoming a public company begins with the search for a qualified underwriter who can lead the company through the maze of steps needed to go public. An underwriter is an entity that sells company shares either directly to individual investors or to institutional buyers, such as mutual fund managers. The largest underwriters operate on an international scale, while others have a regional focus or only concentrate their attention on specific market niches in which they have built up a considerable degree of expertise. A major underwriter may have built up a large retail brokerage operation as well as have significant institutional sales capacity, though some of these underwriters have elected to focus more on one of the two sales channels over the other.

It is better to use underwriters with an established reputation, despite their higher cost, because investors tend to trust them more, which can result in a higher stock price.

Conversely, using an underwriter with a poor reputation (i.e., for drumming up the price of stocks that later crash) is much more likely to result in unhappy investors, potential investor lawsuits, and a thinly traded stock. It is also important to use an underwriter with a strong research capability and a commitment to use this resource to distribute information about the company and its industry to investors. A good way to determine who has the best analyst coverage of an industry is to ask investors and other brokerage houses whose reports they feel are the most complete and accurate.

Underwriters have a tendency to sell shares to institutional investors, because these are sophisticated investors who buy in large volumes, thereby reducing the sales efforts of the underwriters. This can be a problem if a large percentage of the company's shares are being sold to the public, because institutional investors are much more likely to either gain control over the company or at least gain a formidable block of voting stock that can be used to influence the company's direction.

If an IPO is a small one, an underwriter may handle the entire issuance itself. However, it more commonly leads a team of underwriters as the managing underwriter if there is a substantial amount of stock to be sold to the public. It creates this syndication not only to spread its own risk in the transaction, but also to ensure that shares are sold to a wide cross section of the investing public, which is critical for creating a strong market for the company's stock.

A larger company with a strong track record will attract the attention of a number of underwriters who are eager to take it public. When selecting from among this group, one should look for a business with a strong reputation for successfully bringing new offerings to market, which can be easily discerned by reviewing the business press for the last few years. Another key factor should be its distribution capacity, since the company will want a broad range of investors, rather than a small number of powerful institutional investors. The underwriter should also be able to commit to the creation of a strong aftermarket in the company's stock, which can be verified by making reference calls to the CFOs of other companies that it has already taken public as the managing underwriter. These reference calls should include queries about the level of service provided, the level of underwriter expertise, the breadth of share placement among investors, and subsequent promotion through research reports. If the underwriter already employs an analyst for the company's industry, this is a strong indicator of the underwriter's commitment to an aftermarket. Further, one should ask if the analyst plans to issue regular research reports to the underwriter's clients about the company. Of particular concern should be the underwriter's history of bringing companies public as the *managing* underwriter, rather than as one of a large syndicate. If the underwriter has primarily been a syndicate member, this is a strong indication that it lacks experience in managing the IPO process.

Unfortunately, most companies are too small to attract a flurry of underwriter interest. Instead, they must work hard to attract the attention of just one or two. To do so, the owner should have already accomplished all of the long-range targets noted in the last section. In addition, the management team should construct a detailed business plan that dovetails with prior company results, while also showing exactly how it plans to use the cash received from the stock offering to achieve future growth and profitability. The plan should most certainly *not* describe any intent by management to sell off its shares, since this tells underwriters that they want to cash out of the company, potentially leaving investors to shift for themselves. This document should include a detailed description of all key members of the management team, since underwriters are well aware of the importance of a strong team. Further, the plan should itemize all risk areas and how the company plans to hedge those risks while pursuing its growth plans. Above all, the plan must present a compelling story that will attract a quality underwriter.

If an underwriter is sufficiently interested in the company, it will conduct an exhaustive due diligence process to verify that what the company says about itself is true. This is likely to include interviews throughout the company, a detailed analysis of all operations, company tours, and reference calls to company suppliers and customers. In particular, the underwriter will investigate the background of each key executive in detail to be sure that their published resumes are accurate. The underwriter must conduct this level of detailed review in order to protect itself in case problems arise after the IPO that it should have seen prior to the stock offering. If there is even a hint of the company trying to mislead the underwriter about material issues, the underwriter will walk away, so be certain to verify all information in the business plan prior to releasing it to the underwriter.

If the underwriter remains interested in the company after the due diligence phase, it will sign a letter of intent with the company. This letter outlines the following issues:

- *Type of agreement.* The letter will state if the arrangement with the underwriter will be a "firm commitment" deal or a "best efforts" deal. The firm commitment approach is used by most large underwriters and requires them to purchase a fixed number of shares from the company at a fixed price, which is discounted from the price at which they will then sell the shares to investors. This is the preferred approach, since a company will be guaranteed a fixed amount of cash. The alternative is a best efforts deal, under which the underwriter merely tries to sell as many shares as it can, and takes a commission on those shares it sells. This alternative does not guarantee a company any cash yet still requires it to meet with the various requirements of being a publicly held entity, so is much less preferable. A best efforts deal is most common when a company's prospects are considered sufficiently risky such that the underwriter is uncomfortable purchasing the entire stock offering and putting itself at risk of being unable to resell them.

- *Expenses.* The underwriter will outline the expenses it expects to charge the company. The largest portion of these costs will be a percentage of the stock offering. More information about this is listed in the earlier "Cost of an IPO" section. This is a good time for the CFO to consider swapping an issuance of warrants to the underwriter in exchange for a lower commission rate. Another significant cost listed in the agreement will be the legal expenses incurred by the underwriter for its legal counsel to review state "blue sky" laws to see how they apply to the offering. The CFO should insist on a cap to these expenses, which can be substantial. The underwriter may also require the company to pay for any out-of-pocket expenses incurred by the underwriter if the company withdraws from the IPO—if so, be sure to insert a maximum expense cap in the agreement. There should be no expense reimbursement requirement if the underwriter is the party who withdraws from the offering.

- *Overallotment option.* This option is another manner in which the underwriter can profit from a potentially lucrative stock offering. It allows the underwriter to purchase additional shares from the company, up to a specified maximum amount, within a short time period following the IPO date. If the underwriter feels that it can sell additional shares at a high price, it will buy the extra shares from the company, sell them to investors, and pocket the difference. The overallotment option is usually acceptable to company management, unless the additional shares sold might potentially interfere with their control of the company.

- *Expected stock price.*   The agreement will list a price at which the underwriter expects to sell the company's shares, though this is strictly a preliminary number that can vary considerably, depending on market fluctuations and the receptiveness of institutional investors to the proposed price during the subsequent road show.

During the period between when the company engages the services of an underwriter and 25 days after its securities begin trading, the company is in a so-called quiet period, when it should not issue any marketing statements or materials that could be construed as an attempt to promote the stock. For example, no projections about expected company performance should be issued. To avoid any chance of breaking the SEC's quiet period regulations, any company communications during this period should be cleared by legal counsel prior to release.

Once the letter of intent is signed by both parties, they jointly move forward into the IPO registration process, which is described in the next section.

REGISTERING FOR AND COMPLETING THE IPO

Registering for and completing the IPO process usually takes three to four months. The basic steps in the process are due diligence investigations of a company's operations and finances, followed by the creation of a registration statement, whose contents are then updated based on SEC comments. This is followed by a road show, final pricing of the stock, filing of the final prospectus with the SEC, and then closing the deal with the underwriter. The following discussion is based on a firm commitment deal with an underwriter. A best efforts deal differs from this discussion primarily in the length of time required to obtain payment from the underwriter, which may require two to three extra months following the registration effective date.

The due diligence process is conducted by the underwriter and is a vastly expanded version of the due diligence it went through when it was initially investigating the company. In this case, it will require outside auditors to comb the company's financial records at a level of detail significantly greater than a standard audit, and then issue a "comfort letter" to the underwriter, stating the additional procedures it completed at the request of the underwriter. These procedures usually relate to unaudited financial information that is included in the registration statement. The auditors send the comfort letter to the underwriter once the initial registration statement has been filed.

The registration statement is comprised of a prospectus and additional information required by the SEC. The statement is the SEC's Form S-1, which is described in detail in Chapter 8, Reports to the Securities and Exchange Commission. The prospectus portion of the statement is an overview of the company's operations and finances and is carefully designed to be a balance of marketing language intended to bolster the stock and a tedious itemization of every conceivable risk to which the company is or may be subject, with the intent of avoiding liability in case the company's prospects sour after it goes public. It also includes all standard financial reports, such as the balance sheet, income statement, statement of cash flows, and shareholders' equity. It will also include interim financial statements if the registration statement is declared effective (more on that shortly) more than 134 days subsequent to the company's fiscal year-end. The registration statement is a complex document, so the CFO should expect 30 to 60 days to pass before the initial version is ready for review by the SEC.

The registration statement is then forwarded to the SEC, which usually takes about one month to review it, after which it issues a letter of comment containing required changes that must be added to the statement in order to bring it into compliance with SEC regulations. Their comments can include such issues as an expansion of risk disclosures, cross-referencing information within the prospectus, questions about the use of certain accounting policies, and adding information to support claims made. Once these changes are made in an amended filing, the SEC has the right to continue reviewing the document until it declares the statement to be effective.

The company must also submit the registration statement to the National Association of Securities Dealers (NASD), which wants to ensure that the underwriter's compensation is not excessive. The statement must also be sent to each state in which the company plans to offer its shares for sale, so they can verify that the offering meets individual state reporting requirements.

The prospectus portion of the registration statement is then sent to prospective investors. This "red herring" version of the statement may not yet have been approved by the SEC and will not include a final stock price, but will list a range within which the final price will fall. This version is used to educate investors in advance about the offering, but is not used to solicit the sale of stock. It is also sent to the syndicate of other underwriters that the primary, or "managing," underwriter will assemble to help sell the stock.

After filing the registration statement and prior to its effective date, the CEO and CFO (sometimes accompanied by other members of management) go on a road show to visit a number of key institutional investors and analysts, where they make a sales pitch about the company but do not attempt to sell any shares. This is a physically exhausting process that typically lasts about two weeks. As an example of just one day in a typical road show circuit, the CEO of a Silicon Valley company boarded a private jet in San Francisco at 5 A.M. and flew to five cities across the United States, stopping for a one-hour presentation in each city (several being on the East Coast), before flying back to San Francisco—the same day. He did this for nine days in a two-week period. Preparing for the road show also requires long hours, frequently including training by speech coaches and even etiquette consultants.

While the management team is conducting the road show, its legal counsel will file an application with the stock exchange on which it wishes to be listed, while also selecting a registrar (who tracks all stock, pays out dividends of various types, and mails reports to shareholders) and a transfer agent (who handles the transfer of shares between parties) to handle subsequent stock-related issues. It will also submit filings in accordance with the securities laws of all states in which the company expects to sell shares.

Once the SEC is satisfied with all changes made to the registration statement, company management meets with the underwriter to set the final price of the stock. Price setting is part science and part art form. Ostensibly, the price should be based on a quantitative measure, such as the existing price/earnings multiple or price/revenue multiple for similar companies. Other operational issues may also be considered that will modify the price to some extent, such as backorder volume, sales trends, the proportion of expenses to sales, the quality of management, the outlook for the entire industry, the severity of current or potential competition, pending pollution issues, or the presence of valuable patents. However, the comments of institutional investors who were contacted during the road show will have a strong bearing on the final price. They are usually relied on to purchase a significant proportion of the company's stock, and if they show resistance to purchasing stock at a specific price, then the underwriter will recommend a price reduction. In addition, the underwriter will underprice the issuance slightly in order to ensure a complete sale of all shares offered to the public, while also giving it some grounds for avoiding a lawsuit in case the stock price later declines and investors claim that the initial price was too high. The extent of the underpricing tends to be greater during the IPO in comparison to secondary offerings, so management may want to consider selling slightly fewer shares at this time in order to avoid dilution.

Underwriters like to price IPO shares in the range of $10 to $20, on the grounds that this avoids penny stock status (which is $5 or less), and the perception that investors will be less likely to buy shares priced above $25. To achieve this range, the company may have to conduct either a stock split or a reverse stock split. For example, if the underwriter decides that a company's total valuation is $50,000,000 and that the stock price will be $20, then there should be 2,500,000 shares outstanding in order to achieve the designated price per share. If the company actually has 10,000,000 shares outstanding, then it must conduct a 4-for-1 reverse stock split in order to bring the number of outstanding shares down to the required 2,500,000 level.

The underwriter will also want to sell in excess of one million shares during the IPO, not only to create an active trading market for the stock, but also to meet the minimum outstanding shares rules of the stock exchanges (as noted further in the "Trading on an Exchange" section).

Once all parties agree to the stock price, this is included in the registration statement as an amendment along with the net proceeds by the company resulting from the offering and the underwriter's commission. The company then asks the SEC to declare the registration statement "effective." This request is typically accompanied by a request to accelerate the SEC's standard 20-day waiting period between the filing date of the last amendment and the date when the registration is declared effective, which the SEC generally agrees to as long as the prospectus has already been sufficiently widely circulated to prospective investors in its "red herring" format. After the registration is declared effective, the company issues the prospectus to the investors who previously received the "red herring," as well as to any others who wish to review it.

The underwriter and the company will then sign a "lockup agreement," under which management restricts itself from selling any company shares it owns for a minimum period, usually of at least a half-year.

Finally, at a closing meeting that usually takes place about one week after the registration effective date, the underwriter hands over payment for all shares proffered under the IPO offering in exchange for the share certificates. This delay of a few days is needed for the underwriter to collect cash from its investors, who will then receive the stock from the underwriter. The company is now officially a public entity.

ALTERNATIVES FOR SELLING SECURITIES

A traditional IPO may not be available to a company for a variety of reasons. Potential underwriters may feel that a company's underlying technological prowess is too unproven to make a convincing case to potential shareholders. The same reasoning may apply to its rate of growth or the perceived quality of its management team. Or, the market may be saturated with other IPOs, so there is no room for another one without accepting an unreasonably low price. If any of these circumstances apply, a company may consider using the options listed in this section—an "Open IPO" offering, the purchase of a shell corporation, or a SCOR offering.

Open IPO.   One alternative to the traditional sale of stock through an underwriter is to use an "Open IPO" auction. Under this approach, potential investors download a prospectus over the Internet from an underwriter that specializes in this type of offering. If they wish to bid on the shares, they open an account with the underwriter, select a bid price and the number of shares desired, and send the underwriter a check for that amount. This bid can be withdrawn at any time prior to the offering date. Based on the range of bids received, the underwriter then creates a public offering price at which share purchases will be accepted (which matches the price of the lowest bid received, below which all other bids exceed the number of shares to be offered). All investors bidding above this price will be issued their full share allocations, while those whose bids were below the price will be refunded their money. Those investors bidding the exact amount of the public offering price will receive some portion of their requested number of shares, depending on how many other investors requested shares at that price and how many shares are still available for sale. This approach tends to result in higher share prices, resulting in either more proceeds flowing to the company or fewer shares being sold (resulting in more control by the original shareholders).

For example, a company wishes to sell 1 million shares to the public. Investors bid for 500,000 shares at $14 each, while bids are also received for 300,000 shares at $13.50 and 600,000 at $12.00. Since the entire offering can be sold at a price of $12, this becomes the public offering price. All investors bidding at prices of $14 and $13.50 per share will receive their full allocations of shares and will pay $12 per share. Of the 600,000 shares bid at $12, investors will receive only one-third of their requested amounts, since this will result in 1 million shares being sold, which was the original target.

Reverse Merger.   An initial public offering is extremely expensive and requires a great deal of management time to initiate. An alternative that uses less of both resources is the reverse merger. With this approach, a company buys the shell of a company that has already gone public, and merges itself into the shell. A corporate shell is an entity that has suspended ongoing operations, and which generally has few assets.

The cost of a reverse merger ranges from $100,000 to $300,000, plus the cost to obtain the shell corporation (which will vary widely, depending on the value of its assets and the presence of any liabilities or other legal issues). A reverse merger can be completed in as little as 45 to 90 days, which allows management to rapidly return to a focus on operational issues.

Another advantage of the reverse merger is that the shell company has usually sustained losses in the past, resulting in a sometimes sizeable net operating loss (NOL) that can be used to offset the earnings of the acquiring company. However, the use of these NOLs will likely be restricted if there is a change in control of the shell, which is the usual scenario.

However, a shell may have unsettled legal claims that could be brought against the acquiring company. A considerable amount of due diligence is needed to locate potential or existing claims, which also increases the cost of the reverse merger.

Another problem is that the shell may not have kept up its required filings with the SEC, in which case they must be brought up to date before the reverse merger can be completed.

Further, the acquiring company must issue some stock to the shareholders of the shell corporation to pay for the acquisition, possibly as much as 20% of all shares, resulting in dilution of the ownership interests of shareholders in the acquiring company, and possibly of the value of their stock.

A very likely additional problem is that the shell's original shareholders may sell their shares as soon as possible following the reverse merger, resulting in a sudden decline in the traded stock price. This issue can be mitigated by incorporating timing restrictions on stock sales into the acquisition agreement.

Finally, companies that go public through reverse mergers tend to have only modest revenues and growth prospects, and so are ignored by stock analysts and brokers who might otherwise increase investor interest in the stock.

To summarize the key issues, the reverse merger is an attractive alternative to the IPO, but the potential for hidden liabilities requires in-depth due diligence to ensure that the acquiring company does not become mired in lawsuits and the settlement of other liabilities.

SCOR

Another alternative is to file for a small corporate offering registration (SCOR). This is a simplified registration used by companies that want to raise up to $1 million within a 12-month period. One must complete the 50-question Form U-7 and file it with the state securities commission for the state in which the company operates. The form requires no review by the SEC, but must be reviewed by the state securities commission. This form can then be used as a prospectus by the company in its search for investors (since this approach does not normally involve an underwriter). This approach can be taken by any entity incorporated in either the United States or Canada, except for investment or public companies.

The SCOR approach falls under the restrictions of Rule 504 of the SEC's Regulation D, which governs private and limited stock offerings. Rule 504 allows a company to sell shares to an unlimited number of investors, who do not have to meet any accreditation standards. It also allows the company to advertise the stock offering and does not restrict the resale of stock in any way. In short, the SEC is unusually liberal in its regulation of small stock offerings in the size range of a SCOR.

Though the SCOR approach is far less expensive than an IPO, it carries other risks and uncertainties. First, a company using this approach may try to avoid expenses by not using legal counsel. This approach may lay it open to potential shareholder lawsuits due to some unexpected oversight in the registration and solicitation process. The obvious mitigation approach to this risk is to bring the best legal counsel into the SCOR filing process as soon as possible and to solicit its advice at every step of the offering. Also, the management team must sell the shares to investors, an activity that may not fall within its range of expertise. Finally, due to the lack of an underwriter, there will not be a ready market for subsequent sales of the stock, making investment liquidations a chancy affair for investors.

TRADING ON AN EXCHANGE

Though a company has successfully completed an IPO, its stock is not yet traded on a stock exchange. If a company is not listed on an exchange, its securities will be designated as over-the-counter (OTC) stocks and will most likely appear in the Pink Sheets. The "pink sheet" name is derived from the color of stock price sheets that were distributed by the National Quotation Bureau starting in 1904, and which served as a pricing reference for stock trades through local stock dealers. The paper-based service recently expanded into the Internet-based "Electronic Quotation Service," which provides real-time price quotes for over-the-counter securities to market makers and brokers. This market is a dangerous one for investors, who must conduct their own research into prospective investments and are at considerable risk of losing their entire investments in companies that may be in distressed circumstances, or whose stocks are so thinly traded that they are subject to large price swings. Consequently, avoiding OTC status by enrolling in a stock exchange is considered highly advantageous.

Gaining entry to a stock exchange requires an application to it, in which the company states that it meets or exceeds all entry requirements of the exchange. These requirements are not just financial—for example, the major stock exchanges all require a listed company to have an audit committee, usually with at least a majority of the directors being independent of the company. If the exchange accepts an application, the company's shares are listed on the exchange and an exchange representative is assigned to the company in order to advise it on exchange rules and how to market itself most effectively to investors through the exchange. This service comes at a cost—both an initial listing fee and an ongoing annual charge.

There are six stock exchanges of any size in the United States: the American Stock Exchange, Chicago Stock Exchange, NASDAQ Stock Market, New York Stock Exchange, Pacific Stock Exchange, and the Philadelphia Stock Exchange. Of this group, the largest are the American Stock Exchange (AMEX), the NASDAQ Stock Market (NASDAQ), and the New York Stock Exchange (NYSE). Each of the three major exchanges have differing requirements for entry, with the AMEX and NASDAQ SmallCap being the easiest to enter and the NYSE being the most difficult. An increasingly popular alternative is the Alternative Investment Market (AIM) of the London Stock Exchange, which allows companies to avoid many of the onerous rules required by U.S. exchanges.

There is an ongoing international trend for stock exchanges to adopt electronic trading systems; in this more efficient market, there will be a natural trend for the exchanges to compete on price, which will drive down their earnings. To avoid this, exchanges are already differentiating themselves by having different tiers of listings that are based on varying degrees of financial soundness and corporate governance. Thus, the CFO can now find listings that are closely tailored to the needs of his or her firm.

The AMEX allows companies to list their stock on it if they qualify under any of three criteria. All three criteria share common requirements, which are either 800 public shareholders and 500,000 shares held, or 400 public shareholders and 1 million shares publicly held, or 400 public shareholders, 500,000 shares publicly held, and an average daily trading volume of 2,000 shares for the past six months. In addition to these common requirements for trading volume, a company can qualify to be traded on the exchange if it meets any one of the following three sets of criteria:

1. *Income basis of qualification.*   If a company has only a short operating history but significant earnings, then this is the best set of qualification criteria to use. It requires a company to have $4 million of shareholders' equity, as well as $750,000 in pre-tax income in the last fiscal year or in two of the last three years. Also, the stock price must be no lower than $3.00, while the market value of the shares held by the public must be no lower than $3 million.

Number of Shares	Initial Listing Fee	Annual Fee
Up to 5 million	$45,000	$16,500
5+ to 10 million	55,000	19,000
10+ to 15 million	60,000	21,500
15+ to 25 million	70,000	24,500
25+ to 50 million	70,000	32,500
More than 50 million	70,000	34,000

EXHIBIT 16.1   AMEX LISTING AND ANNUAL FEES

2. *Historical basis of qualification.*   If a company's operating results are not exceptional, but it has a multiyear operating history, this is the best set of qualification criteria to use. It requires a company to have shareholders' equity of at least $4 million, plus two years of operational history, a stock price of no less than $3.00, and a market value of shares held by the public of at least $15 million.

3. *Capitalization basis of qualification.*   This set of criteria works best if a company has poor operating results and a minimal operating history but is well capitalized. Under this approach, a company must have shareholders' equity of at least $4 million, a total market capitalization of at least $50 million, and a market value of shares held by the public of at least $15 million.

The AMEX charges a one-time $5,000 application fee. In addition, Exhibit 16.1 shows the rates it charges for an initial listing and on an annual basis.

The NASDAQ is divided into the National Market and the Capital Market. Both markets use an approach similar to the AMEX's in setting listing requirements (which is no surprise, since they have the same corporate parent!). The National Market requires a company to have 1.1 million publicly held shares, a minimum bid price of $5.00, and at least 400 shareholders. In addition to these basic requirements, the National Market allows one to choose from the following three listing criteria:

1. *Income basis of qualification.*   A company must have income from continuing operations pre-tax of at least $1 million in two of the last three years, plus $15 million in stockholders' equity, and maintain a minimum market value of publicly held shares of at least $8 million.

2. *Historical basis of qualification.*   A company must have an operating history of at least two years, but have a much higher stockholders' equity of $30 million and maintain a higher market value of publicly held shares of at least $18 million.

3. *Capitalization basis of qualification.*   A company must have either total revenues, total assets, or total market value of at least $75 million, plus a market value of publicly held shares of at least $20 million.

In short, the National Market makes it easier for profitable companies to be listed and raises the listing requirements substantially if this is not the case.

The National Market charges a $5,000 application fee. Also, it charges a fee of $100,000 for the first 30 million shares registered on the exchange, plus another $125,000 incrementally for the next layer of 20 million shares, and another incremental $150,000 for any additional shares listed. Annual fees are substantially lower than the initial fees, and follow the pricing schedule listed in Exhibit 16.2.

Total Shares Outstanding	Annual Fees
Up to 10 million	$24,500
10+ to 25 million	30,500
25+ to 50 million	34,500
50+ to 75 million	44,500
75+ to 100 million	61,750
Over 100 million	75,000

EXHIBIT 16.2   NASDAQ NATIONAL MARKET ANNUAL FEES

The NASDAQ also maintains the Capital Market. This market is designed for smaller companies with smaller market capitalizations, lower revenues, and reduced profits. If a company later expands in size and wishes to shift over to the National Market, its annual fee for the year in which it switches will be credited toward its (higher) fees on the National Market.

The Capital Market has a simpler set of listing requirements than the National Market. Upon initial listing, a company must have at least 1 million publicly held shares, as well as a market value of $5 million in publicly held shares, and minimum bid price of $4.00. There must also be at least 300 shareholders. The company must also meet one of three capitalization requirements: either (1) $5 million in stockholders' equity, (2) $50 million in the market value of listed securities, or (3) $750,000 in net income from continuing operations in the last fiscal year or in two of the last three fiscal years. These are significantly lower entry requirements than those for the National Market, which makes this a good entry market for a newly public company.

On a continuing basis, a company listed on the Capital Market must maintain either (1) $2.5 million in stockholders' equity, (2) $35 million in the market value of listed securities, or (3) $500,000 in net income from continuing operations in the last fiscal year or in two of the last three fiscal years on a continuing basis, the market value of publicly held shares can drop to $1 million, while the minimum bid price can decline to as low as $1.

The Capital Market also charges lower fees than the National Market. Its application fee is the same $5,000, but its fee schedule for the initial listing of shares is reduced, as noted in Exhibit 16.3. The Capital Market's annual listing fees range from $100,000 to $150,000, depending on the number of shares listed.

The NYSE has the toughest listing requirements of the exchanges, which gives it a reputation for listing companies in only the best possible financial condition. Its listing requirements fall into the categories of distribution, size, and financial criteria. Under its distribution criteria, a company must either have at least 2,200 shareholders and an average monthly trading volume of at least 100,000 shares, or at least 500 shareholders and average monthly trading volume of at least 1,000,000 shares. The latter criterion is

Total Shares Outstanding	Entry Fees
Up to 10 million shares	17,500
Over 10 million shares	21,000

EXHIBIT 16.3   NASDAQ CAPITAL MARKET INITIAL LISTING FEES

Number of Shares	Initial Listing Fees per Share
Up to 75 million	$0.0048
75+ to 300 million	0.00375
More than 300 million	0.0019

EXHIBIT 16.4 NYSE LISTING AND ANNUAL FEES

more helpful to companies with a larger proportion of institutional investors, who tend to trade in much larger blocks of shares. In addition, a company must maintain a minimum of 1.1 million outstanding public shares, plus a market value of public shares of at least $100 million. The last criterion bars smaller companies with lower market capitalizations from listing on the NYSE.

Under its financial criteria, a company must aggregate pre-tax profits of at least $10,000,000 over the last three years, which must include a minimum of $2,000,000 in profits in the most recently completed year. Alternatively, a company must have at least $750 million in market capitalization and $75 million in revenue during the most recent 12 months, and aggregate operating cash flow for the last three years of at least $25,000,000. These criteria are designed to block out companies experiencing continuing losses in profits or cash flows, though it does provide an escape clause if a company maintains a high market capitalization.

The NYSE charges a one-time application fee of $37,500. The rates it charges for an initial listing can be seen in Exhibit 16.4.

Note that the fees shown in Exhibit 16.4 are incremental. For example, a company listing 5 million shares on the NYSE would be charged as follows:

1st million shares	$14,750
2nd million shares	14,750
3rd million shares	7,400
4th million shares	7,400
5th million shares	3,500
Total fee	$47,800

The NYSE's minimum fee for an initial listing is $150,000, while its maximum fee is $250,000. In addition, it charges $0.00093 per share on an annual basis. Its maximum charge for annual fees is $500,000.

The preceding list of listing requirements and fees may leave one wondering why anyone would list their shares on the much more expensive NYSE. There are several good reasons for doing so. Besides having the prestige of listing on the best-known stock exchange in the world, a company's shares will be linked to that prestige, which may command a slight stock price premium. In addition, many institutional investors are not allowed to invest in the shares of any company that is *not* listed on the NYSE, so a company can access a whole new group of sophisticated investors by being listed on the NYSE. Thus, it is better to think of the various exchanges as a progression for a public company—starting with the less prestigious NASDAQ SmallCap or AMEX exchanges and gradually working up to the NASDAQ National Market and then the NYSE as the company grows in revenue, profitability, and market capitalization.

A popular alternative to these major U.S. exchanges is the London Stock Exchange's Alternative Investment Market (AIM). By using this exchange, a company can avoid a multitude of U.S. regulations, which greatly reduces the cost of being a public company. This is particularly appealing for smaller companies, for whom the costs of being publicly held constitute a burdensome percentage of their total costs. AIM fees are also low, with an admission fee of $7,900 and an annual fee of the same amount. Key aspects of the AIM's listing requirements are:

- There is no minimum market capitalization requirement.

- There is no minimum number of shares that must be held by the public.

- Interim financial reports are only required every six months, rather than the three months required in the United States.

- A nominated advisor (Nomad) must be appointed. A Nomad warrants to the AIM that the company is appropriate for trading on the exchange, and also provides ongoing advice to the company regarding AIM regulations. The exchange maintains a list of approved Nomads from which a company can make a selection. A company must be associated with a Nomad at all times.

OVER-THE-COUNTER STOCKS

If a publicly traded company cannot meet the listing requirements of a stock exchange, then it can choose to have its shares traded over-the-counter. The best two vehicles for such trading are Pink Sheets LLC and the OTC Bulletin Board, which is operated by NASDAQ.

The OTC Bulletin Board operates an electronic exchange that handles bid and price information on about 3,300 securities of various kinds. For a company to have its securities quoted in the OTC Bulletin Board exchange, it must first find at least one market maker who is willing to quote the stock; this person must be an SEC-registered broker-dealer. Listing also requires that a company be registered with the Securities and Exchange Commission (SEC), which lends considerable credence to securities quoted on this exchange. The exchange charges no fees for a security to be quoted in its system.

Pink Sheets LLC (www.pinksheets.com) operates an Internet-based, real-time quotation service for over-the-counter equities and bonds, of which about 5,000 are currently traded. It is not a registered stock exchange. For a company to have its securities quoted in the Pink Sheets exchange, it must first find at least one market maker who is willing to quote the stock; this person must be an SEC-registered broker-dealer. Pink Sheets LLC does not require that a company register with the SEC before being listed in its exchange service. Because of the lack of registration requirements, being listed by Pink Sheets LLC tends to give a company the reputation for having questionable financial results.

Pink Sheets LLC is attempting to improve the reputation of a selection of the companies it lists by categorizing them in a premium listing called the OTCQX (Over-the-counterquality exchange). To be listed in the OTCQX, here are some of the requirements that a company must meet:

- Have audited financial statements.

- Conduct an annual shareholders' meeting.

- Maintain a minimum share bid price of $1.

- Post quarterly and annual reports on www.otcqx.com.

- Have ongoing operations (e.g., not a shell company).
- Make interim disclosure of material events.
- Have at least 100 shareholders.

To be listed on the OTCQX also requires a $5,000 application fee and a monthly listing fee of $950.

RESTRICTIONS ON STOCK IN A PUBLICLY TRADED COMPANY

If one acquires securities in unregistered, private sales from the stock issuer, they are considered to be "restricted" shares. This definition typically includes all securities issued as part of private placement offerings, employee stock benefit plans, or in exchange for "seed money" used to start a business. A restricted share usually contains a stamp indicating its status and stating that it cannot be resold in the marketplace unless it is registered with the SEC. A stock transfer agent will not allow a share to be sold unless it receives an opinion letter from the issuer's legal counsel stating that the share can be traded. Once this opinion is received, the transfer agent will remove the stamp, allowing it to be traded in a normal manner.

If this type of security is obtained through a nonpublic offering, the shareholder cannot sell it until one year has elapsed from the date of acquisition. The date of acquisition is considered to be when the securities are bought and fully paid for, which means that taking out a loan from the issuing company in order to pay for the shares is not considered full ownership until the date when the loan is paid off. After that time, one can sell portions of the securities held during successive three-month periods. During each such period, the shareholder cannot sell more than the greater of 1% of the class of security that is outstanding or the average weekly trading volume for the preceding four calendar weeks. When sold, these sales must be handled as routine trading transactions, with brokers receiving the standard commission rate for them. Further, neither the shareholder nor the broker is allowed to solicit orders to purchase the tendered restricted shares.

Before a shareholder sells restricted shares, he or she must file a Form 144 notice with the SEC if the sale is for more than 500 shares or if the total amount of such share sales exceeds $10,000 in any three-month period. Once filed, the reported shares must be sold within three months, or else an amended notice must be filed that describes a later transaction. When completing the form, the shareholder must also state that he or she is not aware of any material adverse information regarding the company that has not already been disclosed to the public.

SUMMARY

The objective of many successful business owners is to take their companies public, so they can eventually sell off some portion of their shares in the business and retire. However, this reasoning does not always work out in practice because of the considerable expense of the IPO, the ongoing cost of reporting to the public, ongoing exchange listing fees, potential investor lawsuits, and the risk of loss of control of the business. Consequently, an increasing number of business owners have concluded that they would rather take their companies private. Doing so requires special reporting requirements, which are discussed in Chapter 17, Taking a Company Private.

TAKING A COMPANY PRIVATE

Many companies find that the cost and liability of operating a publicly owned business is not worth the hassle, and elect to remove themselves from public trading. This involves the filing of a lengthy schedule with the Securities and Exchange Commission (SEC), which is described in this chapter.

GOING PRIVATE TRANSACTION

If a publicly held company wishes to go private, it must disclose information that is itemized under the SEC's Rule 13E-3. This rule applies to situations where a company plans to buy back its securities, as described in the next section.

The information required under these circumstances must be filed on Schedule 13E-3, to which amendments must be added if there are material changes to the information presented on it. The primary information listed on the schedule includes complete company financial statements and various financial information on a per-share basis. The company must also include information regarding the identity of the persons filing the schedule, terms of the arrangement, future plans, the reason for going private, and the source and financing terms for the funding required to complete the transaction.

RULE 13E-3

The SEC's Rule 13E-3 applies to any transaction where equity securities are being purchased by their issuer or when a tender offer for those securities is being made by their issuers or an affiliate. Such a transaction must result in having less than 300 people hold the equity security or the removal of that class of equity securities from being listed on a national exchange.

When an equity security is withdrawn from circulation by the issuer, the rule also states that information about the withdrawal shall not be misleading or attempt to defraud a security holder.

The rule requires the issuer to file Schedule 13E-3 (see next section) prior to withdrawing a class of securities, as well as to file amendments to it to reflect any material changes in the information itemized in the original filing. These amendments will be concluded with an amendment reporting the final results of the withdrawal transaction.

The rule further requires that the security issuer disclose to security holders the following information:

- A summary term sheet
- The purposes, alternatives, reasons for, and effects of the transaction
- Fairness of the transaction to the security holder

- Reports, opinions, appraisals, and negotiations related to the transaction
- Information concerning the rights of the security holders to conduct appraisals
- All other information listed in Schedule 13E-3, except for exhibits. A "fair and adequate summary" can be substituted for this information.

If there are changes to the information offered to security holders, then the rule requires that these changes be promptly reported to them. In any event, the original set of disclosures must be issued to the security holders no later than ten business days prior to any withdrawal transaction. If securities are held in trust for securities holders by a broker-dealer, then the issuer must forward these information materials to the broker-dealer, with instructions to forward it to the security holders.

These reporting requirements are not necessary if the issuer offers security holders another equity security in exchange for the one being retired, but only if the replacement security has essentially the same rights as the old security, including voting, dividends, redemption, and liquidation rights, or if common stock is offered. The reporting is also not required if the security withdrawal is already allowed under the specific provisions itemized in the instrument creating or governing that class of securities.

FILLING OUT SCHEDULE 13E-3

Schedule 13E-3 must be filed with the SEC prior to the withdrawal of securities by the issuer. Some elements of this schedule may also be sent to the security holders, as noted in the last section. This schedule is essentially a full and complete disclosure of the withdrawal transaction.

The lead page of the schedule requires one to note the name of the issuer, the name of the person filing the statement, and the title of the class of securities to be withdrawn under the terms contained within the schedule. The contents of the remaining sections of the report are:

1. *Summary term sheet.* This term sheet must describe the primary terms of the proposed transaction, yielding sufficient information for security holders to understand the basic structure and terms of it. All information in this summary should reference a more detailed discussion in a separate disclosure statement that is sent to the security holders.

2. *Subject company information.* State the name and address of the company. In addition, note the exact title and number of shares outstanding in the security class to be retired. Further, describe the market in which the securities are traded, as well as their high-low sale prices for each quarter in the past two years. Point out the frequency and amount of any dividends paid during the past two years, as well as any restrictions on the company's ability to pay dividends. Also, note the date and size of any public offering of the securities to be retired, if they occurred within the past three years. Finally, mention any prior purchases of the subject security within the past two years, including the amount and range of prices paid.

3. *Identity and background of filing person.* State the name and contact information for the person filing the schedule. Also list the person's current occupation and the name of his or her place of employment, as well as this information for the past five years. Finally, state whether the person was convicted of a criminal activity in the past five years, and if so, when and where the court proceedings took place.

This includes any judgment blocking the person from future activities subject to federal or state securities laws.

4. *Terms of the transaction.*   List the primary terms of the proposed purchase transaction, which should include the total number and class of securities that the company wishes to buy, the price offered for them, and the expiration date of the offer. Also, note if the offering period will be repeated or extended, and the date ranges when current security owners can withdraw from sale any securities they have tendered under the terms of this agreement. Further, describe the procedures to be used by security holders for tendering and withdrawing securities. If the company only intends to purchase some of the outstanding securities, then describe how purchases will be made on a pro rata basis, as well as what will happen in the event of an oversubscription. In addition, point out any material accounting treatment or income tax consequences as a result of the transaction. Also, list any variations on the standard set of purchase terms if they differ by security holder. For those security holders who may object to the transaction, itemize any appraisal rights they may have. Finally, if other securities are being offered as a trade for the subject securities, describe any arrangements the company may have to offer them for public trading.

5. *Past contacts, transactions, negotiations, and agreements.*   List any transaction occurring in the past two years between the filing person and the company if they comprise more than 1% of the company's revenue, or between the filing person and an officer of the company if they comprise more than $60,000. Also, describe any transactions or discussions between the filing person and the company during the past two years that addressed any merger or acquisition, tender offers, director elections, or significant asset sales. Finally, as a blanket disclosure, note any other arrangements between the filing person and any other person regarding the company's securities, which can include security transfers, security votes, joint ventures, loan arrangements, and loan or loss guarantees. This notation should include securities that are pledged in any manner, such that a different person could obtain security voting rights.

6. *Purposes of the transaction and plans or proposals.*   Describe how any acquired securities will be treated, such as retirement or being held in treasury. Also, cover any plans for the company's subsequent merger, liquidation, or sale of major assets, as well as any prospective changes in the company's dividend policy, debt level, or capitalization. Further, note any planned changes in the size or structure of the Board of Directors, as well as any changes in the management team or its employment contracts. Finally, as a blanket disclosure, note any other prospective material changes to the company's structure or business.

7. *Purposes, alternatives, reasons, and effects.*   Describe the underlying reason for the transaction, as well as any alternatives to it that were considered and why they were rejected in favor of the proposed transaction. Further, note the impact of the transaction on the company, which should include its federal tax consequences.

8. *Fairness of the transaction.*   State whether the company thinks the proposed transaction is fair or not to those security holders not affiliated with the company, as well as the factors considered in determining fairness. If any company director either abstained from or rejected the vote for this transaction, list that person's name and the reason for his or her vote. In addition, state if the transaction was approved by a majority of the unaffiliated directors. Further, note whether or not the unaffiliated

directors have retained an unaffiliated person who represents the interests of the unaffiliated security holders in constructing the terms of the transaction. Also point out if the transaction requires the approval of a majority of the security holders.

9. *Reports, opinions, appraisals, and negotiations.*   State whether the company has received an outside party's appraisal of the proposed transaction; if so, list the appraiser's name, as well as his or her qualifications, and any material relationship between the appraiser and the company, either in the past or prospectively. Also, describe the method used to select the appraiser, and if the appraiser recommended the amount of consideration to be paid as part of the transaction. Further, summarize the contents of the appraisal report, including the procedures followed, its findings and recommendations, and any limitations imposed on the appraiser by the company. Finally, state that the full appraisal report is available for review by security holders.

10. *Source and amounts of funds or other consideration.*   Note the source and amount of funds that will be used in the proposed transaction, as well as any material conditions that will be imposed on the company in order to obtain the required funds. Also, describe any alternative financing plans that have been arranged in case the primary source does not work. If the required funds are coming from a borrowing arrangement, then summarize the loan agreement. Further, describe all costs to be incurred as part of the transaction, such as legal, accounting, and appraisal costs.

11. *Interest in securities of the subject company.*   List the number and percentage of the subject securities owned by each company officer or director. Also, describe all transactions involving the subject securities within the past 60 days, including the persons involved, the transaction dates, the amounts of securities involved, and the price per share.

12. *The solicitation or recommendation.*   State if any company officer or director intends to sell securities owned by that person, as well as how each of these people intends to vote their securities in regard to this transaction. Also, state if any person listed in this section has made a recommendation in regard to this transaction, and the reasons therefore.

13. *Financial statements.*   If this information is sent to security holders, one can instead include summarized financial information. If so, instructions must be included in the schedule for how the security holders can obtain more detailed financial information.

14. *Persons/assets retained, employed, compensated, or used.*   List all people who will make solicitations related to the proposed transaction, including the terms of their employment and compensation. This should include any company officers or employees working on the transaction.

15. *Additional information.*   Provide any additional material information that will keep the information contained in the schedule from being misleading to the reader.

16. *Exhibits.*   There are a number of exhibits to be attached to the schedule. They should include any additional disclosure materials issued to the security holders, such as going private disclosure documents, related loan agreements, appraisals, and a detailed discussion of security holder appraisal rights.

The statement must be signed by the filing person or that person's representative (including the representative's authorization to sign). Once completed, the CFO must file eight copies of the schedule with the SEC.

INTENTIONAL DELISTING

The extensive control and reporting requirements of the Sarbanes-Oxley Act may drive companies into going private, but there is an alternative—to intentionally delist from an exchange and deregister with the Securities and Exchange Commission. By doing so, none of the Sarbanes provisions will apply, and company shares can still be traded over-the-counter on the Pink Sheets.

To intentionally delist requires a letter to the exchange on which a company is registered, as well as completion of the one-page Form 15 for the SEC. No investor approval is required for delisting. However, the total number of shareholders must be less than 300 in order to take this approach.

International firms that are listed outside the United States can simply delist from an American stock exchange in order to avoid the Sarbanes provisions.

SUMMARY

Filling out the Schedule 13E-3 described in this section is a time-consuming process. The Internal Revenue Service (IRS) estimates that an appropriate interval for doing so is 150 hours, so the CFO would be well advised to use a project team to work through this lengthy document. Also, be sure to have legal counsel review it, and also subject it to accuracy reviews, so that security holders cannot later claim there are any inaccuracies in the schedule that give them a reason to sue for damages of any kind. If done properly, the schedule is the foundation document for a successful withdrawal of securities from public ownership, so a company can go private.

PART 5

MANAGEMENT

CHAPTER 18

RISK MANAGEMENT*

Some well-managed companies have fallen because they did not pay attention to risk. For example, it is difficult to recover from a fire that destroys a data center or production facility, or from the theft of all one's securities and cash. Though rare, these occurrences can be so catastrophic that it is not possible to recover. An otherwise healthy organization is destroyed, throwing many people out of work and eliminating the equity stake of the owners.

On a lesser scale and much more common are the lawsuits that nearly every company must face from time to time. These may relate to employee injuries, customer or supplier claims regarding contracts, or perhaps sexual harassment or some form of discrimination. These lawsuits do not normally end a company's existence, but they can cripple it if awards are excessive or the company is not in a solid financial position to begin with.

This chapter covers the risk management planning, policies, and procedures that keep a company from being seriously injured by these and other types of risk-related problems. In addition, it notes the role of the risk manager in mitigating a company's risk by modifying internal systems as well as by purchasing insurance. The types of insurance that a company can buy are also discussed, as well as how to select a broker or underwriter to help service a company's needs and how to evaluate the health of an insurance carrier. The chapter concludes with coverage of how to administer insurance claims, and how to write a risk management report that clearly identifies a company's risks and how they are being addressed.

RISK MANAGEMENT POLICIES

A company must determine the amount of risk that it is willing to undertake. When the Board of Directors attempts to quantify this, it frequently finds that it is uncomfortable with the level of risk that it currently has and mandates more action—through new policies—that reduce the level of risk. The policies can include a number of risk management issues, such as the financial limits for risk assumption or retention, self-insurance parameters, the financial condition of insurance providers, and captive insurance companies. The policies do not have to cover some issues that are already required by law, such as workers' compensation insurance. An example of a comprehensive insurance policy is noted in Exhibit 18.1.

There are several key points to consider in the exhibit. First, a company may be tempted to purchase very inexpensive insurance, which typically comes from an insurance provider that is in poor financial condition. If the company subsequently files a claim on this insurance, it may find that the provider is not in a position to pay it. Consequently,

---

* Reprinted with permission from pp. 1117–1126 of *Controllership* by Roehl-Anderson and Bragg (John Wiley & Sons, 2004).

1. ABC Company will obtain insurance only from companies with an A.M. Best rating of at least B+ + .

2. All self-insurance plans will be covered by an umbrella policy that covers all losses exceeding $50,000.

3. No insurance may be obtained from captive insurance companies.

4. The company must always have current insurance for the following categories, and in the stated amounts:

    - Director's and officer's insurance, $5 million.
    - General liability insurance, $10 million.
    - Commercial property insurance that matches the replacement cost of all structures and inventory.
    - Business interruption insurance, sufficient for four months of operations.

EXHIBIT 18.1   A COMPREHENSIVE POLICY FOR RISK MANAGEMENT

the first policy item defines the minimum financial rating that an insurance provider must attain before the company will purchase insurance from it. Another is that a company wants to put a cap on the maximum amount of all risks that it is willing to tolerate so that it cannot be blindsided by a large loss that is not covered by insurance. The second policy point, which requires a cap on self-insured risks, covers this problem. Finally, the Board may feel more comfortable defining the precise amount of insurance coverage needed in specific areas. Though the policy shows a few specific insurance amounts, it is usually better to define a formula for calculating the appropriate amount of insurance, such as commercial property insurance, that will cover the replacement cost of structures and inventory. This keeps the amount defined on the policy from becoming outdated due to changing business conditions. These are some of the most important insurance issues that a risk management policy should cover.

There is a growing understanding that the use of insurance is essentially a direct substitute for a company's equity. If a company were to self-insure its risks and then incur losses, the loss coverage would be extracted from equity in the form of losses. If, however, insurance were to be used to cover selected risks, then a very large loss, paid by the insurer, acts as a low-cost alternative to the equity that would otherwise have been depleted. The cost of the insurance "capital" would have been the insurance premium and any co-pay or risk sharing, divided by the amount of the claim paid by the insurer. Using this logic, another way of deciding upon how to handle a risk is to self-insure when the insurance premium divided by the most likely loss payout is greater than the incremental cost of capital, and vice versa. However, if there is a chance of an extremely large loss that could wipe out all equity, then this logic breaks down, and purchasing insurance, irrespective of cost, may be the more appropriate choice.

RISK MANAGEMENT PLANNING

Companies have a bad habit of structuring their risk planning to deal with events that have occurred before, rather than what may happen in the future. For example, if a lawsuit had previously been brought against a company for illegal software copying, the company will probably implement a comprehensive software auditing system, but make no plans to deal with the earthquake fault line running directly under corporate headquarters, because there has been no earthquake in the past century.

Risk management planning needs to encompass considerably more than systems that were installed to deal with past events. Even if it has not occurred yet, one should be aware of any significant risk of a possible natural disaster that could affect the company. This does not just mean earthquakes, fires, hail storms, floods, and tsunamis that can impact company facilities, but also their impact on key customers and suppliers and what that would mean for the company in terms of lost sales or reduced supplies.

Another problem area is catastrophes caused by complex system failure. For example, an airline manufacturer may need to consider the stresses caused on existing airframes if it installs satellite television reception nodules on the airframes; the airframes were not designed to have additional items bolted onto them, so the level of complexity has increased, resulting in a heightened chance of system failure (airframe cracking). The same concept applies to any business engaged in highly complex systems, such as chemical processing facilities, oil pipelines, and cruise ships. The same concept can even apply to the rewiring of an office building with additional cabling for a variety of purposes—power running through nearby cables may interfere with the data in a communications cable that was inadvertently run alongside it. The solution is to bring together engineers and maintenance personnel who are responsible for these systems, and have them review problem scenarios, as well as review ongoing incident reports to see if they are a prelude to a potential major problem.

Yet another risk area is acts of internal sabotage or terrorism from outside organizations, which can involve product tampering, theft of information, computer viruses, or even employee kidnappings. In this case, it is useful to have technical specialists from both within and outside of the company devise scenarios for destroying or at least penetrating company assets, and then have them create countermeasures to reduce the likelihood of an actual attack.

To coordinate the analysis of the above scenarios, it is useful to create a crisis management team (CMT) that determines which risks are most likely to happen. It can do this by creating a questionnaire that asks recipients, in a broad-based format, where they feel the company is most at risk. The questionnaire should be distributed to both managers and specialists in key operational areas throughout the company, so that responses represent a wide cross-section of the company. The result may be too many identified risks to properly address, so the CMT should then reduce the list to a more manageable size, perhaps the top one or two dozen, based on such issues as probability of occurrence and impact on the company. Given the large number of potential risks, it is useful to categorize the risks visually with a matrix such as the one shown in Exhibit 18.2, where each risk is identified by a letter (N = natural disaster, S = systemic problem, and X = external threat), and a number, both of which are identified in a table below the matrix. The table also identifies graphically how each risk is addressed; a square indicates a risk transfer through insurance, while a circle indicates a retained risk. For example, kidnapping is assigned the code X2 as an external threat, and has been mitigated through the use of kidnap and ransom insurance, so it is situated in a square. This is an easy way to visualize the status of a company's principal risks.

The CMT should also create monitoring systems to spot the targeted risks as soon as they occur (or if events occur that make them more likely), and actively create

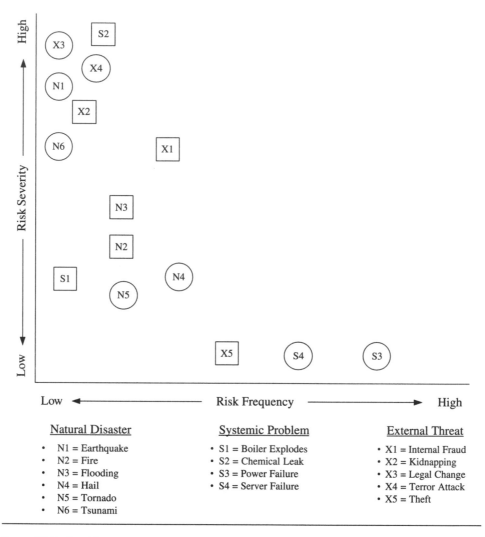

EXHIBIT 18.2 RISK MATRIX

---

systems to either prevent or deal with the selected set of risks. This group should regularly reevaluate its chosen set of most likely risks to see if they must be modified to deal with changing circumstances, which may include a new company strategy, sales into a politically at-risk country, a major acquisition, and so on.

Once the basic risk management system is in place, the CMT must ensure that risk examination becomes an ongoing process, which calls for policies and procedures as well as a monitoring system to verify that all parts of the company are regularly updating risk information. For larger entities with additional funding, it may also be possible to create computer systems that regularly extract data elements from legacy systems that are key indicators of risk factors, and present them in summary format to the CMT and the senior management team.

MANAGER OF RISK MANAGEMENT

In most large companies, the risk management function is assigned to a manager who reports to the chief financial officer, treasurer, or controller. This executive is charged with the responsibility of implementing procedures consistent with the corporate risk management policy (as noted earlier in Exhibit 18.1). This person works closely with other functional areas, such as engineering, safety and health, personnel and industrial relations, production, plant security, legal, and accounting. It is important that this person have a thorough knowledge of the company's operations, products, and services, as well as risk history, so that he or she can evaluate risks and exposure properly. Within these constraints, the job description of the typical risk manager is:

- Ascertain and appraise all corporate risks
- Estimate the probability of loss due to these risks
- Ensure compliance with state, federal, and local requirements regarding insurance
- Select the optimum method for protecting against losses, such as changes to internal procedures or by acquiring insurance
- Work with insurance agents, brokers, consultants, and insurance company representatives
- Supervise a loss prevention program, including planning to minimize losses from anticipated crises
- Maintain appropriate records for all aspects of insurance administration
- Continually evaluate and keep abreast of all changes in company operation
- Stay current on new techniques being developed in the risk management field
- Conduct a periodic audit of the risk management program to ensure that all risks have been identified and covered

RISK MANAGEMENT PROCEDURES

Once the risk management policies have been defined, it is necessary to determine a number of underlying procedures to support them. These guide the actions of the risk manager in ensuring that a company has taken sufficient steps to ensure that risks are kept at a minimum. The procedures follow a logical sequence of exploring the extent of risk issues, finding ways to mitigate those risks internally, and then using insurance to cover any risks that cannot otherwise be reduced. In more detail, the procedures are:

1. *Locate risk areas.* Determine all hazards to which the company is subject by performing a complete review of all properties and operations. This should include a review of not only the physical plant but also of contractual obligations, leasehold requirements, and government regulations. The review can be completed with insurable hazard checklists that are provided by most insurance companies, with the aid of a consultant, or by reviewing historical loss data provided by the company's current insurance firm. However, the person conducting this review must guard against the FUD Principle (Fear, Uncertainty, and Doubt) that is cheerfully practiced by all insurance companies. That is, they tend to hone in on every conceivable risk and amplify the chance of its occurrence, so that a company will

purchase lots of unnecessary insurance. The best way to avoid this problem is to employ an extremely experienced risk manager who knows which potential risks can be safely ignored. The following areas, at a minimum, should be reviewed:

- *Buildings and equipment.* The risk manager should list the type of construction, location, and hazards to which each item is exposed. Each structure and major piece of equipment should be listed separately. The current condition of each item should be determined and its replacement cost evaluated.

- *Business interruption.* The risk manager should determine the amount of lost profits and continuing expenses resulting from a business shutdown as the result of a specific hazard.

- *Liabilities to other parties.* The risk manager should determine the risk of loss or damage to other parties by reason of company products, services, operations, or the acts of employees. This analysis should include a review of all contracts, sales orders, purchase orders, leases, and applicable laws to determine what commitments have been undertaken and what exposures exist.

- *Other assets.* The risk manager should review cash, inventory, and accounts receivable to determine the possible exposure to losses by fire, flood, theft, or other hazards.

2. *Determine the risk reduction method.* Match each risk area with a method for dealing with it. The possible options for each risk area include avoidance, reduction of the hazard, retaining the hazard (i.e., self-insurance), or transferring the risk to an insurance company. Note that only the last option in this list includes the purchase of insurance, for there are many procedures that a company can implement to reduce a risk without resorting to insurance. The selection of a best option is based on a cost-benefit analysis that offsets the cost of each hazard against the cost of avoiding it, factoring in the probability of the hazard's occurrence. The general categories of risk reduction are:

- *Duplicate.* A company can retain multiple copies of records to guard against the destruction of critical information. In addition, key systems such as local area networks, telephone systems, and voice mail storage can be replicated at off-site locations to avoid a shutdown caused by damage to the primary site. For example, airlines maintain elaborate backup systems for their seat reservation databases.

- *Prevent.* A company can institute programs to reduce the likelihood and severity of losses. For example, some companies invite the Occupational Safety and Health Administration (OSHA) to inspect their premises and report on unsafe conditions; the companies then correct the issues to reduce their risk of loss. If a company requires employees to wear hard hats in construction areas, then a falling brick may still cause an accident, but the hard hat will reduce the incident's severity. Examples of prevention techniques include improving lighting, installing protective devices on machinery, and enforcing safety rules.

- *Segregate.* A company can split up key assets such as inventory and distribute it to multiple locations (e.g., warehouses). For example, the military maintains alternate command centers in case of war.

3. *Implement internal changes to reduce risks.* Once the types of risk avoidance have been determined, it is time to implement them. This usually involves new procedures or installations, such as fire suppression systems in the computer processing facility or altered cash tracking procedures that will discourage an employee from stealing money. Changes to procedures can be a lengthy process, for it includes working with the staff of each functional area to create a new procedure that is acceptable to all users, as well as following up with periodic audits to ensure that the procedures are still being followed.

4. *Select a broker.* Every company will require some insurance, unless it takes the hazardous approach of self-insuring virtually every risk. It is necessary to select a broker who can assist the company in procuring the best possible insurance. The right broker can be of great help in this process—not just in picking the least expensive insurance, but also in selecting the correct types of coverage, determining the financial strength of insurers, post-loss service, and in its general knowledge of the company's business and of the types of risk that are most likely to occur in that environment. Unfortunately, many companies look for new brokers every few years on the principle that a long-term broker will eventually raise prices and gouge the company. In reality, a long-term relationship should be encouraged, since the broker will gain a greater knowledge of the company's risks as problems occur and claims are received, giving it a valuable insight into company operations that a new broker does not have.

5. *Determine the types of insurance to be purchased.* Once the broker has been selected, the risk manager can show the preliminary results of the insurance review to the broker, and they can then mutually determine the types of insurance that are needed to supplement the actions already taken internally to mitigate risk. The types of insurance include:

   - *Boiler and machinery.* Covers damage to the boilers and machinery, as well as payments for injuries caused by the equipment. Providers of this insurance also review the company's equipment and issue a report recommending safety improvements.

   - *Business interruption.* Allows a company to pay for its continuing expenses and in some cases will pay for all or part of its anticipated profits.

   - *Commercial property.* The minimum "basic form" of this insurance covers losses from fires, explosions, wind storms, hail, vandalism, and other perils. The "broad form," which is an expanded version, covers everything in the basic form plus damage from falling objects, the weight of snow, water damage, and some causes of building collapse. Optional coverage includes an inflation escalator clause, replacement of destroyed structures at the actual replacement cost, and coverage of finished goods at their selling price (instead of at their cost).

   - *Comprehensive auto liability.* This coverage is usually mandatory and requires a minimum level of coverage for bodily injury and property damage.

   - *Comprehensive crime.* Covers property theft, robbery, safe and premises burglary, and employee dishonesty; in the case of employee dishonesty, the company purchases a fidelity bond, which can cover either a named individual, a specific position, or all employees. Some policies will also cover ransom payments.

- *Directors and officers.*   Provides liability coverage to corporate managers for actions taken while acting as an officer or director of the corporation. D&O insurance includes three types of agreements: the Side A agreement provides coverage to directors and officers for which the company cannot pay, while the Side B agreement reimburses the company for any payments it makes to directors and officers for the cost of claim settlements and legal defense work. The Side C agreement provides coverage to the company for claims made against the corporate entity. D&O insurance is increasingly difficult to obtain, due to massive insurer payouts in recent years, which obligates companies to accept large risk retentions or loss sharing, as well as the obligation to actively and materially assist the insurer in the defense of any litigation. There are also several clauses to be aware of in a D&O contract that can void or reduce coverage. Always look for the following clauses, and attempt to strike them from the contract or at least reduce their impact:

  ▷ Claims caused by fraudulent acts are not covered. Only allow this clause if the fraudulent acts are based on criminal activity, since a claim settlement that does not include the admission of guilt will retain insurance coverage.

  ▷ If the corporate financial statements are considered part of the company's D&O application, then any restatement of the financial statements can result in voided coverage.

  ▷ If the D&O policy includes coverage for other types of risks, then the total policy limit may be exceeded by other types of claims, leaving no coverage for the directors and officers. Accordingly, always specify separate policy limits just for the D&O coverage.

  ▷ Coverage could be terminated by the bankruptcy of the company.

  ▷ Coverage could be denied if a claim is based on the release of pollutants.

- *General liability.*   Covers claims involving accidents on company premises, as well as those caused by its products, services, agents, or contractors. An umbrella policy usually applies to liability insurance and provides extra coverage after the primary coverage is exhausted. An umbrella policy has few exclusions.

- *Group life, health, and disability.*   There are several types of life insurance: *split-dollar life insurance* covers an employee, and its cost is split between the company and the employee; *key person insurance* covers the financial loss to the company in case an employee dies; and a *cross-purchase plan* allows the co-owners of a business to buy out the share of an owner who dies. *Health insurance* typically covers the areas of hospital, medical, surgical, and dental expenses. Disability insurance provides income to an individual who cannot work due to an injury or illness. The disability insurance category is subdivided into *short-term disability* (payments made while recovering one's health following an injury or illness) and *long-term disability* (continuing payments with no anticipation of a return to work).

- *Inland marine.*   Covers company property that is being transported. Examples of covered items include trade show displays and finished goods being shipped.

- *Ocean marine and air cargo.*   Covers the transporting vehicle (including loss of income due to loss of the vehicle), liability claims against the vehicle's owner or operator, and the cargo.

- *Workers' compensation.* Provides medical and disability coverage to workers who are injured while performing duties related to their jobs. The insurance is mandatory, the employer pays all costs, and no legal recourse is permitted against the employer. There are wide variations in each state's coverage of workers' compensation, including levels of compensation, types of occupations that are not considered, and the allowability of negligence lawsuits.

These steps allow a risk manager to determine the types and potential severity of a company's risks, as well as how to reduce those risks, either through internal changes or by purchasing various types of insurance coverage.

TYPES OF INSURANCE COMPANIES

There are several types of insurance companies. Each one may serve a company's insurance needs very well, but there are significant differences between them that a company should be aware of before purchasing an insurance contract. The types of insurance companies include:

- *Captive insurance company.* This is a stock insurance company that is formed to underwrite the risks of its parent company or in some cases a sponsoring group or association.

- *Lloyds of London.* This is an underwriter operating under the special authority of the English Parliament. It may write insurance coverage of a nature that other insurance companies will not underwrite, usually because of high risks or special needs not covered by a standard insurance form. It also provides the usual types of insurance coverage.

- *Mutual.* This is a company in which each policyholder is an owner, and where earnings are distributed as dividends. If a net loss results, policyholders may be subject to extra assessments. In most cases, however, nonassessable policies are issued.

- *Reciprocal organization.* This is an association of insured companies that is independently operated by a manager. Advance deposits are made, against which are charged the proportionate costs of operations.

- *Stock company.* This is an insurance company that behaves like a normal corporation—earnings not retained in the business are distributed to shareholders as dividends and not to policyholders.

Another way to categorize insurance companies is by the type of service offered. For example, a *monoline* company provides only one type of insurance coverage, while a *multiple line* company provides more than one kind of insurance. A *financial services company* provides not only insurance but also financial services to customers.

A company can also use *self-insurance* when it deliberately plans to cover losses from its own resources rather than through those of an insurer. It can be appropriate in any of the following cases:

- When the administrative loss of using an insurer exceeds the amount of the loss.

- When a company has sufficient excess resources available to cover even the largest claim.

- When excessive premium payments are the only alternative.
- When insurance is not available at any price.

A form of partial self-insurance is to use large deductibles on insurance policies, so that a company pays for all but the very largest claims. Finally, a company can create a *captive insurer* that provides insurance to the parent company. Captive insurers can provide coverage that is tailored to the parent organization, making it less dependent on the vagaries of the commercial insurance market. A variation on the captive insurer concept is a *fronting program*, in which a parent company buys insurance from an independent insurance company, which then reinsures the exposure with a captive of the parent company. This technique is used to avoid licensing the captive insurer in every state where the parent company does business, though the captive insurer must still be authorized to accept reinsurance. Fronting also allows the parent company to obtain local service from the independent insurance company while shifting the exposure to the captive company. Whatever form the self-insurance may take, the risk manager should work with the controller to determine the amount of loss reserves to set aside to pay for claims as they arise.

In some states, a company can become a self-insurer for workers' compensation. To do this, a company must qualify under state law as a self-insurer, purchase umbrella coverage to guard against catastrophic claims, post a surety bond, and create a claims administration department to handle claims. The advantages of doing this are lower costs (by eliminating the insurer's profit) and better cash flow (because there are no up-front insurance payments). The disadvantages of this approach are extra administrative costs as well as the cost of qualifying the company in each state in which the company operates.

These are some of the variations that a company can consider when purchasing insurance, either through a third party, a controlled subsidiary, or by providing its own coverage.

EVALUATING THE HEALTH OF AN INSURANCE CARRIER

A company that depends on an insurance carrier to mitigate significant portions of its risk must be aware of the financial health of the carrier. Otherwise, the insurer may fail, forcing the company to assume risk itself or find coverage elsewhere on short notice—and quite possibly at a higher price. Though there are rating systems for insurance carriers (such as those issued by A. M. Best, located at www.ambest.com), the CFO can also gain an understanding of the operating characteristics of a carrier that indicate future problems, ideally before its official rating changes to reflect those characteristics.

A key warning sign is when a carrier concentrates an excessively high proportion of its insurance line in an area suffering from high payouts, such as California earthquake coverage, pollution coverage, or directors' and officers' liability insurance. This is a strong indicator that its reserves are being drained, which may lead to a ratings drop and perhaps a decision by the carrier to exit certain types of insurance coverage.

When reviewing an insurer's financial statements, earnings volatility is a general indicator of trouble. This is most common with smaller carriers, who have concentrated their business in too small a geographic area or only in a few insurance lines, so they have not spread their risk sufficiently in the event of major problems in one or two areas. This leads to wild gyrations in earnings, which is a strong indicator of future bankruptcy. Also, even if there is minimal earnings volatility, watch out for low net income or minimal cash flows, which indicate poor management. Even worse, cash outflows will eat into the carrier's reserves, leaving less money available for future payouts. Another issue when reviewing financials is significant charges to earnings. Though a carrier should be credited with recognizing insurance losses when it posts a large write-down, the fact remains that the carrier expects significant losses in the near term. When all of these factors are considered together—earnings volatility, low or negative income or cash flows, and write-downs—a clear picture emerges of the true financial condition of an insurer.

Insurers are having increasing difficulty recovering receivables from reinsurers, who have tightened their reviews of potential payouts considerably. Thus, an increase in reinsurance receivables over several years is an indicator of potential trouble, especially if management confirms this in its discussion of financial results in the carrier's 10-K report.

A final cause for concern is an excessively high rate of growth in an insurer's policyholders. This is a difficult issue to evaluate, for high growth may simply mean that an insurer has developed an entirely new type of insurance, and is rapidly acquiring market share before anyone else begins to compete. However, the more common scenario is that the insurer is essentially buying market share with excessively low policy pricing, which will eventually cut into its net income, cash flow, and reserves when it begins to experience high payout levels in proportion to its income from those policies.

Unfortunately, there is no completely quantitative way to evaluate the financial health of an insurer—an examination of its business practices is also necessary to understand what its near-term financial condition is likely to be. As noted in this section, there are a number of ways in which a watchful CFO can gain a general understanding of the short-term problems of an insurer, which may allow enough time to shift insurance coverage to a new carrier who is likely to remain in a better financial position.

CATASTROPHE BONDS

The catastrophe bond, more commonly known as a cat bond, is a new type of financial instrument designed to raise money in the event of a major catastrophe, which is usually defined as an earthquake, hurricane, or windstorm. If the issuer suffers a loss from a predefined catastrophe, then its obligation to repay the interest or principal is either deferred or canceled. Some cat bonds are indemnity-based, which means that they pay out based on actual claims stemming from the catastrophe; these bonds are considered more risky for bond purchasers, since a wide variety of claims may be brought. Another type of cat bond is based on parametric data, so they only pay out if precise physical measurements of the actual event occur, such as wind speed or earthquake magnitude exceeding a threshold level.

Large cat bonds are almost always issued by reinsurance companies, and are typically rated as junk bonds. The only recent exceptions have been the Oriental Land Company (Japanese earthquake), Vivendi Universal (California earthquake), and FIFA (terrorism during the 2006 World Cup). The most recent information about cat bond issuances and risk profiles by country is listed in the excellent "World Catastrophe Reinsurance Market" report, which is available for free from Guy Carpenter at www.guycarp.com.

Cat bonds are also available in smaller sizes for individual corporations, though these are usually specially designed private placements to one or two investors. This approach to catastrophe coverage is especially useful when traditional insurance coverage is too expensive, allowing issuers to essentially extract insurance coverage from the securities market.

CLAIMS ADMINISTRATION

Some insurance companies take an extremely long time to respond to claims, and may reject them if they are not reported in a specific format. To avoid these problems, thereby receiving the full amount of claims as quickly as possible, the risk manager must implement a strict claims administration process, as described in this section.

The risk manager should assemble a summary of information to review whenever a claim is filed. By having this information in one place, the risk manager avoids missing any steps that might interfere with the prompt settlement of a claim. The summary should include:

- *Instructions for itemizing damaged items.* Be sure to compile a complete list of all damaged items, including their inventory values, estimates, appraisals, and replacement costs. This assists the claims adjusters in determining the price they will pay to compensate for any claims.

- *Claims representatives.* There should be a list of the names, addresses, and phone numbers of the claims adjusters who handle each line of insurance. This usually requires a fair amount of updating, since there may be a number of changes to this information every year, especially if a company uses a large number of insurance companies for its various types of risk coverage.

- *Key internal personnel.* Company policy may require that the risk manager notify internal personnel if claims have been filed or payments received on those claims. For example, the accountant may want to know if payment for a large claim has been received, so that an entry can be made in the accounting records.

- *Underlying problems.* The risk manager should have a standard group of follow-up steps to review whenever a claim occurs, so that there is a clear understanding of why a claim occurred, as well as how the underlying problem that caused the claim can be avoided in the future. Without these instructions, it is possible that a company will repeat the problem over and over again, resulting in many claims and a vastly increased insurance premium.

- *Instructions for safeguarding damaged items.* If material has been damaged, it is the responsibility of the company to ensure that it is not damaged further, which would result in a larger claim. For example, a company must protect the materials in a warehouse from further damage as soon as it discovers that the roof has leaked and destroyed some items. If it does not take this action, the insurer can rightly claim that it will only pay for the damage that occurred up to the point when the company could have taken corrective action.

The above information is necessary for the filing of every insurance claim. In addition, there are two steps related to claims administration that the risk manager should attend to on an ongoing basis:

1. *Accounting techniques.* The risk manager should work with the accountant to develop a standard set of accounting entries that are used for insurance claims as well as summarize the cost of risk management. These relate to accumulating cost information for each claim so that the risk manager can easily summarize the appropriate information related to each claim and use it to file for reimbursement. This information should include the costs of claims preparation, security and property protection, cleanup, repair costs, property identification, and storage costs.

2. *Audit program.* No matter how good the procedures may be for the claims administration process, it is common for the claims administration staff to forget or sidestep some procedures. This is especially common when there is frequent employee turnover in this area, with poor training of the replacement staff. To identify procedural problems, it is useful to conduct a periodic review of the claims administration process. To ensure consistency in this audit, there should be a standard audit program that forms the minimum set of audit instructions (to be expanded on as needed) for use in conducting each audit.

It can be cost effective to have some claims administered by outside service companies, quite often by the insurance carrier itself. Usually high-volume, low-cost-per-unit items such as medical claims are in this category. When outside services are used, the accountant must establish with the provider the controls to be followed and the reports to be prepared. Periodic audits of the outside claims processing operation should be made by the company to ensure that claims are being handled in a controlled and effective manner.

INSURANCE FILES

Insurance record keeping is vital to ascertain that adequate insurance coverage has been obtained and is being administered properly. The primary risks that this record keeping avoids are inadvertently dropping insurance through lack of renewal and having inadequate insurance given a company's actual claims record. The layout of insurance records described in this section helps a company to avoid these problems.

There are several main categories of insurance records. The first section identifies each policy. The next section is a tickler file that lists key due dates for each policy. This is useful for ensuring that all policy payments are made on time, so that they do not lapse. The next section is the activity file, which describes the claim history and open claims for each policy. Finally, there is the value file, which itemizes the insurable values covered by each policy. The activity and value files are needed to determine the size of claims or the value being covered, so the risk manager can see if each policy provides a sufficient amount of coverage. When properly maintained, these files give the risk manager a basis for sound management of his or her function. The contents of each type of file are:

- *Identification file.* Lists key information on each policy:

    — Abstract of coverage, showing exclusions
    — Broker
    — Effective dates
    — Insurer
    — Policy number
    — Rates, premiums, and refunds
    — Type of insurance coverage

- *Tickler file.* Lists key dates for each policy:

    — Inspection dates
    — Policy expiration date
    — Premium payment dates
    — Reporting dates

- *Activity file.* Describes the claim history and open claims for each policy:
  - Historical comparison of premiums to losses
  - History file on closed claims
  - Reserves established
  - Status of each claim
  - Support and documentation of each claim

- *Value file.* Itemizes the insurable values covered by each policy:
  - Detail of actual cash value of each item covered by a policy
  - Detail of replacement cost of each item covered by a policy
  - Summary of insurable values listed on each policy

ANNUAL RISK MANAGEMENT REPORT

The risk manager should issue a risk management report to the Board of Directors every year. This document reviews all perceived risks to which a company is subject, and then describes the steps taken to mitigate those risks. It is of great value to the Board, because it needs to know the extent of potential risks and how they can impact company operations. Unfortunately, not many controllers or chief financial officers are aware of what should go into the annual risk management report. This presents a problem if the Board asks either of these managers, to whom the risk manager usually reports, about the contents of this document. To avoid this problem, the contents of a typical risk management report are described in this section, including an example based on an organization that provides training in high-risk outdoor activities.

The risk management report contains four sections. The first is an overview that describes the contents of the report, the timing of when it is issued, and to whom it is delivered. The second section itemizes all risks that are perceived to be significant. If every possible risk were to be listed, the document might be too voluminous for easy reading. These risks should be grouped with subheadings rather than appear as an enormous list that is difficult for the reader to digest. The third section notes the ways to cover those risks, *excluding insurance* (which is addressed in the fourth section). These are operational changes such as altered procedures or processes, or additional training. Finally, the fourth section notes the insurance that has been purchased to provide additional coverage to those risk areas that cannot be adequately covered by internal changes. These four sections give the Board an adequate knowledge of a company's efforts in the risk management area.

The example in Exhibit 18.3 presents an extract from the risk management report of an organization that provides outdoor training classes. The example skips the overview section and proceeds straight to the enumeration of risks, how they are covered, and what types of insurance are also needed. This is a good example of the format that a CFO should look for in a risk management report.

KEY-MAN LIFE INSURANCE FOR THE CFO

It is common for companies to take out key man life insurance policies on their chief executive officers or the holders of key product knowledge—but what about the CFO?

Section II: Review of Risks

- *Risk related to education:*

  1.   Risk of school equipment failing

  2.   Risk of accidents due to improper instruction

Section III: Ways to Cover Risks

- *Risk of school equipment failing.* School equipment is reviewed and replaced by the school governing committees on a regular basis. Instructors are also authorized to immediately remove equipment from use if they spot unusual damage that may result in equipment failure.

- *Risk of accidents due to improper supervision.* School instructors must first serve as assistant instructors under the supervision of a more experienced instructor, who evaluates their skills and recommends advancement to full instructor status. The typical instructor has previously completed all prerequisite courses, and has considerable outdoor experience. All instructors must have taken a mountain-oriented first aid class within the last year.

Section IV: Supplemental Insurance Coverage

- *Risk of school equipment failing.* The general liability policy covers this risk for the first $500,000 of payments to a claimant. The umbrella policy covers this risk for an additional $5 million after the coverage provided by the general liability policy is exhausted.

- *Risk of accidents due to improper instruction.* Same insurance coverage as for the risk of school equipment failing.

Exhibit 18.3   Example of a Risk Management Report

First, let us look at the reasons for key-man insurance. It is intended to at least cover the cost of recruiting and training a replacement, and can also be used to fulfill any contractual pay or benefit obligations to the person's surviving spouse. The most justifiable use of this insurance is when the partners in a partnership need the resources to buy out the shares of any partner who dies.

These traditional reasons do not warrant the purchase of key-man insurance for the CFO. Companies should have a sufficiently deep management team to be able to promote a CFO from within, or at least adequately backfill the position until an outsider is hired.

However, there is a scenario when such insurance might make sense. If the current CFO is deeply involved in financing arrangements and there is a serious risk that the financing could be lost in the event of the CFO's demise, then the insurance proceeds could compensate for the lost funds. If this scenario is the reason for having key-man life insurance, then the amount of the insurance should approximate the amount of funding at risk of being lost.

SUMMARY

In a larger company, there is usually a risk manager who identifies and finds ways to mitigate risk, either through internal changes or by purchasing insurance. Because this manager frequently reports to either the controller or CFO, it is important for these people to have an overall knowledge of how risk management works. This chapter answered the need by describing the risk planning, policies and procedures used by a risk manager and that person's job. The types of insurance companies, the paperwork handled by the risk manager, and the annual risk management report were also described.

CHAPTER 19

OUTSOURCING THE ACCOUNTING AND FINANCE FUNCTIONS*

The accounting function is commonly outsourced, though this is usually limited to only a few tasks within the function. There are opportunities to outsource a wide array of services in this area, if a CFO is willing to work with multiple suppliers to achieve this goal. This chapter describes the advantages and disadvantages of using outsourcing for a variety of accounting services. There are also several points regarding contract clauses that the reader should know about before signing any contracts with suppliers. In addition, a section covers the various transition steps needed to hand over an in-house accounting function to a supplier. Many ways to control and measure the performance of suppliers are also revealed, as well as how this information can be used by the managers of the accounting and treasury functions. Finally, there are a number of issues to be aware of that can cause problems when a company wants to terminate a supplier relationship—these issues are described, along with possible solutions. After reading this chapter, a CFO should have a good grounding in the fundamental issues surrounding outsourcing the accounting function and will know how to negotiate contracts with suppliers, transition tasks to them, measure their performance, manage them, and sever relationships if necessary.

ADVANTAGES AND DISADVANTAGES OF OUTSOURCING

This section presents a series of advantages and disadvantages for outsourcing many of a company's accounting functions. Areas covered include accounts receivable collections, internal auditing, payroll, taxation, financial statement reporting, pension administration, transaction processing, and cash management. Each area covered places both the advantages and disadvantages in close proximity so the reader can compare and weigh the benefits and associated problems of using outsourcing.

Several points in favor of outsourcing are not covered for each of the accounting topics, since there would be considerable duplication. Those points are that many of these accounting areas are clerical or subject to automation—such as transaction processing, pension administration, and payroll—and are therefore nonstrategic. Because they are not important to a company's overall strategic direction, they should be outsourced so the CFO can focus on more important tasks that will impact its profitability or position in the marketplace.

The best reason for outsourcing the collections function is that the supplier may pursue those customers who refuse to pay with greater energy than would the in-house

---

* Adapted with permission from Chapter 6 of *Outsourcing*, 2nd edition, by Bragg (John Wiley & Sons, 2006).

collections staff. Particular skill is required in persuading companies to pay for old invoices, and good collection companies employ people of this type. The downside of using collection agencies is that they can be so aggressive with customers that they will refuse to ever do business with the company again; however, since the company had to refer the customer's account to the supplier anyway, the company may not want to pursue further business relations. Also, a collections agency is typically paid a large percentage of each bill collected, normally about one-third of the total. However, a company usually passes along a bill to the collection supplier only at the point when it does not believe it can collect the bill itself, so any collection, even if not for the full amount, is better than what the company had before. Furthermore, many companies write off accounts receivable that must be handed over to collection agencies, so there is no expectation of ever collecting the funds. Also, a company can sometimes work with collection agencies who are willing to be paid by the hour rather than on a percentage basis. The alternative reduces the high cost of collection, but also converts the collection cost from a highly desirable variable cost to a fixed cost. In short, it is very useful to switch the most difficult accounts receivable collection items over to a collections supplier, since they are better at persuading customers to pay their bills.

Companies are now outsourcing their internal audit functions. The following set of reasons for taking this approach should be compared to the list of disadvantages that follow in order to fully understand the ramifications of using outsourcing in this area. Arguments in favor of outsourcing the internal audit function are:

- *Mix of skills*. If the auditing firm doing the work is a large one, the auditors provided can be changed for each audit, only using those people who are most skilled in the requirements of each audit.

- *Management ability*. The supplier can manage the audit for the company; since this is all the supplier does, it should be quite good at managing audits, and can probably do so better than an in-house staff.

- *Knowledge of best practices*. An auditor who reviews the functions of many companies will build up a knowledge base of how processes can be performed most efficiently and effectively, or has access to that knowledge through other auditors at the firm, and can therefore recommend changes to the company. Many internal audit staffs have been with their companies for years and have not acquired this same range of process knowledge due to a lack of exposure to other businesses.

- *Variable cost*. The company only pays for audits performed by the supplier, so the auditing cost can be switched from a fixed one for in-house staff to a variable one for outside staff.

- *Quick access*. The company has the option to quickly bring in an experienced audit team if it acquires a new business in a foreign location that is inconvenient for its internal staff to reach.

- *Reduced travel costs*. The company must fly its internal audit staff to any company location that needs an internal audit, whereas a large auditing firm can assign staff from its regional offices to go to those locations, thus avoiding the excessive travel costs incurred by the internal audit staff. This cost reduction only works if the auditing firm has regional offices near the company's locations.

- *No downtime*. Bringing in an audit team only for specific tasks allows the company to avoid the kind of nonproductive downtime that sometimes occurs with an in-house staff, such as the interval between the end of one audit and the beginning of the next.

- *No hiring and training costs*. A company can avoid the substantial hiring and training costs needed to staff and retain a top-of-the-line in-house audit team.

There are several important reasons why the internal auditing function should *not* be outsourced in some circumstances. Management should be aware of these reasons before making the decision to outsource. Some of the concerns with outsourcing are:

- *Cost*. A major downside of using an outside auditing firm for internal audits is their substantial cost, which includes overhead costs and a healthy profit margin. There may be an additional concern that fees will be low-balled until the company has disbanded its internal auditing staff and has become reliant on the supplier for this work, at which point the supplier will increase its fees.

- *Training*. Some companies use the internal audit function to train their managers, since the job gives a good overview of many company functions. By taking away this job, a company loses its training ground for future managers. One solution is to team these personnel in training with the supplier's audit teams in order to provide ongoing training.

- *Experience*. The perceived quality of the auditors provided by the supplier may be lower than anticipated, since most auditing firms have very high turnover and also like to bring in junior employees in order to give them experience with different accounting systems. This problem can be avoided by previewing the qualifications of each person assigned to internal audits by the supplier.

- *Responsibility*. Management must still realize that it is responsible for the establishment and maintenance of internal controls and the audit of those controls. If the company is sued over a lack of controls, it cannot point to the internal audit supplier as the culprit—management will still be held accountable.

- *Independence*. An auditing firm is supposed to create "walls" within its own company that keep its internal audit work from interfering with the independence of its financial statement audit work. This is an especially difficult task for smaller firms, where there may not be enough people to separately assign to both the internal audit work and the periodic external audit.

The most commonly outsourced accounting function is payroll. Some of the advantages of outsourcing it are to:

- *Avoid filing tax payments*. A company can shift the burden of making timely tax filings to the supplier. The government requires rapid tax filings, and has imposed stiff penalties if taxes are not filed on time. For those companies with a chronic tax-filing problem, handing over this task to a supplier may save the company more money in tax penalties avoided than the entire cost of outsourcing.

- *Avoid paying for software updates*. Companies do not want to pay their software providers for new tax tables every year so they can correctly calculate payroll taxes through their in-house software packages. Since there are some incremental local tax rate changes somewhere every year, a company that runs its payroll on an in-house software package must incur this expense every year in order to stay current.

- *Avoid creating W-2 forms.* A payroll supplier will accumulate all annual payroll information into W-2 tax reports and even mail them to employees for the company. Otherwise, the in-house system would produce these documents and send them to employees.

- *Avoid printing paychecks.* A payroll printing can tie up a printer for a long time if there are many employees, and it must be closely monitored in order to avoid jamming. By using outsourcing, neither the printer nor the employee are needed for this task.

- *Use direct deposit.* Many in-house payroll systems do not allow direct deposit, whereas this service is offered by all major payroll suppliers. Direct deposit is most useful for companies whose employees are constantly traveling and who are therefore not on site to pick up and deposit their paychecks.

- *Use check stuffing.* A supplier can automatically stuff paychecks into envelopes for delivery to employees, removing a clerical task from the accounting staff.

- *Use check delivery to multiple locations.* Though most payroll services will not mail checks to individual employees, they will send batches of checks to multiple company locations for distribution to employees.

- *Stamp signatures on checks.* The supplier stamps an imprint of an officer's signature on all payroll checks, thereby keeping someone from having to perform this boring task.

- *Use custom and standard reports.* Most payroll suppliers provide a plethora of reports that cover the needs of most companies. For special reporting needs, there is usually a custom report-writing tool available that allows the company to create any additional reports it needs.

- *Link to 401(k) plan.* A few payroll suppliers can make automatic deductions from paychecks and deposit this money directly into a 401(k) plan on behalf of the company, thereby eliminating a great deal of paperwork associated with this function.

Despite the formidable array of advantages just noted, some companies do not outsource the payroll function, usually for one or more of the following reasons:

- *Cost.* Payroll suppliers can be quite expensive if all possible payroll services are used. The most typical supplier ploy is to initially charge very low rates for the basic service of printing paychecks. However, once a company has signed up for this service, it will find that additional services may easily exceed the cost of the basic service. For example, additional fees will be charged for automatic signature stamping, check stuffing, delivery to multiple locations, access to custom reporting software, and direct deposits.

- *Conversion problems.* There are a number of data items that must be properly converted over to the supplier's database to ensure that employees will continue to receive paychecks in the correct amounts and with accurate deductions removed. If the conversion to the supplier's database does not go well, the company may become so disenchanted with the supplier that it converts back to an in-house solution. Conversions can be a problem in part because so many companies want to switch to outsourcing at the beginning of the calendar year, which creates a major work overload for the system-conversion staff of the supplier.

- *Create manual paychecks.* It can be difficult to determine the correct amount of tax deductions when cutting a manual check for an employee. However, many payroll suppliers now offer either automated call-in or Internet-based calculations that provide this information.

- *Must send in payroll information.* The payroll supplier does not collect payroll information. The company must still do this, organize it, and submit it to the supplier for wage and tax calculations. As this may be the primary source of clerical time in computing payroll, one may not see how to save costs by shifting to a supplier. This is less of an issue if most company employees are salaried, since there is little timekeeping data to collect. Also, some payroll suppliers offer bar-coded time clocks that can be linked directly into their software, so there is little clerical effort required.

Taxation can be outsourced when a company is not big enough to support the full-time services of a tax department of its own. This is frequently split into two pieces, with state and federal taxation reporting going to a supplier and local taxation being kept in house. The reason for this split is that many taxation firms are experts at state and federal issues because they have their own teams of experts who advise them on these issues; however, they have little incentive to develop an expertise in limited locals areas, such as enterprise development zones.

A company has a supplier create financial statements for it when its in-house accounting staff is not large or experienced enough to do so correctly in a timely manner. This can be a good idea if the accounting firm used is a large one, for its staff will have an excellent knowledge of all reporting requirements needed for financial statements, especially for all required footnotes. A popular variation on this approach is to have an outside firm verify the accuracy of the financial statements that were produced by the in-house staff, especially if the company is a public one and its reports are going to the Securities and Exchange Commission (SEC), which requires a very detailed knowledge of the SEC's reporting requirements. The downside of this approach is that accounting firms usually charge high rates for this service. Thus, one must decide if the improved level of reporting is worth the additional cost.

The advantage of using a supplier to handle a company's 401(k) plan includes reducing the paperwork associated with tracking investments for employees and changing the cost of this function from the fixed cost of an in-house staff to the variable cost of having a supplier do it. This becomes a variable cost because the pricing structures of most suppliers are on a per-person basis. For example, there is a per-person setup fee, an annual per-person maintenance fee, and a per-person fee to remove someone from the plan. If the company's headcount changes, the cost of the supplier will vary with the headcount level. The primary disadvantage of this approach is the risk of hiring a bad supplier who does a poor job of accurately investing funds for each employee. This problem can be partially mitigated by requesting references and contacting them for detailed information about the supplier's performance.

Transaction processing can also be outsourced. One advantage is that the supplier may have a better knowledge of world-class processes that allows it to complete transactions faster than the company's in-house staff. Also, if the company has a widely dispersed transaction-processing function, a supplier can consolidate these locations into a single, highly efficient location to reduce costs. In addition, a company may be able to replace poor in-house management with (presumably) top-notch supplier management. The downside of outsourcing transaction processing includes the cost of doing so; unless they can use their greater knowledge of processes to cut costs, suppliers will be more expensive than the in-house function.

The cash management function can also be outsourced. One reason is that a company manually moves funds between accounts and manually records this information, whereas a bank can automatically consolidate the cash in various accounts and sweep it all into an interest-bearing account without any manual interference at all. This allows one to reduce the fixed cost of the in-house staff it uses to track the flow of cash through its accounts in exchange for a per-transaction fee from the bank for performing the same service. Also, since the bank can fully automate this work, the company has a much lower risk of having any errors in moving funds between accounts. The only disadvantage is that the company is forced to use the same bank for all of its accounts, which does not allow the company to use the services of multiple banks and have them compete against one another in offering the best prices to the company.

CONTRACTUAL ISSUES

This section covers a variety of contract-related issues that a company should be aware of before signing a contract with a supplier to take over an accounting or finance task.

A contract for payroll services will only be negotiable on price, because a payroll supplier has thousands of clients and prefers to use a standard contract for all of them—it cannot begin to track slight contract changes for all of those companies, so it does not allow them. However, suppliers have modified their computer systems to allow for different prices for each company, so this one area is subject to negotiation. Pricing is typically on a per-person basis, plus a fixed baseline fee for various services. A company has the most negotiating power if it has a large number of employees to put on the supplier's payroll system; the prospect of losing all of that revenue will normally elicit price cuts by the supplier. A small company will likely have no luck in negotiating reduced prices, for it has no leverage for doing so.

A contract for tax work is negotiable on price and the supplier staff to be used. Any tax supplier charges a basic hourly rate for work performed, and then discounts this rate for any number of reasons. One can reduce this per-hour rate through negotiation, or can convert the tax work to a fixed fee for a baseline level of work performed, with an hourly rate to be charged for any additional work that falls outside of the deliverables noted in the original contract. If a specific supplier employee does especially good work, one can specify that all tax work will be completed by that person, or at least that the company can reject supplier personnel whom it feels are unsuitable for doing any of its tax work.

A contract for cash management services is sometimes not even negotiable on price—and certainly not on any other contract points—because this service is offered by banks to thousands of customers; given the number of customers, banks cannot keep track of slight contract variations, and thus offer no negotiation options at all. Pricing tends to be fixed because this service does not generate much profit for the bank from a single customer. Only in the case of a large company with thousands of cash management transactions will there be enough leverage to force a price reduction.

A contract for collections work focuses on reimbursement. A typical collections agency wants to keep a large percentage of all money it collects on a company's accounts receivable. This percentage typically varies between one-quarter and one-third of the amount collected. If a company gives a large dollar volume of its business to a collections agency, it may be possible to negotiate this number down. If this price is too high, a company can ask a law firm to collect the largest receivable debts in exchange for per-hour compensation. The only other negotiation point is whether the collection agency should be allowed to finish collecting any accounts receivable it has in its possession at the time when the company decides to stop using the agency. In most cases, the agency is allowed to finish this work, since it may have already invested considerable effort in attempting to collect them. If the collections agency is a law firm working on an hourly basis, then one can take back the accounts receivable at any time.

A contract for internal auditing must target hourly fees, the specific staff to be used, and the methodology that will form the underpinnings of all internal audit work. The hourly fees are subject to considerable negotiation, with price cuts based on the anticipated number of staff to be used as well as on the time of year when the supplier's staff will be used. Since most suppliers who provide internal audit work are also auditing firms, they have poor staff utilization during the summer and fall periods and are most likely to accept lower pricing during those periods. A company may have developed its own detailed internal auditing methodology and wants the supplier to continue using it—this is rarely a problem for the supplier. A typical contract clause addressing this issue should, however, allow the supplier to recommend changes that will bolster the methodology to help provide more complete audit results. Finally, the contract should contain a clause permitting the company to accept or reject personnel who are assigned to its audits.

A contract for pension management tends to have rigid pricing, but does allow some movement on the types of investments offered to employees. Pricing normally includes both baseline fees and per-person fees that are not negotiable unless the company has a large pension plan that can be highly profitable for the supplier. The more common point of negotiation is in having the supplier create a mix of investment vehicles, normally ranging from conservative to speculative, that the company's employees can select from.

A contract for transaction processing has the largest number of clauses open to negotiation. One point is that the company should push to have as many services as possible covered by the baseline or per-transaction fee. Otherwise, the supplier will charge much higher add-on fees for any extra services. Also, if the company's staff is being transferred to the supplier, the contract should specify the minimum time period for retaining these employees (in order to give them some job security), or at least the minimum percentage of employees who will be kept by the supplier. The contract should also specify a minimum time period during which the supplier must keep key personnel working on company business; otherwise, suppliers may take the best of the transferred staffs and move them off to work on projects for other clients. Another issue is that the company should have control over the implementation of new efficiencies by the supplier. This may seem like no control is required—just do whatever it takes to cut costs—but there may be political reasons within the company for keeping the methods of transaction processing the way they are. If this control proves to be a difficult negotiating point, then a fallback position is to require company approval over any transaction-processing changes that impact other areas of the company.

TRANSITION ISSUES

This section covers the specific transition issues associated with each of the accounting tasks that can be outsourced. For the payroll function, the first transition step is to meet with the supplier about one month in advance of the conversion date (or earlier if the payroll system to be converted is especially large or complex). This meeting should cover all key conversion dates and who is to perform which tasks by those dates. Since the payroll function must usually be brought on-line with the supplier as of the first day of the year, this is a very time-sensitive process, so the initial meeting with the supplier is especially important. If various extra payroll features, such as automated check signing, are to be added to the payroll later on, these dates should also be agreed on by both parties during the meeting. The next transition step will be to transfer all payroll information for all employees to the supplier at the end of the year or slightly prior to that date. This may require either the conversion of existing computer data to a format that is readable by the supplier's computer system or a large rekeying effort by the company's payroll staff. It is particularly important during this step to provide time and personnel resources to review all rekeyed information to ensure that it is correct. There must also be enough time to adequately train the staff who will be inputting information into the payroll system on an ongoing basis. Supplier representatives should be on hand during the first few data-entry sessions to ensure that all problem areas are adequately addressed.

The transition of cash management to a supplier begins with a review by the cash management consulting division of the bank to see where lockbox accounts should be set up. The company then has the bank create these accounts, and the bank sets them up to automatically sweep cash receipts into a single account that provides interest income. The company should then create an audit program for periodically reviewing the contents of each account to ensure that cash balances have indeed been shifted to the investment account. Once these steps have been taken, the company must send a mailing to all customers, informing them of the address of the lockbox nearest them to which they should send remittances. Finally, the company should have a procedure in place for reminding companies where to send their payments, since many will ignore the request to send cash to a lockbox and instead will continue to send it to the old remittance address.

Handing over the financial reporting task to a supplier is one of the easier tasks to transition. A quality accountant can produce a financial statement directly from a general ledger report and can add notes to the financial statements based on periodic interviews with company management. The only transition steps required here are to go over with the supplier how individual accounts are to be rolled up into financial statement line items and then to monitor the supplier's financial reports for several months to ensure that the reporting is being completed properly.

The internal audit function requires several extra transition steps to complete. Since the quality of the supplier's audit staff has a strong impact on the speed and in-depth analysis that will characterize each internal audit, the CFO should carefully review the qualifications of all auditors proposed by the supplier and feel free to reject any who appear to have too little experience. Next, the supplier's staff should be thoroughly trained in the company's policies and procedures, meet key employees, and be set up in permanent offices with ready access to office equipment. This step is necessary to ensure that the auditors start off as efficiently as possible. Next, if the company wants to continue with its own internal auditing methodology, it can train the supplier's staff in its use. This is of particular interest in those industries where a standard audit program would not work; for example, the gambling industry requires intensive and frequent reviews of all controls over the cash function, which would not receive much attention under a standard audit program. The CFO and the supplier's management must then agree on an audit program for the upcoming year. The CFO has primary control over the contents of this plan, but the supplier is certainly welcome to recommend changes that will give a more rounded review of as many control points as possible, or which will take advantage of the particular skills of the supplier's staff. It is also helpful to arrange for periodic review meetings in which the supplier's audit staff goes over the findings from each of its audits and the CFO asks for further reviews based on these findings, or modifies the schedule of remaining audits based on time or cost constraints. The final transition step is to arrange for other means of training future company managers if this function had previously been used for that purpose.

Turning over the taxation function to a supplier is one of the easiest accounting tasks to outsource. The supplier who normally takes over this work is the company's current audit firm. The CFO merely needs to authorize the audit firm to begin tax work, so it can review the audit workpapers in its possession to begin work. However, if the CFO has chosen a supplier other than the company auditor for this work, the company must send written permission to the auditor to copy audit files and send them to the tax preparer. Finally, though most tax preparers are too expert in their field to make mistakes, most companies will review the tax forms they have prepared prior to sending them on to the government.

The most difficult accounting task to outsource is transaction processing, because the task may involve large numbers of employees, custom software, supplier training, and a risk of task interruption. However, if the transition of this task is properly carried through, the company's customers will notice no change in the accounting function's services to them. The first task in this area is to transfer the company's staff to the supplier. Since the supplier may not have chosen to hire all of the existing staff, it may also be necessary to train new staff in how to run the company's transaction-processing systems. This training task may extend to the supplier's management team, who may not have hired the company's management team to oversee the area. Also, if the supplier decides to set up an off-site facility, the company's existing hardware and software may have to be removed to that location. An alternative is to load the company's software and related database of information into the supplier's computers at a preexisting location. In either case, the company will have to transfer the software license for the software it uses to process transactions from the company to the supplier, which may involve a substantial payment to the software provider. Once all of these steps have been taken, the supplier should run through a set of sample transactions to ensure that the system is operating properly, prior to processing any real transactions.

The transition process for pension management starts with sending all account information for each participant to the new supplier. Since the current supplier may have the most up-to-date form of this information, written permission may be needed for its release to the new supplier. This information must be loaded into the supplier's database and checked for accuracy. Next, the company must transfer all fund balances to the supplier. Sometimes the money is invested in specific stocks or third-party funds, so simply transferring the power to invest this money to the new supplier is a sufficient way to transfer the funds, which do not really move from where they have been invested. However, if the new supplier has its own funds in which pension investments are to be made, then the money must be extracted from the original supplier and given to the new supplier for reinvestment. In this second case, the company must have all plan participants choose new investment vehicles in which to invest their funds—assuming that the pension plan is a 401(k) plan where employees make their own investment decisions. This paperwork must go to the new supplier, who uses it to apportion the transferred funds to its investment vehicles. Also, the company's in-house human resources personnel must be given adequate stocks of the supplier's investment forms and be instructed in their use. These forms are needed on an ongoing basis to allow employees to enter or exit the plan, or to alter their mix of investments or amount of funds invested. Also, the supplier commonly has its own proprietary software that it gives to the company to input new pension contribution information for each employee following each pay period; the employees who will do this inputting must be trained in how to use the software and allowed practice sessions with test data. Finally, it is advisable to closely review all pension statements for each employee following the first few months of the transition to ensure that all information was correctly converted to the new supplier.

CONTROLLING SUPPLIER PERFORMANCE

This section covers the variety of control points available to a company that wants to ensure that suppliers are completing their designated accounting tasks as efficiently and effectively as possible. Most companies will not have the resources to implement all of the controls noted in this section, but a mix of selected controls should be sufficient to maintain adequate control over accounting suppliers.

The primary control point is the internal audit. The internal audit team should follow an audit program that takes it through a review of each supplier's activities regularly enough for the suppliers to know that they will be undergoing an audit at least once a year. A few of the more common audit objectives are to:

- Verify that supplier invoices have an attached approval signature or purchase order.
- Verify that expense reports are approved and have supporting documentation for expenses of $25 or more.
- Verify that all accounts receivable credits have been approved.
- Verify that appropriate sales tax amounts are charged on invoices.
- Verify that invoices were mailed in a timely manner.
- Verify that payroll taxes are being deposited.
- Verify that tax returns have no material errors.
- Verify that financial statements and accompanying financial notes have no material errors.
- Verify that the cash in all lockbox accounts is being swept into an interest-bearing account.

Once the audit team has completed its audit program for a supplier, it should go over its findings with the management of the supplier to verify that all audit findings are accurate and then meet with company management to present its findings and recommendations. A key consideration when using an audit team is whether it should be outsourced. If the company has an outside audit firm take over this key function, that firm should not be allowed to take over any other accounting tasks—otherwise the audit team will be reviewing the work of its employer, which will not result in an independent review of operations.

Bonuses and penalties are one of the most effective ways to control suppliers. To begin, the company must create target goals for suppliers to achieve. The suppliers must sign off on these goals in advance, so there is no conflict over the nature of each goal, how it is measured, who measures it, and the size of the penalties or bonuses that will result from the measurements. The company must track the measurements, not the suppliers, so that suppliers will not be tempted to skew the results. If the penalties or bonuses tied to these measurements are large, then the measurement results should be given to suppliers during formal meetings, so they can defend the measurement results. When suppliers can gain or lose significant amounts of money through performance measurements, their performance will improve dramatically.

There should be a separate line item in the budget that shows the cost of each accounting supplier. When this information is listed in the monthly financial statements, company management gains a clear understanding of the cost of each supplier and how that cost is changing in comparison to the budget. If there are significant cost overruns appearing in the financial statements, management can take action to reduce them, either through negotiations, less use of supplier services, or by switching to a new supplier.

The final control area is the schedule review meeting. This is useful for going over the results of internal audits, reviewing progress toward predetermined goals, and discussing any problems that have arisen since the last meeting. An agenda should be distributed in advance and strictly followed to ensure that all major areas are addressed. The company should have a meeting secretary record the minutes of each meeting, distribute them to participants, and require that the chief representatives from each side sign off on the meeting minutes as being accurate (or modify them as necessary and then sign off). These minutes should be kept on file in case there are questions later on about what was agreed on during meetings. The number of meetings per year will vary greatly with the type of accounting function being reviewed. Some of the more automated accounting tasks, such as payroll, need as few as one review meeting per year, though many more may be required while the area is first being implemented. Other areas that require constant interaction between the staffs of the company and supplier may require monthly review meetings. The one area that must be reviewed frequently is transaction processing, because problems in this area that are not quickly addressed will cause problems with the company's accounts payable and receivable, which can irritate customers or suppliers.

MEASURING OUTSOURCED ACTIVITIES

Given the large number of tasks within the accounting function that can be outsourced, there are many measurements needed to properly keep track of them all. In this section, the measurements are listed in alphabetical order by task.

CASH MANAGEMENT

- *Earnings rate on investments*. Banks can differentiate themselves by offering higher investment rates on various investments, which they do by keeping less profit on these investments for themselves and giving the forgone profits to the company. Though there is not normally a large basis point spread between the investment rates offered, one could still realize some improvement in investment income with a large cash balance to invest. Thus, the average earnings rate on investment is a useful performance measurement. It can be derived from the monthly bank statement, where one can take the total investment income for the month and divide it by the total average balance invested to derive the earnings rate on investment. One concern here is that a company may try to improve its earnings rate on investment by parking its funds in riskier investment vehicles; this measurement does not factor in the investment risk element, so a company should adopt an investment policy that restricts investments to only specific areas that have limited and acceptable levels of risk.

- *Transaction fees*. A bank will charge a per-transaction fee on every transfer of cash between accounts. Though this fee may be absorbed by credits earned from having excessive cash balances, the fee is still charged and should be tracked in case the company decides to eliminate its excess cash balances, which would result in these fees actually being paid. The information for the measurement is easily obtained from the bank's monthly reporting statement. It is more important to track the per-transaction fee than the total fee, since the total fee will be skewed by the volume of transactions.

COLLECTIONS

- *Percentage collected of dollar volume assigned*. The primary performance measure for any collections agency is the amount of money collected out of the accounts transferred to it. An ineffective agency is one that cannot collect at least a portion of each account receivable turned over to it. Since the company wants to work with only those agencies that can convert the highest possible proportion of accounts receivable into cash, this is the primary measurement to use. The calculation is to divide the total cash received from the agency by the total amount of accounts receivable assigned to it. Since there may be a large time gap between when the agency receives the account and when the cash comes in, it is better to annualize this measurement in order to more closely match inflows and outflows.

FINANCIAL STATEMENTS

- *Accuracy of accruals*. Most suppliers of financial statements only take a set of reports supplied by the company and use them to construct financial statements—they do not get into any journal entries, such as accruals. However, for those that do, it is important that accruals be made correctly. Incorrect accruals lead to inaccurate financial statements, not only for the month in which the accruals are made, but also for the month when the accruals are reversed. This measurement is derived by having the internal audit team periodically review the calculations used for each accrual and then come up with its own accruals. The net variance between the two sets of accruals is the percentage by which the supplier's accruals are inaccurate.

- *Number or percentage of material irregularities*. A supplier must be able to restate a company's reports into an accurate set of financial statements. Any material irregularities in the numbers or accompanying financial notes may cause problems with the company, since lending, investment, and regulatory bodies rely on this information. This can be a difficult measurement to derive. The internal audit team should periodically review the statements for material irregularities, wade through the claims and accusations between the company and supplier regarding how the irregularities occurred, determine the amount by which the financial statements are incorrect, and derive a percentage of inaccuracy based on how far off the profits are from what they should have been. If the problem lies in the accompanying notes, then the measurement is purely qualitative and should be reported as a discussion of how the notes are incorrect.

- *Time to release statements.* A supplier may take its time in preparing and mailing out a company's financial statements. This can be a major problem for the SEC, banks, and investors, who require this information by specific deadlines. Banks frequently require that financial statements be delivered by specific dates—no financial statement, no loan. To measure this item, designate to whom financial statements are to be sent by the supplier, and have that person record the number of days lag between the end of the reporting period and the receipt date.

INTERNAL AUDITING

- *Cost per audit.* Suppliers of internal audits are usually much more expensive on a per-hour basis than an in-house staff. However, this should not be the way to measure the cost effectiveness of an internal audit supplier. Due to the increased experience and training of many supplier employees, internal audit engagements can be completed quite quickly and result in more suggestions for improvements. Since suggestions for improvement are difficult to quantify, it is better to measure the supplier based on just the cost of the audit (as taken from its billing statement to the company), and then evaluate this information in light of the perceived value of suggestions made.

- *Percentage of audits completed.* When a company brings in a supplier to conduct a series of internal audits, it usually starts with a plan of audits to be conducted over the upcoming year. If the supplier cannot complete all of the audits that it agreed to, it is not being efficient and may be replaced in favor of someone else who can do so. This item is easily measured by dividing the total number of audits completed (defined as having been signed off on by all parties) by the total number of audits listed in the annual audit plan.

INVESTMENTS

- *Accuracy of trades.* If the company has a supplier handling all investment trades for it, the company wants some assurance that the trades are being handled properly. For example, authorizations to purchase or sell specific bonds or stocks should be carried through with total accuracy. The company's internal audit team or a staff person can regularly measure this by comparing the company's records of what it authorized for trades to the supplier's periodic statements showing what it actually did. Any problem trend should prompt a discussion with the supplier, if not its immediate firing—a company cannot run the risk of having its funds improperly stored in the wrong investment vehicles.

- *Brokerage fees as a percentage of the amount invested.* A company conducting large numbers of trades should be able to negotiate very good brokerage rates from its supplier. Companies with smaller trading volumes may pay higher rates, since the supplier has no incentive to offer lower prices to retain their business. Brokerage fees are usually located on the periodic brokerage billing statements. If not, the supplier may be hiding excessive fees. If the supplier is unwilling to change its statement format, the company may be better served by switching its business to a more open supplier.

PAYROLL

- *Proportion of fees for extra services.* A payroll supplier likes to gain business by charging low fees for basic payroll-processing services, since companies make the decision to use suppliers based on these initial fees. The suppliers then charge exceedingly high rates for all additional services, which companies ask for after they have enrolled with the supplier and are "locked in." A company should separate these extra fees from the baseline fees to gain an understanding of incremental costs. The calculation should be the total additional fees per reporting period, divided by the total fees during that period.

- *Proportion of payrolls delivered to correct locations.* One service provided by payroll suppliers is guaranteed delivery of payrolls to the company's various locations by payday, usually using overnight mail delivery. If a payroll is sent to the wrong location or lost, this causes major personnel problems (since employees are not being paid), and therefore should be measured. The measurement is to summarize all instances when payroll was incorrectly delivered and to divide this by the total number of payroll deliveries in the reporting period. There is never a problem with collecting the information for missing payrolls—company employees will bring this problem to your attention very quickly.

- *Timeliness in paying payroll taxes.* One of the primary tasks of the supplier is to pay all payroll taxes on behalf of the employer. This greatly reduces the labor and risk of penalties for nonpayment by the company. It is a simple measurement to track, for the government will notify the company of any late payments. If there are no notifications, then the supplier has filed tax payments at the appropriate times. The measurement is to divide the total number of missed tax payments by the number of payrolls per year to determine the average timeliness in paying payroll taxes.

- *Transaction fees per person.* A payroll supplier's services are billed as a mix of per-person costs and fixed costs that are not linked to headcount. The bulk of these fees are based on per-person costs, however, and are therefore an excellent way to determine the per-unit cost of this service. Most payroll providers send out highly detailed billing statements after each payroll, so the information used to derive this measurement is usually easily obtained. To calculate it, summarize all costs per payroll for each person for whom a paycheck was created. This may include fees for check preparation, stuffing, extra calculations for vacations or 401(k) deductions, and wire transfers. All of these per-person fees should be compiled when deriving the transaction fee per person. The total fees are then divided by the total number of employees paid in the period to come up with the per-person amount. If a company has different payrolls of different lengths (i.e., once a week or twice a month), the costs should be annualized to properly account for the costs of all payrolls.

PENSION

- *Investment return.* A typical pension plan will allow a participant to choose from a variety of funds, each of which has a different level of return and risk. To a large extent, the desired return is up to the participant and not the supplier. However, the supplier may do a poor job of managing the funds or extract too large a portion from each investment in the form of management fees, resulting in low returns. If so, it may be time to try a new pension supplier. This is measured by having the supplier provide a quarterly statement of investment return for each fund in the pension plan.

- *On-time release of funds.* Pension suppliers are in charge of disbursing funds to plan participants. These payments normally go straight from the supplier to the participant, so it is difficult for the company to determine if there are any problems with the release of funds on time. However, if there is a pattern of employee complaints in this area, there may be grounds for further investigation.

- *Release of statements on time.* Most pension suppliers issue investment statements to plan participants once a quarter. The in-house pension coordinator will receive many employee complaints if these statements are not released on time, since employees want to know how much money they earned in the last quarter. Also, any supplier that cannot get this simple report out on time may have other administrative problems related to tracking the investments, so not being able to release statements on time may be a sign of other problems at the supplier. This measurement is tracked by comparing the date when statements are received to the date when they are due.

TAXES

- *Absence of penalties.* One of the main reasons for employing someone else to prepare a company's taxes is to avoid tax penalties. These penalties can be caused by either filing tax returns too late or by filing incorrect returns. In either case, the company pays the penalties. This measurement is simply the total of all penalties and related charges paid to tax authorities in a given time period. If company management finds that the tax preparer's fee plus the tax penalties sum to more than the company was spending internally to prepare the tax returns, it may be time for a new supplier.

- *Timeliness of filing.* A tax preparer must be able to file all tax returns on time. This is a large chore if the preparer is filing returns on behalf of the company for a large number of states, perhaps including quarterly returns of various kinds, as well as those tax filings sent to the federal government. Nonetheless, despite the volume, it is the tax preparer's responsibility to send out all tax returns on time. Otherwise, the company may have to pay penalties for late filings. This measurement is easy to track, since the company will be notified by the various government authorities whenever a filing is late—usually by sending a penalty notice. The number of these late filings can be divided by the total number of tax filings to determine the proportion of late filings. One consideration here is that a tax preparer may be late with a variety of inconsequential tax filings but on time with the more important income tax returns. In these cases, due consideration should be made for the importance of the filings that are late.

TRANSACTIONS

- *Average employee expense report turnaround time.* One of the most sensitive accounting issues is the review, approval, and payment of employee expense reports. If payments are made incorrectly or late, employees will be more irate than if the accounting function were to have problems in any other area—after all, it is their money. This problem can be avoided by periodically reviewing the time required to pay employees after they submit expense reports. The sampling method can be either to submit sample expense reports and track the time required to receive payment back or to have an audit team review the supplier's payment records to determine the average turnaround time.

- *Average time to resolve errors.* Once an error is found, it is important to fix it as soon as possible. Otherwise, the paperwork associated with it is relegated further back in the archives area and is more difficult to research and correct. Also, there may be problems caused by an error that will magnify over time and involve considerable effort to correct—angry business partners certainly being the greatest danger to avoid. This is a difficult measure to derive, since a transaction-processing supplier can easily hide the existence of mistakes or mask the amount of time it took to handle them. The best approaches are either to rely on the supplier to track this measure or to send in an audit team. The audit team can find evidence of error correction by looking for journal entries or unusual debits or credits in the accounts payable and receivable journals—these are normally added to the records to fix a previous problem.

- *Cost per transaction.* The cost of a transaction-processing supplier can vary dramatically based on the volume of transactions processed. During a month when there are many invoices to process or bills to pay, the apparent cost of the supplier increases dramatically. However, it is misleading to look at the total cost of such a supplier, since the cost of using one is so dependent on processing volume. Instead, the cost per transaction should be used. This cost does not vary much, unless there is a significant change in the volume of transactions. This cost is easily obtained from the supplier billing statements, and should be tracked on a trend line to spot any changes to the per-unit cost.

- *Error rate on processing.* It is very expensive to use staff to research and resolve any problems caused by incorrect transaction processing. It can also anger customers who may be incorrectly billed, or suppliers who are incorrectly paid. To determine the extent of this problem, the company should schedule periodic audits of all processed transactions to determine the percentage of errors in such areas as billing addresses, accounts payable matching, and tax rates on billings.

- *Percentage of payment discounts taken.* Any supplier who takes over the accounts payable function should certainly be able to process payments fast enough to take all early payment discounts. If not, the company may be losing more money in discounts lost than it is saving by using the supplier. The easiest way to measure this item is to have the supplier generate a monthly report listing all payments made and those for which discounts were taken. An audit team can then sample the payments listed on this report to verify that all discounts were taken, as well as to verify that all payments made during the month were listed on the report. This review can verify that the reported percentage of payment discounts taken is correct.

- *Timeliness of processing.* Some transactions must be processed on time, or they impact company cash flows. A prime example of such a transaction is billing, which should be conducted every day to avoid a reduction in the inflow of cash payments from customers. An internal audit team can measure this item by comparing the arrival of paperwork at the supplier to initiate the transaction processing (with the date of receipt presumably being stamped on the document by the supplier) with the date when the transaction was completed.

The measurements noted in this section focus on the timeliness, accuracy, and cost of each accounting task—the same items that are of concern for an in-house accounting department. Though using all of these measurements at once would be quite a data-collection and analysis burden, a blend of some portion of the measures would be an effective means of monitoring the outsourced accounting tasks.

MANAGING SUPPLIERS

Outsourcing the accounting function almost always occurs in a piecemeal fashion, with one task going to a supplier, followed by a lengthy evaluation period, followed by outsourcing another task. Rarely does an accounting function ever reach the point of being totally outsourced. Instead, a number of key functions, such as cost accounting and financial analysis, are always kept in house. This means that an accounting manager must also be kept to manage the remaining functions. Typically, the in-house accounting manager (usually the controller) will oversee the activities of suppliers dealing with accounting transactions, internal audits (though this may shift to the CFO or the Board's audit committee), collections, financial reporting, taxation, and payroll. Also, the corporate treasurer will oversee the activities of suppliers dealing with investment management, cash management, and pension management. In a smaller company without a treasurer, the suppliers dealing with all of these functions will usually be overseen by the controller. The outsourcing portion of a controller's job description is shown in Exhibit 19.1.

DROPPING SUPPLIERS

With a few exceptions, a company can remove itself from an accounting outsourcing arrangement quite easily, since there are minimal supplier investments involved and the transfer of staff and fixed assets is small. This section points out the areas where this is not so easy, as well as the issues to deal with when this is the case.

One of the more difficult tasks to take away from a supplier is pension management, because it is costly for the supplier to enroll employees in investment funds and to set

---

Employee Title: Controller
Reports to: Chief Financial Officer
Responsibilities:
- Sign off on all agreements with the various accounting suppliers.
- Authorize the release of funds for payment of suppliers.
- Compare actual costs charged to costs listed in contracts to determine the causes of variances; follow up on these variances with suppliers.
- Measure service levels for all accounting areas and resolve any problems.
- Authorize the movement of cash between accounts.
- Approve the transfer of large accounts receivable to collection agencies.
- Review and approve supplier-generated financial statements.
- Review and approve supplier-generated tax returns.
- Approve the internal audit program, and review the findings of completed reviews.
- Approve investment criteria.
- Manage the transfer of functions from the company to suppliers.
- Manage any tasks within the accounting function that have been kept in house.

EXHIBIT 19.1 OUTSOURCING PORTION OF THE CONTROLLER'S JOB DESCRIPTION

them up in their computerized asset-tracking systems. If the company pulls its business away from the supplier after a short time, the supplier will probably not earn any profit at all, since it earns its profit after start-up costs have been covered by a number of periodic maintenance payments. It may take more than a year before profits begin to flow in for the pension supplier. Thus, suppliers like to charge per-person and lumpsum exit fees to keep a customer from pulling out and also to recoup their costs if companies pull out despite the fees.

If a company wants to pull its business away from a collections agency, it is customary to let the agency finish collections work on any accounts receivable that the company has already given to it. This prevents the collections agency from complaining that the company is trying to avoid paying collection fees on any accounts receivable that the agency was on the verge of receiving. If the company feels that the collections agency must stop all work on behalf of the company at once, then an alternative is to pay the agency a negotiated fee in exchange for handing back any accounts receivable that it has not yet collected. This fee should be included in the initial contract with the agency, thereby avoiding any bickering about fees later on.

Canceling an outsourcing contract with a payroll supplier is easy to do, but a CFO should think through the ramifications before going forward with this step. The main problem involves tax and pay accumulators. If a single payroll supplier accumulates all of this information for a full calendar year, it will agree to issue W-2 forms to the company for its employees at the end of the year. However, if the supplier is taking over for only part of a year, it will either not guarantee the accuracy of the W-2 forms or will not agree to issue the forms at all. This means that the company must manually produce W-2 forms at the end of the year, which can be a considerable chore if there are many employees. The best way to avoid this problem is to only switch payroll suppliers at the end of the calendar year, when payroll and tax accumulations are complete and can be reported as such on employee W-2 forms.

The most difficult area to terminate is transaction processing, because the supplier may have hired the company's staff and purchased its computer processing equipment, and will want to return both. If the company does not want to hire back all of the staff it sent to the supplier, it may have to negotiate payment of some portion of the severance payments to them. The company will also need to pay for any equipment previously purchased from it by the supplier; if so, there should be a clause in the original contract stating the prices at which the equipment will be repurchased. The company may also need to transfer back the license to any transaction-processing software that the supplier took over. Also, all transaction information must be sent back to the company and closely reviewed to ensure that no accounts payable or receivable transactions are missed.

Terminating the cash management services of a bank is much more difficult than a company may initially realize. The problem is that the company has gone to some lengths to notify all of its customers regarding the correct address of the nearest bank lockbox to which they should mail in their payments. When those lockboxes are shut down as part of the termination, customers will find that their payments are being returned to them. The customers must then call the company to determine the new lockbox address. This problem reduces the speed with which cash comes to the company, and may require additional debt to tide the company over the period of lengthened cash flow. One way to avoid this problem is to keep the lockboxes open for a substantial period of time after the company has moved its business to a new bank, thereby keeping payments from being sent back to customers. The other option is to contact all customers well in advance of the termination of all lockboxes, so they know where payments should be sent. The best approach is to use both options.

SUMMARY

Accounting outsourcing is unique because there are so many functions to outsource—no one supplier does all of them, but a number of them can be used in concert to shift essentially all accounting functions away from an in-house department. Tight control and carefully planned, sequential transitions by the CFO are the keys to successfully outsourcing the accounting function.

CHAPTER 20

OPERATIONAL BEST PRACTICES*

All accounting processes can be improved in some manner in order to increase the overall efficiency and effectiveness of the accounting department. Such improvements are known as best practices. They can range from such simple expedients as the creation of a signature stamp to increase the speed of check signing to the installation of advanced document management systems that allow one to avoid most records management issues. The full range of best practices would encompass an entire book (and does: for a full treatment of this topic, refer to Bragg, *Accounting Best Practices*, Wiley: 2005). This chapter contains a number of the more common best practices, listed in alphabetical order by functional area, as well as a graphical representation of the approximate cost and implementation time needed to install each one. Any best practice that requires a high cost has a notation beneath it of three stacks of money, while those best practices requiring fewer funds have a correspondingly smaller number of stacks. Similarly, a best practice requiring a lengthy installation time has a notation beneath it containing three alarm clocks, while those with shorter installation times have a smaller number of clocks.

BEST PRACTICES

- *Accounts payable: accept electronic data interchange invoices*. Many larger companies with advanced operational capabilities prefer to issue invoices to their customers by electronic data interchange (EDI), rather than with a paper invoice, because of the increased transaction speed and reduced cost of this approach. A company can alter its internal systems to accept these invoices by creating an interface between its accounting system and its packaged EDI acceptance software, so that an incoming EDI transaction will be sent directly to the accounting system in the correct format without the need for any manual reentry by a key-punching staff. Though a very efficient approach to the entry of supplier invoices, the creation of a customized interface is both lengthy and expensive.

  Cost: 💵 💵 💵

  Installation time: ⏰ ⏰ ⏰

- *Accounts payable: audit expense reports*. Rather than review every line item on every expense report submitted, the accounting manager can schedule a random audit of a small number of expense reports, which will be indicative of any

---

* Adapted with permission from Chapter 25 of *Ultimate Accountants' Reference* by Bragg (John Wiley & Sons, 2005).

problems that may be present in other, unaudited reports. If so, either the scope of the audit can be expanded or else the accounting staff can focus on just those issues that are uncovered in a broader sample of expense reports. Also, if the audits of certain employees continue to reveal ongoing problems, these individuals can be scheduled for full reviews of all expense reports submitted. By taking this approach, a company can still spot the majority of expense report exceptions, while expending much less effort in finding them.

Cost:

Installation time:

- *Accounts payable: automate recurring payments.* A few payments, such as space rental, copier lease, and subscription billings, are the same every month, and are likely to last for some time into the future. To avoid the repetitive entry of these items into the accounts payable database, many off-the-shelf accounting packages allow one to set up automatically recurring payments that must only be entered in the system one time. This option should only be used if it allows for a termination date, since automated payments may otherwise inadvertently pass well beyond their actual termination dates.

Cost:

Installation time:

- *Accounts payable: automate supplier query responses.* The accounts payable staff can spend a large part of its time answering queries from suppliers who want to know when they will be paid. The staff time devoted to this activity can be sharply reduced by installing a computerized phone linkage system that steps suppliers through a menu of queries so that they can find out the status of payments directly from the computer system. It is also possible to do this through an Internet site. Some employee interaction with suppliers will still be necessary, since there will be cases where invoices are not recorded in the system at all, and so will require manual intervention to fix.

Cost: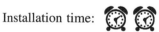

Installation time:

- *Accounts payable: automate three-way matching.* The most labor-intensive effort by the accounts payable staff is to manually compare receiving documents to supplier invoices and internal purchase orders to ensure that all payments made to suppliers are both authorized and received in full. To avoid much of this work, a number of high-end computerized accounting systems will conduct the comparison automatically and warn the staff when it finds inconsistencies. However, this means that the purchasing staff and the receiving staff must enter their purchase orders into the same system, which requires extra coordination with these departments.

Cost:

Installation time:

- *Accounts payable: create an on-line purchasing catalog*. Employee purchases of office supplies and maintenance items comprise a large part of the purchases made by most companies, as well as a correspondingly large part of the accounts payable transactions that it must handle. To avoid this payable work, an on-line purchasing catalog can be created that itemizes all company-approved items; employees can select items directly from this catalog and place an on-line order. These orders will be batched by the computer system and automatically sent to suppliers, who will ship directly to the ordering personnel. Suppliers will then issue summarized invoices to the company, which greatly reduces the paperwork of the accounting staff. It will also reduce a large part of the work of the purchasing staff. However, setting up the system and coordinating its installation with suppliers results in a very lengthy installation interval.

Cost:

Installation time:

- *Accounts payable: eliminate manual check payments*. There are some instances when checks are needed on such short notice that they cannot be included in the scheduled check runs of the accounting staff. Instead, someone must obtain approval on short notice, cut a manual check, have it signed, and log it into the computer system. To avoid these time-consuming steps, one can promulgate a general prohibition on issuing this sort of payment, and can increase the use of petty cash if this will allow the accounting staff to replace manual check payments with cash payments.

Cost:

Installation time:

- *Accounts payable: issue payments based on purchase order approval only*. The typical company payment requires multiple approvals: on the purchase requisition, the purchase order, supplier invoice, and check. A much simpler approach is to require a single approval on the purchase order and ignore all other required approvals. By doing so, the amount of time required to complete accounting transactions can be substantially reduced, since documents must no longer be sent to managers for approval and sit in their in-boxes. However, this means that the controls over purchase order approvals must be iron-clad, so that there is no chance of a supplier payment being sent out without some sort of authorized approval.

Cost:

Installation time:

- *Accounts payable: issue payments based on receipts only.* As previously noted in a preceding best practice, one of the most time-consuming aspects of the accounts payable function is the matching of receiving documents to purchase orders and supplier invoices. To avoid this entire approach, a company can have the receiving staff access purchase orders through a computer terminal and approve received items on the spot through the terminal. The company then issues payments to suppliers based on the prices listed on the purchase orders, rather than waiting for a supplier invoice to arrive. This completely eliminates the matching process. However, this approach requires a great deal of computer software customization, the integration of sales tax tables into the software, and the cooperation of suppliers in accepting payments from the system. This should be considered an advanced best practice that requires great expertise to install.

  Cost:

  Installation time:

- *Accounts payable: pay via automated clearing house transactions.* The check payment transaction involves printing checks, attaching backup materials to the checks, sending them out for signatures, then attaching check stubs to supporting documents and filing them away while the checks are mailed. A much simpler approach that avoids all of these steps is to obtain the bank routing numbers and account numbers from all suppliers and then send payments directly to these accounts with automated clearing house transactions. This can be accomplished with customized accounting software, but is much easier if the software already contains this feature; it is normally only found on more expensive packages.

  Cost:

  Installation time:

- *Accounts payable: pay with purchasing cards.* The bulk of all paperwork dealt with by the accounts payable staff is for small-dollar items. Many of these purchases can be consolidated by distributing purchasing cards (e.g., credit cards) to those employees who most frequently make purchases. By doing so, a company can reduce the amount of paperwork to a single supplier statement each month. Furthermore, some cards can be set to only allow a certain dollar amount of purchases per day, purchases from only certain types of stores, and even to show daily purchases on an Internet site, so that a supervisor can immediately restrict purchasing levels if spending habits appear to be a problem. On the downside, it can be difficult to report use taxes based on purchasing card receipts, which may lead to slightly higher use tax remittances.

  Cost:

  Installation time:

- *Accounts payable: send supplier invoices to an EDI data entry shop.* When a company creates the capability to accept on-line invoices from suppliers via EDI transmissions, it will find that it must still maintain a clerical staff in order to conduct data entry on those paper invoices still being mailed to the company by some suppliers. It can avoid this expense by remailing the invoices to a data entry outsourcing shop that will reenter the invoices into an EDI format and transmit them to the company, thereby ensuring that 100% of all invoices will be received in the EDI format. A good way to avoid the time delay associated with remailing invoices to the data entry supplier is to have all suppliers (those not using EDI) send their invoices to a lockbox that is accessed directly by the supplier. It may also be possible to charge suppliers a small fee if they do not use EDI, thereby covering the cost of the data entry work.

Cost:

Installation time:

- *Accounts payable: sign checks with a signature stamp.* One of the slowest parts of the check creation process is finding an authorized check signer and waiting for that person to sign the checks (which could be days if the person is busy). A better approach is to purchase a signature stamp and have someone on the accounting staff stamp the checks. However, the stamp must be kept locked up in a secure location, so that no unauthorized check signing occurs. Also, since there will no longer be a review of checks before they are sent out, there must be a strong control over payments earlier in the process by requiring purchase order authorizations before any goods or services are ordered from suppliers.

Cost:

Installation time:

- *Collections: approve customer credit prior to sales.* The accounting or finance staff will sometimes find that it is put under considerable pressure by the sales staff to give credit approval to sales that they have already made to prospective customers. Since the sales staff will earn a commission on these sales, the pressure to approve credit can be quite intense, even if the customer does not have a sufficient credit history to deserve it. This can result in an excessive amount of bad debt write-offs. To avoid this situation, the sales and accounting departments can work together to create a list of sales prospects and determine credit levels for them, based on publicly available credit information, before the prospects are ever contacted. However, this is not a cost-effective solution if new customers are of the walk-in variety or if average per-customer sales are so low that the cost of conducting credit checks makes this best practice too expensive to implement.

Cost:

Installation time:

- *Collections: authorize small balance write-offs with no management approval.* Customers will occasionally pay for slightly less than the amount of an account receivable, leaving a small balance cluttering up the accounts receivable database. It can be quite time-consuming to create a permission form for signature by an accounting manager that will lead to the elimination of these small balances. A better approach is to create a policy that allows the collections staff to write off small balances without any permission from management personnel.

Cost:

Installation time:

- *Collections: automate fax delivery of dunning letters.* A computer can be attached to the accounting computer system that is dedicated to sending faxes. This machine is quite useful if it is linked to the collections database, so that reminder faxes can be sent to those customers whose payments are overdue. The severity of the wording on these faxes can increase over time as the number of days late increases. Faxes can even be sent slightly prior to payment due dates, to jog the memory of customers in regard to payment. However, this can be a very expensive option if a customized software linkage must be created between the collections database and the automated faxing system.

Cost:

Installation time: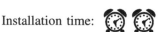

- *Collections: automate fax delivery of overdue invoices.* The preceding best practice for faxing dunning letters can be expanded to also send customers copies of their overdue invoices. In addition, it can be used by the collections staff to only send invoices to those customers to whom collection calls have been made, and who do not have the invoice in hand already. The same software customization issues apply to this best practice as the last one.

Cost:

Installation time: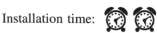

- *Collections: freeze pending customer orders.* If a customer is not paying its overdue invoices, then it certainly makes no sense to send more goods to it, so that even more accounts receivable can become overdue. Consequently, the collections staff should have access to the database of pending customer orders, with authority to halt any further shipments until payment is received for prior shipments. This process can be automated through many accounting systems by setting up maximum credit levels for each customer and allowing the system to automatically freeze shipments once those credit limits are reached. However, some recurring manual review of frozen shipments should be made in order to keep from reducing relations with key customers.

Cost:

Installation time:

- *Collections: receive bankruptcy notices from collection agency.* A company may not realize that a customer has declared bankruptcy, and so will not assert its rights in regard to unpaid invoices, while also continuing to ship to the customer (thereby putting even more accounts receivable at risk of not being paid). To avoid this problem, the Dun & Bradstreet credit agency has an automated bankruptcy notification service that will fax bankruptcy notices to a company for selected customers as soon as a bankruptcy filing becomes public knowledge.

Cost: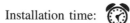

Installation time:

- *Collections: print separate invoices for each line item billed.* Sometimes customers will take issue with one line item on an invoice and refuse to pay the entire invoice until the pricing on that one line item has been resolved, which lengthens the overall interval for collections. To avoid this problem, a company can consider issuing a separate invoice for each line item, rather than clustering them onto a single invoice. This will reduce the average collection period, but may not be cost-effective if the average price for each line item is quite small. It can be a very effective approach, however, for large-dollar line items.

Cost:

Installation time:

- *Collections: send out repeating invoices before the scheduled date.* If a company has a database of prices that it knows it will charge customers on set dates, such as for subscriptions or ongoing standard maintenance fees, it can create and mail the invoices a few days prior to the dates on which they are scheduled to be sent. By creating invoices early, the receiving companies have more time to route the invoices through their internal approval processes, resulting in slightly earlier payments to the issuing company. This is a very inexpensive way to improve the speed of cash flow.

Cost:

Installation time:

- *Collections: stratify required collection calls.* There can be an overwhelming number of potential collection calls to make, and not enough employees to make the calls. In these situations, one should sort the overdue invoices by dollar size, and target the largest ones for the bulk of all calls. This means that the collections staff will focus its efforts on those invoices with the greatest potential dollar return in exchange for the effort put into the calls. This does not mean that small-dollar invoices will be ignored, but the related calls may be delayed or fewer in number.

Cost:

Installation time:

- *Commissions: automate commission calculations*. The calculation of commissions can be a painful process of ascertaining the latest commission deals struck by the sales manager, combing through all of the invoices from the latest month to calculate the preliminary calculation, sending the resulting commission reports to the sales staff, and then dealing with irate sales personnel who think that they have not been fully compensated. A better approach is to first standardize the commission calculation system so that it can be automated through the accounting computer system. By doing so, there will be far fewer complaints from the sales staff about supposedly incorrect commission calculations, no chance of the accounting staff making calculation errors (since the computer is now doing it for them), as well as a much faster completion of this key step in the month-end closing process.

Cost:

Installation time:

- *Commissions: calculate commissions based on cash received*. The sales staff is most concerned with completing a sale to a customer, which it usually defines as the moment when the customer signs a purchase order. However, this ignores the ability of the customer to pay for what it has ordered, which can result in a high level of bad debts. To avoid this problem, the sales staff should be compensated based on cash received from customers. By doing so, the sales staff will be more likely to verify the creditworthiness of customers before selling to them, and will also be more likely to assist in collection efforts.

Cost:

Installation time:

- *Commissions: simplify and standardize the commission payment structure*. As noted earlier in the "automate commission calculations" best practice, a company's commission structure can be an extremely complex one that is difficult to calculate, and which can take a considerable amount of practice to calculate properly. Even if automation of the process is considered too difficult, one can still work with the sales manager to improve the simplicity of calculations. This results in much less review time for the calculations, as well as a more understandable system, which the sales staff will be less likely to make inquiries about.

Cost:

Installation time:

- *Filing: create a document archiving and destruction system*. The operations of the accounting department can be significantly slowed if there is either some difficulty with finding documents or if there are so many stored in the department that it is difficult to rapidly locate the correct items amid the proliferation of paper. The accounting department can set up and follow a detailed set of policies and procedures that are designed to codify and streamline the storage of documents. Such a system can also ensure that stored documents are tagged with destruction dates, as per a standard document retention policy, so that they can be removed from storage on the predetermined dates, thereby creating more room for the accounting department.

Cost:

Installation time:

- *Filing: install a document imaging system*. The problems that a company experiences with missing documents, excessive amounts of space devoted to document storage, and attendant filing costs can largely be eliminated by installing a document imaging system. This involves digitizing documents through a scanner and storing them in a high-capacity storage device on a computer network so that employees can call up images of the documents on-line. This eliminates the risk of lost documents and vastly reduces the amount of required document storage space. However, there may still be a need for off-site storage of some documents if there is a legal requirement for their retention. Also, this system can be very expensive, especially if employees requiring access to it do not already have computer terminals for access to the image database and must be so equipped.

Cost:

Installation time:

- *Filing: stop attaching payment information to checks*. The review of payment information associated with checks by an authorized check signer is considered a key control over the proper disbursement of funds. However, many check signers sign checks with no review at all, considering this step to be a nuisance. If so, an alternative that streamlines the check creation process is to require approval of expenditures earlier in the process, thereby eliminating the need for a check signer (see the previous best practice related to the use of a signature stamp). If there is no check signer, then there is no need to attach related paperwork to checks. An alternative is to have check signers request additional paperwork for only those checks that they wish to inquire more closely about, which relieves the accounts payable staff of the chore of attaching paperwork to the vast majority of all checks.

Cost:

Installation time:

- *Filing: stop storing computer reports*. It is common practice to store paper copies of all computer reports, even when the information is still available either in the computer system or on archiving tapes. One can greatly reduce the amount of required document storage space by only printing out reports for archiving purposes when the related computer files are about to be deleted. Also, there should be a standardized list of reports whose paper copies must be archived—by doing so, a number of unnecessary reports will be kept out of the archives. To make this best practice work properly, there must be sufficient control over the deletion of computer files to ensure that information is not deleted before related reports that are required for archiving have been printed.

Cost:

Installation time:

- *Filing: store canceled checks on CD-ROM*. Canceled checks that are returned by the bank are stored with the bank statement by the month in which the checks cleared the bank, rather than by the month in which the checks were created. This can make it difficult to quickly locate checks. A number of national and regional banks are now offering to store check images on CD-ROMs, which makes it much easier to find canceled check information. It also eliminates the need to store the actual checks. Further, the information on the CD-ROMs can be sorted with a variety of indexes, which makes it very easy to look up information.

Cost:

Installation time:

- *Filing: store records for more time periods in the computer system*. The typical packaged accounting computer system allows for the on-line storage of information for the current and immediately preceding years. The detailed information pertaining to all years prior to these dates will be eliminated, which means that this information must be converted to a paper format and archived. To avoid the associated cost of storing these files, some accounting packages are now offering the option to store records for more accounting periods on-line. Though there can be a considerable additional storage cost associated with this activity, plus a slower computer access speed, this can greatly reduce the need to store archived paper documents. An additional benefit is that accounting reports can be created that will automatically generate comparison reports from many years of on-line data, which eliminates the need to do so manually with information gleaned from paper documents.

Cost:

Installation time:

- *Finance: collect invoice payments through a lockbox.* A company with a large quantity of accounts receivable will lose a day or two of interest income on funds that cannot be invested, because the checks from customers are slowly wending their way through the check-posting process in the accounting department. A better approach is to have customers send their checks directly to a lockbox that is opened by the company's bank, which will cash the checks and then forward the related materials to the company, from which it can post cash payments to the accounting system at its leisure. This process can be quite sophisticated, for a company can operate multiple lockboxes, setting them up in those regions where customers are most densely concentrated. This reduces the lag time caused by mail deliveries. There is some consulting cost associated with determining the correct configuration of lockboxes as well as the cost of notifying customers that they must change the addresses to which they have been sending payments.

Cost:

Installation time:

- *Finance: consolidate bank accounts.* Bank accounts tend to increase in number over time, especially if a company has many stores or subsidiaries. If so, each account will accumulate bank service charges, which can add up if there are many accounts. Also, stray funds may reside in low-interest or no-interest bank accounts for long periods. To avoid these problems, a company should periodically schedule a review of all open accounts and eliminate those that are no longer needed.

Cost:

Installation time:

- *Finance: pay through automated clearing house transactions.* There is a significant cost associated with creating checks, such as buying the check stock and a printer on which to print them, staff time to conduct printing, envelope stuffing, and mailing. All of these costs can be eliminated if payments are instead made through ACH (Automated Clearing House) transactions, which sends funds straight from the company's bank account to the accounts of its suppliers. This can be difficult to set up unless a company's accounting system is already preconfigured to issue payment transactions to its bank. This best practice works best if there are a small number of suppliers, since it can take a considerable amount of effort to collect bank account information from many suppliers and set them up for ACH payments.

Cost:

Installation time:

- *Finance: set up a zero balance account.* In order to invest the maximum amount of excess funds, a company must clear the cash out of all of its checking accounts every day and shift the funds into some sort of interest-bearing account. This is a very labor-intensive task and also is likely to be forgotten from time to time, resulting in less income from invested funds as well as a high cost associated with the transaction. A better approach is to have the bank set up a zero balance account, which parks all funds in an interest-bearing account that is tied back to the corporate checking account. Only enough funds are automatically shifted into the checking account to ensure that those checks being presented for payment each day will be cleared. By using this automated approach, a company can avoid the cost of manually shifting funds between accounts and also benefit from increased investment income.

Cost:

Installation time:

- *Financial statements: automate recurring journal entries.* Some journal entries that are created each month as part of the financial statement production process are unlikely to change from month to month. For example, a standard amortization or depreciation expense will not change from period to period unless the underlying amount of assets is altered. Rather than manually reentering these journal entries in each accounting period, one can use a common feature in most accounting software packages that provides for the repetitive automatic creation of selected journal entries for as far into the future as specified. This reduces the labor associated with the closing process, and also ensures that recurring entries will not accidentally be skipped.

Cost:

Installation time:

- *Financial statements: conduct an on-line bank reconciliation.* Some of the larger national and superregional banks have created either dial-up or Internet access to detailed bank account information for their customers. This is a considerable benefit from the perspective of completing the monthly bank reconciliation, since the accounting staff can now review the bank's detailed records as frequently as each day and conduct an ongoing bank reconciliation. This will not only ensure that company records exactly match bank records at all times, but also eliminates the need to wait for the formal bank statement to be mailed to the company at the end of the month before the closing process is completed, thereby speeding up the production of accurate financial statements.

Cost:

Installation time:

- *Financial statements: create a closing itinerary*. The production of financial statements in an orderly manner requires a tightly scheduled process that interlinks the activities of a number of people. It is very difficult to manage this process without a formal document that itemizes each step in the process, who is responsible for each step, and when each step should be completed. Particular emphasis should be placed on shifting closing tasks into the days prior to the period-end close, automating steps to be completed after the period-end, and shifting nonessential work to later time periods. One should also regularly revise the closing itinerary to reflect ongoing changes in the closing process that are improving its speed and accuracy.

Cost:

Installation time:

- *Financial statements: reduce the number of accruals*. An accounting staff that is excessively focused on achieving perfect accuracy in its financial statements can create a large number of accruals. However, accruals can take a great deal of research to prepare, and interfere with the timely closing of the accounting records. It is better to ignore those smaller accruals that will have only a minimal impact on the financial statements, and concentrate on completing a smaller number of key accruals, thereby improving the overall speed of closing.

Cost:

Installation time:

- *Financial statements: reduce the number of variances investigated*. Whenever a preliminary version of the financial statements is completed, there will be a large number of possible variances from the budget or historical records that the accounting staff could investigate before closing the accounting books. Such investigation takes a great deal of time, so pursuing all possible variance analyses will interfere with the timely closing of the books. To avoid this trouble, the accounting manager should create a rule that forbids all variance analysis if variances fall below a standard dollar or percentage amount. If there still appears to be reason for further review of smaller variances, this can be done *after* the financial statements have been produced, with any resulting changes being recorded in the next accounting period.

Cost:

Installation time:

- *Financial statements: use standardized journal entries.* The majority of journal entries that are made each month are similar in format to those made in previous months; they involve the same account numbers, and may even use the same debits and credits, though the dollar figures may change. Recreating these entries every month requires time and runs the risk of making an error. To avoid these problems, one can create either automated or paper-based standard journal entry forms that are cross-referenced in the closing checklist. By doing so, the accounting staff can verify that all required journal entries have been completed and that the same journal entry format is used during every closing process.

Cost:

Installation time:

- *General ledger: copy the chart of accounts for all subsidiaries.* The consolidation of accounting results for all corporate subsidiaries can be quite a chore if each one uses a different chart of accounts. A mapping table is needed to convert each subsidiary's results into the format used by the corporate parent. Though the mapping table can be incorporated into a reasonably advanced computerized general ledger, it is much simpler to require all subsidiaries to use the same chart of accounts. However, this best practice requires a considerable amount of time to implement, since all subsidiaries must have input into the account structure used; just because the corporate parent prefers to use a particular format does not mean that the businesses it owns can easily dovetail the results of their operations into the same format.

Cost:

Installation time:

- *General ledger: eliminate small-balance accounts.* Over time, there is a tendency to add accounts to the general ledger in order to track special types of expenses. However, many of these expenses are so small in amount that the resulting information does not justify the added cost of tracking the additional account. Consequently, it is best to periodically review the amount of funds being stored in all accounts and eliminate those that are too small.

Cost:

Installation time:

- *General ledger: reduce the number of line items in the chart of accounts.* As noted in the preceding best practice, one can regularly eliminate accounts that experience excessively small amounts of activity. This process can be taken a step further by merging larger accounts together if there is no good reason for separating the information contained within the accounts. For example, there may be a dozen different types of work-in-process inventory that are recorded in different accounts, but the separated information is not used by anyone. Consequently, a general ongoing best practice is to continually examine the chart of accounts with the objective of shrinking it down to only those accounts that are necessary for significant reporting purposes.

Cost:

Installation time:

- *General ledger: store operating data in the general ledger.* When financial statements are produced, they frequently contain operating data, such as headcount, sales backlog dollars, and production capacity. To ensure that this information is reliably stored and readily accessible, extra fields can be created in many general ledger software packages that allow for the storage of alphanumeric information. One can then store operating data in these fields. This is an inexpensive form of data warehouse.

Cost:

Installation time:

- *Inventory: institute cycle counting.* When inventory balances are continually inaccurate, the accounting manager may be uncomfortable with the concept of reporting financial results without first conducting a complete inventory count. This is a very time-consuming and expensive approach that also does not yield completely accurate information. Moreover, it slows down the production of financial statements. A better approach is to authorize the warehouse manager to send a counting person through the warehouse on a continual basis to compare perpetual inventory records to what is physically on hand and to delve into the reasons why there are differences between the two types of data. By doing so, the level of inventory accuracy will always be sufficiently high to avoid the need for a physical inventory count, while there will also be much more attention paid to the reasons why inventory accuracy errors are occurring.

Cost:

Installation time:

- *Inventory: measure inventory accuracy.* The accounting staff will never be sure of the extent to which the inventory is accurate unless it conducts periodic measurements. To do so, someone must select a random sample of inventory items in the warehouse and trace them back to the perpetual inventory database, and vice versa. Any errors in quantity, location, unit of measure, or description should be counted as an incorrect inventory record. By calculating this measurement at a minimum of once a month, the accounting staff will know if the accuracy level has fallen to the point where a physical inventory count will be needed in order to ensure accurate financial results.

Cost:

Installation time:

- *Inventory: move inventory to floor stock*. Counting the entire inventory in the warehouse is a substantial chore. The most difficult items to count tend to be the smallest and least expensive, such as fittings and fasteners. To avoid counting these items, one can expense them when purchased and shift them to inventory storage bins near the manufacturing area. By doing so, the production staff will have much better access to the parts, and will no longer waste time requisitioning them from the warehouse. Offsetting these advantages is the added cost of some pilferage of the items (since they are no longer protected within the confines of the warehouse), as well as some increased tracking difficulty by the purchasing staff, which can no longer rely on perpetual inventory records to determine when additional fittings and fasteners must be purchased.

Cost:

Installation time: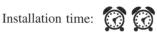

- *Inventory: report on part usage levels*. The most common way to determine inventory obsolescence is to query the warehouse staff about which inventory items appear to be the oldest. This is a decidedly nonscientific approach. A better method is to create several computerized reports that are linked to the perpetual inventory records and the bills of material. These reports will reveal the time period since the last inventory item was requisitioned from stock, as well as the parts that are not used on any bills of material. Both reports clearly indicate which inventory items are at risk of obsolescence, and are also an excellent tool for determining which items are candidates for returns to suppliers.

Cost:

Installation time:

- *Inventory: restrict access to the warehouse*. When the warehouse is open to all employees, it is essentially impossible to maintain an accurate inventory. The reason is that employees with no responsibility for inventory accuracy will take parts without removing them from the inventory database. Consequently, a fence must be constructed around the entire warehouse area, with access being strictly limited to warehouse personnel at all times of the day and night. This is an essential requirement for inventory accuracy.

Cost: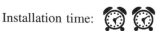

Installation time:

- *Inventory: segregate customer-owned inventory.* The total inventory valuation can be overstated if customer-owned inventory is mixed into it. This occurs when a company manufactures products that require attachments provided by customers. To avoid the problem, it is best to create a fenced-off area within the warehouse whose only use is to store customer-owned inventory. Another option is to create a different set of inventory identification codes for this inventory, so that all inventory valuation reports will automatically set the valuation for these items at zero.

  Cost:

  Installation time: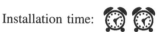

- *Inventory: update bill of material records based on extra warehouse issuances and returns.* Bills of material are commonly used as the basis for issuing parts from the warehouse to the production floor. For example, if ten units of a product are to be created, then the warehouse multiplies all of the parts listed on that product's bill of materials by ten and issues that many items to the production department. However, this can cause problems for the production staff if the bills of material are inaccurate. A good way to correct the bills is to carefully track the number of special requisitions made by the production staff for additional parts, as well as returns from them, since this is a clear indicator of inaccuracies in the bill of material records. By doing so, a company can also eliminate production delays due to parts shortages, while also avoiding rush delivery costs to bring in additional parts on short notice.

  Cost:

  Installation time:

- *Invoicing: computerize the shipping log.* There can be a delay of one or more days in invoicing customers because of the time required for the shipping staff to complete its shipping documentation and deliver it to the accounting department. There is also a risk that some of the paperwork will be lost in transit. To avoid these problems, the shipping staff should be equipped with a computer terminal that allows them to directly enter shipping information into the accounting database. Armed with this data, the accounting staff can issue invoices much more quickly.

  Cost: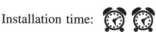

  Installation time:

- *Invoicing: delivery person creates the invoice.* Invoices sent to customers may require subsequent correction with credits if the customer disagrees with the quantity delivered or rejects some items based on quality issues. Since these corrections take a great deal of time by the accounting staff to complete, a better approach is to have the delivery person create an invoice at the point of delivery that contains the quantities to which the customer has already agreed. This eliminates the need for subsequent adjustments. However, this best practice requires a company to have its own employees make deliveries, and also calls for a portable computer and printer for the use of each delivery person. There can also be control problems, since the delivery person may collude with the recipient to bill for a smaller quantity than is actually delivered.

Cost:

Installation time:

- *Invoicing: issue electronic data interchange invoices*. Sending a paper invoice requires that it be sent through the mail, which introduces a time lag before it reaches the recipient. In addition, it may be lost in the mail, misrouted once it arrives at the target company, or some data on it may be incorrectly keyed into the customer's accounts payable system. To avoid all of these problems, one can issue invoices by electronic data interchange (EDI), which involves filling out a standardized transaction form and e-mailing it either directly to the customer or to a third-party organization that maintains an electronic mailbox on behalf of the customer. This approach ensures that invoices will reach customers at once, and can be verified by the return transmission of an acknowledgment of receipt. This method works best when EDI transmission software is directly linked to the billing system, so that invoices will be issued automatically.

Cost:

Installation time:

- *Invoicing: issue single-period invoices*. When a company sells products at very low prices, such as nuts and bolts, the cost of the invoice to the customer may be more than the cost of the products. In these instances, it makes more sense to only issue a single invoice at the end of each month, rather than a series of small invoices. Though this saves on invoicing costs, it will shift cash flows from accounts receivable further into the future, due to the delay in billings. To avoid this problem, one should also look into shortening the payment terms listed on the invoices.

Cost: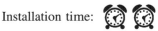

Installation time:

- *Invoicing: reduce the number of invoice parts printed*. When invoices are printed, there may be several copies that go to the customer, another that is filed alphabetically, another that is filed numerically, and yet another that is sent to the collections staff. This requires an expensive multipart form, as well as greater filing costs and a virtual blizzard of paperwork within the accounting department. It is better to reduce the number of invoice parts to the absolute minimum required.

This may include sending just one invoice copy to the customer and retaining another copy for internal reference purposes.

Cost:

Installation time:

- *Management: create a policies and procedures manual*. Though a highly experienced accounting staff may know its tasks by heart and require no written manual, this is not the case when new employees are added to the department or tasks are swapped within the existing staff. When this happens, there is no documentation available that can be used as a basis for training, resulting in slow improvements in knowledge and lots of mistakes in the interim. A policies and procedures manual also improves the level of transactional consistency between the accounting operations of multiple subsidiaries, since their procedures would otherwise tend to diverge over time. It is also possible to issue the manual over the company intranet, which greatly reduces the cost of distribution and the frequency of updates.

Cost:

Installation time:

- *Management: create a staff training schedule*. When new employees are hired into the accounting department, they are typically given enough training to perform their jobs, and nothing more. Instead, a training schedule should be tailored to the needs of each employee so that they are cross-trained in the tasks of other employees. In addition, employees should learn about process improvement so that they are constantly enhancing the transactions for which they are already responsible. This does not mean that all employees require extensive funding to take college courses, but rather that a company develop a mix of seminars, readings, and outside courses to meet its own particular training needs.

Cost: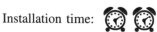

Installation time:

- *Management: issue a monthly schedule of activities*. The accounting staff is driven by a specific schedule of activities to an extent greater than any other department— it must pay taxes on certain dates, process payroll on other dates, issue financial statements on still other dates, and so on. It is a rare case when all of these dates can be memorized, and so some items will occasionally not be completed on time. To avoid this situation, there should be a standard calendar of activities that is updated at the end of each month and issued to the entire accounting staff, with the due dates of each recipient highlighted on it. This requires constant updating as requirements change.

Cost:

Installation time:

- *Management: measure key departmental performance items*. The accounting manager does not have any idea if the performance of the accounting department is improving or degrading over time unless there is a set of measurements that can be used to create a trend line of performance. This may involve meeting due dates earlier—such as issuing financial statements in two days instead of three—or creating fewer transactional errors. The measurement list should be relatively short so that attention can be focused on just those few issues that are most crucial to departmental performance. Other measures can be added over time, as original measurement targets are met or exceeded. This can also be a useful tool for setting up performance-based pay changes for employees.

Cost:

Installation time:

- *Management: outsource selected functions*. Some accounting functions are of such a technical nature or are so prone to error that it may be easier to let an experienced supplier handle them instead. A commonly outsourced function is payroll, which can be shifted to a supplier who will not only calculate payroll and issue checks, but also issue management reports related to payroll, as well as pay various governing authorities all associated payroll taxes. Other functions that can be outsourced include collections, accounts payable, the production of financial statements, and local, state, and federal taxes. The downside to these services is that they cost more than would be the case if handled internally, and they require some oversight by the accounting manager to ensure that they are handled properly.

Cost:

Installation time:

- *Management: review process flows*. Most processes are altered over time as variations occur in the way a company does business. The result is a patchwork of inefficient steps that increase both the time and cost of doing business. This can be avoided by flowcharting the process behind each accounting transaction and then reviewing it over time to see if it can be streamlined. Though this requires some skill in examining process flows, the result can be significant reductions in the cost of transaction processing.

Cost:

Installation time:

- *Payroll: automate vacation accruals.* Accruing and tracking vacation time for employees can be full of errors, for each employee may have been awarded a different vacation period, become employed at a different date during the year, or have some vacation carryforward from the previous year. To avoid these problems, some payroll outsourcing companies and most high-end payroll software packages contain features that allow one to set up standard vacation accruals for each employee. They can factor in vacation carryforwards as well as individual employee start dates. The only trouble with this best practice is that a company must still manually accumulate and deduct vacation time taken so that employees can see their net vacation time available. This information will typically be added to their pay stubs.

Cost: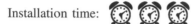

Installation time:

- *Payroll: collect time worked data through a computerized time clock.* The collection of hours worked by hourly employees for the purposes of paying them and tracking hours charged to specific jobs is among the most time-consuming and error-filled transactions in the accounting profession. These problems are caused by the manual time card entries that must be interpreted by payroll clerks into hours worked for each employee—frequently involving missing, false, or unreadable entries. To avoid these problems, a company can invest in computerized time clocks. Under this system, employees are issued bar-coded or magnetic stripe cards, which they slide through a slot on the clock when they are clocking in or out. This action triggers a time entry that is sent to a central payroll computer, where the time entries are stored. Missing scans are noted on management reports, so that they can be fixed before the payroll processing date. By using this approach, there is only a minimal need for data correction, thereby eliminating much of the work by payroll clerks. However, these clocks can cost $2,000 each, and so can only be justified if there are currently many payroll errors or a large staff of payroll clerks that can be eliminated.

Cost: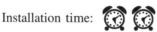

Installation time:

- *Payroll: eliminate deductions from paychecks for employee purchases.* Employees sometimes buy products for themselves through the company's purchasing department in order to take advantage of the lower prices offered to the company. When this happens, they may ask that the cost of the purchased items be gradually deducted from their paychecks. This means that the accounting staff must determine the amount of periodic deductions, as well as when the deductions must stop—all of which takes up valuable accounting time. It is better to create a policy that no employee purchases will be allowed (or at least that employees must pay for all purchases themselves, without deductions), thereby keeping extra deduction-related work away from the payroll staff.

Cost:

Installation time:

- *Payroll: integrate the 401(k) plan into the payroll system.* The typical 401(k) plan is operated separately from the payroll system, so either the accounting or human resources staffs must manually compile payroll and 401(k) participation information, summarize this data into a separate spreadsheet, and send it to the 401(k) administration firm. To avoid this task, some payroll outsourcing companies now offer 401(k) plans that are integrated into their payroll systems. This means that all data collection tasks for 401(k) reporting are fully automated and handled directly by the supplier, rather than the accounting department. However, switching this task to the payroll supplier can be expensive, since it will charge a setup fee as well as ongoing administration fees.

Cost:

Installation time:

- *Payroll: pay employees with direct deposit.* There is no significant difference in efficiencies when a company pays its employees with a check or direct deposit, since the company must still deliver to each employee either a paper check or a deposit advice. Direct deposit may even be slightly more expensive, since there may be a small Automated Clearing House transfer fee associated with each deposit. Nonetheless, the use of direct deposit is generally welcomed by employees, who appreciate not having to physically travel to a bank to deposit payments. It is particularly useful for employees who travel, since they may not be in a position to cash their checks until well after pay dates, and no longer have to worry about cash shortages when direct deposits are used.

Cost:

Installation time:

- *Payroll: reduce the number of payrolls per year.* Every time that a payroll cycle is processed, the payroll staff must accumulate all hours worked, deduction information, and other payroll data, summarize it into either an in-house payroll system or send it to a supplier, and then issue checks to employees. This effort can be reduced by shrinking the number of payrolls that are processed each year. The best alternatives are to process either 24 or 26 payrolls per year. Processing 26 payrolls tends to work better if there are a number of hourly employees, since payrolls will correspond to their weekly timekeeping system. If there are mostly salaried employees, then 24 payrolls can be used, since processing dates will correspond to the end of each month, making it unnecessary to create a salary accrual for hours worked but not paid at the end of each month.

Cost:

Installation time:

- *Payroll: restrict prepayments*. Some employees who travel will request an advance on their paychecks prior to taking trips, so that they will have enough funds to pay for travel costs. This requires that the accounting staff track the amount of all advances, as well as their later deduction from expense reports. It is a system that is highly subject to abuse, since employee advances may never be deducted from expense reports or employees may leave without reimbursing the company. The same problem arises when employees request advances on their paychecks for personal reasons. To avoid these problems, a policy can be created that forbids the use of prepayments. Instead, company purchasing cards can be issued to employees who travel, so that all travel charges are paid directly by the company. If employees want advances on their pay, the company can direct them to a local finance company.

Cost:

Installation time:

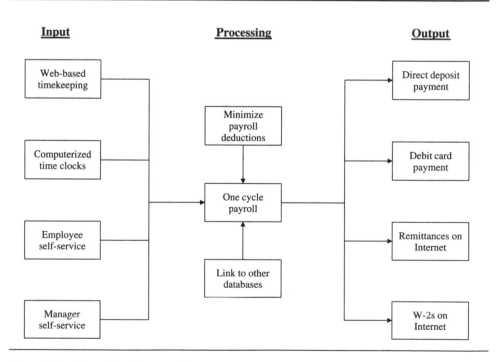

Input **Processing** **Output**

EXHIBIT 20.1 PAYROLL BEST PRACTICES FLOWCHART

The traditional payroll function can be completely overhauled with best practices to achieve a system that requires minimal data entry labor by the payroll staff, simplified processing activities, and the transmission of both electronic payment and remittance information to employees. This ideal situation is portrayed in Exhibit 20.1.

In the flowchart, employees enter their own timekeeping and related payroll information directly into the payroll computer system, using web-based timekeeping, computerized time clocks, and a self-service portal. Similarly, managers can enter employee pay rate changes through a separate self-service portal. This information feeds into a payroll processing function that is consolidated into a single cycle, and which is streamlined through the elimination of as many payroll deductions as possible. Outputs from the system are entirely electronic, with payments being made either with direct deposit or debit card payments, while remittance and W-2 information is posted on a secure web site for employees to access at their leisure. This consolidated group of best practices allows the payroll department to shift into a monitoring and error-correction role, rather than its more traditional role of data entry, payroll calculation, and pay distribution.

SUMMARY

There are thousands of best practices that a company can use to enhance its accounting operations. The best practices noted here are only some of the more common ones currently in use. To acquire information about additional best practices, one can attend seminars that deal specifically with this issue. Another source of information is accounting periodicals, which sometimes contain articles about how other companies have implemented improvements to their systems. This source is particularly useful, because the articles may include information about how to reach the author, so that additional information can be gleaned about specific best practices. Also, local accounting organizations may sometimes sponsor presentations from members at other companies who have installed system enhancements. Finally, a multidivision company may contain a number of accounting departments, any of which may have unique best practices that would be useful. Thus, one must tap into a number of data resources in order to obtain information about additional best practices.

CHAPTER 21

MERGERS AND ACQUISITIONS

There are a great many kinds of analysis needed when a company is contemplating an acquisition. For a full acquisition, involving the assumption of all financial, environmental, and legal liabilities, as well as all assets, there are a great many subsets of analysis to perform. However, for a lesser acquisition, such as the purchase of all or specific assets, the number of analyses is substantially less. In this chapter, the types of acquisition analysis are broken down into a wide range of categories, which makes it easier for a CFO to select just those needed for a specific type of acquisition. In addition, a complete checklist of merger and acquisition analysis questions is included in Appendix C.

Once due diligence is complete, the CFO must estimate the valuation of the acquiree, which can result in a broad range of possible prices. Several methods are described for making this determination.

The CFO must account for merger and acquisition transactions. The only allowable method used is the purchase method. There are also many situations where a company merely makes a small investment in another company, rather than making an outright purchase. This requires three possible types of accounting, depending on the size of the investment and the degree of control attained over the subject company—all three methods, which are the cost, equity, and consolidation methods, are described here. We also delve into special topics associated with mergers and acquisitions, including contingent payments, push-down accounting, leveraged buyouts, spin-off and intercompany transactions, and the proper treatment of goodwill.

When reading this text, one should keep in mind that the terms merger and acquisition are not the same thing. An *acquisition* is when both the acquiring and acquired company are still left standing as separate entities at the end of the transaction. A *merger* results in the legal dissolution of one of the companies, and a *consolidation* dissolves both of the parties and creates a new one, into which the previous entities are merged.

EVALUATING ACQUISITION TARGETS*

The analysis of an acquisition is like no other type of financial analysis—not because the analysis itself is different, but because of the logistics of the situation. Typically, a potential acquisition situation arises suddenly, requires the fullest attention of the accounting staff for a short time, and then subsides, either because the acquisition is judged to not be a good one, or because the deal is completed and management takes over the activities of melding the organizations together. In either case, the CFO is ensconced in the front end of the process, rendering opinions on any possible corporate purchase that the Chief Executive Officer (CEO) sees fit to investigate.

---

*   Compiled with permission from Chapter 6 of *Financial Analysis: A Controller's Guide* by Bragg (John Wiley & Sons, 2000).

Because of the suddenness of an acquisition evaluation, the CFO must be fully pre-pared to switch from any current activities into full-bore analysis mode. To do so, this chapter includes the bulk of analyses that one should pursue in order to determine if the condition of an acquiree is as it purports to be. However, much more than a checklist is required. A CFO and his or her staff have other duties, and cannot let them lie in order to conduct an investigation. Accordingly, the capacity of the accounting department to complete a potentially massive analysis chore may not be possible if the department is still to operate in anything close to a normal and efficient manner. Accordingly, a CFO has three choices to make. First, if there are very few acquisition evaluations to make and the potential acquirees are small ones, then it may be possible to accept some degree of disruption in the accounting ranks and perform all the work with the existing staff. A second alternative is to form an acquisition analysis group that does nothing but evaluate potential candidates on a full-time basis. This is an excellent approach if a company is embarked on the path of growth by acquisition and is willing to buy as many corporations as possible. The third alternative is to hire an outside auditing firm to conduct the financial analysis on behalf of the company. This is a good alternative if the in-house staff does not have the time or training to conduct the work, and if there are not enough acquisitions to justify hiring a full-time team of analysts. However, using outside auditors can be an expensive proposition, and one must be careful to ensure that the audit staff used is of a high enough level of training and experience to conduct a thorough review. Thus, the number of potential acquisitions and the ability of the internal accounting staff to complete acquisition analysis work will dictate the method a CFO uses to obtain sufficient analysis assistance.

With the acquisition analysis team in place, a CFO can proceed through the remainder of this section to determine the precise sets of analysis questions to answer in order to ensure that the type of acquisition being contemplated is fully analyzed—without wasting time on any additional analysis work. The main analysis areas are:

- *Personnel.* If a company has need of employees with great experience or skill, it can fill the need by buying a company that employs them. This is a rare cir-cumstance when only a few people are involved, since it is easier to hire them away with employment offers. However, if a potential acquiree has one or more departments that are justly famous for their work, then buying the company may be worthwhile in order to obtain those specific departments. This situation arises most frequently with engineering or research firms. The main analysis needed here is to determine the current compensation levels of the people being acquired and how these pay levels compare to both internal and industry pay standards. Additional considerations include the presence of any long-term compensation agreements and their net present value.

- *Patents.* A target company may possess one or more valuable patents, especially ones that can be used to enhance the value of the acquiring company's products. This approach is most common with research and drug firms. In this case, the primary analysis focuses on the cost of maintaining those patents, the number of years remaining prior to expiration, and (especially) the expected cash flows to be obtained from them prior to their expiration.

- *Brands.* A brand name is immensely valuable if it has been carefully maintained for many years, has been strongly supported with proper marketing, and represents excellent products. This is a good reason to acquire a target company, and is most common in the consumer goods field. The analysis for this type of acquisition focuses on the incremental profits to be gained by use of the brand name in relation to the cost of maintaining the brand.

- *Capacity.* If a company is faced with a long lead time or technological challenges to acquire greater production capacity, it may be worthwhile to purchase a production facility from another company. The analysis for this type of acquisition focuses on the age and usefulness of the machinery and facility purchased.

- *Assets and liabilities.* When an entire company is purchased, the acquiring organization is taking over virtually all assets, as well as all associated risks. In this instance, a comprehensive review of all balance sheet line items is mandatory.

- *Profitability.* A company may be bought because it has a greater percentage of profitability than the acquiring company, which increases the acquiring company's combined profitability. For this acquisition, a close review of the income statement and balance sheet is necessary.

- *Cash flow.* If a company has a large store of cash or continuing cash flows, it is a prime target for purchase by companies that need the cash, possibly to fund further acquisitions. For this type of acquisition, an intensive review of the balance sheet, income statement, and funds flow statement are necessary.

If a company is involved in a friendly acquisition, then the target company is generally willing to open its accounting books for inspection. The exception to the rule is that, if the target company is a direct competitor to the acquiring organization, then it will resist discussions of trade secrets or processes that will allow it to continue to effectively compete against the acquiring company in case the acquisition does not occur. Also, if an acquisition is of the unfriendly variety, then the opposing company will be quite active in denying access to any information whatever. This is an especially serious problem when a company is privately held, since very little information will be publicly available. In these situations where information is not readily obtainable, how can a CFO find a sufficient amount of information to conduct an analysis?

The first step is to dredge up all possible sources of information. One possibility is the target company's credit report, which may list a recent financial statement (though it may not be remotely accurate since it is usually supplied by the target company, which may not be interested in publicly displaying its financial health). Other sources are articles in trade journals about the organization, as well as a simple review of the facility. By counting the number of cars in the parking lot, one can make a rough estimate, based on the industry average of sales per employee, of the amount of company sales. It may also be possible to talk to former or current employees about the company, as well as its customers or suppliers. Another option is to talk to local recruiters about the positions for which they have been asked to recruit, which may indicate problems that have resulted in employee turnover. Also, the credit report will list all assets against which lenders have filed security claims, which shows the degree to which the target company is using financial leverage to fund its operations. It may also be possible to hire an investigative agency to acquire more information. Finally, reviewing public records about lawsuit filings will reveal if there is any outstanding litigation against the firm. Here is a list of additional outside information sources that may be of use in compiling a comprehensive set of data for a prospective acquisition:

- *Stock transfer agent.* This entity can verify the target company's outstanding capitalization.

- *Title search company.* These organizations, of which Dun & Bradstreet is the best known, will review all public records for the existence of liens on the assets of the target company. The list of liens should be compared to any outstanding debt schedules provided to the buyer to see if there are any discrepancies.

- *Patent/trademark search company.* This type of company reviews all legal filings to see if there are infringement lawsuits against the patents or trademarks of the target company, and can also obtain copies of the original patents or trademarks.

- *Appraisal companies.* An appraisal company can provide a list of the appraised value of a target company's assets, though it will not reveal this information without the prior approval of the target company.

If the target company is diligent in blocking attempts at obtaining information about it, and this results in a significant loss of information, the CFO will not be able to complete a full analysis of the situation. If so, it is very useful to make a list of what information has *not* been obtained, and what the risk may be of not obtaining it. For example, if there is no information available about a company's gross margin, then there is a risk of making too large an offer for a company that does not have the margins to support the price. Once all these risks are assembled into a list, one should determine the level of risk the company is willing to bear by not having the information or in deciding to invest the time and money to obtain the information. This will be an iterative process, as the number of questions posed by the CFO gradually decreases and the cost and time needed to find the answers to the remaining questions goes up. At some point, the CEO will decide that enough information is available to proceed with making an offer or that the work required is excessive and stop any further investigative efforts, proceeding instead to the investigation of other target companies for whom information is easier to obtain.

If the main reason for acquiring a target company is to hire away a specific person or group of people who are deemed to have valuable skills, a CFO has one of two analysis options to pursue. The first is that, if the company has chosen to purchase the entire target company, then a full-blown analysis of all assets, liabilities, controls, and legal issues must be conducted. The analysis for those categories is noted under the following sections of this chapter. However, if the company has persuaded the target company to accept payment in exchange for the transfer of some smaller portion of the company that includes the targeted employees, then the analysis work becomes much more specific.

An example of a partial purchase to obtain employees is when a target company decides to eliminate one of its lines of business and sells the related customer list and assets to the acquiring company. As part of the transaction, the target company lays off its employees that were associated with the line of business that is being transferred to the new company. The acquiring company obtains a list of these employees from the selling company and contacts them to offer them jobs. Because of the nature of this transaction, there is essentially nothing more than a transfer of assets, which greatly reduces the amount of analysis required of the CFO. Only the following analyses should be conducted that are specifically targeted at the employees to be hired, with an emphasis on their quality, cost, and turnover:

- *Investigate employee names listed on patents.* If individual employees are named on patents or patent applications filed by the target company, then it is a good bet that those employees may be in a revenue-sharing agreement with the company employing them. If so, the CFO must research further to determine the amounts paid to the employees for use of the patents, such as a fee per unit sold or an annual payment. These patent payments must be added to the employee salaries to determine the true cost of bringing in the new personnel.

- *Interview customers and suppliers about employees.* If there are problems with the desired employees, the target company is almost certainly not going to reveal this information, since it is trying to obtain payment for "selling" them to the acquiring company. Accordingly, it may be necessary to call the target company's suppliers or customers to see if they have had dealings with the people under consideration and what their opinions may be.

- *Compare employee pay levels to industry and internal averages.* Obtain the pay rates for the entire department to be acquired, and determine the distribution of pay through the group to see if there are any inordinately highly paid people. Then compare these rates not only to the industry average, but also to the acquiring company's average, to determine the difference between the pay levels about to be brought in and the existing rates. If there is a major difference between the two pay rates, then an additional cost of the acquisition may be to bring the pay levels of the in-house staff up to match those of the incoming personnel in order to avoid turmoil caused by the pay differential.

- *Determine the current turnover rate in the targeted department.* If there is a high turnover rate in the department being acquired, then the cost of acquisition may not be worthwhile if there is a high risk of losing the entire group.

- *Review long-term compensation agreements.* If a target company has obtained the services of a number of exceptional employees, it is quite possible that it has done so by offering them expensive, long-term employment contracts. The CFO should review them not only for the projected payment amounts, increases, and net present value, but also for golden parachute clauses that pay these employees exorbitant amounts if the target company is purchased.

The upshot of what a CFO is looking for when reviewing the acquisition of personnel is the actual cost of those employees and the potential impact on their counterparts. The first item is purely financial in nature, while the second is a matter for conjecture regarding the impact of a group of higher-paid employees on the existing, in-house group that is paid less. The CFO can only provide the information regarding pay disparities to the CEO and human resources director and let them determine what to do to boost the morale of the existing staff when they learn about the higher wages being paid to the newly arriving personnel. An example of the analysis report that the CFO should issue for an acquisition based on personnel is shown in Exhibit 21.1.

Note that the cost of acquisition has been converted at the bottom of the example into a cost per employee, which is then compared to the average market rate. The premium to be paid over the market rate gives management its best idea of the true cost of the staff it is acquiring, and whether or not it is a good idea to proceed with the acquisition.

If a company wants to acquire a patent from another company, it does not usually go to the extreme of buying the whole company. Instead, it negotiates for the patent itself, which makes the analysis work substantially easier for the CFO. There are few measures to investigate, with an emphasis on the existing costs and revenues currently experienced by the holder of the patent. Management may require additional analysis to include the estimated additional revenues and costs that will subsequently be incurred by its use of the patent, which may vary from the use to which it has been put by the current patent owner. The primary analyses are:

Description	Additional Information	Summary Costs
Total cost of incoming staff (15 staff)		$1,237,500
Average cost of incoming staff	$82,500	
Average cost of in-house staff	73,000	
Prior year employee turnover level	10%	
Additional cost to match in-house salaries to incoming salaries (13 staff)		123,500
Net present value of projected patent payments to employees		420,000
Cost of employment contract buyouts		250,000
Total cost of employee acquisition		**$2,031,000**
Total cost per employee acquired (15 staff)		**$135,400**
Industry average pay rate per person		$80,000
Percentage premium over market rate		**69%**

EXHIBIT 21.1   ANALYSIS REPORT FOR ACQUISITION OF PERSONNEL

- *Determine annual patent renewal costs.* Annual patent costs are quite minimal, but should be included in any patent analysis, such as the one noted in Exhibit 21.2, in order to present a comprehensive set of cost information.

- *Determine current patent-related revenue stream.* This information is needed to determine the amount of money that the company is willing to pay for a patent; however, if the company wants to shift the focus of the patent to a different application, then this number has less use. Without cooperation from the target company, this can be a very difficult number to determine, since the only alternative is to contact those companies that are licensed to use the patent and see if they will reveal the per-unit payment they are required to make to the target company for use of their patent. If the target company is willing to reveal this information, then also obtain it for the last few years to see if there is an upward or downward trend line for the revenues; if the trend is downward, then the revenue stream for which the company is paying is worth less.

- *Ascertain extent of current litigation to support patent.* A major issue for any patent holder is the amount of money it must spend to keep other entities from encroaching on the patent with parallel patents or just by issuing products that illegally use technology based on the patent. These legal costs can be enormous. If a company wants to take over a patent, it must be aware of the extent of encroachment and the cost of legally pursuing the encroachers.

An example of the analysis report that the CFO should issue for a patent purchase is shown in Exhibit 21.2. The bottom line of the patent acquisition analysis report is the net present value of all cash flows, which the CEO and CFO can use as the highest recommended amount to pay for the patent. However, given alternative uses for the patent that they may be contemplating, they may anticipate a higher cash inflow that will allow them to pay a higher price for the patent.

The analyses needed to review a brand name are relatively simple from the financial perspective, though somewhat more involved from the legal side, since one must conduct research to ensure that there is a clear title to the trademark, as well as ascertain the extent

Description	Additional Information	Summary Revenues and Costs
Years left prior to patent expiration	10 years	
Net present value of cash inflows		$1,200,000
Discounted cost of remaining filing costs		− 42,000
Discounted cost of expected annual legal fees		− 375,000
Net present value of patent		**$783,000**

Exhibit 21.2   Analysis Report for Patent Acquisition

of possible infringements on the brand name and the extent and recent history of litigation needed to support the brand. The primary analyses are:

- *Determine the amount of annual trademark fees.* This is a very minor item, but can grow to considerable proportions if the trademark is being maintained world-wide, which requires filings and maintenance fees in a multitude of jurisdictions.

- *Determine clear title to the brand name.* This is not just a matter of paying for a small amount of research by a legal firm to determine the existence of any countervailing trademarks, but also requires a search in multiple jurisdictions if the buying company wants to expand the brand to other countries.

- *Ascertain the amount and trend of any current cash inflows from the brand name.* The two best analysis options are either to measure just that portion of sales that is specifically due to licensing agreements (and therefore easily traceable) or to measure the incremental difference in cash flows from all products under the brand name in comparison to those of the industry average or specific competitors.

- *Note the amount and trend of any legal fees needed to stop encroachment.* A quality brand frequently attracts a number of companies that build inexpensive knockoffs and illegally sell them for vastly reduced prices. Given the reduced quality and prices, the net impact of these fake goods is to cheapen the brand's image. Consequently, constant legal pursuit of these companies is the only way to keep imitating products off the market. The CFO should roughly estimate the cost of current lawsuits by either reviewing all current lawsuits that are public record or asking the target company. If the acquiring company wants to maintain the brand image, it must be willing to continue to use legal alternatives so the current legal cost can be used as a reasonable benchmark of future costs as well.

- *Note any challenges to use of the brand name.* Yet another legal issue is that there may be lawsuits pending that claim the trademark of another person or corporation supersedes the one about to be purchased. If so, a search of all open lawsuits should reveal this information. Once again, if the company contemplates worldwide usage of the brand name, then a much more extensive search for competing trademarks in other locations is necessary. If there are cases where someone else has filed for the right to use the brand name in another country, then the CFO should calculate the estimated cost of acquiring the rights to that name.

In Exhibit 21.3, we itemize the financial analysis associated with a brand-name acquisition that a CFO should expect to issue to management.

Description	Additional Information	Summary Revenues and Costs
Net present value of current cash inflows		$500,000
Discounted cost of annual trademark fees		− 65,000
Cost of trademark search (for clear title)		− 175,000
Discounted cost of annual legal fees		− 780,000
Cost to purchase competing brand names	See note	− 2,250,000
Total net cost of brand name		**$ − 2,770,000**

Note: A competing trademark has already been filed by company XYZ in all countries of the European community and Japan. The cost required to purchase this trademark is included in the analysis.

EXHIBIT 21.3   ANALYSIS REPORT FOR BRAND ACQUISITION

When a company purchases a specific manufacturing facility from another company, it is usually doing so to increase its capacity. With this end in mind, the key analyses revolve around the condition and cost of the facility so that one can determine the amount of replacement machinery to install as well as the actual production capacity percentage, the cost per percent of capacity, and the facility's overhead cost. For many of the analyses, the information the CFO assembles must be for three activity levels—minimum, normal, and maximum capacity levels. The reason for the threefold format (as also shown in Exhibit 21.4) is that management may not use the facility as much as it anticipates, in which case it must be aware of the minimum costs that will still be incurred, as well as the extra costs that must be covered if the facility runs at the highest possible rate of production. The primary analyses are:

- *Determine the facility overhead cost required for minimum, standard, and maximum capacity.* Any facility requires a minimum cost to maintain, even if it is not running. Such costs include taxes, security, insurance, and building maintenance. Management must know this minimum cost level in case it does not use the facility, but must still pay for the upkeep. Also, current accounting records will reveal the overhead needed to run the facility at a normal level, while the industrial

	Costs at Minimum Capacity Usage	Costs at Normal Capacity Usage	Costs at Maximum Capacity Usage
Facility overhead cost	$1,000,000	$3,500,000	$5,000,000
Capital replacement cost*	0	0	400,000
Equipment maintenance cost	0	450,000	600,000
Cost of environmental damage insurance	50,000	50,000	50,000
Cost to investigate possible environmental damage	100,000	100,000	100,000
Facility modification costs	0	0	700,000
Total costs	**$1,150,000**	**$4,100,000**	**$6,850,000**
Percent capacity level	0%	50%	85%
Cost per percent of capacity	**N/A**	**$82,000**	**$81,000**

*Represents the depreciation on capital replacement items.

EXHIBIT 21.4   ANALYSIS REPORT FOR CAPACITY ACQUISITION

engineering or production personnel can estimate the additional costs needed to run the plant at full capacity.

- *Ascertain the amount of capital replacements needed.*   Some machinery will be so worn out or outdated that it must be replaced. This information is beyond the knowledge of a CFO, but not of an industrial engineer or production manager, who can walk through the facility and determine the condition of the equipment. If this is not readily apparent, then perusing the maintenance records will reveal which machines require so much continuing work that a complete replacement is a more efficient alternative.

- *Find out the periodic maintenance cost of existing equipment.*   Even if equipment does not require replacement, it must still be maintained, which can be a considerable cost. This information should be obtained for the normal run rate and estimated for the maximum capacity level.

- *Determine the maximum production capacity.*   The industrial engineering staff must estimate the maximum capacity level at which the facility can run, subject to expenditures for equipment replacements and facility modifications.

- *Investigate any environmental liabilities.*   Sometimes the target company is more than willing to get rid of a facility if it suspects there is environmental damage that must be fixed. This can be an extraordinarily expensive item, and can sometimes exceed the cost of the entire facility. To guard against this problem, a CFO should determine the cost of conducting an environment investigation, as well as the cost of insurance to provide coverage in case such damage is discovered after the purchase date.

- *Determine the cost of modifications needed to increase the capacity of the facility.*   Unless a facility has been very carefully laid out in the beginning for the highest possible maximization of throughput, it is likely that it can use a significant overhaul of its layout. To do this, the industrial engineering staff must review the current situation and recommend the shifting of equipment and installation of additional materials movement capabilities.

The preceding analyses are summarized in the sample capacity analysis report shown in Exhibit 21.4, which includes low-medium-high categories for costs that are based on projected capacity utilization levels. At the bottom of the example, all costs are converted into a dollar amount for each percent of capacity used. Note that there is no utilization listed for the minimum level, since the facility is shuttered under this assumption.

A company will sometimes acquire just the assets of another organization. This is most common when there is some risk associated with the liabilities of the target company, such as lawsuits or environmental problems, or an excessive amount of debt. When assets are purchased, the buyer can be quite selective in buying only those assets that are of the most value, such as patents, brands, or personnel, which have been covered in previous sections. At this point, we note only the following additional analyses needed to ensure that all other assets are properly reviewed prior to an acquisition:

- *Conduct a fixed asset audit.*   Before paying for an asset, make sure that the asset is there. The fixed asset records of some companies are in such poor condition that assets still on the books may have been disposed of years before. An appraiser or an internal audit team can conduct this review.

- *Appraise the value of fixed assets.*   Even if an asset exists, it may have far less value than the amount listed in the fixed asset database. To be sure of the current value of all assets, have an appraiser review them and determine their value. The final appraisal report should contain two values for each asset—the rush liquidation value and a higher value based on a more careful liquidation approach. These two values can be the focus of a great deal of negotiating between the buyer and the target company, since the buyer will want to pay based on the rush liquidation value, and the target company will prefer to sell at the price indicated by the slower liquidation approach.

- *Ascertain the existence of liens against assets.* A company should not purchase an asset if there is a lien against it. This usually occurs when the target company has used the asset as collateral for loans or used leases to finance the purchase of specific assets. The standard procedure in an acquisition is to have lenders remove liens prior to the completion of an acquisition, which frequently requires paying off those lenders with a new "bridge" loan that covers the period of a few weeks or days between the removal of liens and the transfer of payment from the buyer to the target company, which is then used to pay off the bridge loan.

- *Determine the collectibility of accounts receivable.* If the purchase includes all current accounts receivable, then trace the largest invoices back to specific shipments, and confirm them with the customers to whom the invoices were sent. Also, be sure to trace the history of bad debt write-offs to determine an appropriate average amount that will reflect the amount of the current accounts receivable that will become bad debt.

- *Verify the bank reconciliation for all bank accounts.* For any checking or investment account, verify the amount of cash at the bank and reconcile it to the amount listed in the corporate accounting records. Also, investigate any reconciling items to ensure that they are appropriate.

- *Audit the existence and valuation of remaining assets.* There are usually a number of smaller-dollar assets on the books, such as the payoff value of life insurance, deposits on rentals and leases, and loans to employees or officers. All of these items must be audited, both through investigation of the original contracts on which they are based and through confirmations from those entities who owe the target company money.

- *Determine the value of any tax loss carryforward.* If the buyer is acquiring a tax loss carryforward from the target company, it can use this to reduce its own tax burden. The CFO should use either the corporate tax staff or outside auditors to review not only the validity of the target company's tax returns to ensure that the reported loss on which the carryforward is based is valid, but also the (ever changing) tax laws to ensure that the company is qualified to use the loss carryforward (which, under current laws, can only be recognized over a very long time period).

A sample of an analysis report for assets is noted in Exhibit 21.5.

In Exhibit 21.5, only the appraised rapid liquidation value of the assets to be purchased is listed in the "Valuation Summary" column, whereas two other forms of asset valuation are noted in the "Additional Information" column. The reason for this treatment of asset values is that the CFO is presenting to management the lowest possible asset value, which it will use to determine its lowest offering price for the purchase of the target company's assets. The other higher asset values are included as notations, in case management wants to bid a higher dollar amount and needs to determine its upper boundaries for a reasonable

	Additional Information	Valuation Summary
Appraised value of assets (rapid liquidation)		$16,000,000
Appraised value of assets (slow liquidation)	$18,500,000	
Book value of assets	19,000,000	
Book value of assets with outstanding liens	19,000,000	
Book value of accounts receivable		5,500,000
Recommended bad debt reserve		− 150,000
Value of cash and investments		750,000
Net present value of remaining assets	Discount rate is 13%	629,500
Net present value of tax loss carryforwards	Discount rate is 13%	2,575,000
Total asset valuation		**$25,304,500**

EXHIBIT 21.5   ANALYSIS REPORT FOR ASSETS

offer price. In addition, the value of remaining assets and the tax loss carryforward are both listed at their net present values. The reason for using discounting for these two items is that they may not be readily liquidated in the short term. For example, other assets may include loans to employees or officers that will take several years to collect, while only a portion of a tax loss carryforward can usually be used in each year. Accordingly, the discount rate for the net present value calculation for each of these line items is noted in the "Additional Information" column in the example. Also, the bad debt deduction from the accounts receivable is not the one used by the target company, but rather the one compiled by the CFO's staff, following its review of the history of bad debt write-offs and the risk of bad debt occurrences for the current group of accounts receivable.

If a company decides to purchase a target company as a complete entity, rather than buying pieces of it, then the liabilities side of the balance sheet will also be part of the purchase, and will require analysis by the CFO. The main liability analyses are:

- *Reconcile unpaid debt to lender balances.*   There may be a difference between the amount recorded on the company's books as being the debt liability and the lender's version of the amount still payable. If there is some doubt regarding whose version is correct, one should always use the amount noted by the lender, since this entity will not release its lien on company assets until it believes itself to be fully paid.

- *Look for unrecorded debt.*   A target company may have incorrectly reported a capital lease as an operating lease, or is recording some other form of debt payment as an expense without recording the underlying debt liability. One can review the target company's stream of payments to see if there are any continuing payments—most likely in the same amount from period to period—that indicate the presence of a debt paydown.

- *Audit accounts payable.*   One should also verify that all accounts payable listed on the target company's books are actual expenses and not duplications of earlier payments. Also, one should investigate the unvouchered accounts payable to see if these are all approved and binding expenses, and if there are additional receipts for which there are no existing accounts payable listed in the accounting records.

- *Audit accrued liabilities.*   A target company that wants to obtain the highest possible selling price will downplay these expenses, so one must be careful to verify the existence of all possible accrued expenses and then recalculate how the accruals

Description	Additional Information	Summary Revenues and Costs
Book balance of debt		$3,750,000
Add: Additional lender balance due	See Note 1	15,000
Add: Unrecorded capital leases	See Note 2	175,000
Book balance of accounts payable		2,200,000
Add: Unrecorded accounts payable	See Note 3	28,000
Subtract: Duplicate accounts payable	See Note 4	− 2,000
Book balance of accrued liabilities		450,000
Add: Additional accrual for property taxes	See Note 5	80,000
Add: Accrual for workers' compensation insurance	See Note 6	15,000
Total liabilities valuation		$6,711,000

Note 1: Company recorded $15,000 in late interest payments as a debt reduction.
Note 2: Capital leases for six forklifts recorded as expenses.
Note 3: No supplier invoice recorded for maintenance supplies received on last day of the month.
Note 4: Supplier invoices for in-house construction work recorded under both vouchered and unvouchered accounts payable.
Note 5: Original accrual did not reflect an increase of 2.3% in the tax rate.
Note 6: Original accrual based on a payroll level that is 15% lower than the actual payroll amount.

Exhibit 21.6 Analysis Report for Liabilities

were derived to ensure that the underlying expenses that these accruals will eventually offset are accurate. The following accruals are among the more common ones:

— Income taxes

— Payroll taxes

— Personal property taxes

— Warranty costs

— Product recalls

All of the above analyses are summarized into the sample analysis report for liabilities, which is described in Exhibit 21.6. Of particular interest are the line items for reconciliation problems, such as extra debt and accounts payable, as well as corrections to the accrued expenses. All of these adjustments are used to negotiate a lower price for the target company, since the higher liabilities reduce its net value.

There are several methods a CFO should use when reviewing the profitability of a target company. One is to track the trends in several key variables, since these will indicate worsening profit situations. Also, it is important to segment costs and profits by customer, so that one can see if certain customers soak up an inordinate proportion of the expenses. Further, it may be possible to determine the headcount associated with each major transaction, so that one can determine the possibility of reducing expenses by imposing transaction-related efficiencies that have worked for the acquiring company. The intent of these analyses is to quickly determine the current state and trend of a target company's profits, as well as to pinpoint those customers and costs that are associated with the majority of profits and losses. The main analyses are:

- *Review a trend line of revenues.* If there has been a decline in the rate of growth or an overall decline in revenues, then review the company's percentage of the total market to see if the cause might be a shrinkage in the overall market. If not, then review sales by product and customer to determine the exact cause of the problem.

- *Review a trend line of bad debt expense.* As a market matures and additional sales are harder to come by, a company's management may loosen its credit terms, allowing it to increase sales at the cost of a higher level of bad debt, which may exceed the additional gross margin earned from the incremental sales that were added. To see if a target company has resorted to this approach to increasing sales, review the trend line of bad debt expense to see if there has been a significant increase. Also, review the current accounts receivable for old invoices that have not yet been written off as bad debt, and also see if there are sales credits that are actually bad debts. The sum of these items constitutes the true bad debt expense.

- *Review a trend line of sales discounts.* As a follow-up to the last item, management may offer discounts to customers in advance for additional sales, or add customers who are in the habit of taking discounts, whether approved or not. These issues are most common when a company's sales are no longer trending upward and management is looking for a new approach to spur sales, even at the cost of reduced margins due to the discounts. These discounts may be stored in a separate account for sales discounts, or mixed in with sales credits of other kinds.

- *Review a trend line of material costs.* For most organizations outside of the service sector, this is the largest cost, and so requires a reasonable degree of attention. The CFO cannot hope to delve into all possible aspects of material costs during a due diligence review, such as variances for scrap, purchase prices, or cycle counting adjustments. However, it is easy to run a trend line of material costs for the last few years, just to see if these costs are changing as a proportion of sales. Due to the large overall cost of materials, a small increase in costs here can relate to the entire cost of a department in other areas of the company, so a change of as little as 1% in this expense category is a cause for concern.

- *Review a trend line of direct labor costs.* One should review the trend line of direct labor costs in much the same manner as for material costs. Though this is usually a much smaller cost than for materials, it is still sufficiently large to be a cause for concern if there is a significant trend line of increasing expenses.

- *Review a trend line of gross margins.* This measure is worthy of comparison to industry averages or to the gross margins of specific competitors so the acquiring company can gain some idea of the production efficiencies of the company it is attempting to purchase.

- *Review a trend line of net margins.* If the gross margin looks reasonable, then proceed to a trend-line analysis of net margins. If there is a declining trend here that was not apparent in the preceding gross margin analysis, then one can focus on the sales, general, and administrative expense areas to see where the cost increase has occurred.

- *Ascertain the gross profit by product.* Review the gross profit for each product at the direct cost level to determine which ones have excessively low profit levels and are targets for either withdrawal from the market or a price increase. If possible, also determine the cost of fixed assets that are associated with each product (i.e., product-specific production equipment), so that the buyer can budget for an asset reduction alongside any product terminations.

- *Review a trend line of overhead personnel per major customer.* One can determine the overhead needed to support a profitable base of customers with a ratio of overhead personnel to the number of major customers. This review can extend much more deeply to determine which customers require inordinate amounts of time by the support staff, though this information is rarely available.

- *Review a trend line of overhead personnel per transaction.* Determine the number of personnel involved in all major transactions, such as accounts payable, accounts receivable, receiving, and purchasing, and divide this number into the annual total of all these transactions. If there appears to be an excessive number of employees per transaction, then the acquirer may be able to reduce personnel costs in these areas.

As part of a due diligence analysis, these measures and trend lines will tell a CFO where to focus the bulk of the analysis team's attention in determining the extent of problem areas and their impact on profitability. In the example analysis report shown in Exhibit 21.7, a qualitative review of each analysis area is noted, since this review is intended to find further problems, not to devise a valuation for the target company.

The analysis of a target company's cash flows is a critical item if the entire organization is to be purchased. If a CFO were to miss this item, the buying company could find itself

Type of Analysis Conducted	Notes
Review a trend line of revenues	Percentage rate of growth has declined in last two years.
Review a trend line of bad debt expense	Bad debt expense has increased, due to relaxation of credit standards.
Review a trend line of sales discounts	80% of the newest customers have all been given sales discounts of 10 to 15%.
Review a trend line of material costs	No significant change.
Review a trend line of direct labor costs	No significant change.
Review a trend line of gross margins	The gross margin has dropped 13% in the last two years, entirely due to increased bad debts and sales discounts.
Review a trend line of net margins	Slightly worse reduction than indicated by the gross margin trend-line analysis.
Ascertain the gross profit by product	All products experienced a reduction in gross profit in the last two years.
Ascertain the gross profit by customer	Sales to older customers have retained their gross margin levels, but newer customers have substantially lower margins.
Review a trend line of overhead personnel per major customer	There has been a slight increase in the collections staffing level in the last two years, due to the difficulty of collecting from newer customers.
Review a trend line of overhead personnel per transaction	No significant change.

Conclusion and recommendations: The target company has experienced flattening sales, and so has shifted new sales efforts to low-end customers who cannot pay on time and will accept only lower-priced products, which also increases the overhead needed to service these accounts. Recommend dropping all low-margin, low-credit customers, as well as all associated overhead costs to increase profits.

EXHIBIT 21.7 ANALYSIS REPORT FOR PROFITABILITY

paying for an organization that must be supported with a massive additional infusion of cash. The key cash flow analyses to focus on are:

- *Review trend line of net cash flow before debt and interest payments.* Begin with the cash flows shown on the statement of cash flows. Then ignore the impact of debt and interest payments, since inordinately high cash flows to pay for these two items may mask a perfectly good underlying business. If there is a pronounced additional requirement for more cash to fund either the acquisition of fixed assets or working capital, then identify the culprit and proceed with the following cash-flow analyses. This first trend line, then, was to determine the existence of a problem and to more precisely define it.

- *Review trend line of working capital.* Poor customer credit review policies or inadequate collection efforts will lead to an increased investment in accounts receivable, while excessive production or product obsolescence will increase the inventory investment. Also, a reduction in the days of credit before payments are made to suppliers will reduce the free credit that a company receives from them. To see if there is a problem in this area, add the total accounts receivable to inventory and subtract the accounts payable balance to arrive at the total working capital amount. Then plot this information on a trend line that extends back for at least a year. If there is a steady increase in total working capital, determine which of the three components have caused the problem.

- *Segment working capital investment by customer and product.* One should focus on the accounts receivable and finished goods inventory investments to see if there is a specific customer who is responsible for a working capital increase or review just the inventory investment to see if a specific product is the cause. This information should be cross-referenced against analyses for profitability by customer and product to see if there are any combinations of low-profit, high-investment customers or products that are obvious targets for termination.

- *Review trend line of capital purchases.* This is a simple matter to investigate by general fixed asset category, since this information is reported on the balance sheet. However, there may be good reasons for large increases in fixed asset investments, such as automation, the addition of new facilities, or a general level of competitiveness in the industry that requires constant capital improvements. Only by being certain of the underlying reasons for cash usage in this area can one suggest that cash can be saved here by reducing the volume of asset purchases. The report that a CFO issues as part of the cash-flow analysis is primarily composed of judgments regarding the need for historical cash flows, estimates of future cash flows, and how the acquiring company can alter these flows through specific management actions. A sample of such a report is shown in Exhibit 21.8.

Besides purely financial issues, there are a wide array of legal issues that one's legal staff must peruse. In most cases, the analysis issues noted here are related to various kinds of contracts. When these arise, a key analysis point is to see if they can be dissolved in the event of a corporate change of control. Many contracts contain this feature, so that onerous agreements will not cause a potentially high-priced purchase to fall apart. Key legal reviews are:

- *Bylaws.* This document will include any "poison pill" provisions that are intended to make a change of control very expensive.

Type of Analysis Conducted	Notes
Review trend line of net cash flow before debt and interest payments	The target company is experiencing a massive cash outflow in both the working capital and fixed assets areas.
Review trend line of working capital	There is a severe cash outflow, due to $2,000,000 in accounts receivable invested in the Gidget Company, as well as a large investment in five distribution warehouses for its Auto-Klean product, each of which requires $1,500,000 in inventory.
Segment working capital investment by customer and product	The main cash outflows are due to the Gidget Company customer and the Auto-Klean product.
Review trend line of capital purchases	Has purchased $10,000,000 of automation equipment to improve margins on its sales to the Gidget Company.

Conclusions and recommendations: There is a major investment in sales to the Gidget Company, which is not justified by the 5% return on sales to that customer. The receivable investment of $2,000,000 can be eliminated by stopping sales to this customer, while $5,000,000 can be realized from the sale of automation equipment used for the production of items for sale to it. Also, the number of distribution warehouses for the Auto-Klean product can be reduced by two, which will decrease the inventory investment by $3,000,000. The amount of cash investment that can be eliminated as a result of these actions is $10,000,000.

Exhibit 21.8   Analysis Report for Cash Flow

- *Certificate of incorporation, including name changes.* This is used to find the list of all names under which the target company operates, which is needed for real estate title searches.

- *Employment contracts.* Key employees may be guaranteed high pay levels for a number of years, or a "golden parachute" clause that guarantees them a large payment if the company is sold.

- *Engineering reports.* These documents will note any structural weaknesses in corporate buildings that may require expensive repairs.

- *Environmental exposure.* Review all literature received from the Environmental Protection Agency, as well as the Occupational Safety and Health Administration, and conduct environmental hazard testing around all company premises to ascertain the extent of potential environmental litigation.

- *Insurance policies.* Verify that the existing insurance policies cover all significant risks that are not otherwise covered by internal safety policies. Also, compare these policies to those held by the buyer to see if there can be savings by consolidating the policies for both companies.

- *Labor union agreements.* If the target company is a union shop, the union contract may contain unfavorable provisions related to work rules, guaranteed pay increases, payouts or guaranteed retraining funds in the event of a plant closure, or onerous benefit payments.

- *Leases.* Creating a schedule of all current leases tells a buyer the extent of commitments to pay for leased assets, as well as interest rates and any fees for early lease terminations.

- *Licenses.* A license for a target company to do business, usually granted by a local government, but also by another company for whom it is the distributor or franchisee, may not be transferable if there is a change of ownership. This can be quite a surprise to a buyer that now finds it cannot use the company it has just bought.

- *Litigation.* This is a broad area that requires a considerable amount of review before legal counsel can be reasonably satisfied as to the extent and potential liability associated with current and potential litigation. This review should encompass an investigation of all civil suits and criminal actions that may include contract disputes, fraud, discrimination, breach of employment contract, wrongful termination, inadequate disclosure issues, deceptive trade practices, antitrust suits, or other issues. It should also include tax claims and notices of potential litigation received from any of the following government agencies:

  — Department of Justice

  — Department of Labor

  — Equal Employment Opportunity Commission

  — Federal Trade Commission

  — Internal Revenue Service

  — Securities and Exchange Commission (applies only to a publicly held entity)

- *Marketing materials.* The target company's advertising of its product capabilities can be a source of potential litigation if the publicized product claims are overstated.

- *Pension plans.* Determine the size of the employer-funded portion of the pension plan. This will require the services of an actuary to verify the current cost of required future funding.

- *Product warranty agreements.* Review the published warranty that is issued alongside each product to verify its term as well as what specific features it will replace in the event of product failure.

- *Sponsorship agreements.* A target company may have a long-term commitment to sponsor an event that will require a significant expenditure to maintain or terminate.

- *Supplier or customer contracts.* A target company may be locked into a long-term agreement with one or more of its suppliers or customers, possibly guaranteeing unfavorable terms that will noticeably impact profits if the buyer purchases the company.

Though the above nonfinancial issues are primarily related to the legal liabilities of a corporate entity, there are a few cases where the CFO may be called on to provide an estimate of possible attendant costs. For example, one can quantify the extra cost required to fulfill any poison pill provisions. One can also determine the net present value of all employment, labor union, and lease provisions that require a specified minimum set of payments for a designated time period. An example of the format used to summarize these expenses is shown in Exhibit 21.9.

Description	Additional Information	Summary of Costs
Poison pill payout provision	Bylaws section 2, clause 14	$12,500,000
Golden parachute provision	For all officers	3,250,000
Discounted cost of all lease provisions	Copiers, forklifts	320,000
Discounted pension plan funding requirements		4,750,000
Discounted cost of sponsorship agreement		220,000
Termination payment for long-term supplier contracts		540,000
Total cost of contractual and legal issues		**$21,580,000**

Exhibit 21.9 Analysis Report for Contractual and Legal Issues

COMPLEXITY ANALYSIS

The primary objective of complexity analysis is to determine if it will be too difficult to integrate an acquiree, with a secondary objective of determining the level of risk posed by the acquiree's general level of complexity.

One area to consider is the sources of the acquiree's revenue. The level of complexity and risk is increased when revenue is derived from multiple businesses, since the acquirer must devote additional levels of management resources to each of those businesses. Complexity and risk also increase when a significant percentage of revenue is derived from a small number of large transactions that are custom-tailored to individual customers. These transactions tend to be highly volatile in their amount and frequency, making it difficult to estimate future revenue levels and attendant cash flows.

The tax rate can also contribute to complexity and risk. This is especially true if the acquiree has located its headquarters in a tax haven, since this indicates a strong interest in tax avoidance that has likely led to the use of a variety of complicated tax avoidance schemes. A further indicator of tax complexity is a substantial difference between the reported level of book and tax income. Finally, a volatile effective tax rate indicates that the acquiree is engaged in a variety of one-time tax dodges. While all of these issues may be caused by completely legal transactions, it clearly indicates that the company has altered its operations in a variety of ways to take maximum advantage of the tax laws, and this will require considerable ongoing effort to maintain.

Another indicator of complexity is the presence of off-balance-sheet assets and liabilities, such as variable-interest entities, research and development partnerships, and operating leases. While the intent of these transactions may have little to do with dressing up the balance sheet and may be based on solid operational reasons, they are still more likely to cause sudden changes in the reported condition of the company if underlying accounting rules are altered to require their full presentation.

Finally, a key area that many acquiring companies completely neglect is the consideration of cultural differences. Though difficult issues to quantitatively analyze, they can be the primary issue that results in a failed merger, and so are worth considerable review time. Some of the key factors to consider are:

- What is the company's intent in forcing the acquired company to use its business practices?

- What are the key differences in the decision-making processes of the companies?

- What are the differences in the performance monitoring and bonus payment systems of the companies?
- How do the companies resolve conflicts?
- What types of formal and informal communication systems are used by the companies?
- What is the command structure of the companies?

If there are significant differences between the companies in more than one of the above areas, then the success of the merger will be at risk. If so, the management team should consider in detail what changes will be needed in order to make the two company cultures work together, or scrap the merger entirely.

EVALUATE ACQUISITION TARGETS WITH ALLIANCES

Acquiring any company can be a significant risk, no matter how detailed the level of due diligence used. The problem is the difficulty of determining how the acquiree's employees handle themselves with customers, how they develop products, their level of ethics, and many other intangible issues that are critical to the success of an acquisition, but which are nearly impossible to measure. In addition, a company may pay for an acquisition based on the acquiree's technology, only to find that the market shifts in a different direction, rendering its investment worthless.

The solution in some cases is to first enter into a business alliance with a potential acquiree. By entering into a number of alliances, a company can essentially keep tabs on several potential acquisitions while a new market develops, and then make offers to selected alliance partners depending on the direction in which the market eventually turns. This is less of an advantage in industries where there is little technological innovation, in which case the acquirer can skip the alliance approach and proceed directly to an acquisition.

In addition, if a company makes a substantial investment in the potential acquiree as part of the alliance agreement, then it may obtain a Board seat. By doing so, it has full access to the acquiree's financial information, and will have ready access to any financial or operational issues to which the acquiree is being subjected.

The most important point in favor of the alliance approach is that the two companies have a chance over an extended period of time to examine any potential pitfalls that would interfere with an eventual acquisition, including issues with employees and a variety of communications-related topics. This approach also allows the acquiree's employees to get to know their counterparts in the acquiring firm, which may reduce the amount of employee turnover that sometimes accompanies an acquisition.

The downside of the alliance approach is that a potential acquiree may gain some prestige through the alliance, which can raise the price of the eventual acquisition. Also, taking the additional time to work through an alliance arrangement gives the potential acquiree time to be purchased by a competitor or at least set up a bidding war, though this danger can be eliminated by including a right of first refusal in the alliance agreement.

VALUING THE ACQUIREE

A company's valuation is a highly subjective calculation. All of the following issues must be considered when determining worth:

- *Type of business.* The market assigns a different value to different types of companies. For example, service businesses that survive based on the hourly billings of their employees tend to be valued at one times their annual revenues or less, while product-driven companies are frequently valued at four times revenues or more. A good recent example is computer system security companies, whose valuations were briefly driven up to 17 times revenues following the September 11 attacks.

- *Market timing.* A company's value is strongly impacted by the timing of market conditions. During the recent business bubble, valuations were several times higher for all types of businesses than is currently the case. Market timing can vary by the sector in which a company is located; for example, telecommunication companies have minimal valuations now, while companies in other industries have comparatively higher valuations.

- *Cash flow.* One of the most important foundations of valuation is cash flow, since an acquirer can use this information to estimate the time period that will be required to earn back the price of the acquisition. This is generally considered to be a much better indicator of valuation than profits, which can incorrectly reflect a business's true financial condition.

- *Revenue.* Revenue is certainly a major driver of valuation, since it gives a rough estimate of a business's scale of operations. However, a careful acquirer will also review a company's cost structure to see if the business has essentially "bought" sales by lowballing its products or services or if the corresponding cost structure appears bloated.

- *Product versus service revenue.* Product-based companies typically command much higher valuations than service-based companies, even if they have the same revenue levels. This valuation variation, which may be as high as five to one, is based on the higher margins, branding opportunities, and competitive positioning that can be achieved with products, while, conversely, a services company can suffer a drastic decline in revenues if key service personnel leave its employment. Also, an acquirer usually has a much easier time integrating product sales into its operations than the large staffs required for a services business, since corporate cultures may clash.

- *Technology.* A company that has achieved unusually high efficiencies in its sales or operational capabilities through the use of technology will usually command a higher valuation multiple. This does not necessarily mean that the most cutting-edge technology has been implemented, but rather that key technological innovations have been woven into the operational fabric of the entity, resulting in clearly identifiable cost reductions or improved processes.

- *Sales capability.* A company will earn a higher valuation if it has an exceptional ability to land sales. This may involve excellent knowledge of government contracting requirements, the development of key contacts within major accounts, joint sales relationships with other entities, the employment of well-known experts as salespeople, or the use of highly efficient sales support structures.

- *Difficulty of duplication.* If an acquirer perceives that the barriers to entering a company's field of operations are high, or if the cost of duplicating the company's operations is excessive, the acquirer may be more inclined to pay a premium for the business. For example, a proprietary database may take so long to duplicate that an acquirer will value the acquiree just based on the cost it would otherwise incur to create the database from scratch.

- *Risk of expiring contracts.*   A company whose revenues are tied to short-term sales, without immediate prospects for renewing the backlog, will be perceived to have a lower valuation than an entity possessing a strong backlog and clear evidence of long-term sales agreements with its customers.

- *Fixed expense obligations.*   A company's valuation can be seriously impacted by the presence of long-term payment obligations. The most common example of this issue is a lease of property or equipment, though one can also find long-term employment contracts that guarantee payments. A suitor wants maximum flexibility to improve a company's cost structure, which will be hampered by these obligations.

- *Capital expenditures.*   If a company is in a capital-intensive business, or if the existing asset base is old and will require replacement in the short term, an acquirer will be forced to make these expenditures, and so will subtract the anticipated expenditure from the valuation.

- *Business plan.*   If a company's planning processes are first-rate, and appear to be steering it into profitable market segments, this can increase the corporate valuation. Alternatively, a business that is improperly positioned in the marketplace may have trouble obtaining any valuation.

- *Level of competition.*   A company's valuation will suffer if there is a great deal of competition in the industry. This is particularly true if the level of competition is adversely impacting price points or causing the company to lose business.

- *Management.*   A company's cost structure, perception in the marketplace, and customer relations are driven in large part by the quality of its management team. If this group is perceived to be first-class, it can increase the corporate valuation, since these people typically have exceptional skill in growing businesses and in anticipating and overcoming operational problems.

- *Client base.*   A significant factor in determining valuation is the size, type, and distribution of clients. For example, a company with a single client will be perceived to be at great risk of losing all of its sales if the client is dissatisfied. Alternatively, a broad mix of clients, particularly those large enough to support multiple sales, will reduce the perceived risk of sales loss.

- *Inherent risk.*   A company whose financial performance can be dramatically impacted by adverse situations will have a comparatively lower valuation. For example, farm businesses can be severely impacted by drought conditions.

- *Lawsuits.*   Nothing will drive a suitor away faster than an unresolved lawsuit, especially one with a demand for a large settlement. Even if there is no lawsuit, the prospect of one, as evidenced by lawsuits targeted at others in the same industry, can have a negative impact on valuation.

- *Patents.*   If a company has established key patents or processes that give it a clear competitive advantage, this can increase its valuation level.

- *Branding.*   If a company has invested a great deal of time and effort in creating brands for its products or services, this can give it a significant boost in valuation.

- *Key metrics.*   Some metrics are good indicators of excellent operational performance, showing that a company is probably such a sparing user of assets and expenses that it is worthy of some increase in its valuation. Measures that can be used for this purpose are profits per full-time-equivalent employee, cash-flow return on sales, sales to fixed assets ratio, days of receivables, and days of inventory.

No matter which of the above valuation techniques are used, the present value of any debt and other payables at the time of the acquisition must be deducted from the valuation, since the acquirer would otherwise be obligated to pay off these liabilities.

Though all of the preceding issues are useful for fine-tuning a business valuation, the following quantitative methods are used to create a general high-low price range within which to negotiate with the buyer:

- *Revenue multiple.* As long as some profits are reported, buyers will frequently focus on a comparison of prices paid to revenues for other recent acquisitions in the same industry. This tends to result in a higher valuation. It is an easy way to generate a general price range, though close attention to a selection of the previous qualitative measures is needed to determine if the acquiree is a good fit with the buyer. As an example, if a company with $7 million in revenues is purchased at a revenue multiple of 2, then the purchase price is $14 million.

- *Resale value of assets.* A set of appraisers (usually one paid by the buyer and one by the seller) can review the acquiree's assets to determine the amount of money that the buyer would obtain by selling all assets. Since this approach does not take into account any intangible assets, such as the value of brands, patents, trademarks, special knowledge, and so on, it results in a low valuation of the acquiree's business. The buyer and seller can then argue over the value of these intangibles to arrive at some higher price for the business.

- *Underlying real estate values.* Some acquisitions are entirely contingent on the value of the property owned by the acquiree, and not on the other valuation methodologies covered in this section. For example, in the retailing industry, where some chains own the property on which their stores are situated, the value of the real estate is greater than the cash flow generated by the stores themselves. In cases where the business is financially troubled, it is entirely possible that the purchase price is based entirely on the underlying real estate, with the operations of the business itself being valued at essentially zero. The buyer then uses the value of the real estate as the primary reason for completing the deal. In some situations, the prospective buyer has no real estate experience, and so is more likely to heavily discount the potential value of any real estate when making an offer. If the seller wishes to increase its price, it could consider selling the real estate prior to the sale transaction. By doing so, it converts a *potential* real estate sale price (which might otherwise be discounted by the buyer) into an achieved sale, and may also record a one-time gain on its books based on the asset sale, which may have a positive impact on its sale price. An acquiree's real estate may even be the means for an acquirer to finance the deal. For example, if the acquiree owns property, it may be possible to enter into a sale-and-leaseback transaction which generates enough cash to pay for the acquisition. Another possibility is to look for property leases held by the acquiree that are below current market rates, and sublease them for a profit. Finally, it may be possible to consolidate acquiree locations and sell any remaining properties that are no longer needed.

- *Present value of cash flows.* The most practical approach to valuing a business from the perspective of the buyer is to determine the amount of cash that the target company spins off, adjust it for any likely changes resulting from an acquisition, and then calculate the net present value of the cash flows for several years. This tells the buyer how much cash the acquisition will likely spin off in the near term, which it can use to pay off the purchase price. However, this approach has several flaws. First, the selling company puts itself up for sale at the point when it feels its reported level of cash flows are maximized, such as when sales are peaking. If the buyer assumes that these sales levels will continue for the purposes of the present value calculation, it will seriously overvalue the price of the buyer. Second, the seller is likely to overestimate the number and amount of nonrecurring expenses that can be stripped away from current earnings in order to arrive at a higher level of cash flow. Once again, reliance on these figures can result in an excessive purchase price. Third, the discount rate used to derive the present value of cash flows will be debated by the seller, who wants to use a low discount rate that results in the highest possible valuation. The buyer will want to use a higher discount rate that reflects the risk of reduced returns in future years, and which will also result in a lower price. The usual result is the establishment of a low and a high discount rate, which are used to calculate a bracketed range of possible prices within which the buyer and seller negotiate the final price. Finally, the seller will want to capitalize cash flows from many years into the future in order to pile up the largest possible valuation; the buyer should resist this and limit the period of analysis to five years and certainly no longer than ten, on the grounds that financial results too far in the future are extremely uncertain. An example of how to adjust an acquiree's reported cash flows to arrive at long-term probable cash flows is shown in Exhibit 21.10.
- *Stock valuation.* An increasingly common ploy for companies wanting to be acquired is to file for an initial public offering while also being courted by an acquiring company. By doing so, the acquirer is forced to make an offer near the market valuation at which the acquiree expects to go public. If the prospective acquirer does not bid that high, then the acquiree still has the option of going public. However, given the liabilities of the Sarbanes-Oxley Act and the stock lockup periods required for many new public companies, an acquiree's management is usually more than willing to accept a buyout offer if the price is reasonably close to the acquiree's expected market value.

To continue with the example in Exhibit 21.10, we will assume that the buying entity estimates an ongoing improvement in cash flows after the first year of 20% annually.

Adjustment Description	Adjustment Amount	Reasoning
Reported cash flow	$250,000	
Excess owner salary	+ 150,000	Local manager will replace owner
Owner car payments	+ 45,000	
Interest expense	+ 72,000	Buyer will pay off debt
Capital purchases	− 120,000	Ongoing replacement of assets
Net cash flow	**$397,000**	

EXHIBIT 21.10   ADJUSTING REPORTED CASH FLOWS

Year	Annual Cash Flows	Present Value of 1 Due in N Periods at 12%	Present Value of Cash Flows
1	$397,000	0.8929	$354,481
2	$476,400	0.7972	$379,786
3	$571,700	0.7118	$406,936
4	$686,000	0.6355	$435,953
5	$823,200	0.5674	$467,084
			$2,044,240

Exhibit 21.11   Present Value of Cash Flows Calculation

Also, the buyer and seller have settled on a discount rate of 12%. Using this information, we arrive at the total present value of cash flows of $2,044,240 shown in Exhibit 21.11.

There are times when the buyer and seller of a business have entirely different concepts of the valuation to be used for the acquisition, usually because the buyer is basing its valuation on the acquiree's historical performance, while the seller is using a much higher forward-looking view of the acquiree's prospective performance. The earnout is frequently used to bridge the valuation perception gap between the two parties. Under an earnout, the acquiree's owners will be paid an additional amount by the acquirer if it can achieve specific performance targets (usually the same ones it has already claimed it will achieve during the acquisition negotiations).

The earnout is also a useful tool for the acquirer, because the acquiree's management team has a strong incentive to grow the business for the next few years. In addition, the acquirer can shift a portion of its purchase price into a future liability that can likely be paid from cash earned in the future by the acquiree. It is also useful for the selling party, since it defers income taxes on the payment.

However, many earnouts also result in lawsuits, because the acquiring company merges the acquired company into another business unit, charges corporate overhead to it, or shifts key staff elsewhere in the company—all factors making it extremely difficult for the acquiree's management team to still earn the additional payment, or even to determine what the performance of the acquiree has become. Even if there are no lawsuits, the acquiree's management team may be so focused on achieving their earnout that they do not assist the rest of the company with other matters, so that corporate-level goals are not reached. Also, if the earnout award is based strictly on the achievement of revenue rather than profit, then the acquiree's management team may pursue unprofitable sales in order to meet their earnout goals.

The problems with earnouts can be mitigated by continuing to track the acquiree's performance separately in the financial statements, carefully defining the earnout calculation in the original acquisition document, requiring earnouts to be based solely on net income achieved, and by adding an additional layer of compensation that is based on working more closely with the rest of the company, such as commissions for cross-selling. Also, to keep the acquiree happy, do not institute a "cliff" goal, where no bonus is paid unless the entire target is reached. Instead, use a sliding scale, so that some bonus is paid even if only a portion of the target is achieved.

The determination of the purchase price of an acquiree is more art than science. The methods described in this chapter are the ones most easily supported by calculations, but buyers have been known to pay far more than the prices that would be suggested by these methods. The grounds for doing so usually involve the perception that the acquiree represents a good strategic fit with the acquirer that may result in major increases in profitability. Acquirers must be especially careful with their due diligence efforts when prices are driven very high by this perception of a strategic fit, so that there is very little question that the acquirer can achieve startling profit jumps as a result of the purchase. Otherwise, the buyer is headed for a major write-off of its purchase price. To avoid excessively high bid prices, it is useful to set a maximum price cap prior to the start of negotiations. Another approach is to not allow the buyer's chief negotiator to price an acquisition because this person may become excessively involved in the deal, resulting in overpayment.

DETERMINING THE VALUE OF SYNERGIES

A key part of the pricing calculation used to create a bid price for an acquiree is the value the buyer assigns to any synergies expected from the acquisition. The buyer can locate synergies in any of the following areas:

- *Cost reduction.* The most common synergy is cost reduction through the elimination of various types of duplication, such as overhead staff, facilities, insurance, and so on. Cost reductions can also be achieved through the use of centralized purchasing to buy in larger quantities for the combined companies. These savings can be especially large if the two companies have the same customers or operate in the same geographic region, so that duplicative staff or facilities are obvious and can be quickly eliminated. When calculating synergies through cost reduction, be sure to include the time period over which these reductions are to be achieved, since some costs may take a considerable amount of time to eliminate.

- *Best practices cross-pollination.* Either the buyer or acquiree may have used best practices to develop extremely efficient processes in a number of areas, such as new product development, customer support, or manufacturing. An acquisition allows these best practices to be cross-pollinated between the two companies. In practice, both companies may have areas of particular expertise, so both companies can benefit from each other's specialized knowledge.

- *Treasury enhancements.* A buyer can achieve an immediate savings by replacing the high-cost debt of an acquiree with its own lower-cost debt, though this approach is usually only available to highly regarding buyers who have a strong balance sheet. It is also possible to reduce hedging costs by combining the regular business transactions of both companies to achieve natural hedges that have no cost.

- *Tax reductions.* Careful tax planning can result in an average tax rate that is below the rate paid by the buyer. This can be achieved by shifting centralized administrative functions to low-tax areas, selective transfer pricing strategies, and shifting debt to subsidiaries located in high-tax areas.

- *Revenue expansion.* It may be possible to increase sales as the result of an acquisition because the combined sales force can sell each other's products, and because the company may now have enough mass to make its products more acceptable to prospective buyers. Revenue expansion is especially likely if the buyer has a distribution system in place where the acquiree's products are not currently sold (or vice versa), so there is a reasonable expectation that the newly acquired products can be sold in greater volume fairly quickly. However, estimating revenue increases is notoriously difficult, so it is best to exclude all but the most minimal revenue expansion estimates from any synergy models.

Clearly, there are a number of areas in which synergies can occur. However, it is extremely difficult to accurately estimate the dollar amount of likely synergies due to the time pressures associated with an acquisition and the degree to which confidentiality rules limit the amount of detailed acquiree information to which the acquisition team has access. Thus, it is best to rely more upon conservative estimates of potential synergies, thereby avoiding the risk of paying too much based on overly optimistic synergy estimates that cannot be realized.

FORM OF PAYMENT FOR THE ACQUISITION

It is extremely common for a buying company to offer a variety of types of noncash consideration when extending an offer to purchase another company. They do this in order to preserve cash, which is not always easy to replenish, especially if the buyer is a privately held entity that does not have access to the public capital markets. If the buyer offers a high-value bid that contains a large proportion of stock, it may be surprised to find that the potential acquiree rejects the bid, and perhaps accepts a lower bid from a competing buyer whose offer contains a different mix of consideration, as well as different terms. Some issues to consider regarding the type of payment to be offered to a prospective acquiree are:

- Attempt to obtain information regarding the terms offered by competing bidders, and revise your bid to include a higher proportion of cash. This may result in acceptance by the acquiree, even if the total bid is less than competing bids.
- If the offer must contain a high proportion of stock, then consider including a price protection clause in the offer, so the acquiree's shareholders will be given additional shares if the buyer's stock price declines within a specified time period following the acquisition.
- Structure an offer that gives the acquiree the best possible tax advantages.
- Consider accepting weaker representation and warranty terms in exchange for a smaller amount of consideration.

TERMS OF THE ACQUISITION AGREEMENT

An acquisition agreement is a lengthy document requiring expert legal assistance. This book cannot begin to address all aspects of the acquisition agreement, but will address two areas in which the acquiring company can mitigate its risks.

First, the acquisition agreement should contain indemnification rights. This is the buyer's right to obtain payment from the acquiree if the buyer finds that the acquiree's finances and operations are not as described to the buyer by the acquiree. Indemnification rights usually include a buyer deductible of between one-half and one percent of the entire transaction value, which means that the buyer must absorb the amount of the deductible before claiming any excess amount—the deductible is designed to avoid frivolous claims by the buyer. When negotiating the acquisition agreement, it is possible to modify indemnification rights so that the buyer can claim payment of the deductible amount if a claim exceeds the amount of the deductible. Another point of negotiation is the duration of the indemnification rights, which should last from one to two years. Furthermore, the deductible can be eliminated for certain types of risks, or increased for yet other risks. Also, the maximum possible amount of indemnification is subject to considerable negotiation.

Second, it is useful to obtain clearly defined representations and warranties regarding specific risk areas. Acquirees are reluctant to grant wide-ranging "blanket" representations and warranties, but are more likely to accede to more tightly defined areas. This approach allows the buyer to concentrate representations and warranties primarily on those areas in which it feels the greatest levels of risk are concentrated.

In both of these areas, sharp negotiation can be expected, so the buyer should clearly prioritize which contract clauses must be obtained, and which can be bartered away.

WHEN TO USE AN INVESTMENT BANKER

An investment banking house provides services in the areas of locating both acquirees and acquirers, formulating complex deals, valuing deals, and providing an outside opinion on prospective deals. These are valuable services, but can come at a considerable cost. To avoid investment banking fees, some CFOs bring all or portions of the investment banking services in-house.

The investment banking function most commonly performed internally is the search for acquisitions, on the grounds that a company that is even remotely active in its chosen industry should be aware of its competitors and be able to scout them without outside help. This is not always the case if an investment banker can provide a key contact at a prospective acquiree.

For less complex deals, especially using purchase or sale terms that a CFO has used before in previous deals, there is no overriding need for an investment banker. However, even in this situation, it is useful to occasionally have an investment banker review a prospective deal, just to see if changes in the tax laws or new, innovative acquisition structures have recently arisen that could apply to the company's situation. Conversely, an overly complex acquisition deal is the ideal place to use an investment banker, since this is where they have the greatest expertise.

Finally, the Board of Directors may insist on using investment bankers for larger deals because they want outside verification of the deal valuation, and also to protect themselves from shareholder lawsuits. This is less of a concern in a closely held company with few shareholders.

ACCOUNTING FOR THE ACQUISITION

Having completed discussions of the due diligence process and valuing an acquiree, the discussion turns to the accounting methods to be used to record an acquisition on a company's books. Though most accounting issues are pushed down to the company controller or a general ledger specialist, the CFO will want to review this area of accounting, since a mistake here can have a major impact on overall corporate results. The remaining sections of the chapter deal with the purchase method of accounting for an acquisition, as well as the cost, equity, and consolidation methods, which are used to describe purchases of varying proportions of another entity. We also address how to account for intercompany transactions between the acquirer and acquiree after the purchase is completed, plus contingent payments, push-down accounting, leveraged buyouts, and spin-off transactions.

PURCHASE METHOD*

In brief, this approach to accounting for a business combination assumes that the acquiring company spreads the acquisition price over the assets being bought at their fair market value, with any remaining portion of the acquisition price being recorded in a goodwill account. The company being purchased can be bought with any form of consideration, such as stock, cash, or property.

There are three primary steps involved in accounting for a purchase transaction. The first is to determine the purchase price, the second is to allocate this price among the various assets of the company being purchased, and the third is to account for the first-year partial results of the purchased entity on the buyer's financial statements. The issue with the first step is that the purchase price is based on the fair market value of the consideration given to the seller. For example, if the purchase is made with stock, the stock must be valued at its fair market value. If treasury stock is used as part of the consideration, then this must also be valued at its fair market value. If the buyer's stock is thinly traded or closely held, then it may be necessary to obtain the services of an investment banker or appraiser, who can use various valuation models and industry surveys to derive a price per share.

The second step in the purchase method is to allocate the purchase price among the acquired company's assets and liabilities, which are then recorded in the buyer's accounting records. The method of valuation varies by line item on the acquired company's balance sheet. Key valuation rules are:

- *Accounts receivable.*   Record this asset at its present value, less the allowance for bad debts. Given the exceedingly short time frame over which this asset is outstanding, there is generally no need to discount this valuation, unless there are receivables with very long collection terms. Also, since the acquisition transaction is generally not completed until several months after the acquisition date (given the effort required to make the accounting entry), the amount of the allowance for bad debts can be very precisely determined as of the acquisition date.

- *Marketable securities.*   These assets should be recorded at their fair market value. This is an opportunity for the buyer to mark up a security to its fair market value (if such is the case), since generally accepted accounting principles (GAAP) normally only allows for the recognition of reductions in market value. For this reason, this is an area in which there is some opportunity to allocate an additional portion of the purchase price beyond the original cost of the asset. However, since most companies only invest in short-term, highly liquid securities, it is unlikely that there will be a large amount of potential appreciation in the securities.

- *Inventory—raw materials.*   These assets should be recorded at their replacement cost. This can be a problem if the acquiree is in an industry, such as computer hardware, where inventory costs drop at a rapid pace as new products come into the marketplace. Consequently, the buyer may find itself with a significantly lower

---

* Compiled with permission from Chapter 6 of *Financial Analysis: A Controller's Guide* by Bragg (John Wiley & Sons, 2000).

inventory valuation as a result of the purchase transaction than originally appeared on the accounting records of the acquiree.

- *Inventory—finished goods.*   These assets should be recorded at their selling prices, less their average profit margin and disposition costs. This can be a difficult calculation to make if the finished goods have variable prices depending on where or in what quantities they are sold; in such cases, the determination of selling price should be based on a history of the most common sales transactions. For example, if 80% of all units sold are in purchase quantities that result in a per-unit price of $1.50, then this is the most appropriate price to use. This rule can be avoided, however, if the acquiree has firm sales contracts as of the date of the acquisition with specific customers that can be used to clearly determine the prices at which the finished goods will actually be sold.

   If the acquirer had been using a last-in, first-out (LIFO) inventory valuation system, then the newly derived valuation for the finished goods inventory shall be used as the LIFO base layer for all inventory obtained through the purchase transaction.

- *Inventory—work-in-process.*   These assets receive the same valuation treatment as finished goods, except that the cost of conversion into finished goods must also be subtracted from their eventual sale price.

- *Property, plant, and equipment (PP&E).*   These assets should be recorded at their replacement cost. This can be a difficult task that lengthens the interval before the acquisition journal entry is completed, because some assets may be so old that there is no equivalent product currently on the market, or equipment may be so specialized that it is difficult to find a reasonable alternative on the market. This valuation step frequently calls for the services of an appraiser.

- *Property, plant, and equipment to be sold.*   If the buyer intends to sell off assets as of the acquisition date, then these assets should be recorded at their fair market value. This most accurately reflects their disposal value as of the acquisition date.

- *Capital leases.*   If the acquiree possesses assets that were purchased with capital leases, then the CFO should value the asset at its fair market value, while valuing the associated lease at its net present value.

- *Research and development (R&D) assets.*   If any assets associated with specific R&D projects are part of the acquiree, the CFO should charge these assets off to expense if there is no expectation that they will have an alternative future use once the current R&D project has been completed. The precise allocation of assets to expense or asset accounts can be difficult, since the existing projects may be expected to last well into the future, or the future use of the assets may not be easy to determine. Consequently, one should carefully document the reasons for the treatment of R&D assets.

- *Intangible assets.*   These assets are to be recorded at their appraised values. If the buyer cannot reasonably assign a cost to them or identify them, then no cost should be assigned.

- *Accounts and notes payable.*   Accounts payable can typically be recorded at their current amounts as listed on the books of the acquiree. However, if the accounts payable are not to be paid for some time, then they should be recorded at their discounted present values. The same logic applies to notes payable; since all but the shortest-lived notes will have a significantly different present value, they should be discounted and recorded as such. This treatment is used on the assumption that the buyer would otherwise be purchasing these liabilities on the date of the acquisition, not on a variety of dates stretching out into the future, and so must be discounted to show their value on the acquisition date.

- *Accruals.* These liabilities are typically very short-term ones that will be reversed shortly after the current accounting period. Accordingly, they are to be valued at their present value; discounting is rarely necessary.

- *Pension liability.* If there is an unfunded pension liability, even if not recognized on the books of the acquiree, it must be recognized by the buyer as part of the purchase transaction.

- *Stock option plan.* If the buyer decides to take over an existing stock option plan of the acquiree's, then it must allocate part of the purchase price to the incremental difference between the price at which shares may be purchased under the plan and the market price for the stock as of the date of the acquisition. However, if the buyer forced the acquiree to settle all claims under the option plan prior to the acquisition, then this becomes a compensation expense that is recorded on the books of the acquiree.

If the acquiring company (Charleston Corporation) buys the acquiree's (Denton Corporation's) stock with $500,000 of cash, the entry on Charleston's books would be:

	Debit	Credit
Investment in Denton Corporation	$500,000	
Cash		$500,000

Alternatively, if Charleston were to make the purchase using a mix of 20% cash and 80% for a note, the entry would be:

	Debit	Credit
Investment in Denton Corporation	$500,000	
Cash		$100,000
Note payable		400,000

Another approach would be to exchange 5,000 shares of Charleston's $1 par value stock for that of Denton as a form of payment. Under this method, the entry would be:

	Debit	Credit
Investment in Denton Corporation	$500,000	
Common stock—par value		$5,000
Common stock—additional paid-in capital		495,000

The result of all the preceding valuation rules is shown in Exhibit 21.12, where we show the calculation that would be required to adjust the books of an acquiree in order to then consolidate it with the results of the acquiring company. The exhibit shows the initial book cost of each account on the acquiree's balance sheet, followed by a listing of the required valuation of each account under the purchase method, the adjustment

Account	Acquiree Records	Purchase Method Valuation	Required Adjustment	Adjusted Acquiree Records
Assets				
Cash	$1,413	$1,413	$0	$1,413
Receivables	4,000	4,000	0	4,000
Receivables, long-term	1,072	(NPV) 808	(CR) 264	808
Marketable securities	503	(FMV) 490	(CR) 13	490
Inventory— raw materials	921	(RC) 918	(CR) 3	918
Inventory— WIP	395	(SLM) 429	(DB) 34	429
Inventory— finished goods	871	(SLM) 950	(DB) 79	950
Property, plant, & equipment	6,005	(RC) 7,495	(DB) 1,490	7,495
Equipment for sale	803	(FMV) 745	(CR) 58	745
Capital lease assets	462	(FMV) 500	(DB) 38	500
Goodwill	0	0	(DB)4,677	4,677
Investment in acquiree	0	0	(CR)14,600	− 15,000
Intangibles	593	(AV) 650	(DB) 57	650
Total assets	$17,038	$18,398	(CR)$8,563	$8,075
Liabilities				
Accounts payable	$3,992	$3,992	$0	$3,992
Notes payable, long-term	3,300	(NPV) 2,950	(DB) 350	2,950
Accrued liabilities	325	325	0	325
Capital lease liabilities	450	(NPV) 400	(DB) 50	400
Pension liability	408	408	0	408
Total liabilities	$8,475	$8,075	(DB) $400	$8,075
Shareholders' Equity				
Common stock	$4,586	—	(DB)4,586	$0
Paid-in capital	100	—	(DB) 100	0
Retained earnings	3,877	—	(DB)3,877	0
Total equity	$8,563	—	(DB)$8,563	$0
Total liabilities & equity	$17,038	—	(DB)$8,963	$8,075

EXHIBIT 21.12   ADJUSTMENTS TO THE ACQUIREE'S BOOKS FOR A PURCHASE CONSOLIDATION

required, and the new account valuation. The new account valuation on the right side of the table can then be combined directly into the records of the acquiring company. Under the "Purchase Method Valuation" column, a designation of "NPV" means that the net present value of the line item is shown, a designation of "FMV" means that the fair market value is shown (less any costs required to sell the item, if applicable), "RC" designates the use of replacement cost, "SLM" designates the use of sale price less the gross margin, and "AV" designates an asset's appraised value.

In the exhibit, debits and credits are specified for each adjusting entry listed in the "Required Adjustment" column. The amount of goodwill shown in the "Required Adjustment" column is derived by subtracting the purchase price of $15,000 from the total of all fair market and other valuations shown in the "Purchase Method Valuation" column. In this case, we have a fair market valuation of $18,398 for all assets, less a fair market valuation of $8,075 for all liabilities, which yields a net fair market value for the acquiree of $10,323. When this fair market value is subtracted from the purchase price of $15,000, we end up with a residual of $4,677, which is listed in the goodwill account. Note that the "Adjusted Acquiree Records" column on the right side of the exhibit still must be added to the acquirer's records to arrive at a consolidated financial statement for the combined entities.

The third step in the acquisition process is to account for the first year partial results of the acquired company on its books. Only the income of the acquiree that falls within its current fiscal year, but after the date of the acquisition, should be added to the buyer's accounting records. In addition, the buyer must charge all costs associated with the acquisition to current expense—they *cannot* be capitalized. These acquisition costs should be almost entirely for outside services, since any internal costs charged to the acquisition would likely have been incurred anyway, even in the absence of the acquisition. The only variation from this rule is the costs associated with issuing equity to pay for the acquisition; these costs can be recorded as an offset to the additional paid-in capital account. An additional item is that a liability should be recognized at the time of the acquisition for any plant closings or losses on the dispositions of assets that are planned as of that date; this is not an expense that is recognized at a later date, since we assume that the buyer was aware at the purchase date that some asset dispositions would be required.

If the acquirer chooses to report its financial results for multiple years prior to the acquisition, it does *not* report the combined results of the two entities for years prior to the acquisition.

A *reverse acquisition* is one where the company issuing its shares or other payment is actually the acquiree, because the acquiring company's shareholders do not own a majority of the stock after the acquisition is completed. Though rare, this approach is sometimes used when a shell company with available funding buys an operating company, or when a publicly held shell company is used to buy a nonpublic company, thereby avoiding the need to go through an initial public offering (IPO) by the nonpublic company. In this case, the assets and liabilities of the shell corporation are revalued to their fair market value and then recorded on the books of the company being bought.

COST METHOD

The cost method is used to account for the purchase of another company's stock when the buyer obtains less than 20% of the other company's shares and does not have management control over it. The buyer does not have control if it cannot obtain financial results from the other company that it needs to create entries under the equity method (see next section), or if it fails to obtain representation on the Board of Directors, or is forced to relinquish significant shareholder rights, or the concentration of voting power is clearly in evidence among a different group of shareholders.

Under this method, the investing company records the initial investment at cost on its books. It then recognizes as income any dividends distributed by the investee after the investment date.

EQUITY METHOD

The equity method of accounting for an investment in another company is used when the investor owns more than 20% of the investee's stock, or less than 20% but with evidence of some degree of management control over the investee, such as control over some portion of the investee's Board of Directors, involvement in its management activities, or the exchange of management personnel between companies. The method is only used when the investee is a corporation, partnership, or joint venture, and when both organizations remain separate legal entities.

Under the equity method, the acquirer records its initial investment in the investee at cost. For example, if the initial investment in Company ABC were $1,000,000 in exchange for ownership of 40% of its common stock, then the entry on the books of the investor would be:

	Debit	Credit
Investment in Company ABC	$1,000,000	
Cash		$1,000,000

After the initial entry, the investor records its proportional share of the investee's income against current income. For example, if the investee has a gain of $120,000, the investor can recognize its 40% share of this income, which is $48,000. The entry would be:

	Debit	Credit
Investment in Company ABC	$48,000	
Investment income		$48,000

The credit in the last journal entry can more precisely be made to an Undistributed Investment Income account, since the funds from the investee's income have not actually been distributed to the investor.

The investor should also record a deferred income tax expense based on any income attributed to the investee. To continue with the preceding example, if the incremental tax rate for the investor is 38%, then it would record the following entry that is based on its $48,000 of Company ABC's income:

	Debit	Credit
Income tax expense	$18,240	
Deferred taxes		$18,240

If the investee issues dividends, then these are recorded as an offset to the investment account and a debit to cash. Dividends are not recorded as income, since income was already accounted for as a portion of the investee's income, even though it may not have been received. For example, if dividends of $25,000 are received from Company ABC, the entry would be:

	Debit	Credit
Cash	$25,000	
Investment in Company ABC		$25,000

If the market price of the investor's shares in the investee drops below its investment cost, these are not normally any grounds for reducing the amount of the investment. However, if the loss in market value appears to be permanent, then a loss can be recognized and charged against current earnings. Evidence of a permanent loss in market value would be a long-term drop in market value that is substantially below the investment cost, or repeated and substantial reported losses by the investee, with no prospects for an improvement in reported earnings. For example, if the market price of the stock in Company ABC necessitated a downward adjustment in the investor's valuation, the entry would be:

	Debit	Credit
Loss on investments	$50,000	
Investment in Company ABC		$50,000

If, after making a downward adjustment in its investment, the investor finds that the market price has subsequently increased, it cannot return the carrying amount of the investment to its original level. The new basis for the investment is the amount to which it has been written down. This will increase the size of any gain that is eventually recognized on the sale of the investment.

If the investee experiences an extraordinary gain or loss, the investor should record its proportional share of this amount as well. However, it is recorded separately from the usual investment accounts. For example, if Company ABC were to experience an extraordinary loss of $15,000, the entry would be:

	Debit	Credit
Undistributed extraordinary loss	$15,000	
Investment in Company ABC		$15,000

If the investee experiences such large losses that the investor's investment is reduced to zero, the investor should stop recording any transactions related to the investment in order to avoid recording a negative investment. If the investee eventually records a sufficient amount of income to offset the intervening losses, then the investor can resume use of the equity method in reporting its investment.

If the investor loses control over the investee, then it should switch to the cost method of reporting its investment. When it does this, its cost basis should be the amount in the investment account as of the date of change. However, the same rule does not apply if the investor switches from the cost method to the equity method—in this case, the investor must restate its investment account to reflect the equity method of accounting from the date on which it made its initial investment in the investee.

When reporting the results of its investment in another company under the equity method, the investor should list the investment in a single Investment in Subsidiary line item on its balance sheet and in an Investment Income line item on its income statement.

CONSOLIDATION METHOD

When a company buys more than 50% of the voting stock of another company, but allows it to remain as a separate legal entity, then the financial results of both companies should be combined in a consolidated set of financial statements. However, if the companies are involved in entirely different lines of business, it may still be appropriate to use the equity method; otherwise, the combined results of the two enterprises could lead to misleading financial results. For example, if a software company with 90% gross margins combines with a steel rolling facility whose gross margins are in the 25% range (both being typical margins for their industries) the blended gross margin presents a misleading view of the gross margins of both entities.

Another case in which a 50%+ level of ownership might not result in the use of a consolidation is when the investing company only expects to have temporary control over the acquiree (perhaps because it is reselling the acquiree) or if the buyer does not have control over the acquiree (perhaps because control is exercised through a small amount of restricted voting stock). In either case, the equity method should be used.

When constructing consolidated financial statements, the preacquisition results of the acquiree should be excluded from the financial statements. If there is a year of divestiture, the financial results of the acquiree in that year should only be consolidated up until the date of divestiture.

INTERCOMPANY TRANSACTIONS

When the acquirer elects to report consolidated financial information, it must first eliminate all intercompany transactions. By doing so, it eliminates any transactions that represent the transfer of assets and liabilities between what are now essentially different parts of the same company. The transactions that should be eliminated are:

- *Intercompany sales, accounts receivable and payable.* The most common intercompany transaction is the accounts receivable or payable associated with the transfer of goods between divisions of the parent company. From the perspective of someone outside the consolidated company, these accounting transactions have not really occurred, since the associated goods or services are merely being moved around within the company and are not caused by a business transaction with an outside entity. Accordingly, for consolidation purposes, all intercompany accounts receivable, accounts payable, and sales are eliminated.

- *Intercompany bad debts.* A bad debt from another division of the same company cannot be recognized, since the associated sale and accounts receivable transaction must also be eliminated as part of the consolidation process. In short, if the sale never occurred, then there cannot be a bad debt associated with it.

- *Intercompany dividend payments.* This is merely a transfer of cash between different divisions of the corporate parent, and so should be invisible on the consolidated statement.

- *Intercompany loans and any associated discounts, premiums, and interest payments.* Though there are good reasons for using intercompany loans, such as the provision of funds to risky subsidiaries that might not be able to obtain funds by other means, this is still just a transfer of money within the company, as was the case for intercompany dividend payments. Thus, it must be removed from the consolidated financial statements.

- *Intercompany rent payments.* This is a form of intercompany payable, and so is not allowed.

- *Fixed asset sale transactions.* When fixed assets are sold from one subsidiary to another, the selling company will eliminate the associated accumulated depreciation from its books as well as recognize a gain or loss on the transaction. These entries must be reversed, since the fixed asset has not left the consolidated organization.

- *Intercompany profits.* A common issue for vertically integrated companies is that multiple subsidiaries recognize profits on component parts that are shipped to other subsidiaries for further work. On a consolidated basis, all of these intercompany profits must be eliminated, since the only profit gained from the consolidated perspective is when the completed product is finally sold by the last subsidiary in the production process to an outside entity.

- *Intercompany investments.* The corporate parent's investment in any subsidiaries is removed from the consolidation. For example, if a corporate parent created a subsidiary and invested a certain amount of equity in it, this investment would appear on the books of both the parent (as an investment) and the subsidiary (as equity). In a consolidation, both entries are removed.

All intercompany eliminations are recorded on a separate consolidation worksheet. They are not recorded on the books of any of the subsidiaries or the parent company. In essence, these transactions are invisible to all but the CFO, who is responsible for the consolidation reporting.

CONTINGENT PAYMENTS

A contingent payment is one that is made subsequent to the conclusion of a merger or acquisition, where the buying party may be obligated to make additional payments to the selling party, based on future events. For example, if the sold company produces profits that meet a certain benchmark, then the buyer must pay the seller an additional amount.

These types of transactions cause problems for the CFO, because they cannot be firmly determined as of the date on which the merger or acquisition occurs. Accordingly, one should only record the firm price associated with the transaction at the time of purchase. The CFO can recognize the payments associated with any contingencies as soon as they appear to be highly likely. When this entry is made, the CFO should use the current risk-free interest rate to discount the expected contingent payment down to its net present value and record this reduced amount as the payment amount.

Since there may be a potentially large contingent payment hanging over the buying company, it is important to mention its existence in the footnotes attached to the buying company's financial statements so that readers will at least be aware of the potential need to make additional payments.

The buying company may guarantee to the selling company a minimum price for the stock that it gives to the seller as part of the initial sale transaction. If the price does drop below this point, the buyer will hand over additional shares of stock to make up the difference. In this case, the contingent payment can be easily calculated by the CFO simply by comparing the stock's market price to the minimum required price. Accordingly, this difference can be incrementally accrued in each accounting period up until the date on which the additional payment of stock must be made, rather than waiting until the payment date to record any additional liability. Also, if the payment is made in stock, then the CFO should record its full value as a liability, rather than its discounted value.

The offsetting account to which contingent payments should be charged is the goodwill account. However, if there is reasonable evidence that the contingent payment will only be made if specific employees are required to continue working for the company, then it can be reasonably construed to actually be a compensation expense; if so, a compensation expense should be recognized in the current period for the full amount of the contingent payment, instead of recording an increase in the goodwill account.

PUSH-DOWN ACCOUNTING

Push-down accounting is the inclusion of acquisition accounting adjustments in the books of the acquired company. These may be recorded separately in a worksheet that is used to create financial statements or directly in the accounting records of the acquiree. The use of worksheet adjustments, rather than direct changes to the acquiree's accounting records, is preferable when the historical records are needed either for tax reporting purposes or to determine the amount of a minority interest share in the acquiree.

When push-down accounting is used, the acquiree can alter the valuation of all of its assets and liabilities to reflect those made by its corporate parent as part of the purchase method of accounting used to account for the consolidation. This will also result in a change in depreciation expense to reflect any changed fixed asset valuations (and possible changes in the expected useful lives of some assets).

There are several objections to push-down accounting. One is that it eliminates the use of the historical basis of accounting for transactions, which is one of the foundations of accounting theory. Another problem is that, in cases where an acquirer gradually buys an acquiree through a series of stock purchases, the use of push-down accounting would result in a series of revaluations that would create multiple changes in the financial statements of the acquiree. Given that the American Institute of Certified Public Accountants (AICPA) has not given an authoritative guidance on this issue, *privately* held companies may use it or not, as they so choose.

Push-down accounting is strongly favored by the Securities and Exchange Commission (SEC) for *publicly* held companies that have concluded acquisitions under the purchase method of accounting that result in wholly owned subsidiaries. The SEC requires that the subsidiary also include in its financial statements the cost of any debt used by the acquirer to purchase it if the acquiree guarantees the debt, the acquiree plans a debt or equity offering to retire the existing debt, or if there are plans for the subsidiary to assume the debt.

If there are minority interests in the acquiree or if there is outstanding public debt or preferred stock issued by the subsidiary, then the SEC does not insist on the use of push-down accounting.

LEVERAGED BUYOUTS

A leveraged buyout occurs when funding, which is largely based on debt that is secured by the assets of the acquiree, is used to buy the acquiree. In such cases, it is useful to form a holding company, which buys the stock of the acquiree and becomes its corporate parent. A holding company is particularly useful if the acquiree is publicly held, since it can become the repository for any shares tendered by shareholders of the acquiree in the event of a tender offer.

The acquiree's management team is frequently part of the leveraged buyout, either because it has initiated the buyout itself, or because the investors buying the acquiree realize the importance of keeping the management team in place and offer it either shares or stock options as an incentive to stay. If the management team already owns stock in the acquiree, it can avoid taxes by exchanging this stock for the stock of the holding company that is conducting the buyout.

Of particular concern to whoever is initiating a leveraged buyout is the type of accounting basis that it will be allowed to use when recording the transaction. If there is a change in voting control (which is governed by exceedingly complex rules), then the buyout must be recorded under the purchase method of accounting (see earlier section); this approach results in the recording of all acquiree assets and liabilities at their fair market values, with any remaining unallocated purchase price being recorded as goodwill. If there is a lesser degree of change in the amount of voting control (common enough when the management team is simply increasing its level of ownership), the buyout is considered to be a financial restructuring; in this case, there is no change in the accounting basis. The latter case has the advantage of resulting in no goodwill amortization over many future years, as would be the case under the purchase method, and so yields better financial results in later years.

SPIN-OFF TRANSACTIONS

A company may find it necessary to transfer an operating division directly to company shareholders as a separate entity. If so, it should be transferred at the book values of all assets and liabilities related to the division as of the date of transfer. If the net amount of all assets and liabilities to be transferred is a positive book value, then this amount is to be offset against the company's retained earnings account. Alternatively, if the division being transferred has a negative book value, then the offset (which will be an increase) is to the additional paid-in capital account; the change in account is based on the assumption that investors have essentially paid the company to take the negative net worth division off the company's hands, so they are contributing capital to the company for this privilege.

If the company only owns a small minority interest in the division, then the transaction should be considered a property dividend. Under this concept, the company's share in the division must be transferred at its fair market value, rather than at its book value.

Another consideration is that the corporate parent must continue to track the financial results of the division being spun off up until the date of spin-off and record the results of the division's operations through that date on its books.

SUMMARY

In many organizations, the CFO is primarily rated on his or her ability to find, evaluate, and purchase other companies. Accordingly, this chapter has focused to a considerable extent on the due diligence process (which can be supplemented by the due diligence checklist in Appendix C), as well as on the most common valuation techniques and the large array of qualitative factors that can influence the purchase price. Also, a large number of accounting issues associated with an acquisition transaction were noted. A CFO should be aware of the proper reporting methods, because an incorrect transaction can result in a significant misstatement of the buying entity's results.

CHAPTER 22

ELECTRONIC COMMERCE

Though e-commerce no longer enjoys the fanatical following it had during the technology bubble of a few years ago, it remains a unique approach to developing a new sales channel. As such, it would be incorrect strategy for the CFO to completely ignore e-commerce as a new sales medium without some prior knowledge of its advantages, architecture, business model, and related issues, which include required structural changes and legal and insurance problems. This chapter provides that information.

ADVANTAGES OF ELECTRONIC COMMERCE

When the possibilities of e-commerce in relation to the Internet were first considered, pundits constructed an extraordinarily long list of supposed advantages to this new sales channel. Many of these "advantages" have proven to be false advertising, but the following list of advantages has generally proven to be true for most e-commerce applications:

- *Obtain customers from outside normal geographic sales region.* If a company sells through fixed retail locations, e-commerce can be used to obtain direct access to customers outside of those locations, while avoiding any "bricks and mortar" investments.

- *Offer more products.* The range of products that can be offered through a web site can be far greater than what one could find in a traditional retail location, thereby giving customers a clear reason to prefer this sales channel.

- *Eliminate sales staff.* On-line customers are used to doing their own shopping without any salesperson assistance, so this cost is eliminated.

- *Avoid excessive finished goods.* A company with traditional retail sales channels must stock a full selection of finished goods at each location. In comparison, an e-commerce channel requires one to stock finished goods at only a single location, which dramatically reduces a company's total inventory investment. However, this advantage only works if e-commerce becomes the sales channel of choice, allowing a company to dismantle its other retail locations and realize actual savings on its inventory investment.

- *Avoid the middleman.* An e-commerce solution allows manufacturers to sell directly to end users, rather than to a distributor, who sells it to a retailer, who sells it to a customer—with each one marking up the price along the way. This is not a perfect advantage, since a manufacturer who follows this approach will be using the e-commerce sales channel to sell around the middlemen in its other sales channels, which will not please them. Also, manufacturers may not have experience in dealing directly with customers.

- *Gain immediate payment.* Since many customers buy on-line with credit cards, a company will not only experience accelerated cash flow, but can also avoid the clerical labor associated with processing payments, since customers perform this chore themselves.

- *Eliminate transactional errors.* Under a traditional sales approach, a salesperson writes down an order, which is transcribed into the company computer system, which is used to create and ship an order to the customer. By having customers enter orders themselves directly into the corporate computer system through an e-commerce site, a company can avoid the transactional errors that would otherwise arise, resulting in more accurate orders.

- *Maintain better pricing control.* Companies have pricing problems with catalog sales because some customers retain the catalogs for long time periods and then order items at the old prices, leaving the company in the uncomfortable position of having to decide if it should honor the old price. This is never an issue on an e-commerce web site, where one can instantly alter a price, leaving no old prices for anyone to see.

- *Sell until inventories are gone.* One can withdraw an item for sale from an e-commerce site at the exact point when the last of the associated finished goods inventory is gone, resulting in no leftover inventory.

- *No mail float.* E-commerce improves on the sales catalog approach, since a customer does not rely on mailing in an order—instead, the order is instantly placed in the corporate computer system, which eliminates the float time that would otherwise be imposed on an order by the postal service.

- *Better customer information.* By identifying customers and tracking what web pages they review and which products they buy, a company can develop an extremely detailed database of information about each customer, allowing it to offer tailored sales deals to each customer every time they arrive at the web site.

- *Avoid customer service.* Depending on the situation, customers can avoid calling the customer service staff and instead go straight to the information they need, such as a downloads page for accessing patch or upgrade files, or an FAQs (Frequently Asked Questions) page. However, the e-commerce channel can also result in more questions from customers on entirely new topics, which can *increase* the amount of required customer service support.

The CFO must not react with too much glee to this lengthy list of advantages, for e-commerce also presents a number of problems. The foremost of these issues are lack of site maintenance and the lack of integration between the e-commerce site and corporate back-office systems. The CFO must work through these issues in detail in order to arrive at the true cost-benefit relationship for an e-commerce sales channel.

E-COMMERCE BUSINESS MODEL

The first use to which a company is likely to put an e-commerce site is the simple duplication of its primary sales activity. For example, if it sells television sets, then the site will carry a picture of each television and a price. This approach treats an e-commerce site as an electronic extension of the existing sales effort without regard for the special aspects of this channel. There are other sales models that can be adopted to make an e-commerce site a more effective sales channel.

A minor extension to the basic sales model just noted is a massive increase in the number of products sold over what could possibly be found in a retail location. This approach works because there is no need to stock vast quantities of finished goods at multiple retail locations. This approach attracts more customers because they know the selection improves their chances of finding the exact product they need.

Another modest improvement over the standard sales channel is the provision of much more information about each product sold. This can include detailed product specifications, as well as comments from other buyers, using a rating system. This approach takes the place of a salesperson and goes one step further by giving much more product information than a salesperson would normally be able to impart to a buyer.

A company can take a more radical approach to selling its products by avoiding distributors and retailers entirely and selling its products straight to buyers through the e-commerce channel. Though this seems like an easy way to pass a much larger proportion of profits back to the manufacturer through the elimination of middlemen, the manufacturer may find that it is not structured to deal with consumers. It will need a customer service function, the ability to respond quickly to customer questions, and to service products on short notice—all tasks that the newly eliminated middlemen would have accomplished on its behalf.

One can depart from these variations on the sale of products to attempt much more different business models on an e-commerce site. One such approach is the advice site, where a fee can be charged to either dispense advice from human personnel who research and respond to submitted inquiries or from an automated system that performs the same task. This approach only applies to very specialized niche markets where user-specific knowledge is hard to come by and where it must be tailored to individual needs. An obvious example is in the medical field. However, even in this area, enough free data is available that potential customers may prefer to conduct a general review of free data rather than pay for more specific information.

A more wide-ranging approach to the advice business model is to simply provide access to general types of information for free. For example, one could provide daily updates on the weather, snow conditions, and ticket prices at every ski resort in the country. Revenue would come from the ski resorts, who would pay a fee to have links to their web sites installed on the site. This approach can work, but the barriers to entry are so low that the sponsoring organizations can pick and choose among a variety of competing web sites, thereby driving down the cost of the fees they pay.

Another approach is to be a portal through which customers must go as they enter the Internet. The portal can charge users directly for this service as well as charge a variety of other sites in exchange for being listed on the portal site as direct links, thereby feeding large numbers of customers to them. The problem with this approach is that portals are expensive to ramp up, because several powerful portal brands are already well established, making this a difficult model to successfully follow.

One can also attempt to follow the eBay model and create an auction site for customers, where the company takes a transaction fee on all successful auctions conducted. As was the case with a portal, this can be a difficult and expensive business model to follow, for there are many competitors in the marketplace already, and the cost of attracting auction participants is substantial. The best approach here is to adopt a small niche (such as the sale of oil and gas leases) for which the number of participants can be clearly identified, and work diligently at servicing the needs of that small target population.

A very simple use of e-commerce is not to sell anything to anyone, but rather to speed the flow of transactions electronically between the company and its business partners. This can be accomplished with electronic data interchange (EDI), which has been available since the 1970s. Simply put, a company using EDI loads a business transaction into a standard format and e-mails the transaction to a value-added network (VAN), which is a third party that stores incoming messages in electronic mailboxes. The receiving party automatically polls the mailbox from time to time and extracts the transaction message, which it then forwards to its internal business systems for further processing. In its most elementary form EDI just takes the place of a fax machine with the sender manually reformatting a transaction to meet the transmission format, and the recipient manually reformatting it to fit into its internal computer systems. However, its true value appears when all manual portions of the process flow are automated, resulting in the elimination of transcription and input errors and faster just-in-time ordering. The trouble with this technology is its considerable cost to implement in an automated manner, which tends to restrict its use to a few businesses that order in large quantities from one another or situations where large companies can force its implementation on a group of smaller, dependent suppliers.

The CFO can recommend any of these business models for implementation, or even follow multiple paths by setting up separate web sites for each one. A key factor in any selection will be the amount of change required of the enterprise as a whole in order to make the business model a success. Those factors are discussed in the next section.

RESTRUCTURING THE ORGANIZATION FOR E-COMMERCE

When e-commerce is implemented, the customer service function can expect a rapid increase in its workload, especially if the company is following a business-to-consumer (B2C) model. The jump in workload may be caused by (hopefully) a rapid increase in the number of customers. Even if this does not occur, the customer who uses an e-commerce channel is the type who wants to be well-informed about products and who may have exchanged information about the company with other potential users through various electronic bulletin boards—characteristics that lead to customer inquiries of a much more detailed variety than would be the case through other sales channels, and that require a very high level of product knowledge to answer. This can require additional hiring within the customer support function, routing customers through a phone number for a more interactive experience with the support staff or leading customers through a series of questions to narrow down their issues and route them more accurately to the correct person within the company.

Another area that can experience significant change is the order fulfillment process. E-commerce customers are accustomed to immediate deliveries of ordered goods, which means that there should be a linkage between the e-commerce site and the in-house legacy systems that manage the production and shipping functions, so that deliveries are made with the greatest possible speed. If this linkage does not occur, customers are likely to flood the customer service staff with order status inquiries. Another result of this situation may be a drive toward just-in-time manufacturing systems, so that orders can be fulfilled on very short notice. A company must also prepare itself to use overnight delivery services to a much greater extent than was previously the case with other sales channels.

A fully integrated e-commerce system allows customers to completely avoid the human interface and directly access real-time data themselves, including account status, current pricing, and stock availability. This requires a dedication to the storage of extremely accurate information by the company, since customers combing through the database will certainly spot errors, which can lead to embarrassing problems with pricing and delivery.

The information technology (IT) staff may also find itself working with an outside payment processing company that provides it with a fully configured linkage to a credit card verification and processing facility. It is not difficult to connect to such systems, but an IT department that is accustomed to developing all of its own applications may react adversely to integrating such a system into the in-house legacy systems.

E-COMMERCE ARCHITECTURE

The simplest possible architecture for an e-commerce site is to manually convert information from an in-house computer system to web page format and transmit it to an outside web host, which posts the pages to an Internet site. Under this approach, some web presence is obtained, but there is no interaction with potential customers. The next most complex approach is to program the in-house computer system to automatically publish a new web document at timed intervals, and load it to a company-controlled server that is blocked by a firewall. This approach certainly provides more up-to-date information to customers, but there is still no customer interaction.

To provide interaction, the next highest level of e-commerce architecture is to allow customers to query the central database by issuing queries through the firewall to an application server, which in turn locates the information on the in-house database and issues it back to the Web site. While this approach certainly results in a more informed customer, it does not result in one that can transact business through the e-commerce channel. To do that, the architecture must also include access by the application server to multiple databases, such as customer credit, inventory, and payment systems. At this level, the application server can coordinate complete business transactions with customers, including a search for available inventory, a price quote, payment, and issuance of a shipment order to the in-house order fulfillment system.

Availability is also a key concern of the e-commerce architecture. Unlike a regular business, where work stops after an eight-hour day, customers are liable to access an e-commerce site at any time of the day or night, and on any day of the week. This is particularly true when customers are located in many time zones. This enhanced availability requirement forces a company to adopt redundant equipment, possibly sited in multiple locations, as well as maintain continual backup and restore facilities. The exact amount of investment in these added systems will, to some extent, be driven by the type of service offered through the e-commerce site (e.g., 24-hour food delivery requires 24-hour access), as well as management's decision to either make substantial investments up-front in this channel or to incrementally add systems as the volume from the channel ramps up.

Another architectural concern is scalability, which is the ability of a system to smoothly handle a shift from few to many transactions. If it cannot, users will experience much slower response times or simply not be able to access the system. Though this issue can be dealt with in advance by making a major investment in the hardware and software platform, a CFO may find that the resulting transaction volume never justifies the investment. Instead, it is generally best to begin with a modest investment in systems that are somewhat scalable until the new sales channel has proven that a larger investment is required. One should monitor system response times, especially during peak access periods, to determine when this additional investment must be made.

Another e-commerce issue is how to identify the returning customer. One approach is to plant an identification file, called a "cookie," on the user's computer. This is accessed the next time the customer arrives at the company web site, so the company's e-commerce system knows who he or she is. However, there has been an outcry over the ethics of storing files on customer computers, which has led to many people destroying all cookies they find on their computers. The only alternative is to ask customers to identify themselves when they reach the e-commerce site, usually by signing in. Since many people prefer to operate anonymously, they will back out of the site rather than identify themselves. Thus, this is a problem without a simple solution.

E-COMMERCE SECURITY*

When a business contemplates adding web interfaces to its mission-critical systems, significant security questions often arise. The best approach to security is to implement a range of security features designed to protect sensitive data and systems from the constant barrage of attacks on the Internet. Possible security options are:

- *Access control.* E-commerce applications provide a gateway to information that is to be exchanged between parties. These applications must contain access control mechanisms to ensure that each party has access to only the appropriate functions and data. These controls can be based on the identity of the client. For example, a software supplier's support site may permit anyone who can demonstrate that he or she has a valid software license to download upgrades or patches. This type of site may not identify users by name, but rather requires users to enter a license number embedded in the software to prove that they possess a copy.

- *Authentication.* In e-commerce, each party wants some assurance that it is dealing with the correct party. This can be accomplished for low-value transactions with a user identification number and password. However, users tend to duplicate the same password all over the Internet in order to avoid having too many passwords, which means that if someone can determine a party's password elsewhere on the Internet, the password may give the perpetrator access to other web sites. A business that runs an e-commerce web server will not want an imposter to route customers away from the site, so it can purchase a server certificate from a third party; this is a form of digital passport—difficult to forge and easily recognizable. During the initiation of an SSL connection between a web browser and a web server, the server sends its digital credentials to the client browser. The browser checks these credentials to be sure they are valid and that they correspond to the web site requested by the user. The browser also checks the certificate to be sure a known certificate authority issued it. Web browsers have a database of certificate authorities whose certificates they will recognize automatically.

- *Encryption.* This is the mathematical scrambling of data. The most widely used encryption technique on the Internet is the Secure Sockets Layer protocol (SSL); it allows the selection of various encryption algorithms and strengths (determined by the length of the encryption key) to accommodate different security levels. It is designed specifically for the type of adhoc transactions common in e-commerce where neither party is known to the other at the start of a transaction.

---

*   Adapted with permission from Chapter 49A of *Controllership, 2003 Cumulative Supplement* by Willson, Roehl-Anderson, and Bragg (John Wiley & Sons, 2002).

- *Firewalls.* Firewalls were originally invented to provide protection to Internet connections. By funneling all communications to and from the Internet through a single gateway, a single device can protect many unsecured inside systems. A firewall intentionally restricts data flow based on certain rules of acceptable and unacceptable communications. Because the type of communication that is required between zones varies greatly from system to system, all firewall products are highly configurable. A firewall must be built on a secure host computer to ensure that an attacker does not defeat the firewall by attacking the computer on which the firewall software runs.

- *Host hardening.* The servers that host e-commerce applications must be sufficiently robust to withstand attack from the Internet. This requires "hardening" to add to any default security already provided by the hardware supplier. Some companies also perform host hardening on all production systems, even if not Internet-accessible, to protect against insider attack. This process involves the following configurations:

  — Removal of all unneeded services and protocols
  — Elimination of unneeded user accounts or privileges
  — Enabling audit logging
  — Installing upgrade patches to fix known security vulnerabilities
  — Setting of various operating system parameters to a secure setting

- *Intrusion detection.* Internet-connected systems are typically probed by hackers every day, using automated scanning tools to search for vulnerable systems that they can then go back and penetrate. Intrusion detection software is designed to recognize both scanning probes and actual attacks. In all cases, intrusion detection software will alert a network administrator as to the presence of an attack. A network-based intrusion detection product watches all the data that flow into or out of a network, comparing each data packet to a database of known attack signatures. A host-based intrusion detection product is deployed directly on a server and is configured to watch critical operating system parameters and system log files for conditions that might indicate an attack. Either type of detection product generates large amounts of event data and voluminous reports.

- *Vulnerability testing.* Vulnerability tests simulate the type of probing commonly performed by hackers to detect system vulnerabilities. System administrators can also purchase vulnerability scanning tools that automatically check systems against a database of thousands of possible security flaws. When this type of testing discovers a flaw in the system, it means that hackers could identify the same flaw and exploit it to gain unauthorized access. Consequently, one must then implement fixes to any discovered vulnerabilities. For systems that are not directly accessible via the Internet, one may fix only the most serious flaws, since the cost of fixing minor flaws is usually outweighed by the reduced risk that someone would find a way to exploit them.

E-COMMERCE INSURANCE

When a CFO considers the security of an e-commerce solution, it is usually in terms of the issues noted in the preceding section, not the insurance coverage that is a measure of last resort in case the other security measures fail. Insurance coverage for e-commerce typically falls outside bounds of general liability insurance, because payments under that type of coverage are triggered by property damage to tangible assets or bodily injury, neither of which occurs in an e-commerce environment.

In order to obtain coverage that is tailored to an e-commerce operation, a company must first go through an IT (information technology) security appraisal, whose cost is footed by the company, not the insurer. Depending on the results of the audit, one can then purchase any of the following policies:

- *Business interruption insurance.* If a company based a large part of its revenues on e-commerce, and there were a gap in system security that led to a shutdown in computer operations, it would immediately halt its revenue stream. Business interruption insurance would pay for lost profits under this scenario.

- *Contractual obligation insurance.* If a company is an application service provider, this insurance provides coverage against claims that the company does not deliver on promised services.

- *Data extortion insurance.* Hackers can extract information from a company's computer systems and threaten to use or expose it to the public unless they are paid a fee. Data extortion coverage compensates the company for this damage.

- *Internet liability insurance.* This policy is a variation on errors and omissions insurance, providing coverage against claims of patent or trademark infringement, defamation, and the invasion of privacy that are caused by a company's Internet operations.

A CFO should review these insurance options and only select the most cost-effective alternatives to those areas of potential risk that a company cannot substantially provide against by other means. Thus, only one or a few of these policies will be required for most Internet operations.

E-COMMERCE LEGAL ISSUES

The key legal issue related to e-commerce is sales taxes. The same rule of nexus applies to an e-commerce sale as to any normal sale. Under the nexus concept, a company with a presence in a state must pay sales taxes within that state. "Presence" means having some form of business operation there, such as a sales office, headquarters, training facility, or warehouse. For example, if the ABC Company has a sales office in Colorado, then any purchases made on-line by a customer in Colorado must be charged a sales tax. Worse, some case law indicates that simply outsourcing a server operation to another state will create nexus in that state, requiring one to pay sales taxes for sales made into that state—so be careful about the states to which you outsource server operations!

A major issue for any company offering software downloads over the Internet is to require customer approval of an "Agreements" on-line document. This document should include a general waiver of liability clause, as well as an abbreviated warranty period. The exact wording used can be found on the back of any "shrink-wrapped" software that you physically purchase. The intent of requiring this approval prior to a download is to limit the company's liability in case downloaded software causes significant problems for a customer, such as the loss of data or a system crash.

A final concern is the domain name. Though one can use any domain name that has not been allocated elsewhere, it still may not be used if the domain name matches or is very similar to that of a business name that has been trademarked by another entity. In one recent example, a company took a business name that was closely related to that of another business that had fully established trademark protection. The protected company threatened to sue, and required the first company to shut down its web site on the grounds that the domain name was too similar to its own. The first company complied, though it had already prepaid several years of domain name maintenance for the site.

SUMMARY

This chapter was intended to give the CFO a general overview of e-commerce issues of a business nature. It generally avoided commentary on the technical aspects of creating an e-commerce channel, partially because the CFO is rarely involved in that type of decision, and because the technology underlying these systems changes so rapidly that any advice given here would be somewhat outdated by the time of publication. Nonetheless, the CFO can use this chapter to structure an e-commerce business plan that incorporates risk management, process changes, and security issues, which are key areas for which he or she has direct responsibility.

PART **6**

OTHER TOPICS

CHAPTER 23

EMPLOYEE COMPENSATION

The CFO frequently supervises the human resources department, and so is responsible for a variety of employee compensation topics. While this chapter is not intended to be a comprehensive overview of the entire compensation area, it does provide useful information on several compensation topics for which the CFO is frequently expected to have direct responsibility—deferred compensation plans, life insurance, stock appreciation rights, and stock options. These topics tend to fall outside the range of day-to-day activities of the human resources department, because they tend to be granted only under special circumstances and with greater frequency to the executive team.

An additional topic is the use of a bonus sliding scale. The human resources department manages the bonus plan, but the CFO should be aware of the sliding scale system, since it has a significant impact on the behavior of anyone subject to the bonus plan. Finally, we address the use of captive insurance companies, which can profoundly reduce the cost of employee benefits.

DEFERRED COMPENSATION*

There are a variety of deferred compensation plans used by CFOs who attempt to lock in the services of company employees as far into the future as possible. Under any of these plans, an employee's tax objective is to only pay a tax when the compensation is actually received, while the employer wants to receive a full expense deduction for any amounts paid—and the sooner, the better.

If a plan meets enough criteria to be classified as an *exempt trust* or *qualified plan*, then a company can immediately recognize the expense of payments made into it, even though the employees being compensated will not be paid until some future tax year. Also, the value of funds or stock in the trust can grow on a tax-deferred basis, while participants in the plan will not be taxed until they are paid from it. In addition, the funds paid from such a plan may be eligible for rollover into an IRA, which results in an additional delay in the recognition of taxable income. While the funds are held in trust, they are also beyond the reach of any company creditors.

In order to become a qualified plan, it must meet a number of Internal Revenue Service (IRS) requirements, such as a minimum level of coverage across the companywide pool of employees, the prohibition of benefits under the plan for highly compensated employees to the exclusion of other employees, and restrictions on the amount of benefits that can be issued under the plan. Since many employers are only interested in creating deferred compensation plans in order to retain a small number of key employees, they will instead

---

* Adapted with permission from Chapter 40 of *Ultimate Accountants' Reference* by Bragg (John Wiley & Sons, 2005).

turn to a *nonqualified plan*, which avoids the requirement of having to offer the plan to a large number of employees.

If the plan is nonqualified, then the employer can only record the compensation expense at the same time that the employees are compensated. A company that only wants to extend deferred compensation agreements to a few select employees will tend to use this type of plan, since it does not require payments to a large number of employees and also allows the company to increase the amount of per-person compensation well beyond the restricted levels required under a qualified plan.

A useful variation on the nonqualified plan concept is the *rabbi trust*, which is an irrevocable trust used to fund deferred compensation for key employees. Under this approach, a company contributes stock to a third-party trustee, such as a bank or trust company, with the stock being designated for eventual payment to a few key employees. Employee vesting can take seven years or even longer in a few instances, which gives companies an excellent tool to lock in key employees over long periods of time with such plans. Employees can be paid from the trust either in stock or cash, and will recognize income at the time of receipt. The company can recognize an expense at the same time that the employee recognizes income; however, if the employee gradually vests in the plan, the expense can be proportionally recognized by the company at the time of vesting. If the payments made into the trust are in the form of company stock, then the company must only record as an expense the value of the stock at the time of grant, and can ignore any subsequent changes in the stock's value. A company that uses a rabbi trust does not have to make extensive reports to the government under Employee Retirement Income Security Act (ERISA) rules; instead, it is only necessary to make a one-time disclosure of the plan within four months of its inception. It is also necessary to initiate the plan prior to the start of any services to which the payments apply, or at least include in the plan a forfeiture clause that is active throughout the term of the deferred compensation agreement.

The terms of a rabbi trust must also state that a key employee's benefits from the plan cannot be shifted to a third party. It must also state that the trust be an unfunded one for the purposes of both taxes and Title I of ERISA. Further, the plan must define the timing of future payments, or the events that will trigger payments, as well as the amount of payments to be made to recipients.

A key consideration for any company contemplating the creation of a rabbi trust is that the plan assets must be unsecured and cannot unconditionally vest in the employees who are beneficiaries of the plan. This requirement is founded on the economic benefit doctrine, which holds that the avoidance of taxation can only occur if the receipt of funds is subject to a substantial risk of forfeiture. To this end, the plan document must state that plan participants are classed with general unsecured creditors in terms of their right to receive funds from the plan. The contractual obligation to pay employees from the plan cannot be secured by any type of note, since this defeats the purpose of having the assets be available to general creditors. However, just because the funds can be claimed by general creditors does not mean that they are available for other company uses—payment obligations to targeted employees must be made before any funds may be extracted for other company uses.

The unsecured status of a rabbi trust can be a cause of great concern for employees being paid under its terms. Not only are the funds contributed to the trust at risk of being claimed by general creditors, but so too are all salary deferrals made by the targeted employees into the trust. This is a particular problem in the event of corporate bankruptcy, since secured creditors will be paid in full before the key employees can claim any remaining funds from the trust, which may result in a small payment or none at all. When a bankruptcy occurs or seems likely, the company is required to notify the trustee, which must halt all subsequent scheduled payments to plan participants and hold all remaining funds for distribution to secured creditors. Further, a change in control may result in a new management team that is not inclined to honor the terms of a deferred compensation agreement that require additional payments into the trust, in which case the recipients under the plan may sue the company for the missing benefits. There is some protection for key employees in this case, however, because the terms of the deferred compensation agreement will require the third-party trustee to make payments to employees as they become due; the main problem is that the funds for these payments will only continue to be available if the company pays funds into the trust.

If the perceived risk to plan participants outweighs the advantages of having a rabbi trust, it is also possible to create a *secular trust*. Under this approach, plan participants will have their assets protected in the event of corporate insolvency, but the reduced level of risk is offset by current taxation of the deferred compensation, which defeats the purpose of having the plan. A combined version of the two plans, called a *rabbicular trust*, starts as a rabbi trust, but then converts to a secular trust if the company funding the plan approaches bankruptcy. However, this approach will still result in the immediate recognition of all income at the time of conversion to a secular trust.

Though the rabbi trust concept can result in substantial benefits to both an employer and key employees, it is not allowed in some states, or only in a modified form. Also, rabbicular trusts must be carefully written to comply with all deferred compensation laws at both the state and federal levels. Consequently, the CFO should obtain the assistance of a qualified taxation professional before setting up either type of deferred compensation plan.

LIFE INSURANCE

It is common practice for a company to provide group term life insurance to its employees as part of a standard benefit package. This requires some extra reporting from a tax perspective, however. If the amount of the life insurance benefit exceeds $50,000, the company must report the incremental cost of the life insurance over $50,000 (to the extent that the employee is not paying for the additional insurance) on the employee's W-2 form as taxable income. In the less common case where the company provides life insurance that results in some amount of cash surrender value, then the cost of this permanent benefit to the employee must also be included in the employee's W-2 form. The only case in which these costs are not included in an employee's W-2 form is when the company is the beneficiary of the policy, rather than the employee. The opposite situation arises if the company is providing life insurance only to a few key employees, rather than to all employees; in this case, the entire cost of the insurance must be reported on the employee's W-2 form as taxable income.

STOCK APPRECIATION RIGHTS

A Stock Appreciation Right (SAR) is a form of compensation that rewards an employee if there is an increase in the value of a company's stock, without the employee actually owning the stock. For example, an employee is given 1,000 SARs at the company's current stock price. When the stock price later increases, the employee exercises the SARs at his or her option, resulting in a cash payment by the company to the employee for the net amount of the increase. No stock actually changes hands.

The employee recognizes no income and the company no expense at the time the SARs are granted. Tax recognition only occurs for both parties once the employee chooses to exercise the SARs and the company issues a payment for them. The company will treat this cost as a salary or bonus expense.

STOCK OPTIONS

A stock option gives an employee the right to buy stock at a specific price within a specific time period. Stock options come in two varieties: the *incentive stock option* (ISO) and the *nonqualified stock option* (NSO).

Incentive stock options are not taxable to the employee at the time they are granted, nor at the time when the employee eventually exercises the option to buy stock. If the employee does not dispose of the stock within two years of the date of the option grant or within one year of the date when the option is exercised, then any resulting gain will be taxed as a long-term capital gain. However, if the employee sells the stock within one year of the exercise date, then any gain is taxed as ordinary income. An ISO plan typically requires an employee to exercise any vested stock options within 90 days of that person's voluntary or involuntary termination of employment.

The reduced tax impact associated with waiting until two years have passed from the date of option grant presents a risk to the employee that the value of the related stock will decline in the interim, thereby offsetting the reduced long-term capital gain tax rate achieved at the end of this period. To mitigate the potential loss in stock value, one can make a Section 83(b) election to recognize taxable income on the purchase price of the stock within 30 days following the date when an option is exercised and withhold taxes at the ordinary income tax rate at that time. The employee will not recognize any additional income with respect to the purchased shares until they are sold or otherwise transferred in a taxable transaction, and the additional gain recognized at that time will be taxed at the long-term capital gains rate. It is reasonable to make the Section 83(b) election if the amount of income reported at the time of the election is small and the potential price growth of the stock is significant. However, it is not reasonable to take the election if there is a combination of high reportable income at the time of election (resulting in a large tax payment) and a minimal chance of growth in the stock price, or if the company can forfeit the options. The Section 83(b) election is not available to holders of options under an NSO plan.

The alternative minimum tax (AMT) must also be considered when dealing with an ISO plan. In essence, the AMT requires that an employee pay tax on the difference between the exercise price and the stock price at the time when an option is exercised, even if the stock is not sold at that time. This can result in a severe cash shortfall for the employee, who may only be able to pay the related taxes by selling the stock. This is a particular problem if the value of the shares subsequently drops, since there is now no source of high-priced stock that can be converted into cash in order to pay the required taxes. This problem arises frequently in cases where a company has just gone public, but employees are restricted from selling their shares for some time after the IPO date and run the risk of losing stock value during that interval. Establishing the amount of the gain reportable under AMT rules is especially difficult if a company's stock is not publicly held, since there is no clear consensus on the value of the stock. In this case, the IRS will use the value of the per-share price at which the last round of funding was concluded. When the stock is eventually sold, an AMT credit can be charged against the reported gain, but there can be a significant cash shortfall in the meantime. In order to avoid this situation, an employee could choose to exercise options at the point when the estimated value of company shares is quite low, thereby reducing the AMT payment; however, the employee must now find the cash to pay for the stock that he or she has just purchased, and also runs the risk that the shares will not increase in value and may become worthless.

An ISO plan is only valid if it follows these rules:

- Incentive stock options can only be issued to employees. A person must have been working for the employer at all times during the period that begins on the date of grant and ends on the day three months before the date when the option is exercised.

- The option term cannot exceed ten years from the date of grant. The option term is only five years in the case of an option granted to an employee who, at the time the option is granted, owns stock that has more than 10% of the total combined voting power of all classes of stock of the employer.

- The option price at the time it is granted is not less than the fair market value of the stock. However, it must be 110% of the fair market value in the case of an option granted to an employee who, at the time the option is granted, owns stock that has more than 10% of the total combined voting power of all classes of stock of the employer.

- The total value of all options that can be exercised by any one employee in one year is limited to $100,000. Any amounts exercised that exceed $100,000 will be treated as a nonqualified stock option (to be covered shortly).

- The options cannot be transferred by the employee and can only be exercised during the employee's lifetime.

If the options granted do not include these provisions, or are granted to individuals who are not employees under the preceding definition, then the options must be characterized as nonqualified stock options.

A *nonqualified stock option* is not given any favorable tax treatment under the Internal Revenue Code (hence the name). It is also referred to as a *nonstatutory stock option*. The recipient of an NSO does not owe any tax on the date when options are granted, unless the options are traded on a public exchange. In that case, the options can be traded at once for value, and so tax will be recognized on the fair market value of the options on the public exchange as of the grant date. An NSO option will be taxed when it is exercised, based on the difference between the option price and the fair market value of the stock on that day. The resulting gain will be taxed as ordinary income. If the stock appreciates in value after the exercise date, then the incremental gain is taxable at the capital gains rate.

There are no rules governing an NSO, so the option price can be lower than the fair market value of the stock on the grant date. The option price can also be set substantially higher than the current fair market value at the grant date, which is called a *premium grant*. It is also possible to issue *escalating price options*, which use a sliding scale for the option price that changes in concert with a peer group index, thereby stripping away the impact of broad changes in the stock market and forcing the company to outperform the stock market in order to achieve any profit from granted stock options. Also, a *heavenly parachute* stock option can be created that allows a deceased option holder's estate up to three years in which to exercise his or her options.

Company management should be aware of the impact of both ISO and NSO plans on the company, not just on employees. A company receives no tax deduction on a stock option transaction if it uses an ISO plan. However, if it uses an NSO plan, the company will receive a tax deduction equal to the amount of the income that the employee must recognize. If a company does not expect to have any taxable income during the stock option period, then it will receive no immediate value from having a tax deduction (though the deduction can be carried forward to offset income in future years), and so would be more inclined to use an ISO plan. This is a particularly common approach for companies that have not yet gone public. On the other hand, publicly held companies, which are generally more profitable and so must search for tax deductions, will be more inclined to sponsor an NSO plan. Research has shown that most employees who are granted either type of option will exercise it as soon as possible, which essentially converts the tax impact of the ISO plan into an NSO plan. For this reason also, many companies prefer to use NSO plans.

BONUS SLIDING SCALE

A reasonably progressive budgeting model will include a direct link into the corporate bonus plan, with staff being paid bonuses based on their achievement of certain goals. Though the intention is good—to create incentives to achieve the budget—it actually tends to create more problems than it solves.

One problem is that if employees realize they will fall short of their bonus targets, they will be more likely to hoard their resources or possible sales for the next period when they will have a better opportunity to achieve better performance and be paid a bonus. The result is wild swings in corporate performance from period to period as employees cycle through the hoard-to-splurge cycle.

Another problem is that if the bonus target cannot be attained by normal means, employees will stretch or break the accounting rules in a variety of ways to achieve the target. By doing so, a lower level of ethics is introduced into the company, while also likely saddling the company with a variety of accounting problems that must be addressed in future periods.

The solution is to link the budget to a sliding performance scale that contains no "hard" performance goals. The best example of the sliding bonus scale is what it is *not*—there are no specific goals at which the bonus target suddenly increases in size. Instead, the bonus is a constant percentage of the goal, such as 1% of sales or 5% of net after-tax profits. Also, there should be no upper boundary to the sliding scale, which would present employees with the disincentive to stop performing once they have reached a maximum bonus level. Similarly, there should theoretically be no lower limit to the bonus either, though it is more common to see a baseline level that is derived from the corporate breakeven point, on the grounds that employees must at least ensure that the company does not lose money. The sliding scale approach also makes it much easier to budget for the bonus expense at various activity levels, rather than trying to budget for the more common all-or-nothing bonus payment.

CUT BENEFIT COSTS WITH A CAPTIVE INSURANCE COMPANY

It is possible to reduce employee benefit costs by 5 to 10% by creating a captive insurance company. The basic process is to have a regular insurance company underwrite all of the company's benefits-related insurance (LTD, STD, medical, and so on) for a fee, while the captive can either bear all of the risk or apportion some of it elsewhere by purchasing reinsurance. The cost savings comes from the elimination of third-party profits and overhead charges. Also, since this creates a direct correlation between insurance costs and insurance claims, the company will probably become highly interested in controlling its insurance claim experience.

To legally operate a captive for this purpose, the Department of Labor must issue an exemption from some aspects of the ERISA legislation, which usually calls for clear evidence that employee benefits increase or costs decrease as a result of using the captive (though this does not have to take away all of the savings!). Also, the captive must be licensed in the United States (about half of the states have enacted laws beneficial to captives, so there are plenty of choices), have at least one year of audited financial statements, and be fronted by an insurance company with at least an "A" rating.

Operating a captive is expensive; expect to pay an absolute minimum of $100,000 to set one up, and a minimum of another $50,000 per year to operate it. Thus, savings will only begin to occur for larger companies whose current insurance expense exceeds $1 million.

SUMMARY

The chapter covered only those employee compensation issues with which the CFO tends to become involved. Other issues, such as determining pay scales for employees, dealing with labor unions, and creating performance bonus plans can usually be safely delegated to the human resources department, whereas the topics covered here are more likely to be the responsibility of the CFO and may have to be presented by that person to the Board of Directors.

CHAPTER 24

BANKRUPTCY

Though no CFO ever wants to be involved in a corporate bankruptcy, circumstances may dictate otherwise. The road through the bankruptcy process absolutely requires the best possible legal counsel; this person can advise on a wide range of possible strategies to take in dealing with creditors and the bankruptcy court and the myriad of claims and counterclaims that can arise over the (sometimes) multiyear course of a bankruptcy case. Before calling in legal counsel, the CFO should read this chapter to gain a basic understanding of the main players in the bankruptcy drama, how the bankruptcy process works, creditor priorities, tax issues, and other related issues.

APPLICABLE BANKRUPTCY LAWS

All applicable laws related to bankruptcy are issued by the federal government and are contained within Title 11 of the U.S. Code, which is referred to as the Bankruptcy Code. Chapter 3 of the Code describes how to file for bankruptcy, while Chapter 5 covers debtor and creditor relations, Chapter 7 describes a corporate liquidation, and Chapter 11 itemizes the steps involved in a corporate reorganization.

A Chapter 7 liquidation is a relatively passive affair for the CFO, who essentially watches while a court-appointed trustee sells off business assets and distributes the resulting cash to creditors and stockholders in a carefully prescribed order of payment (see the "Creditor and Shareholder Payment Priorities" section). A Chapter 11 reorganization generally allows management to remain in control while the company negotiates with its creditors to settle outstanding claims.

The Code allows any company to file for bankruptcy at any time. There is no requirement to have a negative net worth, only that a company have a place of business in the United States.

The decision to voluntarily enter bankruptcy is the Board of Directors'. This group must approve a motion, such as the one noted in Exhibit 24.1, which should be retained in the corporate minute book. Alternatively, any group of creditors can jointly file an involuntary bankruptcy petition, thereby forcing a company into bankruptcy against its will.

PLAYERS IN THE BANKRUPTCY DRAMA

A company files a bankruptcy petition with the local *bankruptcy court*. This court is a division of the U.S. District Court, so there is at least one bankruptcy court in each state to mirror the organizational structure of the district court system. There are no juries in the bankruptcy court—instead, all decisions are made by the *bankruptcy judge*. The judge is appointed to a 14-year renewable term. Though bankruptcy cases are assigned to individual judges on a random basis, certain district courts have a reputation for

WHEREAS, the Board of Directors of the Corporation has determined that the Corporation must file a voluntary Chapter 11 petition in bankruptcy court;

BE IT RESOLVED, that the Corporation's officers and any member of its law firm _____ are hereby authorized and directed to deliver all documents needed to effect the filing of a Chapter 11 petition on behalf of the Corporation;

RESOLVED IN ADDITION, that the Corporation's officers are hereby authorized and directed to represent the Corporation in all bankruptcy proceedings, and take all necessary actions on behalf of the Corporation in connection with this petition;

RESOLVED IN ADDITION, that any actions taken by the Corporation's officers prior to the date of this resolution in regard to the bankruptcy petition are hereby approved by the Corporation;

RESOLVED IN ADDITION, that this consent, when signed by the Board members, shall be effective as of [date].

EXHIBIT 24.1   EXAMPLE OF A BOARD'S BANKRUPTCY RESOLUTION

containing a high proportion of business-friendly judges, so companies may attempt to file for bankruptcy in those districts in order to increase their odds of being assigned a "good" judge.

An *examiner* may be assigned by the bankruptcy court to conduct an investigation of a company's finances. This is usually an outside audit firm that does not have previous ties to the company. An examiner must be appointed if the total amount of company debt exceeds $5 million, and is frequently appointed if there is evidence of extensive insider transactions, fraud, or incompetence.

If the company files for liquidation under Chapter 7 of the Code, the court will assign a *trustee* to oversee the liquidation. A trustee is usually not assigned to a Chapter 11 reorganization, since the current management team is assumed to be running the reorganization process. However, a trustee will be assigned to a Chapter 11 reorganization if there is proof of fraud or gross incompetence by the existing management team. The trustee's fees are paid from the assets of the bankrupt company.

If a trustee is not assigned to a Chapter 11 reorganization, then the *existing management team* is assigned to manage the bankruptcy. At this point, the role of the management team shifts from attaining a high return on equity for shareholders to ensuring that creditors are paid back to the greatest extent possible—essentially, the management team's boss has changed to a new group of entities. If the management team continues to make decisions that place shareholders ahead of creditors, they stand a good chance of being replaced by the bankruptcy court with a trustee. The management team is obligated to work with creditors to devise a repayment plan that is acceptable to all key parties, while also keeping the bankruptcy court informed of its progress with monthly operating reports.

The *secured creditors* and the *unsecured creditors committee* must work with the management team or trustee in devising a plan of reorganization. The secured creditors will be primarily interested in obtaining the full value from any collateral that has been assigned to them. Usually, only the seven largest unsecured creditors are included in the unsecured creditors committee, since the inclusion of all creditors would make for a most unwieldy group. Members of this committee are supposed to represent all other unsecured creditors before the bankruptcy court.

Finally, there are a number of advisers that a company or the bankruptcy court may employ. *Lawyers* who specialize in bankruptcy proceedings should be asked to advise on the timing, location, and structure of the bankruptcy filing at the earliest possible date. As previously noted, *auditors* may be called in by the court to examine the corporate books, while *accountants* may be hired by the company to prepare for the auditors' arrival. It is also useful to hire a *public relations* firm that can put a favorable spin on the bankruptcy proceedings with a company's business partners. If creditors are wary of the management team's ability to return a company to solvency, they may insist on the hiring of a *turnaround specialist* who either fills the president position or becomes an adviser to that person. *Appraisers* may also be employed to determine the market value of secured creditor collateral, as well as the overall value of the company as a going concern. Finally, in a worst-case scenario, an *auction house* may be brought in to liquidate all corporate assets.

CREDITOR AND SHAREHOLDER PAYMENT PRIORITIES

The Bankruptcy Code lists a specific order in which bankruptcy claims will be paid, which is:

1. *Secured claims.*   A creditor who has obtained collateral against a company liability will be paid up to the liquidation value of the collateral. Any excess amount owed will then be shifted to the unsecured creditor claims category.

2. *Administration costs related to the bankruptcy.*   Any legal, trustee, or other advisory fees related to the bankruptcy.

3. *Employee payroll.*   Unpaid wage and salary expenses incurred within 90 days of the bankruptcy filing date.

4. *Taxes.*   Any unpaid taxes owed to government entities, which can include corporate income, sales, payroll, and personal property taxes.

5. *Unsecured creditor claims.*   All claims not previously specified that are not secured by any form of collateral. This tends to comprise the bulk of creditor claims in a bankruptcy. Distributions to this group are made on a pro rata basis if there are not sufficient funds available to pay off 100% of all claims.

6. *Shareholders.*   Any equity holder will only be paid if the claims of all entities previously noted on this list have been satisfied, which frequently leaves nothing at all. Also, any shareholder who obtains a favorable court judgment in relation to a securities fraud claim will have the amount of the judgment clustered into this category—which means that the judgment may never be paid.

BANKRUPTCY SEQUENCE OF EVENTS

If a company decides to enter Chapter 11 bankruptcy, it must complete a petition to the bankruptcy court that is accompanied by a Board-approved bankruptcy resolution (as described earlier in Exhibit 24.1). The first order of business when filing this petition is determining the best court to which it will be submitted. Though all bankruptcy judges operate under the same guidelines and therefore should issue the same opinions when presented with the same facts, this is not quite the case. Some bankruptcy judges are considered to be more friendly to debtors, while others may be swayed by the potential loss of jobs if a company has a large number of employees working near the court. Thus, a company incorporated in Delaware may elect to file for bankruptcy there, due to the business-friendly reputation of its judges, but could instead file for bankruptcy in the district where its largest base of employees is located. Other reasons for picking a specific venue are the familiarity of the company's counsel with a specific court, or simply the expense of having to frequently travel to a distant venue for bankruptcy hearings.

The filing itself requires a great deal of manual labor, though some of its components can be delayed a number of days after the initial bankruptcy filing. The most labor-intensive parts of the filing are:

- *Schedules of Assets and Liabilities.* This is essentially a very detailed balance sheet that itemizes all types of property (such as individual accounts receivable and all fixed assets), as well as listings of all creditors having secured and unsecured claims, and the amounts of those claims. It is very important to note whether each claim is disputed, uncertain in amount, or contingent on some event. By doing so, all possible creditors will be added to the court's notification list of bankruptcy actions, so they cannot claim they were never notified. This keeps the company from dealing with additional undocumented claims once it departs bankruptcy protection. These schedules also include lists of unexpired contracts and co-debtors. A company will almost certainly never arrive at a complete list of all assets and liabilities on its first filing of these schedules with the bankruptcy court, but it can file updated schedules at a later date as more information becomes available.

- *Statement of Financial Affairs.* This is a very detailed income statement for the year-to-date and the two preceding years. Of particular interest is an additional schedule detailing all payments to creditors in the 90 days immediately preceding the bankruptcy filing, which is used to determine if the company is entitled to retrieve payments made to creditors. Another schedule itemizes all gifts paid out within the past year, which can be used to find any fraudulent transfers that may be recovered by the company.

The company is officially in bankruptcy as of the time when the filing is date-stamped by a clerk of the court. As of this date and time, creditors are barred from taking further action against the company to collect funds or other assets owed to them, which includes collection calls, taking possession of collateral, lien enforcement, canceling insurance, withholding tax refunds, initiating lawsuits, or setting off outstanding debtor debts against debts by them to the company. However, outside entities can still proceed with criminal prosecution, and landlords can evict debtors if the terms of their leases expired prior to the bankruptcy filing.

The company must also file a petition for the retention of professionals to assist it in the bankruptcy case. This can include lawyers, accountants, special managers to assist in operations, appraisers, and a public relations firm. The petition may include a provision to pay these professionals for any assistance already given to the company prior to the bankruptcy petition.

Once the bankruptcy petition has been filed, the first order of business is to apply for *first day orders*. These are court orders for the company to pay preexisting claims by employees (primarily wages and salaries) and key suppliers, so there is no significant short-term disruption in company business in the early days of the bankruptcy. Though employee wages and salaries are routinely allowed in first day orders, supplier payments will only be allowed if the suppliers are difficult to replace or would cause major disruption to the business.

The court must also confirm the result of negotiations the company will undertake with any utilities. A utility is required by law to continue providing services to a bankrupt company for only the first 20 days of its bankruptcy, after which it can cut off service if the company cannot provide additional assurance of payment, such as a large deposit. Given the need for continued service by such suppliers, the court is typically most willing to approve of any reasonable arrangements that will provide utilities with some assurance of payment.

The court may also confirm retention bonuses to key personnel, which are especially important for those who have key business knowledge or contacts and whose departure might result in a major business disruption. Courts may also confirm modest severance packages for key personnel, but are unlikely to do so for exorbitant "golden parachute" deals.

The next key step in the bankruptcy process is to secure sufficient financing to keep the company operating. Though it may be possible to carefully manage working capital to such an extent that no other financing is needed, a company should at least obtain a line of credit to tide it over any unforeseen cash-flow dips. The simplest approach is to continue an existing line of credit, though this will certainly require additional negotiations with the lender, who may want additional collateral, frequent operational reports, periodic loan payments, and considerable input into an operating budget. If a new lender must be found to extend a line of credit, then the company can offer it collateral, as well as a "super priority" over other administrative expenses, so that the lender will be paid in full prior to any other administrative expense claims. In rare cases, it is also possible to offer "super priority" to a lender on assets that have already been encumbered by other liens. This last approach only works if the company can prove that the amount of collateral encumbered by existing creditors exceeds the value of their claims, in which case the difference can be offered (with court approval) to the new lender.

With financing taken care of, the company must then stabilize its operations. A key area to address is maintaining reasonable credit terms with suppliers, whose first knee-jerk reaction to the bankruptcy filing will be to switch over to cash on delivery payment terms. This can be done by keeping suppliers appraised of the progress of the bankruptcy case, as well as by following through on payment commitments on an ongoing basis. A good approach is to negotiate good payment terms with suppliers subsequent to the bankruptcy filing in exchange for attempting to convince the court that the suppliers should be paid in full as part of the first day orders. Even if a supplier does switch to cash on delivery terms, the CFO can attempt to reestablish credit in small amounts and on short payment intervals, and then gradually improve these terms by proving the company's ability to follow through on the reduced terms.

Operational stabilization activities do not require court approval, though management can have its collective hand slapped by the court if it engages in activities that fall outside the bounds of normal business activities, such as the sale of assets or any activity that can be perceived as paying off a creditor's prebankruptcy claims. The unsecured creditors committee will be rightfully concerned about the amount of asset sales, since they are a source of funds that can be used to pay off the creditor's claims. The court will want to obtain the best possible price for any assets that management wants to sell, so it may require considerable shopping around among potential buyers in order to secure a good sale price.

As the company proceeds through the various stages of the bankruptcy, it must also file a monthly operating report with the bankruptcy court. This report is generally due 15 days after the end of the month, and should include detailed financial statements as well as such supporting documents as bank statements, accounts receivable and accounts payable aging reports. The standard contents of such a report are:

- Current month receipts and disbursements matrix, by bank account
- Accounts receivable aging
- Accounts payable aging
- Cash disbursements report
- Balance sheet matrix, by subsidiary
- Postpetition income statement, by subsidiary
- Year-to-date income statement, prepetition by subsidiary
- Year-to-date income statement, postpetition by subsidiary
- Schedule of additions to and deletions from fixed assets
- Schedule of payments to insiders and professionals
- Schedule of changes in employee headcount
- Schedule of current insurance policies and periods of coverage
- Discussion of progress toward the filing of a plan of reorganization

Relatively early in the bankruptcy process, the company should ask the court to issue a *bar date order*. This order states that creditors must file a claim by a specific date or be unable to file a claim thereafter. By publicizing this court order extensively with all creditors (a good idea is to send it to everyone in the supplier address database, even if there is no evidence of a claim), a company can ensure that it is at minimal risk of having any additional claims arise after the bankruptcy case has been completed.

If a company is publicly held, it must also notify the Securities and Exchange Commission (SEC) of the intended filing, as well as of the progress of the bankruptcy case at regular intervals. These regular notifications may be accompanied by ongoing discussions with the SEC about the potential delisting of the company's stock and securities. Also, the SEC may wish to conduct its own investigation into the reasons for the bankruptcy filing, since there may be charges of fraud from investors to which it may wish to respond, or it may wish to file charges of its own.

In addition to the SEC, a publicly held company may find itself negotiating with the stock exchange where its shares are listed for sale. An exchange usually has a rule that a company's stock will be delisted if its price drops below $1 for a period of at least 90 days, though the exchanges typically offer prolonged grace periods while companies find a way to increase the price (such as through a reverse stock split).

A key benefit to a bankrupt entity is its legal right to review all executory contracts and unexpired leases, and either accept or reject them. An executory contract is one where there is enough unfinished activity related to the contract by both parties that if either party were to halt its activities, the other party could claim a breach of contract. A lease is any series of ongoing payments in exchange for the use of property, such as a copier, vehicle, or facility. These two contract definitions will address many types of contracts, leaving a company with an exceptional ability to reconsider a large proportion of its legal agreements, which can result in a significant reduction in its liabilities.

Though a company has the right to accept or reject these types of contracts, it should take its time in doing so, until it is certain of having a viable business plan that can reasonably be expected to take it out of bankruptcy. Otherwise, all payments under an accepted contract will fall into the administrative expense category, where they will be ranked ahead of unsecured creditor claims (which is why the unsecured creditors committee tends to protest contract acceptances). The only downside of waiting to confirm a contract is that the company is still obligated to make payments under the contract's terms while the decision is being made. In short, it is best to string along any contracts that management is fairly sure it *will* confirm, and cancel any that it clearly *does not* want.

If management chooses to reject a contract, the remaining payments under the contract do not disappear—instead, they are shifted into unsecured creditor claims, where they may have a significantly lower chance of being paid. Since some leases have extremely long terms, the total amount of these rejected payments can be so large that they are a substantial proportion of all unsecured claims, thereby reducing the value of all other claims in cases where the amount of eventual payout by the company is limited. To prevent a lessor from being in such a dominant payment position, the bankruptcy law restricts lease claims to the lesser of 15% of all remaining rent payments or one year's rent.

If management chooses to accept a contract, the other party may choose to breach it, using the bankruptcy as an excuse. If so, management can offer to place a large deposit with the other party or take some other similar action in order to give it assurances of being able to complete the contract.

Company management is allowed four months from the bankruptcy petition date to come up with a plan of reorganization, and another two months to have it approved by the court. These time intervals can be extended, sometimes for many additional months, as long as the management team is clearly attempting in good faith to complete a plan. If it does not do so, other parties are allowed to file reorganization plans instead, essentially working around the company.

Devising a reorganization plan can be exceedingly difficult, and certainly time-consuming, because the company must work with the various creditor groups and equity holders in order to gain general agreement to the plan. The cause of the difficulty is the differing objectives of the various groups. For example, secured creditors are primarily concerned with retaining the full value of their collateral and thereby gaining full payment of their claims. Alternatively, "vulture" investors, who have bought the company's debt at a steep discount, are more likely to want a portion of company stock so they can gain operating control. Unsecured creditors generally want a cash payment, even if only for a small percentage of their claims, while shareholders are happy to retain even a small amount of equity. Clearly, gaining any sort of agreement from this diverse group can be quite a chore, and usually only occurs after negotiations have gone on for many months.

The reorganization plan is likely be a variation on one or a combination of several payment options, which are:

- *Long-term cash payments.* Secured lenders are the chief beneficiaries, since it may be years before the company can generate enough cash to pay them off and finally get to the unsecured creditor group. Shareholders can do well under this approach, and may team with the secured shareholders in approving it.

- *Asset liquidation.* Though not necessarily a complete liquidation of the business, this approach is designed to pay off creditors in the near term, leaving a much smaller company. Both the secured and unsecured creditors are likely to support this approach.

- *Debt or capital infusion.* This approach works where there is a general recognition that the company will be of the most value to all parties if it continues to exist to pay off its debts. However, adding equity will dilute the shareholders and adding debt will introduce new secured creditors, so this approach is not highly favored by anyone.

- *Convert debt to equity.* This approach is used when there is no source of cash with which to pay off creditors. Shareholders may be diluted in the extreme, so they will not vote for it. Creditors only use this option as a last resort, since they will not receive any cash payment.

No matter what form of payment is used to satisfy creditors, the plan will follow the same general structure. First, the plan will describe how the various creditors are classified in voting blocks. Similar types of claims are clustered together for voting purposes, so a secured creditor might be grouped into a secured creditor voting block and also in an unsecured creditor voting block to the extent that any of its claim is not supported by collateral. The next section describes how each class of creditor will be treated. For example, secured creditors will be paid in full, while unsecured creditors will receive one-fourth of the amounts owed to them. The plan next describes exactly how the management team proposes to accomplish this payout, which may include a complete operational budget as well as an organizational restructuring, securing new loans, merging with another entity, and so on. There is also a section that specifies exactly which leases and contracts the company has decided to either accept or reject, so there is a formal record in the event that another party brings suit over the issue at a later date.

Next, the management team creates an executive summary of the reorganization plan, called a disclosure statement. This statement is issued to creditors and is used to convince them to vote in favor of the reorganization plan. The contents of the disclosure statement are quite similar to those of an offering memorandum that one would create for an equity offering, as is described in Chapter 15, Obtaining Equity Financing.

Following approval by the court of the disclosure statement, the company then sends it, along with a voting ballot, to those creditors whose claims are impaired (i.e., their claims are unlikely to be paid off in full). The package is not sent to anyone whose claims will be paid in full (e.g., a secured creditor), since the court assumes that they will approve the plan. Creditors will be divided into classes for voting purposes. A class is construed as a group of creditors whose claims will be paid off in the same manner. For example, one group may be offered 30 cents on the dollar, while another group may be offered stock in the company in exchange for the amounts owed to them. In order for the plan to be approved by the creditors, at least one-half of all voting creditors in each class must vote in favor of it, as well as two-thirds of the dollar value of all claims being voted within that class. This is called the *one-half/two-thirds requirement*. For example, if there are 50 creditors within a class and only 8 of them vote, then the one-half/two-thirds rule will only apply to those 8 votes. Thus, a very small fraction of just one class of creditors could potentially have control over whether a plan is accepted.

With the voting completed, the plan will then go to the court for final approval. There are a number of regulatory tests that the court will apply to the plan prior to final approval. Of particular interest to the management team is a "best interests of creditors" test, which must show that the creditors will be better off through the approval of the presented plan than they would be if the company simply liquidated. The management team must have this concept firmly in mind when it first drafts the reorganization plan, so the plan is not ultimately rejected by the court.

If all creditor classes have approved of the plan and all regulatory hurdles have been passed, then the court is likely to approve the plan of reorganization. However, if a creditor class has rejected the plan, the management team has the option of requesting that the plan be accepted by the court anyway, which is called a "cramdown." Under this scenario, at least one creditor class must have approved of the plan, and the management team must provide for full payment of the claims of the creditor classes that have rejected it. This typically means that the claims of any classes having a lower priority than those of the rejecting class will not be paid. In particular, equity holders, who have the lowest priority, will almost certainly receive nothing. In short, a cramdown can only be accomplished by probably eliminating the equity stakes of the original shareholders.

Once the plan is approved, the court officially discharges the company from all the debts that the reorganization plan does not require it to pay. If the company later goes into bankruptcy again, it will only owe creditors for the reduced amount of the debts that were itemized in the reorganization plan.

Given the large number of steps required for a company to complete before a discharge can be obtained from a bankruptcy court, it is obvious that the cost of professional fees through this lengthy process will be substantial, and may consume a large proportion of the estate. Consequently, the management team should be careful not to wait too long before entering bankruptcy protection, while it still has enough funds on hand to pay the professionals and enough money left over to see it through the process. This means that entering bankruptcy is not a last-minute affair, but rather one that is discussed well in advance with legal counsel regarding the appropriate timing of the event.

TAX LIABILITIES IN A BANKRUPTCY*

Taxes are not usually discharged as a result of a bankruptcy filing. Most prepetition tax debts are classified for payment purposes within the creditor and shareholder payment priority list. They are as follows:

- Income taxes for years prior to the bankruptcy
- Income taxes assessed within 240 days prior to the bankruptcy filing
- Income taxes not assessed, but assessable as of the petition date
- Withholding taxes for which the company is liable
- The employer's share of employment taxes on wages
- Excise taxes on any transactions occurring prior to the bankruptcy date

If a company files for liquidation under Chapter 7 of the bankruptcy law, then these taxes will be paid out of whatever company assets are left, once the claims of creditors with a higher priority have been fulfilled. If the entity is under Chapter 11 bankruptcy protection, then it can pay these taxes to the IRS over six years; this will include an interest assessment.

Any taxes that arise during the period when a company is in bankruptcy are considered to be ongoing administrative expenses, and so will be paid at once.

If a company is late in paying the state unemployment tax, it is normally restricted to making a 90% deduction of the amount paid into the federal unemployment fund against the state tax. However, this penalty is waived in the case of a bankrupt company, so that

---

* Adapted with permission from p. 611 of *Ultimate Accountants' Reference* by Bragg (John Wiley & Sons, 2005).

the full amount of the federal unemployment payment can still be taken against the state unemployment tax.

In some cases, the amount of debt canceled while in bankruptcy is considered to be taxable income to the bankrupt entity. If so, the amount of the debt reduction can be used to reduce the basis of any depreciable property (but not more than the total basis of property held, less total liabilities held directly after the debt cancelation). As an alternative, it can be used to (1) offset any net operating loss for the year in which the debt cancellation took place, (2) offset any carryovers of amounts normally used to calculate the general business credit, (3) offset any minimum tax credit, (4) offset any net capital loss and any capital loss carryover, and then (5) offset any passive activity losses. These offsets can be dollar-for-dollar for canceled debt, except for the reduction of *credit* carryovers, which can be reduced at the rate of 33 1/3 cents for every dollar of canceled debt.

A special concern to corporate officers is the payment of payroll withholding taxes. These taxes are held in trust by the company until they are turned over to the government, and so are not considered to be part of the bankrupt company and must still be paid in full even after the bankruptcy filing. The government can bypass the company and collect these funds from the company's officers (which can include anyone who signs the payroll checks, even though this person may not be an officer!). Thus, to avoid personal liability, officers must be sure to remit withheld taxes when due, both before and during a bankruptcy proceeding.

SPECIAL BANKRUPTCY RULES

A company is authorized (and required) to collect payments made to creditors in the 90 days prior to the bankruptcy filing that constitute a larger payment than the creditor would have received if it had been reimbursed with other unsecured creditors subsequent to the bankruptcy. An unsecured creditor who is sued for repayment in this manner then has its claim clumped in with all other unsecured creditors, and will be paid on a pro rata basis along with the others. This rule does not include secured creditors, since they would have been paid the same amount if they had waited until after the bankruptcy for reimbursement. The 90-day period used for this rule is extended to a full year for cases where payments were made to company insiders.

Part of the process of operational stabilization is a review of all liens on company property. If a creditor has publicly registered a notice with a state official, such as the secretary of state, that it has a lien on company property, then the company is obligated to acknowledge the lien and categorize the creditor as a secured creditor. This person is much more likely to receive full reimbursement for all collateralized debts. However, if the creditor has not publicly registered such a notice, then any lien it has on company property will be stripped away, leaving the creditor no better off for reimbursement purposes than the other unsecured creditors. This rule applies even if company management *knows* that the creditor has a lien on company assets.

One crucial instance where creditors are not barred from further collection activity is when a secured creditor claims that further use by the company of its collateral will gradually diminish the amount of its security interest. For example, a loan that is collateralized by a company's inventory will gradually become more at risk of not being repaid if the level of inventory drops subsequent to the bankruptcy filing. In this case, the creditor can require the company to replace the diminished collateral with other forms of collateral by cash payments that reduce the amount of debt or by some other negotiated solution.

THE BANKRUPTCY ACT OF 2005

The Bankruptcy Act of 2005 was primarily intended to modify personal bankruptcy situations, but also contains several provisions that have a strong impact on corporate bankruptcies. First, a company entering bankruptcy must propose a reorganization plan within 180 days, after which creditors can propose a plan. Second, a company has a maximum of 210 days in which to assume or reject a lease. Third, retention pay for executives is capped at 10 times the average amount earned by company employees; and such retention pay can only be granted if an executive has proof of a job offer that pays at least as much as his or her current compensation. Finally, suppliers who are not paid for goods they shipped to the company within 20 days of its bankruptcy filing can obtain a priority claim on those goods, requiring them to be paid in full before a court accepts a reorganization plan. Suppliers can also reclaim any unpaid goods that were shipped to the company within 45 days of its bankruptcy filing.

In short, this law clearly puts more power in the hands of creditors, while also making it more difficult for companies to reorganize themselves in bankruptcy. Instead, it is now more likely for companies to liquidate themselves, since they are more likely to lose key executives, make rushed decisions on lease retentions, and lose key inventory to suppliers.

ALTERNATIVES TO BANKRUPTCY

Bankruptcy is an exceedingly expensive undertaking, so the CFO may want to consider alternatives prior to taking the plunge. One option is to ask creditors for *extensions* on payments. Creditors who grant this request may ask for collateral in return, which may cause a chain reaction of additional negotiations with other entities that already have senior collateral positions on assets. The CFO may wish to deal with creditors individually in regard to extensions, in case some can be persuaded to accept longer payment terms than others. If creditors band together into a creditor's committee, then a standard repayment period is the more likely result.

A slightly more drastic alternative (for creditors) is for the CFO to approach them about a *composition*, which is their acceptance of partial payment on debts owed. Though creditors will obviously not be paid in full, they may accept this alternative over the company's bankruptcy, on the grounds that they will gain a greater distribution than would be the case in bankruptcy. This approach is least acceptable to secured creditors, who may stand to gain full payment on debts owed if they wait for bankruptcy proceedings, on the assumption that the resale value of their attached collateral at least matches the amounts owed to them.

Creditors may require some representation in management affairs or on the Board of Directors in exchange for these reductions or delays in payments. Though the CFO may experience some loss of control, this is typically well worth the reduction in expenses associated with a bankruptcy.

SUMMARY

The CFO should come away from this chapter having learned two key points. First, bankruptcy can be very expensive, due to the number of bankruptcy professionals who must be employed. Second, the number of steps and outside parties involved in a bankruptcy make this a very long process to successfully conclude. For both of these reasons, it is critically important that a company enter bankruptcy with enough cash to see it through the process. This means that a bankruptcy should be planned well in advance, perhaps as one of a variety of strategic alternatives, and entered as soon as it becomes the most viable approach to resolving business issues. Conversely, the worst way to enter bankruptcy is after having unsuccessfully tried all other alternatives, used up all cash, and obtained (and exhausted) every possible form of credit. This latter approach nearly always results in a company's eventual liquidation rather than its successful emergence from bankruptcy at some point in the future.

PART 7

APPENDICES

NEW CFO CHECKLIST

A person who has been newly hired into the CFO position may feel overwhelmed by the vast number of tasks to be completed, and may wonder where to begin. The attached list gives some guidance about the priority of tasks.

The first few priorities are heavily stacked in favor of creating and improving the accuracy of a cash forecasting system, which requires a detailed knowledge of payables, receivables, debt payments, contracts, and capital expenditures. The new CFO must have a firm grasp of this information before proceeding to any other steps, since a company without cash will not survive long enough for the CFO to address anything else.

A key priority falling immediately after the cash forecasting system is a detailed review of all current contracts. The CFO should read these personally, with the objective of finding any contract terms that have a potential to put the company in jeopardy or at least have a significant downward impact on its profitability.

The next group of priorities involve the establishment of measurement systems, so the CFO can see what problems are likely to arise and how this can impact the priority of his or her future activities.

Next in line is a complete review of the CFO staff's capabilities, work schedules, and training requirements. Though an inexperienced CFO may be tempted to advance this task to the topmost priority, it is listed lower here because staff development is more of a mid-range to long-term goal. It has little impact on the very short-term performance of the CFO's assigned areas, whereas the preceding items must be completed very quickly, so the CFO can see which areas are at risk and require the most immediate attention.

Activities following the staff development priorities can be shifted in priority, depending on the company-specific situation. However, it is highly recommended that the CFO follow the exact priorities through and including the staff development action items, since completing these tasks will likely give the CFO the best possible handle on the critical short-term needs of the organization.

Priority	Action	Description
1	Forecast cash	Any other action is useless if the company runs out of money, so immediately create a cash forecast and initially revise it on a weekly basis. Continually modify the model to improve its accuracy.

Priority	Action	Description
2	Establish daily bank reconciliations	The cash forecast will not be too accurate if the underlying bank balances are inaccurate, so arrange to have Internet access to daily bank balances and ensure that a daily reconciliation is made with this information.
3	Review payables	Go over not only all current payables, but conduct a full one-year review of the vendor ledger with the payables staff. The objective is to understand the nature, amount, and timing of payments. This information is very useful for increasing the accuracy of the cash forecast.
4	Review collections	Go over all current accounts receivable with the collections staff, and then expand the review to all major customers, even if there are no receivables currently outstanding. This gives an excellent overview of cash inflows for the cash forecast.
5	Review debt agreements	Personally review the debt agreements to verify the dates when payments come due, the applicable interest rates, and particularly any covenants that can result in the debt being called by the lender. This knowledge prevents any unexpected surprises from occurring in the cash forecasting system.
6	Review capital expenditures	The last priority that feeds into the cash forecasting system is capital expenditures. This has the lowest priority of the cash-related activities, since this is typically a discretionary payment. The CFO should be aware of which expenditures are critical short-term items that probably cannot be delayed, and which can potentially be shifted further into the future.
7	Review contracts	The CFO and legal counsel should obtain copies of all current contracts and review them in great detail to ensure that there are no hidden surprises, such as unexpected liabilities or potential lawsuits. This is a problem in a large number of situations, and is worthy of review very early in a CFO's tenure.
8	Establish metrics	Establish a set of initial metrics on a multimonth trend line in order to determine the company's performance in a number of areas. This should certainly include days of receivables, payables, and inventory, as well as gross and operating margins, the overall breakeven point, and any metrics required by loan covenants. The exact measures used will vary by industry. The intent is to give the CFO early knowledge of potential performance issues.
9	Create sales report	The CFO must be aware of anticipated sales for at least the current month, as well as changes in the backlog. This should be included in a weekly sales report that goes not only to the CFO but to the entire management team.
10	Create flash report	The CFO should incorporate the total periodic sales listed on the sales report in a flash report that itemizes the latest expectation for total financial results for the reporting period. As was the case for the sales report, this should be issued weekly, and should go to the entire management team. By completing these top ten priorities, the CFO has gained a knowledge of all aspects of cash flow, any contractual problems, and short-term financial results.

Priority	Action	Description
11	Review the staff	With short-term issues taken care of, it is now time to deal with the CFO's primary long-term asset— the staff. This review should include an examination of all resumes for employees reporting either directly or indirectly to the CFO, face-to-face meetings with them, and group sessions. The outcome should be a clear understanding of each person's capabilities and aspirations, training needs, and weaknesses.
12	Review department efficiencies	Develop metrics for those functions reporting to the CFO, and determine where efficiencies are in the most need of improvement. Based on the initial staff review, create a plan to improve efficiency levels and begin its implementation.
13	Establish training schedules	Based on the staff review and departmental efficiency plans, create a training schedule for each employee that is precisely tailored to how that person fits into the CFO's plans for increasing departmental efficiency.
14	Delegate tasks	Based on information gleaned from the last three tasks, the CFO should consider a gradual shifting of selected tasks to subordinates, allowing him or her more time to delve into the priorities yet to come. If there are no competent staff to whom anything can be delegated, then the next step will be staff replacement in order to upgrade staff quality. With these basic staff-management priorities initiated, the CFO can shift to the identification and resolution of risk issues.
15	Review auditors' management letter	Outside auditors usually issue a letter to management at the conclusion of each audit that itemizes control and other problems that they feel should be addressed. This is an excellent source of information for the new CFO who wants a quick grasp of potential problem areas.
16	Review internal audit reports	Internal audit reports are similar to the auditors' management letter in providing information about potential areas of risk, though many firms do not have internal audit teams or target the activities of their teams at only a small number of areas each year. If available, the CFO should obtain and read these reports.
17	Review controls	The CFO should conduct a general overview of all financial controls, based on the information contained in the last two priority items, plus an examination of control flowcharts for all key accounting and financial processes. This should result in the identification of control weaknesses that the CFO can fix.
18	Review insurance policies	The CFO should retain legal counsel to review all outstanding insurance policies, as well as to conduct an assessment of all liabilities for which additional insurance coverage may be required. This is a technical area for which the CFO will probably not be entirely qualified, hence the need for an expert. The CFO should evaluate the expert's report and change insurance as necessary.

Priority	Action	Description
19	Review other risks	The CFO should meet with other department managers to assess any other types of risk to which the company is subject, and devise a risk management strategy to compensate for each one. This concludes the priorities addressing risk management. The CFO can then turn to the creation of better reporting systems.
20	Review financial disclosures	If the company is publicly held, the CFO should compare all current SEC filing requirements to what the company is actually reporting and adjust reports as necessary. This chore can be given to a qualified subordinate or even the outside auditors.
21	Revise management reports	The CFO should now have enough preliminary knowledge of company operations to see if the management reports being issued by the accounting and finance departments contain the right kind of information needed to properly run the company. It is likely that a substantial overhaul of the existing reporting system will be necessary.
22	Review computer system requirements	The creation of new management reports may uncover flaws in the underlying computer systems, such as data storage capacity problems or the inability to automatically collect various types of key information. This is a good time for the CFO to assess the requirements of these systems and initiate their long-term overhaul, if necessary.
23	Conduct cost review	The CFO should use group and individual sessions with the accounting staff, as well as with most department managers, in order to walk through the entire income statement and devise both short- and long-term plans for reducing costs.
24	Review finance policies	Company profits can be linked to the finance department's policies on the extension of credit, allowed investment options, and taxation issues. The CFO should work with impacted departments (such as the credit policy with the sales manager) to determine the appropriate policies to use in these areas.
25	Create budgeting process	The priority for budgeting may be accelerated if the CFO begins work near or in the midst of the standard budgeting period. This process should include an evaluation of how well the process has worked in the past, how it supports company strategy, and how it supports the management compensation plan. A key aspect is the creation of a financing plan, so the CFO has some idea of the timing and amount of funds that may be needed.
26	Meet with lenders	This priority may be substantially accelerated if the company is in substantial difficulties when the CFO is hired. Otherwise, the CFO should first create a financing budget and then meet with lenders to see how they can assist in accommodating the company's needs.
27	Meet with investment bankers	The result of the budgeting process is not just a plan for obtaining debt (see last two priorities), but also the acquisition of more equity, if necessary. The CFO should work with the company's investment bankers to determine the state of the equity markets and the cost to obtain more equity.

Priority	Action	Description
28	Review inventory aging	If the company has substantial assets tied up in inventory, the CFO should take a significant amount of time to physically review the state of the inventory, where it is stored, how old it is, and how much appears to be reduced in value. These steps are necessary because inventory is subject to reporting fraud and shrinkage, can be grossly overvalued, and in short can cause reporting nightmares for the CFO if not properly kept track of.
29	Review document retention systems	Last in priority is a review of document retention systems. Some CFOs may ignore this item entirely, but inadequate paperwork storage can cause major problems in the event of any type of audit, which may result in fines by government entities. Though a low priority, it must be addressed at some point.

The preceding priority list should not lead one to believe that an item, once completed, does not have to be addressed again. On the contrary, additional problem areas will likely be revealed during the completion of each priority item that will require additional work to address. In addition, any system is likely to degrade over time, requiring repeated reviews by the CFO to ensure that it is operating properly. In short, the new CFO will find that he or she will repeatedly cycle through this list.

PERFORMANCE MEASUREMENT CHECKLIST*

This appendix contains all of the measurements that a CFO would need in order to determine the financial condition of a company as well as the operational performance of the accounting department. It is intended to be a quick reference for the reader who needs to find a formula as soon as possible.

The following measurements are listed in alphabetical order within these general categories:

- Asset utilization
- Operating performance
- Cash flow
- Liquidity
- Capital structure and solvency
- Return on investment
- Market performance
- Measurements for the accounting/finance department

In some cases, multiple variations on the same measurement are shown.

Name	Formula
Accumulated Depreciation to Fixed Assets Ratio	$\dfrac{\text{Accumulated Depreciation}}{\text{Total Fixed Assets}}$
Asset Utilization Measurements	
Breakeven Point	$\dfrac{\text{Total Operating Expenses}}{\text{Average Gross Margin Percentage}}$
	$\dfrac{\text{Total Operating Expenses} - (\text{Depreciation} + \text{Amortization} + \text{Other Noncash Expenses})}{\text{Average Gross Margin Percentage}}$

---

* Adapted with permission from Appendix B of *Business Ratios and Formulas* by Bragg (John Wiley & Sons, 2002).

Name	Formula
Foreign Exchange Ratios	$$\dfrac{\text{Foreign Currency Gains and Losses}}{\text{Net Income}}$$
	$$\dfrac{\text{Foreign Currency Gains and Losses}}{\text{Total Sales}}$$
Fringe Benefits to Wages and Salaries Expense	$$\dfrac{\text{Life Insurance} + \text{Medical Insurance} + \text{Pension Funding Expense} + \text{Other Benefits}}{\text{Wages} + \text{Salaries} + \text{Payroll Taxes}}$$
Goodwill to Assets Ratio	$$\dfrac{\text{Unamortized Goodwill}}{\text{Total Assets}}$$
Interest Expense to Debt Ratio	$$\dfrac{\text{Interest Expense}}{(\text{Short-Term Debt}) + (\text{Long-Term Debt})}$$
Investment Turnover	$$\dfrac{\text{Sales}}{\text{Stockholders' Equity} + \text{Long-Term Liabilities}}$$
Margin of Safety	$$\dfrac{\text{Current Sales Level} - \text{Breakeven Point}}{\text{Current Sales Level}}$$
Overhead Rate	$$\dfrac{\text{Total Overhead Expenses}}{\text{Direct Labor}}$$
	$$\dfrac{\text{Total Overhead Expenses}}{\text{Total Machine Hours}}$$
Overhead of Cost of Sales Ratio	$$\dfrac{\text{Total Overhead Expenses}}{\text{Cost of Goods Sold}}$$
	$$\dfrac{\text{Total Overhead Expenses}}{\text{Direct Materials} + \text{Direct Labor}}$$
	$$\dfrac{\text{Total Overhead Expenses}}{\text{Direct Materials}}$$
Repairs and Maintenance Expense to Fixed Assets Ratio	$$\dfrac{\text{Total Repairs and Maintenance Expense}}{\text{Total Fixed Assets Before Depreciation}}$$
Sales Backlog Ratio	$$\dfrac{\text{Backlog of Orders Received}}{\text{Sales}}$$
	$$\dfrac{\text{Total Backlog}}{\text{Annual Sales/360 Days}}$$
Sales Expenses to Sales Ratio	$$\dfrac{\text{Sales Salaries} + \text{Commissions} + \text{Sales Travel Expenses} + \text{Other Sales Expenses}}{\text{Sales}}$$
Days of Working Capital	$$\dfrac{(\text{Accounts Receivable} + \text{Inventory} - \text{Accounts Payable})}{\text{Net Sales}}$$
Sales per Person	$$\dfrac{\text{Annualized Revenue}}{\text{Total Full-Time Equivalents}}$$
Sales Returns to Gross Sales Ratio	$$\dfrac{\text{Total Sales Returns}}{\text{Gross Sales}}$$

Name	Formula
Sales to Administrative Expenses Ratio	$$\dfrac{\text{Annualized Net Sales}}{\text{Total General and Administrative Expenses}}$$
Sales to Equity Ratio	$$\dfrac{\text{Annual Net Sales}}{\text{Total Equity}}$$
Sales to Fixed Assets Ratio	$$\dfrac{\text{Annualized Net Sales}}{\text{Total Fixed Assets}}$$
	$$\dfrac{\text{Annualized Net Sales}}{\text{Total Fixed Assets Prior to Accumulated Depreciation}}$$
Sales to Working Capital Ratio	$$\dfrac{\text{Annualized Net Sales}}{(\text{Accounts Receivable} + \text{Inventory} - \text{Accounts Payable})}$$
Tax Rate Percentage	$$\dfrac{\text{Income Tax Paid}}{\text{Before-Tax Income}}$$
	$$\dfrac{\text{Income Tax Expense}}{\text{Before-Tax Income}}$$

Operating Performance Measurements

Name	Formula
Gross Profit Index	$$\dfrac{\dfrac{\text{Gross Profit in Period Two}}{\text{Sales in Period Two}}}{\dfrac{\text{Gross Profit in Period One}}{\text{Sales in Period One}}}$$
Core Growth Rate	$$\dfrac{((\text{Current Annual Revenue} - \text{Annual Revenue 5 Years Ago} - \text{Acquired Revenue} - \text{Revenue Recognition Changes}))/(\text{Annual Revenue 5 Years Ago}}{5}$$ $$- \text{Average Annual Price Increase}$$
Gross Profit Percentage	$$\dfrac{\text{Revenue} - (\text{Overhead} + \text{Direct Materials} + \text{Direct Labor})}{\text{Revenue}}$$
	$$\dfrac{\text{Revenue} - \text{Direct Materials}}{\text{Revenue}}$$
Investment Income Percentage	$$\dfrac{\text{Dividend Income} + \text{Interest Income}}{\text{Carrying Value of Investments}}$$
Net Income Percentage	$$\dfrac{\text{Net Income}}{\text{Revenue}}$$
Operating Assets Ratio	$$\dfrac{\text{Assets Used to Create Revenue}}{\text{Total Assets}}$$
Operating Leverage Ratio	$$\dfrac{\text{Sales} - \text{Variable Expenses}}{\text{Operating Income}}$$
Operating Profit Percentage	$$\dfrac{\text{Sales} - (\text{Cost of Goods Sold} + \text{Sales, General and Administrative Expenses})}{\text{Sales}}$$

Name	Formula
Profit per Person	$$\frac{\text{Net Profit}}{\text{Total Full-Time Equivalents}}$$
Sales Margin	$$\frac{\text{Gross Margin} - \text{Sales Expenses}}{\text{Gross Sales}}$$
Sales to Operating Income Ratio	$$\frac{\text{Operating Income}}{(\text{Net Sales} - \text{Investment Income})}$$

Cash-Flow Measurements

Name	Formula
Cash Flow Coverage Ratio	$$\frac{\text{Total Debt Payments} + \text{Dividend Payments} + \text{Capital Expenditures}}{\text{Net Income} + \text{Noncash Expenses} - \text{Noncash Sales}}$$
Cash Flow from Operations	$$\frac{\text{Income from Operations} + \text{Noncash Expenses} - \text{Noncash Sales}}{\text{Income from Operations}}$$
	$$\frac{\text{Net Income} + \text{Noncash Expenses} - \text{Noncash Sales}}{\text{Net Income}}$$
Cash Flow Return on Assets	$$\frac{\text{Net Income} + \text{Noncash Expenses} - \text{Noncash Sales}}{\text{Total Assets}}$$
Cash Flow Return on Sales	$$\frac{\text{Net Income} + \text{Noncash Expenses} - \text{Noncash Sales}}{\text{Total Sales}}$$
Cash Flow to Debt Ratio	$$\frac{\text{Net Income} + \text{Noncash Expenses} - \text{Noncash Sales}}{\text{Debt} + \text{Lease Obligations}}$$
	$$\frac{\text{Net Income} + \text{Noncash Expenses} - \text{Noncash Sales}}{\text{Total Long-Term Debt Payments for the Period}}$$
Cash Flow to Fixed Asset Requirements	$$\frac{\text{Net Income} + \text{Noncash Expenses} - \text{Noncash Sales}}{\text{Budgeted Fixed Asset Purchases}}$$
	$$\frac{\text{Net Income} + \text{Noncash Expenses} - \text{Noncash Sales} - \text{Dividends} - \text{Principal Payments}}{\text{Budgeted Fixed Asset Purchases}}$$
Cash Receipts to Billed Sales and Progress Payments	$$\frac{\text{Cash Receipts}}{\text{Billed Sales} + \text{Billed Progress Payments}}$$
Cash Reinvestment Ratio	$$\frac{\text{Increase in Fixed Assets} + \text{Increase in Working Capital}}{\text{Net Income} + \text{Noncash Expenses} - \text{Noncash Sales} - \text{Dividends}}$$
Cash to Current Assets Ratio	$$\frac{\text{Cash} + \text{Short-Term Marketable Securities}}{\text{Current Assets}}$$

Name	Formula
Cash to Current Liabilities Ratio	$$\frac{\text{Cash} + \text{Short-Term Marketable Securities}}{\text{Current Liabilities}}$$
Cash to Working Capital Ratio	$$\frac{\text{Cash} + \text{Short-Term Marketable Securities}}{\text{Current Assets} - \text{Current Liabilities}}$$
Dividend Payout Ratio	$$\frac{\text{Total Dividend Payments}}{\text{Net Income} + \text{Noncash Expenses} - \text{Noncash Sales}}$$
Expense Coverage Days	$$\frac{\text{Cash} + \text{Short-Term Marketable Securities} + \text{Accounts Receivable}}{\text{Annual Cash Expenditures } 360}$$
Fixed Charge Coverage	$$\frac{\text{Fixed Expenses} + \text{Fixed Payments}}{\text{Cash Flow from Operations}}$$
Stock Price to Cash Flow Ratio	$$\frac{(\text{Stock Price}) \times (\text{Number of Shares Outstanding})}{\text{Earnings Before Interest, Taxes, Depreciation, and Amortization}}$$

Liquidity Measurements

Name	Formula
Accounts Payable Days	$$\frac{\text{Accounts Payable}}{\text{Purchases}/360}$$
Accounts Payable Turnover	$$\frac{\text{Total Purchases}}{\text{Ending Accounts Payable Balance}}$$
Accounts Receivable Investment	$$\frac{\text{Average Days to Payment}}{360 \text{ Days}} \times \frac{\text{Annual Credit Sales} \times (1 - \text{Gross}}{\text{Margin \%}) \times (\text{Cost of Capital})}$$
Accounts Receivable Turnover	$$\frac{\text{Annualized Credit Sales}}{\text{Average Accounts Receivable} + \text{Notes Payable by Customers}}$$
Altman's Z-Score Bankruptcy Prediction Formula	$(\text{Operating Income}/\text{Total Assets}) \times 3.3$ $+$ $(\text{Sales}/\text{Total Assets}) \times 0.999$ $+$ $(\text{Market Value of Common Stock} + \text{Preferred Stock}/\text{Total Liabilities}) \times 0.6$ $+$ $(\text{Working Capital}/\text{Total Assets}) \times 1.2$ $+$ $(\text{Retained Earnings}/\text{Total Assets}) \times 1.4$
Average Receivable Collection Period	$$\frac{\text{Average Accounts Receivable}}{\text{Annual Sales}/365}$$
Cash Ratio	$$\frac{\text{Cash} + \text{Short-Term Marketable Securities}}{\text{Current Liabilities}}$$
Current Liability Ratio	$$\frac{\text{Current Liabilities}}{\text{Total Liabilities}}$$
Current Ratio	$$\frac{\text{Current Assets}}{\text{Current Liabilities}}$$

Name	Formula
Days Delinquent Sales Outstanding	$$\frac{365 \text{ Annualized Credit Sales from Delinquent Accounts}}{\text{Average Delinquent Accounts Receivable}}$$
Days' Sales in Receivables Index	$$\frac{\dfrac{\text{Accounts Receivable in Period Two}}{\text{Sales in Period Two}}}{\dfrac{\text{Accounts Receivable in Period One}}{\text{Sales in Period One}}}$$
Defensive Interval Ratio	$$\frac{\text{Cash} + \text{Marketable Securities} + \text{Accounts Receivable}}{\text{Expected Daily Operating Expenses}}$$
Ending Receivable Balance	$$\text{Average Receivable Collection Period} \times \frac{\text{Sales Forecast for Period}}{\text{Days in Period}}$$
Inventory to Sales Ratio	$$\frac{\text{Sales}}{\text{Inventory}}$$
Inventory to Working Capital Ratio	$$\frac{\text{Inventory}}{\text{Accounts Receivable} + \text{Inventory} - \text{Accounts Payable}}$$
Collection Effectiveness Index	$$\frac{\text{Beginning Receivables} + \text{Credit Sales} - \text{Ending Total Receivables}}{\text{Beginning Receivables} + \text{Credit Sales} - \text{Ending Current Receivables}} \times 100$$
Inventory Turnover	$$\frac{\text{Cost of Goods Sold}}{\text{Inventory}}$$ $$365 / \frac{\text{Cost of Goods Sold}}{\text{Inventory}}$$ $$\frac{\text{Direct Materials}}{\text{Raw Materials Inventory}}$$
Liquidity Index	$$\frac{(\text{Accounts Receivable} \times \text{Days to Liquidate}) + (\text{Inventory} \times \text{Days to Liquidate})}{\text{Accounts Receivable} + \text{Inventory}}$$
Noncurrent Assets to Noncurrent Liabilities Ratio	$$\frac{\text{Noncurrent Assets}}{\text{Noncurrent Liabilities}}$$
Quick Ratio	$$\frac{\text{Cash} + \text{Marketable Securities} + \text{Accounts Receivable}}{\text{Current Liabilities}}$$
Required Current Liabilities to Total Current Liabilities Ratio	$$\frac{\text{Current Liabilities with Required Payment Dates}}{\text{Total Current Liabilities}}$$
Risky Asset Conversion Ratio	$$\frac{\text{Cost of Assets with Minimal Cash Conversion Value}}{\text{Total Assets}}$$
Sales to Current Assets Ratio	$$\frac{\text{Sales}}{\text{Current Assets}}$$

Name	Formula
Short-Term Debt to Long-Term Debt Ratio	$\dfrac{\text{Total Short-Term Debt}}{\text{Total Long-Term Debt}}$
Working Capital Productivity	$\dfrac{\text{Annual Sales}}{\text{Working Capital}}$
Working Capital to Debt Ratio	$\dfrac{\text{Cash} + \text{Accounts Receivable} + \text{Inventory} - \text{Accounts Payable}}{\text{Debt}}$

Capital Structure and Solvency Measurements

Accruals to Assets Ratio	$\dfrac{\text{Change in Working Capital} - \text{Change in Cash} - \text{Change in Depreciation}}{\text{Change in Total Assets}}$
Asset Quality Index	$\dfrac{1 - \dfrac{\text{Current Assets in Period Two} + \text{Net Fixed Assets in Period Two}}{\text{Total Assets in Period Two}}}{1 - \dfrac{\text{Current Assets in Period One} + \text{Net Fixed Assets in Period One}}{\text{Total Assets in Period One}}}$
Debt Coverage Ratio	$\dfrac{\text{Earnings Before Interest and Taxes}}{\text{Interest} + \dfrac{\text{Scheduled Principal Payments}}{(1 - \text{Tax Rate})}}$
Debt to Equity Ratio	$\dfrac{\text{Debt}}{\text{Equity}}$
Funded Capital Ratio	$\dfrac{\text{Stockholders' Equity} + \text{Long-Term Debt}}{\text{Fixed Assets}}$
Issued Shares to Authorized Shares	$\dfrac{\text{Issued Shares} + \text{Stock Options} + \text{Stock Warrants} + \text{Convertible Securities}}{\text{Total Authorized Shares}}$
Preferred Stock to Total Stockholders' Equity	$\dfrac{\text{Preferred Stock}}{\text{Stockholders' Equity}}$
Retained Earnings to Stockholders' Equity	$\dfrac{\text{Retained Earnings}}{\text{Total Stockholders' Equity}}$
Times Interest Earned	$\dfrac{\text{Average Cash Flow}}{\text{Average Interest Expense}}$
Times Preferred Dividend Earned	$\dfrac{\text{Net Income}}{\text{Preferred Dividend}}$

Return on Investment Measurements

Book Value per Share	$\dfrac{\text{Total Equity} - \text{Cost to Liquidate Preferred Stock}}{\text{Total Number of Common Shares Outstanding}}$
Dividend Payout Ratio	$\dfrac{\text{Dividend per Share}}{\text{Earnings per Share}}$

Name	Formula
Dividend Yield Ratio	$\dfrac{\text{Dividend per Share}}{\text{Market Price per Share}}$
Earnings per Share	$\dfrac{\text{Net Income} - \text{Dividends on Preferred Stock}}{\text{Number of Outstanding Common Shares} + \text{Common Stock Equivalents}}$
Economic Value Added	(Net Investment) × (Actual Return on Investment − Percentage Cost of Capital)
Equity Growth Rate	$\dfrac{\text{Net Income} - \text{Common Stock Dividends} - \text{Preferred Stock Dividends}}{\text{Beginning Common Stockholders' Equity}}$
Financial Leverage Index	$\dfrac{\text{Return on Equity}}{\text{Return on Assets}}$
Net Worth	Total Assets − Total Liabilities
	$\dfrac{\text{Total Assets} - \text{Total Liabilities} - \text{Preferred Stock Dividends}}{\text{Total Outstanding Common Shares}}$
Percentage Change in Earnings per Share	$\dfrac{\text{Incremental Change in Earnings per Share}}{\text{Earnings per Share from Previous Period}}$
Return on Assets Employed	$\dfrac{\text{Net Profit}}{\text{Total Assets}}$
Return on Common Equity	$\dfrac{\text{Net Income} - \text{Preferred Stock Dividends}}{\text{Common Stockholders' Equity}}$
Return on Equity Percentage	$\dfrac{\text{Net Income}}{\text{Total Equity}}$
Return on Operating Assets	$\dfrac{\text{Net Income}}{\text{Assets Used to Create Revenue}}$
Tangible Book Value	Book Value − (Goodwill + Other Intangibles)

Market Performance Measurements

Name	Formula
Capitalization Rate	$\dfrac{\text{Earnings per Share}}{\text{Market Price per Share}}$
Cost of Capital	$\dfrac{\text{Interest Expense} \times (1 - \text{Tax Rate})}{\text{Amount of Debt} - \text{Debt Acquisition Fees} + \text{Premium on Debt} - \text{Discount on Debt}}$ $+$ $\dfrac{\text{Interest Expense}}{\text{Amount of Preferred Stock}}$ $+$ Risk-Free Return + (Beta × (Average Stock Return − Risk-Free Return))
Insider Stock Buy-Sell Ratio	$\dfrac{\text{Number of Stock Sale Transactions by Insiders}}{\text{Number of Stock Purchase Transactions by Insiders}}$

Name	Formula
Market Value Added	(Number of Common Shares Outstanding $\times$ Share Price) + (Number of Preferred Shares Outstanding $\times$ Share Price) $-$ (Book Value of Invested Capital)
Price/Earnings Ratio	$$\frac{\text{Average Common Stock Price}}{\text{Net Income per Share}}$$
Enterprise Value/Earnings Ratio	$$\frac{(\text{Total Shares} \times \text{Stock Price}) + \text{Debt} - \text{Cash} - \text{Marketable Securities}}{\text{Net Income} - \text{Interest Expense}}$$
Sales to Stock Price Ratio	$$\frac{\text{Annual Net Sales}}{\text{Average Common Stock Price}}$$
Stock Options to Common Shares Ratio	$$\frac{\text{Total Stock Options}}{\text{Total Common Shares Outstanding}}$$ $$\frac{\text{Total Vested Stock Options}}{\text{Total Common Shares Outstanding}}$$ $$\frac{\text{Total Vested Options in the Money}}{\text{Total Common Shares Outstanding}}$$

Measurements for the Accounting/Finance Department

Name	Formula
Average Employee Expense Report Turnaround Time	(Date of Payment to Employees) $-$ (Date of Expense Report Receipt)
Average Time to Issue Invoices	$$\frac{(\text{Sum of Invoice Dates}) - (\text{Sum of Shipment Dates})}{\text{Number of Invoices Issued}}$$
Bad Debt Percentage	$$\frac{\text{Total Bad Debt Dollars Recognized}}{\text{Total Outstanding Accounts Receivable}}$$ $$\frac{\text{Total Bad Debt Dollars Recognized}}{\text{Total Credit Sales}}$$
Borrowing Base Usage Percentage	$$\frac{\text{Amount of Debt Outstanding}}{(\text{Accounts Receivable} \times \text{Allowable Percentage}) + (\text{Inventory} \times \text{Allowable Percentage})}$$
Brokerage Fee Percentage	$$\frac{\text{Bank/Broker Transaction Fees Charged}}{\text{Total Funds Invested}}$$ $$\frac{\text{Bank/Broker Transaction Fees Charged}}{\text{Number of Bank/Broker Transactions Processed}}$$
Cost of Credit	Discount % / (100 $-$ Discount%) $\times$ (360/(Full Allowed Payment Days $-$ Discount Days))
Earnings Rate on Invested Funds	$$\frac{\text{Interest Earned} + \text{Increase in Market Value of Securities}}{\text{Total Funds Invested}}$$
Internal Audit Efficiency	$$\frac{\text{Number of Internal Audits Completed}}{\text{Number of Internal Audits Planned}}$$

Name	Formula
Internal Audit Efficiency	$\dfrac{\text{Number of Internal Audits Completed}}{\text{Number of Internal Audits Planned}}$
Internal Audit Savings to Cost Percentage	$\dfrac{\text{Internal Audit Recommended Savings}}{\text{Internal Audit Expense}}$
Payroll Transaction Fees per Employee	$\dfrac{\text{Total Payroll Outsourcing Fee per Payroll}}{\text{Total Number of Employees Itemized in Payroll}}$
Percent of Cash Applied on Day of Receipt	$\dfrac{\text{Dollars of Cash Receipts Applied on Day of Receipt}}{\text{Total Dollars of Incoming Cash on Day of Receipt}}$
Unmatched Receipts Exposure	$\dfrac{\text{Total Balance in Unmatched Receipts Suspense Account}}{\text{Total Accounts Receivable Balance}}$
Percent of Receivables Over XX Days Old	$\dfrac{\text{Dollar Amount of Outstanding Receivables } \rangle \text{ XX Days Old}}{\text{Total Dollars of Outstanding Receivables}}$
Percentage Collected of Dollar Volume Assigned	$\dfrac{\text{Cash Received from Collection Agency}}{\text{Total Accounts Receivable Assigned to Collection Agency}}$
Percentage of Payment Discounts Missed	$\dfrac{\text{Number of Payment Discounts Missed}}{\text{Total Number of Payment Discounts Available}}$
Percentage of Tax Filing Dates Missed	$\dfrac{\text{Total Number of Tax Returns Filed Late}}{\text{Total Number of Tax Returns Filed}}$
Proportion of Products Costed Prior to Release	$\dfrac{\text{Number of Products Costed Prior to Release}}{\text{Total Number of Products Released}}$

DUE DILIGENCE CHECKLIST

The general topic of mergers and acquisitions was covered in Chapter 21, including a lengthy discussion of the key topics to address in a due diligence proceeding. This appendix includes a more detailed checklist that one can use as a master list, picking only those topics that appear to be relevant to the due diligence tasks at hand. They are:

INDUSTRY OVERVIEW

1. What is the size of the industry?
2. How is the industry segmented?
3. What is the industry's projected growth and profitability?
4. What are the factors affecting growth and profitability?
5. What are the trends in the number of competitors and their size, product innovation, distribution, finances, regulation, and product liability?

CORPORATE OVERVIEW

1. When and where was the company founded, and by whom?
2. What is its history of product development?
3. What is the history of the management team?
4. Has the corporate location changed?
5. Have there been ownership changes?
6. Have there been acquisitions or divestitures?
7. What is its financial history?

ORGANIZATION AND GENERAL CORPORATE ISSUES

1. Obtain the articles of incorporation and bylaws. Review for the existence of pre-emptive rights, rights of first refusal, registration rights, or any other rights related to the issuance or registration of securities.

2. Review the bylaws for any unusual provisions affecting shareholder rights or restrictions on ownership, transfer, or voting of shares.

3. Review the terms associated with any preferred stock or unexercised warrants.

4. Describe any antitakeover provisions.

5. Obtain certificates of good standing for the company and all significant subsidiaries.

6. Obtain the minutes from all shareholder meetings for the past five years. Review for proper notice prior to meetings, the existence of a quorum, and proper voting procedures; verify that stock issuances have been authorized; verify that insider transactions have been approved; verify that officers have been properly elected; verify that shares are properly approved and reserved for stock option and purchase plans.

7. Obtain the minutes of the executive committee and audit committee for the past five years, as well as the minutes of any other special Board committees. Review all documents.

8. If the company is publicly held, obtain all periodic filings for the past five years, including the 10-K, 10-Q, 8-K, and Schedule 13D.

9. Review all annual and quarterly reports to shareholders.

10. Obtain a list of all states in which the company is qualified to do business and a list of those states in which it maintains significant operations. Determine if there is any state where the company is not qualified but should be qualified to do business.

11. Review the articles of incorporation and bylaws of each significant subsidiary. Determine if there are restrictions on dividends to the company. For each subsidiary, review the minutes of the Board of Directors for matters requiring disclosure. Also review each subsidiary's legal right to do business in each state in which it operates.

12. Review the company's correspondence with the SEC, any national exchange, or state securities commission, other than routine transmittals, for the past five years. Determine if there are or were any enforcement or disciplinary actions or any ongoing investigations or suggestions of violations by any of these entities.

13. Review all corporate insurance, using a schedule from the company's insurance agency. If there is material pending litigation, determine the extent of insurance coverage and obtain insurance company confirmation.

14. Review all pending and threatened legal proceedings to which the company or any of its subsidiaries is a party. Describe principal parties, allegations, and relief sought. This includes any governmental or environmental proceedings. Obtain copies of existing consent decrees or significant settlement agreements relating to the company or its subsidiaries.

15. Review the auditors' letter to management concerning internal accounting controls and procedures, as well as any management responses.

16. If there has been a change in accountants during the past five years, find out why.

17. Review any reports of outside consultants or analysts concerning the company.

18. Review any correspondence during the past five years with the EPA, FTC, OSHA, EEOC, or IRS. Determine if there are any ongoing investigations or suggestions of violations by any of these agencies.

19. Research any press releases or articles about the company within the past year (see Bloomberg.com, NEXIS, Equifax, etc.).

20. Review all contracts that are important to operations. Also review any contracts with shareholders or officers. In particular, look for the following provisions:

- Default or termination provisions

- Restrictions on company action

- Consent requirements

- Termination provisions in employment contracts

- Ownership of technology

- Cancellation provisions in major supply and customer contracts

- Unusual warranties or the absence of protective provisions

21. Review any required regulatory compliance and verify that necessary licenses and permits have been maintained, as well as ongoing filings and reports.

22. Review all current patent, trademark, service mark, trade name, and copyright agreements, and note renewal dates. Determine which patents have commercial applications. Estimate the possibility of extending the duration of patent protection.

23. Review all related-party transactions for the past three years.

24. Review the terms of any outbound or inbound royalty agreements.

25. Was any company software (either used internally or resold) obtained from another company? If so, what are the terms under which the code is licensed? Are there any associated royalty payments?

26. Review all legal invoices for the past two years.

27. Obtain a copy of any factoring agreements.

28. Obtain copies of all outsourcing agreements.

CAPITALIZATION AND SIGNIFICANT SUBSIDIARIES

1. Review all Board resolutions authorizing the issuance of stock to ensure that all shares are validly issued.

2. Review debt agreements to which the company or any subsidiary is a party, as well as all debt guarantees. Note any restrictions on dividends, on incurring extra debt, and on issuing additional capital stock. Note any unusual consent or default provisions. If subordinated debt securities are being issued, compare new subordination provisions with the provisions for other agreements for compatibility. Review the latest borrowing base certificates. Inquire whether there are any defaults or potential defaults.

3. Review any disclosure documents used in the private placement of securities or loan applications during the preceding five years.

4. Review all documents affecting ownership, voting, or rights to acquire the company's stock for required disclosure and significance to the purchase transactions, such as warrants, options, security holder agreements, registration rights agreements, shareholder rights, or poison pill plans.

EMPLOYEES

1. Obtain copies of any employment agreements, and document any change in control clauses that will trigger the cancellation of employee loans, severance payments, or the acceleration of vesting in such benefits as stock options.
2. Obtain copies of any noncompete agreements.
3. Obtain copies of any salesperson compensation agreements.
4. Obtain copies of any director compensation agreements.
5. Obtain copies of any option plans.
6. Summarize any loan amounts and terms to officers, directors, or employees.
7. Obtain any union labor agreements.
8. Determine the number of states to which payroll taxes must be paid.
9. Obtain a copy of the employee manual.
10. Obtain a list of all employees, their current compensation, and compensation for the prior year.
11. Summarize the names, ages, titles, education, experience, and professional biographies of the senior management team.
12. Obtain copies of employee resumes.
13. What has been the employee turnover rate for the past two years?
14. Obtain a copy of the organization chart.

REVENUE

1. Summarize sales by customer for the current and past year.
2. Summarize sales by product for the current and past year.
3. Summarize the backlog by customer.
4. Summarize the backlog by custom work and standard products.
5. Determine how much staffing is required to complete the existing backlog of custom work.
6. Determine the seasonality of revenue.
7. Determine the amount of ongoing maintenance revenue from standard software products.
8. Obtain copies of all outstanding proposals, bids, and offers pending award.
9. Obtain copies of all existing contracts for products or services, including warranty and guarantee work.

ASSETS

1. Obtain copies of all asset leases, and review for term, early payment, and bargain purchase clauses.

2. Obtain copies of all office space lease agreements, and review for term and renewal provisions.

3. Review the title insurance for any significant land parcels owned by the company.

4. Obtain current detail of accounts receivable.

5. Obtain a list of all accounts and notes receivable from employees.

6. Obtain a list of all inventory items, and discuss the obsolescence reserve.

7. Obtain the current fixed asset listing, as well as depreciation calculations.

8. Review the bad debt reserve calculation.

9. Obtain an itemized list of all assets that are not receivables or fixed assets.

10. Obtain any maintenance agreements on company equipment.

11. Is there an upcoming need to replace assets?

12. Discuss whether there are any plans to close, relocate, or expand any facilities.

13. Itemize all capitalized R&D or software development expenses.

LIABILITIES

1. Verify wage and tax remittances to all government entities and that there are no unpaid amounts.

2. Obtain a list of all accounts payable to employees.

3. Review the sufficiency of accruals for wages, vacation time, legal expenses, insurance, property taxes, and commissions.

4. Review the terms of any lines of credit.

5. Review the amount and terms of any other debt agreements.

6. Review the current accounts payable listing.

7. Obtain copies of all unexpired purchasing commitments (purchase orders, etc.).

FINANCIAL STATEMENTS

1. Obtain audited financial statements for the last three years.

2. Obtain monthly financial statements for the current year.

3. What are the revenues and profits per employee?

4. What is direct labor expense as a percentage of revenue?

5. Obtain copies of federal tax returns for the last three years.

6. Verify the most recent bank reconciliation.

7. Determine profitability by product, by customer, and by segment.

8. Obtain a copy of the business plan and budget.

INTERNET

1. Does the company use the Internet for internal use as an interactive part of operations? What functions are used in this manner?

2. Has the company's firewall ever been penetrated, and how sensitive is the information stored on the company network's publicly available segments?

3. Does the company provide technical support information through its web site?

4. Are web site usage statistics tracked? If so, how are they used for management decisions?

5. In what way could operational costs decrease if the company's customers interacted with it through the Internet?

SOFTWARE DEVELOPMENT

1. Who are the key development personnel involved with the creation, coding, and evaluation of software products? What is their tenure and educational background?

2. How much money is invested annually in development? As a proportion of sales?

3. What is the strategic plan for the development of new products? What is the timeline for their introduction? To what markets are they targeted?

4. How many patches were required to make the last major software release stable and commercially viable?

5. What was the average time required to resolve customer software problems?

6. How many customer accounts have been lost due to a software upgrade? What reasons did they give for dropping maintenance?

7. What operating system platforms are the target for the company's software products? Is there a plan to port any company products to other platforms? For what proportion of existing products has this been done?

8. Does the company use structured programming techniques that allow for easy software updating, maintenance, and enhancement?

9. What development languages and tools does the development staff use now? Are there plans to change to other languages and tools?

10. What are the attributes that make the company's products unique?

11. What is the company's strategy in designing new products (e.g., quality, support, special features).

MARKETING

1. What types of advertising and promotion are used?

2. Does the company have a web site? Who owns the site and how is it hosted?

3. Does the company use e-mail for marketing notifications to customers?

4. What are the proportions of sales by distribution channel?

5. How many customers can the company potentially market its products to? What would be the volume by customer?

6. What is the company's market share? What is the trend?

7. Are there new markets in which the products can be sold?

SALES

1. What is the sales strategy (e.g., add customers, increase support, increase penetration into existing customer base, pricing, etc.).

2. What is the structure of the sales organization? Are there independent sales representatives?

3. Obtain the sales organization chart.

4. How many sales personnel are in each sales position?

5. What the sales force's geographic coverage?

6. What is the sales force's compensation, split by base pay and commission?

7. What was the sales per salesperson for the past year?

8. What was the sales expense per salesperson for the past year?

9. What is the sales projection by product for the next 12 months?

10. Into what category do customers fall—end users, retailers, OEMs, wholesalers, and/or distributors?

11. Who are the top 10 customers, based on sales volume?

12. What is the historical sales volume to all customers for the past three years?

13. How many customers are there for each product, industry, and geographic region?

14. What is the average order size?

15. Does the company have an Internet store? Does the site accept on-line payments and orders? What percentage of total sales come through this medium?

16. How many customers have current subscriptions or maintenance for the company's software? What is the dollar amount per customer? What is the growth rate in the number of customers?

17. What is the structure of the technical support group? How many people are in it, and what is their compensation?

18. Obtain a list of all customers who have stopped doing business with the company in the last three years.

RESEARCH AND DEVELOPMENT

1. Obtain a summary of all R&D projects currently underway, including their current status, estimated time and cost to complete, and estimated unit costs as compared to target costs.

2. Determine the need for key staff positions to complete current R&D projects.

3. Estimate the worst-case, average-case, and best-case scenarios for revenue streams resulting from current R&D projects.

4. Estimate the types of patents that may be filed as a result of current R&D projects, and determine how these patents could be used to enhance the company's competitive position and/or block the positions of competitors.

PAYROLL

1. Verify if any special bonuses are to be paid to acquiree employees in the event of a merger or acquisition, and quantify the amount.

2. Determine if the acquiree has agreed to an extension of the IRS's statute of limitations for reviewing the acquiree's tax records, and adjust the review period for the following items to match the resulting longer period subject to IRS audit.

3. Verify that employees are properly categorized as contractors versus employees, as well as exempt versus nonexempt.

4. Verify compliance with filing dates for federal, state, and local payroll tax deposits.

5. Verify that all payroll tax returns have been filed by the required dates.

6. Verify that annual state unemployment rate notices have been incorporated into unemployment tax remittances.

7. Reconcile wages reported on quarterly Forms 941 to year-end Forms W-2 for both federal and state reporting.

8. Search for payroll tax liabilities recorded in the general ledger that have not been cleared by scheduled payment due dates.

9. Examine the number and size of payroll tax remittance penalties paid to determine if the remittance process has significant ongoing weaknesses.

10. Determine if the acquiree is being audited for various payroll taxes, and determine the size of the tax amounts under review.

11. Match the employee benefits listed in the employee handbook to benefits expenditures and related employee deductions actually being made.

HUMAN RESOURCES

1. Review the unemployment rate notices and reserve balances for every state in which the acquiree has employees.

2. Determine the matching contribution levels for pension plans.

3. Determine the pension plan eligibility criteria and vesting period.

TREASURY

1. Document banking relationships, available credit lines, and collateral.

2. Document all hedging activities and identify areas of risk.

3. Document transfer pricing policies and note government audits in this area.

4. Identify all funds invested in nonliquid assets, and determine their first possible liquidation dates and associated penalties for early liquidation.

5. Determine the extent and accuracy of cash forecasting systems.

CULTURE

1. What is the company's intent in forcing the acquired company to use its business practices?

2. What are the decision-making processes of the company?

3. What are the performance monitoring and bonus payment systems of the company?

4. How does the company resolve conflicts?

5. What types of formal and informal communication systems are used by the company?

6. What is the command structure of the company?

COMPLEXITY

1. Evaluate the number and variability of revenue sources.

2. Review the size and volatility of individual revenue transactions.

3. Review the volatility of the effective tax rate.

4. Investigate differences between tax and book income.

5. Review off-balance-sheet assets and liabilities.

OTHER

1. Discuss revenue recognition policies.

2. Construct a cash forecast through the end of the year.

3. Obtain a copy of the chart of accounts.

4. Determine risk management strategies and insurance coverage.

5. Is there a 401(k) plan? Any company contribution? Who manages it? Are contribution payments current?

6. Evaluate the company benefit plan to determine its cost, as well as the amount of employee participation.

7. Obtain a list of all significant accounting policies.

Index

A

401(k)
  Deductions, 327
  Plan, 238–239
A.M. Best, 280
Accounting department measurements, 412–413
Accounts payable
  Audit tasks, 120
  Best practices, 306–310
  Controls, 103–105
  Days, 82–83
  Factory, 21–22
  Payment delay, 213
  Payment terms, 18
  Prepayments, 18
  Review, 400
Accounts receivable
  Audit tasks, 120
  Collection acceleration, 213–214
  Controls, 99–100
  Factoring, 17, 215
  Reduction of, 17
Accrual reduction, 318
Accumulated earnings tax, 43–44
Acquiree valuation, 348–354
Acquisitions, *See* Mergers
Alliances, use of, 348
Alternative Investment Market, 261–262
Alternative minimum tax, 382
American Stock Exchange, 258–259
Anticipation survey, 189
Arithmetic mean, 172–173
Asset
  Analysis report, 340
  Due diligence, 417–418
  Impairment testing, 103
  Resale value, 351
  Utilization measurements, 68–72, 404–40406

Audit
  Committee, 113–115
  Opinions, 116
Auditor management letter, 401
Auditor roles,
  External, 115–117
  Internal, 119–122
Authentication, 373
Automated Clearing House (ACH) payments, 17, 309, 316
Average receivable collection period, 80

B

Bad debt, approval of, 99
Bank account consolidation, 316
Bank reconciliations, 97–98, 201, 317–318, 400
Bank relations, 211–212, 402
Banking relationship, 14–15
Bankruptcy
  Act of 2005, 396
  Alternatives, 396
  Notices, 312
  Process, 386–397
  Reorganization plan, 392–393
  Resolution, 387
  Schedule of assets and liabilities, 389
  Statement of financial affairs, 389
Bar date order, 391
Best practices, 306–329
Bill of materials
  Accuracy, 18, 100
  Record access, 100
  Updating, 322
Billing
  Audit tasks, 121
  Best practices, 322–324
  Errors, 201
  Recurring, 17
Blanket purchase orders, 107